AF715023

Environmental Law in Montenegro

Environmental Law in Montenegro

Dragoljub Todić
Mihajlo Vučić

This book was originally published as a monograph in the International Encyclopaedia of Laws/Environmental Law.

Founding Editor: Roger Blanpain
General Editor: Frank Hendrickx
Volume Editor: Kurt Deketelaere

Wolters Kluwer

Published by:
Kluwer Law International B.V.
PO Box 316
2400 AH Alphen aan den Rijn
The Netherlands
E-mail: lrs-sales@wolterskluwer.com
Website: www.wolterskluwer.com/en/solutions/kluwerlawinternational

Sold and distributed by:
Wolters Kluwer Legal & Regulatory U.S.
920 Links Avenue
Landisville, PA 17538
United States of America
E-mail: customer.service@wolterskluwer.com

DISCLAIMER: The material in this volume is in the nature of general comment only. It is not offered as advice on any particular matter and should not be taken as such. The editor and the contributing authors expressly disclaim all liability to any person with regard to anything done or omitted to be done, and with respect to the consequences of anything done or omitted to be done wholly or partly in reliance upon the whole or any part of the contents of this volume. No reader should act or refrain from acting on the basis of any matter contained in this volume without first obtaining professional advice regarding the particular facts and circumstances at issue. Any and all opinions expressed herein are those of the particular author and are not necessarily those of the editor or publisher of this volume.

ISBN 978-94-035-4936-1

e-Book: ISBN 978-94-035-4946-0
web-PDF: ISBN 978-94-035-4956-9

This title is available on www.kluwerlawonline.com

© 2023 Kluwer Law International BV, The Netherlands

All rights reserved. No part of this publication may be reproduced, stored in a retrieval system, or transmitted in any form or by any means, electronic, mechanical, photocopying, recording, or otherwise, without the prior written permission of the publisher.

Permission to use this content must be obtained from the copyright owner. More information can be found at: www.wolterskluwer.com/en/solutions/legal-regulatory/permissions-reprints-and-licensing

The Authors

Dr Dragoljub Todić received his PhD and Master's from the University of Belgrade, Faculty of Law, Serbia, and Diploma from the Faculty of Political Sciences from Belgrade University, Serbia.

Currently he is employed at the Institute of international politics and economics, Belgrade, Serbia. A professor at Megatrend University in Belgrade, Serbia, Todic's fields of interest include environmental law and policy, international law, sustainable development, human rights, the European Union (EU) environmental policy and law, and migration law. He is a member of several professional and Non-governmental Organizations (NGOs) in the field of law and the environment.

Author or co-author of twenty books, two guidance publications, two dictionaries, one collection of laws and more than two hundred articles and other shorter works, Dr Todic has participated in a number of conferences in Serbia and abroad and in several domestic and international projects. Email: d.todic@diplomacy.bg.ac.rs; dtodic@ymail.com.

Dr Mihajlo Vučić is a senior research fellow at the Institute of International Politics and Economics (IIPE) and an associate professor at the Faculty of Diplomacy and Security where he teaches the subject 'European Union studies'. He holds a PhD in public international law and a Master's degree in European integration. He authored several monographies and articles in the field of environmental law. Email: mihajlo@diplomacy.bg.ac.rs; mihajlovucic@gmail.com.

The Authors

Table of Contents

Table of Contents

List of Abbreviations

BAT	Best Available Techniques
CDM	Clean Development Mechanism
CE	Council of Europe
CETI	Centre for Ecotoxicological Research
CFCs	Chlorofluorocarbons
CITES	Convention on International Trade in Endangered Species
CLRTAP	Convention on the Long-Range Transboundary Air Pollution
EAR	European Agency for Reconstruction
EBRD	European Bank for Reconstruction and Development
EC	European Commission/Commission of the European Communities
EEA	European Environmental Agency
EIA	Environmental Impact Assessment
EMS	Environmental Management System
EMEP	Protocol on Long-Term Financing of the Cooperative Programme for Monitoring and Evaluation of the Long-range Transmission of Air Pollutants in Europe
EPA	Environmental Protection Agency of Montenegro
EU	European Union
FAO	Food and Agriculture Organization
FDI	Foreign Direct Investment
FRY	Federal Republic of Yugoslavia
GEF	Global Environmental Facility
GMNE	Government of Montenegro
GLP	Good Laboratory Practice
GDP	Gross Domestic Product
GMO	Genetically Modified Organisms
GNI	Gross National Income
Hydromet	Hydrological and Meteorological Service of Montenegro

List of Abbreviations

IAEA	International Atomic Energy Agency
IDPs	Internally Displaced Persons
IMF	International Monetary Fund
IMPP	Institute of International Politics and Economics
IPPC	Integrated Pollution Prevention and Control
KAP	Kombinat Aluminium Podgorica
MAFWM	Ministry of Agriculture, Forestry and Water Management
MARD	Ministry of Agriculture and Rural Development
MC	Ministry of Culture
MCI	Ministry of Capital Investments
ME	Ministry of Economy
MEAs	Multilateral Environmental Agreements
MED	Ministry for Economic Development
MEDPOL	Programme for the Assessment and Control of Pollution in the Mediterranean Region
MES	Ministry for Education and Science
MESPU	Ministry of Ecology, Spatial Planning and Urbanism
MF	Ministry of Finance
MFAEI	Ministry of Foreign Affairs and European Integration
MHLSW	Ministry of Health, Labour and Social Welfare
MH	Ministry of Health
MI	Ministry of the Interior
MNE	Montenegro
MONSTAT	Statistical Office of Montenegro
MoU	Memorandum of Understanding
MP	Member of Parliament
MPPEP	Ministry of Physical Planning and Environmental Protection
MSDT	Ministry of Sustainable Development and Tourism
MTEP	Ministry of Tourism and Environmental Protection
MTMA	Ministry of Transport and Maritime Affairs
NATO	North Atlantic Treaty Organization
NCSD	National Council for Sustainable Development
NGO	Non-governmental Organization
NEPA	Nature and Environmental Protection Agency
NPI	National Programme for Integration with European Union
NSBS	National Bio Safety Council
NSSDM	National Strategy of Sustainable Development of Montenegro
OSD	Office for Sustainable Development

OJ MNE	Official Journal of Montenegro
OJ MNE – IT	Official Journal of Montenegro – International Treaties
OSCE	Organization for Security and Cooperation in Europe
PET	Polyethylene Terephthalate
PHRF	Protector of Human Rights and Freedoms
PIC	Rotterdam Convention on the Prior Informed Consent Procedure for Certain Hazardous Chemicals and Pesticides in International Trade
POPs	Stockholm Convention on Persistent Organic Pollutants
RM	Republic of Montenegro
RS	Republic of Serbia
SAA	Stabilization and Association Agreement
SEA	Strategic Environmental Assessment
S&M	Serbia and Montenegro
SFRY	Socialist Federal Republic of Yugoslavia
SPM	Spatial Plan of Montenegro until 2020
SRM	Socialist Republic of Montenegro
SY MNE	Statistical Yearbook of Montenegro
UN	United Nations
UNCCD	Convention UN Convention to Combat Desertification in Countries Experiencing Serious Drought and/or Desertification, Particularly in Africa
UNDP	United Nations Development Programme
UNECE	United Nations Economic Commission for Europe
UNEP	United Nations Environment Programme
UNESCO	United Nations Educational, Scientific and Cultural Organization
UNFCCC	United National Framework Convention on Climate Change
UNIDO	United Nation Industrial Development Organization
UNMIK	United Nations Interim Administration Mission in Kosovo
WB	World Bank

List of Abbreviations

Acknowledgements

The author would like to thank Dr Vid Vukasovic+ (Scientific Adviser, Institute of International Politics and Economics, Belgrade), Ms Mladenka Ignjatić (M.Sc. independent consultant) and Ms Ksenija Maltez (Senior English Language Teacher, Megatrend University, Belgrade) for their suggestions and contributions.

Acknowledgements

[illegible]

General Introduction

§1. General Information

I. Geography and Population

A. Geography

1. Geographically, Montenegro belongs to the region of the Western Balkans, while its coast lies on the eastern part of the Adriatic Sea.[1] So, Montenegro is a Mediterranean country in Southeastern Europe, located between 41°52' and 43°32' of northern latitude and between 18°26' and 20°21' of eastern longitude, with total area of 13,812 square kilometres (km^2).[2] Its neighbouring countries are Bosnia and Herzegovina and Croatia to the west, Serbia to the north and Albania to the south-east and east.[3] Montenegro has 293.5 km of Adriatic Sea coastline.[4]

2. Montenegro's location in the Mediterranean has marked its historic and cultural development. The position provides numerous advantages, first of all for development of tourism and a maritime economy.[5] Another important feature of its position is the link with Serbia which lies at the crossroads of European main road corridors VI and X linking Central and Southern Europe.[6]

1. MESPU. EPA (2022a), p. 77.
2. 'The distance between the southernmost and northernmost point of the mainland of Montenegro is 192 km, as the crow flies, and between the westernmost and the easternmost points is 163 km.' MSDT (2020), p. 18.
3. SY MNE-2021, 18. Nevertheless, in relation to these data it should be kept in mind that Montenegro recognized Kosovo as an independent and sovereign state by the Decision of Government adopted on 9 Oct. 2008. Diplomatic relations between Montenegro and the Republic of Kosovo were established on 15 Jan. 2010. *See* https://www.gov.me/en/diplomatic-missions/embassies-and-consulates-of-montenegro/kosovo (16 Dec. 2022).
4. SY MNE-2021, 18. There are nine islands in the Bay of Kotor, and the other four are located along the southern part of the coast. EPA (2021), p. 136.
5. 'The sea is a very important touristic, economic and biological resource for Montenegro. … The costal area of Montenegro is one of the most valuable national resources'. MESPU, EPA (2022a), p. 77.
6. GMNE (2008C), 35.

3. Approximate total territory of the country for structural use (13.812 km^2) is woods approximately 45%; agricultural land approximately 37%; and settlements, roads, stony areas and other categories approximately 18%.[7]

4. Climate conditions in Montenegro are predominantly influenced by the Adriatic Sea and mountain massifs.[8] There are four distinctive climatic zones in Montenegro which are as follows: (1) the coastal area with a salubrious climate; (2) High Dinaric Limestone mountains (Rumija, Sutorman, Orjen and Lovćen) with patches of fertile land in karst depressions, in one of the rainiest areas in Europe; (3) the Central depression of Montenegro, with altitudes between 40 and 500 m. The Zeta River valley and Nikšić are the only plain areas in Montenegro that constitute the two largest cities with high population density: the capital city of Podgorica (population 169,132) and Nikšić (population 75,282); (4) the high mountain ranges of over 2,000 m of northern Montenegro with sub-alpine, cold, snowy winters and moderate summers.[9]

5. The country has seven main rivers: Lim (123 km in Montenegro), Tara (141 km), Çehotina (100 km), Moraca (99 km), Piva (78 km), Zeta (65 km) and Bojana (30 km).[10] There are also forty lakes.

6. Montenegro has significant reserves of bauxite, lead, zinc, coal, ornamental stones, sea salt, gravel, sand and other construction materials. The most significant are red bauxite and coal which are strategic mineral raw materials in Montenegro.[11] In the territory of Montenegrin Littoral deposits of mineral raw materials have been discovered.[12] The main industries are aluminium smelting, lumber milling, salt and tobacco processing. Major agricultural crops include cereals, tobacco, vegetables and fruits.

7. Generally, 'geographic position, climate conditions[13] and spatial characteristics, natural resources and their distribution are what make Montenegro an extraordinary state for various reasons. The territory of Montenegro falls within two basic

7. *Ibid.*, 32.
8. The average annual air temperature ranges from 4.6°C in the area of Žabljak which is 1,450 m above sea level, to 15.8°C on the coast. The average annual precipitation ranges from 800 mm in the far north to around 5,000 mm in the far southwest. MSDT.(2020), p. 37.
9. The highest peak is Bobotov Kuk at 2,522 m, of Durmitor Mountain. SY MNE- 2021, 19. In this area two national parks are situated: Biogradska Gora (5,650 ha) and Durmitor (39,000 ha).
10. SY MNE-2021, 19.
11. UNECE (2003), 111; Oil and gas are still under research. For more details on mineral resources *see*: GMNE (2008C), 37–41.
12. *See* extensively, GMNE (2007D), 19.
13. However, 'there is no comprehensive model on economic impacts from climate change for Montenegro. The project-based "Technology Needs Assessment for Climate Change Mitigation and Adaptation for Montenegro – National Strategy and Action Plan" (TNA) gives an indication of costs for priority measures of adaptation for the sectors most relevant: health sector, €1.8 million; water sector, €4.3 million; agriculture sector, €2.1 million; coastal area, €1.9 million; and forestry sector, €1.4 million'. UNECE (2015), 99.

biogeographical regions (Mediterranean and Alpine).[14] The nature of Montenegro, including biological diversity, as well as characteristic landscapes and cultural values are some of the greatest treasures of Montenegro. Forests and water resources, including the sea and a coast around 300 km long, are among the most important natural and development resources of the country'.[15] The conclusions in the Report on national consultations regarding Post-Millennium Development Goals Montenegro 'identify environment as one of the greatest advantages and opportunities of the country. However, it is noted that the potentials of the environment are not only underutilized, but its qualitative properties are also rapidly disrupted'.[16]

B. *Population*

8. According to 2011 census,[17] Montenegro had 620,029 inhabitants with an average density of 44.9 inhabitants per km^2.[18] During the period between two censuses (1991–2003) population of Montenegro increased by 4.8%, having an annual growth rate of 0.34%. Population growth had slowed down in this period, compared with the previous time frame with ageing in the general population.[19] In addition, during the period between the last two censuses (2003–2011), the total population increased by 1.3%.[20]

9. With respect to demographic problems following basic factors should be mentioned.[21] The increase in the total number of inhabitants continued but at a slower rate due to the abrupt increase in mortality.[22] As a result of such a situation there was a decrease in the vital index (from 2,852 in 1980 to 1,458 in 2003 or 1.95 times lower);[23] a decrease in the number of marriages and an increase in the number of divorces (4.1 per family member according to census in 1981, 3.7 in 1991 and 3.5 in 2003).[24] Also, migration of the younger population from rural into urban zones

14. For more details *see*: MSDT (2014), 5.
15. GMNE, NCSD (2011), 9. 'Taking in consideration the size and population, Montenegro, with its geographical position and characteristics of natural potentials, is one of the countries with favourable climate geodiversity, due to land configuration, vicinity of the sea and natural features (apart from belonging to the Mediterranean seismic zone).', *Ibid.*, 9.
16. MSDT (2016c). p. 33.
17. In order to organize and conduct the next census, the Parliament of Montenegro adopted the Law on the Census of Population, Households and Dwellings (12 Dec. 2022). *See*: https://www.skupstina.me/me/sjednice/pretraga-dokumenata (24 Dec. 2022).
18. SY MNE-2021, 39.
19. Participation of population above sixty years of age increased from 13.3% in 1991 to 16.8% in 2001, while the participation of population aged 0 to 19 decreased from 33.9% to 28.8%. At the same time, the percentage of people aged 20 to 59 increased by 1.6%. GMNE (2008C), 61.
20. MSDT (2016b). https://www.gov.me/en/documents/6852d215-af43-4671-b940-cbd0525896c1 (16 Dec. 2022), 29.
21. GMNE (2008C), 62.
22. In 2010, 7,420 children were born. There were 5,633 deaths. Natural increase rate (per 1,000 inhabitants): 2,9. MONSTAT (2011e), 1 and 2.
23. In 2010, vital index (live births per 100 deaths): 131.7. *Ibid.*, 2.
24. In 2010 there were 3,675 marriages. Marriage rate (marriage per 1,000 inhabitants) in 2010 was 5.9. There were 520 divorces. *Ibid.*, 5.

continued, and the reverse led to the changed structure of settlements. In most of the municipal centres the number of inhabitants increased migration from the northern to the southern region continued,[25] and each coastal municipality had a positive migration balance except Ulcinj.[26] The trend of ageing in population has continued[27] and so has further depopulation in rural areas.

10. The wave of migration from the Middle East, Central Asia and North Africa to Europe began in 2011, intensified in 2014, and reached unprecedented proportions in 2015. For the mentioned period, 9,000 asylum applications were submitted in Montenegro, and the largest number were citizens of Syria, Eritrea, Somalia, Afghanistan, etc.[28]

11. Number of persons with university degrees increased from 5% in 1991 to 7.5% in 2003 and with college degrees from 3.8% to 5.09%. Simultaneously, number of persons who graduated from secondary schools increased from 34.9% to 48.44%, and the illiteracy rate decreased from 5.6% in 1991 to 2.5% in 2003.[29] According to the results of the Census of Population, Households and Dwellings in 2011, in Montenegro there are 232,010 active population, i.e., 46% of the total number of population aged fifteen years and over. Number of inactive population is 268,288, i.e., 54% of the total number of population aged 15 years and over.[30] Furthermore, there are 17% of population with higher or high school attainment, both by old and new Bologna educational system. Of the total number of population 15 years of age and over, there are 260,277, i.e., 52%, of persons with secondary school completed. But, of that number, there are 27,285 persons currently attending university.[31] In addition, there are 542,649 persons of age 10 years and over, of which 8,149 are illiterate persons, i.e., 1.5%. The average age of illiterate person is 62 years.[32]

12. The ethnic composition of Montenegro is as follows: ethnic Montenegrins fell by 107,000 between 1991 and 2003 to 267,669 (43.16% of the population), ethnic Serbs rose, during the same period, from 57,000 to 198,414 (31.99%). Other ethnic groups include Bosniaks (48,184 or 7.77%), Albanians (31,163 or 5.03%), Muslims by nationality (24,625 or 3.97%), Croats (6,811 or 1.1%) and some other small ethnic groups.[33] According to the 2011 Census of Population: Montenegrins

25. Internal migrations are intensive. Due to that in several municipalities in the north (Šavnik, Žabljak, Plužine, Berane, Andrijevica and Pljevlja) number of inhabitants is continually decreasing, while the capital city of Podgorica and coastal municipalities have a continuous population influx in each census conducted after World War II.
26. In 2010, of twenty-one municipalities, more persons immigrated than emigrated in ten municipalities, while a negative net migration was recorded in eleven municipalities (Internal migrations). MONSTAT (2011e), 6.
27. The average age of the population of Montenegro is 37.2 years. MONSTAT (2011f), 5.
28. MI (2021), 47.
29. GMNE (2008C), 62.
30. MONSTAT (2012a), 2.
31. MONSTAT (2012b), 1.
32. *Ibid.*, 4.
33. UNECE (2007), 5. *See also* SY MNE-2008, 44.

278,865 (44.98%), Serbs, 178,110 (28.73%), Bosniaks, 53,605 (8.65%), Albanians, 30,439 (4.91%), Muslims, 20,537 (3.31%), Croats, 6,021 (0.97%), etc.[34] In 2003, 63.5% of the population declared Serbian as their mother tongue, while almost 22% spoke Montenegrin language.[35] According to the 2011 Census of Population: Serbian mother tongue – 42.88%; Montenegrin mother tongue – 36.97%, etc.[36] In regard to religion, according to 2003 census, 74.2% of the population are Orthodox Christians, 17.7% Sunni Muslims and 3.5% Roman Catholics.[37] According to the 2011 Census of Population: 72.07% are Orthodox; 15.97% Islam; 3.14% Muslims; 3.44% Catholics, etc.[38]

13. The fall of former Yugoslavia, wars in the Balkans, United Nations' (UN) sanctions and constant economic decline caused huge population movement across the whole former Yugoslav territory and out of it.[39] There were, as a consequence, nearly 18,000 refugees (mainly ethnic Serbian or members of the Roma community) from Kosovo and more than 8,000 from Bosnia and Croatia.[40] In the period from 7 November 2009 (date of entry into force of the Law Amending the Law on Foreigners) to 1 January 2018, Internally Displaced Persons (IDPs) submitted a total of 8,428 requests for approval of permanent residence; 8,181 cases are resolved; 7,120 requests are approved (granted permanent residence).[41]

II. Legal and Political Structure

14. Montenegro is an independent and sovereign state, as stated in Article 1 of its Constitution (OJMNE, Nos 1/2007, 38/2013), 'the [a]republican form of government and a civil, democratic, ecological society with the state of social justice, based on the rule of law'. According to Article 11 of the Constitution, principle of the division of powers into the legislative (exercised by the Parliament), executive (exercised by the Government) and judicial (exercised by the Courts)[42] is applied in the country. The relationship among the powers is based on balance and mutual control.[43]

34. SY MNE-2011, 46.
35. UNECE (2007), 6. According to the 2011 Census of Population: Serbian mother tongue – 42.88%; Montenegrin mother tongue – 36.97%, etc.
36. MONSTAT (2011a), 12.
37. UNECE (2007), 5. *See also* SY MNE-2008, 244.
38. MONSTAT (2011a), 15.
39. According to the best estimates, in the period 1990–1995, more than 2,000 personnel (mostly electrical engineering experts, civil engineers and technicians) left Montenegro. UNDP (2005a), 30.
40. UNECE (2007), 6. In 2005, the Government of Montenegro adopted a National Strategy for the solution of the IDPs' and Refugees' issue. On this subject, *see also* GMNE (2008d).
41. Report on Implementation of Measures from the Action Plan for the Implementation of the Strategy for Durable Solutions Issues Relating to Displaced and Internally Displaced Persons in Montenegro, with particular reference to the area of Konik for 2017, p. 4. *See*: https://www.gov.me/en/documents/d0bb7427-0e0c-43b7-b1aa-6e6f1c019375 (21 Nov. 2022).
42. The power shall be limited by the Constitution and the law (Art. 11, para. 3).
43. From 2002, Montenegro has entered into a period of fundamental political transformation. It went through two substantial changes in its internal structure and organization, from the Federal Republic of Yugoslavia into the State Union of Serbia and Montenegro in 2003, and to its full independence

15. Article 82 of the Constitution provides that the Parliament[44] shall: (1) adopt the Constitution; (2) adopt laws; (3) adopt other regulations and general acts (decisions, conclusions, resolutions, declarations and recommendations); (4) proclaim a state of war and a state of emergency; (5) adopt the budget and the final statement of the budget; (6) adopt the National security strategy and Defence strategy; (7) adopt the Development plan and Spatial plan of Montenegro; (8) decide on the use of units of the Army of Montenegro in the international forces; (9) regulate the state administration system; (10) perform supervision of the army and security services; (11) call for a national referendum; (12) elect and dismiss from duty the Prime Minister and members of the Government; (13) elect and dismiss from duty the President of the Supreme Court, the President and the judges of the Constitutional Court; (14) appoint and dismiss from duty the Supreme State Prosecutor and State Prosecutors, the Protector of human rights and liberties (Ombudsman), the Governor of the Central Bank and members of the Council of the Central Bank of Montenegro, the President and members of the Senate of the State Audit Institution and other officials stipulated by law; (15) decide on immunity rights; (16) grant amnesty; (17) confirm international agreements; (18) announce public loans and decide on borrowings by Montenegro; (19) decide on the use of state property above the value stipulated by law; and (20) perform other duties stipulated by the Constitution or law.[45]

16. The President of Montenegro is elected by a popular vote for a five-year term and can serve two terms in office. He/she has, in accordance with Article 95 of the Constitution, following functions: he/she represents Montenegro in the country and abroad; commands over the Army on the basis of the decisions of the Defence and Security Council; proclaims laws by Ordinance; calls for the elections for the Parliament; proposes to the Parliament: candidates for the Prime Minister, after consultations with the representatives of the political parties represented in the Parliament; President and judges of the Constitutional Court; and the Protector of human rights and liberties; appoints and revokes ambassadors and heads of other diplomatic missions of Montenegro abroad at the proposal of the Government and after obtaining the opinion of the Parliamentary Committee responsible for international relations; accepts letters of accreditation and revocation of the foreign diplomats;

---

in 2006. Apart from that, another area of fundamental transformation is privatization of state assets, a process that is deeply influencing the political, economic, social and environmental sectors. UNECE (2007), 29.

44. The Parliament of the present convocation was constituted on 2 Oct. 2006. It is composed of eighty-one deputies, i.e., members of the Parliament from sixteen political parties. Eight clubs have been constituted and eleven permanent working bodies established. The work of the Parliament is organized through parliamentary boards (one of them is Board for Tourism, Agriculture, Ecology and Physical Planning) and in plenary sessions.
45. The Rules of Procedure of the Parliament of Montenegro (Official Journal of RM, Nos 51/06 and 66/06, OJ MNE, Nos 88/09, 80/10, 39/11, 25/12, 49/13) have been applied since the Constitution of the new parliamentary convocation.

awards medals and honours of Montenegro; grants amnesty; performs other tasks stipulated by the Constitution or the law.[46]

17. Montenegrin presidential election was held on 6 April 2008. Candidates for Montenegrin president are proposed by political parties, coalitions or citizens' groups. Each president has a term of five years in office. The ruling Democratic Party of Socialists nominated the current president of Montenegro, Milo Đukanović.[47]

18. The executive branch of state authority is the Government, headed by the Prime Minister. He/she submits to the Parliament the Government's programme including a list of proposed ministers. His/her resignation causes the fall of the Government. The responsibility of the Government is prescribed by Article 100 of the Constitution.[48]

19. It is prescribed by Article 22 of the Constitution that 'the right to local self-government shall be guaranteed'. The right to local self-government shall incorporate the right of the citizens and local self-government authorities to regulate and manage specific public and other affairs based on their own responsibility and in the interest of the local population (Article 113, paragraph 2). Municipality is the basic form of local self-government although it is also possible to establish other forms of local self-government (Article 114).[49]

20. Parliamentary and local elections were held in Montenegro on 10 September 2006,[50] in the wake of independence euphoria.[51] The Democratic Party of Socialists (DPS) won the elections, and ensured, in a coalition with a smaller Social

---

46. In case of cessation of mandate of the President of Montenegro, until the election of the new President, as well as in the case of a temporary impediment of the President to discharge his/her duties, the Speaker of the Parliament shall discharge this duty (Art. 99 of the Constitution).
47. *See*: http://www.predsjednik.me/ (22 Nov. 2022).
48. *See also* Introduction – Part devoted to the Role of Government Institutions in the Shaping and Administration of Environmental Law and Policy in this Monograph.
49. Spatial Register covers the territory of Republic of Montenegro, divided into units of spatial register by municipalities, villages, local communities, cadastral municipalities, statistical and enumeration areas. According to present status the territory of Montenegro has a total of: Administrative centre, the capital and 19 municipalities, 1,256 settlement, (40 urban and 1,216 other types of settlements). *See*: Law on territorial organization (Official Journal of MNE, No. 54/11); Law on self-government (Official Journal of RM, Nos 42/03, 28/04, 75/05, Official Journal of MNE, Nos 88/09, 3/10); Law on unique records and register of spatial units ('Official Journal of SRM 43/90' and 'Official Journal of RM 27/94'); Law on Settlements ('Official Journal of SRM 29/90' and 'Official Journal of RM 48/91, 17/92 and 27/94').
50. According to Art. 14 of the Constitutional Law for the implementation of the Constitution of Montenegro (Official Journal of MNE, No. 1/07) elections for the Members of the Parliament of Montenegro shall be held latest by the end of 2009.
51. Montenegro officially declared independence on 3 Jun. 2006. 'Despite the success of the referendum, voting patterns suggest that the electorate is to some extent split across regional lines. Much of the population identifying itself as ethnic Serb, particularly in the poorer northern region of the country, remains sceptical of the benefits of independence.' WB (2007), 2.

Democratic Party (SDP), forty-one seats in an eighty-one-seat Parliament.[52] The same coalition won in **eleven** out of the fourteen municipalities at the local election. The other party, gaining a significant number of Parliamentary seats in the elections, was the Movement for Change (PZP or *Pokret za Promjene*). Last parliamentary elections were held in 2020 and resulted in the transfer of power from the DPS to the wide-ranging coalition of opposition parties.[53]

21. European integration has been declared by the government as one of the strategic priorities for the republic. The Montenegrin Parliament acted similarly by confirming in its Declaration of Independence 'as its strategic priority an accelerated integration into the European Union … '.[54]

22. The significant progress and important steps have been made in the European integration process of Montenegro. On 15 December 2009, Montenegro submitted application for EU membership. On 23 April 2009 the Council of the EU decided to invite the European Commission (EC) to prepare its opinion on Montenegro's application for membership and Montenegro received the Questionnaire of the EC containing over 4,000 questions from all chapters of the *Acquis communautaire* of the EU. On the basis of the Questionnaire the EC prepared its opinion and submitted recommendation to the Council to grant the candidate status to Montenegro. Montenegro gained official status of 'candidate' for membership in December 2010. In its 2011 Enlargement Strategy Paper, based on the analysis in the 2011 Progress Report,[55] the Commission concluded that:

> Montenegro has successfully addressed the key priorities set out in 2010 by the EU as a prerequisite to opening accession negotiations. The December 2011 European Council welcomed the Commission's assessment on the good progress made by Montenegro, which has achieved overall satisfactory results.[56]

23. On 29 June 2012 the European Council endorsed the earlier decision of the General Affairs Council to open accession negotiations with Montenegro and the first meeting of the Accession Conference was held on the same day. As of, November 2022, all 33 screened chapters have been opened, three of which are provisionally closed (25 – Science and Research, 26 – Education and Culture, 30 – External Relations), Chapter 27 (Environment and Climate Change) was opened in December 2018. In February 2020, a revised methodology was presented by the

52. EBRD (2007), 8.
53. See the complete election results at: https://dik.co.me/ukupni-rezultati-izbora-za-poslanike-u-skupstinu-crne-gore-2/ (22 Nov. 2022).
54. Deklaracija o nezavisnosti Republike Crne Gore (Declaration of the Independent Republic of Montenegro), point 2.
55. *See*: EC (2011).
56. EC (2012), 2. 'During the accession negotiations' process, the Commission will continue to put particular focus on the area of rule of law and fundamental rights, especially the fight against corruption and organised crime, so as to ensure a solid track record. It will make full use of the tools available at all stages of the accession process.' *Ibid.*, 12.

Commission, intended to drive forward the enlargement process with a stronger political steer and in a more credible, predictable and dynamic way. Since then, two Political Intergovernmental Conferences under the revised enlargement methodology were held to provide political steer to the accession process (June and December 2021).[57]

24. Montenegro became a full member of the North Atlantic Treaty Organization (NATO), on 5 June 2017.[58]

III. Economic Characteristics

25. According to Article 139 of the Constitution of Montenegro (OJ MNE, Nos 1/2007, 38/2013) 'economic system shall be based on a free and open market, freedom of entrepreneurship and competition, independence of the economic entities and their responsibility for the obligations accepted in the legal undertakings, protection and equality of all forms of property'. Property rights[59] and freedom of entrepreneurship[60] are guaranteed by Articles 58 and 59 of the Constitution. Pursuant to Article 61 a foreign national may be the holder of property rights in accordance with the law. In addition, economic rights defined by the Constitution include, *inter alia*, right to succession, right to work, prohibition of forced labour, rights of the employed, strike, social insurance, protection of persons with disability.

26. Montenegro is currently undergoing the final stage of transition that had been initiated in the early 1990s and that had been gradually reforming and preparing the economic system for the approaching EU accession stage. Economic recession of the 1990s together with inefficiencies and structural inadequacies inherited from the period of centrally planned economy and internationally imposed sanctions against – at the time – a newly established Federal Republic of Yugoslavia (FRY) (in May 1992) had contributed to the dissatisfactory condition of the Montenegrin economy.[61] 'So far, transition-related reforms have advanced well in

---

57. https://neighbourhood-enlargement.ec.europa.eu/enlargement-policy/montenegro_en (22 Nov. 2022).
58. *See*: https://www.nato.int/cps/su/natohq/topics_49736.htm# (16 Dec. 2022).
59. No one shall be deprived of or restricted in property rights, unless when so required by the public interest, with rightful compensation (Art. 58, para. 2). However, it is necessary to have in mind that property rights relations in Montenegro have not been comprehensively regulated by law. Currently, the old Law on Basis of Ownership and Proprietary Relations is still in force (Official Journal of SFRY, Nos 6/80 and 36/90 and Official Journal of SRY, No. 29/96).
60. Yet, freedom of entrepreneurship may be limited only if so necessary in order to protect the health of the people, environment, natural resources, cultural heritage or security and defence of Montenegro (Art. 59, para. 2).
61. GMNE (2007C), 23–24. In 1999, Montenegro introduced a foreign currency as the legal tender (Deutsche mark) as a parallel currency with the Yugoslavian Dinar. When the European Union adopted the Euro in 2002, Montenegro also changed its official currency to Euros.

several areas – notably price and trade liberalization, privatization[62] and banking sector reform – but only limited progress has occurred when it comes to deeper institutional reforms.'[63]

27. 'Montenegro is a small, open, middle-income economy. In 2006 total Gross Domestic Product (GDP) was approximately USD 2.4 billion'.[64] Latest data shows that the GDP totals approximately EUR 4,95 billion.[65] The GDP (in US dollars) has grown since 2002 and average GDP per capita has more than doubled between 2000 and 2005, increasing by 11.2%.[66] GDP per capita is comparable to or higher than other Western Balkan countries and per capita incomes remain well below recent EU members except for Bulgaria.[67] Estimated GDP for 2015 is EUR 3.595 million with real growth rate of 3.2%. GDP/pc is EUR 5.784. Measuring GDP/pc in PPS, Montenegro is 41% of the EU average in 2014.[68]

28. The economy of Montenegro is mainly based on services, including tourism, and specializes in the manufacture of a few products, notably aluminium. Power generation,[69] mining and metal processing account for around 70% of industrial output. Other industries include wood, textiles and food processing and manufacturing. The agricultural sector's share of GDP is insignificant.

29. Public debt of Montenegro (without public enterprises) is EUR 782.2 million (34.3% of GDP). The main share of the public debt is foreign debt of EUR 478.1 million (21.3% of GDP) while the internal public debt is EUR 285.1 million (12.9% of GDP).[70] As of 31 January 2012, the government debt of Montenegro was EUR 1,473.2 million or 43.4% of GDP. Internal debt was EUR 419 million or 12.3% of GDP, while the foreign debt was EUR 1,054.2 million or 31.0% of GDP. Deposits of the Ministry of Finance (MF) as of 31 January 2012 were EUR 57.1 million, including also 38,477 ounces of gold, and thus the net amount of the government debt was at approximately 41.6% of GDP.[71] Over the period of 2014–2017, General government debt grew from 59.9% to 65.1% of GDP.[72]

---

62. The privatization process in Montenegro can be considered 'as one of the most successful in the region'. More than 85% of state-owned capital has been privatized. GMNE (2008b), 69. On the other hand, 'the ongoing privatization process, not being subject at present to any legal environmental constraints, is causing deep concern in respect of big polluting enterprises'. UNECE (2007), 2. *See also* pp. 89–90.
63. EBRD (2007), 11–13.
64. WB (2007), 3–6, *see also* SY MNE-2008, 71.
65. SY MNE 2021, 69.
66. UNECE (2007), 7. Real GDP growth amounted to 8.6% in 2006, and was primarily driven by increasing demand in construction, tourism, the banking system and FDI, GMNE (2008b), 72.
67. For regional review *see*: Matijas (2007), 5–29.
68. MSDT (2016c), 3. https://sustainabledevelopment.un.org/memberstates/montenegro (3 Mar. 2018).
69. Energy efficiency is ranked among the lowest countries in the world. Montenegro has a very high energy consumption rate compared with countries with similar GNI levels. UNECE (2007), 7.
70. GMNE (2008b), 65.
71. MF (2012), 1.
72. MF (2018), 10.

30. Significant regional differences in the level of development are one of the characteristics of Montenegro (underdeveloped northern region and more developed central and southern regions):[73]

> In order to reduce significant regional disparities, which is a very large problem with numerous difficult consequences on the state as a whole, the Law on Regional Development was adopted after the Strategy, which created certain preconditions for adoption and implementation of effective measures in that area. Because of their overall characteristics, in order to achieve visible results in these regions that should serve as a test of effectiveness and applicability of the concept of 'green economy' it is necessary to prepare programmes and specific measures, as well as sufficient funds, through support and favourable loans.[74]

31. The rate of unemployed people on the records of the Employment Agency reduced from 18.5% in 2005 to 11.9% in 2007. The number of employees increased from 145,261 to 159,223 in 2008.[75] According to the data for four quarters of 2017, there were 273,200 active population in Montenegro, out of which there were 229,300 employed persons or 83.9% and 43,900 unemployed or 16.1%. The number of persons in employment in comparison with the previous year has increased by 2.3% and the number of unemployed has decreased by 9.1%.[76] The latest data for 2021 shows the number of employed persons is 176,693.[77]

32. 'The labour market dynamics during the first three quarters of 2017 were characterized by a continuous increase in employment and a reduction in the number of unemployed. According to data from the Labour Force Survey (LFS), employment grew by 3.2 per cent in the third quarter year-on-year, and unemployment grew by 2.1 percentage points. The unemployment rate in the third quarter was 14.8 per cent.'[78]

33. 'Absolute poverty line for Montenegro in 2013 was €186.45 per equivalent adult, which is approximately €4 more than in 2012. In 2013 8.6% of the population had equivalent consumption below the absolute poverty line'.[79] Total poverty rate in 2013 decreased, while depth and severity also decreased. Portion of persons in the poverty decreased from 11.3% in 2012 to 8.6% in 2013. 'There are significant differences in the extent of poverty in the region between the North and other

---

73. For more details *see* GMNE (2007C), 24–25.
74. GMNE, NCSD (2011), 18.
75. GMNE (2008b), 73. However, in SY MNE-2008 the following data have been cited: 144340 (2005), 156408 (2007), SY MNE-2008, 60.
76. MONSTAT. *Labour Force Survey 2017*, Podgorica, 2 Apr. 2018, 1.
77. SY MNE 2021, 57.
78. GMNE (2018). Economic Reform Programme for Montenegro 2018–2020, Government of Montenegro. 14. https://www.gov.me/en/documents/f81d3b15-83a5-484f-9ece-d6e882aaf2b6 (22 Nov. 2022).
79. MONSTAT (2014). Poverty analysis in Montenegro in 2013, Podgorica, December 2014. p. 3. https://www.monstat.org/userfiles/file/analiza%20siromastva/2013/ENGLESKI-%20ANALIZA%20SIROMA%C5%A0TVA%20U%20CRNOJ%20GORI%20U%202013___.pdf (13 Jan. 2023).

parts of the country.'[80] 'The at-risk-of-poverty rate, i.e. share of population with an income below the national poverty threshold (€2,347 for a one-member household) dropped to 22.6% in 2020.' A positive trend has been recorded for poverty, social exclusion and material deprivation of children, 'but the rate (38.6%) remains high and worrying.' Poverty is increasing in the north with the at-risk-of poverty rate being four times higher than in the southern region.[81]

34. On 12 January 2012, the Government of Montenegro (GMNE) adopted the pre-accession economic programme (PEP),[82] a fiscal surveillance procedure, for the period of 2012–2014.

35. The GMNE adopted the Economic Reform Programme for the period of 2018–2020, as the most important document in the economic dialogue with the EC and the EU Member States, whose goal is sustainable and inclusive economic growth and improvement of the quality of life of citizens of Montenegro.[83]

36. The Economic Reform Programme for period 2022–2024 was adopted in January 2022. It describes how after a period of growth in the second half of the twenties, Montenegro experienced the deepest recession in Europe in 2020. The COVID-19 pandemic, coupled with restrictions that followed it, took a huge toll on the country that strongly depends on tourism for its economic well-being. GDP fell 15.3% and the public debt burden expanded. However, in 2021, the economy bounced back, with tourism leading the recovery. GDP again rose approximately 13.4%. In the short term, Montenegro has the potential to develop its touristic, energy, agricultural and information-communication sectors further.[84]

IV. Social and Cultural Characteristics

37. The commitment of the citizens of Montenegro to live in a state in which the basic values are multiculturalism, freedom, peace, tolerance, respect for human rights and liberties, democracy and the rule of law is expressed in the Preamble of the Constitution of Montenegro (paragraph 2). Montenegro is defined as 'the state

---

80. *Ibid.*, p. 5. The poverty rate in North region is almost three times higher than poverty rate in Southern region. Poverty rate in North region was 10.3% in 2013. In that region there is 25.0% of the total population of Montenegro, but there is also 30.1% of all the poor. Poverty rate in Central region is 10.3%, and in South 3.8%.
81. GMNE (2022d), p. 12. 'Achievement of SDG 1 requires effective interventions in the field of social policy and regional development policy.' For more information, *see also*: Golubovic, et al., (2022).
82. The PEP aims at preparing the EU candidate countries for the participation in the multilateral surveillance and economic policy coordination procedures currently in place in the EU as part of the Economic and Monetary Union. *See*: https://ec.europa.eu/economy_finance/international/enlargement/pre-accession_prog/pep/2014-pep-montenegro_en.pdf (22 Nov. 2022).
83. *See*: https://www.gov.me/en/article/montenegro-economic-reform-programme (20 Nov. 2022).
84. GMNE (2022c), pp. 1–2.

of social justice' (Article 1, paragraph 2). Economic, Social and Cultural Rights and Freedoms are defined under Chapter IV of the Constitution of Montenegro.[85]

38. Nevertheless, changes brought about by transition led to negative trends regarding exercise of equal rights (including the right to employment, right to development and other fundamental human rights), to social stratification and the emergence of the category of 'losers of transition'.[86] Some of the problems of social inequality, however, have deeper and systemic roots.[87] Protection of children and youth deserves special attention.[88]

39. The public sector has a dominant role in the organization and financing of the healthcare system. This represents a significant challenge in light of conditions such as a low GDP and considerable pressures on public spending. Goals of the reform of the health protection system[89] are 'integration of private and public sectors, and overcoming the problems of the healthcare system inherited from the past'.[90]

40. Historically, the cultural space of Montenegro has been developed under the influence of the different civilizations and cultures (Mediterranean, Central European, East European and Oriental). It could be said that multiculturalism is, 'an intrinsic feature of the cultural heritage and the life style, which, together with the rich natural heritage, makes one of the most significant comparative advantages. At the same time, cultural heritage management and preservation of cultural identity constitute significant challenges in the transition period'.[91]

41. Article 13 of the Constitution of Montenegro provides that Montenegrin is the language in official use[92] and Cyrillic and Latin alphabet are equal. Religious

---

85. It includes *inter alia*: Property rights (Art. 58), Entrepreneurship (Art. 59), Right to work (Art. 62), Prohibition of forced labour (Art. 63), Rights of the employed (Art. 64), Social council (Art. 65), Strike (Art. 66), Social insurance (Art. 67), Protection of the persons with disability (Art. 68), Health protection (Art. 69), Consumer protection (Art. 70), Family (Art. 72), Protection of mother and child (Art. 73), Rights of a child (Art. 74), Freedom of creation (Art. 76), Science, culture and arts (Art. 77), Minority rights (Arts 79–80), etc.
86. *See* generally MHLSW (2007). *See also* The Belgrade Centre for Human Rights (2006).
87. For example, the problems related to gender inequality and social exclusion of Roma. From the equity standpoint, refugees and displaced persons represent a particularly vulnerable category, whose difficult economic situation is frequently related to the issues of social marginalization. GMNE (2007C), 55.
88. *See* extensively GMNE (2008e).
89. Montenegro has joined an unique international process implementing papers of the World Health Organization 'Health for all in XXI Century' and '21 objectives for the 21st Century' by adopting Health policy in the Republic of Montenegro until 2020. *See* on these issues GMNE (2003b).
90. GMNE (2007C), 54.
91. *Ibid.*, 57. Transitional changes significantly influenced culture, first in terms of ownership and organizational restructuring of some types of cultural production and in particular informative activity. Private initiative is especially visible in publishing activity, literature, painting and theatre activities. GMNE (2008C), 77. For more details *see also* CE, Steering Committee for Culture (2004).
92. Serbian, Bosnian, Albanian and Croatian languages shall also be in official use (Art. 13, para. 3 of the Constitution).

communities are equal and free in the exercise of religious rites and religious affairs and they are separated from the state (Article 14 of the Constitution).

42. In accordance with Article 75 of the Constitution of Montenegro the right to education 'under same conditions is guaranteed and elementary education is obligatory and free of charge'.[93] However, a number of problems identified in the past were and still are the subject of the ongoing comprehensive education sector reform.[94] From the point of view of sustainable development, a special problem is the fact that environment and sustainable development were not properly and sufficiently included in the old curricula.[95]

V. Main Environmental Problems

43. Montenegro got its first Indicator-based State of the Environment Report, covering the period from 2009 to 2012.[96] The last report refers to the period 2017–2020.[97]

44. According to available data on the state of the environment in Montenegro[98] it could be concluded that 'the quality of environment has been preserved, which enables a comprehensive and dynamic sustainable development of Montenegro'.[99] However, it can be said that there are several systemic environmental problems[100] that deserve special attention in environmental policy and law.

93. At the same time, the autonomy of universities, high education and scientific institutions is guaranteed (Art. 75, para. 3).
94. 'Total budgetary spending on education in the past has not been adequate to cover the needs and ensure the development of modern education system'. At the same time, the expenditures for research and development were 'very low'. GMNE (2007C), 52.
95. GMNE (2007C), 52. On this subject *see*: GMNE (2007b).
96. *See*: EPA, Indicator-based State of the Environment Report of Montenegro, Environmental Protection Agency of Montenegro, Podgorica, 2013. https://epa.org.me/wp-content/uploads/2018/03/Izvjestaj-final-engl.pdf (5 Dec. 2022). For more information on monitoring, *see*: UNECE (2015), 69–84.
97. *See*: EPA (2021).
98. Although there are several strategic documents which contain data on state of the environment in Montenegro and which should be kept in mind, Information on the state of environment in Montenegro is the most important. Last Information that was 'Information published refers to the state of the environment for 2021. *See*: MESPU, EPA (2022a); Apart from that, Reports on the implementation of some international agreements are an important source of information about the state of the environment.
99. GMNE (2008C), 92.
100. It is necessary to keep in mind all events that happened during last decade of the twentieth century (sanctions of the international community, NATO bombing, etc.). The NATO reports that (during bombing of Yugoslavia from March to June 1999) rounds of DU ammunition were fired at one site in Montenegro in addition to ten sites in Serbia. Depleted Uranium in Kosovo, Post-Conflict environmental assessment, UNEP, 2001, 32, *See* more extensively, 70–78. On this subject *see also* Federal Ministry for Development, science and the environment (2000).

45. 'It is the overwhelming opinion that rapid destruction of natural resources is taking place,'[101] because of several reasons (uncontrolled and illegal construction, construction that is not in line with the natural surroundings, industry that produces pollution (harbours that are major polluters, ship construction sites, etc.), fishery sites (that have a negative effect on the coastal flora and fauna), pollution of the sea by ships that were not supposed to be granted access to the bay without certificates proving that they are environment-friendly, etc).

46. Key environmental problems include air and water pollution, land degradation, loss of biodiversity and ecosystems, especially in forest areas and in the coastal zone and poor waste management.[102]

47. 'Air quality is affected the most by industrial activity and emissions resulting from the combustion of fuels in large and small furnaces, and internal combustion engines. In addition to emissions, concentrations of air pollutants depend on the geographic and climatic characteristics. This is mostly reflected in the concentration of PM particles, which is the biggest problem for the air quality in Montenegro'.[103] During 2021, a slight improvement in air quality in comparison with 2020 was detected, especially in urban areas in the Northern and Central zone, while in the Southern zone, the air was of high quality during the whole monitoring period, with only five days of exceeding the medium daily concentration of PM10 particles.[104] In the period October–April, high-air pollution in Northern and Central zone, primarily by PM10 and PM2.5 particles, comes as a result of fossil fuels burning (coal and wood) used for heating purposes. Frequent temperature inversions prevent the emissions dispersion and cause the retention of pollutants that emanate from fossil fuel burning, traffic emissions, and similar sources, directly above the soil, resulting in high concentrations of polluting substances in the atmosphere. As for sulphur dioxide (SO_2) concentrations, the industrial region of Pljevlje experienced the improvement of the situation in 2021, while in other measure stations, the values of this pollutant were significantly lower than the threshold values.[105]

---

101. O. Komar & P. Gegaj (2015). *The Montenegro I Want*, Report on Post-2015 National Consultations in Montenegro, The United Nations System in Montenegro, Podgorica, 20.
102. In addition, low level of the energy efficiency should be added as one of environmental problems of Montenegro. UNECE (2007), 1, 7, 91. *See also* GMNE, NCSD (2011); EPA (2010a); EPA (2011a); EPA (2012b), UNECE (2015), 4, 101; ME (2019). GMNE (2022d), 97.
103. EPA (2013), p. 7. High concentrations and a large number of exceeded permitted daily mean concentrations were most pronounced during the heating season, mainly due to the use of solid fuels (coal and wood). The air quality assessed in terms of the concentration of SO_2, NO_2 and O_3 is within the prescribed threshold limit value, with no major concentration variations on an annual basis.
104. MESPU, EPA (2022b) p. 6.
105. *Ibid.*

48. Water resources (and particularly water resources management) is another potential area of concern. Most industrial and communal waste waters[106] are discharged into natural recipients without any treatment, the exception being certain industrial facilities and communal wastewaters in eleven municipalities.[107] Untreated waste waters from industries are also discharged into the public sewage systems. 'Of the total water used in the industry, there is 99.8% of water used in sector Electricity, gas and steam supply, air-conditioning, while there are 0.2% of water used in sectors Mining and Manufacturing'.[108] Of the total industrial waste water, there is 79.1% from Manufacturing sector, and the rest 20.9% is from Mining and Electricity, gas and steam supply, and air-conditioning supply. Untreated industrial and municipal waste waters present key sources of water pollution in Montenegro. It can be said that one of the most significant causes of pollution of surface and groundwater is inadequate state of infrastructure and inadequate collection and waste water treatment.[109] The quality of surface water resources is a matter of concern – out of twenty-eight riverine localities examined in 2021, only 1 (3.6%) had satisfying parameters in terms of quality and status of water.[110] The situation with ground waters is slightly more positive – out of forty-eight examined localities, only thirty satisfied the status conditions.

49. There are serious problems with the water distribution system. Compared with the resources available, water consumption levels are too high,[111] especially during the summer when water resources are limited.[112]

50. The coastal area of Montenegro is exposed to numerous and diverse pressures and different sources of pollution. This includes the impacts of pollution from untreated municipal wastewater (in municipalities where there are no modern devices for wastewater treatment), solid waste, shipbuilding/repair of ships, from ports and marinas (which are not sufficiently equipped to receive waste from vessels), from vessels and from industry.[113]

---

106. Approximately 60% of urban population discharges waste water in public sewage networks, or 37% of the total population of Montenegro, which is far from satisfactory. GMNE (2008C), 89. *See also* UNECE (2015), p. 121.
107. MESPU, EPA (2022a). p. 76.
108. MONSTAT (2017). Water use and protection against pollution in the industry 2016, Podgorica, 3 Nov. 2017. p. 1. https://www.monstat.org/userfiles/file/ziv%20sredina/2016/Water%20use%20and%20protection%20against%20pollution%20in%20the%20industry%202016.pdf (Apr. 12, 2018).
109. EPA (2012b), 44.
110. Information on the state of environment in Montenegro 2021, p. 76, *see*: https://epa.org.me/wp-content/uploads/2022/11/Informacija-o-stanju-%C5%BEivotne-sredine-jun-2022.pdf (19 Dec. 2022).
111. It should be emphasized that the average consumption in Montenegro is extremely high, twice that of Western Europe. GMNE (2008C), 104.
112. UNECE (2007), 9.
113. MESPU, EPA (2022), p. 136.

51. Montenegro is facing considerable problems with managing all types of waste. 'Most of the collected waste ends up in municipal landfills.'[114] The operational and financial effectiveness of waste sorting and processing is low in Montenegro because of a lack of adequate waste inputs.

52. 'The share of Montenegro's population covered by public waste collection services has been slightly increasing over the last 5 years, from 82 % in 2015 to 86 % in 2019, although there are differences within the country.'[115] Montenegro possesses several regional dumps of non-dangerous waste in the largest cities of Podgorica and Bar; recycling centres in four municipalities; and several other recycling facilities (vehicle waste, electrical and electronic waste and medical waste).[116]

53. The destruction of good-quality soil is caused by a number of human activities such as sand and gravel extraction, exploitation and processing of minerals (bauxite, coal, stone, zinc, lead), solid waste and tailings disposal, and production of brick and roof tiles from raw material collected by surface excavations in Tivatsko field, Berane, Kolašin and Pljevlja.[117]

54. Biodiversity, landscape values and coastal zones are pressed by intense development of tourism, urbanization, pollution from waste water and solid waste, etc. The principal reasons for the decline in biodiversity fall into a few broad categories: habitat degradation, illegal use of natural resources or poaching, and pollution.[118] There is no biodiversity inventory or monitoring, and therefore no red books on flora and fauna, an issue of concern that was already pointed out in the first Environmental Performance Review in 2002.[119]

---

114. EEA (2021), p. 4. *See also*: GMNE, NCSD (2011), 20.
115. *Ibid.*
116. Information on the state of environment in Montenegro 2021, p. 115, *see*: https://epa.org.me/wp-content/uploads/2022/11/Informacija-o-stanju-%C5%BEivotne-sredine-jun-2022.pdf (19 Dec. 2022).
117. According to performed monitoring, increased quantity of polluters (organic and non-organic) has been recorded in seven municipalities (Podgorica, Herceg Novi, Ulcinj, Bar, Pljevlja, Plužine). This is a result of inadequate discharge of communal waste although in most of the municipalities there is an influence of the traffic caused by emission of exhaust gases through increased quantity of both organic and non-organic polluters. GMNE (2008C), 93. 'When it comes to land degradation and devastation, the following problems are emphasized: taking over fertile land by unregulated construction, mostly in tourist areas on the coast, as well as in mountains that became popular for tourism and around big urban and industrial centres, and by planned expansion of city areas. Fertile land is also lost due to construction of roads and other infrastructural facilities. This unfavourable development is further on affected by covering of the land and its pollution from landfills of communal and industrial waste surrounding all settlements; by soil erosion; chemical degradation due to unregulated use of chemicals, lead and mineral oil pollution around roads, electrical substations, warehouses, etc. This is aggravated further by the deagrarianization and depopulation of large areas, which caused many plots of arable land to be abandoned and neglected.' GMNE, NCSD (2011), 10.
118. GMNE (2008c), 93. *See also* MSPE (2010b), 10–24. GMNE, NCSD (2011), 9.
119. UNECE (2007), 10.

55. Outside of protected zones, the pressures on the environment are diverse and serious. Forest ecosystems are today exposed to multiple pressures through uncontrolled and excessive exploitation, for instance, by hunting, fishing, tourism, harvesting of medicinal and aromatic plants, and agroforestry. Coastal areas are losing habitats and species due to eutrophication and problems caused by the rapid growth of the tourism industry. The unregulated – and sometimes illegal – fishing and hunting are causing significant damage to the animal populations. Pressure on biodiversity caused by pollution is centred on some hotspots such as gravel mining in the Moraca River, and waste water from Kombinat Aluminium Podgorica (KAP) and the Nikšić steelworks.[120]

56. 'From the long list of new and emerging challenges that are expected to put sustainable development on test globally, the following have been recognized as the most relevant ones for Montenegro: Climate change; Sustainable land use/ management of space and linkages with biodiversity conservation, water management and energy; Inefficient and harmful consumption and production patterns; Degradation of coastal zone and marine ecosystems; Further progress towards fulfilment of Millennium Development Goals, particularly regarding the position of vulnerable groups and regional development, since these are areas of particular interest in the national context; the unfolding of global financial crisis and recession and related negative impacts on the national economy.'[121]

57. The analysis shows that the ecological footprint in Montenegro for the period 2006–2015 has notable increase (+ 45%) in environmental footprint of Montenegro (2.7–3.9 gha per capita) compared to the almost constant biocapacity (2.70–2.67 gha per capita). 'Discrepancy between the ecological footprint and biocapacity of Montenegro indicates that demand for energy, fossil fuels and energy-intensive goods (i.e., carbon footprint component) accounts for about 45% of the footprint Montenegro, while forest ecosystems account for over 75% of the total biocapacity of the country'.[122]

§2. Basic Principles of Environmental Law

I. Definitions and Notions

58. In almost all basic environmental laws, important definitions and basic principles relevant to environmental protection have been established. Definition of the 'environment' is very broad. The Law on Environment (OJ MNE, Nos 52/16, 73/19) defines, for example, environment as space, i.e., natural environment, air, land,

120. *Ibid.*, 10.
121. GMNE (2011a), 9.
122. MSDT (2016c). p. 79. 'In 2015, the production from the biocapacity of the ecosystem represented 70% of the demand of population for renewable energy sources and services. Results also show that, during the observed period, the gap between the resources and services that Montenegro provides and resources that citizens of Montenegro use has increased, thus increasing the dependence from biocapacities imported from abroad.' *Ibid.*

water and sea, plant and animal world, phenomena and activities: climate, ionizing and non-energizing radiation, noise and vibration, and the environment created by man: cities and other settlements, cultural-historical heritage, infrastructure, industrial and other facilities (Article 2).[123]

II. Basic Principles

59. Several environmental laws contain basic principles in accordance with modern trends in the field of environmental policy.[124] Following environmental policy principles are mentioned in Article 5 of the Law on Environment:

– the principle of sustainable development;
– the integration principle;
– the principle of preservation of natural resources;
– the principle of cooperation;
– the polluter-pays principle;
– the principle of user pay;
– the obligatory insurance;
– the principle of preventive action;
– the principle of precaution;
– the principle of subsidiary responsibility;
– the principle of incentive measures;
– the principle of access to information and public participation; and
– the principle of the protection of the right to a healthy environment and access to justice.

60. The Law on Strategic Environmental Assessment (SEA) (OJ RM, No. 80/05, OJ MNE, Nos 73/10, 40/11, 59/11, 52/16) contains in Article 3 following basic principles of strategic assessment:

– the principle of sustainable development;
– the integrity principle;
– the principle of precaution;

123. Apart from that, the Law on Environment contains forty-three definitions, including following: environmental protection, quality of the environment, standard of the quality of environment, sustainable development, sustainable management, natural resources, natural goods, protected natural goods, public natural goods, ecosystem, biodiversity, landscape, environmental pollution, polluter, polluted substances, cadastre of polluters, capacity of the environment, waste, load, load to the environment, monitoring, emission, domino effect, imission, risk, accident, dangerous substances, degradation of environment, environmental information, environmental information in the possession of state administration bodies, administrative bodies or local government bodies, public, geological storage of carbon-dioxide.

124. *See also* Art. 3 (Main principles of water management) of the Law on Waters (Official Journal of RM, No. 27/07, Official Journal of MNE, Nos 32/11, 47/11, 48/15, 52/16, 55/16, 2/17), Art. 7 (Basic principles) of the Law on Waste Management (Official Journal of RM, No. 80/05), Arts 6–9 (Principles of the GMO Management) of the Law on Genetically Modified Organisms (Official Journal of MNE, No. 22/08, 40/11), etc.

– the principle of hierarchy and coordination; and
– the principle of public.

61. The Law on Spatial Development and Construction of Structure (OJ MNE, Nos 64/17, 44/18, 63/18, 11/19-corr, 82/20) spatial development contains in Article 3 following basic principles: integral approach in the planning process; spatial sustainability of development and quality of planning and construction; compliance of planning documents with confirmed international treaties, declarations and conventions; horizontal integration; vertical integrations; preventing or mitigating the effects of climate change; realization and protection of public and individual interests; reductions in seismic risk; transparency and prohibition of discrimination in accordance with special regulations.

62. It should be added that some strategic documents adopted by competent bodies also contain principles relevant to the environmental policy and law. National Strategy on Sustainable Development of Montenegro is, for example, based on the globally accepted principles of sustainable development, defined in the Rio Declaration and Agenda 21, Johannesburg Declaration and Implementation Plan, as well as on the principles of the UN Millennium Declaration (from which the Millennium Development Goals – MDGs – were derived).[125]

63. The Spatial plan of Montenegro (2008) should also be mentioned. It establishes two types of principles: global development principles and specific principles and objectives of the National Spatial Plan by sectors (Economic development: Industry and mining, Agriculture, forestry and fishery, Tourism, Maritime economy and traffic; Social development: Pedagogical educational activities, Science, Physical culture, Healthcare, Social and children care; Technical infrastructure systems: Traffic infrastructure, Telecommunication infrastructure, Postal network, Energy infrastructure, Hydro-technical infrastructure, Waste management; Specific aspects of spatial development; Protection against natural hazards and industrial damage, Seismic risks, Defence and protection; Development of settlement structure: Cultural heritage, Natural heritage).[126]

64. The Spatial Plan of Montenegro contains following general principles:

---

125. In the document titled, Visions of Sustainable Development of Montenegro, these principles are summarized as follows: Integration of environmental concerns into development policies; Internalization of environmental costs (i.e., conversion of external costs of environmental degradation into internal costs of polluters/users) through the implementation of polluter/user pays principles; participation of all the stakeholders in the decision-making, consultations, dialogue and partnerships; access to information and justice; equity among generations and equity within the same generation (including gender equality); the precautionary principle that is requirement to safeguard natural equilibrium in the absence of certainty; the principle of subsidiarity and interdependency between local and global levels; and access to services and financial resources necessary to meet basic needs. GMNE (2008b), 10–11.
126. GMNE (2008C), 110–137.

- Spatial development structures foster and improve the status of 'Montenegro – an ecological State' by ensuring a rational use of land and space and by the valorization of landscapes.
- The application of the principles of sustainable development, defined in the National Strategy of Sustainable Development, based on the Rio Declaration, Millennium Declaration and Johannesburg Plan for Implementation, is promoted consequently in all aspects concerning spatial development.
- All groups of the population are the target group for economic and social development; socially and spatially marginalized groups will be integrated.
- The spatial development contributes to the conservation and enhancement of the identity of its population, in particular regarding its cultural heritage.
- The widespread unplanned construction and misuse of land will be fought by the elaboration of more appropriate legal instruments and by improvement of control mechanisms and their enforcement.[127]

III. Constitutional Provisions

65. The Constitution of Montenegro (OJ MNE, Nos 01/07, 38/13) was adopted on 19 October 2007 and promulgated by the Constituent Assembly on 22 October 2007.[128] The Constitutional Law for the enforcement of the Constitution of Montenegro (OJ MNE, Nos 01/07, 9/08, 4/09, 71/09, 22/10) prescribed obligations of the Parliament concerning the legislative activities in the ensuing period.

66. According to Article 1, paragraph 2 of the Constitution, 'ecological' character of the State has been mentioned in the same way and together with other basic characteristics of the State like 'civil', 'democratic', 'state of social justice' and 'rule of law'.[129] In the preamble part of the Constitution it is proclaimed 'that the state is responsible for the preservation of nature, sound environment, sustainable and balanced development of all its regions and the establishment of social justice' (al. 4).[130]

---

127. *Ibid.*, 110.
128. According to the GMNE (2008b) 'the Constitution has been drawn up in full coordination with relevant international institutions, such as the Council of Europe, OSCE and particularly the Venetian Commission as a body of the European Commission for Democracy through Law. The Constitution has been compiled fully in compliance with the European standards' GMNE (2008b), 9. For historic review *see* Vujošević, M (2005).
129. In addition, Montenegro is defined as 'an independent and sovereign state, with the republican form of government' (Art. 1, para. 1).
130. Importance of this formulation becomes more obvious from the fact that this formulation is placed together with several other fundamental phrases expressed in the other four items of the Preamble, which read: 'Stemming from: The decision of the citizens of Montenegro to live in an independent and sovereign state of Montenegro, made in the referendum held on 21 May 2006; The commitment of the citizens of Montenegro to live in a state in which the basic values are freedom, peace, tolerance, respect for human rights and liberties, multiculturalism, democracy and the rule of law; The determination that, as free and equal citizens, persons belonging to nations and national minorities living in Montenegro: Montenegrins, Serbs, Bosnians, Albanians, Muslims, Croats and others,

67. Certainly, the most important provision of the Constitution can be considered the provision of Article 23 which reads: 'Everyone shall have the right to a healthy environment'. Everyone shall have the right to receive timely and full information about the status of the environment, to influence the decision-making regarding the issues of importance for the environment, and to legal protection of these rights. Everyone – the state in particular – shall be bound to preserve and improve the environment.[131]

68. In the part of the Constitution which refers to the economic, social and cultural rights, it is proclaimed that everyone is obliged to preserve the natural and cultural heritage of general interest and that the natural and cultural heritage is protected by the State (Article 78).

69. Besides the above-mentioned provisions, environment has also been mentioned in Articles 59 and 133 of the Constitution. Article 59 provides that freedom of entrepreneurship is guaranteed and it can be limited only if that is deemed necessary for the protection of citizens' health, environment, natural resources, cultural inheritance or security and defence of Montenegro. Article 133 of the Constitution stipulates that the state of emergency may be proclaimed in the territory or part of the territory of Montenegro in case of the 'technical-technological and environmental accidents and epidemics'; as well as in following cases: (1) big natural disasters; (2) greater disruption of public peace and order; and (3) violation or attempt to abolish the constitutional order.

we are loyal to the democratic and civil state of Montenegro; … The dedication to cooperation on equal footing with other nations and states and to the European and Euro-Atlantic integrations …'.

131. Old Constitution (Official Journal of RM, No. 48/92) contained following provisions: 'Montenegro is a democratic, social and ecological state' (Art. 1, para. 1); 'Everyone shall have the right to a healthy environment and shall be entitled to a timely and complete information on its state. Everyone has the duty to preserve and promote the environment' (Art. 19); 'The state shall protect environment. Freedom of earning and free entrepreneurship shall be restricted by environment protection' (Art. 65 'state and environment'). In relation to the provisions of the old Constitution the following comments should be kept in mind: 'Unfortunately, the constitutional declaration of the "ecological" state of Montenegro appears to have become just empty words.' UNDP (2005a), 19. At the same time in Strategic Master Plan for Waste Management on the Republic Level, Art. 1 of the Constitution (Montenegro is designated as a 'democratic, social and ecological state') had been interpreted in the following way: 'This must be understood as recognition and a directive for all-inclusive protection of environment and nature in the broadest sense and as a valuable constitutional rank.' EAR (2004), 29. The conclusion that can be made is 'that the Parliament's adoption of the Declaration of Montenegro as an Ecological State and the Constitutional enforcement of such a commitment, even though positively seen by the broad public and outside of Montenegro, mostly had a promotional, and only partly an encouraging and action-based character, both on internal and external levels. The act, however, was not the basis for adoption, or implementation of integral, clear and time-bound measures of economic, social, educational, scientific and any other policy that would lead to the reinforcement of this idea. That is why the twentieth anniversary of the adoption of the decision on Declaration of Montenegro as an Ecological State is an opportunity to consider the situation and make a choice'. GMNE, NCSD (2011), 17.

§3. HISTORICAL BACKGROUND OF ENVIRONMENTAL LAW

70. Natural resources and care for them were mentioned in some of the medieval written documents (end of the fifteenth century),[132] for example, in Hrisovulje of Ivan CrnojeviÇ the ruler of Zeta. Another example is description of fauna of LovÇen Mountain by BoliÇ in his documents from 1614, where he mentioned specific and medicinal herbs. First Montenegrin legal act, called 'Stega', was adopted in 1796 by the Assembly of the Montenegrin and highlander chiefs. In his book on Montenegro *Napoleon's Colonel, Viale de Somera*, published in Paris in 1820, a special chapter had been dedicated to Montenegrin forests, which he described as 'perfect vegetation', outlining the first known division according to altitude of habitats.[133]

71. Most important event for development of the legal culture in Montenegro that significantly influenced the development of law as a whole was the General Property Law for the Principality of Montenegro,[134] drafted by the famous European legal expert, Valtazar BogišiÇ, and adopted in 1888.[135]

72. A more comprehensive legal regulation of natural resources started in the early years of the twentieth century and was undertaken by the Ministry of Interior in 1904[136] with adoption of a number of legal acts, which regulated many aspects of utilization and protection of natural resources (Circulars on Forests, Hunting Law, Fishery Regulations, etc.).[137]

73. Between two world wars a number of legal acts were regulated in the Kingdom of Yugoslavia[138] – issues which would now be regarded as environmental, for

132. Montenegro was a sovereign country from the Middle Ages, during the governance of Zeta rulers Balšići and Crnojevići, before the period of Turkish rule. On Montenegrin history until the end of the nineteenth century *see*: Kokel Pol, (1998), 43–108, 193–480; For more details on general history of Montenegro *see:* Stivenson S. Frensis (2001). *See also* Jovanović, J., (2001).

133. MAFWM (2008b), 8.

134. The country was in the nineteenth century a semi-sovereign principality, gaining full independence in 1878. According to the provisions of Berlin Congress (1878), Montenegro was fully recognized as an independent state at an international level.

135. This Law represents codification and synthesis, and a classical work in the development of our legal tradition. From the point of view of its suitability, compactness and comprehensiveness, this Law outgrew and exceeded legal practice of that time, also outside the borders of Montenegro, and civilized world of that time was proud of it.

136. The first National Assembly of Montenegro was constituted on 31 Oct. 1906. For more details *see*: https://www.skupstina.me/me/skupstina/istorijat-parlamentarizma (5 Dec. 2022). For history of Governments of Montenegro *see*: D. Koprivica, & M. Kovačević (2010), 6–21 (10 May 2012).

137. The Circular (order) on forests which was adopted in 1904 is the first comprehensive state act on regulation of forest-related activities. A more comprehensive and more precise Circular on Forests was adopted in 1909 by Montenegrin Parliament, and it will remain applicable until 1918. MAFWM (2008b), 9.

138. After World War I, it became a part of the so-called first Yugoslavia (which was formed in 1918 as the Kingdom of Serbs, Croats and Slovenians). 'This act was conducted in an illegal manner when Petrović-Njegoš Dynasty was driven from a throne.' MAFWM (2006a), 20.

example Law on sea fishing (1922); Law on Forestry (1929); Regulations on drinking water quality (1931); Law on the use of hydro-energy (1931); Law on hunting (1931); Regulations on regulatory Plans (1932).

74. Development of environmental law in Montenegro was steadily progressing after World War II[139] and especially in the late 1960s and after the 1972 Stockholm Conference. In 1974 some provisions on environmental protection were introduced even in the new Constitution of the Socialist Federative Republic of Yugoslavia (for instance, Articles 87, 192, 193, etc.) as well as constitutions of the republics.[140]

75. Article 1 of the (1992) Constitution of Montenegro (OJ RM, No. 48/92) states that Montenegro is an 'ecological state' as well as 'democratic' and 'social'. In accordance with Article 19, everyone had the right to a healthy environment and shall be entitled to timely and complete information on its state. On the other hand, everyone has the duty to preserve and promote the environment. Besides the Constitution, principles of environmental protection were established by the first environmental framework law – Law on Environment – adopted in April 1996.[141] It established the obligation of the Republic to care about preservation of resources and improvement of the quality of environment, reducing the risk to peoples' life and health, removal and prevention of detrimental effects on environment with a view to providing for higher quality of living.

76. In the period from 2000 to 2008,[142] several key legal instruments in the field of environmental protection, Environmental Impact Assessment (EIA), Strategic

139. Between 1945 and 1991 Montenegro was one of the six constituent republics of the former Socialist Federal Republic of Yugoslavia, and had, especially after 1974, high competencies in different fields including environmental matters. Introduction of multiparty system and first parliamentary elections in 1990 brought significant progress on the political scene. In April 1991, Montenegro was declared a Republic and in 1992 Montenegro and Serbia jointly proclaimed the new Federal Republic of Yugoslavia (so-called Third Yugoslavia), which had some competencies in environmental field (mainly related to the international aspects).
140. In this period several environmental regulations had been adopted in Montenegro. For example: Law on Air Protection (Official Journal of SRM, No. 14/80) and its subsequent Regulations on admissible concentrations of harmful substances in the air (OJ SRM, Nos 4/82 and 8/82) set ambient air maximum allowable concentrations (MAC) for various sectors such as the metal and chemical industries, and energy production. Besides that, during the 1980s, spatial planning and development in Montenegro was based on a system of self-governing social planning. The Law on spatial planning and development was based on the system of social planning with complete planning of the economic and social development, primarily through the rules for planning development of activities in the space and protection of the public property. GMNE (2008C), 29. For more information on environmental regulations in some other member republics of the former Yugoslavia, See: Vukasović, V., Todić, D (2021). *Environmenal Law in Serbia*, Wolters Kluwer; Todić, D., Ignjatić, M., Vukasović, V (2022). *Environmental Law in Bosnia & Herzegovina*. Wolters Kluwer.
141. OJRM, No. 12/96. This Law laid down the main principles, such as polluter pays, environmental impact assessment, data transparency, and user pays, for environmental protection.
142. Belgrade charter was signed on 4 Feb. 2003 and proclaimed the State Union of Serbia and Montenegro. Finally, a referendum on sovereignty was held on 21 May 2006, on which the majority of voters voted in favour of independence. On the basis of it the Parliament of the Republic of Montenegro adopted the Decision on Proclamation of Independence of the Republic of Montenegro on 3 Jun. 2006. The new (2007) Constitution of Montenegro has been adopted, too.

Environmental Impact Assessment (SEIA) and integrated prevention and pollution control were adopted. Besides that, sectoral regulations have also been adopted (air, water, waste management, noise protection, nature protection, mining, fishing, sea, spatial development and constructions of structures, etc.).

77. It should be added that some strategic documents relevant for development of environmental policy and law have been adopted, too. In June 1998 development of the Spatial Plan for the area for a special purpose for the Coastal Zone of Montenegro was initiated.[143] Based on the Decision of the Parliament of the Republic of Montenegro (RM) from September 2001 (OJ RM, No. 45/01), elaboration of the Spatial Plan of Montenegro started in 2002 and was adopted in 2008.[144] National Biodiversity Strategy with Action Plan for 2016–2020 has been adopted.[145]

78. First Montenegro report on the State of the Environment was published in November 2000,[146] and in March 2003, the GMNE adopted the study – Directions of the development of Montenegro – ecological state, as a long-term development document of strategic character. In 2006, the final draft of the Montenegro National Sustainable Development Strategy based on the concept of sustainable development, identification of environmental problems, natural resources management and economic and social development was completed.[147] In December 2015, the GMNE adopted the National Strategy for Sustainable Development (NSSD) until 2030.[148] The United Nations Economic Commission for Europe (UNECE) published in 2007, the Second EPR of Montenegro which 'takes stock of the progress made by Montenegro in the management of its environment since the country was first reviewed in 2002, when the country was part of Yugoslavia'.[149] The third UNECE EPR report was released in 2015.[150]

79. The Government adopted in 2008 the National Programme for Integration of Montenegro into the EU (NPI) for the period of 2008–2012 establishing priorities in the different relevant fields, including adoption of the Acquis relevant to the environment.[151] The main characteristic of the country's evolving legal framework in all the areas pertinent to environment and sustainable development is its progressive harmonization with the EU acquis, as a part of the accession process. 'The EU

143. GMNE (2007D), 8. Adopted 2007. Apart from this, National Strategy for Integrated Management of Costal Zone has been prepared (2007).
144. GMNE (2008C), 16. In addition, several sectoral strategic documents were adopted. For example: Energy Development Strategy, Agriculture Strategy, Food Safety Strategy, National Forest Policy, Fishery Development Strategy, Traffic Development Strategy, Strategy on Tourism, Strategy for the Development of Small Hydropower Plants and so on.
145. *See*: https://www.gov.me/dokumenta/632aa485-839f-47a6-aa10-9b180aba31bc (6 Dec. 2022).
146. UNECE (2007), 20. Besides that, Millennium Development Goals Progress Report in Montenegro has been published 2005. UNDP (2005a).
147. GMNE (2007C), 20. First National Strategy for Sustainable Development had been adopted in April 2007, together with a corresponding Action Plan for the period of 2007–2012.
148. *See*: MSDT (2016b).
149. UNECE (2007), iii.
150. *See*: UNECE (2015).
151. *See* GMNE (2008b), 516–554.

integration is a strong driver for implementation of sustainable development concepts in Montenegro as European regulations and policies are seen as one of the most progressive ones worldwide, striving to achieve goals of competitive- and knowledge-based economy, equitable and inclusive society and preserved natural environments'.[152]

80. The National Strategy with Action Plan for transposition, implementation and enforcement of the EU acquis on Environment and Climate Change 2016–2020 is adopted (2016) in order to achieve gradual and complete transposition of the entire EU acquis for Chapter 27 – Environment and Climate Change into the legal system of Montenegro. In November 2013 based on the Screening Report presented by the EC, Council decided that Montenegro needs to fulfil the opening benchmark in order to open the negotiations with the EU for Chapter 27 (Environment and Climate Change).[153] In 2021, the Government adopted the Programme for the Accession of Montenegro to the European Union for the period 2021–2023 as a strategic document covering all thirty-three negotiation chapters.[154]

§4. Role of Government Institutions in the Shaping and Administration of Environmental Law and Policy

I. The Governmental Institutions and Their Competences

81. Responsibility of the Government[155] is prescribed by Article 100 of the Constitution and includes the following obligations of the Government: (1) manage internal and foreign policy of Montenegro; (2) enforce laws, other regulations and general acts; (3) adopt decrees, decisions and other acts for the enforcement of the laws; (4) sign international agreements; (5) propose the Development plan and Spatial plan of Montenegro; (6) propose the Budget and the Final Statement of the Budget; (7) propose the National Security Strategy and Defence Strategy; (8) decide on the recognition of states and establishment of diplomatic and consular relations with

152. GMNE (2011a), 3. 'In addition to intensive work on aligning national with the EU legislation, a large number of strategic documents were adopted during the past five years for areas and sectors significant for sustainable development, including *inter alia* spatial planning, energy, transport, waste and waste water management, climate change, biodiversity, forestry, agriculture, regional development and others. Furthermore, much has been done to improve policy and strategic frameworks for public participation, development of partnerships among stakeholders, application of principles of solidarity and equity (within current generation and among generations), equal access to resources and services (including health and education), poverty reduction and similar. As for the local level, a limited number of municipalities have developed local sustainable development strategies, environmental action plans and similar documents addressing sustainability issues.' *Ibid.*, 3.
153. MSDT (2016a).
154. For Ch. 27, *see*: GMNE (2021), pp. 123–131.
155. The current, 43rd Government of Montenegro, consists of President, 4 Vice presidents, 16 ministers to head their ministries and 2 minister without portfolio. *See* https://www.gov.me/en/organizational-units (20 Dec. 2022).

other states; (9) nominate ambassadors and heads of diplomatic missions of Montenegro abroad; and (10) perform other tasks stipulated by the Constitution or the law.[156] Pursuant to Article 111 of the Constitution, the duties of the civil service shall be discharged by the ministries and other administrative authorities. Particular public administration activities are performed by the local self-government bodies, institutions and legal entities, when these activities have been assigned to them.[157]

82. The main objectives and measures of the reform process for public administration and therefore for the state administration, defined by Administrative Reforms Strategy of Montenegro (2002–2009),[158] were, *inter alia*: delegation of significant amount of authorization to the lower system levels enabling higher flexibility of the entire administrative system; ensuring better quality in performing tasks assigned, introducing specific control mechanisms and encouraging efficient responsibility establishment on all levels; public services development and services for the final users – citizens and companies; modern information technology optimal usage; raising the quality level of legal regulations, conducting deregulation in specific over-regulated areas and strengthening monitoring function of the administrative system.[159]

Government at its session in April 2011 adopted the new Strategy for Public Administration Reform for the period 2011 to 2016 with the Framework Action Plan for its implementation. The goal of the Strategy of Public Administration Reform for 2011–2016 was: efficient, professional, and service-oriented public administration serving the needs of citizens and other social and business entities. Based on this primary goal the following specific objectives have been identified: strengthening of rule of law by strengthening legality and predictability of administrative procedures and decisions; improving efficiency and cost-effectiveness of public administration; improving the business environment while improving the quality of public services and reducing the administrative burden; raising the level of ethics in public administration; improving transparency and accountability of public administration; integration of Montenegro's public administration in the European Administrative Space.[160]

83. According to obligations and deadlines established by Administrative Reforms of Montenegro Strategy 2002–2009, new normative-legislative framework

156. On this subject *see* D. Koprivica & M. Kovačević (2010).
157. Individual duties of the civil service may be delegated to the local self-government or some other legal entity by the law, as well as by the regulation of the Government (Art. 112 of the Constitution).
158. *See*: GMNE (2003a) 14.
159. Good governance across a broad spectrum of policy, administrative and institutional dimensions is now widely recognized as a key factor in attracting investment, increasing growth and reducing poverty. 'Despite considerable legislative reform, enforcement remains limited. Vigorous efforts to implement the new legislative framework and build institutional capacity will be needed. An EBRD-World Bank Business Environment and Enterprise Performance Survey (BEEPS) shows that corruption continues to be a problem for doing business in Montenegro, as it is throughout Central and Eastern Europe.' WB (2007), 6–7.
160. GMNE (2011c), 9.

was created for changes in public administration work and functioning. The new Strategy of Public Administration Reform 2011–2016:

> defines the process of administrative reform as a long-term development process which entails continuing development and upgrading of the administrative system. This Strategy is not a point where one strategy ends and a completely new one begins but rather a continuity of the Government's reform efforts. The areas with further reform of public administration system are: public administration, local government and public services and other organizations exercising public authority.[161] The latest Strategy of Public Administration Reform (2022–2026) was adopted in December 2021.[162] It listed five main strategic reform goals: (1) to organize public administration as a service of civil needs; (2) to raise the quality of administrative services for citizens and economy; (3) to further professionalize the administrative sector; (4) to improve the transparency and openness of the administrative services; (5) to make citizens both the active participants in administrative procedures and primary beneficiary of administrative services.

84. Thus, legislative framework consists of Law on State Administration (OJ MNE, No.78/18), Law on Civil Servants and Government Employees (OJ MNE, Nos 2/2018, 34/2019, 8/2021),[163] The Law on salaries of employees in the public sector (OJ MNE, Nos 16/16, 83/16, 21/17, 42/17, 12/18, 39/18 - CC, 42/18, 34/19), Law on General Administrative Procedure (OJ MNE, Nos 56/14, 20/15, 14/16, 37/17),[164] Law on Inspection Control (OJ RM, No. 39/03, OJ MNE, Nos 76/09, 57/11, 18/14, 11/15), Law on the Protector of Human Rights and Freedoms (PHRF) of Montenegro (OJ MNE, Nos 42/11, 42/14), Decree on the Government of the RM (OJ MNE, Nos 80/08, 14/17), Rule of Procedures of the Government of the RM (OJ MNE, No. 3/12),[165] Decree on state administration organization and operations (OJ MNE, Nos 118/2020, 121/2020, 1/2021, 2/2021); Decree on General Secretariat (OJ MNE, Nos 47/09, 30/12, 3/13, 26/13, 39/15, 19/17,33/18, 39/18,62/18), etc.

161. *Ibid.*, 10.
162. *See*: https://www.gov.me/dokumenta/823842f4-2ffd-4a0d-936e-c1b00c669115 (12 Dec. 2022).
163. On the basis of this Law, the following by-laws have been enacted: Decree on the Manner and Procedure of Evaluation Trial Work in the Government Bodies (Official Journal of RM, No. 51/12), Decree on the Criteria for Evaluating Work of Managers in the Government Body (Official Journal of RM, No. 33/13), Decree on the type, the content, the method of preparation, the adoption and the methodology for the development of a programme of professional training of civil servants and employees (OJ MNE, No. 58/13), Decree on the Procedure for Testing Competencies for Performing Work of Government Employees (Official Journal of RM, No. 4/13), Code of Ethics for Government Employees and Civil Servants (Official Journal of RM, No. 20/12). *See*: http://www.uzk.co.me/images/stories/dokumenti/2013/Eticki%20kodeks2013.pdf (31 Mar. 2018).
164. Decree on Compensation of Costs in the Administrative Procedure (Official Journal of RM, No. 6/04) has been enacted for the implementation of this Law.
165. Rule of Procedures of the Government of Montenegro (Official Journal of MNE, No. 3/12) closely regulate organization, work manner and decision-making of the Government, commission work and other issues relevant for the Governmental work.

85. According to Article 1 of the Law on State Administration (OJ RM, No. 38/03 and OJ MNE, Nos 22/08, 42/11, 54/16), the state administration performs administrative affairs within the scope of rights and obligations of the RM.[166] The affairs of state administration shall be performed by the ministries[167] and other administrative authorities (state administration authorities).[168] Certain affairs of state administration may be performed, as public authorities, by local self-government authorities, institutions and other legal persons, when these affairs are delegated or entrusted to them (Article 3).

86. The affairs of state administration are proposing internal and foreign policy; conducting developmental policy; normative affairs;[169] enforcing laws and other regulations;[170] conducting administrative supervision; deciding on administrative procedures on rights and obligations of citizens and legal persons; proceeding in misdemeanour procedures; ensuring public interest affairs performance; other affairs of the state administration set forth by the law and other regulations (Article 11).

87. In order to implement this Law on State Administration, the following by-laws have been enacted: Decree on Organization and Manner of Work of the Public Administration (OJ MNE, Nos 5/12, 25/12, 61/12, 20/13, 17/14, 35/16, 73/16, 3/17, 19/17) and Decree on Job Groups, Criteria for Internal Organization and Systematization, Job Nomenclature and Draft Number of Executors in the Public Administration Bodies (OJ RM, No. 54/04).

88. Decree on the Government of the RM (OJ MNE, Nos 80/08, 14/17) regulates transparency (Article 4), position of members of the Government (Articles 5–7), work and government decision-making (Articles 8–16), acts of government (Articles 17–23), relationship with public administration (Article 24), relationship with the President of Montenegro and the Assembly (Articles 25–29), official identification card (Article 30), general secretariat and government offices (Article 31).

---

166. The state administration shall perform the affairs by virtue of the Constitution, the law and other regulations and general acts (Art. 2).
167. Ministries are established for one or more connected administrative domains, depending on the character, significance and scope of these affairs, and on the need for providing a development strategy (Art. 26).
168. The state administration authorities are established by the Government of the Republic of Montenegro (Art. 24).
169. Normative affairs comprise the preparation of draft texts and proposals of laws and other regulations and the passing of secondary legislation (Art. 14).
170. Enforcement of laws and other regulations comprises administrative procedures, issuing and executing decisions and other individual acts, undertaking of administrative measures and actions, monitoring of their execution, giving explanations, issuing professional instructions for work, as well as offering professional assistance (Art. 15).

II. The Actual Role of the Governmental Institutions

89. The main authorities competent for the protection of the environment in Montenegro are the Ministry for Ecology, Spatial Planning and Urbanism (MESPU) and Environmental Protection Agency (EPA).[171] According to Article 13 of the Decree on state administration organization and operations (OJ MNE, Nos 118/2020, 121/2020, 1/2021, 2/2021) the Ministry for Ecology, Spatial Planning and Urbanism[172] shall conduct administrative activities with regard to, *inter alia*: integrated spatial development and management, sustainable development, assistance to National Council for Sustainable Development (NCSD), strategic policy in the field of construction, energy efficiency in planning and construction, tourism, housing, integrated system of environmental protection; sustainable use of natural resources; EIA and SEA, integrated prevention and control of pollution, nature protection, air quality, climate change and ozone layer; noise and vibration, chemicals, protection from radiation and ionized radiation, non-ionized radiation, land protection, integrated coast management and integrated protection of sea, industrial pollution control and risk management, new and clean technologies, waste and water waste management, system of communal activities, regional water systems, Genetically Modified Organisms (GMO) in the area for which the Ministry is established, hydrographic affairs, environmental standards, monitoring of the state of environment, cooperation with international institutions and EU funds, cooperation with NGO, harmonization of the national legislation with EU legislation, administrative supervision in the area for which the Ministry is established and other activities delegated to its competency.

90. Pursuant to the same Decree the MESPU shares some of the environmentally important competencies with some other ministries:

- Ministry of Agriculture and Forestry and Water Management (Article 12).
- Ministry of Economic Development (Article 11).
- Ministry of Health (MH) (Article 10).
- Ministry of Capital Investment (Article 14).
- Ministry of the Interior (MI) (Article 4).
- Ministry of Justice, Human and Minority Rights (Article 3).
- Ministry of Finance, and Social Welfare (Article 6).
- Ministry of Foreign Affairs (Article 7).

171. Instead of the EPA, the Nature and Environment Protection Agency (NEPA) (OJ MNE, No. 19/27) was formed by the modifications of the Decree on Organization and Manner of Work of the Public Administration (March 2017).

172. Until November 2006, the Ministry of Environmental Protection and Physical Planning (MEPPP) mainly was in charge of environmental issues. The Sector for Environmental Protection within the Ministry was responsible for supervising the following public enterprises: The Centre for Ecotoxicological Research (CETI), responsible for air monitoring, monitoring of water, soil, waste, radiation and food; National Parks of Montenegro, responsible for the management of national parks. UNECE (2007), 15.

– Ministry of Education, Science, Culture and Sports (Article 9).
– Ministry of Public Administration, Digital Society and Media (Article 8), etc.

91. According to Article 65 of the Law on State Administration (OJ RMNE, No. 38/03, OJ MNE, Nos 22/08, 42/11, 54/16) the ministries shall cooperate and inform each other on their work, especially on issues of significance to their work. Ministries shall jointly implement activities, if the Government should decide so, or if it derives from their stipulated duty. A ministry may call for another ministry to involve it in the performance of specific affairs that are of interest to that ministry.[173]

92. In accordance with Article 21a of the Decree, Nature and Environmental Protection Agency (NEPA) shall perform administrative affairs related to the following: organization, planning and participation in the environmental monitoring in the field of air quality (including monitoring of airborne pollen), the content of dangerous and harmful substances in the soil, the state of the ecosystem of the coastal sea, the state of biodiversity, environmental noise, ionizing and non-ionizing radiation; reporting on the state of the environment, proposing measures to reduce the negative impact on the environment; issuing an act on nature protection requirements for the purpose of drawing up plans, bases and programmes; drafting of the Protection Study for the Designation of a Protected Natural Property; permits (Integrated Pollution Prevention and Control (IPPC), permits for the cross-border movement of waste, processing and/or removal of waste; permits for carrying out maintenance and/or repair activities, as well as exclusion from the use of products containing substances that damage the ozone layer and/or alternative substances; permits for monitoring fuel quality, air quality; permits for measuring emission of pollutants from polluting substances in the air, permits for import or export of ozone-depleting substances, alternative substances and products containing them; permits for measuring the noise level in the environment and to develop strategic noise maps; permits based on the law regulating the nature protection; permits for the production, circulation and use of sources of ionizing radiation and radioactive materials; permits for conducting professional activities of non-ionizing radiation protection, use of electromagnetic field sources, devices emitting optical radiation or containing optical radiation sources and ultrasound transmitting devices as well as a professional qualification permit for persons responsible for carrying out protection measures against non-ionizing radiation; permits for import and export of chemicals listed on the List of Classified Substances, permits for importing and exporting detergents, permits for performing hazardous chemicals activities, permits for importing and exporting biocidal products); conducting a SEA and EIA procedure; conducting a procedure for identifying immediate danger to environmental harm and responsibility for environmental damage; consent to waste management

173. In preparing and passing regulations, strategic, plans and analytical documents the ministries shall cooperate with each other respectively obtain the opinions of other interested ministries (Art. 66). When the performance of certain affairs is in the competence of two or more ministries, the execution of these affairs shall be administered by the ministry in whose purview lays the predominant part of affairs to be executed (Art. 67).

plans; opinions in the process of issuing licences; keeping records on production and waste management; estimation of radiological population load; drafting a quality monitoring programme for liquid fuels of petroleum origin; gathering data to update LRTAP and GHG Inventory; reporting to international organizations (the European Environment Agency, Programme for the Assessment and Control of Pollution in the Mediterranean Region (MEDPOL) United Nations Environment Programme (UNEP/MAP)); monitoring of the condition and vulnerability of habitat types, number and status of wild bird populations, as well as other indicator of species indicating and enabling the status of nature to be assessed; conducting the PIC procedure; the implementation of international treaties under the authority of this body; preparation of expert backgrounds for drafting regulations in the field of environmental protection; maintains an environmental information system; polluters cadastre; opinions on the planning documentations and the nature protection measures that these documents should contain; as well as other tasks assigned to it by the competent authority.

93. Several other institutions (administrations, secretariats, directorates, bureaus, agencies, etc.) have competencies relevant for achieving environmental policy and law goals. Administrations[174] are, *inter alia*: Maritime Safety Department and Port Authority of Montenegro (Article 40 of the Decree on Organization and Manner of Work of the Public Administration),[175] Administration for food security, veterinary and phytosanitary policy (Article 33),[176] Police Administration (Article 17),[177] Civil Aviation Agency,[178] Department of Revenues and Customs (Article 9),[179] Administration for the protection of cultural property of Montenegro (Article 29), Montenegro Transport Administration (Article 41),[180] Directorate for inspection affairs (Article 33),[181] Forest Administration (Article 34),[182] Water Administration (Article 20),[183] Secretariat for Legislation[184] (Article 43), etc.

174. Administrations are authorities which immediately implement the laws and other regulations and decide on rights and liabilities of private and legal persons and other entities (Art. 31 of the Law on State Administration).
175. 'The basic activity of the Maritime Safety Department is to ensure conditions for, and actual performance of, tasks stemming from the international obligations that the State has agreed to by signing conventions, agreements and protocols, related to the safety and security of navigation in the area of responsibility of the Contracting Government.' *See*: https://www.gov.me/ups (12 Dec. 2022).
176. https://www.gov.me/ubh (5 Dec. 2022).
177. https://www.gov.me/mup/policija (5 Dec. 2022).
178. https://www.caa.me/ (5 Dec. 2022).
179. https://www.gov.me/upravaprihoda (5 Dec. 2022).
180. https://www.gov.me/uzs (5 Dec. 2022).
181. https://www.gov.me/uip (8 Dec. 2022).
182. http://www.upravazasume.me/prva.php (12 Dec. 2022).
183. https://www.gov.me/uprava-za-vode (12 Dec. 2022).
184. https://www.gov.me/szz (12 Dec. 2022). Secretariats are authorities performing chiefly professional affairs with the potential to perform certain administrative and other affairs (Art. 31 of the Law on State Administration).

94. Relevant bureaus[185] are, *inter alia*: Statistical Office of Montenegro (MONSTAT) (Article 24),[186] Bureau for Metrology (Article 32),[187] HydroMeteorological and Seismological Bureau (Article 38),[188] etc.

95. Directorates[189] are, *inter alia*, Directorate for Public Works,[190] Agency for personal data protection and free information access,[191] and Directorate for Public Procurements (Article 31).[192]

96. Office for Sustainable Development (OSD) was established in 2005 in cooperation with the United Nations Development Programme (UNDP). The Office operates within the General Secretariat of the GMNE, outside ministries and deals with all pillars of sustainable development. Office is responsible directly to the Prime Minister, who also chaired the work of the Council.[193]

97. Other bodies and institutions that have competencies relevant for sustainable development include Public Enterprise National Parks;[194] Public Enterprise for Public Maritime Domain;[195] Centre for Eco-toxicological Research;[196] Public Health Institute;[197] Real Estate Administration;[198] and others.

98. At local-level municipal environmental offices are in charge of environmental policy.[199] Also, they are responsible for adoption and implementation of their own environmental protection programmes and plans in compliance with national

185. Bureaus are authorities performing professional and related administrative affairs by applying scientific methods and knowledge (Art. 32 of the Law on State Administration).
186. *See*: https://www.monstat.org/ (12 Dec. 2022).
187. *See*: https://metrologija.me/ (12 Dec. 2022).
188. Responsible for air quality monitoring, as well as surface and underground water quality monitoring. *See*: Hydrological and Meteorological Service of Montenegro (http://www.meteo.co.me/index.php, 12 Dec. 2022) and Montenegro Seismological Observatory (http://www.seismo.co.me/Home.htm, 12 Dec. 2022).
189. Directorates are authorities performing mainly professional and related administrative affairs in the field of economy (Art. 33 of the Law on State Administration).
190. *See*: http://www.djr.gov.me/en/directorate?alphabet=lat (31 Mar. 2018).
191. *See*: https://www.azlp.me/me/agencija (12 Dec. 2022).
192. *See*: https://ujn.gov.me/ (12 Dec. 2022).
193. The main objectives of the OSDare as follows: (1) secretariat of the NCSD; (2) monitoring of the National Strategy of Sustainable Development, and drafting of annual implementation reports (The *First annual Report was adopted in October 2008, while the second one is currently being prepared)*; (3) monitoring and drafting of annual reports on implementation of the Millennium development Goals in Montenegro; (4) coordination of actors from various fields of sustainable development in Montenegro; and (5) international cooperation with organizations and networks dealing with sustainable development issues and fostering of bilateral relations in these areas. *See*: https://www.gov.me/vlada-crne-gore/odrzivi-razvoj (12 Dec. 2022).
194. *See*: http://www.nparkovi.me/ (12 Dec. 2022).
195. *See*: https://www.morskodobro.me/ (12 Dec. 2022).
196. *See*: https://mne.ceti.me/ (12 Dec. 2022).
197. *See*: https://www.ijzcg.me/ (12 Dec. 2022).
198. *See*: https://www.gov.me/en/cadastre-and-state-property-administration (12 Dec. 2022).
199. However, their capacities for laws for implementation are very limited, explaining why compliance with environmental legislation is not at a satisfactory level. UNECE (2007), 18.

environmental strategic documents.[200] In accordance with the EIA, SEA and Industrial Emissions Law, they are responsible for implementation of procedures that are not of national importance, communal waste management and for implementation of protection measures against erosion and noise. 'Since 2007, the competences of local self-government authorities on environmental matters have increased. They were assigned new responsibilities and were also provided with a range of opportunities to improve environmental policy at the local level. However, local self-government authorities dealing with environmental issues are poorly staffed and trained, and face difficulties in coping with their environment-related responsibilities'.[201]

99. Generally, '... Montenegro has the basic organizational infrastructure to deal with environment and sustainable development issues, as well as to implement strategic documents in this field. However, it is not fully adequate and sufficient. In case of the main state body in charge of environment, both the name and jurisdictions of the institution have been changed very often in the past (only environment; environment and spatial planning; environment and tourism; sustainable development and tourism). Establishment of the Environment Protection Agency in 2008 is a positive development, even though a certain time is needed to strengthen human resources and other capacities'.[202] It will also be necessary to make additional changes in the distribution of authorities among government bodies and public institutions, in order to unite all areas of environmental protection under the same umbrella (water, forests, sea protection, etc.), and to improve organizational, professional and technical skills of municipal bodies.

100. 'In general, the institutions responsible for policy development, implementation and enforcement are in place, but need to be strengthened considerably. The

200. Pursuant to Art. 31 of the Law on Local Self-Government (Official Journal of RM, Nos 42/03, 28/04, 75/05, 13/06, Official Journal of MNE, Nos 88/09, 3/10, 38/12, 10/14) the Municipality, in accordance with the law and other regulations, shall adopt, *inter alia*, 'other act, in accordance with its jurisdiction' (point 6). In the Local Communities the citizens shall be entitled to decide and take part in decision-making processes in order to address local needs and interests in the following fields: organization of settlements, housing, consumer protection, culture, physical education, protection and improvement of environment, as well as in other spheres of life and work, in accordance with the municipal statute (Art. 95, para. 1).

201. UNECE (2015), p. xx.

202. GMNE, NCSD (2011), 11. 'The lack of clearly specified jurisdictions as well as adequate skills and readiness to execute a strict enforcement of laws is present in many areas, including: devastation of national parks; illegal construction; illegal waste disposal; changing the purpose of agricultural land; unsustainable forest logging; lack of law enforcement in terms of air, water and soil pollution, etc.' There is also a significant problem of inadequate organization and insufficient organizational, professional, technical and financial skills of local authorities to perform their obligations in the field of environmental protection and sustainable development. It should be kept in mind that the capacities of local authorities are basic conditions for successful management of numerous issues related to environment, spatial planning and sustainable development, all falling in their jurisdiction. There are also insufficient scientific and research technical capacities for many new and complex issues regarding environment, climate changes and sustainable development, which are necessary to provide a reliable support to institutions, organizations and bodies in Montenegro and to establish cooperation with scientific and research centres and programmes on the international level. *Ibid.*, 12.

administrative capacities and staffing levels for environmental issues are low, both at national and local level and across the entire environment and climate action sectors'.[203]

§5. Sources of Environmental Law

101. Depending on the subject, there are several different sources of environmental law. The broadest review of relevant legal and sub-legal acts and about the state of compatibility with EU legislation is given to the NPI adopted by the GMNE in 2008.[204]

I. International Sources of Environmental Law

102. The Constitution of Montenegro (OJ MNE, No. 1/2007) explicitly prescribes in Article 9 that ratified and published international agreements and generally accepted rules of international law make an integral part of the internal legal order, are supreme over the national legislation and are applied directly when they regulate relations in a way different from national legislation.[205] Article 17 of the Constitution also prescribes that rights and liberties shall be exercised on the basis of the Constitution and confirmed international agreements.[206]

103. The procedure for conclusion of international treaties is regulated by the Law on conclusion and implementation of international treaties, adopted by the Parliament on 16 December 2008 (OJ MNE, No. 77/2008).[207]

104. In the period after independence (2006) Montenegro has become a contracting party to a number of multilateral treaties concerning the environment.[208] It is party to the following environmental treaties ratified by the former Yugoslavia and the State Union of Serbia and Montenegro (S&M): Convention on Long-range Transboundary Air Pollution (CLRTAP) and the Protocol on Long-Term Financing of the Cooperative Programme for Monitoring and Evaluation of the Long-range

203. EC (2013b), p. 21.
204. *See*: GMNE (2008b), 516–554. For more information *see also* Todić, D. (2011a).
205. According to Art. 15 of the Constitution, Montenegro shall cooperate and develop friendly relations with other states, regional and international organizations, based on the principles and rules of international law.
206. In addition, international treaties, law and obligations have been mentioned in following articles of the Constitution: Arts 12, 56, 81, 82, 100, 118, 129, 145, 149, 152.
207. For historic review *see*: Milojević (2005), 1–5.
208. For an overview of international agreements and the situation for the period before independence, *see*: Todić (2002).

Transmission of Air Pollutants in Europe (EMEP),[209] Basel Convention on the Control of Transboundary Movements of Hazardous Wastes and their Disposal, Convention for the Protection of the Ozone Layer, Montreal Protocol on Substances that Deplete the Ozone Layer with all amendments, United National Framework Convention on Climate Change (UNFCCC), Convention on Biological Diversity, Convention on Wetlands of International Importance especially as Waterfowl Habitat (Ramsar Convention), Convention on International Trade in Endangered Species of Wild Fauna and Flora (CITES Convention) and the Cartagena Protocol, UN Convention on the Law of the Sea, International Convention relating to Intervention on the High Seas in Cases of Oil Pollution Casualties, Protocol of the International Convention relating to Intervention on the High Seas in Cases of Pollution by Substances other than Oil, 1973, as amended, Convention on the Prevention of Marine Pollution by Dumping of Wastes and Other Matter, 1972, as amended (LC (amended) 1972), International Convention for the Prevention of Pollution from Ships, 1973 (MARPOL, 1973) as modified by the Protocol of 1978 relating thereto, and its annexes from I to VI (MARPOL 73/78), etc.[210]

105. The country has also become a party to the following conventions: Vienna Convention on Civil Liability for Nuclear Damage, 1963; The Convention on Physical Protection of Nuclear Material, 1980; Convention on Early Notification of a Nuclear Accident, 1986; Convention on Assistance in the Case of Nuclear Accident or Radiology Emergency, Vienna, 26 September 1986; MAAE Technical Assistance Agreement signed in 1983.[211]

---

209. Aimed at full implementation of the CLRTAP, midterm priorities refer to the continuation of adoption of: the Protocol on the Long-range Transboundary Air Pollution concerning the Control of Emission of Nitrogen Oxides (NOx) or their Transboundary Fluxes Sofia, 1988; Law on the Ratification of the Protocol on the Long-range Transboundary Air Pollution concerning the Reduction of Sulphur Emissions (SO_2) by 30%, Helsinki, 1985; Law on the Ratification of the Protocol on the Long-range Transboundary Air Pollution concerning Heavy Metals, Aarhus, 1998; Law on the Ratification of the Protocol on the Long-range Transboundary Air Pollution concerning Persistent Organic Pollutants (POPs), Aarhus, 1998; Law on the Ratification of the Protocol on the Long-range Transboundary Air Pollution to Abate Acidification, Eutrophication and Ground-level Ozone, Gothenburg, 1999; Law on the Ratification of the Protocol on the Long-range Transboundary Air Pollution concerning the Control of Emissions of Volatile Organic Compounds, Geneva, 1991; Law on the Ratification of the Protocol on the Long-range Transboundary Air Pollution concerning Further Reduction of Sulphur Emissions, Oslo, 1994. GMNE (2008b), 524–525. In the meantime, Montenegro become party of the Protocol on the Long-range Transboundary Air Pollution concerning Heavy Metals, Aarhus, 1998, and Protocol on the Long-range Transboundary Air Pollution concerning Persistent Organic Pollutants (POPs), Aarhus, 1998.
210. For more details *see*: Akcioni plan za imlementacju preporuka Evropskog partnerstva (Action Plan for Implementation of Recommendation of the European Partnership), Vlada Republike Crne Gore, Podgorica, 2007. Aneks I – Lista medunarodnih konvencija i medunarodnih organizacija kojima je Republika Crna Gora pristupila (Annex I – List of international conventions and international organization to which Republic of Montenegro has acceded to).
211. In 2006 Montenegro notified officially the depositories (Russian Federation and United Kingdom) on acceptance of following international agreements: Treaty Banning Nuclear Weapon Tests in the Atmosphere, in Outer Space and Under Water of 5 Aug. 1963; Treaty on the Prohibition of the Emplacement of Nuclear Weapons and Other Weapons of Mass Destruction on the Sea-Bed and the Ocean Floor and in the Subsoil Thereof of 14 Feb. 1971; Treaty on Non-Proliferation of Nuclear Weapons, 1 Jul. 1968; Treaty on the Non-Proliferation of Nuclear Weapons, London, Moscow and

106. Montenegro ratified key environmental treaties like Kyoto Protocol (OJ RM, No. 17/07), UN Convention to Combat Desertification (UNCCD) in Those Countries Experiencing Serious Drought and/or Desertification, Particularly in Africa (OJ RM, No. 17/07), Convention for the Protection of the Marine Environment and the Coastal Region of the Mediterranean (Barcelona Convention), along with four supporting Protocols (OJ RM, No. 64/07),[212] Convention on the Conservation of European Wildlife and Natural Habitats (OJ MNE – International Treaties, No. 7/08), Convention on Transboundary Effects of the Industrial Accidents (OJ MNE – International Treaties, No. 9/08), Convention on the Conservation of Migratory Species of Wild Animals (Bonn Convention) (OJ MNE, No. 06/08), Agreement on the Conservation of Cetaceans Whales and Dolphins in the Black Sea, Mediterranean Sea and Contiguous Atlantic area (ACCOBAMS) (OJ MNE, No. 07/08),[213] Convention on Persistent Organic Pollutants (POPs) (OJ MNE – International Treaties, No. 16/2010),[214] Rotterdam Convention on the Prior Informed Consent Procedure for Certain Hazardous Chemicals and Pesticides in International Trade (PIC) (OJ MNE – International Treaties, No. 3/2011), International Convention on the Control of Harmful Anti-fouling Systems on Ships (OJ MNE – International Treaties, No. 7/2011) and Convention on International Hydrographic Organization (OJ MNE – International Treaties, No. 8/2013).

107. Montenegro also ratified Convention on the Protection and Use of Transboundary Watercourses and International Lakes – Helsinki Convention (OJ MNE – International Treaties, No. 1/2014), and Convention on the Law of Non-Navigational Uses of International Watercourses (OJ MNE – International Treaties, No. 6/2013). Montenegro signed Memorandum of Understanding (MoU) between the International Sava River Basin Commission and Montenegro at Belgrade on 9 December 2013,[215] and The Energy Charter Treaty (OJ MNE – International Treaties, No. 9/2015).

108. Montenegro membership in international organizations and activity in other institutional arrangements also influences the country's environmental policy and

Washington, 1 Jul. 1968; Treaty on the Prohibition of the Emplacement of Nuclear Weapons and Other Weapons of Mass Destruction on the Sea-Bed and the Ocean Floor and in the Subsoil Thereof, London, Moscow, Washington of 11 Feb. 1971; Treaty Banning Nuclear Weapon Tests in the Atmosphere, in Outer Space and Under Water, Moscow, of 5 Aug. 1963. GMNE (2008b), 328–329.

212. Protocol on Integrated Coastal Zone Management in the Mediterranean (OJ MNE – International Treaties, No. 16/2011) is, also, ratified.
213. And Amendments to the Agreement on the Conservation of Whales and Dolphins (CETACEA) in the Black Sea Mediterranean Sea and Contiguous Atlantic Area (OJ MNE – International Treaties, No. 4/2014).
214. And Amendments to the POPs (OJ MNE – International Treaties, Nos 4/2014), and 9/2017.
215. *See*: https://www.savacommission.org/UserDocsImages/05_documents_publications/basic_documen
ts/memo_of_understanding_between_isrbc_and_montenegro.pdf (12 Dec. 2022).

law. It is conducting numerous activities at the international level concerning cooperation with relevant international organizations in the environment field and on global and regional levels;[216] relevant for the process of accession of Montenegro to the EU; bilateral cooperation; projects financed from credit funds, etc.

109. During the past decade, the UN assistance was to a large degree extended through UNDP office in Montenegro and was referring to issues such as establishment and operation of the OSD, functioning and reform of NCSD as well as the preparation of NSDS. Assistance from UN DESA was received in improving the existing set of core indicators of sustainable development.[217]

II. National Sources of Environmental Law

110. The basic provisions establishing rules relating to the role of legal and sub-legal acts and procedures for their adoption are contained in the Constitution of Montenegro (OJ MNE, No. 1/2007). Article 16 of the Constitution prescribes that the law[218] regulates: (1) the manner of exercise of human rights and liberties when this is necessary for their exercise; (2) the manner of exercise of the special minority rights; (3) the manner of establishment, organization and competences of the authorities and procedure before those authorities, if so required for their operation; (4) the system of local self-government; and (5) other matters of interest for Montenegro. Article 147 prescribes that law and other regulations do not have retroactive effect.[219]

111. It is prescribed by Article 38 of the Law on State Administration (OJ RM, No. 38/2003, OJ MNE, Nos 22/2008, 42/2011) that by-laws,[220] orders[221] and

216. *See*: on this subject: GMNE (2008a), 31–36; MTEP (2008b). *See also* D. Todić, V. Vukasović, M. Ignjatić, A. Čavoški, (2011), D. Todić, (2011b), 54.
217. Furthermore, the UN system provided an essential support to Montenegro in the areas of: Climate change (strengthening capacities to address climate change and analyze its impacts on people, economy and environment); Biodiversity (building capacities for development and implementation of adequate policies, improving management of protected areas); Monitoring and reporting on the implementation of Millennium Development Goals and preparation of Human Development Reports; Preparation of strategic documents for regional development, public administration reform, etc. GMNE (2011a), 6.
218. Article 145 of the Constitution prescribes that the law has to be in conformity with the Constitution and confirmed international agreements. Other regulations have to be in conformity with the Constitution and the law. In addition, any individual legal act has to be in conformity with the law (Art. 148). Any person may file an initiative to start the procedure for the assessment of constitutionality and legality (Art. 150). For more details *see* Part V devoted to the Juridical Actions of Individuals.
219. If required so by the public interest established in the process of law adoption, individual provisions of the law may exceptionally have retroactive effect. Provision of the Criminal code may have retroactive effect only if it is more lenient for the perpetrator of a criminal offence (Art. 147, paras 2 and 3).
220. The by-laws shall elaborate specific provisions of laws and other regulations (Art. 39, para. 1).
221. The orders shall order or prohibit the proceeding in a specific situation that is of public significance (Art. 39, para. 2).

instructions[222] for the enforcement of laws and other regulations are adopted by the ministries. However, according to Article 40 of the same law, regulations of ministries may not establish rights and obligations for private and legal persons.

A. *Procedure of Adoption of Laws*

112. It is in competence of the Parliament of Montenegro, in accordance with Article 82 of the Constitution, to adopt laws and other regulations and general acts (decisions, conclusions, resolutions, declarations and recommendations). It is prescribed by Article 93 of the Constitution that the right to propose laws and other acts is granted to the Government and to members of the Parliament. The right to propose laws is also granted to 6,000 voters through the Member of the Parliament they authorized.[223]

113. Preparation of the acts and other materials for consideration in the session of the Government is regulated by Chapter VI of the Rules of Procedure of the Government (OJ MNE, Nos 3/2012, 31/15, 48/17):[224] Articles 32–49.

114. Proposition of the law, other regulations or general acts which the Government submits to Assembly are prepared in accordance with provisions of the Rules of Procedure of the Assembly (Article 37).[225] Proposition of the law, other regulation or general act which the Government adopts needs to be explained.[226]

115. According to Article 34, material for consideration and decision by the Government shall be submitted in the form of: (1) the proposition of the law, other regulation or general act which the Government submits to the Assembly; (2) the proposition of the law on: Budget, Budget of Montenegro and the final accounts of Montenegro; (3) the proposal of decrees, decisions and other general acts adopted by the Government; (4) the basis of proposals for international meetings in the country and abroad, and the basis of proposals concerning negotiations and conclusion of treaties with other countries and international organizations; (5) the proposals of the Government's opinion on the propositions of laws, other regulations or by-laws whose proponent is not the Government; (6) the preposition of the

222. The instructions shall prescribe the manner of work and performance of affairs of administrative authorities, as well as of local self-government authorities, institutions and other legal persons in performing delegated, respectively entrusted affairs (Art. 39, para. 3).
223. The proposal to call for the national referendum may be submitted by: twenty-five Members of the Parliament, the President of Montenegro, the Government or minimum 10% of the citizens with the right to vote (Art. 93, para. 3).
224. Upon entry into force these Rules shall supersede previous Rules of the Government of Montenegro (Official Journal of MNE, No. 48/09) (Art. 72).
225. *See*: 12 Dec. 2022).
226. With the proposition of the regulation, the proponent shall submit the text of provisions that are proposed to be changed or supplemented if it would lead to an amendment to the regulations (Art. 37 para. 3).

strategies, plans, programmes, contracts, reports, information, ratings, opinions and conclusions of the Government on certain issues; (7) the proposition of answers or opinions that the Government submits to the Constitutional Court of Montenegro, as well as the preposition on the measures for the implementation of decisions of the Constitutional Court of Montenegro; and (8) the preposition of the decisions and other rulings made by the Government.[227]

116. In accordance with the provisions of Article 33 in the process of drafting the laws and regulations, the proponent shall conduct an analysis of regulatory impact assessment (RIA)[228] in accordance with the regulations of the Ministry of Finance.[229] In addition to the proposition of law, the proponent shall submit a report on the public hearing, which was conducted in accordance with Government regulation. If public hearing has not been conducted the proponent shall, with the proposition of the law for which was not conducted a public hearing, provide reasons for why the public hearing was not conducted (Article 35, paragraph 2).[230]

117. The solutions from the proposition of law, other regulations and general acts, before submission to the Government, are coordinated with the attitudes of the Secretariat for Legislation and the ministries of which were previously obtained

227. The materials should as well include the propositions of evaluation and conclusions that the government should adopt. The preposition of conclusion contains precisely determined particular obligation, the holder and the deadline for the execution of the duties. With the preposition of the law, other regulations or legislation, which the Government proposes to the Assembly, the proponent submits to the Government a proposal for delegation of representatives of the Government who should participate in the Assembly and its working bodies (Art. 34 paras 2, 3).
228. '*The implementation of regulatory impact assessment (RIA),* i.e., a system controlling the quality of regulation, imposes the obligation on legislators to take a set of standardized questions before adoption and implementation of the regulation in question. Legislators will thus be obliged to explain what effects the regulation will have on the business setting, environment, social policy, etc. In order to institutionalize regulatory impact assessment and point out the significance of RIA institutional setting as the foundation for decision-making and quality regulations, the following activities must be initiated: identify the areas that resources and analysis would focus on; identify adequate methodology for *ex ante* and *ex post* assessment; conduct *ex post* assessment of the results achieved by implementation of regulation to test whether the desired outcomes defined in *ex ante* analysis have been achieved; organize training for drafters of legislation to develop their analytical and decision-making skills; identify clear criteria for the assessment of impact on the economy, environment, social status of specific population groups, as well as RIA procedures; provide support and a system of coordination for the sake of quality regulations that are acceptable to all the other institutions, easy to implement, and in line with Montenegro's policy of sustainable development.' GMNE (2011c), 27 and 28. *See also* Guidance on compilation of reports on the conducted regulatory impact assessment (OJ MNE, No. 9/12), and Guidance on instruments for harmonization of the regulations of Montenegro with the legal acquis of the European Union (OJ MNE, No. 15/12).
229. If the proponent considers that in the drafting of laws or regulations there should not be conducted RIA, he/she is obliged to give reasons in particular (Art. 33, para. 2).
230. In this case, as well as in the cases of considerations regarding other draft documents, strategic and planning documents for which was not conducted a public hearing, the Government may determine the proposition of the law or the other document as a draft document and demand on proponent to conduct a public hearing in accordance with the government regulations (Art. 35, para. 3).

opinions (Article 42).[231] With the proposition of law and other legislation, as well as strategic and planning documents, the proponent shall submit a report on executed intergovernmental consultations, which will contain the views, opinions and suggestions outlined in the consultation, unless the consultation has been carried out during the public hearing, what must be specifically stated in the statement of the public hearing (Article 40, paragraph 2).

118. Article 40 regulates that the proponent is required to, in addition to the proposed law, regulation or by-laws, provide the following: (1) opinion of the Secretariat for Legislation on the compliance of the proposed act with the Constitution and legal system of Montenegro; (2) a statement of compliance of the proposed act to the relevant EU regulations, with accompanying compliance table, drawn up in accordance with the instructions of the Ministry of Foreign Affairs and European Integration (MFAEI), and confirmed by the ministry;[232] (3) opinion of the Ministry of Justice to the proposed legislation regulating the proceedings in the courts, as well as the provisions of the proposed act regulating sanctions and the infringement procedure; (4) opinion of the Ministry of Interior Affairs on proposed legislation regulating the procedure of the authorities, the organization of state and local governments; (5) RIA form, prepared in accordance with the regulations of the Ministry of Finance, as well as the opinion of the Ministry of Finance on whether the position of the proponent is not required to perform RIA and whether the RIA conducted by the proponent is adequate; (6) The opinion of the MFAEI on the proposed law on ratification of a treaty, on the proposed basis for concluding international agreements and materials referred to in Article 39 of the Rules; and (7) the opinion of the staff of the Directorate for Human Resources on the proposed regulation on internal organization and systemization of the administrative authority's organs.[233]

119. The government has jurisdiction over the permanent working bodies of the Government (Committee on Political System, Internal and Foreign Policy Commission for economic policy and financial system), and among other things, on the consideration of the proposed laws, other regulations and general acts and other

231. If the proponent does not accept the views of the Secretariat for Legislation and Ministries included in their opinions, and if does not agree with them, the proposal of the act cannot be put on the agenda of the Commission while, at the request of the proponent, the disputable issues are not resolved with the competent vice president of the Government (Art. 42 para. 2).

232. With the proposition of the law, the proponent is required under para. 1, line 2 of this Article to deliver to the ministry the regulations of the European Union and ratified international treaties to which the act is complied with (Art. 40 para. 5).

233. With the preposition of the law, the proponent is required to submit the analysis of the situation and the occurrence of problems regulated by the law. With the proposition of the law and other legislation, as well as strategic and planning documents, the proponent shall submit a proposal thesis communications (Art. 40 paras 3 and 4). Besides this, the proponent is required to submit the proposition of the act and electronic data of a contact person to the ministries and other bodies referred to in para. 1 above.

materials (Articles 15 and 16). At the preparation committee meeting, chairperson of the Commission, on his/her own initiative or at the conclusion of the commission, may organize meetings with authorized representatives of the ministries, other administrative agencies, state authorities or other legal entities (Article 22). The Commission shall submit a report on the reviewed material to the Government, which includes: evaluation and findings and conclusions of the proposal (Article 23).

120. The proponent shall, within seven days after receiving the decision of the Government, prepare a regulation or other general act in a text adopted by the Government and submit it to the Secretariat for Legislation (Article 65, paragraph 1).[234]

121. The proponent shall, within seven days after receiving the decision of the Government, prepare the proposition of the law or other document in a text established by the Government (Article 67). Proposition of the law or other document with the form of regulations for the classification and declaration of conformity referred to in Article 40, paragraph 1, line 2 of the Rules, with a cover letter that the minister has made that statement in a text established by the Government, the proponent shall submit to the General Secretariat of the Government in two copies, to prepare the supporting documents for the Assembly, signed by the Prime Minister.[235]

122. According to the Rules of Procedure (of Parliament),[236] the procedure for enactment of laws is initiated by submission of proposed law which is submitted in the form in which the law should be enacted and must be accompanied by the rationale. The Speaker sends the proposed law to the Member of Parliament (MP), competent committees and Government (if the Government is not the proposer of that piece of legislation).[237] The deliberation of the proposed laws is conducted in three

234. The Secretary General of the Government submits the regulation or other general act, prepared in the manner specified in Art. 65 of the Rules, to the signature of the Prime Minister and after that to the Secretariat for Legislation, which takes care of its publication in Official Journal of MNE (Art. 66).
235. After signing, the supporting document shall be submitted to the petitioner who, along with the proposition of the law or other document, and in the form of classification of rules and a declaration of conformity referred to in Art. 40, para. 1, line 2 of the Rules, copies and submits it to the Assembly in the appropriate number of copies and in electronic form, and gives one copy also to the General Secretariat of the Government (Art. 67 para. 3).
236. The Rules of Procedure (of Parliament) regulates, *inter alia*, the procedures in Parliament (procedures in deliberating upon certain matters), organization and functioning of Parliament, the relations between Parliament and other state bodies, principles of organization of the Parliamentary Service, rights and duties of the MP, etc.
237. The proposed law may not be placed on the agenda of a sitting of Parliament prior to the expiration of the period of fifteen days from its delivery to members of Parliament, unless in case of shortened procedure for enactment of laws.

readings.[238] The adoption of other acts is carried out in accordance with the provisions of the Rules of Procedure on the procedure for adopting a law, although only a single debate is held.[239]

123. Article 146 of the Constitution prescribes that laws and other regulations have to be published prior to coming into effect,[240] and they can come into force no sooner than the eighth day from the day of publication.[241] The President of Montenegro proclaims the law within seven days from the day of adoption of the law (Article 94), that is, within three days if the law has been adopted under a speedy procedure or sends the law back to the Parliament for new decision-making process.[242]

124. The local self-government adopts regulations which are made public in the Official Journal. Provisions relating to the affairs performed by the Assembly of the local self-government are prescribed by Article 45 of the Law on Local Self-Government (OJ RM, Nos 42/03, 28/04, 75/05, 13/06, OJ MNE, Nos 88/09, 3/10, 38/12, 10/14, 57/14, 3/16)[243] and it includes, *inter alia*, adoption of regulations and other general acts, adoption of plans and programmes of municipal development, adoption of plans of ambient and urbanism, establishment of the level of municipal taxes and fees and charges. According to Article 57, the Mayor can, *inter alia*: propose regulations and other regulations to be adopted by the Assembly, as well as methods of solving specific issues from the jurisdiction of the Assembly; take care and be responsible for implementing laws, other regulations and general regulations, etc. The Mayor can, temporarily, pass regulations that fall within the jurisdiction of the Assembly if the Assembly is unable to hold a session or its work is made impossible, and when the failure to adopt such regulations could affect the lives of citizens or property of an important value (Article 58).[244]

---

238. The First reading includes the familiarization of the MP with the proposed law and its deliberation in the competent committees. Second reading includes the general debate on the proposed law. Third reading constitutes the debate of the proposed law in detail which entails debate on provisions in the proposed law, submitted but disputable amendments and stands, as well as proposals of committees.
239. On the reports submitted to the Parliament by individual bodies, the Parliament may adopt the assessment, stands and conclusions.
240. In accordance with Art. 2 of the Law on the promulgation of the regulations and other acts (Official Journal of RM, No. 5/08), laws and other regulations enacted by the competent authorities of Montenegro, as well as other acts when the law prescribes that or when competent organs decide that have to be published in the Official Journal of Montenegro. For other acts competent organs determine the manner of their publication.
241. Exceptionally, when the reasons for such action exist and have been established in the adoption procedure, law and other regulation may come into effect no sooner than the date of publication thereof (Art. 146, para. 2 of the Constitution of Montenegro).
242. The President of Montenegro shall proclaim the readopted law (Art. 94, para. 2).
243. Pursuant to the Art. 115, para. 2 of the Constitution 'municipality shall adopt the Statute and General Acts'.
244. The Mayor must submit to the Assembly this regulation for certification at the first session following its adoption. If the Assembly does not certify this regulation, or the Mayor fails to submit it, the adopted regulation shall cease to be valid on the date the session of the Assembly terminates (Art. 58, paras 2 and 3).

125. Over the past decade Montenegro has taken significant steps towards regulatory reform and development of the legal system. The legislative drafting now incorporates the assessment of fiscal impact and compliance with *Acquis communautaire*. Intensive legislative activity is expected over the coming years too with the aim to finalize the reforms and harmonies the national legislation with international standards, with *Acquis communautaire*. In this regard, nomotechnical rules have already been adopted together with the guidelines for harmonization of Montenegro's legislation with that of the EU.[245]

B. *The List of Basic Environmental Laws*

126. The list of Montenegrin environmental legislation includes significant number of sources of law that could be classified according to different criteria. Following are basic groups of regulations:

(1) Horizontal legislation: Law on Environment (OJ MNE, Nos 52/16, 73/19); Law on Strategic Impact Assessment (OJ RM, No. 80/05, OJ MNE, Nos 73/10, 40/11, 59/11, 52/16); Law on Environmental Impact Assessment (EIA) (OJ MNE, 75/18); Decree on the National List of Environmental Protection Indicators (OJ MNE, No. 19/13).
(2) Air Quality: Law on Air Protection (OJ MNE, Nos 25/10, 40/11, 43/15, 73/19).
(3) Soil Protection: Law on agricultural land (OJ RM, Nos 15/92, 59/92, 27/94, OJ MNE, Nos 73/10, 32/11); Law on Forests (OJ MNE, Nos 74/10, 47/15); Law on spatial development and construction of buildings (OJ MNE, Nos 64/17, 44/18, 63/18, 11/19-corr, 82/20); Law on geological research (OJ RM, Nos 28/93, 42/94, 26/2007, OJ MNE, No. 28/11); Law on mining (OJ MNE, Nos 65/08, 74/10).
(4) Water management: Law on Waters (OJ RM, No. 27/07, OJ MNE, Nos 32/11, 47/11-corr, 48/15, 52/16, 55/16, 2/17, 80/17, 84/18); Law on the financing of Water Management (OJ MNE 65/08, 74/10, 40/11, 82/20), Law on Municipal Wastewater Management (OJ MNE, No. 2/17); Law on hydrometeorological affairs (OJ RM, Nos 26/10, 30/12).
(5) Sea and Coastal Zone: Law on the Protection of the Marine Environment (OJ MNE 73/19), Law on marine protection from the pollution from vessels (OJ RM, Nos 20/11, 26/11, 27/14), Law on hydrographical activities (OJ RM, Nos 26/10, 30/12), Law on ports (OJ MNE, Nos 51/08, 27/13, 18/19), Law on

245. GMNE (2011c), 26. 'Comparative analysis of legislative drafting practices in Montenegro and European Union Member States shows that drafts and bills in Montenegro are generally prepared without previous analysis. Certain areas are manifestly over-regulated and therefore their respective regulations and administrative procedures must be either abandoned altogether or simplified.' *Ibid.*, 26. For removal of business barriers, as one of regulatory reform priorities, a broader spectrum of regulatory instruments must be applied, such as the *Guillotine of existing regulations*. Regulatory reform will repeal or amend in a single action the regulations that are obsolete and/or harmful to the economy. This process will include a compilation of a list of applicable laws of Montenegro as well as of all administrative procedures enforced in public administration. *Ibid.*, 27.

Yachts (OJ RM, No. 46/07, OJ MNE, Nos 73/10, 40/11, 42/15), Law on the Sea (OJ MNE, Nos 17/07, 6/08, 40/11); Law on Waters (OJ RM, No. 27/07, OJ MNE, Nos 32/11, 47/11, 48/15, 52/16, 55/16, 2/17, 80/17, 84/18).

(6) Waste management: Law on Waste Management (OJ MNE, Nos 64/11, 39/16), Law on Utility Activities (OJ MNE, Nos 55/16, 74/16), Law on Municipal Wastewater Management (OJ MNE, No. 2/17).

(7) Nature conservation: Law on nature protection (OJ MNE, Nos 54/16, 18/19); Law on National Parks (OJ MNE, Nos 28/14, 39/16), Law on Alien and Invasive Alien Species of Plants, Animals and Fungi (18/19), Decision on Placing under Protection Rare, Thinned, Endemic and Endangered Plant and Animal Species (OJ SRM, No. 76/06); Declaration on the Protection of River Tara (OJ RM, No. 78/04).

(8) Monuments and Landscape: Law on the protection of cultural property (OJ MNE, No. 49/10, 44/17, 18/19), Law Culture (OJ MNE, No. 49/08), Law on Museum Activities (OJ MNE, No. 49/10), Law on Archiving Activities (OJ MNE, No. 49/10).

(9) Industrial Pollution: Law on Industrial Emissions (OJ MNE 17/19).

(10) Chemicals: Law on Chemicals (OJ MNE, No. 51/17). Law on Biocidal Products (OJ MNE, No. 54/16).

(11) Energy efficiency: Law on energy (OJ MNE, Nos 5/16, 51/17, 82/20), Law on energy efficiency (OJ MNE, Nos 57/14, 3/15, 25/19).

(12) Genetically Modified Organisms: Law on Genetically Modified Organisms (OJ MNE, Nos 22/08, 40/11).

(13) Noise Protection: Law on Environmental Noise Protection (OJ MNE, Nos 28/11, 1/14, 2/18); Rulebook on Limit Values for the Environmental Noise Levels (OJ RM, No. 74/06).

(14) Radiation: Law on ionizing radiation protection and radiation safety (OJ MNE, Nos 56/09, 58/09, 40/11); Law on protection from non-ionizing radiation (OJ MNE, No. 35/13).

(15) Agriculture: Law on Agriculture and Rural Development (OJ MNE, Nos 56/09, 18/11, 40/11, 34/14, 1/15, 30/17, 51/17), Law on Plant Health Protection (OJ RM, Nos 28/06, 28/11), Law on means for plant protection (OJ MNE, Nos 51/08, 40/11, 18/14), Law on Agricultural Plant Seeds (OJ RM, No. 28/06, OJ MNE, Nos 73/10, 40/11, 61/11, 48/15), Law on Plant Variety Protection (OJ RM, Nos 48/07, 76/08, 73/10, 40/11), Law on Organic Agriculture (OJ RM, No. 56/13), Law on Veterinary Medicine (OJ MNE, Nos 30/12, 48/15, 52/16, 43/18), Law on Protection of Animal Welfare (OJ MNE, Nos 14/08, 40/11, 47/15), Law on Agricultural Land (OJ RM, Nos 15/92 and 59/92, OJ MNE, No. 32/11), Food Safety Law (OJ MNE, No. 57/15), Law on Animal Identification and Registration (OJ RM, No. 48/07, OJ MNE, No. 73/10), etc.

(16) Forestry: Law on Forests (OJ MNE, Nos 84/10, 40/11, 47/15); Law on Forest Trees Reproductive Material (OJ RM, No. 37/07); Law on Game and Hunting (OJ MNE, Nos 52/08, 40/11, 48/15).

(17) Fishery: Law on the Marine Fisheries and Mariculture (OJ MNE, Nos 56/2009, 47/15), Law on the Freshwater Fisheries (OJ MNE, Nos 11/07, 40/11).

(18) Minerals: Law on geological research (OJ RM, Nos 28/93, 42/94 and 26/2007, OJ MNE, No. 28/11), Law on mining (OJ MNE, Nos 65/08, 74/10), Law on *See* (OJ RM, Nos 17/07, 6/08, 40/11), Law on research and production of hydrocarbons (OJ MNE, Nos 41/10, 40/11, 62/13), Law on Concession (OJ MNE, Nos 8/09, 73/19).

(19) Zoning and land-use planning: Law on spatial development and construction of buildings (OJ MNE, Nos 64/17, 44/18, 63/18, 11/19-corr, 82/20), Spatial Plan of Montenegro (Official Journal RM, No. 45/01, OJ MNE, No. 24/08), Spatial plan of the Coastal Zone of Montenegro, etc.

(20) Climate: Law on the Protection from the Negative Impact of Climate Change (OJ MNE 73/19).

Part I. Pollution Control

Chapter 1. General Law

127. General framework for the protection of the environment is determined by several legal acts and strategic documents. Constitution of Montenegro (OJ MNE, No. 01/07)[246] has basic character, while the so-called horizontal regulations include several laws and by-laws. The new Law on Environment has been adopted in July 2016 and following two laws were adopted in 2005 and entered into force on 1 January 2008. These are Law on EIA and Law on Strategic Impact Assessment. In addition, Montenegro adopted Law on liability for environmental damage (2014)[247] and Law on infrastructure of spatial data (2017).

§1. Law on Environment

128. The Law on Environment (OJ MNE, Nos 52/16, 73/19)[248] contains the following fifteen parts: Part I – General Provisions (Articles 1–7), Part II – Subject of the environmental protection (Articles 8–14), Part III – Segments of the environment (Articles 15–21), Part IV – Protection from the impact of the environmental loading (Articles 22–28), Part V – Documents of the sustainable development and environmental protection (Articles 29–37), Part VI – Environmental protection instruments (Articles 38–45), Part VII – Special measures of the environmental protection (Articles 46–53), Part VIII – Monitoring of the state of the environment (Articles 54–59), Part IX – Reporting on the state of the environment (Articles 60–61), Part X – Information system of the environmental protection (Articles 62–65),[249] Part XI – Informing the public, participation of the public and the interested public and the right to legal protection in the environmental protection issues

246. For more details *see* chapter devoted to 'Basic Principles' (Constitutional provisions).
247. *See* the Chapter on Liability Questions.
248. On the day when this Law entered into force, the old Law on Environment (Official Journal of M, Nos 48/08, 40/10, 40/11, 27714), provisions of Art. 35, para. 2, Art. 36 and Arts 38 to 41 of the Law on the Environment (Official Journal of the RM, No. 12/96) and Art. 154 of the Law on Amendments to the Law, which provide for fines for offences (Official Journal of MNE, No. 40/11) have ceased to apply (Art. 94).
249. Important by law adopted on the basis of the Law on the Environment include the Rulebook on the method of keeping, maintenance, input methodology and data processing for the environmental protection information system (OJ MNE, No. 80/20).

(Articles 66–73), Part XII – Financing (Articles 74–79), Part XIII – Supervision (Articles 80–86), Part XIV – Penalties (Article 87), Part XV – Transitory and final provisions (Articles 88–95).

129. According to Article 1, the Law on Environment regulates the principles of environmental protection and sustainable development, instruments and measures of environmental protection and other issues of importance for the environment.[250]

130. Goals of environmental protection (subject of protection) have been defined by Article 4. Environmental protection is being implemented with the aim of: (1) the protection of life and health of people; (2) protection of plant and animal world, biological and landscape diversity, as well as the preservation of ecological sustainability; (3) protection and improvement of the quality of certain segments of the environment; (4) the protection of ozone layer and reduction of climate change; (5) the protection and renewal of cultural and aesthetic values of landscapes; (6) prevention and reduction of environmental pollution; (7) sustainable use of natural resources; (8) the rational use of energy and to encourage use of renewable energy sources; (9) removing the effects of environmental pollution; (10) improvements of disturbed natural balance to re-establish its regenerative abilities; (11) to achieve sustainable production and consumption; (12) reducing the use and substitution of chemicals, which can endanger the environment and human health; (13) sustainable use of natural resources; and (14) improving the state of the environment and ensuring a healthy environment.[251]

131. In accordance with Article 6 of the Law 'environmental protection and sustainable development are regulated by this Law and by special laws which regulate the individual segments of the environment'.[252]

132. Basic principles of environmental protection are the following: principle of sustainable development, principle of integrated approach to environmental protection, principle of conservation of natural resources, principle of cooperation, principle of polluter pays, principles of user pays, principle of compulsory insurance, principle of prevention, precautionary principle, principle of subsidiarity, principle

250. *The environment* is the space, i.e., the natural environment, the air, the soil, the water and the sea, the flora and fauna, phenomena and activities: climate, ionizing and non-ionizing radiation, noise and vibrations, as well as the environment created by man: cities and other settlements, cultural and historical heritage, infrastructural, industrial and other facilities (Art. 2).

251. All defined objectives are being achieved by applying the principles of environmental protection, instruments and measures of environmental protection prescribed by this Law and special regulations (Art. 4, para. 2).

252. These are: (1) EIA, SEA; (2) responsibility for environmental damage; (3) IPPC; (4) nature protection; (5) protection of air, water, sea, land, forests and geological resources; (6) chemicals; (7) waste management; (8) protection from negative impacts of climate change; (9) ionizing and non-ionizing radiation; and (10) noise protection.

of incentive measures, principle of access to information and public participation and principle of protection of the right to a healthy environment and access to justice (Article 5).[253]

133. Subjects of environmental protection are the following: the state authorities, local governments, legal and natural persons,[254] NGOs, citizens and associations of citizens[255] (Article 8). In accordance with the provision of Article 8 of the Law, subjects of environmental protection are obliged to, within their rights and obligations, provide control and prevention of all forms of pollution and degradation of the environment, and their reduction to the minimum possible extent. In addition, they are obliged to provide rehabilitation of parts or segments of the environment whose quality is disturbed due to pollution and other forms of degradation, providing the way to sustainable use of natural resources as the basic conditions for sustainable development.[256]

I. Documents of Sustainable Development and Environmental Protection

134. Pursuant to Article 29 of the Law, documents of sustainable development and environmental protection are national strategy of sustainable development;[257] climate change strategy; low-carbon development strategy; climate change adaptation plan; national plan for the fight against desertification; strategy for the protection of the marine environment; national strategy for integrated coastal management; local environmental protection plans;[258] strategies, plans and programmes that are made, or which are issued according to special regulations in certain areas for certain segments of the environment.

135. Two types of reports have to be prepared and adopted: report on the state of the environment (Article 60), and report on the state of the environment of the unit of local self-government (Article 61).

253. For more details *see* chapter devoted to 'Basic Principles' (Introduction, Ch. 2).
254. Natural and legal persons are obliged to carry out their activities in a manner that ensures the rational use of natural resources, internalization of the costs of environmental protection in the investment and production costs, the application of regulations, and/or undertaking measures to protect the environment in accordance with this Law and other regulations (Art. 10).
255. Non-governmental organizations participate in the preservation of the environment in accordance with their programmes and in the manner established by special regulations. The state encourages the participation of NGOs in process of decision-making and implementation activities which are of importance for environmental protection (Art. 14).
256. Besides that, subjects of environmental protection have obligation to cooperate and have mutual communication in accordance with special regulations (Art. 8, para. 3).
257. Strategy, for the period of fifteen years, has to be adopted by the Government (Art. 30, para. 6).
258. Measures from the National Environmental Protection Programme which relates to the area, in accordance with the local characteristics and specifics of areas for which the plan is being adopted, are elaborated by the Local plan of environmental protection (Art. 37, para. 1). Goals and tasks of importance for environmental protection and sustainable development at the local level are established by the Local plan (Art. 37, para. 2).

136. Several strategic documents, plans or programmes for specific areas of the environment have been adopted including National Strategy with Action Plan for Transposition, Implementation, and Enforcement of the EU Acquis on Environment and Climate Change 2016–2020, National Strategy on Sustainable Development 2030, National Biodiversity Strategy with the Action Plan 2016–2020, National Strategy for Integrated Coastal Zone Management, National Strategy on Climate Change until 2030, National Strategy for Air Quality Management with the Action Plan 2013–2016, National Strategy on Waste Management until 2030, National Plan on Waste Management 2015–2020, National Strategy on Chemical Management 2015–2018, National Action Plan for the Implementation of Stockholm Convention, National Action Plan for Fight Against Desertification, etc.

137. 'Implementation of some strategic documents, e.g. the Biodiversity Strategy, encounters difficulties because of poor financing. The development of strategies, plans and programmes at the local level faces significant delays'.[259]

II. Instruments of Environmental Protection

138. Article 38 of the Law on Environment defines instruments of environmental protection. These are (1) environmental quality standards; (2) the technical standards of environmental protection; (3) a SEA; (4) EIA; (5) eligibility assessment; (6) responsibility for environmental damage; (7) IPPC; (8) prevention and control of accidents involving dangerous substances; (9) spatial plans; (10) environmental management system (EMS);[260] (11) use of an eco-label; and (12) other instruments of environmental protection set forth in special regulations.[261]

139. According to Article 46 of the Law special environmental protection measures are taken to prevent, reduce or mitigate the negative impacts of long-term organic pollutants, asbestos, mercury and carbon-dioxide emissions into the environment.

III. Sustainable Development and Environmental Protection Documents

140. Chapter V of the Law is devoted to the sustainable development and environmental protection documents (Articles 29–37). It includes (1) National Strategy

259. UNECE (2015), xx.
260. The Government adopted in 1994 and revised in 1999 and 2003 the Quality System Implementation Strategy. It created incentives by allocating resources to enterprises willing to implement ISO 9000 and ISO 14000 standards voluntarily. UNECE (2007), 26.
261. According to Art. 31 strategic environmental assessment, environmental impact assessment, integrated prevention and pollution control, urban planning, environmental protection measures for projects for which obligation of the environmental impact assessment has not been prescribed have to be carried in accordance with special regulations.

for Sustainable Development of Montenegro;[262] (2) Climate Change Strategy; (3) Low-carbon development strategy; (4) Plan for adaptation to climate change; (5) National plan to combat desertification; (6) Strategy for protection of the marine environment; (7) National Strategy for Integrated Coastal Zone Management; (8) local environmental plans; (9) strategies, plans and programmes that are adopted, or which are adopted according to special regulations in certain areas for certain segments of the environment.

IV. Financing of Environmental Protection

141. Funds for the financing of environmental protection are provided from the state budget; budget of the local self-government; Fund for Environmental Protection; eco-tax, loans, donations and assistance; instruments, programmes and funds of the EU, the United Nations and international organizations; foreign investment intended to protect the environment; and other sources in accordance with special regulations (Article 75).

142. Units of local self-government may, within their rights and responsibilities, prescribe a fee for the protection and improvement of the environment in accordance with its needs and characteristics (Article 79).

V. Ecological Sign

143. The ecological sign is established for products intended for general consumption, with the exception of food products, agricultural and other products obtained in accordance with the regulations regulating organic production, beverage production, pharmaceutical products and medical equipment which, compared to similar products, are less polluting the environment during the production, placement, traffic, consumption and disposal or they are obtained by recycling of waste (Article 44).[263] An interested person shall submit an application for obtaining an eco-sign to the Agency (Article 45, paragraph 2).[264]

262. *See*: MSDT (2016b). For the first review of the implementation of the National Strategy for Sustainable Development by 2030, adopted by the Government in 2016, *See*:.
263. Conditions and procedures for obtaining the rights to the use of ecological sign, the amount of costs incurred by assigning the rights to the use of ecological sign, appearance and use of ecological sign for products, processes and services have to be prescribed by the Ministry (Art. 45, para. 4).
264. The right to use the ecological sign is given for a period of three years (Art. 45, para. 1). The right to use the ecological sign can be cancelled if a product, or service fails to meet the prescribed conditions (Art. 45, para. 4).

§2. Environmental Impact Assessment[265]

144. Law on Environmental Impact Assessment (OJ MNE, No. 75/18) consists of forty articles divided into six chapters: Chapter I – Basic Provisions (Articles 1–6), Chapter II – EIA Procedure (Articles 7), Chapter III – Notification, Recording and Publication of Data (Articles 8–31), Chapter IV – Supervision (Articles 32–34),[266] Chapter V – Penal Provisions (Articles 35–36) and Chapter VI – Transitional and Final Provisions (Articles 37–40).

I. Basic Provisions

145. According to Article 1, the law regulates the manner and procedure of the EIA for projects that might cause a significant impact on the environment, the creation end evaluation of the EIA study, and other issues of interest to the EIA. The EIA procedure encompasses the preparation of the EIA study, participation of stakeholders, study evaluation and its confirmation or denial, as well as the elaboration of significant environmental impacts on which the decision is based, taking into account the results of public consultations (Article 2).

146. EIA is conducted for assessment of direct and indirect impacts of planned projects on (1) population and human health, where it includes also risk assessment from great disasters and accidents; (2) biodiversity, in particular on protected plant, animal and fungi species, and their habitats; (3) soil, water, air, climate, and landscape; (4) material goods and cultural heritage; and their mutual interactions (Article 3).

---

265. According to the Old Law on the environment (1996) an obligatory preliminary assessment procedure of the environmental impact of the planned activity had been prescribed as one of the basic principles of environmental protection (Art. 7, para. 4). By Arts 17, 18, 19 and 20 of the same Law, the framework for the assessment procedure of the environmental impact of the planned activities had been prescribed. It was the obligation of the investor to carry out the preliminary assessment procedure before the commencement of the realization of the planned activities, which could pollute or create the risk of pollution of the environment. Apart from that, it had been prescribed that direct and indirect possible impacts on the environment in general should be identified in the assessment, as well as the specific segments of the environment. The Ministry was entitled to grant approvals to the EIA statements (Art. 19, para. 1). Besides, it had been prescribed that in spatial planning the capacity of the environment had to be taken into account and especially its sensitivity in specific areas, its relation to natural resources, cultural heritage, renewable and non-renewable natural resources etc (Art. 20, para. 1). The Sector for Environmental Protection issued 145 EIA permits in 2005 and 260 in 2006 for projects that require EIAs according to the currently implemented 1997 Regulation on Environmental Impact Assessment (Official Journal of RM, No. 14/1997), and the 1997 Guidelines on EIA Study Content (Official Journal of RM, No. 21/1997). UNECE (2007), 24.
266. Supervision over the implementation of this Law and regulations made on its basis, within the jurisdiction established by this Law, shall be carried out by the body of the state administration responsible for environmental protection and body of local government responsible for environmental protection. Inspection's supervision, within the jurisdiction of the state administration responsible for environmental protection, shall be carried out by ecological inspections in accordance with law (Art. 33).

147. The EIA's object is projects being planned or realized that might significantly impact human health or the environment from various fields of economic activities: industry, mining, energy, transport, tourism, agriculture, forestry, water management, communal services, and projects planned in protected natural areas or locations of immovable cultural good. Projects in the field of defence, natural disaster, and natural hazard consequences removal are exempted from the EIA obligation (Article 4).

148. Responsible authorities for the EIA are: (1) the administrative organ responsible for environmental affairs if project documentation and permits are confirmed and provided by state administration or (2) the municipal administrative organ responsible for environmental affairs if project documentation and permits are confirmed and provided by the municipal administration (Article 5).

II. The EIA Procedure

149. The projects that need obligatory EIA study are defined by the Government, while those projects that only optionally require the study would be decided by the responsible authority on a case-by-case basis (Article 8).

150. The project instigator must acquire the EIA consent decision. The law defines the project instigator as any domestic or foreign legal person, entrepreneur, or natural person that requests a permit or consent for a project (Article 6(3)). A project is defined as any construction, reconstruction, installation, removal, or dismantling of objects, facilities, or systems, repair, and other activities in nature or the natural environment including the exploitation of mineral resources (Article 6(4)).

151. Article 8 provides for the application of the Law on nature's protection if the EIA includes the procedure of project applicability assessment. Other project-related procedures provided for in other legislation should be coordinated with the EIA procedure. The study and consent decision form a part of the documentation requested for construction permit grant, object construction application and construction start consent.

152. The EIA encompasses: (1) a decision on the need for a study; (2) dfinition on the scope and contents of the study; (3) a consent decision (Article 9). On the request of the project instigator, state and local authorities are obliged to deliver the necessary data and results of EIA within fifteen days from the date of request receipt or inform the instigator of the lack of such information (Article 10).

153. The law prescribes the necessary supporting documentation to be provided with the request for a decision on the need for the study: (1) location description; (2) project description; (3) possible significant environmental impacts description; (4) information sources. The request might be sent via the e-government portal or e-mail (Article 11)

154. The law describes the following procedure upon the request receipt in Article 12. The responsible authority checks the documentation and in case it is incomplete informs the project instigator within three days to provide the missing documents. If the missing documents are not sent within the designated period, the request is denied.

155. Interested organs and organizations (stakeholders) have the right to be informed of the request and its contents by the responsible authority within three days to offer their opinion on the matter within five days (Article 13).

156. After the expiry of this period, the responsible authority is granted four days to decide on the request, taking into consideration the stakeholders' opinions, and to inform them and the public of its decision within three days of its adoption. If the decision is positive, elaborate on the reasons for the need to conduct a study, project description, location description, and possible significant environmental impact description. If the decision is negative, reasons shall be offered why the authority believes the study is not needed, and measures of protection for the mitigation of negative environmental impact shall be suggested. The decision can be appealed to the Ministry (Article 14).

157. The project instigator might additionally request a decision on the study's scope and contents (Article 15). Besides the usual documentation from previous articles, the instigator must deliver the report on the existing environmental segments for projects in areas of protected natural and cultural goods, tourism, and complex engineering projects. This report is prepared by the legal entity, entrepreneur, or natural person authorized for monitoring certain environmental segments under existing regulations.

158. The procedure for the decision on the study's scope and contents is similar to the previously described procedure. In Article 16 it is stated that the responsible authority checks the documentation and passes the complete request to the EIA Commission (*see* below Article 21). The EIA Commission is obliged to make a report suggesting the scope and contents of the study back to the authority. The stakeholders and the public, besides the project instigator, are informed about the Commission's report. The stakeholders and the public can offer their opinions on the matter, which the authority has to consider. Once the decision is adopted, it also might be appealed to the Ministry.

159. Article 17 regulates the procedure for the consent decision. The request for a consent decision should be delivered by the project instigator within two years of the decision on the need for the study, or a decision on the scope and contents of the study.

160. Article 18 defines the necessary elements of the study's contents. The study is an analysis and evaluation of the quality of certain environmental segments and their impact on a certain area, of mutual interaction between existing and planned activities, of direct and indirect environmental impacts and measures for prevention, restitution, mitigation, and remedy of harmful impacts on the environment and human health.

161. The study can be prepared by a legal person or an entrepreneur, registered in the Central register of economic entities for project and engineering activities, development of studies, and analysis. They must hire competent persons for certain environmental segments, depending on the project contents with at least VII-1 level of national education and at least five years of working experience, and designate the study coordinator. For projects realized in protected areas a person with level VII-1 in biology has to be hired additionally (Article 19)

162. Within five days of the request for a consent decision receipt, the responsible authority is obliged to organize a public discussion and invite all the stakeholders to offer their opinions. The project instigator and at least one person that participated in the study's development are obliged to attend a public hearing organized as a part of this discussion. Otherwise, the hearing has to be repeated. The discussion shall last at least thirty days (Article 20).

163. The EIA Commission is formed from the employees of the responsible authority and other competent persons with at least VII-1 level of education and five years of experience in environmental affairs. Persons that have participated in the study development or are employed with the project instigator or study developer cannot become members of the Commission (Article 21). The study, along with objections expressed during the public discussion is delivered to the Commission by the responsible authority within three days of the end of the discussion. The Commission can return the study to the project instigator twice at most to make necessary changes and additions. If the project instigator fails to respond, the Commission decides based on available documentation. After it finishes work, the Commission delivers the report with the study's evaluation and the proposal of the decision within twenty-five days to the responsible authority (Article 22). The project instigator covers all the costs of this procedure (Article 23).

164. The consent decision is made based on the EIA Commission's report and proposal. The decision contains an explanation of the reasons and a description of all project components and measures that the project instigator is obliged to perform to prevent, evade, remove or mitigate the harmful effects and to perform environmental monitoring. The decision is delivered to the project instigator within five days of the Commission's report and proposal receipt. The stakeholders must be informed on the web page of the responsible authority or the Government's electronic portal on the decision contents, the Commission's report, and the study. The environmental inspection should be informed within five days of the decision's adoption as well. The decision might be appealed to the Ministry (Article 24).

165. The decision will expire if the project instigator fails to acquire the construction permit or the consent for project implementation, or submit the application for the start of the construction within two years of the decision's receipt (Article 25).

166. The project instigator is obliged to implement measures prescribed in the study or the decision on the lack of need for a study. The environmental inspector supervises these measures and reports on its findings to the responsible authority (Article 26).[267]

III. Notification, Recording, and Publication of Data

167. Public notification, as part of the EIA procedure, is conducted through printed and electronic media accessible to the area impacted by a planned project. The stakeholders are notified through the mail, telefax, web page of the responsible authority, or e-mail. The data processing, exchange, and publication are conducted following regulations on the e-government, electronic identification, electronic signature, e-trade, and informational security (Article 28).

168. If the project might significantly impact another state's environment or another state requests to be notified of the project, the Ministry delivers to that state the data on the project and its possible impacts, the nature of the decision that might be adopted, and the period within which that state can express the intention to participate in the EIA procedure.[268] The Ministry informs the state that decided to participate in the decision contents and conditions, the justifications for the decision, and most important measure that the project instigator has to perform concerning harmful effects. The law offers the possibility of creating a common body (bilateral or multilateral) with interested states to conduct the process of notification and consultation (Article 29).

169. The responsible authority is responsible for recording the decisions on consent or denial. The evidence thus made is open to the public (Article 30).

170. The responsible authority is obliged to answer the stakeholder's request for insight into documentation related to the EIA procedure, except for documents designated with a proper level of confidentiality within fifteen days of the request's

267. If the project instigator is at the same time the responsible authority, its organizational unit responsible for the EIA procedure is prevented from participating in the project and must conduct the procedure objectively, to prevent a conflict of interests (Art. 27).

268. The International Court of Justice has debated the extent of the concept 'significant impact' in relation to the transboundary EIA procedures in several cases. It is important to note that the ICJ argues the risk from significant damage encompasses all activities that are inherently risky, regardles of them being of industrial or other nature (Vučić 2016b, 87). However, in one of its decisions, the ICJ argued the risk assessment depends also on the 'scope and context of the project' (Vučić 2016b, 90).

receipt. The confidentiality does not relate to documentation on the harmful emissions, risk of accidents, monitoring results, or inspectional supervision (Article 31).

IV. Supervision

171. The supervision over the implementation of this law and the by-laws adopted under it is in the purview of the Ministry for environmental affairs and the local administrative organ responsible for environmental affairs. Inspectional supervision is conducted by the environmental inspection in general or other responsible inspections where needed and following specific regulations (Article 32).

172. The environmental inspector controls whether the project instigator: (1) possesses the decision on the need for the study development; (2) or the consent decision; (3) realizes measures from the study; (4) or measures from the decision on the lack of need for the study (Article 33).

173. In the course of this process, the environmental inspector is authorized to perform administrative actions and measures prescribed by law and if it finds a breach of law, it is specifically authorized: (1) to order the project instigator to acquire the decision on the need for a study; (2) or the consent decision; (3) or to realize the measures from the study; (4) or measures contained in the decision on the lack of need for a study; (5) order the implementation of the environmental impact monitoring programme; (6) prohibit the project instigator from starting project activities until it acquires the consent decision or the decision on the lack of the need for a study.

V. Penal Provisions

174. The law provides for financial sanctions for a legal entity or a responsible person in this entity found to be in breach of certain provisions ranging from EUR 2,000 to EUR 40,000. Listed breaches include: (1) the start of the project implementation or the acquisition of consent for the performance of activities without the consent decision or a decision on the lack of need for a study; (2) failure to hire competent persons for certain environmental segments with a prescribed level of education and experience or to designate a coordinator; (3) failure to hire a competent person from biology field for the project realized in the protected area; (4) failure to perform measures prescribed in the EIA study that was given the consent or measures prescribed in the decision on the lack of need for a study (Article 35).

175. A responsible person in the central or local administrative organ can be penalized with a financial sanction ranging from EUR 500 to EUR 4,000 in the following cases: (1) if it fails to organize the public discussion or notify the public and stakeholders; (2) fails to publish the starting date of the public discussion; (3) fails to form the EIA Commission in a prescribed manner; (4) fails to publish consent or denial decision, report on the acceptance or denial of stakeholder and public opinions in the prescribed term; (5) fails to lead the register of decisions; (6) fails to enable the access to documentation.

VI. Other EIA Regulations

176. EIA by-laws include one Decree and three regulations. These are:

- The Decree on Projects Subject to an EIA (OJ RM, No. 20/2007, OJ MNE, Nos 47/13, 53/14).
- Rulebook on content of documentation that is submitted with the application for a decision on the need for environmental impact assessment (OJ RM, No. 14/07).
- Rulebook on content of documentation that is submitted with the application for a decision on the need for the determination of the scope and content of environmental impact assessment (OJ MNE, No. 19/19).
- Rulebook on the Contents of EIA Study[269] (OJ RM, No. 14/07).

177. The Decree on Projects Subject to an EIA defines the projects for which the EIA is mandatory and the projects for which EIA may be required. Projects for which the EIA is obligatory are established in List I of this Decree (Article 2, paragraph 1). Projects for which EIA may be required are prescribed in List II of this Decree (Article 2, paragraph 2).

178. As already mentioned, the Law on EIA was adopted at the end of 2005, and their implementation started on 1 January 2008. During the first eleven months of 2008, over seventy-five applications were processed for the decisions to be made with regard to the requirement of EIA, twenty out of which were completed in the first phase, that is, the decision was made that the EIA was not required. About thirty decisions were made to approve EIA for projects.[270]

§3. Strategic Environmental Assessment

179. Law on SEA (OJ RM, No. 80/05, OJ MNE, Nos 73/10, 40/11, 59/11, 52/16)[271] is the basic legal instrument which defines the complete SEA procedure,

269. According to Art. 2, EIA study includes the following elements: (1) general information; (2) description of location; (3) a description of the project; (4) a description of considered alternatives; (5) description of the segments of the environment; (6) a description of the possible significant influence of the project on the environment; (7) a description of the foresaw measures in order to prevent, reduce or remove significant harmful impact on the environment; (8) monitoring programme of impact on the environment; (9) a summary of information from items 2 to 7 of this paragraph; and (10) information about the possible difficulties encountered by the project developer in the process of data collection and documentation.

270. GMNE (2008a), 16.

271. The Law on Strategic Environmental Impact Assessment was adopted at the end of 2005, and their implementation commenced on 1 Jan. 2008 (Art. 29). During 2006 and 2007 an initial project on

from screening to approval, including public participation and transboundary effects. The Law has twenty-nine articles grouped in the following five chapters: Chapter I – Basic Provisions (Articles 1–7), Chapter II – Procedure of SEA (Articles 8–26), Chapter III – Supervision (Article 27),[272] Chapter IV – Penal Provisions (Article 28) and Chapter V – Final Provision (Article 29).

180. According to Article 3 of the Law the basic principles of SEA[273] are the principle of sustainable development, the principle of integration, the principle of precautions, the principle of hierarchy and coordination and the principle of the public.

181. SEA is carried out for plans or programmes when there is a possibility that their implementation challenges consequences for the environment (Article 5, paragraph 1). Plans and programmes are subject to a mandatory SEA if they are prepared for sectors specified in the Law[274] and/or if they set the framework for future development projects that are subject to the EIA and could affect protected areas, natural habitats and preservation of wildlife plant and animal species (Article 5, paragraph 2).[275]

182. In cases of minor modification to plans and programmes as well as for programmes and plans at local level, SEA may be required. This also refers to the plans and programmes which are not referred to in paragraph 2, item 1, indent 1 of this Article, but which provide a framework for the development of projects subject to EIAs.

I. SEA Procedure

183. The SEA procedure is composed of the following stages:

---

strengthening capacities for strategic assessment, supported by the World Bank, was conducted. Besides, multi-year (for the period 2007–2011) Strategy for Strengthening Capacities for Strategic Assessment was developed. GMNE (2008b), 501.

272. Supervision over the implementation of this Law, within the established jurisdiction, has to be carried out by the authority of state administration responsible for environmental protection and authority of local government responsible for environmental protection. Inspection's supervision has to be carried out by ecological inspections (Art. 27).

273. Strategic environmental assessment of the certain plans and programmes is assessment of the possible impact on the environment including human health which implies the preparation of the report on the status of the environment, implementation of the consultation procedure, taking into account the report and results of consultations in the decision-making procedure and procedure of enactment or adoption of certain plans and programmes, as well as providing information and data related to the adopted decisions (Art. 7, point 2).

274. These specified sectors are agriculture, forestry, fisheries, energy, industry including mining, transport, telecommunication, waste management, management of sea goods, water management, regional development, tourism, town and country planning or land use.

275. The provisions of this Law shall not apply to plans and programmes designated to the national defence purposes, plans of mitigation and elimination of consequences of natural disasters and financial and budget plans (Art. 5, para. 2, point 3).

– the decision on the need for a SEA;
– the definition of the content and scope of the report on SEA; and
– the decision on the approval of the report on SEA (Article 8, paragraph 2).

184. In accordance with Article 9 for the plans and programmes referred to in Article 5, paragraph 2, item 1 of this Law, the body responsible for preparing the plan shall make a decision on the preparation of a strategic assessment.[276]

185. The Law regulates what the proposal for a decision on the development of the strategic assessment referred to in Article 9 of this Law contains (Article 10).

186. Participation of interested bodies and organizations is defined by several provisions of the Law in several different phases of the procedure. Proposal for the decision has to be submitted to the competent authority for environmental protection, the body responsible for health and other interested bodies and organizations (Article 12). Deadline for submission of the opinion is fifteen days from the date of receipt of request (paragraph 2).

187. In accordance with Article 17 body responsible for the preparation of plans or programmes has the obligation to submit to interested agencies and organizations a report on the strategic assessment of Article 15 of this Law. Interested parties can submit their opinion within thirty days (Article 17, paragraph 2).

188. The competent planning authority has to inform the public and interested public about the method and deadlines for insight into the content of the report and submission of opinions, as well as about the time and venue of public debate (Article 19).

189. The competent planning authority shall compile the report on participation of authorities and organizations and the public concerned, which shall include all the opinions submitted in accordance with Article 17, paragraph 2 of this Law, as well as opinions submitted during the public insight and public debate on the strategic assessment report referred to in Article 19 of this Law (Article 20).

190. The body responsible for the preparation of the plan and programme decides on the choice of the head of the strategic report assessment (Article 16, paragraph 1). The principal author of the report referred to in paragraph 1 of this Article may be a domestic or foreign legal entity or an entrepreneur registered in the Central Register of Economic Entities or in an appropriate register of the competent body of the parent state of a foreign legal person or an entrepreneur, for

276. The decision referred to in para. 1 of this Article shall be adopted at the same time as the decision to draw up a plan and programme (para. 2).

the activities regarding planning documents, studies and environmental impact analysis (Article 16, paragraph 2).

191. Organ responsible for the preparation of plans or programmes has to submit to the competent authority for environmental protection the report on strategic assessment, with a report on the participation of interested bodies and organizations and on the public hearing referred to in Article 20, paragraph 1 of this Law (Article 21).

192. Assessment of the report has to be made on the basis of several criteria related to the plan and programme, state of the environment, variant solutions, assessment of impact on the environment, measures and the status of the environment, report on the strategic assessment and participation of interested bodies and organizations and the public (Article 21, paragraph 3). On the basis of the evaluation referred to in Article 21 of this Law, the organ responsible for environmental protection approves or rejects the request for giving consent to the report on strategic assessment (Article 22).[277]

II. 'Transboundary' Arrangements

193. Provisions for procedures in cases of potential transboundary effects follow the SEA Directive and the Convention on Environmental Impact Assessment in a Transboundary Context. The SEA procedure is the responsibility of the respective environmental authority (Article 23, paragraph 1).[278]

194. In July 2009, Parliament of Montenegro ratified the Protocol on SEA to the Convention on Environmental Impact Assessment in a Transboundary Context 2008 (OJ MNE – International Treaties, No. 2/09) and Montenegro is member of this Protocol since 2 November 2009.[279]

§4. Industrial Emissions

195. The Law on Industrial Emissions (OJ MNE, No. 17/19) regulates measures for prevention and control of emissions originating from industrial facilities, which

277. The deadline for deciding on the consent is thirty days from the date of the receipt of request from the competent authorities for the preparation of plan or programme (Art. 22, para. 2).
278. The strategic assessment report and results of participation of the authorities and organizations and the public concerned and other states in cases of transboundary impact make integral parts of the documentation basis of plans and programmes. The competent planning authority provides for the access to relevant data after the adoption of plans and programmes under the conditions set forth by the Law (Art. 24).
279. Http://treaties.un.org/Pages/ViewDetails.aspx?src=TREATY&mtdsg_no=XXVII-4-b&chapter=27 &lang=en (26 Apr. 2108).

might have negative impact on human health, environment, material goods and other issues of interest to the integrated pollution prevention and control (Article 1). The Law contains the following eleven chapters with total of seventy-six articles: Chapter I – General Provisions (Articles 1–6), Chapter II – Integrated Permit (Articles 6–31), Chapter III – Facilities for Combustion (Articles 32–42), Chapter IV Incineration and Co-Incineration (Articles 43–51),[280] Chapter V Organic Solvents (Articles 52–56), special chapters dedicated to Titanium Dioxide and Mercury (VI and VII), Chapter VIII – Reporting (Article 61), Chapter IX – Supervision (62–68), Chapter X – Penal Provisions (69–70 and finally Chapter XI – Transitional and Final Provisions (Articles 71–76).

196. The Law does not apply to facilities used for research, development, and examination of new products and procedures (Article 2). It lays down several principles well-known in the doctrine of the practice of international environmental law: (1) the precautionary principle; (2) the principle of integrated management of licenses; (3) the principle of sustainable development; (4) the principle of hierarchy in waste management; (5) the polluter pays principle; (6) access to information and public participation principle (Article 4).

I. Integrated Permit and Permit Granting Procedure

197. The permit is issued for both new and existing facilities and any changes in their operations.[281] The permit regulates measures for the protection of soil, air, and sea, depending on the facility's location and type of technological processes, under the Best Available Techniques (BAT), for ten years, by the administrative organ responsible for environmental protection (Article 7).

198. The operator is obliged to request the permit and to submit the information on itself, the facility (location, type of activity), types of materials and energy used in the facility, polluting substances that emanate from the facility's activities, sources of pollution, nature, and quantity of emissions that enter the soil, water and

280. Supervision over the implementation of this Law and regulations adopted on the basis of this Law has to be carried out by the organ of state administration responsible for environmental protection and authority of local government responsible for environmental protection. Inspection's supervision, within the jurisdiction of the state administration responsible for the environmental protection, performs ecological inspections (Art. 26).

281. The Law on Industrial emissions is still a relatively recent edition to Montenegrin legal system. Elsewhere in the neighbourhood, it was noted that these type of laws come across several obstacles for successful implementation: 'the lack of capacities on the part of the state administration competent for implementing these legislations, combined with difficulties sustained by the addressees (the operators of installations) in times of deep economic crisis, as well as the general technical complexity of the legislation and the lack of awareness of the addressees about their obligations, along with short periods for the implementation which do not take into account real possibilities of the adaptation of the national economy, all these factors taken together led to difficulties in reaching the aim of pollution prevention and control, and ultimately paralyze the application of the law' (*see* Vučić 2016b, 303 – discussing the Serbian law in the same field).

air from the facility, all the identified significant impacts on the environment, technologies used for emissions mitigation, BAT applied by the operator for pollution prevention or mitigation, measures performed for the abatement of waste, measures for energy efficiency, manner of emissions monitoring, alternative technologies, techniques and measures that the operator intends to perform (Article 8).

199. The operator must attach the following documentation with the permit request: (1) main facility project; (2) report on the last technical inspection; (3) monitoring plan, pollution, and other measured parameters during the trial operation; (4) waste management plan accepted by the responsible authority; (5) plan of energy efficiency measures; (6) plan on prevention from accidents accepted by the responsible authority; (7) greenhouse gasses emission permit; (8) plan for environmental protection measures after the closure of the facility; (9) the proof of right to exploit natural resources. In the case of a new facility, an environmental impact assessment accepted by the responsible authority is needed. In the case of an existing facility, the operator needs to submit a plan of measures for environmental protection and the programme of adaptation of the existing activities to the law's conditions (Article 9).

200. The administrative organ responsible for the granting procedure is obliged to publish received permit requests on its web-page and to inform on its contents the stakeholders among state authorities and the public. Interested stakeholders might forward their opinions on the request to the administrative organ (Article 12). The same applies to the draft permit issued by the organ (Article 13). If the stakeholders have some comments, the administrative organ can consult with the operator on them.

201. Permit requests, draft permits, and stakeholders' opinions shall then be forwarded to the Expert Commission, whose members are employees of the administrative organ, employees of other state institutions, or independent experts with necessary qualifications. Persons that participated in the elaboration of the environmental impact assessment for the permit request, the operator, and its employees and relatives are banned from membership in the Expert Commission (Article 14). The Commission analyses the documentation and issues a report with the evaluation of conditions contained in the draft permit (Article 15).

202. The administrative organ is obliged to issue a decision on the permit request in thirty days. If it finds that the facility does not fulfil the law's conditions, or the environmental standards contained in other legislation, or is inaccurate, it can deny the request and must inform of its decision the operator and the stakeholder within eight days. The decision can be appealed to the Ministry of Ecology, Spatial Planning, and Urbanism (Article 16).

203. The permit contains several elements: (1) Threshold values of polluting substances; (2) Measures for the protection of soil and groundwater; (3) Measures for waste management; (4) Monitoring modes; (5) Measures for transboundary pollution mitigation; (6) extraordinary measures needed in case of accidents, stoppages, discharges, breaks and discontinuations of activities and manner of facility's removal once it ceases the activities (Article 17).

204. Threshold emission values in normal conditions of a facility's operation are assessed under the BAT. The operator is obliged to measure emissions and to report on them yearly to the administrative organ (Article 19). In case of disproportionate costs for operators concerning the purpose of environmental protection, the administrative organ can, with the authorization of the expert commission, assess higher threshold values than those assessed under BAT. These costs must be due to the geographical location or environmental conditions of the facility; the facility's technical characteristics. These higher thresholds must not cause significant environmental pollution (Article 20). Threshold emission values for greenhouse gasses are assessed under the procedures of the Law on the Protection from Negative Impact of Climate Change in December 2019 (OJ MNE 73/19) (Article 21).

205. Operators are obliged generally to perform all necessary measures for the prevention of environmental pollution; apply the BAT; refrain from causing significant environmental pollution; minimize or if possible eliminate waste generation; re-use, recycle, treat or dispose of generated waste to minimize or prevent environmental impact; efficiently use energy; perform measures for accident prevention (Article 22). After the grant of the permit, the operator is specifically obliged to inform the administrative organ of the emission monitoring data; enable the inspection's control; promptly inform the administrative organ of any extraordinary event that significantly impacts the environment (Article 23). In the case of an accident with a significant environmental impact, the operator is obliged to promptly inform the administrative organ and the responsible inspection; promptly undertake measures for environmental impact mitigation and further possible accident prevention (Article 24). After the facility ceases operation, the operator is obliged to assess soil and groundwater by the dangerous substances generated during the operation. If the operation caused significant pollution the operator is obliged to promptly perform measures of environmental restitution, as technically feasible, and to report these measures to the administrative organ (Article 29).

206. The permit is regularly reviewed and revised every five years. The administrative organ can further ex officio review and revise the permit due to pollution caused by the facility's operation; possible harm to the environment or human health; new developments in BAT that enable significant emission reductions; introduction of new techniques in the facility's operation; revisions in environmental legislation (Article 26). The permit can be extended on the operator's request under conditions analogous to the issuance of the original permit (Article 27). The permit expires on the operator's request; after twelve months of the day of the permit grant if the operator does not start the activities; if the operator ceases to fulfil any of the conditions set in law; if the administrative organ finds that the permit grant was based on inaccurate or falsified data; if the operator fails to perform monitoring and data provision; on the notice of the responsible inspection to the administrative organ that the operator fails to perform the measures requested by the inspection; in case of operator's bankruptcy or liquidation, if no other operator is continuing with the activity or the continuing operator does not fulfil the conditions from the permit (Article 28).[282]

207. The exchange of information on the transboundary impact is a necessary step in the permit grant procedure if the facility's operation might negatively impact another state's environment or the other state request such exchange. The Ministry of Ecology, Spatial Planning and Urbanism is responsible for providing information to the other state on the permit request, the administrative organ responsible for permit grants, draft permits, the outcome of the public participation process, decision on the permit request, and the contents of the permit itself. The procedure of information exchange is conducted per ratified treaties based on reciprocity (Article 31).

II. Combustion Facilities

208. The law regulates the issue of combustion facilities which are defined as technical devices for fuel combustions with the aim of energy production (Article 5(23)). It differentiates between medium and large combustion facilities depending on the nominal input power (more or less than 50 MW), regardless of the type of fuel used. It also differentiates between medium or large gas turbines depending on the nominal input power (more or less than 50 MW).

209. Facilities excluded from the purview of this Article are (1) facilities for waste incineration and co-incineration (regulated separately in the Articles 43–51); (2) internal combustion motors installed in non-road bound mechanization; (3) combustion facilities at agricultural farms with total input power equal or less than 5 MW if they use exclusively non-treated poultry fertilizer as fuel; (4) combustion facilities that use refinery fuels, alone or in combination with other fuels for the production of energy in the framework of mineral oil and gas refineries; (5) facilities that use combustion products for direct heating, drying or other method of product or material treatment; (6) combustion facilities that use gas products of combustion for direct gas heating of closed spaces to improve working conditions; (7) facilities for eventual combustion constructed for purification of gas wastes by combustion, if they do not operate as a separate combustion facility; (8) facilities for the renewal of catalysts from the process of catalytic cracking; (9) facilties for the extrication of sulfur from the hydrogen sulfide; (10) reactors used in chemical industry; (11) coke coal battery furnaces; (12) Kauper heaters; (13) crematoria; (14) technical devices used as propulsion vehicles for automobiles, sailing crafts or aircrafts; (15) turbines, gas or diesel engines used in sea platforms; (16) utility boilers as part of

282. All the granted permits are inscribed in the public register managed by the administrative organ (Art. 30). For a list of decisions made by the EPA, *see*: https://epa.org.me/wp-content/uploads/2019/01/dozvole_IPPC_sajt.pdf (10 Jan. 2023).

facilities for wood pulp production; (17) facilities that use solid or liquid waste for fuel, except radioactive waste, or waste containing halogen organic compounds or heavy metals (Article 32).

210. The law obliges the operators of combustion facilities to install shafts,[283] with one or more pipes, setting their height in a way that protects human health and the environment.

211. Threshold emission values of combustion facilities shall be assessed based on input thermal power and type of fuel used, except for medium facilities that are specially regulated by legislation on air protection. Threshold emission values, the manner of assessment of values for facilities that use multiple types of fuel, rates of desulfurization, and the manner of emission measurement shall be more closely regulated by the Government (Article 33).

212. The law prescribes certain rules on the accumulation of thermal power input. If one or more separate combustion facilities discharge gas wastes through a common shaft, for the purposes of the law they are treated as one facility, with the total input power being a sum of their separate input powers. Even if two separate facilities do not discharge gas through a common shaft, the administrative organ can treat them as one unit if they are constructed and installed in a way that enables technically and economically the common usage of the shaft. Individual facilities with total input power of less than 15 MW are not taken into consideration in this process. The threshold emission values of these facilities are assessed based on the sum of their input powers (Article 34).

213. The law provides for certain exceptions to the general rule concerning threshold emission values. These limits can be exceeded for sulphur dioxide in case of supply shortages of fuel with low sulfur content, in the maximum period of six months, with the authorization of the administrative organ responsible for energy affairs. Another exemption provided is in case of supply shortages of gas fuel, which leads to the operator having to use other fuels, for a maximum period of ten days, on condition of the operator being equipped for gas waste purification. Only an energy producer can exceed the ten-day limit if the incessant delivery of energy would otherwise be endangered.

214. Furthermore, existing medium combustion facilities can exceed the threshold emission values if they have not operated for more than 500 hours yearly on average in the period of the last five years. The same facilities can be exempted even if they work on average more than 1,000 hours yearly if the main source of energy supply stops working, or in the circumstances of extremely cold weather conditions, but only for thermal energy production purposes. However, in these cases, the medium combustion facilities must not exceed the threshold emission values for

283. A shaft is a structure that contains one or more pipes through which gas wastes pass before being discharged into air (Art. 5(24).

suspended particles of 200 mg/m^3 if solid fuels are used. Facilities that have operated on average less than 500 hours yearly in the last three years can exceed the threshold emission values if these emissions contain less than 100 mg/m^3 of suspended particles. In case the emissions of suspended particles exceed these limits, the operators must promptly report to the administrative organ (Article 33).

215. Combustion facilities that use solid domestic fuel, including co-incineration facilities, might also be allowed to exceed threshold emission values for sulphur dioxide due to the characteristics of this fuel, however, they are allowed to use desulfurization techniques to achieve prescribed minimal rates of desulfurization. When using these techniques they must constantly control the level of sulfur in the used fuel (Article 37).

216. In some cases, the law provides for stricter threshold emission values. In areas where standards of air quality are exceeded, these stricter thresholds might be applied for certain medium combustion facilities if this would lead to efficient improvement of air quality. A special permit is issued in this case for individual facilities (Article 37).

217. Any malfunction of the device for emission mitigation in the combustion facility must be repaired in twenty-four hours, otherwise, the operator must diminish the operation workload or cease the operation of the facility, or switch to the usage of fuel with low emission that causes less air pollution. The malfunction of the device must be reported to the administrative organ within forty-four hours, as well as any cut-off of supply of low-sulfur fuel or gas. The operation during the malfunctioning must not be longer than 120 hours within twelve months. The administrative organ might decide to prolong this limit if the need for energy supply arises or if the alternative facility to the malfunctioning one would cause a general emission increase (Article 38).

218. Emissions monitoring is another obligation on the part of the operator. Operator with a total input of thermal power that exceeds 100 MW is obliged to provide the continuous monitoring of sulfur dioxide, nitric oxide, and suspended particles in gas waste emissions. If the operator uses gas fuels, carbon-monoxide monitoring is obligatory as well. There are several exceptions to this rule: (1) if the facility's lifecycle is less than 10,000 working hours; (2) if it uses natural gas but just for sulphur dioxide and suspended particles; (3) if the facility uses liquid fuel with a known sulfur content and has no desulfurization equipment for sulfur dioxide; (4) for sulfur dioxide when the facility uses biomass if the operator can prove that its emissions cannot under any circumstances exceed the threshold. The measurements must be performed every six months for sulfur dioxide, nitric oxide, suspended particles, and carbon monoxide. Total mercury emissions are measured once a year. Measurements are performed in normal working conditions, during the combustion of fuel likely to result in the highest level of emissions. In other cases of medium combustion facilities, if the nominal input thermal power is over 20 MW measurements of polluting material are taken once a year, and for those between 1 and 20 MW once every three years. Exceptionally, measurements might be less frequent, but once in five years at the minimum (Article 39).

219. Automated emissions monitoring systems are allowed under the law, but they must be checked yearly through parallel measurements by the accredited legal entity, and check results must be reported by the operator to the administrative organ no later than fifteen days after the receipt of results. Results are considered invalid if more than three average hourly measurements are found to be inaccurate during one day due to malfunctioning or servicing of the automated emissions monitoring system. If during one year more than ten daily results are found to be invalid in this way, the operator is obliged to repair the system and report to the administrative organ (Article 40).

220. The operator is obliged to keep the evidence of monitoring results in a manner that would enable the control of their accord with emission limits. In the medium combustion facilities that use secondary emissions mitigation equipment, the evidence should indicate the continuous efficient operation of the equipment. The evidence relates to the following documents: all the permits acquired and related information; monitoring results; working hours if needed;[284] fuel types and quantities and any malfunctioning of the secondary equipment. The evidence shall be kept for at least six years and reported to the administrative organ on notice. In case the limits of threshold emissions are breached, the operator is obliged to promptly decrease the level of activities or cease the operation completely until it performs measures that would normalize the emissions conditions. The stoppages in activities have to be reported to the administrative organ within forty-eight hours. After the continuation of activities emission measurements shall be enabled immediately. The operator should make sure that the periods of switching on and switching off are as short as possible (Article 41).

221. In case of any changes in the combustion facility that might impact the quality of the environment, and if this change impacts the part of the facility with total thermal input power of 50 MW or more, threshold values are modified for the changed part in relation to the total thermal input power. The same rule applies to the case of the combustion facility's enlargement. Any such change, or plan of change, in the combustion facility, must be promptly reported to the administrative organ. The law stipulates that the changes specifically of interest to this provision are those related to fuel and manner of operation (Article 42).

III. Waste Incineration and Co-Incineration

222. The law defines the facilities for waste incineration as stationary or mobile technical unit and equipment intended for thermal waste treatment. These facilities

284. Working hours relate to the time of full or partial activities that cause emissions or pollution, excluding the the switching on and switching off period (Art. 5(25)).

may or may not use the energy produced through incineration. They might incinerate waste through oxidation or other methods of thermal treatment, such as pyrolysis, gasification, or plasma method if the substances created through these methods are later incinerated (Article 5(33)).

223. The co-incineration facility differs from the incineration facility in that its main purpose is the production of energy or material goods, but it uses waste as ordinary or additional fuel, and later disposes of waste through the same incineration methods (Article 5(34)).

224. These facilities encompass waste reception; waste storage; objects for provisional treatment in the location; systems for waste, fuel, and air inlet, boilers, objects for gas waste disposal, objects for treatment or storage of wastewater on the location, shafts, devices and systems for incineration or co-incineration control, evidence and monitoring of incineration or co-incineration (Article 42).

225. Facilities exempted from the law's remit are (1) facilities for gasification or pyrolysis if the gasses that result from their activities are purified before incineration to the level that they do not represent waste and if the emissions they cause are not higher than natural gas incineration emissions; (2) facilities that incinerate or co-incinerate waste created by research and exploitation of gas and oil on the high seas facilities where it was already incinerated, radioactive waste, animal waste not intended for human nutrition, biomass; (3) experimental facilities used for research, development and examination of the advanced incineration methods that incinerate under fifty tons of waste yearly (Article 43).

226. Incineration and co-incineration facilities operate under a special permit that must be requested by the operator. Besides general permit request data, the law stipulates some special data the operator is obliged to submit in Article 44: (1) data concerning the projected facility, equipment, maintenance manner, and categories of waste being incinerated or co-incinerated; (2) manner of thermal energy usage; (3) residue and its minimization treatment and possibilities for recycling; (4) manner of residue disposal (Article 44).

227. The permit provides several conditions for the operator: (1) list of types of treatable waste; (2) total facility capacity; (3) threshold emission values for air and water polluting substances; (4) wastewater discharge conditions (temperature, flow, and PH value); (5) manner of monitoring, methods, and frequency; (6) maximum period allowed for when air emissions and wastewater discharges can exceed the threshold emission values due to inevitable technical breaks or stoppages of the purification or measurement devices. In case of dangerous waste, the permit additionally requires: (1) a list of dangerous waste; (2) minimal and maximal mass flows of dangerous waste, highest and lowest calorific values, and maximal content of certain polluting materials (pentachlorophenol, chlorine, flour, sulfur, heavy metals, and others). The procedure for a permit grant is the same as in the case of a general permit (Article 45).

228. Shafts in these facilities have to be designed with a certain height to protect human health and the environment. Threshold emission values are measured in the place of wastewater discharge. Wastewater must not be diluted. The facility must possess a pool of enough capacity to intake atmospheric water from its location, polluted water, or water created after fire extinguishment, to examine and purify the water before discharge if needed (Article 46).

229. The operator is obliged to monitor emissions from the facility and to keep evidence of emissions for value assessment. Automated monitoring systems, if used, have to be controlled once a year through parallel measurement of the accredited legal entity. The operator must report on the results of this measurement within fifteen days (Article 47).[285]

230. During the waste intake, the operator is obliged to perform precautionary measures to prevent or minimize air, soil, and water pollution, odours, noise, and risks to human health. The operator must assess the waste quantity and categorize it before the intake. It must also collect the data concerning (1) waste origin from the producer's evidence; (2) Physicochemical waste contents to assess the appropriate method of incineration; (3) Dangerous waste characteristics and necessary precautionary measures in its handling. The operator furthermore has to check the waste documentation and take waste samples (Article 49).

231. Residues left after the incineration process in the form of dust must be provisionally stored and transported to prevent dissipation into the environment. Before residue disposal or recycling, physicochemical examinations should be performed to ascertain the total content of solvable fractions and in particular heavy metals solvable fractions (Article 50).[286]

IV. Organic Solvents

232. The law specifically regulates the operation of facilities using organic solvents. They must be registered as facilities using organic solvents or products containing volatile organic compounds at the operator's request by the administrative organ. The Ministry should more closely regulate the type of activities allowed in these facilities, thresholds of organic solvent consumption, the procedure for permit requests, and registry management (Article 52).

233. Substances or mixtures classified as carcinogenic, mutagenic, or toxic for reproduction under chemicals regulations, and designated by warning signs H340, H350, H350i, H360D, or H360F, can be substituted with less harmful substances or mixtures for usage in these facilities. (Article 53)

---

285. In case the facility exceeds the threshold emission values it must stop the incineration process after four hours at most, or sixty hours total per one year (Art. 48).
286. For the incineration and co-incineration facilities with a nominal capacity of fewer than 2 tons per hour, the administrative organ publishes a list on its web page (Art. 51).

234. Emissions from facilities that use organic solvents fall under threshold values. For every substance or mixture designated with a warning sign, the operator is obliged to achieve prescribed threshold values. Total emission threshold values might be exceeded in case this does not endanger human health or the environment (Article 54).[287]

235. Certain significant changes in facilities that use organic solvents require the grant of the general permit from Articles 8 –16. Changes in the maximal intake of organic solvents are deemed significant if they cause emissions of volatile organic compounds for more than 25% if facilities consume less than 10 tons, or 10% in other cases (Article 56).

V. Special Cases of Titanium Dioxide and Mercury

236. Operators that produce titanium dioxide are obliged to perform the monitoring of emissions to air and water from the facilities. The law prohibits disposal of certain categories of waste from such facilities into the water: (1) solid waste; (2) mother liquor created by filtration, after the hydrolysis of the titanyl sulfate solution from the facility that applies the sulfate method, including acid waste related to liquors that contains more than 0.5% of free sulfate acid and various heavy metals in total, including mother liquors diluted to contain 0.5% or less free sulfate acid; (3) waste from facilities that apply the chlorine creation method containing more than 0.5% of free hydrochloric acid and various heavy metals, including waste diluted to contain 0.5% or less of free hydrochloric acid; (4) filtered salt, sludges and liquid waste created through waste treatment (concentration or neutralization) from previous two examples, which contains various heavy metals but not the neutralized and filtered or squeezed waste which contains only traces of heavy metals and which before any dilution had a PH value of more than 5.5 (Article 57).

237. The law prohibits the use of mercury, mercury compounds, and mixtures in the facilities and their production processes, except when they are used in the production of sodium or potassium methylates or ethylates (Article 58).

238. The production and marketing of new products (produced after 1 January 2018) containing mercury or mercury compounds are prohibited except for equipment used for national security purposes (arms, munitions, and military materiel); equipment designed for space launching; technical upgrades or redesign of products produced before 1 January 2018 if these changes result in the decrease of mercury content; if special regulations on the limit of use of certain dangerous products in electronic or electric equipment allow it (Article 59).[288]

---

287. The operator is obliged to perform monitoring, formulate a report on the yearly consumption of organic solvents, and forward it to the administrative authority (Art. 55).
288. Traditional mining and treatment of gold that uses mercury amalgams for the separation of gold from ore are prohibited (Art. 60).

VI. Reporting

239. Reporting obligations on the part of the authorities are contained in Article 61 of the law. The administrative organ creates a yearly inventory of sulfur dioxide, nitrite oxide, suspended particle emissions, and energy consumption for every combustion facility separately. The inventory should contain: (1) total thermal input power; (2) type of facility; (3) date of the start of operations; (4) total yearly emissions of sulfur dioxide, nitrite oxide, and suspended particles in tons; (5) working hours number; (6) yearly energy consumption rate with data on caloric values in terajoules for following fuel categories: coal, lignite, biomass, peat, other solid fuels, liquid fuels, natural gas or other gasses.

240. From the moment of Montenegro's accession to the EU, several obligations concerning the EU institutions would be activated (Article 74).

241. At the request of the European Commission, the administrative organ reports these data to it. Inventory's resume is forwarded to the European Commission every three years, indicating specifically the data on the combustion in refineries.

242. Once a year, the administrative organ sends to the European Commission a report with data on: (1) combustion facilities that apply the desulfurization technique, contents of sulfur in used domestic solid fuel, and the average monthly rate of desulfurization; (2) the yearly number of working hours of combustion facilities that have not worked more than 1,500 working hours on average in last five years; (3) the operations and emissions monitoring of incineration and co-incineration facilities. The first such report contains also data on technical justifications for the desulfurization techniques application. All the exceptions made under Article 35 of the law must be reported to the Commission as well.

VII. Supervision and Penal Provisions

243. The Ministry is responsible for supervising the law's implementation (Article 62). Common inspectional supervision of the law's implementation is the responsibility of the administrative organ for inspectional supervision. Environmental inspection and other inspections responsible for the supervision of specific environmental segments are conducted for all activities of the facilities that impact the environment, including visits to a facility, supervision over emissions monitoring, review of internal reports and annexed documentation, review of monitoring results provided by the operator, review of techniques used and supervision over the management of a facility and its location (Article 63).

244. Inspectors plan the supervision following the yearly plan and programme of work of environmental inspection and other inspections. The plan of work of environmental inspection includes: (1) a general assessment of important relevant environmental issues; (2) a geographic area of inspectional control; (3) the registry of facilities included in the plan; (4) procedures for the creation of programmes of routine environmental inspection control; (5) procedures for non-routine environmental inspection control; (6) cooperation plans among various inspection services, where needed. The plan identifies the frequency of supervision of various facilities and their locations, based on the negative environmental impact assessments. The Ministry coordinates common inspectional supervision with other state authorities responsible for maritime, agriculture, husbandry, veterinary, forestry, water management, mining, fire protection, labour protection, health, spatial planning, construction, thermal energy, electro-energy equipment, and civil protection affairs (Article 64).[289]

245. Environmental inspector controls certain specific aspects of the facility's operation: (1) whether it acquired the permit; (2) whether it satisfies the permit's conditions; (3) the implementation of prescribed measures and conditions of environmental protection; (4) any change in the operation; (5) emissions monitoring process its results and reporting; (6) yearly activities reports; (7) necessary documentation for the grant, extension, change and expiry of the permit. The inspector reports on its findings and measures ordered to the operator within two months of the end of the inspection and publishes the report on its webpage within four months (Article 65).[290]

246. The inspector can prohibit further operations of the facility or its part if it finds out that the operator is: (1) operating without the legal permit; (2) operating with an expired permit; (3) operating with the previous permit although he substantially changed the facility; (4) operating with disrespect to the environmental quality standards or technical standards of environmental protection. When the operator eliminates the obstacles to further operations it must report this to the operator and is then able to continue its activity (Article 67).

247. The administrative organ responsible for inspectional supervision is obliged to inform the public about all the aspects of the supervision. These aspects are provided by the law in detail (Article 68).[291]

289. Extraordinary inspectional supervisions are conducted in cases of serious risk of harm or environmental harm, excesses of threshold emission values, before the granting, revision, or changes or additions to permits and other similar cases Risk assessment is conducted based on: (1) potential and real effects of the facility on human health and the environment; (2) evidence of fulfilment of permit conditions; (3) operator's participation in the environmental management and independent assessment system (EMAS) (Art. 64).

290. The inspector is authorized to order certain measures to the operator if it finds any breaches of provisions (Art. 66).

291. The law stipulates financial sanctions for legal entities found to be in breach of its provisions ranging from EUR 5,000 to EUR 40,000, or EUR 250 to EUR 2,500 for responsible persons in these entities (Arts 69–70).

VIII. Transitional and Final Provisions

248. The operator of a large existing combustion facility that is exempted from the application of threshold emission values by the Decision of the Council of Energy Community until 31 December 2023 is obliged to: (1) deliver to the responsible energy administration the evidence of the number of yearly working hours before 31 March 2023; (2) cease the facility's operation after 20,000 working hours, counting from the 1 January 2018, up until 31 December 2023 (Article 73(1)).[292]

249. Existing medium combustion facilities with input thermal power of more than 5 MW can be exempted from the threshold of emission values for nitrite oxide until the 1st of January 2030 if they are used for the launching of gas compressing cells that secure and protect the gas transport system (Article 73(3)).[293]

IX. Other Relevant Regulations

250. Based on the Law on Industrial Emissions, following regulations were adopted:

- The Regulation on the threshold emission values from combustion facilities and the manner of threshold emission values calculation for facilities that use multiple fuel types (OJ MNE 129/21).
- The Rulebook on the threshold emission values of polluting substances, the method of monitoring performance and conditions of the operation for waste incineration and co-incineration facilities (OJ MNE, No. 79/20).
- The Rulebook on the method of monitoring performance of emissions into water and air from facilities producing Titanium Dioxide (OJ MNE, No. 70/20).
- The Rulebook on the threshold emission values of polluting substances, technical measures for the exemption of the application of threshold values and monitoring method (OJ MNE, No. 61/20).
- The Rulebook on the content and manner of submission of the request for integrated permit (OJ MNE, No. 55/20).
- The Rulebook on the type of activities, threshold emission values and monitoring method in facilities using organic solvents (OJ MNE, No. 30/20).
- The Regulation on types of activities and installations for which an integrated permit is issued (OJ MNE, No. 68/19).
- The Rulebook on conditions for use and discharge of mercury and mercury compound (OJ MNE No. 68/19).

292. Existing medium combustion facilities with input thermal power of more than 5 MW can be exempted from the threshold of emission values until the 1 Jan. 2030, provided at least 50% of useful energy produced in the facility in the last five years was delivered as steam or hot water to the public network for thermal energy delivery and that the sulfur dioxide emissions do not exceed 1.100 mg/m3, or the suspended particles 150 mg/m3 (Art. 73(2)).

293. Medium combustion facilities that use biomass as the main fuel, located in areas not affected by exceeding levels of air pollution, can be exempted from the application of threshold emission values until the 1 Jan. 2030 if the suspended particles emissions do not exceed 150 mg/Nm3.

- The Rulebook on the integrated permit form (OJ MNE, No. 59/19).
- The Rulebook on Criteria for Determining BAT for environmental protection and the list of polluting substances from industrial facilities (OJ MNE, No. 35/19).

Based on the Law on Environment (OJ MNE, Nos 52/16, 73/19), following regulations were adopted:

- Regulations on the quantities of dangerous substances by categories that determine the degree of risk of the Seveso plant[294] (OJ MNE, No. 63/16).
- Regulation on the content of the Prevention Plan and the Accident Prevention Plan (OJ MNE, No. 67/16).
- Regulation on the criteria to be met by a reference laboratory for environmental monitoring (OJ MNE, No. 11/17).

251. So far, seven installations have received integrated permits.[295]

§5. Access to Information and Public Participation in the Field of the Environment

252. Access to Information and Public participation in the environmental field means several different elements.[296] It includes a harmonized system of the regulations in different areas, the corresponding capacities of institutions of public authorities, the appropriate relationship of the business sector,[297] regulated position and role of the NGOs as well as the satisfactory level of the awareness of citizens, etc. The basic framework is the existence of functional regulations which guarantee respect for human rights and their implementation in practice. Currently, this area has been regulated by a large number of general rules and environmental regulations.[298]

294. Seveso plants are facilities with specially issued permits for operation, since they represent a major risk factor from industrial accidents (see more in Vučić 2012b).
295. *See*: https://epa.org.me/wp-content/uploads/2019/01/dozvole_IPPC_sajt.pdf (1 Jan. 2023).
296. One of the fundamental tenets of the idea of public access to environmental information is to provide the citizens with the 'specific technique for the protection of the environment'. This idea is in 'direct connection with the principle of preventive action'. It aims to establish 'an ecologically educated environment' which enables the realization of the ultimate aim of 'sustainable environment for future generations' (Vučić 2011, 450).
297. Generally, 'despite some positive examples during the last few years, the level of involvement of business sector and its contribution to sustainable development goals has remained at relatively low level. Concepts such as sustainable consumption and production and corporate social responsibility are not widely applied. Development of public – private partnerships is still at initial stage.' GMNE (2011a), 6.
298. 'Cooperation with civil society has improved, but further efforts are needed to achieve effective public participation and consultation in decision-making.' EC. *Montenegro 2018 Report*, Accompanying the document Communication from the Commission to the European Parliament, the Council, the European Economic and Social Committee and the Committee of the Regions 2018 Communication on EU Enlargement Policy, Strasbourg, 17.4.2018, SWD(2018) 150 final, 79.

I. Constitutional Provisions

253. Access to environmental information and public participation in environmental decision-making procedures is regulated by several legal and sub-legal instruments. In accordance with Article 51 of the Constitution of Montenegro (OJ MNE, No. 1/2007) 'everyone shall have the right to obtain information held by the state authorities and organizations exercising public authority'.[299] The right to accessibility of information may be limited if this is in the interest of: the protection of life; public health; morality and privacy; carrying of criminal proceedings; security and defence of Montenegro; and foreign, monetary and economic policy (Article 51, paragraph 2). The right of recourse has been stipulated in Article 57 of the Constitution. Pursuant to this article 'everyone has the right of recourse, individually or collectively with others, to the state authority or the organization exercising public powers and the right to receive a response'.[300]

254. In accordance with Article 53 the freedom of association and action, without approval, by the registration with the competent authority, has been guaranteed.[301] Apart from the above-mentioned provisions, Article 23 prescribed that 'everyone shall have the right to receive timely and full information about the status of the environment, to influence the decision-making regarding the issues of importance for the environment, and to legal protection of these rights'.

II. Aarhus Convention

255. Montenegro ratified Convention on Access to Information, Public Participation in Decision-Making and Access to Justice in Environmental Matters (Aarhus, 1998) (OJ MNE – International Treaties, No. 3/09),[302] and Protocol on Pollutant Release and Transfer Registers to the Convention on Access to Information, Public Participation in Decision-Making and Access to Justice in Environmental Matters (Kiev, 2003) (OJ MNE – International Treaties, No. 6/17)[303] but did not ratify Amendment to the Convention (Almay, 2005).[304] Furthermore, Montenegro

299. The right to environmental information was provided for by the provisions of the Art. 19 of the previous Constitution of the Republic of Montenegro (Official Journal of RM, No. 48/1992), too.
300. No one shall be held responsible, or suffer other harmful consequences due to the views expressed in the recourse, unless having committed a crime in doing so (Art. 57, para. 2).
301. The state supports associations when there is a public interest to do so (Art. 53, para. 3).
302. The revolutionary novelty of the Aarhus convention is the line of positive obligations of the state institutions to provide a 'free flow' of the information that can seriously influence the environment (Vučić 2011, 456).
303. *See*: https://treaties.un.org/Pages/ViewDetails.aspx?src=TREATY&mtdsg_no=XXVII-13-a&chapter=27&clang=_en (18 Jan. 2023).
304. *See*: https://treaties.un.org/Pages/ViewDetails.aspx?src=TREATY&mtdsg_no=XXVII-13-b&chapter=27&clang=_en (18 Jan. 2023).

ratified Council of Europe (CE) Convention on Access to Official Documents, CETS No. 205 (Tromso, 2009) (OJ MNE – International Treaties, No. 7/2011).

256. Aarhus Centre Podgorica is founded as the first Aarhus centre in Montenegro. A network of Aarhus centres in Montenegro consists of Aarhus centres Podgorica, Nikšić, Berane and Pljevlja. Aarhus centres Podgorica and Berane are centres formed within government institutions – the MSDT and the NEPA, while the two centres operate within NGOs – Arhus Centar Nikšić – Environmental Movement Ozon and Aarhus Centre Pljevlja – Ecological Society Breznica, Pljevlja. Aarhus centres Podgorica, Nikšić and Berane were opened with the support of the Organization for Security and Cooperation in Europe (OSCE) Mission to Montenegro.[305]

III. General Legislation

A. Law on State Administration

257. The Law on State Administration (OJ MNE, Nos 78/18, 70/21, 50/22) stipulates that 'the work of state administration authorities shall be public.' (Article 6).

258. Chapter VIII of the Law is devoted to the state administration and citizens' issues. Domestic and foreign physical and legal entities have the right to free access to information held by state administration bodies, in accordance with the law (Article 53).

State administration authorities and holders of public authorizations are obligated to possess official website where they publish information on their activities such as: motions of laws and regulations from their jurisdictions; strategies and planning documents, programmes of work and work reports; data on internal organization and contacts of responsible persons; information on their jurisdiction; and other data relevant for rights, obligations and legal interests of citizens (Article 51).[306]

259. State administration authorities have the obligation to provide a book, a box for complaints or other means to facilitate the clients to impart objections and complaints on the work of state administration authorities or an inappropriate attitude of civil servants. State administration authorities are obliged to reply in writing to the submitter within fifteen days of the submission of the complaint if the citizen requires so (Article 55). In preparing laws that shall regulate rights, obligations and legal interests of citizens, a minister shall have the draft law published through

305. For more information *see*: https://aarhus.osce.org/montenegro (18 Jan. 2023).
306. State administration authorities are obliged to promptly and lawfully decide on citizens' requests, and to offer them any relevant data, explanations, notifications and expert advice (Art. 54).

media and invite all stakeholders to present their comments, proposals and suggestions. When preparing other laws a is obliged to implement the procedure of public debate (Article 52, paragraph 1).[307]

260. Relations of State administration Authorities with NGOs are the subject of the regulations of Article 79. State administration bodies cooperate with Non-governmental Organizations (NGOs) by enabling the participation of NGOs in (1) the procedure for conducting a public hearing in the preparation of laws and strategies, in accordance with Article 51 of this law; (2) the work of working groups and other working bodies formed by state administration bodies for the purpose of reviewing issues of common interest or for the normative regulation of relevant issues.[308]

B. *Law on Inspection Control*

261. The Law on Inspection Control (OJ RMN, No. 39/03, OJ MNE, Nos 76/09, 57/11, 18/14, 11/15, 52/16) stipulates that one of the basic principles of the inspection control is principle of publicity. Pursuant to Article 8 of this Law 'the inspection control procedure shall be public'. In the cases of protection of private person's life and health, or in the cases of severe violation of the public interest, inspection authority shall be obliged to inform the public of the factual state and irregularities established during the inspection control procedure (Article 8, paragraph 2).

C. *Law on Local Self-Government*

262. The Law on Local Self-Government (OJ MNE, Nos 2/18, 34/19, 34/20, 50/22)[309] enshrines the principle of publicity of operations of municipal organs, local administrative organs and related services (Article 12).

263. In accordance with Article 170 local self-government bodies have the obligation to provide the citizens, in exercise of their rights and interests, with necessary information, explanation and notification through technical facilities, brochures, and public media. Local administrative bodies and public services have to inform the public about the status of affairs from their scope of jurisdiction and

307. However, in certain situations, a public hearing is not mandatory (Art. 52, para. 2).

308. The criteria and procedure for the selection of representatives of non-governmental organizations in working groups and other working bodies from para. 1 item 2 of this article shall be determined by the Government (Art. 79 para. 2).

309. The Law on local self-government financing (OJ MNE, No. 3/19) regulates the sources of funds, the method of financial equalization and financing of local self-government affairs, namely: municipalities, municipalities within the Capital City, and the Capital City (Art. 1).

report to it on their performance through public media or some other suitable means (Article 193).

264. For the purpose of promoting an open and democratic society, local self-government bodies have the obligation to cooperate with the NGO (Article 174).[310]

265. Methods of citizen participation are defined by Articles 158–168 of the Law. The methods of direct citizen participation in expressing their views and in decision-making shall consist of the initiative,[311] the civil initiative,[312] the assembly of citizens,[313] referendum (at the level of local communities[314] and the Municipality)[315] and other methods of expressing views and decision-making provided for in the municipal statute.

266. Apart from direct decision-making and an expression of views, citizens may also participate in the exercise of the local self-government by lodging

---

310. Cooperation shall be realized through, namely: (1) providing information on all issues that are important for the non-governmental sector; (2) consultation of the non-governmental sector with respect to development programmes of the local self-government and drafts of general regulations to be passed by the Assembly; (3) enabling participation in working groups on drafting normative regulations or preparation of programmes and projects; (4) organizing joint public hearings, round tables, seminars, etc.; (5) financing projects presented by the non-governmental organizations that are of interest for the local population under the conditions and procedures prescribed by a general regulation of the Municipality; (6) providing working conditions for non-governmental organizations, in accordance with possibilities of the authorities of local self-government; (7) through the empty chair institute; and (8) by other methods as set forth in the municipal statute (Art. 116, para. 2).
311. Citizens are entitled to launch an initiative before the competent bodies for the purpose of considering and deciding on certain matters that are of interest for the local population. The competent bodies shall take a position on the submitted initiative within thirty days and inform the submitter on it. If the competent bodies do not take action at the initiative from para. 1 of this article, those who submitted the initiative may refer to the Mayor of Town or the Assembly (Art. 101).
312. The civil initiative shall be launched for the purpose of adoption or amending a regulation that defines important matters falling under the local self-government jurisdiction. The municipal statute shall regulate matters that may be subject of civil initiative, the required number of citizens' signatures for launching the initiative, procedure for conduct of the initiative and other issues that are important for civil initiative. If the competent body does not accept the civil initiative, a matter that was subject of the initiative may be submitted to a referendum that shall be held within ninety days from the date the decision has been passed (Art. 160).
313. The assembly of citizens, by a majority vote of citizens present, shall adopt requests and proposals and forward them to competent bodies. Local self-government bodies shall, within sixty days from the date the assembly of citizens was held, discuss the requests and proposals and inform citizens on it. The procedure of convening the assembly of citizens, methods of work and decision-making shall be regulated by the municipal statute or specific regulation (Art. 161).
314. The matters that citizens of Local Communities may submit to a referendum, as well as the procedure of calling and holding the referendum shall be regulated in the law, that is, the municipal statute (Art. 162, para. 2).
315. Calling for a municipal referendum may give citizens an opportunity to express their views on certain matters that fall under the jurisdiction of the local self-government in the cases, pursuant to methods and following the procedure provided for in the municipal statute, in accordance with the law (Art. 163).

petitions, suggestions and complaints, in accordance with the municipal statute (Article 164).[316]

267. For the purpose of participation of local population in making decisions of direct and common interest, the Assembly shall adopt a special ordinance that regulates the methods and procedure of participation of local population in public affairs conducting (Article 166).[317]

268. Prior to adoption of municipal development programmes, spatial and urban plans, budget and general acts that regulate rights and obligations of citizens, the Municipality shall prepare a Plan for Citizen Participation in Decision-Making and it shall appoint a body that shall hold public hearings. Public hearings may also be held to discuss regulations related to the matters that are important for local population, in accordance with the Statute and Municipal Ordinance. The public hearings may not last less than fifteen days (Article 167).[318]

---

316. Any person may lodge a civil complaint or petition to local self-government bodies, as well as request information concerning the scope of work of these bodies. The municipal statute has to specify the procedure for submitting civil complaints and petitions as well as the methods of action to be taken by the competent bodies. The bodies to whom requests have been referred to shall make a decision, that is, provide information respectively within thirty days from the date that the request was received (Art. 165). *See also* T. Dašić-Raspopović & S. Bajić (2007).
317. The Ordinance in terms of para. 1 of this Article shall regulate: forms, mechanisms (surveys, media plans, notice boards, boxes for remarks, suggestions and proposals, websites, orderly telephone lines, organization of workshops in Local Communities, information centres, visits of lecturers, expert meetings and round tables, etc.), subjects, procedures, deadlines and methods of participation of the local population in public affairs conducting, reporting on success of the procedures and other issues that are important for activities of the local population in decision-making process.
318. Participation of the local population in decision-making process related to affairs from Art. 109 of this law shall be provided, in particular as following: (1) To make available information on activities planned to be carried out at the municipal level during a year to every citizen, administration body, legal entity, person, non-governmental organization, and other interested party (hereinafter 'participants in the public hearings'), before the drafts of municipal development plans and programmes, budget and general regulations that set forth rights and obligations of citizens have been prepared, and their needs in the respective areas have been collected; (2) To make public drafts of municipal development plan and programme, budget and general acts that set forth rights and obligations of citizens shall be publicized in a manner which makes them accessible to all participants in public hearings; programmes of public hearings in every Local Community related to the needs of the local population, in particular in the area of housing, public utilities, urban planning and environment, educational and social affairs, etc.; (3) To give notice on the manner, deadlines, venue and time of holding public hearings which contains the necessary information on the subject to be discussed; (4) In the Municipality where members of minority nations and other minority national communities form a majority or significant number of population, the Plan shall contain a method of providing the participation of minority nations and other minority national communities on their languages, too; (5) To commit local self-government authorities to consider all submitted comments, proposals and suggestions of participants in public hearings, to make a summary of comments and explain their acceptance, i.e., reasons for their rejection, to prepare a report on results of the public hearings, and to convey all of that accompanied with draft municipal development plan and programme, budget and general regulations that regulate rights and obligations of citizens to the applicant; and (6) To make adopted documents available to the public, in particular to persons with special needs who express an interest in it.

D. Law on Free Access to Information

269. The Law on Free Access to Information (OJ MNE, Nos 44/12, 30/17) regulates access to information.[319] Right to access to information held by public authorities[320] shall be exercised in manner and according to procedure prescribed by this Law (Article 1). The right to access to information[321] shall encompass the right to ask for and receive information, regardless to purpose and data consisted of (Article 10, paragraph 2).

270. Pursuant to Article 11:

> The public authority shall develop, publish, and regularly update a guide for access to information held by it (hereinafter referred to as 'the access to information guide') (Para 1). The access to information guide shall contain a catalogue of all types of documents, including public registers and public records, the address and e-mail address for submission of request, contact telephone, information on responsible persons, information on costs of access to information, and other data that are of importance to the exercise of the right of access to information held by the public authority (Para 2).[322]

271. The public authority shall grant the access to information or a part thereof to any physical or legal entity seeking the access to information (hereinafter referred to as 'applicant'), that it holds at the time of dealing with the request, except in cases envisaged by this law (Article 13). According to Article 14 of the Law, access to information may be restricted if it is in the interest of following: (1) protection of privacy from disclosure of personal data envisaged in the law regulating protection of data on individuals,[323] (2) security, defence, foreign, monetary and economic policy of Montenegro, in accordance with the laws regulating the field of data

319. Access to information held by public authorities (hereinafter referred to as 'access to information') shall be based on the principles of free access to information, transparency in work of public authorities, the right of the public to know and equality of requests, and it shall be carried out at the level of standards set out in ratified international agreements on human rights and freedoms and in generally recognized rules of international law (Art. 2).
320. 'Information held by public authorities' shall mean factual possession of the requested information by the public authority (their own information, as well as information reported by other government agencies or third persons), regardless of the grounds and manner of acquisition (Art. 9, para. 2). 'Publication of information' shall mean making the contents of information available (Art. 9, para. 3).
321. 'Information' shall be a document in written, print, video, audio, electronic or any other form, including its copy or part thereof, regardless to content, source (of author), date and time of composing or classification system (Art. 10, para. 1).
322. The public authority shall update 'The access to information guide' at least once a year, or within thirty days following the change of type of information in its possession and data important for access to information. Content of 'The access to information guide' shall not exclude obligation of the public authority to provide access to information that holds and that is not covered by the Guide. The public authority shall appoint and authorize a person responsible for access to information (Art. 11, paras 3–5).
323. Except for data relating to following: persons exercising public function, as well as to incomes, property and conflict of interest of those persons and their relatives covered by the law regulating

secrecy, classified with certain level of confidentiality, (3) prevention of investigation and criminal prosecution,[324] (4) performing the official duty,[325] (5) protection of private and commercial interest from disclosure of data relating to protection of competition and business secret in relation to intellectual property right and (6) if the information is a business or a tax secret in accordance with the law.

272. According to Article 16 access to information shall be restricted if disclosure of information would significantly jeopardize interests referred to in Article 14 herein, or if there is a possibility that disclosure of information would cause harm to interest that is greater than the interest of the public to know that information, unless there is prevailing public interest prescribed by Article 17 of this Law.[326]

273. Procedure for access to information shall be initiated upon a written[327] or verbal request[328] of an individual seeking access to information.[329] One request for information may refer to several pieces of information (Article 18, paragraphs 1, and 2). If the applicant requests the public authority shall issue, or deliver, adequate proof confirming reception of the request for access to information (Article 18, paragraph 5).

274. Pursuant to Article 31 the public authority shall make a decision on the request for access to information and deliver it to the applicant within fifteen working days following the adequate request has been submitted (paragraph 1). If access to information is requested for the purpose of protecting the life or freedom of an individual, the public authority shall make a decision and deliver it to the applicant within forty-eight hours of the hour of submission of the request. The time limit

---

preventing of conflict of interest; resources allocated from the public funds, except those for social security benefits, healthcare, and protection against unemployment.

324. In order to protect from disclosure data referring to following: to prevent committing the criminal act, on reporting criminal act and perpetrator of it, on content of actions undertaken in pretrial and criminal procedure; data collected through observation and investigation, on secret surveillance measures; on protected witness and collaborators of justice; efficient conducting of procedure.

325. in order to protect from disclosure data referring to following: planning of inspection control and supervision by the public authority, consultations within and between public authorities regarding defining the positions and development of official documents and proposals for resolution of a case, work and decision-making by collegial bodies; bringing and conduct of disciplinary proceedings.

326. Prevailing public interest for disclosure of information, or a part thereof, exists when the requested information contains data that evidently refer to following: (1) corruption, non-observance of regulations, unauthorized use of public funds, or abuse of authority in exercising public function; (2) the existence of grounds to believe that a criminal offence has been committed or existence of reasons to challenge a court decision; (3) illegal receiving or spending of funds originating from public revenues; (4) threats to public security; (5) threats to life; (6) threats to public health; and (7) *threats to the environment* (Art. 17, para. 1).

327. The written request for access to information shall be submitted directly to the responsible authority by hand, mail or e-mail (via fax, e-mail, etc) (Art. 18, para. 3).

328. The verbal request shall be submitted to the responsible authority directly to the minutes/record (Art. 18, para. 4).

329. The fee shall not be paid for the submitting the request for access to information. The applicant shall pay costs of procedure for access to information that relate to actual costs incurred by the public authority in relation to copying of documents and delivery of information to the applicant, in accordance with the regulation adopted by the Government of Montenegro (Art. 33, paras 1 and 2).

referred to in paragraph 1 of this Article may be extended for eight days, provided that: (1) the request refers to exceptionally voluminous information; (2) the request for access to information refers to classified information; (3) tracking the requested information entails search through a large volume of information and therefore disturbs performance of regular activities of the public authority.[330]

275. The applicant, or another individual having an interest, may make a complaint[331] against the decision of the public authority on the request for access to information to an independent supervisory authority responsible for protection of personal data and access to information (hereinafter referred to as 'the Agency'), and through the authority that has decided upon request in first instance (Article 34, paragraph 1).[332]

E. Law on Personal Data Protection[333]

276. Protection of data relating to individuals is provided under the conditions and in the way laid down by Law on Personal Data Protection (OJ MNE, Nos 79/08, 70/09, 44/12, 22/17),[334] in accordance with the principles and standards contained in the ratified international human rights treaties and generally recognized rules of international law (Article 1).[335] Pursuant to Article 49 an Agency for Personal Data Protection is hereby set up to perform the tasks of the supervisory authority as laid down by this law.[336]

277. 'It is encouraging that the protection of personal data is more present in public but also encouraging is the statement of the Agency that more people address

330. In the case referred to in para. 3 of this Article, the public authority shall, within three working days after the request has been submitted, inform the applicant in writing of an extension of the time limit in which a decision on the request will be made (Art. 31, para. 3).
331. A complaint may be lodged against the decision on request for access to information for the violation of rules of procedure, incompletely and incorrectly defined factual state, and misapplication of material law (Art. 35).
332. Notwithstanding para. 1 of this Article, complaint may not be filed against decision denying access to information containing data marked as classified, but it is possible to initiate administrative dispute against adopted decision (Art. 34, para. 2).
333. In connection with this Law is the Law on Information Confidentiality (Official Journal of MNE, Nos 14/08, 76/09, 41/10, 40/11).
334. The Law on the Protection of Personal Data (Official Journal of the FRY, No. 24/98) shall be repealed as of the day when this law becomes applicable (Art. 78).
335. Law regulates following issues: processing of personal data (Ch. 2, Arts 10–30), special categories of personal data processing (Ch. 3, Arts 31–40), transfer of personal data from Montenegro (Ch. 4, Arts 41–42), rights of data subjects to protection of personal data (Ch. 5, Arts 43–48), Agency for personal data protection (Ch. 6, Arts 49–64), supervision (Ch. 7, Arts 65–73), penal provisions (Ch. 8, Art. 74).
336. The Agency shall be autonomous and independent in the performance of the tasks falling within its competence and shall have legal personality (Art. 49, paras 2 and 3). For more information *see*: http://www.azlp.me/en/about-agency (2 Apr. 2018).

the Agency asking for opinion, consent and explanations. It also receives requirements for the protection of rights. The Agency announced that higher level of protection of personal data is evident through submission of the Evidence on collections of data on personality through requirements for providing consent for introduction of video surveillance'.[337]

F. Law on Electronic Media[338]

278. Law on Electronic Media (OJ MNE, Nos 46/10, 40/11, 53/11, 6/13, 55/16, 92/17, and 8/20) has been adopted by the Parliament of Montenegro. This Law regulates rights, obligations and responsibilities of legal and physical entities performing the activity of production and providing of audio visual media services (hereinafter referred to as 'AVM service'), and providing of services of electronic publications via electronic communication networks; the law regulates competences, status and financing of Agency for Electronic Media; regulates prevention of illegal media concentration; encouraging of media pluralism; and governs other issues relating to providing of AVM service, in accordance with international conventions and standards (Article 1).[339]

G. Law on NGO

279. Basic legal act regulating NGOs in Montenegro is the Law on NGOs (OJ MNE, Nos 39/11, 37/17).[340] It has the following ten parts: Part I – General Provisions (Articles 1–9), Part II – Foundation (Articles 10–13), Part III – Register of NGOs (Articles 14–20), Part IV – Membership and bodies of the association (Articles 21–24), Part V – Bodies of the foundation (Articles 25–27), Part VI – Property and financing (Articles 28–37), Part VII – Removal from the register and the disposal of assets (Articles 38–40), Part VIII – Supervision (Article 41), IX – Penalties (Articles 42–43) and Part X – Transitional and final provisions (Articles 44–51).[341]

---

337. Youth Initiative for Human Rights, Montenegro (2012) *Human Rights in Montenegro – 2011*, 85 Podgorica. http://gamn.org/files/Izvjestaj%20YIHR%202012%20eng.pdf (10 May 2012).

338. Furthermore, the Montenegrin Parliament adopted the changes to the Law on Electronic Communications (Official Journal of MNE, Nos 40/13, 56/13-corr, 2/17).

339. No provision of this law may be interpreted in a way that gives the right to censorship or restrictions on the rights of freedom of speech and freedom of expression. This law shall be interpreted in accordance with the principles of the European Convention for protection of human rights and fundamental freedoms, and by using case law practices of the European Court for human rights (Art. 2).

340. The Law on Non-Governmental Organizations (Official Journal of RM, Nos 27/1999, 09/2002, 30/2002 and Official Journal of MNE, No. 17/2007) has ceased to be in effect (Art. 50).

341. According to the *Montenegro 2011 Progress Report* 'the legal and regulatory framework for NGO's activities and State financial support to these organizations have been improved, notably through the adoption of a new Law on NGOs.' EC (2011), 17. 'A new law on NGOs, passed in August 2011,

280. This Law regulates the way of establishing, registration and deletion from the register, status, bodies, funding and other issues of importance for status and work of NGOs (Article 1, paragraph 1).[342] NGOs according to this Law are the non-governmental associations[343] and non-governmental foundations[344] (Article 1, paragraph 2).

281. Foreign NGOs (hereinafter 'foreign organizations')[345] can operate in Montenegro to achieve the goals and interests which are not prohibited by the Constitution and the Law (Article 4, paragraph 1). They can operate on the territory of Montenegro if it has subscribed branch office at the Ministry[346] (Article 20, paragraph 1).

282. The NGO is a legal entity. It acquires that status on the entry date into the register in accordance with this Law (Article 6, paragraph 1). The register of associations, the register of foundations and the register of foreign organizations in written and in electronic form keep the government authority in charge of administrative affairs (hereinafter 'Ministry')[347] (Article 14, paragraph 1).

283. NGO is established for an indefinite period or for specified period of time (Article 8, paragraph 1).[348] The association can be established by minimum of three persons, out of which one must have domicile, residence or head office in Montenegro (Article 10, paragraph 1).

---

improved the legislative framework for the establishment and work of NGOs, aligning it with international standards (the European Convention on Human Rights and Freedoms, in particular) and best practices.' Freedom House. (2012).

342. 'Since 2002, the NGO sector has been developing rapidly in Montenegro. NGOs are playing an increasingly significant role in: national environmental and social policy development, environmental decision-making, raising environmental awareness, advocating human rights and promoting sustainable development principles.' UNECE (2007), 34. Today, 'most Montenegrin NGOs are small, characterized by underdeveloped organizational structures and insufficient human resources. However, at the national level there is a small but influential core of well-established, organizationally mature NGOs, engaged mainly in advocacy and research on human rights, good governance, and poverty reduction.' Freedom House (2012).
343. *Non-government association* (hereinafter '*Association*') is a voluntary non-profit membership organization, founded by domestic and/or foreign individuals and/or legal entities, in order to achieve certain common or general goals and interests (Art. 2, para. 1).
344. *Non-governmental foundation* (hereinafter '*Foundation*') is a voluntary non-profit organization without membership, founded by domestic and/or foreign individuals and/or legal persons with or without the initial property, in order to achieve general goals and interests (Art. 3, para. 1).
345. *Foreign organization*, in terms of this Law, is NGO being legal entity, whose headquarter is in another state, established under the regulations of that State in order to achieve common or general goals and interest (Art. 4, para. 2).
346. Branch office of the foreign organization is not a legal entity (Art. 20, para. 3).
347. The content and manner of keeping the registers, and application forms for entry in the registers are prescribed by the Ministry (Art. 14, para. 2). For the list of NGO *see* Register of NGO: http://www.dokumenta.me/nvo/ (1 Apr. 2018).
348. If the statute provides otherwise, it shall be considered that non-governmental organization was founded for an indefinite period of time (Art. 8, para. 2).

284. The state provides support to NGOs through provision of financial resources to support the budget, as well as by introduction of tax and other concessions to NGOs, in accordance with the Law (Article 31, paragraph 1).[349]

285. The role of civil society stakeholders and their contributions to sustainable development need to be further strengthened through continuous efforts to allow for meaningful participation in policy and decision-making. Existing partnerships need to be extended and new ones built to harness potential of this stakeholder group to its full potential. Relative to the role of civil sector in the society, capacities are significant. This is mainly due to flexibility and openness of civil society stakeholders. On the other hand, there is room for improvements. Media, for example, could do more on awareness-raising agenda and with better/more in-depth coverage on all the issues from the sustainable development corpus.[350]

286. 'An important incentive to improved relations between the governmental and non-governmental sector was the signing of the Memorandum on Cooperation between the then Ministry of Spatial Planning and Environment and environmental NGOs, and the selection of the representative of NGO sector for the position of a deputy president of the National Council for Sustainable Development … '[351] 'Relations between civil society and the government have occasionally been overly adversarial and characterized by distrust, especially on the political situation, the rule of law and fundamental rights. NGOs participate in working groups, including for accession negotiations, but are dissatisfied with their level of involvement in policy-making and access to information'.[352]

---

349. Government adopted Decree on the procedure for cooperation between state administration bodies and NGOs (Official Journal of MNE, No. 7/12). On 15 Apr. 2010, the Government of Montenegro adopted a Decision on establishment the Council for Cooperation between of the Government and NGOs. The Council acts as an advisory body to the Government. http://www.gov.me/naslovna/Savjetodavna_tijela/Savjet_za_saradnju_Vlade_Crne_Gore_i_nevladinih_or/97137/Prezentacija-Odluke-o-obrazovanju-Savjeta-za-saradnju-Vlade-Crne-Gore-i-nevladinih-organizacija.html (1 Apr. 2018). '… some of the ministries administer funds that are used for financing of projects conducted by non-governmental organizations. Ministry of Culture has a fund for CSOs with the annual budget of somewhat over 1 million EUR, whereas the Fund of Directorate for sport and youth disburses 150,000 EUR. Ministry for Environmental Protection and Tourism has in 2010 disbursed over 100,000 EUR for NGO projects, and Ministry for Human and Minority Rights slightly below 125,000 EUR.' TACSO, 12.
350. GMNE (2011a), 6.
351. GMNE, NCSD (2011), 13. 'When such cooperation was missing, there were situations when opinions of non-governmental sector and Government were different, as in the case of the construction project of the hydropower plant "Buk Bijela" on Tara River, when the mobilization of the overall non-governmental sector suspended the decision on construction, i.e., prevented non-compliance with the rules of the Convention Concerning the Protection of the World Cultural and Natural Heritage, since Tara is a part of the National Park "Durmitor", as a part of the world heritage, and a reserve within the international "Man and Biosphere" programme. NGOs also criticized the construction project of hydropower plants on Morača River, which did not contain alternative solutions, but solutions that seriously endangered biodiversity and ecosystem of the basin covered by the hydropower plant and accumulations.' *Ibid.*, 13, 14.
352. EC. *Montenegro 2016 Report*, Accompanying the document Communication from the Commission to the European Parliament, the Council, the European Economic and Social Committee and the Committee of the Regions, 2016 Communication on EU Enlargement Policy, Brussels, 9.11.2016,

H. The Law on Voluntary Work

287. Basic legal act regulating voluntary work in Montenegro is the Law on voluntary work (OJ RM, Nos 26/10, 14/12, 48/15) adopted in Parliament on 22 April 2010. It has the following six parts: Part I – General Provisions (Articles 1–11), Part II – Contract on voluntary work (Articles 12–16), Part III – Rights and obligations of volunteers and organizers of volunteer work (Articles 17–23), Part IV – Development and monitoring of volunteerism (Articles 24–30), Part V – Evidence and supervision (Articles 31–34) and Part VI – Transitional and final provision (Articles 35–36).

288. According to Article 1, volunteer work is performed under conditions and in the manner prescribed by this Law. Volunteer work[353] is voluntary and free of charge investment of time, knowledge and skills providing services or activities in favour of another person or for the general welfare of society (hereinafter 'voluntary services') (Article 2, paragraph 1). At the level of territory of Montenegro and at local government level they may establish volunteer services (Article 25, paragraph 1).

289. Providing volunteer services is performed on the basis of the contract on voluntary work (Article 8, paragraph 1). The contract on the voluntary work is concluded in the writing between the volunteers[354] and organizer of the volunteer work (Article 12, paragraph 1).

290. The role and importance of volunteer work, long-term objectives, development priorities and measures for their realization shall be determined by the Strategy for the development of volunteerism (Article 24, paragraph 1), adopted by the GMNE for a period of five years (Article 24, paragraph 2). In accordance with this Strategy, Programmes for development of the volunteerism are adopted at the local level (Article 24, paragraph 3).[355]

SWD(2016) 360 final, p. 9. 'The government needs to find a balance between the requirements of efficient policy-making and the need for transparency and inclusiveness of civil society.'

353. Volunteer work is done without pay for the work performed, fees or some other profit, if not otherwise specified in this Law (Art. 3, para. 1). Volunteer work, according to this Law, shall be (Art. 11, para. 1): (1) training without employment, in accordance with special law; (2) training of apprentices for the period of apprenticeship; (3) provision of services or activities that one person is required to provide to another person on the basis of the laws or other regulations; (4) performing of special duties in accordance with court orders and judgments; (5) performance of services or activities that are common in family, friendly or neighbourly relations.

354. A volunteer is a person who performs voluntary and free-of-charge volunteer services (Art. 4, para. 1).

355. Supervision of the implementation of this Law and regulations governing the voluntary work is done by the Ministry over the labour inspection (Art. 32, para. 1).

I. Criminal Code

291. Criminal Code (OJ RM, Nos 70/2003, 47/2006, OJ MNE, Nos 40/2008, 25/2010, 32/2011, 64/11-corr, 40/13, 56/13-corr, 14/15, 42/15, 58/15, 44/17, 49/18, 3/20, 145/21) contains special criminal offence prescribed in Article 317 (violation of the right to be informed on the state of the environment). Article 317 declares:

> Anyone who contrary to regulations does not provide data or provides untrue data on the state of the environment and the phenomena which are necessary for the assessment of danger for the environment and for taking measures for the protection of life and health of people shall be liable to a fine or imprisonment for a maximum term not exceeding one year.[356]

292. The Code provides clear restrictions and criminal sanctions for non-authorized private, corporate or state data collection, disclosure or dissemination.

IV. Environmental Legislation

293. All relevant environmental regulations contain provisions relating to access to information and public participation in decision-making. These are, *inter alia*: the Law on EIA (OJ MNE, No. 75/18),[357] the Law on SEA (OJ RM, No. 80/05, OJ MNE, Nos 73/10, 40/11, 59/11, 52/16), the Law on IPPC (OJ RM, No. 80/05, OJ MNE, Nos 54/09, 73/10, 40/11, 42/15, 54/16, and 55/18),[358] the Law on Waste Management (OJ MNE, Nos 64/11, 39/16), the Law on Environmental Noise Protection (OJ MNE (OJ MNE, Nos 28/11, 1/14, 2/18), the Law on Waters (OJ RM, No. 27/07, OJ MNE, Nos 32/11, 47/11-corr, 48/15, 52/16, 2/17, 80/17, 84/18), etc.

294. One of the basic principles of the environmental protection stipulated in Law on Environment (OJ MNE, Nos 52/16, 73/19)[359] is the principle of access to

356. Anyone who makes public untrue data on the state of the environment and thereby causes panic or major alarm among citizens shall be liable to a penalty referred to in para. 1 of this article (Art. 317, para. 2).
357. *See* more extensively, subchapter that refers to the general law.
358. The Law on IPPC has ceased to be valid due to the adoption of the Law on Industrial Emissions (OJ MNE, No. 17/19). This law also contains special provisions on access to information and public participation.
359. Also, the first Law on Environment (Official Journal of RM, No. 12/1996) contained several provisions relevant for environmental information and public participation. According to Art. 27, 'The Republic is obliged to provide citizens with timely and complete information about the state of the environment and pollution that may pose a threat to human life or health and/or flora and fauna.' Data on the state and quality of the environment and data on the emission of polluting substances shall be considered as public ones. No one shall be entitled to withhold information or in any other way render them inaccessible to the public (Art. 28).

information and public participation. In accordance with Article 5, point 12 'everyone has the right to be informed about the state of the environment and to participate in the decision-making process which could have an effect on the environment. Information on the state of the environment[360] is public'.[361]

295. Although several other provisions of the Law could be relevant for environmental information and public participation in decision-making process the most important are those related to the monitoring[362] and environmental information system (Chapters VIII and X). In this regard state authorities and units of local self-government have several prescribed obligations. Units of local self-government can organize monitoring of the environment on the territory of the municipality (Article 58). Legal entities and/or entrepreneurs which are the users of the facilities that pollute the environment have the obligation to organize the monitoring of the emission and other sources of pollution (Article 59, paragraph 1).

296. Environmental protection information system has to be established in order to identify effective classifying, processing, monitoring and recording of natural resources and environmental management (Article 62). All subjects of environmental protection (defined in Article 8 of this Law) are obliged, at the request of the Agency, to submit data and information which are necessary for information systems (Article 64). Cadastre of polluters of the environment contains information about the sources, type, amount, manner and place of release, transmission and disposal of polluting matters and waste in the environment (Article 65).

297. The Environmental Performance Review carried out in 2002 recommended to the RM that it should strengthen its environmental policy framework regarding information, public participation and education. These recommendations were addressed to different ministries and government agencies. The whole governance system has been under reform since 2002. This has profound implications for the disclosure of environmental information, public access to this information and public participation in environmental decision-making and highlights the need for more environmental education.[363] In the meantime 'Montenegro has taken some steps to improve cooperation with civil society, but considerable efforts are needed to achieve effective public participation and consultation in decision-making'.[364]

360. 'Environmental information' is any information in written, visual, audio, electronic or any other available form, which is related to the environment (Art. 7, point 12 of the Law on Environment).
361. 'Public' is one or more natural or legal persons, their associations, organizations or groups (Art. 7, point 13 of the Law on Environment).
362. Apart from the Law on Environment, legislative framework regulating environmental monitoring activities include several other laws and by laws in different field as well as international treaties.
363. UNECE (2007), 29.
364. EC. *Montenegro 2016 Report*, Accompanying the document Communication from the Commission to the European Parliament, the Council, the European Economic and Social Committee and the Committee of the Regions, 2016 Communication on EU Enlargement Policy, Brussels, 9.11.2016, SWD(2016) 360 final, p. 75. For more details *see*: UNECE (2015), 75.

298. 'Efforts were made to establish an integrated environmental information system, of which the air quality and water information systems are an integral part. However it has been developed partially, and for the parts available no automatic information flows have been ensured. Data reporting by enterprises is still limited'.[365]

§6. Law on Infrastructure of Spatial Data

299. The Parliament of Montenegro adopted the Law on infrastructure of spatial data (OJ MNE, No. 37/17. This Law regulates the establishment and maintenance of the spatial data infrastructure,[366] as well as other issues of relevance to the spatial data infrastructure (Article 1).

300. The Law contains following thirty articles: object (Article 1); spatial data infrastructure (Article 2); spatial data (Article 3); change of regulations (Article 4); meaning of the terms (Article 5); areas of spatial data (Article 6); obligations of public institutions (Article 7); metadata (Article 8); interoperability (Article 9); network services and technologies (Article 10); geoportal (Article 11); connecting of network services (Article 12); access to network services and exchange of spatial data sets and services (Article 13); cross-border cooperation agreements (Article 14); restriction of access to spatial data (Article 15); fee for usage of network data (Article 16); spatial Data infrastructure council (Article 17); competencies of the council (Article 18); monitoring and reporting (Article 19); cooperation and data delivery (Article 29); financial resources (Article 21); supervision (Article 22); penalties (Article 23); deadline for passing regulations (Article 24); establishing of the council (Article 25); deadlines for harmonizing of spatial data (Article 26); establishing of geoportal (Article 27); beginning of the application (Article 28); termination of application (Article 29); and entry into force (Article 30).

§7. Enforcement and Control

301. Enforcement and control activities have been regulated by several legal regulations. Although general framework has been established by the Law on Inspection Supervision and the Law on State Administration specific environmental legislation contains relevant provisions, too. Inspections are performed by the ecological inspectorate at the state level and inspections at the local self-government level in accordance with defined competencies. In addition, inspections in other areas may be important for the inspection activities in the field of environment (e.g.,

365. UNECE (2015), p. xxii.
366. Spatial Data Infrastructure is a set of technologies, rules and standards for the processing, access, exchange of spatial data and their optimal use (Art. 2, para. 1). Spatial data, within the meaning of this Law, are data that are directly or indirectly related to the geographical location or geographical area (Art. 3, para. 1).

in the field of construction and physical planning, forestry, water management, transport, sanitary,[367] health and tourism).

302. According to the Strategy of public administration reform in Montenegro 2011–2016 'inspection system in Montenegro makes thirty-four inspections, which act within the eleven ministries, and is characterized by redundancy and over-standardize setting. It is necessary to complete the codification system of inspection in order to avoid the current problems over-standardize setting'.[368]

303. In the period from 1 September 2011 to 31 March 2012 environmental inspection, on the basis of valid legal regulations, performed 1,195 inspection supervisions and issued 294 Decisions related to taking measures and actions with the aim of environmental pollution protection and elimination of the determined irregularities.[369] 'Almost 2,500 inspections carried out by seven people in 2013 means that every environmental inspector undertook about 350 inspections per year, which is an unusually high number compared with other inspections. For example, a water inspector conducted 100–150 site visits per year in 2012–2013, while 11 forestry inspectors made about 1,148 checks in 2013'.[370]

304. 'An important organizational change was made in 2012 in order to bring all inspections under a single administrative body, the Administration for Inspection Affairs'.[371] Within the Administration for Inspection Affairs, environmental inspection is currently performed by seven people, whereas twelve inspectors were formerly employed by the EPA.

---

367. On 9 Mar. 2010 Parliament of Montenegro adopted a new *Law on Sanitary Inspection* (Official Journal of MNE, No. 14/10). It has the following twelve Articles: Art. 1 – Subject, Art. 2 – Jurisdiction of the inspector, Art. 3 – Keeping the identity of the initiative submitter, Art. 4 – Areas that are subjects of the inspection, Art. 5 – Facilities that are subject of the inspection, Art. 6 – The authority of the sanitary inspectors, Art. 7 – Obligations of sanitary inspectors, Art. 8 – Sanitary approval, Art. 9 – Evidence, Art. 10 – The deadline for adoption of by-laws, Art. 11 – Cessation of validity and Art. 12 – Entry into force.
368. 'Organizing inspections as internal organizational units of ministries and other government has certain disadvantages and adversely affect the general position of the inspection system, and therefore the general independence which is necessary to perform their functions. Also, analysis of existing inspection organization in the relevant principle, determined the unequal impact of inspections and inspectors. Competences of individual inspections are interwoven, where they appear as positive and negative conflicts of jurisdiction. This is particularly characteristic of utility and sanitary, veterinary and sanitary, health and sanitary inspection, etc., making it necessary to thoroughly examine and clearly delineate the responsibilities of individual inspectors.' GMNE (2011b), 35.
369. GMNE (2012), 97.
370. UNECE (2015), 44. 'A possible root cause of this excessive number of environmental inspections is the definition of inspection and likely inclusion in overall statistics of the small-desk reviews of documentation and administrative checks carried out on site. In any case, current reporting on environmental inspections is limited so the roots of the problem are not understood.' *Ibid.*, 45.
371. For more information *see*: UNECE (2015), p. 34. 'There is no formal methodology behind the current inspection planning approach. No standardized operating procedures for inspections have been adopted to date. The establishment of an efficient enforcement system in the water sector remains a challenge, because of the limited resources of the water inspection, as well as difficulties with data coordination and exchange between the environmental and water authorities.' *Ibid.*, p. xx.

I. General Legislation

305. The general legal provision for enforcement activities is established by the Law on Inspection's Supervision (Official Journal RM, No. 39/03 and OJ MNE, Nos 76/09, 57/11, 18/14, 11/15, 52/16).[372] The Law contains the following thirteen chapters: Chapter I – Basic Provisions (Articles 1–5), Chapter II – Principles of Inspection Supervisions (Articles 6–12), Chapter III – Obligations and Authorities of Inspectors (Articles 13–19), Chapter IV – Rights and Obligations of a Controlled Entity and other Persons (Articles 20–24), Chapter V – Inspection Control Procedure (Articles 25–41), Chapter VI – Specific Action of the Inspection Procedure (Articles 42–55), Chapter VII – Execution (Articles 56–62), Chapter VIII – Relations between Inspection and Other Authorities (Articles 63–65), Chapter IX – Expenses of Inspection Procedure (Article 66), Chapter X – Joint Inspection Control (Articles 67–68), Chapter XI – Inspectors and their Responsibility (Articles 69–72), Chapter XII – Penal Provisions (Article 73) and Chapter XIII – Transitory and Final Provisions (Articles 74–79).

306. The Law set the principles of inspection supervision (i.e., prevention,[373] proportionality,[374] publicity, independence, protection of the public interest, truth and subsidiarity) and the obligations and authorities of inspectors as well as other issues important for performance of inspection control (Article 1). Inspection control, in accordance with the law and other regulations, has to be performed by administrative authorities competent for inspection supervision (hereinafter 'Inspection Body') (Article 2, paragraph 1), although the local self-government authorities have to also apply provisions of this law when they perform inspection control in accordance with the law and other regulations (Article 2, paragraph 6).[375]

307. The obligations and authorities of inspectors and the administrative measures and actions (including fines as an administrative measure) are defined by the provisions of Chapter III (Articles 13–19).[376] According to Article 13 an inspector

372. On the day when this Law entered into force, the Law on Inspection Control (Official Journal of RM, No. 50/92) ceased to be in effect, except the provisions of Art. 26 and Ch. IV on Administrative Inspection (Arts 29–32) (Art. 77). Entering into force of this law, the Law on Inspection Control (Official Journal of RM, No. 50/92), except for the provisions of the Art. 26 and Ch. IV on Administrative Inspection (Arts 29–32), ceases to be in effect (Art. 77).

373. Pursuant to the provision of Art. 6 'priority function of the inspection control shall be a prevention, and inspector shall perform administrative measures and actions only when the preventive function cannot achieve purpose and objective of the inspection control'.

374. In performing inspection control, an inspector shall undertake only those measures and actions that are proportional to the irregularities done, and by which the objective and purpose of inspection control shall be achieved in more convenient way for the controlled entity (Art. 7).

375. Inspection supervision shall be performed by an inspector as a civil servant with specific competences and responsibilities. Exceptionally, the chief of the inspection authority can determine that an inspector may perform inspection control in other administrative area from the competence of that authority (Art. 4).

376. Other issues relating to the inspectors and their responsibility (appointment of inspectors, official identification, responsibilities of an inspector, release of inspectors) are regulated by the provisions of the Arts 69–72 (Ch. X).

is especially obliged to: (1) consider an initiative for starting an inspection procedure and to inform the submitter of the undertaken measures; (2) notify the responsible person on the starting of an inspection control, except if he/she deems that this notification might disparage the effectiveness of the inspection control; (3) point a controlled entity to his/her rights that he/she may exercise during inspection control procedure; (4) make a record on the performed inspection control as well as other prescribed records; and (5) act legally, promptly and in accordance with the civil servants' ethics code.[377]

308. Obligations and authorities in eliminating the irregularities include obligation and authority of the inspector to: (1) indicate the established irregularities and to set a time limit for their elimination; (2) issue an order for appropriate measures and actions within the time limit he/she determines; (3) temporarily prohibit the performing of the activity and other actions; (4) temporarily seize objects or means, which some criminal act has been committed with, until the finalization of the procedure in front of the competent authority; (5) pronounce fines, in accordance with the law and other regulations; (6) submit a demand for starting of an offence procedure;[378] (7) bring criminal or other appropriate charges; and (8) perform other obligations and authorities in accordance with regulations (Article 15).[379]

309. A specific chapter of the Law is devoted to the description of rights and obligations of a body under inspection and other legal persons (Chapter IV, Articles 20–24). A controlled entity is obliged to act in accordance with the proposal or the order of the inspector; to provide the inspector free access for inspection control; to give information and submit documentation for inspection, that is, data needed for the performance of inspection control; to ensure conditions necessary for undisturbed work and establishment of factual state to the inspector. On request or order of the inspector, the controlled entity is obliged to submit or prepare accurate and complete data, documentation or other material needed for the inspection control to

---

377. In performing inspection control, the inspector shall have the authority to: (1) examine: buildings and premises, fields, equipment and appliances, work device and other objects, products that have been put in sale, circulation of goods as well as services, business books, files and registers, contracts, public papers and other business documentation; (2) establish the identity of the controlled entity and other persons; (3) take statements from the controlled entity and other persons; (4) take samples necessary for establishing the factual state; (5) order the performing of appropriate measures and actions for the purpose of providing the inspection control; (6) temporary take-away documentation, objects and other things necessary for establishing the factual state; (7) prohibit the performance of certain activities; (8) provide execution of ordered measures; and (9) undertake other measures by which the performance of the inspection control is ensured (Art. 14).
378. There was only one court case in 2006. UNECE (2007), 24. But, generally speaking, the environmental inspectorate never receives feedback on cases being prosecuted. *Ibid.*, 25.
379. Penalty for offences of a controlled entity – legal person who fails to act in accordance with inspector's order, or does not permit performance of the inspection control, or fails to prepare and deliver the requested data and documentation within a fixed deadline, or fails to allow the inspector undisturbed performance of the control, or fails to provide conditions for undisturbed work and establishment of the factual state has been prescribed by the Art. 73 of the Law.

the inspector on his/her request or order, in determined deadline (Article 21).[380] The person, who has not been a controlled entity in the procedure, has the obligation to permit inspection control when there is considerable doubt that activities have been performed or that there are objects subject to inspection control on these premises (Article 24).[381]

310. The inspection supervision procedures[382] are described in Chapter V of the Law (Articles 25–41). It includes provisions which relate to the following issues: performance of the control in the absence of a controlled entity, disturbing of an Inspector, obligation of the Police to cooperation, cooperation of other institutions and experts, record on the inspection control, exception from the obligation to make a record, establishing facts during the inspection control procedure, signature of the record, inspection control of the unidentified controlled entity, indication, conclusions and decisions during the procedure, appeal and delay of the execution upon appeal. Pursuant to Article 26 the inspection supervision procedure has to be performed, in accordance with this law, other regulations and the Law on General Administrative Procedure.[383]

311. Specific action of the inspection procedure includes provisions which relate to the following: taking samples (Articles 42 and 43),[384] assumption of concord (Article 44), denial of analysis results (Article 45), super analysis (Article 46), expenses of analysis (Article 47), temporary seizure of objects for provision of evidence (Articles 48–53) and obligation to compensation of damage to the controlled entity (Article 54).

380. The responsibility for undisturbed inspection control and the execution of the ordered measures shall lie with the controlled entity and responsible person within the controlled entity. The controlled entity, that is, a responsible person within the controlled entity, shall be obliged to inform the inspector in written form on whether the ordered measures have been executed, in three days from the expiry of the time limit set for the execution of the same (Art. 23).

381. A penalty has been prescribed for a controlled entity – legal person if: (1) he fails to allow the inspector undisturbed performance of the control, or fails to provide conditions for undisturbed work and establishment of the factual state (Art. 21, paras 1 and 2); (2) he fails to prepare and deliver the requested data and documentation within a fixed deadline (Art. 21, para. 3); (3) he does not permit performance of the inspection control (Art. 24, para. 1); and (4) he fails to act on inspector's order, fails to inform the inspector on the execution or he fails to execute an ordered measure, in a fixed deadline (Arts 20, 23, para. 2, Art. 56, para. 1) (Art. 73).

382. An inspection control procedure in the sense of this law shall comprise the performance of inspection control, decision on rights and duties of a controlled entity and execution of administrative measures and actions (Art. 25).

383. Inspections are carried out in various ways; they can: (i) be planned; (ii) be ordered by the Minister or Deputy Minister; (iii) follow complaints; (iv) take place after an accident; and (v) take place at facilities requiring an environmental impact assessment. Inspections are ad hoc, and there is no inventory or list of polluting industries requiring environmental inspections, which implies that the enterprises eligible for inspection are not known. UNECE (2007), 25.

384. The inspectorate entrusts the appointed or accredited laboratories (CETI, Hydromet, Institute of Heath, Institute of Metallurgy for steel and iron) with the analyzing of samples taken during the inspections. Out of three mandatory samples taken, one is kept for further analysis in case of non-compliance. UNECE (2007), 25.

312. Monitoring of execution, administrative execution, execution through other persons, execution through fines, execution through direct coercion, execution of financial obligations[385] and expenses of execution are regulated by Articles 56–62. Pursuant to Article 56 'the controlled entity is obliged to execute a decision, within the deadline determined in the decision. If the controlled entity fails to execute a decision in determined deadline, a decision shall be executed in administrative manner'.[386] If the execution cannot be ensured through other persons or by fines, it shall be ensured through direct coercion (Article 60).

313. Relations between inspections[387] and other authorities are subject to regulations of Articles 63–65 of the Law. Expenses of the inspection procedure are prescribed by Article 66.[388] In performing inspection control, inspection authorities are obliged to mutually cooperate and cooperate with other authorities and organizations. Public administration authorities, local self-government authorities and other organs and organizations, upon demand of the inspector, are obliged to deliver the requested data and information necessary for the achievement of his/her functions (Article 63).

The Law on State Administration (OJ MNE, Nos 78/18, 70/21, 50/22) prescribes, *inter alia*, general rules relating to the administrative supervision activities. Pursuant to Article 9 'the work of state administration authorities is subject to control. The control of the work of state administration authorities shall be realized through administrative and other supervision, judicial control and other forms of control, in accordance with the law'.[389] Inspectional supervision determines whether the subjects of supervision abide by laws, other regulations and general acts. Furthermore, it executes administrative and other measures and actions to remedy the determined illegalities and secure the proper application of acts (Article 20).

(Article 20, paragraph 1).[390]

---

385. Decision and conclusion on financial obligations of the controlled entity shall be executed coercively by the competent authority for public revenues (Art. 61).
386. The administrative act of the inspector shall be administrative executed through other persons, by a fine or direct force (Art. 57).
387. There are other inspectorates at the national level which are relevant for environmental issues and whose activities have been regulated by specific legislation. These are: for mining, energy, forestry, veterinary services and water. Since 2003, there has been efficient cooperation among the different inspectorate bodies. This cooperation is achieved through joint inspections or by other inspectors reporting violations to the relevant inspectorate. UNECE (2007), 25.
388. The expenses of an inspection procedure that was decided upon in favour of the controlled entity shall be borne by the inspection authority, if the law does not provide something else. The expenses of an inspection procedure that was decided upon unfavourably for the controlled entity shall be borne by the controlled entity itself. The expenses of a procedure that arose from illicit activities of the controlled entity shall be borne by the controlled entity; regardless of how the procedure was completed (Art. 66, paras 1–3).
389. The conduct of administrative supervision comprises: (1) supervision over the legality of administrative acts and other administrative activities; (2) supervision of the legality and effectiveness of the work of administrative bodies, local self-government and other legal entities in the performance of transferred or entrusted tasks; (3) inspection supervision (Art. 17).
390. Inspection supervision shall be regulated by a specific law (Art. 20, para. 2).

314. The ministry performs control of general acts adopted by public institutions founded by the state, warns their organs if general acts do not abide by the Constitution or a law and suggests adequate measures for harmonization. If the public institution founded by the state fails to conform to the warning of a ministry, a ministry can ask the Government to suspend the application of the act if its application might cause substantial harmful consequences. A ministry might initiate a procedure for the constitutional revision of the act in front of the Constitutional Court (Article 76).

315. Ministry controls the work of local self-administration in the performance of delegated or entrusted tasks and it has the right and obligation to: (1) issue the obligatory instructions for performance and offer expert advice; (2) warn the local self-administration for the failure to perform the tasks and oblige it to secure the completion of tasks in a certain time-frame; (3) warn the local self-administration to execute certain measures for the performance of tasks; (4) issue the preliminary consent on the acts and regulations of local self-administration adopted in relation to delegated or entrusted tasks; (5) execute measures of responsibility.

316. If the local self-administration fails to act upon the warning to execute certain measures for the performance of tasks, the Ministry can execute these measures on its own, with the costs being borne by the local self-administration (Article 39).[391]

II. Specific Environmental Legislation

317. All basic laws in the field of environmental protection (Law on Environment, Law on EIA, Law on SEA, Law on IPPC, etc.) contain special provisions concerning implementation mechanisms as well as control of the functioning of the mechanisms. Specific provisions for environmental inspections are set in media-oriented laws, too. Besides that, it must be kept in mind that certain acts, very relevant to the protection of the environment, have been sanctioned by the criminal law as criminal acts.

318. The Law on Environment (Official Journal MNE, No. 52/16)[392] contains special chapters devoted to supervision (Chapter XI), liability for pollution of the environment (Chapter VII), as well as the division with penal measures (Chapter

391. The Ministry might suggest to the Government to initiate the procedure for divestment of the local self-administration from delegated or entrusted tasks, if, after being warned, it still fails to perform them legally or promptly (Art. 40).

392. By the old Law on the environment (Official Journal of RM, Nos 12/1996 and 55/2000) it had been prescribed (Art. 43) that the inspection of the implementation of the Law itself, and of regulations based on it, had been entrusted to the environmental inspection of the Ministry for inspection and supervision. According to the same Law there were certain issues for which 'the environmental inspector is primarily competent' (Art. 44), but a procedure had also been given in cases when other laws or regulations had been violated if the violation could have had an impact on the environment.

XIII).[393] In addition, it should have in mind the provisions relating to the monitoring of the state of the environment (Chapter VIII). Supervision over the implementation of this Law and regulations adopted on the basis of this law has to be carried out by the Ministry and other competent state organs in accordance with law (Article 80). However, inspection supervision over the implementation of laws and regulations adopted on the basis of this law is made by the inspections, in accordance with the law and the law that regulates the inspection.

319. The rights, duties and competencies of the inspectors are stipulated in Articles 80–86 of the Law. Pursuant to Article 33 of the Law on EIA (OJ RM, No. 80/05, OJ MNE, Nos 40/10, 27/13, 52/16) supervision over the implementation of this Law and regulations adopted on the basis of this law made has to be carried out by 'government agencies responsible for environmental protection and authority of local government responsible for environmental protection'.

320. Inspection within the jurisdiction of the state administration responsible for environmental protection is carried out by the environmental inspections in accordance with law.[394] If the rules prescribed by the law or other regulations are injured, the environmental inspector has obligation to undertake the following administrative measures and actions:[395] (1) order the project developer to acquire decisions of the competent authorities on the need for impact assessment; (2) order the project developer to obtain the consent of the EIA study; (3) order the project developer to implement measures determined by the EIA study; (4) order the project developer to implement the programme of the project's impact on the environment; and (5) prohibit the construction of the project developer until the consent of the competent authorities of the EIA study is obtained (Article 34).

321. Supervision of the implementation of the Law on SEA (OJ RM, No. 80/05, OJ MNE, Nos 73/10, 40/11, 59/11, 52/16), within the jurisdiction established by this law, has to be carried out by the body of state administration responsible for environmental protection and authority of local government responsible for environmental protection. Inspection has to be carried out by the ecological inspections in accordance with law (Article 27).[396]

322. In accordance with Article 26 of the Law on IPPC (OJ RM, No. 80/05, OJ MNE, Nos 54/09, 73/10, 40/11, 42/15, 54/16), supervision over the implementation of this law and regulations established on the basis of this law has to be implemented by the state administration responsible for environmental protection and authority of local government responsible for environmental protection. Inspection,

393. Article 87 prescribes a fine for offences for breaches of the relevant articles of the Law.
394. In carrying out the inspection control environmental inspector controls especially: (1) if the holder of the project has the decision of the competent authorities about the need for impact assessment; (2) if the holder of the project has the approval of the EIA study; and (3) if the holder of the project implemented measures from EIA study for which the consent has been issued (Art. 33, para. 3).
395. In addition to administrative measures and actions defined by Law inspection's control.
396. With regard to those issues not regulated by the Law on SEA, provisions of the law which regulates the general administrative procedure will be implemented (Art. 26).

within the jurisdiction of the state administration responsible for affairs of the environment, is performed by ecological inspections,[397] in accordance with the Law on inspection's control.

323. During 2008 the Environmental Inspection conducted 772 inspection supervisions (verbal warning for minor work-related irregularities, preventive instructing with regard to the waste disposal and others); adopted 445 decisions regarding measures and actions to be undertaken with the aim of removal of the established irregularities, monitoring (measurement) of emissions, industrial waste disposal, aberration from the prescribed production process and obtaining environmental consent for the structure. Furthermore, sixty-nine notifications were submitted to other inspection authorities in order for them to undertake measures within their competence and twenty-two misdemeanour citations were also submitted.[398]

324. Generally speaking, 'the institutional framework for compliance assurance remains weak. Communication and coordination among various authorities are not yet effective. Local self-government units have been transferred many responsibilities while their capacity for environmental management is limited, in particular for implementing EIA and IPPC-related legislations'.[399]

397. In performing inspection supervision, ecological inspector controls especially: (1) the work of new facilities in regard to obtaining permits; (2) the work of the existing facilities in regard to compliance with the requirements and conditions for obtaining licences established by this law; (3) implementation of prescribed measures and conditions for environmental protection established by the permit; (4) any change in the work and functioning of plants; (5) implementation of their own monitoring programmes, monitoring results, as well as their submitting; (6) annual reports on the carrying out of activities for which a permit is issued; and (7) documentation of the operator in connection with issuing, extending or changing the dissolution of the validity of permits (Art. 26, para. 3).

398. GMNE (2008a), 42. In 2006 the Ecological Inspectorate: carried out 279 inspections (delivering oral warnings for minor irregularities, and preventive instructions for proper waste disposal); issued 115 decisions on measures to be taken in order to correct certain irregularities regarding emission monitoring, industrial waste disposal, deviation from authorized production processes and a lack of necessary environmental authorization for construction; issued sixteen information notices to other inspectorates about measures undertaken within their area of responsibility; filed thirty-seven law infraction cases (unfulfilled obligations, inappropriate waste disposal, a lack of necessary authorizations, environmental pollution and activities initiated in the protected natural zones); filed one claim for criminal offence due to a pollution discharge on a large scale; issued twelve decisions on withholding of authorizations for activities until corrective measures are implemented; and forced closure of two premises. In addition, in 2006, the ecological inspectorate also carried out: 15,305 controls of radioactivity on imported goods; 123 controls of authorizations for import, export and transit of waste on border crossings; thirty-six controls of authorizations for import, export and transit of goods containing ozone-depleting substances; and twenty controls of ionized emissions at border crossings. UNECE (2007), 25. For the data in the period from 1 Jan. 2004 to 24 Aug. 2006 *see*: Republička ekološka inspekcija (2006).

399. UNECE (2015), 48. For more information *see* chapter 'Compliance and enforcement mechanisms' in UNECE (2015), 33–50.

325. According to the 2018 Progress Report 'significant efforts are still needed on implementation and enforcement, in particular on water quality, nature protection, and waste management'.[400] In addition, the EC Report for 2022 emphasizes climate change.[401]

§8. Legal Harmonization with EU Legislation

326. 'Since 2002, environmental legislation has developed significantly'.[402] The main driving force that explains this progress is the country's overarching priority, accession to the EU.[403]

327. On 22 January 2007, the EU Council passed the Decision on the adoption of a new document on the European Partnership with Montenegro.[404] According to Article 2 of the Decision 'the implementation of the European Partnership with Montenegro shall be examined through the mechanisms established under the stabilization and association process, notably the annual progress reports presented by the Commission'.[405]

328. The Stabilization and Association Agreement (SAA) between the European Communities and Montenegro as well as the Interim Agreement on Trade and Trade-Related Matters been signed by Montenegro on 15 October 2007 in Luxembourg.[406] Issues related to the area of environment are defined in Title VIII – Cooperation Policies, precisely by Article 111 relating to the Environment and Article 97 on Forestry.

329. By signing the SAA, Montenegro has also assumed the obligation to harmonize Montenegrin legislation with *Acquis communautaire*. Pursuant to Article 72 of the SAA, the parties to the Agreement recognize the significance of harmonization of the existing Montenegrin legislation with the legislation of the Community, as well as its efficient enforcement.[407]

---

400. EC (2018). p. 79. For more detailed *see*: MSDT (2016a).
401. EC (2022), p. 112.
402. UNECE (2007), 22.
403. In the European Partnership with the State Union of Serbia and Montenegro, which was adopted by the European Council in June 2004, the main emphasis was given to adjusting the horizontal legislation. *Ibid.*, 22.
404. Council Decision 2007/49/EC of 22 Jan. 2007 on the principles, priorities and conditions contained in the European Partnership with Montenegro (Official Journal L 20, 27 Jan. 2007, 16).
405. Since March 2002, the Commission of the European Communities has reported regularly to the Council and the Parliament on progress made by the countries of the Western Balkans region. Following Montenegro's independence in June 2006, the Commission issued progress reports dedicated entirely to Montenegro in 2006 and 2007. *See*: EC (2006); EC (2007), 38–39.
406. The Agreement on Stabilization and Association has been ratified in the Parliament of Montenegro on 13 Nov. 2007. The consent to the Agreement was given by the European Parliament on 13 Dec. 2007. The implementation of the Interim Agreement has successfully commenced since 1 Jan. 2008. GMNE (2008b), 1.
407. GMNE (2008b), 2–3.

330. At its session held on 21 June 2007, the Government decided to elaborate on the NPI for the period of 2008–2012 which represents a national plan for the adoption of the Acquis.

331. Process of the harmonization of national laws in the area of the Environment with the relevant EU Directives has been intensified and set of new laws in the area of EIA and SEIA, air quality, waste management, water management, industrial pollution control, chemicals and noise were adopted.[408] Further harmonization in these areas will be realized by adoption of secondary regulations. In addition, the process of the ratification of Multilateral Environmental Agreements (MEAs) has been intensified.[409]

332. In the period from 2010 through 2012, full implementation of the legal system of EU regulations in the area of horizontal legislation was envisaged.[410]

333. The Environmental Law (2016) was adopted in order to comply with EU regulations. The major share of the EU horizontal legislation has already been transposed into the legal system of Montenegro. The following directives are fully transposed: Directive 2001/42/EC (SEA); Directive 2011/92/EU (EIA), which codified Directive 85/337/EEC and its amendments by Directive 97/11/EC, Directive 2003/35/EC and Directive 2009/31/EC; Directive 2003/4/EC (access to environmental information); Directive 2003/35/EC (public participation and access to justice in EIA procedures and procedures for the issuance of IPPC permits); Directive 2004/35/EC (environmental liability), as amended by Directive 2006/21/EC (mining waste), Directive 2009/31/EC (geological storage of carbon-dioxide) and Directive 2013/30/EU (safety of offshore oil and gas operations); Directive 2008/99/EC (on the protection of the environment through criminal law).[411]

334. According to the programme for the accession of Montenegro to the European Union 2021–2023 Montenegro plans to implement a total of twenty-seven obligations (five in the strategic and twenty-two in the legislative framework) in 2021. A total of sixteen, or 59.3% (two from the strategic and fourteen from the legislative framework) have been implemented. All planned obligations in the fields of chemicals and climate change have been implemented, and the Government has also

408. All these laws are important steps in the harmonization of the national legislation with the EU environmental acquis. Specifically, the laws on EIA, SEA and IPPC are crucial because of their horizontal character (i.e., relating to general environmental management issues rather than specific media).
409. GMNE (2008b), 497. Serbia is the successor to all international agreements that Serbia and Montenegro (SFRY, FRY – predecessors of Serbia and Montenegro) were party to. Based on submitted statements of succession, Montenegro is now in the process of becoming a party to all the MEAs previously ratified (signed) by Serbia and Montenegro, SFRY and FRY. UNDP (2007), 44.
410. GMNE (2008b), 502.
411. MSDT (2016a), p. 9, 10. The report on the implementation of the Program of Accession of Montenegro to the European Union 2021–2023 for the year 2021, and Montenegro's Program of Accession to the European Union 2022–2023 were adopted by the Government of Montenegro in January 2022. *See:* https://www.gov.me/en/documents/a4fb6c49-bdc4-4880-b978-4b92805d859a (1 Jan. 2023), https://www.eu.me/biblioteka/#1583-1683-ppcg (1 Jan. 2023).

adopted the Financial Assessment of the Action Plan for meeting the final benchmarks in Chapter 27 – Environment and Climate Change.[412]

335. According to the 2022 Progress Report 'limited progress was made in further aligning with the EU acquis, on water, nature protection and climate change.'[413]

§9. Critical Evaluation of the Efficiency of the Existing Montenegrin Environmental Laws

336. Based on the Analysis of available documents in which the assessment of the state of the efficiency of application of environmental regulations and realization of environmental policy objectives has been given it can be concluded that in Montenegro significant progress in the construction of relevant legal frameworks in the field of environment has been made in the last few years.[414] However, in several areas, the need for further upgrading of the system has been identified.

337. Montenegro improved the normative framework in the field of environmental protection and achieved good progress in harmonizing legislation with the *acquis* of the EU. It strengthened the institutional framework for realizing the right to a healthy environment.[415]

338. According to the Montenegro 2022 Progress Report Montenegro 'has some level of preparation in this area.' However, limited progress was made in further aligning with the EU acquis in the following areas: water, nature protection and climate change. It is estimated that it is necessary to make significant progress in terms of implementation and enforcement, in particular on waste management, water quality, nature protection and climate change.[416]

---

412. GMNE (2022a). p. 70, 71. In the coming period, several strategic documents are expected to be adopted, which are extremely important in terms of meeting the final benchmarks in this area, namely: Air Quality Management Strategy with Action Plan, Water Management Plans in the water area of the Danube and Adriatic basins, and Forestry Development Strategy. Also, the adoption of one of the most important systemic regulations – the Law on Waste Management, as well as a series of by-laws in the areas of waste management and nature protection – is expected.
413. *EC (2022),* p. 112. In October 2021, the government adopted the first semi-annual report on the implementation of the action plan for the fulfilment of the closing benchmarks in Chapter 27. Two months later, the government adopted the financial assessment of the action plan for the fulfilment of the closing benchmarks in Chapter 27, covering 2021–2025, indicating financial needs amounting to nearly EUR 483 million. *Ibid.*
414. Project 'Monitoring the Progress in the Environment Sector' has begun in Montenegro in 2006 with the support of the Directorate General for the Environment of the European Commission. GMNE (2009b), 500.
415. PHRF (2022), 103. However, the ecological awareness of institutions about the importance of protecting the environment, climate and human health is still not sufficiently developed, which causes a low level of realization of the right to a healthy life.
416. EC. *Montenegro 2022 Report*, p. 112.

339. Compliance with legally binding rules for the implementation of EIA procedures and implementation of AC 'are key elements of an efficient horizontal sector'.[417] Control of measures in practice is absent. The national EIONET network for monitoring and reporting (on the state of the environment) has not been established. Environmental monitoring is a particular challenge. A collision of laws can lead to inadequate enforcement.[418]

340. 'The institutional framework for compliance assurance remains weak. Communication and coordination among various authorities is not yet effective. Local self-government units have been transferred many responsibilities while their capacity for environmental management is limited, in particular for implementing EIA and IPPC-related legislation.'[419]

341. As for the institutional set-up, competencies and capacity available for efficient transposition and implementation of the EU acquis in the area of horizontal legislation, several key gaps have been identified. These are, *inter alia*: there is no sufficient number of employees to perform tasks; human resource capacity for implementation of the legislation at the national and local levels is quite modest in quantitative terms and poses one of the key barriers to higher quality implementation of the EU acquis, which particularly refers to the legislation on EIA, SEA, and the access to environmental information and public participation.[420] Communication and coordination of activities between authorities competent for implementation of the legislation, as well as with the stakeholders, have to be intensified.[421] 'Capacity and infrastructure for transposition and implementation of the INSPIRE Directive are yet to be developed'. Capacity for the performance of inspection control of implementation of the horizontal legislation is 'quite modest'; it is necessary to build capacity of the authorities in justice sector for conducting administrative procedures in respect of access to environmental justice.[422]

342. 'There are still numerous weaknesses in the EMSs that have been identified in the NSSD from 2007, and most notably those relating to: enabling full harmonization of national legislation with the EU acquis, more effective application of

417. Coalition for monitoring of negotiation process within Chapter 27, *ANALYSIS: Chapter 27-Environment and Climate Change,* – English version, February 2018. http://koalicija27.me/2018/02/08/analysis-chapter-27-environment-and-climate-change-english-version/ (23 Dec. 2022), p. 22. Several deficiencies are evident (unclear level of expertise of persons providing consulting services, lack of criteria for relevance and age of data, inadequate list of projects for which the EIA is mandatory).
418. *Ibid.*
419. UNECE (2015), p. 48. 'There are competency overlaps between the environmental inspection and the communal police. Coordination between environmental and water permitting is weak. The integrated register of environment polluters is not yet operational. Environmental protection and water information systems do not yet exist. Lack of competent staff is sometimes flagrant, with competent authorities failing to recruit a chemicals inspector, for example.' *Ibid.*
420. The lack of sufficient administrative capacities at central and local level and inspection bodies, insufficient interinstitutional coordination and lack of a sustainable financial framework remain challenges to be urgently addressed. EC (2022), p. 112.
421. MSDT (2016a). p. 16.
422. *Ibid.*

regulations, the development of administrative and the overall institutional capacities for management of the environment and natural resources, and enabling for more efficient horizontal and vertical institutional coordination, and especially overcoming inadequate environmental financing from both public and private sources, and the still expressed low level of integration of environmental concerns into sectoral policies'.[423]

343. According to the EC 'Montenegro should considerably step up its ambitions towards a green transition' (intensify implementation and enforcement work for the fulfilment of the closing benchmarks in Chapter 27, in particular in the water, nature protection, and climate change sectors; finalise the waste management law and the national waste management plan; and adopt the national energy and climate plan in line with the EU's 2050 zero emission target and the Green Agenda for the Western Balkans).[424]

423. MSDT (2016c). p. 65.
424. EC (2022), p. 112.

Chapter 2. Air Pollution and Climate Change

§1. The Monitoring System

344. In order to monitor level of air pollution in Montenegro, the Government established a network for air quality monitoring (hereinafter 'The State network')[425] (Article 11, paragraph 1 of the Law on air protection, OJ MNE, Nos 25/10, 40/11, 43/15). Air quality monitoring in the State network shall be performed according to the annual air quality monitoring programme developed by the Agency (Article 12, paragraph 1).

345. The local government may, in accordance with the Law, establish a network for monitoring air quality in their area (hereinafter referred to as 'local area network')[426] (Article 14, paragraph 1). The local authorities body adopts a programme for air quality monitoring in the local network (Article 14, paragraph 3), which is carried out in accordance with the provisions of Article 15 of this Law (Article 14, paragraph 4).

346. The Ministry prescribes terms and method of air quality monitoring, standardization of measurements, the conditions to be met by equipment for assessing of air quality, the reference methods, the criteria for achieving data quality, data quality assurance and data validation and content of assessment results in case that for the assessment of air quality are used other methods than measurements (Article 15).[427]

347. Air quality monitoring, emissions measurement and monitoring of fuel quality can be carried out by legal entities and entrepreneurs[428] registered in the Central Registry of the Commercial Court or in another appropriate register (Article 17, paragraph 1).

---

425. The state network consists of measuring points for measurement of (Art. 11, para. 2): (1) air pollution in settlements and in industrial areas; (2) air quality in protected natural areas, sensitive ecological systems, cultural and natural heritage; (3) background pollution, regional and remote cross-border transmission, and measurements within the international obligations of Montenegro; and (4) the impact of mobile sources of air pollution on air quality.
426. The establishment of local networks is carried out in accordance with the criteria from the Art. 11, para. 3 of this Act (Art. 14, para. 2).
427. Furthermore, the Ministry prescribes method of emissions from stationary sources measurement, procedures for measuring, checking accuracy and calibration of measuring devices, the process of results evaluation and the method for providing air quality data for the information system (Art. 16).
428. The legal persons and entrepreneurs are not allowed to operate without the permission of the Agency (Art. 17, para. 2). The Agency issues a licence on the basis of the relevant certificate issued by the National accreditation body (Art. 17, para. 3).

348. In the vicinity of air pollution stationary sources requiring or which may require environment impact assessment, the polluter monitors air quality in the way laid down in the feasibility study of the environment impact assessment (Article 18, paragraph 1).[429]

349. 'In the first half of 2009 measurements of the air quality were performed on a single automated station in Podgorica, while the other three stationary stations were put into operation in the second half of 2009. This was the most important step in modernizing the monitoring of air quality in Montenegro. ... A number of parameters in the monitoring programme of air quality were reduced according to the "Regulation on determination of Types of Pollutants, Limit Values and Other Ambient Air Quality Standards" (OJ MNE, No. 45/08). The Regulation complies with EU Air quality framework Directive'.[430]

350. Systematic measuring of emissions of basic polluting substances to the air of Montenegro includes continuous twenty-four-hour measuring of: sulphur dioxide (SO_2), total nitrogen oxides (NO_x), tropospheric ozone (O_3), black soot, the overall content of suspended particles including the content of heavy metals and PAHs, and the content of heavy metals in sedimentary materials at fourteen locations in ten settlements of Montenegro. Measurements at these locations have been performed continually since 1998. Since 2007, measurement of particles that have a special impact on human health ($PM_{2.5}$ and PM_{10}) is being performed in one location.

351. 'The network of stationary automatic monitoring stations was developed gradually over a few years with the support of international organizations and donors, except for the station located in Zabljak. The oldest station of the network is that located in Podgorica, which dates from 2006. The stations in Bar, Nikšić and Pljevlja were installed in 2009, and those in Tivat, Golubovci and Gradina were installed in 2012'. In addition, there is a station located in Zabljak for measuring transboundary air pollution in accordance with the requirements of the Convention on the Long-range Transboundary Air Pollution (CLRTAP) and its European Monitoring and Evaluation Programme (EMEP).[431] Today, the state network for continuous monitoring of air quality, which is in charge of the Environmental Protection Agency, consists of nine stationary stations.[432]

429. Polluter is obliged that air quality data obtained from air quality monitoring from para. 1 of this Article are submitted to the Agency and to the relevant local government authority until 31 March of the year for the previous year (Art. 18, para. 2).
430. UNECE, Working Group on Environmental Monitoring and Assessment (2010a), 1.
431. UNECE (2015), p. 69.
432. MESPU, EPA (2022a) p. 8,9. In accordance with the Regulation on the establishment of a network of measuring points for air quality monitoring (OJ MNE, 44/10, 13/11, 64/18), 'optimal territorial coverage with data on air quality has been established.'

§2. State of Air Pollution and Climate Change

352. 'The quality of air in Montenegro exacerbated in time, with most significant causes being: transportation, industry, agriculture, thermoenergetics and some communal activities. Transportation affects air pollution in cities with main transportation roads; industry particularly in Podgorica and Nikšić; energetics in Pljevlja; and certain communal activities in towns'.[433]

353. The highest level of air pollution is connected with the industrial production (Aluminium production, TE Pljevlja and Steel Plant Nikšić, Mojkovac, etc.), uncontrolled combustion of the waste at town landfills and traffic, which significantly pollute the atmosphere of the urban settlements with exhaust gases.[434] So, 'one of the key challenges is achieving a satisfactory air quality in all areas, particularly for the municipalities of Podgorica, Pljevlja and Nikšić, where the concentration of polluting matter frequently goes above threshold values.'[435]

354. The key sources of primary suspended particles smaller than 10 µm (PM10) and particulate matter smaller than 2.5 µm (PM2.5) are non-industrial combustion plants and road traffic. During 2018, 98% of sulfur oxides (SOx) and 31% of nitrogen oxides (NOx) were emitted from the energy production and transformation sector, while road traffic and other traffic, including construction machinery, was the source of about 54% of NOx emissions. The greater part (96%) of the total emission of ammonia (NH3) originates from the agricultural sector.[436]

355. During 2021, a slight improvement in air quality compared to 2020 was recorded. The results of air quality monitoring in the urban parts of cities in the Northern and Central zones lead to this conclusion, while in the Southern zone, as in the previous year, the air was of very good quality during the entire monitoring period, with occasional (rare) exceedances of the average daily concentration of PM10 particles.[437]

---

433. GMNE, NCSD, 10. Sustainable management of these resources is one of the main challenges faced by Montenegro. *See also* GMNE (2007C), 39–40.
434. GMNE (2008C), 93; *See also* CETI (2008a), 18–20.
435. GMNE (2022d), 34.
436. EPA (2021), p. 23. In the period 2005–2018, a slight decrease in PM2.5 emissions of 2.2% was recorded, while PM10 emissions decreased by 3.4% in the observed period. In the period 2005–2018, there was an increase in emissions from energy production and transformation in total SOx and NOx emissions (by 42% and 15%, respectively), a significant reduction in emissions from energy use in industry (over 90% and 40%), while emissions from traffic increased by 3% (SOx) and, depending on the vehicle category, by over 40% in the case of NOx. *Ibid*, p. 25.
437. MESPU, EPA (2022a) p. 26. The presence of PM10 and PM2.5 in concentrations above the prescribed is highest in Pljevlje and Bijelo Polje, but they are also significant in Podgorica and Nikšić. In the Northern Zone, the highest number of days with exceedances of the limit value of the average daily concentration of PM10 particles was registered in Pljevlja (114 days), while in the Central Zone, the highest number of exceedances was registered at the measuring site Podgorica 3 (seventy days).

356. Montenegro is particularly exposed and vulnerable to climate hazards, such as heatwaves, droughts, forest fires, floods, etc. The results from the climate projections show an increase of 1.5° C to 2°C in the mean annual temperature by 2040 throughout the country. By 2070 the mean annual temperature will increase by up to 3°C and by 2100 the increase is projected to be with 5.5°C.[438] The country has committed to reduce by 30% GHG emissions by 2030 (compared to the reference year 1990) as part of its ambitious mitigation target through its NDC. 'The forecast economic growth for 2017–2030 is based around clean energy (hydroelectric power plants (HPPs), wind, photovoltaic, biomass, and energy-efficiency programmes in transportation (building the national highway and other projects), industry (especially the metal industry), tourism (tourist resorts and hotels), and agriculture.'[439]

§3. Competencies

357. According to Article 4 of the Law on Air Protection (OJ MNE, Nos 25/10, 40/11 and 43/15) the effectiveness of protection and improvement of air quality is assured by: public authorities, governmental bodies, local governments, domestic and foreign legal entities and entrepreneurs, NGOs, citizens and citizen associations (paragraph 1).[440] Administrative and professional duties related to protection and improvement of air quality and implementation of measures for protection and improvement of air quality are conducted and provided by: state authorities responsible for environmental protection (hereinafter 'Ministry'),[441] the administrative authority responsible for environmental protection (hereinafter 'Agency'),[442] the administrative authority responsible for meteorological and hydrological activities (hereinafter 'Hydrometeorological Service'),[443] local administrative authority

---

438. MSDT (2020), p. 24.
439. *Ibid.*,p. 23.
440. *See also* the Decree on Organization and Manner of Work of the Public Administration (Official Journal of MNE, Nos 49/22, 52/22, 56/22, 82/22).
441. In performing of the duties the Ministry establishes, coordinates and supervises the implementation of measures for protection and improvement of air quality, coordinates implementation of national air quality management strategy and execution of the commitments arising from international agreements and conducts international cooperation, including cooperation with European Commission and the exchange of data in the field of air quality (Art. 5).
442. In performing its duties the Agency organizes monitoring of air quality. Air quality assessment is performed on the basis of all available air quality data from various data sources determined by this Law and by other regulations. It also checks the accuracy of the measurements and other methods used by the legal persons authorized to monitor air quality, prepares analyzes and reports, informs the public, performs inspection tasks, establishes communication with relevant national and international bodies and organizations and performs other duties prescribed by this law and by special regulations (Art. 6).
443. *Hydrometeorological Service*, within its responsibility, performs observations and measurements of environmental parameters, control and assessment of air quality and rainfalls, and preparation of studies, reports, studies, analyzes and information, as well as the execution of international obligations in the field of air quality (Art. 7, item 1).

responsible for environmental protection (hereinafter referred to as 'a Local authority'),[444] as well as legal persons and entrepreneurs having public authority (Article 4, paragraph 2).

§4. Strategic Documents and Legislation

358. The following strategies and policies were adopted: National Air Quality Management Strategy with Action Plan for the period 2013–2016;[445] the National Climate Change Strategy until 2030 (2015), the Second Report on the Implementation of the National Climate Change Strategy (2022), the Third National Communication, the Third Biennial Update Report on Climate Change and the updated Intended Nationally Determined Contribution (in 2021), which increases the emissions reduction target to 35% by 2030 (compared to 1990 levels). In addition, the National Strategy for Disaster Risk Reduction 2018–2023 was adopted, and the Disaster Risk Assessment of Montenegro (published in 2021).[446]

359. The Draft Air Quality Management Strategy for the period 2021–2029 has been prepared.[447] The document was sent to the European Commission for its opinion in March 2021.

360. When the Law on the Environment (OJ MNE, Nos 52/2016, 73/19) is concerned, specific legal provisions about the air are contained explicitly in several articles (Articles 2, 6, 7, 15, 18, 19, 42, 54, 55, 67, 77). However, the basic law regulating these issues is the Law on Air Protection.

I. The Law on Air Protection

A. *General Remarks*

361. Basic legal act regulating air protection in Montenegro is the Law on air protection (OJ MNE, Nos 25/10, 40/11, and 43/15). It has the following eleven parts: Part I – General Provisions (Articles 1–3), Part II – Competences and obligations (Articles 4–7), Part III – Assessment of air quality (Articles 8–14), Part IV

---

444. *The national accreditation body* is responsible for accrediting of legal entities to carry out monitoring of air quality and emissions into the air (Art. 7, item 2); *Institute for Standardization* transfers to the national-level European and international standards of air quality that are of interest for Montenegro and participates in the preparation of technical regulations (Art. 7, item 3); *Customs administration* controls the import and export of substances that deplete the ozone layer, alternative substances and products containing these substances and other substances and products that affect or may affect air quality in accordance with this law and special regulations (Art. 7, item 4).
445. *See:* https://www.gov.me/dokumenta/5278544d-536e-49c6-ad06-a0476ee715ac (14 Jan. 2023).
446. It was prepared in line with the EU guidelines for risk assessment and mapping for disaster manageme. GMNE (2022d), p. 105.
447. *See*: MESPU (2021).

– Air quality monitoring and emissions in the air (Articles 15–18), Part V – Air quality management (Articles 19–27), Part VI – Air quality improvement (Articles 28–41), Part VII – Informing and reporting (Articles 42–47), Part VIII – Air quality financing (Articles 48–49), Part IX – Supervision (Articles 50–52), Part X – Penalties (Articles 53–54) and Part XI – Transitional and final provisions (Articles 55–59).

362. According to Article 1, the Law on air[448] protection regulates the method of air quality monitoring, protection measures, evaluating and air quality improvement, as well as planning and management of air quality.

363. The air pollution sources are stationary and mobile emission sources, as well as certain products and activities that cause emissions of air pollution (Article 2, paragraph 1). The stationery and mobile emission sources must be built and/or manufactured, supplied, used and maintained in a way that they do not emit pollutants[449] into the air above the emission limit values, or that they do not emit pollutants into the air in quantities that could endanger human health and the environment (Article 2, paragraph 5).

364. The types of pollutants and air quality standards[450] for each type of air pollutant determines the GMNE (Article 8, paragraph 1).

B. Zones of Air Quality

365. In order to control, maintain the conditions and/or improve air quality, the territory of Montenegro is divided into the zones of Air Quality (hereinafter referred to as 'zones')[451] (Article 9, paragraph 1) by the Government of Montenegro (Article 9, paragraph 3). Delineation is made on the basis of air quality assessment, depending on upper and lower limits of grading. Assessment of air quality and air quality management is required in all zones (Article 9, paragraph 2).

---

448. The Air, as the natural value of general interest, is part of the environment and has special protection in Montenegro (Art. 1, para. 2). *The air* is outside air in the troposphere, excluding workplace air, which quality is regulated by regulations on safety at work (Art. 3, para. 1, item 1).
449. *Pollutant* is any substance present in the air, which can adversely affect human health and/or the environment (Art. 3, para. 1, item 2).
450. *Air quality standard* is herewith each determined limit, target value, long-term goal, a critical level, the level of warning or notice, or other value of pollutant concentrations in the air determined in accordance with international standards in order to avoid, prevent or minimize adverse impacts on human health and/or the environment as a whole (Art. 3, para. 1, point 5).
451. Determined zones are reviewed at least once in five years (Art. 9, para. 3). In case of significant changes in activities that affect air quality zones are reviewed in a shorter period (Art. 9, para. 4). *Zone* is a part of the territory of Montenegro, delimited in order to assess the air quality and air quality management.

366. In the zones where the concentration level of pollutants[452] referred to in Article 9, paragraph 4 of this Law exceeds the upper limits for the assessment of these pollutants or long-term objective for ozone, data used for air quality assessment are obtained by fixed measurements that can be complemented by the methods of mathematical modelling and/or indicative measurements (Article 10, paragraph 1). In the zones where the concentration level of pollutants referred to in Article 9, paragraph 4 of this Law is below the upper limit established for these pollutants, for air quality assessment used data obtained by combination of fixed measurement and methods of mathematical modelling and/or indicative measurements (Article 10, paragraph 2). In the zones where the concentration level of pollutants referred to in Article 9, paragraph 4 of this Law is below the lower limit established for the assessment of these pollutants, assessment of air quality using the methods of mathematical modelling and/or other methods of objective assessment in accordance with generally accepted international practice (Article 10, paragraph 3).

C. Air Quality Management and Plans

367. The National Strategy for air quality management (hereinafter 'National Strategy') is adopted in order to preserve and improve air quality and to avoid, prevent or reduce harmful effects on human health and/or the environment (Article 19, paragraph 1).[453] National Strategy aims to integrate the protection and improvement of air quality from planning and strategic documents in this area related to the fulfilment of international commitments and programmes, plans and short-term action plans prepared in accordance with this Law (Article 20, paragraph 1).

368. In the zones where the concentration of polluting substances is beyond any established limit or target value, taking into account the tolerance limits if they are prescribed, the Ministry, in cooperation with the Agency and relevant local authority, adopts the plan of Air Quality (hereinafter 'Plan'),[454] in order to reach as quickly as possible values prescribed in Article 8 of this Law (Article 21, paragraph 1). In case of exceeding the limit values[455] for which the deadline for achieving has already expired, the Plan should contain appropriate measures which reduce the minimum duration of exceeding and measures relating to the protection of particularly vulnerable population groups, especially children (Article 21, paragraph 2).

452. *Level of pollution* is the concentration of air pollutants and their deposition on the surface at a certain period of time (Art. 3, para. 1, point 3).

453. The Government adopts the National Strategy for the period of four years (Art. 19, para. 2).

454. Plan is adopted at latest by 31 January of the current year for the previous year, in which are determined exceedances of the permitted levels of air pollution. (Art. 21, para. 5). Funding for the development and implementation of the Plan shall be provided from the state budget and budgets of the relevant local government (Art. 21, para. 6). If the plan prescribes measures to reduce emissions from stationary sources, these measures are to be funded and implemented by the polluter (Art. 21, para. 7).

455. *Limit* is the level of value established on the basis of scientific knowledge in order to avoid, prevent or minimize adverse impacts on human health and/or the environment as a whole, to be achieved in a given period and that shall not be exceeded (Art. 3, para. 1, Point 6).

D. Short-Term Action Plans

369. The Agency, in cooperation with the local authorities in whose territory is zone situated, adopts short-term action plan in case that in the zones where levels of warning are exceeded and/or notification for sulphur dioxide and nitrogen dioxide are at risk for exceeding these standards (Article 23, paragraph 1).[456] If the short-term action plan prescribes measures for reducing emissions from stationary sources, the polluter is obliged to fund and implement these measures (Article 23, paragraph 5).

370. Short-term action plans contain, in particular, short-term measures taken to reduce the risk or duration of the overdraft (Article 24, paragraph 1).[457] The public, NGOs, environmental protection associations, consumer protection associations, associations for the protection of vulnerable population groups, health institutions and relevant companies are met with short-term action plan and with application of the measures prescribed by the plan (Article 25, paragraph 1).

E. Plans in Case of Transboundary Air Pollution and Preventive Measures

371. The Agency is obliged to notify the Ministry in case the warning threshold limit values and/or targeted values, including tolerance limits, if they are prescribed, or if long-term objective for ozone is exceeded due to a significant transboundary transfer of polluting substances or their precursors (Article 26, paragraph 1).[458]

372. In areas where the concentration of polluting substances does not exceed the prescribed limits or long-term objectives for ozone, the Agency and local authorities on whose territory is the zone are obliged to plan each activity, approve and implement it in accordance with the principle of prevention, in a way to cause the least possible change in air quality, i.e., that has the lowest possible risk to the environment and human health and to prevent or limit the impact on air quality at the source that these values cannot be exceeded, and to endeavour to maintain the best air quality in accordance with sustainable development (Article 27, paragraph 1).

---

456. Funding for the development and implementation of short-term action plan shall be provided from the state budget and budgets of local governments on whose territory a zone is located (Art. 23, para. 2).

457. Depending on each case, by short-term action plan can be undertaken measures to control and if necessary, to suspend activities such as motor vehicles traffic, carrying out of construction works, the activity of anchored ships, the use of industrial plants and products, domestic heating, etc. (Art. 24, para. 2). The measures may include protection of vulnerable groups such as children and the elderly (Art. 24, para. 3).

458. When the concentration of polluting substances in border areas exceed threshold warning and/or notification, the Ministry shall promptly notify the relevant authorities of neighbouring countries (Art. 26, para. 3).

F. Improvement of Air Quality

373. In order to prevent and reduce air pollution and improve air quality, the following measures are taken (Article 28, paragraph 1): determination of emission limit values from stationary sources and mobile sources of pollution;[459] determination of limits of certain polluting substances in certain products; establishing national emission maximum for certain polluting substance; gradual reducing usage of substances that deplete the ozone layer; other measures to prevent and reduce pollution.

374. The limit values for the content of volatile compounds in paints, varnishes and certain products for protection, painting and varnishing of vehicles are prescribed by the Ministry (Article 30, paragraph 1).[460] Technical standards of air protection from fumes of volatile organic compounds[461] arising during the storage, decanting and distribution of motor gasoline are prescribed by the Ministry (Article 31, paragraph 1).

375. Legal entities and entrepreneurs which during their activities affect or may affect the air quality are obliged to provide: technical measures for prevention or reduction of emissions into the air, including air pollution protecting cost in the investment and production costs, and keeping records of spent funds, monitoring the impact of activities on air quality and other protective measures in accordance with this Law and with other regulations (Article 39, paragraph 1).[462]

376. Local authority, on the bases of data from Article 40, paragraph 1 of this Law, keeps a register of sources of air pollution with data on the spatial location and capacities of pollution sources, as well as about all changes and modifications (Article 41, paragraph 1).[463]

---

459. The Government prescribes emission limit values of polluting substances and other measures to protect air emissions from stationary sources and activities that cause polluting substances' emissions into the air (Art. 29, para. 1). Limit values and other protection measures of air from mobile sources emissions are prescribed by the Government (Art. 29, para. 2).
460. The types of liquid fuels of petroleum origin (hereinafter referred to as 'fuel'), the limit values of polluting substances content and other characteristics of the fuel in relation to the environmental protection which are to be met at the time of placing on the domestic market, the method of determining and monitoring of fuel characteristics and conformity assessment are prescribed by the Government (Art. 30, para. 3).
461. *Volatile organic compounds (VOCs)* are organic compounds from anthropogenic and biogenic sources, other than methane, which in the sunlight, in the reaction with nitrogen oxides can form photochemical oxidants (Art. 3, para. 1, point 25).
462. Legal entities and entrepreneurs referred to in para. 1 of Art. 29 shall obtain a permit on permitted emissions of pollutants in the air (hereinafter referred to as 'emission permits') from the Agency (Art. 39, para. 2).
463. These data are to be submitted to the Agency, which keeps an integral cadastre of environmental pollutants (Art. 41, para. 2).

G. Information and Reporting

377. The Agency timely and appropriately informs the public and interested organizations (NGOs and environmental protection associations, consumer protection associations, associations for the protection of vulnerable population groups, health institutions and relevant companies) on air quality, as well as about making plans, programmes and measures for protection and improvement of air quality (Article 42, paragraph 1).[464]

378. On the basis of data obtained during implementation of the annual programme of air quality monitoring and other data, the Agency drew annual information on air quality (hereinafter 'Information') (Article 46, paragraph 1).[465] For achievement of the objectives of the strategic and planning documents determined by this Law and by other documents related to the protection and improvement of air quality, the Agency draws Report on Air Quality in Montenegro, for a period of four years (Article 47, paragraph 1) which is an integral part of the report on the environmental status of Montenegro.

H. Financing of Air Protection and Supervision

379. Funding for the protection and improvement of air quality is assured from: the State budget, the budget of local governments and other sources in accordance with this Law (Article 48).

380. Supervision of implementation of this Law and regulations made under this Act is conducted by the Ministry unless otherwise prescribed by the Law (Article 50, paragraph 1). Inspection supervision on the implementation of this Law and the regulations made under this Law shall be conducted by the Agency in accordance with this Law and the Law regulating the inspection (Article 50, paragraph 2).[466]

II. Law on the Protection from Negative Impact of Climate Change

A. General Remark

381. The Parliament of Montenegro adopted the Law on the Protection from Negative Impact of Climate Change in December 2019 (OJ MNE 73/19). The law

464. Information and data on air quality are free of charge and are available on the media and on websites of the competent authorities (Art. 42, para. 2).
465. Detailed contents and method of making the information is prescribed by the Ministry (Art. 46, para. 4).
466. Article 51 prescribes the right and duties of inspectors, while Art. 52 prescribes inspectors competences.

regulates protection from negative impacts of climate change, the reduction of greenhouse gasses emissions,[467] protection of the ozone layer and other related issues.

382. The Law is divided into 9 chapters and contains 40 articles: Chapter I – Basic Provisions (Articles 1–4); Chapter II – Documents on the Protection from Negative Impacts of Climate Change (Articles 5–10); Chapter III – Achieving the Low-Carbon Development (Articles 11–16); Chapter IV – Emissions Reporting and Verification (Articles 17–22); Chapter V – Geological Storage (Articles 23–27); Chapter VI – Ozone Layer (Articles 28–30); Chapter VII – Supervision (Articles 31–33); Chapter VIII – Penal Provisions (Article 34; Chapter IX – Transitional and Final Provisions (Articles 35–40).

B. Strategic documents

383. The Law obliges the Government to adopt vital documents on the protection from climate change: (1) The strategy on low-carbon development; (2) The plan for the climate change adaptation

384. The Strategy for low-carbon development is adopted for the period of thirty years. It contains the analysis of the socio-economic situation that impacts the emissions level; economic analysis of possible avenues of low-carbon development; proposals of policies and measures required; total targets of emissions source reduction and emissions sink increase;[468] individual sectoral targets of emissions reduction and sink increase; estimates of socio-economic impacts of decarbonization measures; indicators for the Strategy's implementation monitoring. Part of the Strategy is greenhouse gasses emission levels projections that include the existing data on emissions, projections with or without measures and methodology for creation of measures.[469] The projections are separately created for energy, industry, agriculture, forestry and traffic sectors. The Strategy shall be reconsidered every five years and revised if needed. All strategic documents, development plans and programmes must be in accordance with the Strategy. (Article 6).

385. The Strategy is implemented on the basis of the Action Plan, adopted by the Government, for a period of two years. The Action Plan contains measures and

---

467. The Law defines greenhouse gasses as those parts of atmosphere caused by antropoghenic and natural factors that absorb and re-emit infra-red radiation (Art. 4(3)). Emissions are defined as every greenhouse gas discharge from an aircraft or a facility to the atmosphere (Art. 4(8)). Facilities are defined as aby stationary technical unit in which one or more activities are performed, including all the other technically directly related activities, which cause the greenhouse gassess emissions and pollution (Art. 4(19)).
468. The Law defines a sink as any process, activity or mechanism which expels from the atmosphere greenhouse gasses, aerosols or greenhouse gass precursors (Art. 4(18)).
469. The Law defines a projection as a forecast of antropoghenic emissions by sources and removals of greenhouse gasses through sinks or the development of energy system, developed for the period of at least sixteen years, in which the quantitave assesments are accounted for the most proximate four future years that end on the number zero or five (Art. 4(20)).

activities required for the implementation of Strategy's targets; periods and persons responsible for implementation; indicators for the Strategy's implementation monitoring; an assessment of funds required for the implementation. The Ministry of Ecology, Spatial Planning and Urbanism is required to adopt a bi-annual report to the Government on the Strategy and Action Plan implementation (Article 6).

386. The Plan for the Climate Change Adaptation shall be adopted with the aim of identification of sectors vulnerable to climate change and mitigation of negative impacts on these sectors. It has to contain the description of the present state of affairs due to climate change; identification of vulnerable sectors; the analysis of socio-economic situation that impacts the climate change; the analysis of the observed climate change and extreme climate conditions; the overview of expected climate change with the key risks assessment; the analysis of climate change impact; main targets of the climate change adaptation; the description of the institutional framework for climate change adaptation; the overview of existing plans and strategic documents in the field of climate change adaptation with the evaluation of progress in the implementation and the examples of best practice; the assessment of capacities for climate change adaptation; measures for climate change adaptation; priority measures and persons responsible for their implementation; the description of mechanisms and the framework for monitoring and evaluation of the Plan's implementation; the assessment of funds needed for the measures implementation. (Article 9).[470]

387. The Ministry of Ecology, Spatial Planning and Urbanism is required to adopt a bi-annual report to the Government on the Plan's implementation (Article 9). State authorities responsible for energy, industry, agriculture, forestry and transport are obliged to report bi-annually to the Ministry on the measures performed under the strategic documents for the prevention of the negative impacts of climate change, as well as on data on floods, droughts, extreme temperatures and other similar events (Article 10).

388. The Law identifies certain special measures of protection for the agricultural, waste management, energy, industrial processes and product use sectors. The special measures also guarantee that the accounted for greenhouse gas emissions from forestry, land use and land assignment change do not exceed the sectoral emissions sinks. These special measures do not relate to emissions from facilities and the activities for which the greenhouse gas emission permit is issued. In case the special measures fail to decrease the emissions in the prescribed term, the Ministry shall adopt the corrective Action plan with the exact timetable of additional measures implementation (Article 7).

389. The Law lists certain obligations on the part of the stationary facility operator and the aircraft operator (Part III – The Achievement of Low-Carbon Development). The Operator of the stationary facility is defined as any legal person or

470. The Plan for the Climate Change Adaptation shall be adopted for a period of ten years by the Government of Montenegro.

entrepreneur which operates the stationary facility, controls it, or is responsible for decision-making related to the operation of the facility (Article 4(16)). The aircraft operator is any natural or legal person or a state organ that operates the aircraft or intends to operate the aircraft (Article 4(17)).

C. Low-Carbon Development and Permit

390. Operator of the new stationary facility that performs activities which cause greenhouse gas emissions is obliged to acquire a permit for the greenhouse gas emission before the start of the facility's operation. Furthermore, the operator is obliged to acquire the emission credit,[471] for every unit of equivalent carbon dioxide emission that it emits.[472] The permit is issued for a period of ten years, by the local state administrative organ responsible for environmental affairs, for the whole facility, or a part of it, or as one permit for multiple facilities located in the same location and operated by the same operator. The facilities that are operated for the purpose of research, development and analysis of new products and processes, as well as the facilities that use exclusively biomass are not obliged to acquire the permit. The Government shall more closely define the activities and gasses that need to acquire the permit. The Government shall allocate emission credits through public auctions or free allocation (Article 11).

391. The request for the permit should be submitted by the operator of the stationary facility in both written and electronic format. It must contain the name and place of incorporation of the operator; the description of the activities; the facility's location; technology description; data on raw materials whose usage causes the greenhouse gas emissions; data on the type and source of emissions; non-technical resume; the plan for emissions monitoring (in two copies). The Ministry of Ecology, Spatial Planning and Urbanism shall more closely define the contents of the emissions monitoring plan (Article 12).

392. The permit shall be issued in the period of thirty days since the acceptance of the request. The incomplete requests will be denied. The Decision on the permit issuance or denial will be delivered to the applicant within the period of eight days since its adoption. The Decision can be appealed to the Ministry of Ecology, Spatial Planning and Urbanism (Article 13).

393. If the conditions under which the operator performs its activities change over time, it is obliged to report these changes to the organ that issued the permit no longer than sixty days after the changes occur. The changes relate to technical and technological characteristics of the facility; the enlargement of the facility; the

471. The Law defines emission credit as the transferrable permit for the emission of a one ton of equivalent carbon dioxide for a certain time period (Art. 4(2)).
472. During 2022, two permits were issued. *See*: https://epa.org.me/wp-content/uploads/2022/01/dozvole_klimatske_sajt.pdf (10 Jan. 2023).

increase or decrease of the capacities; the type of fuel used; the raw materials used; the caloric input; responsible persons; operator's place of incorporation (Article 15).

394. Aircraft operator is obliged to adopt a plan for aircraft emission monitoring before it starts operating and no longer than sixty days after it receives its operating license, in accordance with the law on air transport. The Civil Aviation Agency should review the plan and give its opinion to the local state administrative organ that issues its acceptance of the plan (Article 16).

D. Emissions Reporting and Report Verification

395. Operators are obliged to submit a verified report on the emissions on the yearly basis to the state organ that issued the permit (Part IV – Reporting on the Emissions and the Verification of the Report). If they fail to perform this obligation, the state organ performs a conservative assessment of the emission level, while the costs of this assessment fall on the operator (Article 17). Only accredited legal entities, capable of verification in terms of human resources and equipment, can verify the reports (Article 18). The operator is responsible for creating a proper evidence of the emissions and the procedures for the conservation of the documentation for the minimal time period of ten years (Article 19). The state administrative authority responsible for permit issuance develops the inventory of emissions, on the basis of data reported by the operators (Article 20). The data from the inventory is related further in the form of an annual report to the Ministry and relevant international institutions (Article 20).

396. The Ministry of Ecology, Spatial Planning and Urbanism prepares a National report on climate change and a Bi-annual updated report, to be adopted at the next session of the Government (Article 21).

397. Legal entities that trade or lease new passenger vehicles are obliged to make accessible to the persons wishing to acquire the vehicle, for every particular model of the vehicle, the data on the fuel consumption and carbon-dioxide emissions through the use of stickers, posters or displays, or the specially prepared guides and other kinds of promotive reading material (Article 22).

E. Geological Storage

398. The Law regulates the issue of the geological storage,[473] of carbon dioxide on the territory of Montenegro through a complete ban on such storage throughout its territorial waters, water courses, exclusive economic zone and continental shelf

473. Geological storage of carbon-dioxide is defined as the storage in underground geological formations, for the purpose of its permanent storage in the fight against the negative impact of climate change. This storage should prevent or minimize as much as possible the risk for environment and human health (Art. 4(5)).

(Article 23). The transboundary movement of carbon dioxide over the territory of Montenegro for storage in another state is allowed if necessary infrastructure exists (Article 24). The operator of industrial facility has a general right of access to the transport network for this purpose. However, this right depends on certain criteria such as the capacity of available or potentially available transport network; the assessment of the decrease of carbon dioxide emissions effectuated through storage in relation to the general obligatory decreases; technical difficulties that oblige the operator to deny the access; the need to respect the rational interests and needs of the network operator and all other network users (Article 25). If the lack of capacity is stated as the excuse for the access denial, the transport network operator is obliged to improve the capacities if economically feasible or if the user is ready to finance these improvements, if these improvements would not negatively impact the transport security related to environmental protection (Article 25(2)).

399. In case of a dispute on the access to transport networks or geolocations for carbon dioxide storage outside of Montenegro's territory, the applicable law will be the law of the state that has the jurisdiction over the transport network or the geolocation in question (Article 26). An independent body for the settlement of the dispute will be formed on the basis of the agreement of all the involved parties and states.

400. Companies that produce electricity in thermo-energetic facilities with the output power of 300 MW or more are obliged to prepare a study on the catchment and take care of carbon dioxide. The study shall describe the manner of taking care of carbon-dioxide, the place of storage, technical and economic feasibility of the construction of the transport infrastructure and catchment devices. This study is an integral part of the environmental impact assessment elaboration (Article 27).

F. Ozone Layer

401. The Law regulates the protection of the Ozone Layer as a separate issue (Part VI). Production, trade, use, export and import of substances, equipment and products that damage the ozone layer, or alternative substances,[474] will be regulated by the Government adopted by-law (Article 28). Only specially permitted legal persons and entrepreneurs can perform activities of maintenance, repair, and decommission of products and equipment detrimental to the ozone layer. The Ministry of Ecology, Spatial Planning and Urbanism issues these permits for a period of five years (Article 29). The Law prohibits production of substances that damage the ozone layer; export/import of substances that damage the ozone layer and products that contain substances enumerated in the Montreal Protocol on the ozone layer to countries that have not ratified this Protocol; export/import of substances that damage the ozone layer or alternative substances with no permission from the administrative authorities; import and trade in new products that contain substances that

474. The law defines them as fluoride gasses or mixes of these gasses whose potential for damage to the ozone layer is equal to none, but they nevertheless contribute to global warming (Art. 4(1)).

damage the ozone layer; discharge into the environment of substances that damage the ozone layer or alternative substances; charging of systems that use alternative substances with substances that damage the ozone layer; rinsing with substances that damage the ozone layer; import and trade in substances that damage the ozone layer and alternative substances in one-use cylinders; import and trade in second hand products and equipment that contains substances that damage the ozone layer or were made by the use of them; import of recycled, used or regenerated substances that damage the ozone layer, with the exception of substances that hail from facilities for regeneration (Article 30).

G. Supervision

402. Implementation monitoring of the Law and by-laws adopted under the law is the responsibility of the Ministry of Ecology, Spatial Planning and Urbanism and local administrative authorities responsible for inspection review (Article 31). The so-called environmental inspector has several responsibilities in this regard. It controls whether the operator has the valid permit; satisfies the conditions for its operations; keeps the evidence and conserves documentation on the emissions; manages the substances that damage the ozone layer or alternative substances in the prescribed manner. The environmental inspector is authorized the prohibit further operations that go against the law, enforce the operator to request the permit, order the operator to keep the prescribed monitoring of emissions, keep the evidence and preserve information on emissions, and prohibit the use of substances detrimental to the ozone layer or alternative substances (Article 32). The market inspector, on the other hand, controls the obligations of the legal entities that trade or lease new passenger vehicles from Article 22 of the Law (Article 33).[475]

III. Other Regulations

403. Following by-laws have been adopted:

- Rulebook on method and procedure for measuring emissions from stationary sources (OJ MNE, No. 39/2013).
- Decree on activities affecting or likely to affect air quality (OJ MNE, No. 61/2012).
- Quality monitoring programme of liquid fuels of oil origin for 2012 (OJ MNE, 23/12).
- Decree on establishment of kinds of polluting substances, border values and other standards of air quality (OJ MNE, No. 25/2012).
- Decree on the maximum national emissions of certain pollutants substances (OJ MNE, No. 3/12).

475. The Law enumerates different fiscal sanctions for the breaches of these obligations which range from EUR 2,000–EUR 40,000.

- Decree on entrusting the part of the activities in the competencies of the Environmental Protection Agency to the Public Institution 'Centre for Ecotoxicological Research of Montenegro' (OJ MNE, No. 62/11).
- Decree on establishment of network of measuring stations for air quality monitoring ('OJ MNE' Nos 44/10, 13/11).
- Decree on the substances which damage ozone layer and alternative substances ('OJ MNE', 5/11).
- Decree on limit values of emissions of pollution materials in the air from stationary sources ('OJ MNE', 10/11).
- Decree on limit values of emissions of pollution substances in the air from stationary sources ('OJ MNE', 10/11).
- Decree on limit values of the content of pollution materials in liquid fuels of oil origin ('OJ MNE', 39/10).
- Rulebook on contents and method for preparation of annual information on air quality ('OJ MNE', 27/12).
- Rulebook on the manner and conditions of air quality monitoring ('OJ MNE', 21/11).
- Rulebook on emission of harmful substances in the air ('OJ the RM', 25/01 and 10/11).
- Air Quality Plan for the Main City Podgorica, 2015.

Several by-laws were adopted under the Law on the Protection from Negative Impact of Climate Change in December 2019 (OJ MNE 73/19):

- The Rulebook on the content of the monitoring plan of greenhouse gasses emissions from facilities (OJ MNE 10/22).
- The Regulation on the substances that damage the ozone layer and alternative substances (OJ MNE No. 79/21).
- The Regulation on aircraft activities excluded from the obligation to submit the plan of greenhouse gasses emissions monitoring (OJ MNE No. 77/21).
- The Rulebook on the form of the greenhouse gasses emission permit and the method of leading the evidence (OJ MNE, No. 13/21).
- The Rulebook on the form, content and method of verification of the greenhouse gasses emissions report (OJ MNE, No. 13/21).
- The Rulebook on the closer conditions for the access to the transport network for carbon dioxide, the procedure and criteria for reception of carbon-dioxide routes (OJ MNE, no. 12/21).
- The Rulebook on conditions for personnel and equipment of a legal entity that verifies the greenhouse gasses emissions report (OJ MNE, No. 12/21).
- The Rulebook on the Plan of greenhouse gasses emissions from the aircraft monitoring (OJ MNE, No. 102/20).
- The Rulebook on the content of the Plan of greenhouse gasses emissions from a facility monitoring (OJ MNE, No. 92/20).
- The Rulebook on the closer method and required documentation for the permit to export/import substances that damage the ozone layer and alternative substances (OJ MNE, No. 69/20).

- The Rulebook on the method of creation and content of the greenhouse gasses emissions inventory (OJ MNE, No. 55/20).
- The Rulebook on the manner of formulation of obligatory targets for greenhouse gasses emissions mitigation (OJ MNE, No. 57/20).
- The Regulation on the activities that cause greenhouse gasses emissions for which the emission permit is issued (OJ MNE, No. 8/20).

IV. International Treaties

404. Montenegro has ratified the Convention on Persistent Organic Pollutants – the Stockholm Convention (POPs) (OJ MNE – International Treaties, No. 16/2010).[476] Through succession from the State Union of S&M, Montenegro took over in 2006 UNECE CLRTAP and the EMEP.[477]

405. Also by succession in 2006, the Convention for the Protection of the Ozone Layer and its Montreal Protocol on Substances that Deplete the Ozone Layer with all amendments[478] and the UNFCCC were taken over.[479]

406. The country also ratified Kyoto Protocol in March 2007 (OJ RM, No. 17/07).[480] Montenegro is a member of the Paris Agreement on Climate.[481] Furthermore, Montenegro ratified Convention on Environmental Impact Assessment in a Transboundary Context (Espoo, Finland, 1991) (OJ MNE, No. 8/08) and the Convention on the Transboundary Effects of Industrial Accidents (Helsinki, 1992) on 27 December 2008.

407. On 22 June 2011, Parliament ratified Protocol to the 1979 Convention on Long-Range Transboundary Air Pollution on Abate Acidification, Eutrophication and Ground-level Ozone (Gothenburg, 1999) and Protocol to the 1979 Convention on Long-Range Transboundary Air Pollution on Persistent Organic Pollutants (Aarhus Protocol, 1998). In addition, the Pollutant Release and Transfer Register Protocol to the Aarhus Convention (PRTR) has been ratified (6/2017).

---

476. And Amendments to the POPs (OJ MNE, IT, No. 9/17).
477. In order to achieve the full implementation of Long-Range Transboundary Air Pollution, the LRTAP, midterm priorities refer to the continuation of adoption of laws on the ratification of other protocols adopted under this Convention.
478. National Programme for the Elimination of Use of Ozone Layer Depleting Substances and the Plan for Phase-out of Chlorofluorocarbons (CFCs) were prepared with the technical and financial support of United Nation Industrial Development Organization (UNIDO) and the Montreal Protocol Multilateral Fund, which were adopted in September 2007. Programme of Institutional Strengthening for the Implementation of the Montreal Protocol and Establishment of the Office for Ozone in Montenegro was also prepared.
479. In 2010, the First National Communication to United Nations Framework Convention on Climate Change has been completed. *See*: http://unfccc.int/essential_background/library/items/3599.php?such=j&symbol=MNE/COM/1%20E#beg (10 Jun. 2012).
480. Designated National Authority for Approval of CDM Projects was established in February 2008, by which the implementation of the Kyoto Protocol begun in Montenegro.
481. *See*: https://treaties.un.org/Pages/ViewDetails.aspx?src=TREATY&mtdsg_no=XXVII-7-d&chapter=27&clang=_en (1 Jan. 2022).

V. Harmonization with the EU

408. According to the 2018 Progress Report, 'the level of legislative alignment shows a good level of preparation'. An action plan to implement the national strategy on air quality management for 2017–2020 was adopted. A short-term action plan to tackle air pollution in Pljevlja was adopted. However, implementation of the adopted action plans and the prescribed measures remains a challenge.[482] The adoption of the strategy on air quality management for the period 2021–2029, as well as of the action plan 2021–2022, remain pending.[483]

409. The National Inventory of Pollutant Gas Emissions into the Air has been updated in accordance with international obligations from the Convention on Long-Range Transboundary Air Pollution (CLRTAP). Montenegro, as a contracting party to the convention, is obliged to apply guidelines on annual reporting on emissions of nitrogen oxides (NOx), sulfur oxides (SOx), non-methane components (NMVOC), carbon monoxide (CO), ammonia (NH3), powdery substances (PM), heavy metals (TM) and persistent organic pollutants (POPs).[484]

410. The level of alignment in the field of climate change remains limited. Montenegro has to intensify its work to ensure consistency with the EU 2030 climate and energy policy framework. It also needs to ensure that its strategy is integrated into all relevant sectoral policies and strategies. In addition, Montenegro needs to enhance its administrative capacity to enable implementation and enforcement of the *acquis*. 'Considerable work is still required to align with the EU *acquis* …'[485]

411. National Inventories of greenhouse gases for the period 1990–2019 were updated as part of cooperation with the Austrian Environmental Protection Agency, Twinning light project Development of integrated Air Emissions Inventory tool and Update of Air Emissions Inventory for the period 2011–2018 with the additional year 2019, as well as for the purpose of updating the National Inventory Report (NIR). To update the inventory time series, the 2006 IPCC international methodology and a specially created tool in Excel were used to calculate GHG emissions, as well as emissions of polluting gases into the air.[486]

482. EC (2018). p. 79. 'Alignment with the EU requirements on sulphur content in liquid fuels further progressed. Work on further improving its monitoring system is ongoing.' *Ibid.*
483. EC (2022), p. 112.
484. MESPU, EPA (2022a) p. 32.
485. EC (2022), p. 113, 114.
486. MESPU, EPA (2022a) p. 47.

Chapter 3. Water Pollution

§1. SURFACE WATER

I. Water Availability and Use

412. Regardless of unbalanced distribution of water, water potentials are among the basic development potentials of Montenegro, since it is very rich in water, and in relation to the overall surface, it is among the richest countries in general,[487] but the uneven distribution of water, together with floods as the main hydrological disaster (Zetska Plain and the area around the Skadarsko Lake), are at the same the limiting development factors.[488] 'Hydrological droughts occurred during 2017, 2018, and 2019, significantly affecting the water levels of important rivers and lakes, such as the Rivers Morača and Zeta, as well as Lake Skadar.'[489]

413. Surface water resources of Montenegro include rivers, lakes and the Adriatic coastal waters. Most important river systems are the Moraca/Zeta, the Lim and the Tara/Piva.[490] Skadarsko Lake, shared with Albania, is the largest lake in the Balkans, with a surface area of 369.7 km^2.[491] Montenegro has good quality and abundant underground and surface waters (unlike most of the other Mediterranean countries, where water shortages are present). Water resources thus represent one of the most important comparative advantages for the country.[492]

414. When drinking water is concerned, out of the total population of Montenegro, 65%–70% are provided with water through communal water supply systems, while a bit more than 30% of population in villages get water from their own water supply systems and individually, by using springs, wells for catchments of ground waters or cisterns for collection of atmospheric water.[493]

415. For the needs of industry and mining, including thermoenergy facilities, which used water for cooling in the period of their most intensive development and work (from 1978 to 1993), between 60 and 142 million m^3 of water was used per year.[494] Hydropower plants are an important source of energy. There are two large plants ('PeruÇica' and 'Piva') on rivers Zeta and Piva and seven small ones ('Glava Zete', 'Slap Zete', on Zeta River, 'Rijeka MušoviÇa' – Kolašin, 'Šavnik', 'Lijeva Rijeka', 'Podgor' on Orahovštica River and 'Rijeka CrnojeviÇa' at Obodsko vrelo). Some 1,665 GWh (average generation for the period 1976–2004) was generated.[495]

487. *Ibid.*, p. 36.
488. GMNE, NCSD (2011), 10.
489. MSDT (2020), p. 166. This resulted in impacts in the fisheries, agriculture, and energy sectors.
490. UNECE (2003), 74.
491. SY MNE-2008, 18.
492. GMNE (2007C), 37.
493. Town water supply systems include, apart from forty town settlements, also 174 suburban and rural settlements – the total of 214 settlements. GMNE (2008C), 87.
494. *Ibid.*, 88.
495. *Ibid.*, 87.

II. Water Pollution Sources

416. The discharge of both municipal and industrial wastewater into natural receivers is done almost without any purification (exceptions are some industrial plants and part of municipal wastewater in Podgorica, Mojkovac, Žabljak, Pljevlja, Nikšić, Šavnik, Budva, Herceg Novi, Kotor and Tivat, A plant in Danilovgrad is under construction and preparation for the construction and construction of a plant for Podgorica, as well as the construction of a plant purification plant for wastewater in Petnjica.[496]

417. Waste water from settlements and industry is prevailing pollutant.[497] 'Waste water has been identified as a main source of pollution'.[498] Water quality (of watercourses, lakes, sea and ground waters) is satisfactory. Groundwater quality in natural conditions, except for coastal aquifers influenced by the sea, is of Class I for the major part of the year. Natural quality of waters in the mainland, in aquifers of intergranular structure, is jeopardized at a few locations, usually downstream from larger settlements and industry.

418. Vulnerability analysis (based on data from the Monitoring Programme of the State of the Coastal Sea Ecosystem of Montenegro, which was implemented in the period from 2008 to 2011), which was implemented through the Coastal Area Management Programme (CAMP Montenegro), showed a very high vulnerability of the sea in Boki, as well as in certain locations in Budva, Petrovac, Sutomor, Bar, Ulcinj, but also in the open sea.[499] Municipal wastewater is the main source of sea pollution in the entire coastal area, also in recent years, plastic waste pollution has become more and more present, which puts additional pressure on the marine ecosystem.[500]

419. In 2007, a systematic research on quantity and quality of surface and underground waters was done by the Hydrological and Meteorological Service of Montenegro (Hydromet), in accordance with Article 30 Law on Water (OJ RM, No. 27/07) and the Regulation on the classification and categorization of water (OJ RM,

496. MESPU, EPA (2022a) p. 76.
497. Industry is mainly supplied with water from its own sources, and total water consumption in recent years amounted between 50 and 60 million m3. More than half of the water consumed by industry comes from underground sources. The biggest industrial consumers of water are: metallurgic facilities (aluminium factory, steel mill) and thermal power plant in Pljevlja. They use around 43 million m3/year, while it is estimated that approximately two-thirds of this water gets recirculated. Agriculture is not a significant consumer. It uses approximately only 6 million m3 per year. GMNE (2007C), 38.
498. EC. *Montenegro 2018 Report*, Accompanying the document Communication from the Commission to the European Parliament, the Council, the European Economic and Social Committee and the Committee of the Regions 2018 Communication on EU Enlargement Policy, Strasbourg, 17.4.2018, SWD(2018) 150 final, p. 80.
499. MESPU, EPA (2022a), p. 77.
500. *Ibid*, p. 78. The pressure generated by improper disposal of waste was miraculously alleviated by putting into operation the Možura sanitary landfill, where approximately 62,000 tons of municipal waste from Bar, Ulcinj, Kotor, Budva and Tivat are currently disposed of annually.

Nos 14/96, 19/96 and 15/97) on the basis of a programme adopted by the Ministry of Agriculture, Forestry and Water Management (MAFWM). The programme defined network stations which cover thirteen rivers with sixty-six measures profile, three lakes with eleven measures profile, maritime sea at nineteen measures profile and underground water plain of Zeta in eight villages.[501]

420. The monitoring of surface and underground waters in 2021 was carried out in accordance with the Framework Directive on Water (ODV), i.e., in accordance with the Rulebook on the method and deadlines for determining the status of surface waters (OJ MNE, 25/2019), and the Rulebook on the method and deadlines for determining status of groundwater (OJ MNE, 52/2019). Water quality testing is performed by the state administration body responsible for hydrometeorological affairs (Institute for Hydrometeorology and Seismology of Montenegro), according to the annual Surface and Groundwater Monitoring Programme issued by the Ministry with previously obtained opinions of the state administration bodies responsible for health and environmental protection.[502]

III. Competencies

421. According to the Law on Waters, the state administration in the area of water is performed by the Ministry, the competent administrative authority, the competent local self-government authority and the competent local government authority, in accordance with the Law. The competent authority in the performance of tasks determined by this Law prepares expert bases for determining waters of importance for Montenegro, the method of categorization and category of water facilities and for regulations, plans and programmes that are passed by the Government and the Ministry. The competent administrative authority may delegate expert tasks in water planning and management to specialized organizations, in accordance with the Law (Article 151, paragraphs 1–3).[503] Supervision over the implementation of the provision of Water Law and the regulations adopted on the basis of this Law is conducted by the Ministry, the Ministry in charge of health, the Ministry in charge of environmental protection, the Ministry in charge of geology and competent authority of the local government (Article 161). The inspection supervision is conducted by the Ministry, through water inspectors.[504]

501. MTEP (2008a), 20. For the assessment of the water quality in several past years *see*: UNECE (2003), 74–76.

502. MESPU, EPA (2022a), p. 47, 48. The network of stations for surface water quality in 2021 included nineteen watercourses with twenty-eight measuring points, four natural lakes with seven measuring points, one artificial lake with one measuring point, five mixed waters with five measuring points and the coastal sea with five measuring points.

503. *See also* the Decree on Organization and Manner of Work of the Public Administration (Official Journal MNE, Nos 49/22, 52/22, 56/22, 82/22).

504. From 2002, water monitoring programmes have been managed by MTEP (former MEPP), CETI and Hydromet. Water monitoring is performed on surface and underground water. The measuring network includes thirty-six stations on watercourses, ten on lakes, twenty on underground reservoirs and seventeen on the coast. CETI is equipped to measure fifty-six chemical and toxicological parameters and certain radiation measurements. The Institute of Public Health is another body

IV. Strategic Documents

422. Water management strategy (June 2017) is the basis of the long-term plan for maintenance and improvement of water.[505] The objective of the Water Management Strategy is to achieve a uniform and fully harmonized water regime in Montenegro, on each of its two river basins – Adriatic and Danube (pursuant to Article 21 of the Water Act).

423. At its session held on 9 February 2017, the GMNE adopted the General Plan for the Protection from the Harmful Impact of Water, for waters of importance for Montenegro, for a period of 2017 to 2022 (OJ MNE, No. 17/17).

424. Ministry of Agriculture and Rural Development (MARD) adopted Operational plan for protection against harmful effects of waters, for waters of importance for Montenegro for 2018 (OJ MNE, No. 4/2018).

V. Legislation

A. *Law on Environment*

425. The Law on environment (OJ MNE, Nos 52/16, 73/19) has general provisions concerning water protection. For example, 'water' is included in the term 'environment' (Article 2), and following articles: special laws (Article 6), notions (Article 7, point 34), protection of environmental segments (Article 15), water protection (Article 17), protective zone (Article 42), geological storage of carbon-dioxide (Article 51), systematic monitoring of the environment (Article 54), manner of monitoring the environment (Article 55), implementation of monitoring (Article 56) and environmental information (Article 67).

426. According to Article 17, water protection includes the implementation of water protection measures and the improvement of the status of water and water ecosystems in order to prevent or reduce the adverse effects on human health, water ecosystems, quality of life and the environment as a whole (paragraph 1).[506] The implementation of water protection measures ensures the prevention or limitation of the introduction into water of hazardous, waste and other harmful substances, the

---

responsible for control of drinking water quality. The Hydromet monitoring network includes forty hydrological stations and thirty-six stations measuring water quality indicators. The Institute of Marine Biology, which is part of the University of Montenegro, monitors a number of organic pollutants and biological components and some specific water phenomena caused by pollution for the purpose of scientific research. UNECE (2007), 31.

505. *See*: https://www.gov.me/dokumenta/c991a55e-cd22-4c46-af58-e3c6cab103a9 (3 Dec. 2022).

506. The protection and use of water is realized within the integral water management system, the implementation of measures for the protection of surface and ground waters and their reserves, quality and quantity, as well as the protection of basins, coastal areas and basins, in accordance with the law regulating water (para. 2).

monitoring and testing of surface and groundwater quality as well as the quality of wastewater and their purification (paragraph 3).

B. Law on Waters

427. Basic legal act regulating water protection in Montenegro[507] is the Law on Waters (OJ RM, No. 27/2007, OJ MNE, Nos 32/11, 47/11, 48/15, 52/16, 55/16, 02/17, 80/17, 84/18). It has following nine parts: Part I – General Provisions (Articles 1–5), Part II – Waters and Water Property (Articles 6–17), Part III – Water Management and Water Facilities (Articles 18–132), Part IV – Water and Water Good Concessions (Articles 133–140), Part V – Limitation of Rights and Obligations of Owners and Users of Land and Water Facilities (Articles 141–150), Part VI – Organization of Water Management (Articles 151–160), Part VII – Supervision (Articles 161–163), Part VIII – Penalty Provisions (Articles 164–167) and Part IX – Transitional and Final Provisions (Articles 168–175).

428. According to Article 1, the Law on Waters regulates the legal status and the manner of integrated management of waters; water and shore land and water-related facilities, conditions and manner for performing water-related activities[508] and other issues important for management of waters and water resources.[509]

429. Article 2 prescribes that this Law applies to surface[510] and ground waters[511] and partly saline waters in mouths of the rivers that run into the sea; mineral[512] and thermal waters;[513] water good; sources of drinking water in the territorial sea; coastal water protection from pollution from the land (Article 2).

---

507. First adopted laws in this field were: Law on Republic water fund (Official Journal of SRM, No. 5/65) and Law on water contribution for year 1966 (Official Journal of SRM, No. 33/65), while soon after that, the first complete Montenegrin Water Law was adopted (Official Journal of RM, Nos 1/67, 20/67, 2/69 and 15/70). Later on Law was amended and upgraded with adoption of Water Law (Official Journal of SRM, No. 22/74), then Water Law (Official Journal of SRM, Nos 25/81, 12/86 and 6/90), Water Law (Official Journal of RM, No. 16/95) and finally valid Water Law (Official Journal of RM, No. 27/07), in a manner that with each new law, the former was repealed. All these laws were followed by appropriate amendments of by-laws adopted for their implementation. Radunović, Lj. M., (2008), 9.

508. The water activity is an activity of general interest for Republic of Montenegro. The water activity includes: water management; ensuring and use of waters with long-term protection of water quality and water source; protection of waters against pollution; regulation of waters and water stream; protection from harmful effects waters (Art. 4).

509. Funds for financing water management operations will be provided in accordance with the special Law on Financing of Waters (Art. 1, para. 1).

510. Surface water means all waters, excluding ground waters, transitional waters, partly saline waters and coastal waters (Art. 5, point 51).

511. Ground water means all waters which are below the surface of the ground (Art. 5, point 48).

512. Mineral water means all groundwater with natural mineral substance in quantity of 1 gm per litre (Art. 5, point 36).

513. Thermal water means all groundwater with natural raise temperature similar or higher then 20° (Art. 5, point 67).

1. Water and Water Good

430. Most important part of the Law contains provisions concerning water management and management of water good, providing in this way the legal prerequisites for organized and appropriate social activity aimed at the maintenance and improvement of water regime in a unique water system. The state owns waters, as a natural wealth and a public good, and they can be used under the terms and conditions fixed by this Law (Article 6). The waters are divided into liquid and standing waters on the surface of the earth and groundwater on land and sea (Article 7). Waters are classified in terms of importance or cross-border impact. There are two groups of water: water of Republican[514] and local importance (Article 8, paragraph 1).

431. Article 3 of the Law stipulated that water management has the following aims: prevents deterioration and protects and enhances the status of aquatic ecosystems, terrestrial ecosystems and wetlands directly depending on the aquatic ecosystem which are directly dependent on water systems; ensures the good status of waters; encourages economic and social development; protects and improves the aquatic ecosystems through specific measures for the progressive reduction of pollutions by the priority hazardous substances; promotes sustainable water use based on a long-term protection of available water resources; ensures the progressive reduction of pollution of groundwater and prevents its further pollution; contributes to mitigating the effects of floods and droughts; contributes to the provision of the sufficient supply of good-quality surface water and groundwater as needed for sustainable, balanced and equitable water use; a significant reduction in pollution of groundwater, the protection of territorial and coastal waters; achieving the objectives fixed by the relevant international agreements; ensures public participation in making decisions related to waters; creates the conditions for meeting international obligations in the area of waters;[515] and prevents and resolves conflicts related to water use and water protection.

432. Water good, in terms of this Law, includes natural and artificial waterbodies and water land (Article 9, paragraph 1). The water good is of general interest and is used in the manner and under the conditions laid down by the Law. Water good, by its significance, is divided into water good of importance for Montenegro

514. Waters of the importance for the Republic have to been determined by the Government, at the proposal of the Ministry (Art. 8, para. 2). The waters of importance for Montenegro shall be entered in the Register maintained by the state administration authority responsible for water management (hereinafter: the competent administrative authority) (Art. 8, para. 3). Waters of local importance shall be entered in the register kept by the competent local authority (Art. 8, para. 5).

515. In line with the established maxim of international law that enables states to control the natural resources on its territory (including water resources) while still respecting internationally accepted obligations, or as stated by Vučić (2019b, 76): 'Theory of limited territorial sovereignty is based on the assertion that every state is free to use shared watercourses flowing on its territory as long as such utilisation does not prejudice the rights and interests of the co-riparians'.

and water good of local importance, according to the division of waters carried out in accordance with Article 8 of this Law (Article 9, paragraphs 3 and 4).[516]

433. For the purposes of this law, the coastal land consists of a 15-m-wide land-line for waters of importance for Montenegro and 10 m for waters of local importance from the boundary of aquatic land, which, as a rule, serves for the maintenance of protective structures and troughs for large water and other activities in water management (Article 10, paragraph 1).[517]

Public Water Good

434. The public water good may be: (1) Natural and (2) Built. The natural public water goods are water and aquatic land (Article 13, paragraphs 1–2). The built public water good is (1) aquatic land due to the displacement or arrangement of natural watercourses, partitioning of running water, extraction of mineral resources and other activities in the area; (2) a facility on aquatic soil (canals, arranged coast, etc.). Public water good is state-owned (Article 13, paragraphs 3–4).[518]

Water Good Usage

435. Public water good is in general use and is used under the conditions defined by this Law, in a way that does not adversely affect water and a coastal ecosystem and does not limit the equal rights of others (Article 15, paragraph 1). The public water good may be acquired for special use (Article 15, paragraph 2).[519]

Water Management and Water Facilities

436. Water management, as good of general interest, is realized in the manner and under the conditions determined by this Law (Article 18, paragraph 1). For the purpose of this Law, the management of waters and aquatic land includes activities and measures taken to maintain and improve the water regime in a unique water system in a particular area in order to: ensure the required quantity of water of the prescribed quality for certain purposes, protection of waters against pollution and protection from harmful effects of water (Article 18, paragraph 2).[520]

437. Following are ten generally accepted principles on which water management and management of water good are based: (1) irreplaceable character of water as a resource and a condition for survival – as a natural public good, water may be used exclusively so as not to endanger its substance and not to exclude its natural

516. Water land can be in private and state property, in accordance with the Law (Art. 9, para. 5).
517. The boundaries of aquatic land shall be determined by the competent administrative authority or the competent local authority. The designations and boundaries of aquatic land at the proposal of the competent authority shall be entered in the real estate cadastre. (Art. 11, paras 1–2).
518. Natural and built public water good shall be entered in the Real Estate Cadastre, on the proposal of the competent authority (Art. 13, para. 7).
519. The right to special use of public water good shall be acquired in accordance with the Law on the basis of the concession contract and the water permit (Art. 15, para. 3).
520. The management of waters and aquatic land, of importance for Montenegro, is under the jurisdiction of Montenegro. The management of waters and aquatic land, of local importance, is the responsibility of the local self-government units, unless otherwise provided by this Law (Art. 18, paras 3–4).

role; (2) completeness – natural processes and water as their significant component as well as the connections and interrelations between aquatic and riparian ecosystems must be respected; (3) integrated water system – the need for integral water management in united water area in line with the development of the Republic and establishment of integrated water information system; respecting the international agreements with other countries in the river basin in area of sustainable water management; (4) sustainable development whereby the needs of the present generations are met without threatening the possibility for future generations to meet their needs; (5) long-term protection of water quality and sustainable use of available water sources; (6) the right on protection against adverse impacts of water following the need to protect the population and their assets, respecting the laws of natural processes, protecting the natural values and economic justifications for the protection; (7) economic valuation of waters which includes full recovery of costs of water production and treatment for different users, water regulation and protection against pollution based on the 'user pays-polluter pays' principle; (8) continuous water management because waters must be managed continuously on all levels of planning and at all stages of water regulation, use and protection; (9) public participation in the processes of preparation and adoption of Water Management Plans; and (10) adoption of the best available technologies and new scientific developments related to the laws of nature (Article 19).

Territorial Basis for Water Management

438. The territory of Montenegro is a unique water area, on which the boundaries of administrative and territorial units cannot limit integrated water management (Article 20). In order to ensure complete water management, while respecting the hydrographic characteristics, uniqueness and connection of the water regime, in the territory of Montenegro water areas are defined as the basic water management units as follows: The water area of the Danube basin and the water area of Jadran sea (Article 21).[521]

Planning Documents of Water Management

439. Water Management Strategy (hereinafter 'the Strategy') is a planning document that determines long-term water management directions (Article 23, paragraph 1).[522] The Strategy contains in particular: (1) assessment of the current situation in the area of water management; (2) objectives and guidelines for water management; (3) measures for achieving the defined objectives of water management; and (4) projection of water management development (Article 23, paragraph 2).[523]

521. Water areas are divided into: (1) Areas of sub-basins and (2) Areas of small basins (Art. 21a, para. 1).

522. The Strategy is adopted by the Government for a period of at least ten years. The strategy shall be reviewed at the expiration of six years from the date of its adoption (Art. 23, paras 3–4).

523. The Ministry monitors the Strategy implementation and prepares an annual report on the implementation of the Strategy that is submitted to the Government no later than 15 April of the current year for the previous year (Art. 23, para. 6).

440. The water management plan determines the water management elements of the river basin (Article 24, paragraph 1). The water management plan shall contain in particular: general description of the space characteristics for which the plan is in operation; presentation of significant impacts of human activities on the status of surface and groundwater; identification and production of maps of protected areas; a map of the monitoring network and a map showing the results of the observation; a list of priority environmental objectives in terms of surface and groundwater and protected areas, with reasons for possible deviations; water balance; identification of water bodies used for water supply, an overview of the programme of measures and the manner and dynamics for achieving established goals in the field of protection against harmful effects of waters, water protection and water use; additional measures for achieving the established environmental objectives; an overview of specific water management plans for particular sub-basins and programme measures, with characteristics or types of watercourses; economic analysis of the use and protection of waters and protection against harmful effects of waters, conducted on the basis of the 'user pay' and 'polluter pays' principle, with recommendation of optimal solutions; a list of bodies and organizations in the field of water management, with their responsibility and status; an overview of the obligations assumed by international agreements related to water management and implementation method; principles for the establishment of an information system for the provision of water management in the water area, or the river basin, etc. (Article 24, paragraph 3).

441. The waters of the international river basin are managed on the basis of the management plan of the states on which territory is located parts of this basin (Article 24a). Water management plans are passed by the Government, at the proposal of the Ministry. The expert preparation of water management plans for river basins is carried out by the competent administrative authority (Article 25, paragraphs 1 and 2).[524]

Special Plans

442. If the implementation of the Strategy cannot be provided for the water management plans referred to in Article 24 of this Law, the Government shall, upon the proposal of the Ministry, adopt a separate water management plan for certain categories of watercourses or for specific water management issues (Article 28, paragraph 1). Expert preparation of a special water management plan shall be carried out by the competent administrative authority. The plan must be in accordance with the water management plan on the river basin, i.e., the water area of the river basin (paragraphs 2 and 3).[525]

524. Water management plans must be reviewed at the expiration of six years from the date of their adoption or review (Art. 25, para. 3).

525. The Government's proposal, upon the proposal of the Ministry, determines the closer content and manner for preparation of the plan (Art. 28, para. 4).

SEA and Public Participation

443. Development of a strategic EIA is mandatory for the water management strategy and plans in the water area, or part of the water area. The strategic assessment shall be carried out in the manner prescribed by the regulations on strategic impact assessment environment (Article 29, paragraphs 1–2).

444. The competent administration body shall be obliged to enable the active participation of the public and interested parties in the process of preparing and adopting water management plan, or its amendment after the conducted review procedure and upon the availability of all the documentation of relevance for its creation. The competent administration body is obliged to inform interested persons and the general public through the public media about the beginning preparation stage of the water management plan (Article 30, paragraphs 1–2).

445. Persons referred to in Article 30 paragraph 1 of this Law may make written comments, proposals and suggestions on the documents referred to in Article 30 paragraphs 3, 4 and 5 of this Law and submit it to the competent administrative authority within six months, and on a special water management plan within one month from the date of publication on the Ministry's website (Article 31, paragraph 1).[526]

Water Facilities and Systems

446. Water facilities and systems, for the purposes of this Law, are considered as construction and other facilities or a set of facilities, with belonging devices, which constitute a technical unit, and serve for performing aquatic activity. Facilities intended for watercourse regulation and protection against harmful effects of water, water monitoring facilities, as well as natural and artificial watercourses included in the water system, constitute a water infrastructure. A more detailed regulation on the composition and content of water infrastructure is issued by the Ministry (Article 34, paragraphs 1–2).[527]

Water Activities

447. Water regulation is a set of measures and works on preservation and regulation of water quantities for the purpose of securing: (1) quantitative, spatial and time distribution of water for supplying legal entities and natural persons; (2) survival of aquatic and coastal ecosystems; and (3) increased quantities of water in the water courses during the low water period. The type and scope of water management measures and measures referred to in paragraph 1 of this Article shall be an

526. The competent administrative body shall be obliged, within three months from the expiration of the deadline referred to in para. 1 of this Article, to prepare a report on the views on the submitted comments, proposals and suggestions (Art. 31, para. 2).
527. Water facilities shall be entered in the Real Estate Cadastre (Art. 36).

integral part of the Strategy and Water Management Plan referred to in Articles 23 and 24 of this Law (Article 39, paragraphs 1–2).[528]

Water Protection from Pollution

448. Protection of water from pollution is regulated by several provisions of this Law (Articles 72–91). It includes a set of measures and actions for improvement of the water quality to an appropriate level (Article 72, paragraph 1) and it is implemented in order to ensure harmless an unobstructed water use, promotion of the public health, protection of flora and fauna and environmental protection (Article 72, paragraph 2).[529]

449. According to Article 73, water protection goals include goals for surface waters, groundwater and for protected areas. Goals for surface waters are necessary measures to prevent deterioration of the status of all bodies of surface water; protect, enhance and restore all bodies of surface water; achieving good surface water status for artificial and heavily modified bodies of water; protect and enhance all artificial and heavily modified bodies of water, with the aim of achieving good ecological potential and good surface water chemical status; acceleration of reducing pollution from priority substances and ceasing or phasing out emission, discharges and losses of priority hazardous substances.

450. Goals for groundwater are following: prevent or limit the input of pollutants into groundwater and prevent the deterioration of the status of all bodies of groundwater; protect, enhance and restore all bodies of groundwater, ensure a balance between abstraction and recharge of groundwater (protect of excessive exploitation), with the aim of achieving good groundwater status; reduction of any significant and sustained upward trend in the concentration of any pollutant resulting from the impact of human activity in order progressively to reduce pollution of groundwater (Article 73, point 2).

---

528. The use of water is allowed under the conditions determined by this Law. Water must be used rationally and economically (Art. 40, paras 1–2).
529. Protection against water pollution is implemented through: bans, limitations and prevention of input of dangerous and harmful substances into the water, prescription and implementation of other measures for water quality preservation and improvement, control and bans on river dam operation in case of adverse modification of watercourses in specific periods of the year (Art. 72, paras 3–4). Apart from that Art. 74 prescribes that protection against water pollution includes following measures: Organizational measures, including the monitoring of water quality and pollution sources, ban and limitation on intake of hazardous and dangerous substances in waters, ban on trading with substances dangerous for water if they can be substituted with more environmentally friendly products, etc.; Economic measures, implying water pollution fines exceeding the cost of water treatment; Technical and technological measures, implying waste water treatment at the point of origin, as well as the introduction of cleaner production technologies; Water measures, implying the improvement of the regime and quality of small waters with special-purpose discharge of clean water for the reservoirs, which is vital for the remediation of the damage caused by pollution accidents.

Areas of Special Water Protection

451. For each water area, areas of special protection of waters (hereinafter 'protected areas') are defined for the protection of surface and ground waters, or the preservation of habitats of plant and animal species directly dependent on water (Article 74a, paragraph 1).[530]

Plan for the Protection of Water from Pollution

452. Water pollution protection is carried out in accordance with the water protection plan for pollution. The water protection plan for pollution is drawn up based on the established water status in accordance with the Strategy (Article 77, paragraphs 1–2). The plan for the protection of waters against pollution is adopted by the Government at the proposal of the Ministry for a period of six years (Article 77, paragraph 4).

Operational Plan for Water Protection from Accidental Pollution

453. Water protection in case of hazardous pollution is carried out in accordance with the operational plan for protection against pollution (Article 78, paragraph 1). The operational plan for protection of water from pollution for waters of importance for Montenegro shall be prepared and implemented by the competent administrative authority, and shall be adopted by the Ministry, with the consent of the ministry responsible for environmental protection, for a period of two years. Operational plan for protection of waters from pollution for waters of local importance,[531] with the consent of the competent administrative body, is adopted and implemented by local self-government units for a period of two years. The operational plan referred must be in accordance with the plan referred to in paragraph 3 of this Article (Article 78, paragraphs 3–4).

Bans and Obligations

454. The Law establishes following prohibitions for the purpose of protection of water quality:

(1) Intake of hazardous and dangerous substances in surface and ground waters that might aggravate the existing status, that is, exceeding the prescribed water quality standards.
(2) Intake of substances that might contaminate water or may cause siltation and salivation of water and settlement of sediments.
(3) Use of fertilizers or herbicides on riparian land, which may exceed a limit of prescribed standard surface water quality.
(4) Discharge into the public sewerage system containing hazardous and dangerous substances that: exceed the prescribed standards, might have an adverse

530. Protected areas are registered in the Register of Protected Areas (hereinafter: the Register), which is kept by the competent administration body. The registry also contains maps indicating the position of each protected area and the name of the acts on the basis of which the protected areas have been declared (Art. 74a, paras 3–4).
531. This plan must be in accordance with the operational plan for protection of water from pollution for waters of importance for Montenegro (Art. 78, para. 5).

effect on the waste water treatment possibility, might damage the sewer works and water treatment plants might have an adverse effect on the health of the sewerage system maintenance workers.

(5) Disposal of communal and other wastes on water land, high river banks, slopes of river canyons, natural pits, valleys and other locations from where they may enter either surface or ground waters and cause water quality degradation.

(6) Disposal of the substances that might contaminate water in the high water beds of natural and artificial streams and lakes, as well as on other lands.

(7) Washing of motor vehicles, machines, equipment and appliances in surface waters and on water land (Article 79).[532]

Obligation of Pollutants

455. If there is an imminent threat of pollution or pollution of surface and groundwater, a company, another legal entity or entrepreneur that caused the danger, i.e., pollution, is obliged to immediately undertake the measures necessary for preventing, reducing and remediation of water pollution, to plan assets and deadlines for their execution, as well as to compensate for the damage.[533] The Ministry shall closely determine the elements for assessing the direct and indirect damage and the measures necessary for their elimination (Article 81, paragraphs 1–2).

Monitoring

456. Monitoring is carried out by systematic monitoring of water status in order to determine the status of water based on the programme from Article 58, paragraph 3 of this Law, which covers all water areas (Article 83, paragraph 1).[534]

457. The monitoring shall be performed by the authority responsible for hydrometeorological operations which is obliged to enable the use of monitoring results to all interested legal entities and natural persons, free of charge. The body responsible for hydrometeorological affairs shall prepare an annual report on the status and changes in the quality and quantity of water and submit it by 1 March at the latest for the previous year to the Ministry, the competent administration body and the state administration body competent for health, environment and geological affairs (Article 82, paragraphs 5–7).

---

532. The Ministry has the obligation to adopt a more detailed regulation on the sanitary technical conditions for the discharge of waste water into recipients and into public sewerage system, with previous opinion of the Ministry competent for environmental protection and Ministry for health (Art. 79, para. 2). According to Art. 91 any citizen, owner, that is user of a stretch of a bank, captain of a vessel, and other responsible person on a vessel have to report immediately to the Ministry in charge of navigation, relevant inspection or policy any identified water pollution in a stream, lake or in the coastal waters.

533. If a company, another legal entity or an entrepreneur fails to act within the meaning of para. 1 of this Article, the implementation of these measures, at its expense, shall be provided by the competent authority, in accordance with the law (Art. 81, para. 3).

534. The monitoring may include: supervisory monitoring; operational monitoring; and research monitoring (Art. 83, para. 3).

Characteristics of the Water Area

458. The characteristics of the water area are determined for each water area or for the part of the international water area belonging to the territory of the area by the: (1) analysis of its characteristics; (2) analysis of the impact of human activity on the status of surface and groundwater; and (3) economic analysis of water use (Article 83a, paragraph 1).[535]

459. The following issues are regulated by the special provisions of the Law: Classification of water bodies (Article 83b), Artificial or highly modified water body (Article 83c), Temporary deterioration of the status of water bodies (Article 83d), Exceptions in achieving goals (Article 83e) and Application of exemption rules (Article 83f).

Protection from Contamination by Mineral Oils

460. Article 87 of the Law stipulates that it is prohibited to discharge, from vessels or from banks or inside of water source zones, following: mineral oils[536] that can directly or indirectly reach waters, mineral oils originating from any equipment for loading or unloading of fright on and from ships, as well as other substances directly originating from or linked to explorations, use and processing of mineral resources extracted from the river bed on the banks.[537]

461. Specified piers and ports have obligation to install the necessary equipment to collect larger volumes of mineral oil waste, oil mixtures, wastewater and other wastes from vessels. It is prescribed by Article 89 that oil pipelines, connections from ships to the equipment on the banks and the equipment for the collection, treatment and storage of mineral oils must be constructed and maintained so as to prevent discharge and spills of oil into the water.[538]

Protection Against Harmful Effects of Water

462. Protection against harmful effects of water includes works and measures for flood protection, protection against river erosion, protection against water erosion, wind and floods, and drainage and elimination of the consequences of these water activities (Article 94, paragraph 1).[539]

535. The analyses referred to in para. 1 of this Article shall be carried out every six years and shall form an integral part of the Water Management Plan (para. 2).
536. For the purposes of this Law, mineral oil means: crude oil, petroleum, petrol, petroleum, diesel fuel, heating oil, lubricating oils and grease (Art. 87, para. 3).
537. In extraordinary circumstances, in case of sudden contamination of a stream with mineral oils, the relevant inspection authority shall inspect each case separately to identify whether all necessary measures for the prevention of pollution have been implemented (Art. 87, para. 2).
538. Owners, that is, users of vessels have to keep a registry of oils for the vessel in accordance with the international and domestic regulation (Art. 90).
539. In order to ensure protection against harmful effects of water for each water area, an area that is endangered due to: (1) flood (hereinafter: flood area); (2) erosion with water and wind (hereinafter: erosive area). Flood and erosive areas are kept in the real estate cadastre (Art. 95, paras 1–2).

Management of Flood Risks

463. Floods are managed to reduce the harmful effects of floods on human health, the environment, cultural heritage and the economy. Flood risks are managed on the basis of a flood risk management plan and other measures prescribed by the Law (Article 95a, paragraphs 1–2).[540]

Plans for Protection Against Harmful Effects of Water

464. Protection against harmful effects of water is organized and implemented in accordance with general and operational plans for protection against harmful effects of waters, which are brought for waters of importance for Montenegro and waters of local importance. The general plan of protection against harmful effects of water, for a period of six years, for waters of importance for Montenegro, at the proposal of the Ministry, is passed by the Government, while for local water bodies the competent local self-government authority, with the previous opinion of the Ministry (Article 100, paragraphs 1–2). The operational plan for protection against harmful effects of water for a period of one year, for waters of importance for Montenegro, is passed by the Ministry and is prepared by the competent administrative body, and for local water bodies the competent local authority, with the consent of the competent administrative body (Article 100, paragraph 4).[541]

465. Obligations of Montenegro and the local self-government unit in the field of protection against harmful effects of water

466. In order to protect against harmful effects of water, Montenegro and the local self-government unit provide planning, construction, maintenance and management of water facilities in the vulnerable area (Article 106, paragraph 1). Water facilities for protection against harmful effects of water are state-owned (Article 107, paragraph 1). Water facilities for protection against harmful effects of water of importance to Montenegro are managed by the competent administration body. Water facilities for protection against the harmful effects of water of local importance are managed by the local self-government unit (Article 108, paragraphs 1–2).[542]

467. The protection against the harmful effects of atmospheric waters in regulated settlements is the responsibility of local self-government units (Article 111).

540. In the process of elaboration of the flood risk management plan and during their updating, the participation of all interested persons and the public must be ensured, in order to provide comments, proposals and suggestions (Art. 95f, para. 1).

541. The operational plan for protection against harmful effects of water, for waters of importance for Montenegro, is adopted no later than 30 November, and for waters of local importance until 15 December of the current year, for the next year (Art. 100, para. 6).

542. The competent administration body is obliged to provide monitoring and measurement of natural and other phenomena (floods, floods, erosion, etc.) in order to provide data for protection against harmful effects of waters. These data referred shall be public (Art. 109, paras 1–2).

Rehabilitation of Consequences of Harmful Effects of Water

468. The rehabilitation of the consequences of harmful effects of water on aquatic soil, water bodies and water facilities is carried out on the basis of a rehabilitation programme that determines the types and extent of the required work. The legal entity or natural person who caused the damage to a state-owned water facility is obliged to execute the rehabilitation or reimburse the costs of remediation (Article 110, paragraphs 1–2).[543]

Water Acts and Other Water Documentation

469. In order to ensure a unique water regime, integral management and fair access to water, the water acts determine the conditions and manner of exercising the right to water (Article 112, paragraph 1). Water acts are (1) water conditions; (2) water consent; (3) water permit; and (4) water order.[544]

Water Conditions

470. The investor is obliged, in order to create technical documentation for the construction of new or reconstruction of existing ones' facilities and carry out geological explorations and other works that can permanently, occasionally or temporarily influence the changes in the water regime, and acquire aquatic conditions (Article 114, paragraph 1).

Water Consent

471. The investor is obliged, prior to the commencement of the construction of new and reconstruction of existing facilities and facilities and works for which water requirements are to obtain water consent. It is determined by water consent that the technical documentation for the objects and works referred to in Article 115 of this Law is made in accordance with determined water conditions. The water consent shall be issued by the authority that has determined the water conditions (Article 118, paragraphs 1–3).

472. The validity period of the water consent cannot be longer than two years from the date of its issuance, that is, the time of construction of the building permit (Article 119, paragraph 3).

Water Permit

473. The investor is obliged to obtain water permit, before using the facilities and plants for which water consent is required, which determines that the facilities and installations have been built in accordance with the water consent (Article 120, paragraph 1).

---

543. The rehabilitation programme shall be prepared by the competent administrative authority or the competent local authority in accordance with the water management plans, unless otherwise provided by Law (Art. 110, para. 4).

544. Water acts must be in accordance with the Strategy, water management plans and appropriate technical documentation (Art. 112, para. 3).

474. A water permit is issued by a body that has issued a water consent, on the basis of a report by an expert, commission or scientific or professional organization, which, depending on the complexity of the case, is determined by that authority. The water permit is issued for a limited period of time, and the longest period is up to ten years (Article 120, paragraphs 3–4).[545]

Water Order

475. In order to eliminate the danger of threatening or disturbances in the water regime, as well as for the establishment of a condition in accordance with the conditions specified by the water permit, the water order determines the holder's obligation to execute or to refrain from certain activities or works within a certain period of time. The water order is issued by the authority that issued the water permit (Article 126, paragraphs 1–2).

Water Documentation

476. Water documentation consists of a water book, a register and a collection of technical rules on the functioning and regime of exploitation of water systems, water cadastres and records of concession contracts on water resources, water facilities and systems. Water documentation shall be kept by the competent administrative authority, as a single register of data (Article 127, paragraphs 1–2).

Concessions in the Area of Water and Aquatic Goods

477. In order to improve water systems, ensure the sustainable use of water based on long-term protection of available water resources,[546] proper, economical and efficient use of public water resources and security financial means for improving water, concessions can be given in the public water good.[547] The concession on the public water good shall be obtained in the manner and according to the procedure established by the law regulating the concession on natural resources unless otherwise provided by this law (Article 133, paragraph 1).

C. The Law on Hydrometeorological Affairs

478. Basic legal act regulating hydrometeorological affairs in Montenegro is the Law on hydrometeorological affairs (OJ MNE, Nos 26/10, 30/12). It has the

545. Water permit for the use of hydro-accumulations for the production of electricity shall be issued for a period of up to thirty years (Art. 120, para. 5).

546. It is important to note in this regard that Montenegro is a part of the Council of Europe's Convention on fundamental human rights and freedom's system of human rights protections. Although lacking in explicit confirmation of the right to water as a human right, the Convention can be implicitly interpreted so to contain important restrictions on concession contracts on water resources with the aim of ensuring 'adequate quantities and qualities of potable water' (Vučić 2017, 521).

547. The concession on the public water good shall be obtained in the manner and according to the procedure established by the law regulating the concession on natural resources, unless otherwise provided by this law (Art. 133, para. 2).

following eight parts: Part I – General Provisions (Articles 1–4), Part II – Hydrometeorological affairs[548] (Article 5), Part III – Way of performing hydrometeorological affairs (Articles 6–16), Part IV – Meteorological and hydrological observation system (Articles 17–23), Part V – Database of meteorological and hydrological data and information (Articles 24–26), Part VI – Supervision (Article 27), Part VII – Penalty provisions (Article 28) and Part VIII – Transitional and final provisions (Articles 29–31).

479. According to Article 1, paragraph 1, this Law regulates hydrometeorological affairs, manner of performing and other issues of importance for conducting hydrometeorological affairs. Hydrometeorological affairs provide scientifically based warnings, forecasts and data on weather and climate, atmosphere and water status[549] in order to protect the natural and by work created material goods and sustainable development (Article 2, paragraph 1). Hydrometeorological affairs shall be conducted in a manner that provides internationally comparable meteorological and hydrological data, including data on air and water quality (Article 3, paragraph 7).[550]

1. Performing of Hydrometeorological Affairs

480. Hydrometeorological affairs from Article 5 of this Law are affairs of national interest for Montenegro. These activities are performed by the administrative authority responsible for hydrometeorological affairs (hereinafter referred to as 'Hydrometeorological service') (Article 6, paragraph 1), on the basis of annual plan of work, adopted by GMNE (Article 9, paragraph 1).

481. Hydrometeorological service is in charge to inform public in electronic and printed media about conditions of weather, climate and water and to publish warnings on atmosphere and hydrological disasters, as well as on disasters at sea (Article 7, paragraph 1).

548. Hydrometeorological affairs, pursuant to this Law, include a set of activities on systematic monitoring, research and forecasting of weather and climate, sea state, air and water quality (Art. 5, para. 5).
549. *The state of the atmosphere* is set of quantitative and qualitative values of physical parameters of atmosphere in certain periods of time or in time intervals, processed and presented in a way which ensures objective assessment on observed components of natural environment (Art. 4, point 10). *The water state* is set of quantitative and qualitative values of surface and ground parameters of water and sea, in certain period of time or in time interval, processed and presented in a way which ensures objective assessment on observed components of natural environment (Art. 4, point 11).
550. Performing of hydrometeorological affairs is based on the following principles (Art. 3, para. 1): The principle of integrity, The principle of continuity, The principle of prevention, The principle of information of public, The principle of validity and The principle of standardization.

482. Hydrometeorological service monitors pollutants' content in atmosphere and in water,[551] and in case of incidental pollution it continuously monitors that appearance and informs the competent authorities and the public (Article 7, paragraph 2). Hydrometeorological service establishes hydrometeorological telecommunication system and ensures its connection with international telecommunication and information system in the field of meteorology and hydrology for the purpose of operational exchange of data and information, in relation to ratified international agreements (Article 8, paragraph 1).

483. Activities from Article 5, point 15, concerning meteorological securing of air traffic perform provider of aviation services,[552] in the manner specified in regulations adopted on the basis of this Law and on Law on the air traffic (Article 10, paragraph 1). Hydrometeorological service performs marine meteorological measurements and observations on vessels in ports and harbours, lighthouses, dams and accumulations (Article 11, paragraphs 1 and 2).

484. Meteorological notifications on adverse and dangerous weather phenomena on the sea and information on sea pollution have priority in the notice of the administrative authority in charge of maritime security operations and electronic and print media (Article 13, paragraph 1).

2. Meteorological and Hydrological Observing System

485. Meteorological observation system consists of a network of meteorological stations,[553] as follows (Article 17, paragraph 1): synoptic stations; climatological stations; agrometeorological stations; precipitation stations; radar stations; maritime stations; phenological stations; stations for measuring and monitoring air quality;[554] and precipitation stations for measuring and monitoring solar radiation and atmospheric ozone etc.

---

551. *Measuring and monitoring of water quality* is the systematic measurement and monitoring of physical–chemical–biological condition of water and sediments, determined by the action of hydrometeorological processes, including spatial–temporal monitoring by hydrological and oceanographic numeric prognostic models (Art. 4, point 5).
552. The provider is in charge to submit reports on meteorological measurements and observations conducted in a way determined in regulations adopted on the base of this Law (Art. 10, para. 2). *Meteorological measurements and observations* are instrumental measurements and/or determination of values of one or more meteorological elements (Art. 4, point 1). *The provider of aviation services* is specialized organization established by the Government of Montenegro for the provision of aviation services (Art. 4, point. 21).
553. *Meteorological station* is a representative space for appropriate facility, instruments and equipment for performing of meteorological measurements and observations, including sampling of air and precipitation (Art. 4, point 6).
554. *Measurement and monitoring of air quality* is the systematical measurement and monitoring of physical–chemical condition of state of air and precipitation, which is determined by the action of meteorological and hydrological processes, including spatial–temporal monitoring by hydrometeorological numeric prognostic models (Art. 4, point 4).

486. Hydrological observation system consists of a network of hydrological stations, as follows (Article 17, paragraph 2): station of surface water; station of underground water; station for quality of surface water; stations for the quality of underground water; mareographic stations; stations for marine water quality.

487. An integral part of the meteorological and hydrological observation system consists of the following accredited laboratories (Article 17, paragraph 3): for water quality control; for air and precipitation quality control; for providing of etalon, methods and measurement techniques of standardizations and calibration of meteorological and hydrological instruments.

488. Local governments and other legal entities[555] may, in accordance with the need, at their own expense, establish additional network of meteorological and/or hydrological stations[556] (Article 21, paragraph 1). Instruments and devices used in complementary networks of meteorological and hydrological stations must meet the metrological requirements established by the Law (Article 21, paragraph 2).

489. Hydrometeorological Institute is obliged to issue the emergency meteorological and hydrological information and warnings in the conditions precedent to the atmospheric and hydrological elementary disasters (emergency), in accordance with the Law (Article 23, paragraph 1).

3. The Meteorological and Hydrological Data and the Information

490. Hydrometeorological service establishes, develops and maintains a unique database of meteorological and hydrological data and information, including information on air quality and water and the radioactivity of air and precipitation (Article 24, paragraph 1).[557]

491. In accordance with the Law, information that Hydrometeorological service has on weather conditions, climate, water, air and water quality[558] are public unless the data are confidential, (Article 25, paragraph 1). Supervision over the enforcement of this Law and regulations enacted under this Law is performed by responsible Ministry (Article 27, paragraph 1).

---

555. Legal entities from para. 21 of this Law performing meteorological and/or hydrological measurements and observations, including measurements of water quality and air pollution, are required to notify the Hydrometeorological service on the commencement of these works, their content and duration (Art. 22, para. 1). The results of measurement and observation referred to in para. 1 hereof shall be submitted for verification to the Hydrometeorological service (Art. 22, para. 2).
556. *Hydrological station* is a place with certain facility, instruments and equipment for performing hydrological measurements and supervision, including sampling of water for physico-chemical and biological analysis (Art. 4, point 7).
557. The Ministry prescribes the content of a unique database on weather conditions, climate and water, including sea water, the mode of their records, verification, storage and use (Art. 24, para. 3).
558. These informations of the Hydrometeorological service include international data exchange and are published in periodical reports (Art. 25, para. 2).

D. Law on Regional Water Supply of the Montenegrin Coast

492. The Law on regional water supply of Montenegrin Coast (OJ MNE, No. 56/16) has the following seven parts: Part I – General Provisions (Articles 1–6), Part II – Activity of regional water supply (Articles 7–19), Part III – Financing (Articles 20–22), Part IV – Obligations of the land owner on the regional water supply system (Articles 23–24), Part V – Supervision (Articles 25–26), Part VI – Penalties (Articles 27–28) and Part VII – Transitory and final provisions (Articles 29–33).

493. This law regulates the manner of organizing and performing activities of regional water supply of the Montenegrin coast[559] and other areas, water capture from regional water supply sources for other purposes and other issues of importance for the performance of these activities (Article 1). Regional water supply is an activity of public interest. For the purpose of providing and protecting the public interest, the GMNE: (1) adopted a development programme of activities of regional water supply and water abstraction for other purposes; (2) approved water prices; and (3) approved the annual work plan of the company that performs the activity of regional water supply (Article 3, paragraphs 1, and 2).

1. Activity of Regional Water Supply

494. The activity of regional water supply is carried out[560] by a company founded by the Government (Article 7, paragraph 1). Water abstraction activities for other purposes may be performed by: (1) a company referred to in paragraph 1 of this Article based on a decision of the Government and (2) another company or entrepreneur, based on a concession contract or a public-private partnership, in accordance with the Law (paragraph 2).[561]

559. Regional water supply of the Montenegrin coast and other areas is the catching of drinking water from the regional water supply, measurement, preparation and treatment of water to the point of connection to the local water supply networks, i.e., the places of connection of other users and the measurement of the supplied water (hereinafter: regional water supply) (Art. 2, para. 1).

560. The activity of regional water supply is based on the following principles: (1) continuity in the supply of drinking water of the appropriate quality; (2) compliance of public and economic interest – water price and the provision of regional water supply services provide income that enables the covering of labour costs and current and investment maintenance of the regional water supply system and repayment of loans for the construction and operation of this system; (3) sustainable development of natural resources and protection of the space and environment; (4) harmonization of the interests of the state and local self-government units; (5) ensuring the priority of regional water supply in relation to water abstraction for other purposes; (6) protection of users; (7) protection of competition; and (8) public work of a company performing regional water supply activities (Art. 5).

561. The activity of regional water supply and water capture for other purposes is carried out on the basis of the activities development programme of regional water supply and water capture for other needs. The programme shall be adopted by the Government for a period of five years (Art. 8, paras 1 and 2).

2. Financing

495. Regional water supply activities are financed from (1) funds generated for the provision of regional water supply services (water supplies); (2) investments by the founder or the owner of the company referred to in Article 7 paragraph 1 of this Law; and (3) donations and other sources in accordance with the Law (Article 20, paragraph 1).

496. Investors who build or reconstruct objects on the Montenegrin coast or in the region pay a special fee on the investment (hereinafter 'special fee') prior to the issuance of the building permit (Article 22, paragraph 1).

497. The special fee is the income of the budget of Montenegro and the income of the municipality, of which: (1) 80% of the budget revenues of Montenegro is paid to the company referred to in Article 7 paragraph 1 of this Law and used for the construction of the regional water supply system and the repayment of loans for this construction and (2) 20% of the municipal budget revenue are used to finance the construction of connections to the regional water supply system and the construction and/or investment maintenance of the local water supply network (Article 22, paragraph 5).[562]

3. Supervision

498. Supervision over the implementation of this Law and regulations adopted pursuant to this Law shall be carried out by the Ministry. The tasks of inspection supervision over the application of this Law and the regulations adopted pursuant to this Law shall be performed by the Ministry and the administrative body in charge of inspection supervision, through inspectors in charge of water, ecology and health protection, within the defined competencies (Article 26, paragraphs 1 and 2).

E. Other Regulations

499. Other relevant regulations include the following:

- Law on Water Management Financing (OJ MNE, Nos 65/08, 82/20).[563]
- Law on Municipal Wastewater Management (OJ MNE, No. 2/17).
- Law on Geological Research (OJ RM, Nos 28/93, 27/94, 42/94, 26/07, 28/11).

562. The manner of calculating special fee is regulated by the Government regulation (Art. 22, para. 7).
563. This Law lays down the sources of funds for water management financing, the method of accounting and payment of charges for protection and use of waters and water estate and applies to waters, water estate and water facilities and systems stipulated by the law regulating the water-related issues (Art. 1). *See also* Decision on the amount and method of accounting the water charges, criteria and method of establishing the degree of water pollution (Official Journal of MNE, No. 29/09).

- Law on Nature Protection (OJ MNE, Nos 54/16, 18/19).
- Law on National Parks (OJ MNE, Nos 28/14, 39/16).
- Law on Concessions (OJ MNE, Nos. 8/09, 73/19).
- Law on EIA (OJ MNE, No, 75/18).
- Law on SEA (OJ RM, No. 80/05, OJ MNE, Nos 73/10, 40/11, 59/11, 52/16).
- Law on Industrial Emissions (OJ MNE, No. 17/19).[564]

500. In accordance with the Law on water, a large number of secondary legislations have been adopted, as follows:

- Decision on the designation of areas at significant risk from floods (OJ MNE 30/22).
- Decision on the determination of sensitive areas in the Adriatic basin (OJ MNE, No. 7/20). – Rulebook on the method and terms for the determination of the groundwater status (OJ MNE, No. 52/19).
- Rulebook on the manner and deadlines for the determination of the surface waters (OJ MNE, No. 25/19).
- Decision on the determination of sensitive areas (OJ MNE, No. 46/17).
- Rulebook on criteria for determining sensitive and vulnerable areas to protect water from pollution (OJ MNE, No. 69/21).
- Rulebook on the closer method of determining and securing the environmentally acceptable surface water flow (OJ MNE, Nos 2/16, 23/16).
- Rulebook on the content of the water management strategy and report on the implementation of the strategy (OJ MNE, No. 17/16).
- Rulebook on the boundaries of the area of sub-basins and areas of small basins (OJ MNE, No. 18/21).
- Decree on the method of determining water land boundaries (OJ MNE, No. 25/12).
- Decree on classification and categorization of surface and ground waters (OJ MNE, No. 2/07).
- Decree on designation of waters of importance to Montenegro (OJ MNE, Nos 9/08 and 28/09).
- Decree on method of categorization and categories of water facilities and their giving over for management and maintenance (OJ MNE, No. 15/08).
- Decree on the contents and method of water information system management (OJ MNE, No. 33/08).
- Rulebook on the method of defining the guaranteed flow minimum downstream from the water intake (OJ MNE, No. 22/08).
- Rulebook on the contents of requests and documentation for the issuance of water rights acts, method of and conditions for mandatory announcement in the procedure of stipulating the water rights terms and the contents of water rights acts (OJ MNE, No. 7/08).
- Rulebook on pattern, more details contents and the method of keeping the water register (OJ MNE, No. 81/08).

564. *See also* regulations in the field of marine protection.

– Rulebook on the quality and sanitary technical requirements for wastewater discharge, the method and procedure of wastewater quality testing and the contents of the report on the determined wastewater quality (OJ MNE, Nos 56/19).
– Decision on designation of sources intended for regional and public water supply (by means of public water supply system) and establishing of their borders (OJ MNE, No. 36/08).

F. International Treaties

501. Montenegro is contracting party to the Convention on Cooperation for the Protection and Sustainable Use of the River Danube (Danube River Protection Convention) from 28 October 2008[565] and the Convention on the Protection and Use of Transboundary Watercourses and International Lakes – Helsinki Convention (1992).[566] In addition, Montenegro is a member of the Convention on the Law of Non-Navigational Uses of International Watercourses (OJ-International Agreements, No. 6/13).[567] Montenegro is not a member of the Framework Agreement on the Sava River Basin (FASRB).[568]

502. Bilaterally, Montenegro concluded an Agreement with Croatia on the mutual relations in the field of water management (OJ MNE, No. 1/2008), Treaty with the Republic of Albania on water-related issues (2001) and the Agreement on Protection and Sustainable Development of the Skadar Lake (2008). 'Moreover, conclusion of agreements on water management of common interest with Serbia and Bosnia and Herzegovina is imminent. For now, the cooperation with these countries is realized according to the need pointed, or on an ad hoc basis'.[569]

VI. Harmonization with EU Legislation

503. In the '2022 Progress Report', it is stated that the level of alignment on water quality 'remains limited.' Significant efforts are still needed to implement the

565. *See*: www.icpdr.org/icpdr-pages/contracting_parties.htm (15 Dec. 2022).
566. *See*: https://treaties.un.org/Pages/ViewDetails.aspx?src=TREATY&mtdsg_no=XXVII-5&chapter=27&clang=_en (15 Dec. 2022).
567. *See*: https://treaties.un.org/Pages/ViewDetails.aspx?src=TREATY&mtdsg_no=XXVII-12&chapter=27&clang=_en (15 Dec. 2022). On the nature and manner of the application of this Convention in member countries, especially in relation to the obligation of equitable and rational use of water resources, sustainable utilization of water resources and the no-harm rule see extensively Vučić, 2018.
568. The status of Montenegro in FASRB has been regulated by the Memorandum of Understanding between the International Sava River Basin Commission and Montenegro (9 Dec. 2014).
569. MPPEP (2009), 152. In addition, the basis for cooperation with Croatia, Serbia and Bosnia and Herzegovina was established by acquiring full membership of Montenegro in the Commission for the Protection of the Danube River, and the inclusion of Montenegro in the work of the Commission for the Protection of the river Sava (Sava Commission) as an observer.

water quality *acquis*.[570] The government adopted (in March 2021) the water management plans for the Danube and Adriatic basins. In addition, in the reporting period an analysis of the existing flood protection infrastructure has been done and a preliminary risk assessment has been carried out.

§2. Marine Pollution

504. The sea of Montenegro consists of interior waters and the territorial sea, 12 NM off the shore. The coastal zone covers some 300 km of the coast and towns and other settlements within six Montenegrin municipalities.[571]

505. The sea is another valuable resource of Montenegro, because of its characteristics, as a foundation for development of tourism, transportation, fishing and the use of other resources. Unfortunately, the narrow coastal area has become more affected in the previous years, especially the shallow coastal area at the mouth of the Bojana River, where, for an ecological state, enormous quantities of waste are disposed from the land to the sea (partly due to disposal of waste from the Bijela Shipyard), as well as the Boka Kotorska Basin, particularly endangered by wastewater which is largely untreated and disposed into the sea.[572]

I. Monitoring and Quality of the Seawater

506. Organized monitoring of seawater quality has been resumed since 1995, on sites mostly situated on the beaches. Seawater tested at these sites generally meets the criteria for Class I bathing water.[573]

507. Research along the Montenegrin Littoral, from the exit of Boka Kotorska Bay to the Bojana River mouth, also covered a part of the inshore sea exposed to the South Adriatic open seawaters. The quality of seawater here is far superior to the inshore seawater quality at Boka Kotorska Bay.[574]

508. According to the 2015 data, 'the measuring network for coastal seawater includes 16 sampling locations with a frequency of eight sampling sessions per year'.[575] With regard to the monitoring of the ecosystems of coastal seawater, there is a comprehensive programme, managed independently, for the monitoring of (i) the quality of coastal, transitional and marine waters; (ii) eutrophication; (iii) biological and ecological indicators; (iv) water quality in aquaculture; (v) hotspots; (vi)

570. EC (2022), p. 113. Further work for alignment with the *acquis* was pursued in the field of water intended for human consumption and for implementing the bathing water directive.
571. GMNE (2007C), 46.
572. GMNE, NCSD (2011), 10.
573. GMNE (2007D), 70.
574. *Ibid.*, 70–72. *See also* MTEP (2008a), 24.
575. UNECE (2015), p. 71.

tributaries; and (vii) effluents. Monitoring for bathing seawater 'has been conducted independently of the formal monitoring of environmental media'.[576]

509. Research carried out within the scope of the Programme of systematic research of contents of radio nuclides in the environment of Montenegro has confirmed that levels of radio nuclides, except for potassium, are far below those specified for drinking.[577]

510. Compared to 2010, there can be noticed certain increased concentrations of phosphate salts in the deeper layers of the Bay of Kotor and Risan especially in summer when the population increases and consequently does the amount of waste water. All the values of nutrient salts including the concentration of chlorophyll are expectedly increased in the Bay of Risan and Kotor. Occasionally, during heavy rains in April and May, Risan shows the characteristics of eutrophic areas, so it would be necessary to repair the sewer drain current situation in Risan Bay, and then it would be needed to control the quality of coastal sea throughout the year. The examined areas that are most susceptible to eutrophication are those of the Kotor (Kotor, Dobrota) and Risan Bay as part of the coast which is strongly influenced by the river Bojana. The most significant impact of such a condition has the combined influx of freshwater and anthropogenic activities. The most significant impact of such a condition, in the coastal region of Montenegro, has the combined influx of freshwater and anthropogenic activities. Proper treatment of the waste water, especially during the tourist season, would greatly decrease the degree of eutrophication, especially in systems such as the Bokorski gulf with poor water flow dynamics.[578]

II. Competencies

511. Competence concerning protection against pollution of seawater belongs to the Ministry of Capital Investment (MCI), MED, MAFWM, MESPU, Maritime Safety Administration, Directorate for Water and Public Enterprise for the Coastal Zone Resources Management, and as a consultative body of experts, the recently formed Coordination Body for the protection of the Marine Environment.[579]

512. The Ministry of Transport and Maritime Affairs (MTMA) performs the administrative activities related to maritime transport, safety of internal and international navigation and safety of maritime transport. It defines indicators, monitors pollution and undertakes urgent measures in cases of pollution. It is in charge of

576. *Ibid.* Public enterprise for coastal zone management realizes annual monitoring programmes of bathing water quality on public beaches during the summer season. For more information *see*: https://www.morskodobro.me/me/kontrola (3 Dec. 2022).
577. GMNE (2007D), 70–72.
578. EPA (2012), 61. It is necessary to bring short- and long-term objectives for environmental protection of the Montenegrin coast and gradually solve the problem of waste water treatment especially in places that are 'naturally sensitive' to eutrophication.
579. See the Decision on its establishment in the OJ MNE 95/21.

ports, marines and shipyards, as well as of administrative supervision of Harbour master office, situated in the city of Kotor, with branch harbour offices in Tivat, Zelenika and Herceg Novi and Harbour master office in the city of Bar with the branch harbour offices in Ulcinj, Budva, and Virpazar as regional organizational units of the Department for Maritime Affairs in the MTMA.

III. Strategic Documents

513. The Spatial plan of the Coastal Zone of Montenegro, as a basic strategic document, has been adopted (2007). It covers the local seawater (about 2,540 km^2), the whole coast (about 310 km) and a narrow part of mainland as defined by the Law on the Coastal Zone (surface of about 58 km^2).[580]

IV. Legislation

514. Protection of the sea is regulated by a number of sources of law. Besides the already mentioned legal and sub-legal acts in the field of water, it should be kept in mind that Montenegro is a contracting party to a number of international agreements concerning protection of marine environment. Domestic regulations related to the protection of marine environment include several laws and by-laws relevant to the sea environment, including regulations related to maritime transport.

A. *International Treaties*

515. The Convention for the Protection of the Marine Environment and the Coastal Region of the Mediterranean (known also as Barcelona Convention) has been ratified in 2007, along with four supporting Protocols (OJ RM, No. 64/07). Implementation of it is important both in terms of the creation of preconditions for the implementation of the EU Marine Strategy and the new Marine Directive.

516. Montenegro acquired membership in the UN Organizations and in a number of international treaties through succession from the State Union of S&M. In this manner, it acquired membership in the International Maritime Organization (IMO) and accession to Conventions which have been ratified in the previous period, including the UN Convention on the Law of the Sea,[581] International Convention relating to Intervention on the High Seas in Cases of Oil Pollution Casualties, 1969 (INTERVENTION 1969), Protocol to the International Convention relating to Intervention on the High Seas in Cases of Pollution by Substances other than Oil, 1973, as amended (INTERVENTION PROT 1973), Convention on the Prevention of Marine Pollution by Dumping of Wastes and Other Matter, 1972, as

580. *Ibid.*, 8.
581. *See*: https://www.un.org/depts/los/convention_agreements/texts/unclos/unclos_e.pdf (3 Dec. 2022.

amended (LC (amended) 1972), International Convention for the Prevention of Pollution from Ships, 1973 (MARPOL, 1973) as modified by the Protocol of 1978 relating thereto, and its Annexes from I to VI (MARPOL 73/78).

517. In 2011, Montenegro ratified following treaties: International Convention for the Control and Management of Ships' Ballast Water and Sediments (2004) (OJ MNE – International Treaties, No. 7/2011), International Convention on the Control of Harmful Anti-fouling Systems on Ships (2001), (OJ MNE – International Treaties, No. 7/2011), International Convention on Civil Liability for Bunker Oil Pollution Damage (2001), International Convention on Civil Liability for Oil Pollution Damage (1992) (OJ MNE – International Treaties, No. 7/2011), International Convention on the Establishment of an International Fund for Compensation for Oil Pollution Damage (1992) (OJ MNE – International Treaties, No. 7/2011), Protocol of 2003 to the International Convention on the Establishment of an International Fund for Compensation for Oil Pollution Damage (OJ MNE – International Treaties, No. 7/2011), International Convention on Liability and Compensation for Damage in connection with the Carriage of Hazardous and Noxious Substances by Sea (1996) (OJ MNE – International Treaties, No. 7/2011) and Convention on International Hydrographic Organization (OJ MNE – International Treaties, No. 8/2013).

B. Law on the Sea

518. The Law on the Sea (OJ MNE, Nos 17/2007, 6/2008, 40/2011) has forty-seven articles divided into following nine chapters: Chapter I – Basic Provisions (Articles 1–3), Chapter II – Internal Sea Waters (Articles 4–12), Chapter III – Territorial Sea (Articles 13–24), Chapter IV – Exclusive Economic Zone (Articles 25–34), Chapter V – Continental Shelf (Articles 35–38), Chapter VI – Right to Persecution (Article 39), Chapter VII – Supervision (Articles 40–41), Chapter VIII – Penal Provisions (Articles 42–43) and Chapter IX – Transitional and Final provisions (Articles 44–47).[582]

519. This Law regulates the marine and submarine areas of the RM and the internal seawater, territorial sea, exclusive economic zone, continental shelf, and prohibition of arrival, stay and expulsion of a ship.

520. Environmental protection (apart from the other relevant issues) is the subject of regulation of several provisions of this Law.[583]

---

582. The Law on coastal zone and continental shelf (Official Journal of SFRY, Nos 49/87 and 57/89) and the provisions of the Arts 38, 39 and 40 of the Law on maritime and inland navigation (Official Journal of FRY, Nos 12/98, 44/99, 74/99 and 73/00) have ceased to apply (Art. 46).

583. Republic protects, preserves and promotes the sea environment (Art. 2, para. 3). In accordance with Art. 2, para. 2 of the Law 'in its exclusive economic zone and continental shelf', Republic has sovereign rights and jurisdiction for the research, exploitation, protection, preservation and promotion of natural marine resources, including resources in the seabed and sea submarine in order to perform other economic activities.

1. Internal Seawater

521. Article 9, paragraph 2 prescribes that domestic and foreign legal and natural persons may carry out the research, recording and Hydrographic survey of the seabed and submarine in the protected parts of the nature of internal seawater[584] for the scientific purposes, with the approval of the Ministry competent for the protection of the environment.[585]

2. Territorial Sea

522. According to Article 16, paragraph 1, the harmless way of sailing in foreign facility includes sailing in the territorial sea[586] without entrance in the internal seawater or sailing to the internal seawater and to sailing from that water in the water of exclusive economic zone, provided that they do not endanger the order, peace, environment or security of the Republic.

523. The Ministry may prohibit sailing in ports of internal seawaters or territorial sea for certain types and sizes of ships and for ships that transport a certain type of cargo because of safety of navigation, protection of the sea from pollution, prevention of the threat to biological species and because of decrease of the risk of major maritime accidents (Article 19, paragraph 2).

3. Exclusive Economic Zone

524. The Assembly of the Republic has the competence of declaring an exclusive economic zone,[587] taking into account cooperation with other Adriatic countries. The zone may be declared, *inter alia*: when it is necessary because of the realization of rights and enforcement of obligations in the protection and preservation of marine environment.[588]

---

584. Internal sea waters include: ports, bays and islands, the mouth of the rivers, parts of the sea between coast and the basic lines of the territorial sea referred to in Art. 14, para. 2, points 2 and 3 of this Law (Art. 4, para. 1).
585. During research in protected parts of nature the foreign scientific research ship, a professional person nominated by the Ministry responsible for environmental protection must be on the ship, at the expense of the person who carried out research (Art. 9, para. 8).
586. According to Art. 13 of the Law territorial sea is the sea area – 12 nautical miles wide, from the basic line in the direction the sea.
587. Exclusive economic zone includes the marine areas from the external borders of the territorial sea in the direction of the sea to its external borders established by agreement, on the basis of international law (Art. 25).
588. Apart from that, other reasons include following: in the areas of management, preservation, research and exploitation of living resources in the sea; in the field of scientific research and, when it is appropriate, taking joint research areas; inviting interested States or international organizations to cooperate in accordance with the provisions of the United Nations Convention on the law of the sea (Art. 25, para. 2).

525. According to Article 28, construction, operation and use of facilities in the exclusive economic zone must be in accordance with law. Legal or natural person whose construction is approved is obliged to, *inter alia*, remove each marine facility that is no longer used or is abandoned,[589] not caused by doing damage to fishing, to environment and to ecological preservation of marine space or other legitimate use of the sea.[590]

526. When sailing in an exclusive economic zone vessels are obliged to respect generally accepted international regulations, standards and domestic regulations on the protection of sea and air pollution from ships and pollution caused by immersion or activities in the submarine (Article 34). Legal and natural persons, who participate in the study or utilize natural resources of exclusive economic zone, are obliged to respect international and domestic regulations, procedures and standards concerning protection of the sea, living marine resources and marine environment.[591]

4. Continental Shelf

527. Pursuant to Article 38 of the Law research and exploitation of natural resources of continental shelf,[592] as well as putting into operation and maintenance of necessary facilities and equipment for research, can be done under the prescribed conditions, regulations issued on the basis of this Law and other relevant regulations. Use and emission of dangerous and harmful substances and oil must be done so as to minimize negative impact on the environment of marine ecosystems of continental belt in accordance with the law and with international.[593]

C. The Law on the Protection of the Marine Environment

528. The law on the protection of the marine environment (OJ MNE 73/19) is compatible with the Barcelona Convention on the protection of the marine

---

589. No later than thirty days from the date of termination of construction or use.

590. Apart from this, obligations include also following: (1) at least thirty days before the commencement of works, through the Ministry – port authorities, to publish information about the place, and manner of construction, dimensions, size, depth and the appearance of marine facility and (2) before the start of construction, on the place where the construction starts, and then on the sea object, set the fixed signal means (Art. 29, points 1 and 2).

591. When it overshoots the exclusive economic zone, aircraft has the obligation to respect the generally accepted international regulations and domestic regulations on the protection of marine pollution from the air or by air (Art. 34, para. 3).

592. Continental shelf includes seabed and sea submarine outside the external borders of the territorial sea in the direction to the sea to the border of continental belt with neighbouring states, established by international agreements (Art. 35).

593. The Ministry will, in cooperation with the Ministry responsible for environmental protection, in accordance with the law and international regulations, undertake measures to prevent pollution, especially protected areas, which appear as a consequence of activities in continental shelf (Art. 38, para. 3).

environment and the coastal region of the Mediterranean,[594] and is implementing several pieces of EU legislation: Directive 2008/56/EZ of the European Parliament and the Council which establishes the framework for the community's action in the field of marine environmental policy, Directive 2017/845/EU of the European Parliament and the Council regarding a framework of elements that have to be taken into consideration in the preparation of strategies for marine environmental protection and the Commission Decision 2017/848/EU on the definition of criteria and methodological standards on the proper state of the marine environment.

529. The law is 33 articles long and divided into seven chapters: Chapter I – Basic Provisions (Articles 1–5); Chapter II – Documents on the Protection of the Marine Environment (Articles 6–9); Chapter III – State of the Marine Environment monitoring (Articles 10–19); Chapter IV – Strategy Revision, Public Notification and Information (Articles 20–25); Chapter V – Marine Environment financing (Article 26); Chapter VI – Supervision (Article 27); Chapter VII –Transitional and Final Provisions (Articles 28–33).

1. Basic Provisions

530. In Article 2, the marine environment is defined as the area of the open sea, river estuaries, coastal region area (including internal waters), territorial waters under Montenegro's sovereignty, seabed and subsoil that represent the living space of organisms and their communities.

531. The Law's stated purpose is to (1) protect, preserve, recover and evaluate, wherever possible, the restoration of structure and function of marine and coastal ecosystems and biodiversity protection; (2) preserve protected maritime areas and environmentally important areas in the framework of Natura 2000 network; (3) prevent, and if possible, mitigate pollution of the marine environment and coastal region, in the manner that secures the mitigation of negative impacts or risks for human health and biodiversity or ecosystem health, or sea and coast use; (4) preserve, upgrade and re-establish the balance between human activities and natural resources in the sea and coastal region; (5) preserve the marine and coastal region for the benefit of present and future generations; (6) sustainably use natural resources in the sea and coastal region, especially maritime and continental water spaces; (7) preserve the integrity of coastal ecosystems, landscapes, and geomorphology; (8) prevent or mitigate natural events' impact, especially climate change, caused by natural or human activities; (9) coordinate public and private needs and decisions on state and local level that impact the use of maritime and coastal regions.

594. Adopted in 1995 in the framework of the Mediterranean Action Plan (MAP), it constitutes the principal regional legally binding Multilateral Environmental Agreement (MEA) in the Mediterranean, *see* https://www.unep.org/unepmap/who-we-are/barcelona-convention-and-protocols (26 Nov. 2022.)

2. Documents on the Protection of the Marine Environment

532. Strategy on marine environment protection is the central document of the law's provisions. It is adopted by the Government for a period of a minimum of ten years, on the proposal of the Ministry for Environmental Affairs. It is based on the ecosystem approach to human activities,[595] integrated management of the coastal region, and with due consideration to the transboundary impacts. The law defines in Article 6 several strategy elements: (1) preliminary assessment of the condition of the marine environment; (2) criteria and methodology for identification of the proper condition of the marine environment; (3) targets and indicators for the preservation of the proper condition of the marine environment; (4) monitoring programme of the marine environment; (5) programme of measures for the preservation of the proper condition of the marine environment (programme of measures). The NCSC, climate change, and integrated management of the coastal region have a right to be consulted by the Ministry on the contents of the Strategy.

533. The first element, the Preliminary Assessment of the condition of the marine environment is a document that contains several analyses and plans: (1) the analysis of basic characteristics of the marine environment (hydrographic, physical and chemical, types of habitats, biological properties, and hydromorphology); (2) the analysis of the state of and main pressure points and impacts on the marine environment, segments of the environment of the coastal region, including human activities; (3) economic and social analysis of the exploitation of the marine environment and coastal region, with costs of recovery; (4) the manner of planning and exploitation of the marine environment and coastal region (Article 7).[596]

534. The second element more closely defined by the law in Article 8 is the Proper condition of the marine environment. This is the condition where the marine environment and coastal region are preserved, environmentally diverse and dynamic, clean, healthy, and productive in their natural conditions, their exploitation is sustainable and thus their potential is preserved both for present and future

595. Ecosystem approach can best be defined by a threefold definition: 'Firstly, the accent of the protection is to be put on the system rather than the individual components. In this systematic view, all the species belonging to the particular ecosystem must be taken in their entire interconnectedness, however complex it might be, since every single connection is important for the functioning of the system as a whole.Secondly, in the ecosystem there are various subsystems which represent their own micro-worlds of interconnectedness. They must be recognized as influencing each other through the mutual interaction, while also responding to the influences coming from the exterior, mainly caused by the human activity.Thirdly, these micro-systems are capable of organizing themselves and with that of further organizing the larger ecosystem to which they belong. Therefore, any human interaction with these self-organized units must take into consideration this ability if it wants to exploit the ecosystem integrity for the success of its purpose' (Vučić 2012a, 199).

596. These analyzes should give an integral picture of the marine environment, that takes into account the structure, function, and processes of maritime ecosystems, together with natural, physiographic, geographic, biological, geologic, and climate factors as well as physical, acoustic and chemical conditions, including conditions caused by human activities inside or outside this area (Art. 7).

generations. In addition, the ecosystems are fully functioning and resistant to man-made changes in the environment, the species and habitats are preserved, the biodiversity decline is prevented and various biological components seem in balance. When all the ecosystem properties are in balance and contribute to the functioning of the ecosystem, the antropoghenic inputs of substances and energy, including noise, do not pollute the marine environment. These legally defined characteristics of the proper condition of the marine environment are established through certain criteria and methodology, more closely defined by the act of the Ministry (Article 9).

3. Condition of the Marine Environment Monitoring

535. The Strategy for marine environment protection is conducted under the monitoring programme and measures programme (Article 10).

536. The Law defines the Monitoring Programme in Article 11. The preliminary assessment of the marine environment's condition as well as targets and indicators for the preservation of this state, methodological standards for ecosystems monitoring, pressure points, and human activities impact on the marine environment serve as the bases for this programme. The programme is an integral part of a yearly environmental monitoring programme, as defined by the law on the environment. Monitoring programme of the marine ecosystem and coastal region is a part of this programme as well. The Programme uses the same methodology as the marine environment monitoring for the marine region and sub region, to enable results comparison. It takes into consideration significant transboundary impacts and marine environment characteristics. The Programme is conducted by the administrative organ responsible for the environment. The administrative organ may choose to hire for certain tasks accredited legal entities. The administrative organ makes a yearly report on the state of the marine environment based on the monitoring results.[597]

537. The Programme of measures is defined in Article 12. This Programme is based on the preliminary assessment of the marine environment's condition, a Monitoring Programme from Article 11, and regulations on water management, communal waste waters, quality of washing water, control of pollution from vessels, and intake and treatment of waste in harbours, under the ratified international agreements. The Programme of measures contains measures related to protected marine areas, ecosystems, and ecologically important areas in the framework of the Natura 2000 network, internationally agreed measures, time and bodies allocated for implementation, and the assessment of required funding. The Programme is based

597. This report is a part of the information on the state of the environment. This information is delivered to the European Environmental Agency and the implementation bodies of the Barcelona convention.

on sustainable development, and social and economic considerations and its measures are proportionate to the costs of realization and technically feasible. The Ministry develops the EIA and cost-benefit analysis in relation to measures. After the start of implementation, the Ministry will adopt a report within three years.

538. The Programme of measures can be altered to remove or mitigate negative impacts and to sustain or renew the integrity, structure, and functionality of the ecosystems if the Ministry decides that human activities can negatively impact the marine environment's condition to a great extent, and especially in protected and environmentally important areas from Article 12. If on the EU or international level, human activities are conducted that can negatively impact to a great extent the marine environment in the sovereign parts of Montenegro's jurisdiction, the responsible bodies of the marine sub region are informed. On the other hand, Montenegro's Ministry responsible for the environment conducts the transboundary impact assessment of the measure for Montenegro's territory, to remove or minimize the danger of harm and negative impact on another state's territory (Article 13).[598]

539. In Article 15, the Law provides for exceptions to the application of the Programme of measures, to be decided by the Ministry and included in the Programme itself. These include (1) actions or omissions for which Montenegro is not responsible; (2) natural phenomenon; (3) force majeure; (4) changes in physical properties of the marine environment caused by activities of public interest; (5) natural conditions that prevent the timely improvements of the marine environment's condition. In the case of (1), the Ministry adopts special, ad hoc measures to prevent negative impacts in the marine region or sub region. Measures from (4) must secure that the changes in physical properties of the marine environment do not permanently disable or endanger the goal of the proper marine environmental condition for other states in the same marine region or sub region.

540. Certain measures of the Strategy for marine environment's protection might be muted if no danger exists or the costs would be disproportionate to risks. This provision does not apply to the preliminary assessment of the marine environment' condition (Article 16).[599]

541. The authorities responsible for marine environment protection are the Ministry and administrative organs for fisheries and water management; marine protection from vessels' pollution; security of navigation and marine transport; protection and rescue; health protection; cultural heritage protection; research and production of hydrocarbons; defence; other affairs related to the marine environment (Article 18).

598. In the case of significant deterioration of the marine environment's condition, the Government adopts a plan of emergency measures. Under this plan, measures of protection stricter than those provided in the Program of measures can be adopted, if this does not prevent the preservation of the proper marine environment condition in the given marine subregion (Art. 14).

599. If the negative impact on the marine environment' condition cannot be removed with measures provided by the law or other compatible measures, the European Commission is informed and measures are recommended to it (Art. 17).

542. Article 19 provides for regional cooperation. It is pursued together with the EU Member States, states parties to the Barcelona convention, and regional bodies for the implementation of the Barcelona convention, including parties to the international agreement on the cooperation for the protection of the Adriatic sea and coastal regions from pollution. Regional cooperation is especially important during the adoption and application of the Strategy, because of possible transboundary impacts. The cooperation is realized also with other states, non-EU members or Barcelona parties if they form a part of the same basin, even if they have no access to the sea.

4. Strategy Revision, Public Notification and Information

543. Strategy revision is conducted every six years or less, following the changes in the marine region, or sub region (Article 20).[600]

544. The Information system for the marine environment is regulated in Article 22. It is established for data collection and reporting by the administrative organ, as a part of the information system for environmental protection. It contains data on the marine environment, data, and indicators on the measures and targets of protection, data from the programme of monitoring, numerical analyses, and models in digital form and databases.

545. Public notification is regulated in Article 23. The Ministry is responsible for publishing in an open-access format the information on the protection of the marine environment. This information includes the Strategy and its components, monitoring data, and reports on the implementation of international treaties and agreements.

546. The Coordination body for the protection of the marine environment is established for the monitoring and improvement of the marine environment. Its functions are enumerated in Article 24: (1) provision of opinions on the proposal of the Strategy and its components; (2) proposition of improvements to marine environment protection; (3) consideration of the report on the implementation of the programme of measures (Article 24). The Coordination body is formed by the Government and its members are the Minister;[601] the representative of the coastal units of local municipalities (proposed by the Community of municipalities for the one-year); representatives of state organs responsible for the protection of the sea from vessels, security of navigation and marine transport; fisheries and water management; protection and rescue; research; protection of cultural heritage; human health protection; research and production of hydrocarbons; defence affairs.

---

600. From the moment of Montenegro's accession to the EU, the Ministry will be responsible for notifying the European Commission of the law's implementation (Art. 21).

601. The Minister is the President of the Coordination body. Working groups might be formed and experts hired to help the body in its work. It is financed from the state budget.

5. Financing and Supervision

547. The financing of marine environment protection is threefold: the state budget – donations – other sources established by law (Article 26). Supervision is conducted by the Ministry and other responsible authorities (Article 27).

548. Several by-laws have been adopted based on this law:

The Rulebook on criteria and methodological standards for defining the proper state and monitoring of the marine environment (OJ MNE, No. 36/21).

The Rulebook on the closer content of the programme of measures for the realization and preservation of the proper state of the marine environment (OJ MNE, No. 36/21).

The Rulebook on the analytical method of properties and characteristics of the current state of the marine environment, qualitative indicators, and the defining method of targets and indicators for the realization and preservation of the proper state of the marine environment (OJ MNE, No. 36/21)

D. The Law on the Sea Good

549. Due to the fact that it is mainly concerned with the environmental issues, the Law on the sea good (OJ RM, No. 14/92) deserves special attention. It has following five chapters: Chapter I – Basic Provisions (Articles 1–6), Chapter II – Utilization of the Sea Good (Articles 7–16), Chapter III – Protection of the Sea Good (Articles 17–22), Chapter IV – Penal Provisions (Articles 23–28) and Chapter V – Transitional and Final Provisions (Articles 29–35).

550. The Law in its Article 2 precisely determines the area, objects and resources which make a part of the coastal zone such as:

> sea shore, ports, breakwaters, slipways, drifts, sand-banks, swimming areas, cliffs, bayous, crag, submarine springs, springs and wells on the shore, river mouths running into sea, channels connected with sea, submarine, seabed and underground as well as the internal seawaters and territorial waters, alive and non-alive resources in them, and alive and non-alive resources of continental zone. The Coastal Zone in the sense of the Law on the Coastal Zone includes shores of the river Bojana in the territory of the Republic of Montenegro.

551. Article 3 of the Law defines the seashore as the:

> zone of mainland bordered with the line that highest waves can reach during the strongest storms as well as the part of the mainland which according to its nature or purpose serves to use of the sea for maritime traffic and maritime

fishing and for other purposes which are related to use of sea, which is at least 6 m wide starting from the line that highest waves reach during the time of strongest storm.[602]

552. According to Article 17, paragraph 1, protection of the sea is considered to be protection from pollution by dangerous and harmful substances[603] from the mainland and from vessels. It is prohibited to threaten sea good with dangerous and harmful substances and other wastes (Article 18).[604] Obligations of different entities are defined in Articles 20–22. It includes obligations of companies, other legal persons and citizens (Article 20), the user of port open to international traffic, shipyards and other users of marine goods (Article 21), captain of ships, crew members, heads of boats and port's authorities (Article 22).

E. The Law on Hydrographical Activities

553. Basic legal act regulating hydrographical activities in Montenegro is the Law on hydrographical activities (OJ MNE, Nos 26/10, 30/12). It has the following five parts: Part I – General Provisions (Articles 1–3), Part II – Performing of hydrographical activities (Articles 4–19), Part III – Supervision (Articles 20–22), Part IV – Penalty provisions (Article 23) and Part V – Transitional and final provisions (Articles 24–26).

554. According to Article 1, paragraph 1, this Law regulates performing of hydrographical activities, with the aim of hydrographic navigation securing the maritime sailing and inland waterways to protect human life and property at sea and inland waterways, research for management of marine resources and environmental protection. Hydrographical activities[605] include: hydrographic[606]–topographic[607] survey at sea and inland waterways, collecting data from hydrography,[608] cartography, navigation, geology, geophysics (sea level fluctuations, waves, sea currents, thermohaline, hydroacoustic and optical properties of the sea, etc.), preparation,

602. Shore of the river Bojana includes the area of mainland which is at least 6 m wide starting from the line which is horizontally distanced from the line of the medium twenty-year-old water level (Art. 3, para. 2).
603. Dangerous and harmful substances are defined as substances which are in sea and which can lead to danger of life and health, and survival of plant and animal or cause a change in physical, chemical or natural properties of water (Art. 17, para. 2).
604. Article 23, para. 1, point 2 provides for the punishment for violation of these provisions.
605. Hydrographic activities are activities of interest for Montenegro (Art. 2, para. 2).
606. *Hydrographic survey* is the survey conducted to determine: water depth, configuration and nature of the seabed, directions and intensity of sea currents, weather and level of performance of high and low water and monitoring of changes in sea level caused by tides, topographic objects position and fixed landmarks for purpose of surveying and navigation sailing (Art. 3, point 2).
607. *Topographic survey is* the recording configuration of the ground surface (relief) and the position of natural objects and facilities built on it (Art. 3, point 9).
608. *Hydrography* includes the measurement and description of the physical characteristics of sea and coastal areas that are primarily used for navigation, exploration and environmental protection (Art. 3, point 1).

issuance and maintenance of navigational charts and publications in accordance with the recommendations of the International Hydrographic Organization (IHO) and the International Maritime Organization (IMO) (Article 2, paragraph 1).

1. Performing of Hydrographical Activities

555. Hydrographical activity of interest for Montenegro performs the administrative authority responsible for hydrographical activity (hereinafter referred to as 'Hydrometeorological service') (Article 4, paragraph 1). Hydrographical activities in the jurisdiction of the Hydrometeorological service are stipulated in Article 5, paragraph 1.[609] Hydrometeorological services can perform hydrographic, cartographic and publishing activities[610] for domestic and foreign entities (Article 5, paragraph 2). The data which are collected and processed by the Hydrometeorological service in carrying out the activities from Article 5 of this Law are official data.[611] The data collected and processed by the legal entities are not considered official data (Article 11, paragraphs 1 and 2).

556. Hydrographic survey of sea and inland waterways, as well as recording of facilities in the coastal area, the seabed and the underwater, for legal entities and natural persons, may carry out domestic and foreign legal entities registered for performing these activities in the Central Registry of the Commercial Court, or in the appropriate Register of competent home country of the foreign legal entity and if they satisfy other conditions stipulated in this Article (Article 6, paragraph 1).[612]

557. Compliance with the conditions for carrying out activities referred to in paragraph 1 of Article 6 shall determine the administrative authority responsible for environmental protection by the decision[613] (hereinafter 'the Agency') (Article 6, paragraph 2). The Agency keeps a record of issued decisions (Article 8, paragraph 1). The content of the Decision is prescribed in Article 8, paragraph 2.

558. The legal entities possessing the decision for performing hydrographical activities from Article 6, paragraph 1, are in charge to perform activities in a manner and under conditions prescribed by this Law and in accordance with the standards of the IHO for Hydrographic survey (standards S-44: special survey, survey I line, surveys of II and III lines)[614] (Article 9, paragraph 1).

---

609. Hydrographic activities from Art. 5 of this Law are performed on the base of five-year work plan determined by the Government (Art. 19, para. 1).
610. The fee for such activities shall be paid into a special account and used for improvement of hydrographic activities (Art. 5, para. 3).
611. The original data referred to in para. 1 of this Article as well as changes in the navigation maps of interest for the defence are published in separate publications by Hydrometeorological service (Art. 11, para. 4).
612. The legal entities are required to obtain a permit from the Agency for carrying out activities referred to in para. 1 of this Article (Art. 6, para. 3).
613. The decision is issued on the request for the period of one year (Art. 7, para. 1).
614. The Ministry shall publish standards from para. 1 of this Article (Art. 9, para. 2).

559. Ships and other vessels registered in the national register of ships and other vessels must have official navigation charts and nautical publications issued by the Hydrometeorological service, in accordance with the SOLAS Convention (Article 12, paragraph 1).

560. Data obtained by performing hydrographical activities of interest for Montenegro may be given to be used, under conditions that they are not declared as a secret by a competent authority and in accordance with the Law (Article 15, paragraph 1). A fee is paid for the usage of information from navigation charts and publications from hydrographic databases (Article 16, paragraph 1). Funds from the fee are income to the Budget of Montenegro and are used for protection, development and improvement of hydrographical activities (Article 16, paragraph 4).[615]

2. Supervision

561. The supervision of this Law and the regulations adopted on the basis of this Law performs the Ministry unless otherwise prescribed by the Law (Article 20, paragraph 1). Inspection supervision over the implementation of this Law and the regulations adopted on the basis of this Law shall be conducted by the Agency in accordance with this Law and the Law regulating the inspection supervision (Article 20, paragraph 2).[616]

F. Maritime Transport Legislation

562. Currently, legal regulation of maritime transport is based on the Law on Maritime and Inland Navigation (OJ FRY, Nos 12/98, 44/99, 74/99 and 73/00) and the Law on Maritime and Inland Navigation (OJ SRM, Nos 17/78, 8/79, 19/87, 22/90 and 13/01).

1. Law on Maritime and Internal Navigation

563. The Law on maritime and internal navigation (OJ FRY, Nos 12/98, 44/99 and 74/99) regulates the safety of navigation at sea and inland waters, waterways in the coastal sea and on inland waters, state affiliation, identification and registration of the ship, basic property-legal relations in terms of ships, shipping, obligation relations regarding the ships, navigation accident, applicable law and competent courts for disputes with international elements (Article 1).

615. Hydrometeorological service represents Montenegro in IHO and other international organizations in the field of hydrography (Art. 18, para. 1).

616. Hydrometeorological service is in charge to notify the Ministry if in performing of activities of state interest, within its responsibilities determined by this Law, finds that legal entities do not perform activities in accordance with this Law and with other regulations (Art. 22, para. 1).

564. Article 72 regulates handling of cargo. It must be loaded within the limits of allowable load of the ship and according to technical rules so that, in all conditions that may appear, it does not threaten the safety of the ship, human life and environment. Capacity of the maritime ship for the transport of bulk, frozen or dangerous goods must be determined and this ship must obtain appropriate documents and books (Article 102).[617]

565. In order to protect the environment, maritime ships have to obtain the appropriate documents and books (Article 112). A crew member is obliged to perform tasks on the ship in accordance with the rules of navigation, in a way that allows safety, which does not damage the ship or cargo on it, and does not endanger the safety of passengers on the boat or other members of the crew and the environment from pollution by hazardous and harmful substances (oil, liquid wastes and their mixture of fuel, wastewater and other wastes, as well as radioactive or other wastes) (Article 136). Moreover, a crew member has the obligation to immediately notify the manager or captain of the ship in following case: about any special event that could threaten the security of the ship, passengers, other persons or cargo on board, as well as to pollute environment by dangerous and harmful substances from ships (Article 147, paragraph 1).[618]

566. Articles 154 and 161 of the Law contain provisions concerning special authority and responsibility of the captain as well as rights and duties concerning performance of supervision activities.[619]

2. The Law on Marine Protection from the Pollution from the Vessels

567. Basic legal act regulating marine protection from pollution from the vessels in Montenegro is the Law on marine protection from pollution from the vessels (OJ RM, Nos 20/11, 26/11, 27/14). It has the following sixteen parts: Part I – General Provisions (Articles 1–3), Part II – Pollution from the vessels (Articles 4–15), Part III – Ship for the transport of oil as load or as a fuel (Articles 16–27), Part IV – Ship for transport of harmful liquids in bulk (Article 28), Part V – Ship for transport of harmful substances in the packed form (Article 29), Part VI – Fecal waste (Articles 30–32), Part VII – Communal waste (Articles 33–34), Part VIII – The emission of harmful substances into the air (Articles 35–39), Part IX – Ballast waters (Articles 40–48), Part X – System anti-fouling ship plating (Article 49), Part XI – Intentionally dumping of the waste (Article 50), Part XII – Reception and handling of waste, waste oil, cargo residues and sludge from ballast tanks in the ports

617. Documents and books confirm that the ship complies with the conditions prescribed for the transport of liquid, chilled or hazardous cargo – in order to protect the ship, persons on the ship, cargo and environment (Art. 102, para. 3).
618. In case of danger, shipwreck or other accident, ship crew members are obliged to support the rescue of the ship, passengers, other persons and cargo on the ship, as well as for environmental protection, while the captain does not order leaving the ship (Art. 147, para. 2).
619. *See also* relevant provisions on supervision: Art. 193, point 1, Art. 195, para. 2, Art. 197, para. 1, point 2, Art. 198, para. 2, etc.

(Articles 51–54), Part XIII – Responsibility and compensation in case of marine pollution from the vessels (Articles 55–58), Part XIV – Supervision (Articles 59–61), Part XV – Penalties (Article 62) and Part XVI – Transitional and final provisions (Articles 63–69).

568. This Law regulates the marine protection from pollution[620] from vessels which sail or which are in the internal seawater and at territorial sea of Montenegro (hereinafter 'the waters of Montenegro'), reception and handling of waste[621] in ports, as well as responsibility and compensation in case of pollution (Article 1, paragraph 1).

569. A ship[622] flying the flag of Montenegro and a ship flying a foreign flag are allowed to sail in the waters of Montenegro in accordance with the provisions of this Law and the Law regulating the safety of navigation, if its constructional and navigable features, machinery, devices and equipment used for the maintenance of maritime ship navigation safety, which according to the technical characteristics, quantity, type and arrangement on the ship, meet the technical requirements of the International Maritime Organization (IMO) (Article 2, paragraph 1).

570. Testing of compliance with the requirements from paragraph 1 of this Article for the ship flying the flag of Montenegro performs the administrative authority responsible for maritime safety (hereinafter 'administrative authority'), or an organization recognized by the International Maritime Organization (IMO) (hereinafter 'recognized organization'), with which Montenegro concludes the contract (Article 2, paragraph 2). On the basis of the performed verification, i.e., compliance with the requirements of paragraph 1 of this Article, the administrative authority or recognized organization shall issue appropriate certificates (shipping documents, testimonies, books, records, etc.) (Article 2, paragraph 3).

a. Pollution from the Vessels

571. According to Article 4 paragraph 4, it is prohibited from the vessel[623] in the waters of Montenegro: to discharge oil, oily mixture, bilge water[624] and oily waste; to discharge harmful substances that are temporarily characterized as such, water

620. *Pollution* is directly or indirectly discharge, dumping or emission of substances into the sea and air as well as maritime accidents that adversely affects or could adversely affect the living beings and marine organisms, pose a threat to human health, hinder marine activities including fishing and other forms of lawful use of the sea, deteriorate the quality of sea water and reduce the possibility of using the sea for recreation (Art. 3, point 52).

621. *Waste* is unnecessary, undesirable or superfluous material left over after the completion of a process at vessel (Art. 3, point 23).

622. *Ship* is a passenger, cargo, fishing, public or scientific research vessel designed to sail the sea, whose length exceeds 12 ms, a capacity of at least 15 tonnes or is intended to carry more than twelve passengers (Art. 3, point 4).

623. *Vessel* is a ship, a floating facility, boat and other object located in the marine environment and include hydrofoil boats, submarines, floating and fixed or floating platforms (Art. 3, point 27).

624. *Oily bilge water* is oily water collected in engine space, as well as water from bilge space of the ship's storage, formed from the remains of cargo and precipitation (Art. 3, point 13).

from the tanks washing or other mixtures containing such substances; to discharge and dispose in the seabed harmful substances in packed form;[625] to discharge communal waste;[626] to discharge pollutants into the air; to discharge ballast water[627] and sediment from ballast tanks if they contain harmful substances, pathogens microorganisms and invasive species; the application of anti-fouling systems against boat fouling if they contain organic biocidal compounds of tin; and to dump, incinerate and bury in the seabed wastes or other substances.

572. The ship carrying harmful substances, when sailing into and sailing out of Montenegro port, is obliged to use a pilot (Article 8, paragraph 1).[628] In the case of marine pollution from the vessel, the administrative authority is obliged to take the necessary measures for the prevention, reduction and elimination of consequences of pollution in accordance with the plan for emergency response (Article 14, paragraph 1).

b. The Ship Used for Transport

573. An oil tanker carrying capacity of at least 5,000 tons, which has not a double plating,[629] tanker category 1, which was built by the end of 1982 and the tankers of categories 2 and 3 which are built up to the end of 1984 were forbidden to sail into the waters of Montenegro (Article 16, paragraph 1).

574. It is forbidden to sail into the waters of Montenegro oil tankers carrying heavy oil fractions as a burden if they do not have double plating (Article 17, paragraph 1).[630]

575. The shipmaster is obliged, the latest twenty-four hours prior to arrival at the port of Montenegro, to submit to the Harbour Master a report on the quantity of heavy oil residues, waste oil,[631] oily mixture and bilge water, as well as the date and place of their last submission (Article 27, paragraph 1).

625. *Packaged form* is a form of packaging that is specifically designated for harmful substances (Art. 3, point 50).

626. *Communal wastes* are all kinds of animal waste, waste from the ship kitchen and waste from the works performed on ship, excluding fresh fish and its parts incurred by regular work, and which may be removed (Art. 3, point 14).

627. *The ballast water* is water taken from the sea, river or lakes to correct longitudinal and cross slope, depth gauge, stability, and pressure vessel, which is not transported as cargo (Art. 3, point 2).

628. The commander of a ship when notices oil pollution or harmful substances at the fairway is obliged, without delay, over communication links to notify the Captains about the perceived pollution (Art. 9, para. 1).

629. *The double plating* is the existence of two plating between cargo which is transported in a ship and the sea, to prevent leakage of cargo into the sea when breaking the outer shell of the ship (Art. 3, point 6).

630. The provisions of para. 1 of this Article shall not apply to the carriage performed on a single port area (Art. 17, para. 1).

631. *Waste oil* is oil, useless, manufactured or created on the vessel (Art. 3, point 24).

576. The ship intended for the transport of harmful liquid substances in bulk must have (Article 28, paragraph 1): (1) international testimony on the prevention of marine pollution by harmful liquid substances in bulk; (2) P&A Manual for the handling of harmful liquid substances in bulk; (3) a book on the cargo; (4) marine plan for emergency response in case of pollution.

577. Harmful substances carried as cargo must be packed in the prescribed manner and labelled (Article 29, paragraph 1).[632]

c. Faecal Waste, Communal Waste and Emission of Harmful Substances into the Air

578. Ship capacity of 400 tons carrying more than fifteen passengers and crew members and ship capacity of a minimum of 400 tons must have an international testimony to the prevention of marine pollution by faecal waste (Article 30, paragraph 1). Food waste from a ship may be discharged into the sea at a distance greater than 3 NM from the land if they are chopped with chopping devices with openings smaller than 25 mm (Article 33, paragraph 1) (Article 33, paragraph 1). It is prohibited to discharge pollutants into the air from the vessel, except in cases of research and exploitation of the seabed and the laying of submarine cables, as well as in the case of imminent danger to life and human health and the environment, on the base of the state administration approval responsible for environmental protection issues, taking care to reduce pollution to a minimum (Article 35, paragraph 1).

d. Responsibility in Case of Pollution from the Vessels

579. The owner of the vessel is responsible for damage caused by the vessel carrying oil as bulk cargo or vessel that transports hazardous materials in bulk and for leakage or discharge of that oil or hazardous substances into the sea unless he proves that the leakage or discharge is caused by: (1) war or force majeure; (2) only by an act or omission of a third person with the intent to cause damage; and (3) only by an act or omission of the Captaincy or administrative body (Article 55, paragraph 1).[633]

3. Law on Yachts

580. The Law on Yachts also deserves to be mentioned (OJ RM, Nos 46/07, 73/10, 40/11, 42/15). It transposes the EU Directive 94/25/EC and Resolution No. 40 (TRANS/SC 3/147) and creates a yacht-friendly legal framework for development of nautical tourism in Montenegro. It regulates flagging, identification of

632. On the packaging of hazardous substances referred to in para. 1 of this Article shall be specified the technical names of substances and placed the mark that packaged substances are pollutants (Art. 29, para. 2).
633. The supervision over the implementation of this Law and the regulations made under this Law shall be conducted by the Ministry (Art. 59, para. 1).

yachts and inscription into yacht register clearance and sailing (manner of arriving, staying and departure) of yachts as well as the rights and obligations in chartering yachts.

581. Following sub-legal acts have been adopted on the basis of the Law: Regulation on Specimens and Manner of Keeping Register of Yachts of Montenegro and Book for Recording Yacht Chartering and the Regulation on the Forms of Registration of Yachts in the Yacht Register and the Stay of Yachts in Montenegrin Waters (OJ MNE, No. 27/08), which are in line with the Directive 2002/6/EU.[634]

4. Law on Ports

582. The provisions on the environment are contained in several Articles of the Law on ports (OJ MNE, Nos 51/08, 27/13, 18/19). These are following: the Concession Act (Article 18), the concession contract (Article 20, paragraph 2, points 10 and 16) and the termination of the concession (Article 22, paragraph 2, point 3).

583. Article 26 defines protection of the sea against pollution. The administration body must ensure the fulfilment of the conditions stipulated by the international and internal regulations which regulate the prevention of the ship-sourced pollution of environment, protection of the marine environment and the coastal zone and civil responsibility for damage caused by pollution (Article 26, paragraph 1). It is prohibited in the port to emit and dispose into the sea and on coast solid and liquid waste, oil and oily water and cargo residues from ships, as well as other substances that pollute the environment, except in places where there are facilities, equipment and devices for receiving and handling these materials.[635] Natural or legal persons who use the facilities, equipment and devices shall take measures to prevent the discharge or outflow of oil and oily water, and prevent the spread of these substances into the sea and onshore. The inspector in charge of security of navigation will order the legal or natural person who pollutes to stop doing it and to eliminate harmful effects.[636]

G. Harmonization with EU Legislation

584. The Law on the Sea (OJ MNE, Nos 17/07, 6/08 and 40/11) is harmonized with the UN Convention on the Law of the Sea and the Convention on Protection of the Mediterranean Sea from Pollution (Barcelona Convention).[637]

---

634. For the list of documents required for registration of a yacht *see*: https://www.registracijaplovila.com/en/registracija-plovila-en/registration-of-the-vessels (3 Dec. 2022).
635. Law prescribes penalty for violation of this provision (Art. 31 para. 1 point 6).
636. If natural or legal person fails to comply with the order, the inspection will order cleaning of the port at the expense of person who pollutes (Art. 26, para. 5).
637. GMNE (2008b), 550.

585. Particularly important for sea and coastal zone protection is further harmonization of the national legislation with the EU Marine Directive. That means introduction of integrated sea protection and management system as a specific ecosystem and special segment of environmental protection. The EU Marine Strategy has been taken into account in planning short-term and midterm measures on the national level.[638]

586. Legal regulation concerning maritime transport is insufficiently harmonized with the conventions of IMO, as well as with the EU *Acquis communautaire*.

Monitoring of seawater quality is still not aligned with requirements of the EU Marine Directive and the Barcelona Convention. It is conducted only as part of regular activities of the Hydrometeorological Institute.[639]

638. There was a plan to adopt new regulations which include, *inter alia*: Law on Protection of the Sea Against Pollution from Watercrafts and Floating Vessels, Law on the Ratification of the Protocol of Integrated Coastal Zone Management in the Mediterranean, Law on the Ratification of the Convention on the Protection and Use of Transboundary Watercourses and International Lakes – Helsinki Convention, Amendments to the Law on Coastal Zone Resources or the development of the new Law on Coastal Zone in accordance with the Barcelona Convention, accompanying Protocols and other international Conventions, secondary regulations under the Law on Coastal Zone, secondary regulations under the Law on Protection of the Sea against Pollution from Watercrafts and Floating Vessels. GMNE (2008b), 551.
639. The existing monitoring is inadequate for many reasons, especially from the aspect of availability of indicators regarding the criteria and indicators of the EEA. Activities for the harmonization of the National Monitoring Programme of State of the Environment with the criteria of the MED POL Programme have been initiated. GMNE (2008b), 531.

Chapter 4. Waste

§1. Waste Pollution

587. Waste is a serious problem in Montenegro, having critical and long-term impact on both the environment and public health. Each urban settlement in Montenegro has at least one main town landfill and several scattered smaller ones.[640] According to the *Information on State of the Environment – 2011*, there were 273 sites with different capacities.[641] Current system of waste collection and disposal is such that it does not provide waste separation and separate treatment of different types of waste, while in principle the disposal of non-hazardous industrial, municipal and hazardous wastes alike do not meet the minimum environmental standards.[642]

588. Industrial and communal wastes are disposed of in many landfills or dumps scattered throughout the country. Estimation is that in 2004 about 85% of solid waste in major towns was collected by a regular service, in comparison with only 15% in rural areas. On average, only about 60% of all communal waste was collected in 2004.[643] Of the total 557,635.81 tonnes of waste generated in the industry (2011), mining sector has generated 1,790.46 tonnes, i.e., 0.3%; manufacturing 60,271.81 tonnes, i.e., 10.8%; and sectors of electricity, gas and steam supply 495,573.54 tonnes, i.e., 88.9%.[644] There was collected 297,428 tonnes of communal waste in Montenegro in 2011. The number of households included in the waste collection increased by 2.7% in 2011 in comparison with 2010.[645]

589. At the beginning of 2008, there was only one sanitary landfill functioning in Montenegro, where the waste collected from territories of local self-government units of Podgorica and Danilovgrad was disposed. It was planned that during 2008 and 2009 remaining six regional sanitary landfills were constructed and six inter-municipal enterprises for managing these landfills were established. Activities on

---

640. GMNE (2008C), 89–90. *See also* GMNE (2007d), 70; 'Situation with waste and waste water in Montenegro is formidable, almost alarming. Unorganized system of waste management is very negatively reflected on water, air, sea and soil, as well as on climate, health and environment. Groundwater is especially affected, as it is the main source of drinking water and the most important national resource.' GME, NCSD (2011), 20.
641. EPA (2012b), 89.
642. GMNE (2007C), 49–50.
643. There is almost no recycling and only 1% of all waste was recycled in 2004. There is no deposit system for PET bottles and packaging material. Waste collection equipment is largely obsolete (75% of equipment is more than ten years old). UNECE (2007), 10.
644. By sectors, the relationship of non-hazardous and hazardous waste is the following: mining sector (31.4% of non-hazardous waste, and 68.6% of hazardous waste), manufacturing sector (90.3% of non-hazardous waste, 9.7% of hazardous waste,) and electricity, gas and steam supply (99.9% of non-hazardous waste, 0.1% of hazardous waste). MONSTAT (2012e), 1.
645. MONSTAT (2012f), 1.

the construction of regional recycling centre on the landfill in Podgorica are undergoing, with the capacity of 90,000 tons/year of unselected communal waste.[646]

590. In the period 2011–2015, the amount of municipal waste generated decreased, while the GDP increased by 3.4%, which indicates the fact that the pressure on the environment was also decreasing. However, in the period of constant GDP growth, 2015–2019, there is a trend of slight fluctuations in the amount of produced waste.[647] According to the latest official data, in 2019, 753,239 tons of industrial waste were produced in Montenegro. This amount is slightly lower compared to the previous year, but higher than all others in the period 2011–2017.[648]

591. Remediation of unorganized waste disposal sites in Montenegro continues to be one of the more prioritized goals. Remediation of large unorganized landfills was carried out ('Čarkovo polje', in the municipality of Žabljak, 'Vrtijeljka', in the municipality of Cetinje, 'Vasove vode', in the municipality of Berane, 'Zauglina', in the municipality of Šavnik and 'Komorača' in the municipality of Plav).[649]

§2. Monitoring System

592. Several provisions of the Law on Waste Management (OJ MNE, Nos 64/11, 39/16) explicitly refer to the monitoring. These are following: the content of the permit for processing and/or removal of waste (Article 32, paragraph 1, pp. 6 and 7), an application for a permit for processing and/or removal of waste (Article 33) and notification to the public (Article 34).

593. Regarding waste statistics, Statistical Office (MONSTAT) collects data both from utilities and from industrial pollutants, on the basis of annual survey. Through a licencing system for handling and storage of hazardous waste as well as inspections that are done, Environmental Protection Agency of Montenegro (EPA) established its own database, starting from 2009.[650]

§3. Competencies

594. The MESPU conducts administrative activities in regard to waste (Article 12 of the Decree on state administration organization and operations (OJ MNE, Nos

646. EAR (2004), 33.
647. EPA (2021). p. 103.
648. *Ibid.*, p. 107.
649. MESPU. EPA (2022a), p. 115. In 2020, the revision of the Main Project for the rehabilitation of the temporary municipal waste disposal site at the location 'Zakršnica' (territory of the municipality of Mojkovac), was completed. The feasibility study for the construction of a regional waste management centre in the municipality of Bijelo Polje, which will serve the municipalities of the northern region of Montenegro, has been completed.
650. UNECE, Working Group on Environmental Monitoring and Assessment (2010b), 2.

49/22, 52/22, 56/22, 82/22). Local self-government units are in charge of development and application of waste management policy on the local level. Activities of waste collection, transport and disposal are organized within public communal services enterprises.

595. Pursuant to the provisions of Article 86 of the Law on Waste Management (OJ MNE, Nos 64/11, and 39/16) supervision over the implementation of Law and regulations adopted on the basis of this law is performed by Ministry, state administration bodies responsible for the fields of agriculture, forestry, energy, mining, traffic, internal trade, collection of taxes and customs clearance and local government authority.[651]

§4. Strategic Documents

596. A Proposal for the Waste Management Strategy of Montenegro until 2030 has been prepared.[652] The basic strategic document in the field of waste management is the National Waste Management Plan in Montenegro 2015–2020. By adopting the new National Waste Management Plan, the previously adopted Strategic Master Plan for Waste Management (2005) and the State Waste Management Plan 2008–2012 cease to be in force. Recently, the MESPU adopted a Decision on the development of a strategic environmental impact assessment for the new National Waste Management Plan 2023–2028 (OJ MNE No. 108/22).

§5. Legislation

597. Montenegro acceded, by succession, to the Basel Convention on the Control of Transboundary Movements of Hazardous Wastes and their Disposal in 2006.[653] Montenegro is a member of the Ban Amendment[654] but it is not a member of the Basel Protocol on Liability and Compensation for Damage Resulting from Transboundary Movements of Hazardous Wastes and their Disposal (1999).[655]

598. Waste in the Law on Environment (OJ MNE, No. 52/16) is mentioned in several provisions (Articles 6, 7, points 25, 17, 25, 26, 44, 49, 54, 63, 65, 67, 77, 82).

651. The jurisdiction of certain types of inspections (ecological, phytosanitary, mining, traffic, communal, etc.) is defined.
652. *See*: https://www.gov.me/en/documents/d8073954-d74f-4398-ba8c-2e6747c153f2 (15 Dec. 2022).
653. *See*: http://www.basel.int/TheConvention/Overview/TextoftheConvention/tabid/1275/Default.aspx (3 Dec. 2022).
654. *See*: http://www.basel.int/TheConvention/Amendments/Overview/tabid/2759/Default.aspx (3 Dec. 2022).
655. *See*: http://www.basel.int/TheConvention/Overview/LiabilityProtocol/tabid/2399/Default.aspx (3 Dec. 2022).

I. Law on Waste Management

599. The Law on Waste Management (OJ MNE, Nos 64/11, 39/16) has been adopted by the Assembly of Montenegro on 24 December 2011.[656] The Law contains 102 Articles divided into following twelve chapters: I basic provisions (Articles 1–5); II waste management (Articles 6–17); III plans and programmes of waste management (Articles 18–30); IV permits and registration (Articles 31–45); V special kinds of waste (Articles 46–64); VI incineration of waste co-incineration of waste (Articles 65–67); VII waste disposal and storage (Articles 68–78); VIII transboundary movement of waste (Articles 79–83); IX financing of waste management (Articles 84–85); X supervision (Articles 86–89), XI penal provisions (Articles 90–91); and XII transitional and final provisions (Articles 92–102).

600. This Law regulates types and classifications of waste, waste management planning, conditions and method of waste management, as well as other issues relevant to waste management[657] (Article 1, paragraph 1). According to provisions of Article 2, this Law is not applied to: (1) gaseous substances emitted in air; (2) ground, including not dug contaminated ground and construction objects permanently attached to the ground; (3) uncontaminated ground and other materials excavated during construction works, if that material is used for construction purposes, in its natural form on the construction site on which it has been dug; (4) radioactive waste; (5) deactivated, or disabled explosives; (6) straw and other harmless agricultural or forest materials, that are found in nature, or that are used in agriculture, forestry or for production of energy by methods that do not have harmful impact on the environment and human health; (7) sediments that are moved within surface water, for the sake of management of waters and watercourses, prevention of floods or alleviation of consequences caused by floods, drought or soil regeneration, if it is proved that these sediments are harmless; (8) electric and electronic products that are used as armament, ammunition or other products necessary for defence and security of Montenegro; (9) batteries and accumulators, armament, ammunition or other products needed for defence and security of Montenegro; (10) waste waters, waste from mining, waste that is generated by navigable vessels, side products of animal origin, including prefabricated products of animal origin, except those intended for incineration, disposal on a dumping site or use in installations using

656. After this Law comes into force, the previous Law on waste management ('Official Journal of RM', No. 80/05 and 'Official Journal of MNE', No. 73/08) ceases to be in force (Art. 101).

657. Waste is any substance or object rejected by the owner, intended to be rejected by the owner or obliged to be rejected in accordance with the Law (Art. 3, point 27). (1) Waste that has passed procedure of processing, including recycling, is not regarded as waste under condition that: that obtained substance or object used in certain purposes; that such substance or object is needed; substance or object fulfils technical conditions for certain purpose in accordance with law; use substance or object will not cause negative impact on the environment or human health. (2) Criteria for cessation of the status of waste for certain kinds of waste, and especially for: aggregate rock, paper, glass, plastic, metal, rubber and textile, including border values for dangerous substances in waste, are regulated by regulation of the Government (Art. 9).

biogas or compost, carcasses of dead animals, including animals killed for sake of wiping out epizootic and faecal matter, if it is not regulated in a different way by a special law.

A. *Waste Management*[658]

601. Waste management is based on following principles: (1) sustainable development, that secures efficient use of resources, reduction of quantity of waste and acting when waste is concerned in a way that contributes to realization of goals of sustainable development; (2) proximity and regional waste management, due to the need to process the waste as near as possible to the site of its origin in accordance with economic viability of location choice, while regional waste management is provided by development and implementation of regional strategic plans based on national policy; (3) precautionary, or preventive actions, undertaking measures for prevention of negative impact on the environment and human health and in case of lacking of scientific and expert data; (4) 'polluter pays', according to which the producer of waste bears expenses of waste management and preventive measures aimed at avoiding negative impact on the environment and human health; (5) hierarchy, that respects the order of priority in waste management: prevention, preparation for reuse, recycling and other methods of prefabrication (use of energy) and disposal of waste (Article 4).[659]

602. Pursuant to Article 6, waste is classified according to groups and subgroups, according to the origin of waste and kinds, depending on dangerous characteristics. Waste is divided into groups and subgroups depending on the activity and method which generated it. Kinds of waste, depending on dangerous characteristics, are dangerous and non-dangerous waste, and when disposal is concerned inert waste.[660]

603. In accordance with provisions of Article 7, characterization of waste comprises determination of groups or subgroups of waste according to the catalogue of waste and kinds of waste depending on dangerous characteristics determined on the basis of examination. Owner of waste is obliged to perform characterization of waste, except communal waste generated in households. Characterization of waste

658. Waste management is prevention of creation, reduction of quantity of waste or reuse of waste and collection, transport, processing and disposal of waste, supervision over these operations and procedures and of subsequent maintenance of dumping sites, including the activities of traders and intermediaries of waste (Art. 1, para. 2).
659. Waste management is conducted in a way that does not cause negative impact on the environment and human health, and particularly to: water, air, land, plants and animals; noise and smell; areas of special interest (protected natural and cultural goods) (Art. 5).
660. Classification of waste, catalogue of waste, procedures of processing of waste, or processing and disposal are regulated by regulation of organs of state administration competent for the environment (hereinafter 'Ministry') (Art. 6. para. 4).

is done on the basis of catalogue of waste.[661] Waste that is not classified as dangerous in the catalogue will be regarded as dangerous if it is found by examination it has one or more dangerous characteristics, in accordance with regulation (Article 7, paragraphs 1–5). Examination of dangerous characteristics of waste may be done by an accredited laboratory, with a capacity of legal person, which meets conditions regarding staff, equipment and space (paragraph 6).[662]

604. The law regulates obligations of original producer of waste (Article 10),[663] extended liability of manufacturers and importers (Article 11),[664] way of collection and processing of waste (Article 13),[665] reuse and recycling (Article 14),[666] prohibition of mixing of dangerous waste (Article 15), obligation of labelling dangerous waste (Article 16)[667] and obligation to remove the waste (Article 17).[668]

605. Commercial society or entrepreneur which produces or upgrades a product, processes, sells or imports a product that generates special kinds of waste has an enhanced responsibility, that includes: (1) being entered into the register of the producers and importers with a duty of extended responsibilities; (2) keeping and saving evidence and registration of quantity of produced or imported products, or equipment in that these products are inbuilt; (3) securing products or waste that remains after use of products; (4) subsequent waste management and financial responsibility for these activities; (5) obligation of disclosing publicly accessible information in what measure the product fit for reuse or recycling and obligation of identification of recyclable components of products; (6) design of products in a way

661. If characterization of waste cannot be done on the basis of catalogue of waste, it will be done on the basis of examination of dangerous characteristics of waste (Art. 7 para. 4).
662. Methods of testing of dangerous characteristics of waste and more precise conditions from para. 6 of this Article are regulated by regulation of the Ministry (Art. 7 para. 7).
663. Original producer of waste is every person whose activity produces waste (Art. 3. Point 11).
664. Owner waste is producer of waste or legal or physical person that owns waste (Art. 3. Point 8).
665. Waste is collected separately, if it is practical in technical and economic sense and from the point of view of protection of the environment justified, in a way that is not mixed with other waste or other material that have different characteristics (Art. 13 para. 1). Notwithstanding para. 1 of this Article, the separate collection of municipal waste shall be mandatory (Art. 13, para. 2). Paper, metal, plastic, glass and biowaste are collected separately, in accordance with the plan from Art. 19 of this Law. Processing of waste is done in a way that provides respect for principles from Arts 4 and 5 of this Law. Method of separate collection and collection of communal waste for processing is prescribed by regulation of the competent organ of unit of local self-government, with prior approval of the Ministry (Art. 13 paras 3–5).
666. Waste management is done in following way: if at least 50% total mass of collected waste, as, e.g., as paper, metal, plastic and glass from households and other sources, is prepared for reuse and recycling; if at least 70% of non-dangerous building waste is prepared for reuse and recycling and other ways of processing, as it is used for substitution of other materials during the process of burying (covering with earth), excluding materials from nature (Art. 14).
667. During collection, transport and temporary storage of dangerous waste is packed and labelled in accordance with the law regulating transport of dangerous substances. Dangerous waste during transport within the state must be accompanied with document on transport of dangerous substances, in accordance with law (Art. 16, paras 1, 2).
668. Disposal of waste is done on location intended for that purpose by certain spatial planning document, as well as in installations or objects that fulfil conditions prescribed by law. Disposal waste is done in accordance with this law. Prohibited is burning of waste in open space and/or plants that do not have a permit under Art. 31 of this Law (Art. 17, paras 1–3).

as to reduce negative impact on the environment, reduction of production of waste and secure that processing and disposal of products that became waste is performed in a way acceptable for the environment and human health, with recommendations for development, production and marketing of products that are fit for multiple use, technically durable and, when they become waste, easy for orderly and secure processing and removal (Article 11, paragraph 2).[669]

B. Plans and Programmes of Waste Management

606. Waste management is performed in accordance with the State plan of waste management (hereinafter 'The State plan') and local plan of management communal waste, and non-hazardous construction waste that does not contain or is not exposed to hazardous substances (hereinafter 'local plan') (Article 18).[670]

607. The State plan of waste management is basic document that regulates long-term goals of waste management and prescribes conditions for rational and sustainable waste management in Montenegro. The State plan gives review of existing state of waste management, with measures which should be undertaken regarding achievement of best conditions for preparation of waste for reuse, recycling and disposal, in a way acceptable for protection of the environment and human health (Article 19, paragraphs 1 and 2).[671]

608. Local plan is adopted by assembly of the unit of local self-government, for a period for which is adopted the State plan (Article 23, paragraph 1). The local plan must be harmonized with the State plan (Article 23, paragraph 3).[672]

609. In addition, the Law regulates issues concerning the Programme of disposal of biologically degradable waste (Article 20, paragraph 1),[673] Programme for prevention of generation of waste (Article 21), Plans of management of medicinal

669. The Register of Manufacturers and Importers with Extended responsibility is managed by the Agency. (Art. 11. para. 3).
670. Prohibited is waste management that is not in accordance with plans of waste management prescribed by this law (Art. 30).
671. The State plan is adopted by the Government, on proposal of the Ministry, for period that is not shorter than five years (Art. 19, para. 5).
672. Competent organ of local self-government informs the public about the drafting of local plan by at least one electronic means of information emitted on the territory of unit of local self-government and printed means of information that is distributed on the territory of Montenegro. For implementation of local plan is responsible executive organ of unit of local self-government (Art. 23, paras 6 and 9).
673. Biologically degradable waste is waste that is suitable for anaerobic or aerobic degradation (bio waste, paper and cardboard) (Art. 3. Point 1).

and veterinary waste and with sewerage sludge (Article 22),[674] Plan waste management of the producer of waste (Articles 26–29),[675] Joint management of communal waste, and non-hazardous construction waste (Article 24),[676] Reporting on implementation of plans (Article 25).

C. Permits and Registrations

610. Processing and/or disposal of waste can be performed by commercial society or entrepreneur if it possesses adequate equipment, installation for processing of waste and needed number of employees, on the basis of permits for processing, or disposal of waste (Article 31, paragraph 1). For commercial society or entrepreneur which performs processing and/or disposal of waste in installation, or site that fulfils conditions prescribed by The Law that regulates integral prevention and control of pollution of the environment, permits from paragraph 1 of this Article is included in integrated permit for installation, in accordance with the Law (Article 31, paragraph 3).[677]

611. Permits from Article 31 of this Law especially contain (1) data on location; (2) quantity and kinds of waste that can be processed and/or removed; (3) technical and other conditions that are important for procedure of processing and/or removal; (4) security and other preventive measures which should be undertaken, or measures of protection from accident and fire; (5) methods to be applied for all procedures of processing and/or disposal; (6) methods of supervision of procedures of processing and/or disposal and monitoring of the environment; and (7) conditions that are related to closure, maintenance and monitoring of the state after closure of dumping sites or installations (Article 32).[678]

612. Collection or transport of waste can be performed by commercial society or entrepreneur if it has the equipment for collection, or transport of waste and needed number of employees (Article 36, paragraph 1). Commercial society or

674. Medical waste is waste that is produced by performing health services and by doing scientific research and experiments in the field of medicine; (Art. 3, para. 17). Sewerage sludge is waste that is generated during the treatment of communal waste water in installations for purification (Art. 3, para. 12).
675. Producer of waste that on annual level produces more than 200 kg dangerous waste or more than 20 tonnes non-dangerous waste is obliged to make waste management plan in accordance with this law. (2) Producer of waste from para. 1 of this Article is obliged to make waste management plan in the period of sixty days prior to commencement of procedure or activities during which is generated waste. (3) Provisions of this Article do not apply on communal waste (Art. 26).
676. Two or more units of local self-government can jointly organize management of communal and non-hazardous construction waste, in accordance with law (Art. 24, para. 1).
677. Fulfilment of conditions for performing activities of processing and/or removal of waste is checked by the Agency which also issues the permit from para. 1 of this Article (Art. 31 para. 4).
678. Permit which is issued for installation for incineration and/or co-incineration, besides the data from para. 1 of this Article, must contain measures for use of energy that fulfil high level of efficiency (Art. 32 para. 2).

entrepreneur which fulfils conditions from Article 36 paragraph 1 of this Law concerning activity of collection or transport of waste is obliged to be registered in the register of collectors and transporters of waste. Realization of conditions from paragraph 1 of this Article is estimated by the Agency (Article 37, paragraphs 1, 2).[679]

D. Special Kinds of Waste[680]

613. In Chapter V, the Law regulates waste management of electric and electronic products (Article 46), System of transfer, collection and processing waste of electric and electronic products (Article 47), Management of waste vehicles (Article 48), Management of waste tires (Article 49), Management of waste batteries and accumulators (Article 50), System of acquisition, collection and processing of waste batteries and accumulators (Article 51), Waste lubricating oils and liquids (Article 52), Waste Packaging waste (Article 53), Building waste (Article 54), Waste that contains asbestos (Article 55), PCB and waste that contains PCB (Article 56), Plan of management of equipment and of waste that contain PCB and evidence of PCB (Article 57), Communal sludge from sewage systems (Article 58), Sludge treatment and use of processed sludge (Article 59), Prohibited use of sludge (Article 60), Obligations of users of treated sludge (Article 61), Medical and veterinary waste (Article 62), Competence of organs of state health administration, for veterinary and for water (Article 63), and Organization of activities of acquisition, collection and processing of special kinds of waste (Article 64).

E. Incineration and Co-incineration of Waste

614. Waste is burnt in installations for incineration and/or co-incineration of waste. Installations for incineration and/or co-incineration waste are projected, built and equipped in a way that secures technical-technological functionality with the least possible quantity of emissions and negative impact of waste on human life, human health and the environment. Besides the conditions from Article 32 of this

679. Furthermore, following issues are also regulated: Content permits for processing and/or disposal waste (Art. 32), Application for issuance of permits for processing and/or disposal of waste (Art. 33), Information of the public (Art. 34), Refusal of application for issuance of permits for processing and/or disposal of waste (Art. 35), Collection or transport of waste (Art. 36), Enrolment in register for collection, or transport of waste (Art. 37), Application for registration in the register of collectors, or transporters of waste (Art. 38), Refusal of application for registration in the register of collectors, or transporters (Art. 39), Registration of traders and intermediaries (Art. 40), Performance of more than one activity (Art. 41), Management of communal waste (Art. 42), Management of biowaste (Art. 43), Evidence of waste (Art. 44), Evidence and registration of data (Art. 45).

680. Special kinds of waste are: waste of electric and electronic products, waste vehicles, waste tires, waste batteries and accumulators, waste oils, waste packing, building waste, waste from mining, waste that contains asbestos, PCB waste, sewerage sludge, medical and veterinary waste (Art. 3 point 37).

Law, permits for processing and/or disposal of waste in installations for incineration and/or co-incineration of waste are prescribed measures for use of energy produced by incineration or co-incineration of waste; reduction of quantity and danger of remnants of incineration or co-incineration of waste; and disposal of remnants of incineration or co-incineration of waste, if these remnants cannot be processed (Article 65, paragraphs 1–3).[681]

615. The Ministry regulates in detail following: (1) waste that cannot be incinerated and/or co-incineration in accordance with this Law; (2) method of processing waste in installations for incineration and/or co-incineration of waste; (3) conditions which should be fulfilled by objects and installations for incineration and/or co-incineration of waste; (4) technical-technological procedures of incineration and/or co-incineration of certain kinds of waste; (5) method of generation and management of waste produced by the process of incineration and/or co-incineration; (6) specialist's training and qualification of managers of installations for incineration and/or co-incineration of waste; and (7) method of functioning of the process of incineration and/or co-incineration of waste in accordance with this Law (Article 67).

F. Dumping and Storage of Waste

616. Dumping sites for waste may be dumping site for dangerous waste;[682] dumping site for inert waste; and[683] dumping site for non-dangerous waste (Article 68, paragraph 1).[684] For dumping sites from paragraph 1 of this Article the Ministry, with consent of competent organ of state administration, by its regulation more precisely prescribes characteristics of the location (geologic, hydrologic, morphologic, meteorological, seismologic and other), conditions of building, sanitary and

681. If in installations for incineration and/or co-incineration of waste is burnt dangerous waste, the permit for processing and/or disposal of waste from Art. 32 of this Law, also regulates: quantity and kinds of dangerous waste, in accordance with the catalogue of waste that can be incinerated; least and greatest mass flow according to kinds of dangerous waste; least and greatest caloric value of dangerous waste; greatest contents of dangerous substances, and particularly of PCB, chlorine, flour, sulphur and heavy metals (Art. 65 para. 4). The Law in Art. 66. regulates obligations of managers of installations for incineration and/or co-incineration.

682. Dangerous waste is waste that contains elements or compounds that have one or more of following dangerous characteristics: explosiveness, reactivity, inflammable, irritable, harmful, toxic, infective, carcinogenic, corrosive, mutagenic, teratogenic, ecotoxic, characteristic of rusting and characteristic of emission of toxic gases by chemical or biological reaction and sensitivity/irritability, as well as the waste from which, after disposal, can be generated another substance that has some of dangerous characteristics (Art. 3, point 25).

683. Inert waste is non-dangerous waste if it is not able to cause significant physical, chemical or biological change, does not dissolve, does not burn, is not biodegradable, does not pollute the environment, has not harmful impact on human health and whose residual waters in contact with other materials do not cause reactions and do not imperil ecotoxic quality of surface or ground waters (Art. 3, point 10).

684. Non-dangerous waste is waste that has not some of characteristics of dangerous waste (Art. 3 point 20).

technical conditions, method of work and procedure of closing the dumping site, professional education and qualification of managers of the dumping sites (Article 68, paragraph 2).[685]

617. Producer of waste is obliged to, within the scope of technological possibilities of the production process, perform physical, chemical, biological and thermal processing and sorting of waste with an aim of reducing its quantity or volume for disposal and of reduction of danger for human health and the environment (Article 70, paragraph 1).[686]

618. Besides above-mentioned, the Law regulates following issues: mixed disposal of waste (Article 71), inert waste (Article 72), mixed communal waste (Article 73), obligations of managerial staff of dumping sites (Article 74), closure of dumping sites (Article 75), financial means for disposal of waste on dumping sites and closure of dumping sites (Article 76), storage of waste (Article 77) and temporary storage of communal waste (Article 78).

G. *Transboundary Movement of Waste*[687]

619. As already mentioned, Montenegro is a member of the Basel Convention on the Control of Transboundary Movements of Hazardous Waste and their Disposal (1989).[688]

620. Import and transit of non-dangerous waste can be performed only on the basis of permits which is, on application of commercial society or entrepreneur, issued by the Agency.[689] Export and transit of dangerous waste can be performed

685. It is prohibited to dispose waste on dumping sites if: (1) it is not in accordance with waste management plans; (2) if it is in liquid state; (3) if it has explosive, oxidizing, very inflammable or inflammable characteristics; (4) if it is unprocessed medical or veterinary waste; (5) if it consists of waste automobile and industrial batteries and accumulators; (6) if the waste consists of whole or crushed waste tires, except bicycle tires and tire with outer diameter greater than 400 mm; (7) that has been produced as a result of scientific research, and which characteristics are not known or are new and its impact on people or the environment are not known; (8) on the area that could cause impact on surface and ground waters. Prohibited is mixing of different kinds of waste, mixing with other substances, dilution and performing other procedures aimed at fulfilling conditions for accepting waste on dumping sites. Kinds of waste and conditions for accepting waste on a dumping site are prescribed by the Ministry (Art. 69, paras 1–3).

686. On inert waste, or on waste which was treated by physical, chemical or biological processing, cannot influence the reduction of quantity or volume for disposal, and on it do not apply procedures from para. 1 of this Article (Art. 70, para. 2).

687. Transboundary movement of waste is import of waste on the territory of Montenegro, transit of waste of foreign origin via territory Montenegro and export of waste from the territory of Montenegro (Art. 79).

688. *See*: *Basel Convention Country Fact Sheet*,http://www.basel.int/Countries/Countryfactsheets/tabid/1293/Default.aspx (3 Dec. 2022).

689. Prohibited is import of dangerous waste. Prohibited is import of non-dangerous waste for disposal or for its use as fuel or in other way for production of energy (Art. 80).

only on the basis of permits that, on application of commercial society or entrepreneur, are issued by the Agency. Permits from paragraphs 1 and 2 of this Article are entered in the registry kept by the Agency (Article 81, paragraphs 1–3).[690]

621. Export of non-dangerous waste can be performed by commercial society or entrepreneur that is registered in the register of Exporters of non-dangerous waste. Registration in the register from paragraph 1 of this Article is done on the basis of application that is submitted to the Agency (Article 82, paragraphs 1–2).[691] Border passages across which may be performed transboundary movement of waste is prescribed by the Government, in accordance with international agreements and this Law (Article 83).

H. Financing of Waste Management

622. Owner of waste shall bear all costs of collection, transport and processing of waste in accordance with the principle 'polluter pays'. Waste management costs are also paid by producers, importers and distributors of products out of which the waste has been generated (Article 84, paragraphs 1–2).

623. Pursuant to Article 85 Special charge is paid for waste management. Special charge for waste management from paragraph 1 of this Article belongs to the budget of Montenegro (Article 85, paragraph 9). This means from paragraph 9 of this Article are paid on a special account used for co-financing of realization of projects from the field of waste management and expenses regarding receiving, collection and recycling of special kinds of waste mentioned in Article 64 of this Law (Article 85, paragraph 10).[692]

II. Law on the Municipal Waste Water Management

624. The Law on the Municipal Waste Water Management (OJ MNE, No. 2/17) regulates municipal (communal) wastewater management, conditions to be met by

690. More detailed contents of documentation which should be submitted with application for issuance of the permit from points 1 and 2 of this Article, list of waste classification and the method of keeping the register from para. 3 of this Article are prescribed by regulation of the Ministry (Art. 81 para. 4).
691. Register from para. 1 of this Article is kept by the Agency. Commercial societies or entrepreneurs that are enlisted in the register from para. 1 of this Article are obliged to submit to the Agency annual report on kinds and quantities of exported non-dangerous waste, till 31 March, of the current year for previous year (Art. 82 para. 3 i 4).
692. Precise criteria, amount and method of payment of the special charge are regulated by regulation of the Government (Art. 85 para. 11).

the collecting systems and municipal wastewater treatment facilities, manner of collection, treatment and disposal of municipal wastewater and other issues of importance for the management of municipal wastewaters (Article 1).[693]

625. Municipal wastewater, within the meaning of this Law, is household wastewater or a mixture of water with industrial wastewater and/or atmospheric waste waters (Article 2, paragraph 1).[694] Communal wastewater management is of public interest (Article 4).

626. Based on the Law on Municipal Waste Water Management several by-laws have been adopted. These are, *inter alia*, following:

- Rulebook on Geographical Boundaries, Number and Capacity of Agglomerations (OJ MNE, No. 78/17).
- Rulebook on monitoring and evaluation of results of quality and quantity of released municipal and biodegradable industrial wastewater effluents (OJ MNE, No. 78/17).
- Rulebook on the content of the records of municipal wastewater discharges and biodegradable industrial wastewater (OJ MNE, No. 78/17).
- Rulebook on the contents of the report on the discharge of municipal wastewater and biodegradable industrial wastewater (OJ MNE, No. 78/17).

III. Other Waste Regulations

627. During the last several years the following sub-legal acts have been adopted:

- National Waste Management Plan in Montenegro 2015–2020.[695]
- Decree on the method and conditions of waste storage (OJ MNE, Nos 33/13, 65/15).
- Decree on conditions to be met by materials or objects arising from the production process for side products (OJ MNE, No. 30/15).

---

693. This law has been harmonized with the Directive 91/271/EEC concerning urban waste water treatment, and 2014/431/EU: Commission Implementing Decision of 26 Jun., 2014 concerning formats for reporting on the national programmes for the implementation of Council Directive 91/271/EEC.

694. Waste water from households, referred to in para. 1 of this Article, is waste water from residential and service facilities, which is originated from human metabolism and home activities (para. 2). Industrial waste water, referred to in para. 1 of this Article, is waste water that is exited from facilities or premises used for performing craft or industrial activities, other than waste water from household and atmospheric waters (para. 3). Atmospheric water, referred to in para. 1 of this Article, is waste water produced by the atmospheric rainfall from public surfaces (streets, canopies, parks, squares and other public surfaces) that dissolve pollutants that are spilled into collector systems or directly into surface and underground water (para. 4).

695. *See*: http://www.komunalnocetinje.me/wp-content/uploads/2019/05/DRZAVNI-PLAN-2015-2020-O-UPRAVLJANJU-OTPADOM.pdf (3 Dec. 2022).

- Decree on criteria, the amount and method of paying a special waste management fee (OJ MNE, No. 39/12).
- Decree on the method and procedure of establishment of the system of taking on, collection and processing of waste of electric and electronic products and functioning of the system (OJ MNE, No. 24/2012).
- Decree on the method and procedure of establishment of the system of taking on, collecting and processing waste vehicles and functioning of the system (OJ MNE, No. 28/2012).
- Decree on the manner and procedure of application for the placement of electrical and electronic products on the market, establishment of the system of taking, collecting and treatment of waste from electrical and electronic products and operations of the system ('OJ MNE', 9/10).
- Decree on the manner and procedure of application for the placement of packaging and packed products on the market, establishment of the system of taking, collecting and treatment of waste packaging material and operations of the system ('OJ MNE', 9/10, 19/11).
- Decree on the manner and procedure of the application for the placement of vehicle on the market, establishment of the system of taking, collecting and treatment of waste vehicles and operations of the system ('OJ MNE', 9/10).
- Decree on the manner and procedure of application for the placement of tires on the market, establishment of the system of taking, collecting and treatment of waste tires and operations of this system ('OJ MNE', 9/10).
- Decree on the criteria, level and method of payment of special waste management fee ('OJ MNE', 11/09, 46/09, 15/11).
- Decree on the manner and procedure of application for the placement of batteries and generators on the market, establishment of the system of taking, collecting and treatment of used batteries and generators and operations of this system ('OJ MNE', 15/10).
- Regulations on classification of waste and on the catalogue of waste (OJ MNE, No. 35/2012).
- Rulebook on criteria for selection of locations, manner and procedure of waste material disposal ('OJ RM', 56/00).
- Rulebook on more detailed characteristics of the location, conditions of construction, sanitary and technical conditions, manner of work and closing of landfills, education and competence of the landfill manager and types of waste and conditions for acceptance of waste at landfills ('OJ MNE', 84/09).
- Rulebook on treatment of waste oil ('OJ MNE', 21/10).
- Rulebook on the form, content and manner of fulfilling the waste material transport form, waste material records, annual waste material report, content and manner of keeping the data registry and content and form of the collective report ('OJ MNE', 46/10).
- Rulebook on treatment of construction waste material, manner and procedure of construction waste material treatment, conditions and manner of asbestos cement waste disposal ('OJ MNE', 60/10).
- Rulebook on incineration of waste ('OJ MNE', 14/11).
- Rulebook on the manner and procedure of treatment of equipment and waste containing PCB ('OJ MNE', 34/11).

- Rulebook on classification of waste material and procedures of its treatment, processing and disposal ('OJ MNE', 68/09 and 86/09).
- Rulebook on the content, form and manner of keeping the register of issued permits for cross-border waste transport ('OJ MNE', 71/10).
- Rulebook on more detailed content of the documents submitted to support the application for issuance of waste import, export and transit licence, and the list of waste classification ('OJ MNE', 71/10).
- Rulebook on more detailed requirements for the sewage mud, amounts, volume, frequency and methods of analysis of the sewage mud for permissible purposes and requirements for the soil intended for its application ('OJ MNE', 89/09).
- Rulebook on equipment and staff in the waste treatment or disposal facility and more detailed content on description of the work process ('OJ MNE', 75/10).

§6. Harmonization with EU Legislation

628. According to the Report of the Commission of the European Community in 2016 the legal framework on waste management is partially aligned.[696] A similar assessment exists in the 2018 Report,[697] and in the 2022 Report.[698]

629. '… Considerable efforts on strategic planning and investments are needed to implement the national strategy for waste management until 2030', and 'a new national waste management plan remains to be drafted.'[699]

696. EC (2016). p. 76.
697. *See*: EC (2018). p. 80.
698. EC (2022)., p. 112.
699. EC (2022), p. 112.

Chapter 5. Soil Pollution

§1. The State of Soil Pollution

630. 'Agricultural land in Montenegro covers the area of 517,136 ha, i.e., 37.4% of the total land area, of which only 36% is arable land and only 23,500 ha are covered by cultivated fields, orchards and vineyards, mostly in private ownership, and those fields are significantly fragmented.[700] The estimation is that only 30% of arable land is used at the moment, and deagrarianization, abandonment and neglect continue, as well as transformation of agricultural into construction land'.[701]

631. One of the problems with soil in Montenegro is the fact that permanent conversion of the agricultural land is done by the change of its purpose through the process of construction in urban and rural settlements, traffic lines, tourist, industrial and other types of facilities.[702]

632. Forests and forest land in Montenegro consist of approximately 738,000 ha or around 53.4% of the overall surface. About 622,000 ha are covered with forest vegetation which forms forested area of 45%. This percentage of forested area is estimated as very favourable, from environmental point of view.[703]

633. The coastal area is used for various economic and other human activities and due to that it has suffered a significant change in natural and landscaping values.[704] Pollution by organic polluting agents in coastal regions is generally below the threshold, while the quantity of inorganic polluting substances (Cr, Ni and B) exceeds the prescribed levels at all sites in this region. There are two possible explanations for such a state of affairs: it could be the consequence of the very nature of the soil in the region or it could be the result of cross-border pollution transfer from maritime side.[705]

634. The programme for testing the presence of harmful substances in the soil of Montenegro in 2011 included ten Montenegrin municipalities. Sampling was

---

700. According to the agricultural census from 2010, KEY VARIABLES – LAND AND LIVESTOCK, family agricultural farms and business entities had a total of 309,240.7 ha of available land. The census included 48,824 family farms with 294,400.7 ha of available land, which is 95.2% of the total available land. An average farm has 6.0 ha of available agricultural land. In total, 48.277 farms covering the area of 22,1297.6 ha of the used agricultural land in total account for 71.6% of the total area of available land. An average agricultural farm has 4.6 ha of land used for agriculture.
701. GMNE, NCSD (2011), 10. *See also* GMNE (2008C), 31–32.
702. This destruction is done through the series of various human activities including: exploitation of sand and gravel at several places in rivers and karst fields (lower watercourse of Moraca – Platije); exploitation of solid mineral resources – bauxite, coal, stone, zinc, lead; processing of mineral and other resources in industrial facilities; production of brick and roofing tile of the resources from the surface mines in Tivatsko polje, Berane, Kolašin and Pljevlja; mining waste disposals. GMNE (2008C), 102–104.
703. GMNE (2008C), 71.
704. *Ibid.*, 102–104.
705. GMNE (2007D), 70.

conducted at thirty-four sites, while the testing was conducted on a total of fifty-eight samples. In addition to the usual locations in the land monitoring programme, this year there were also included locations of the Katun Laticno in Golija, playgrounds in Podgorica, Tivat and Nikšić and mine 'Brskovo' in the municipality Mojkovac. The programme encompasses the physical-chemical testing of most of the pollutants that can show us the real situation of soil pollution, sources of pollution, etc.

635. The programme of investigations of possible soil contamination from the atmosphere (emissions that occur as a result of industrial and technological processes, combustion of fossil fuels in industry, as well as the work of individual and local boiler rooms) includes locations in the three municipalities with industrial hotspots: Podgorica, Nikšić and Pljevlja. In order to achieve a more realistic picture of pollution level, sampling was conducted at three locations in the most representative way to display the influence of the industrial plants in the surrounding soil: Srpska (KAP), Rubeza (Nikšić steelworks) and Komini (TE Pljevlja). Examining was conducted in a total of six samples.[706]

636. Consideration of the impact of emissions from motor vehicles, that use petroleum products as potential sources of pollution of land, was carried out by analysing twenty-three samples of soil sampled byroads.[707]

637. The degree of soil pollution due to indiscriminate and improperly delayed industrial or municipal waste was observed through examination of soil samples near the landfill of municipal waste in Zabljak and Bijelo Polje, as well as samples near the landfill of Steelworks in Nikšić, and Jaloviste in Pljevlja.[708]

706. The influence of plant KAP is seen most prominently in soil samples from locations of the village Srpska, where has been registered an increased concentration of polyaromatic hydrocarbons (PAH). Results of analysis of soil samples in the settlement Rubeza in 2011 did not show the negative effects of the work of the steelworks in terms of increased content of organic and inorganic pollutants in soil. Results of analysis of soil samples in the settlement Komini do not show negative effects of TE Pljevlja in terms of increased content of organic and inorganic pollutants in soil.
707. The results showed that concentrations of lead (which is an indicator of inorganic car exhaust) and polyaromatic hydrocarbons (which are indicators of organic emissions vehicle), in the soil along roads, are within the limits of MAC.
708. Analysis has revealed the increased concentrations of inorganic pollutants (copper, zinc, cadmium and boron) and organic pollutants (PAH congeners and PBC), in soil sampled near the landfill of Nikšić Steelworks, are directly related to its inadequate deposited waste. Also, Jaloviste in Pljevlja is directly related to the increased concentration of inorganic pollutants by nickel in soil sampled in the vicinity. EPA (2012), 75. In order to assess soil contamination due to improper use of agricultural pesticides and the like, there has been executed an analysis of samples from thirteen locations. None of the tested samples of soil show the presence of pollutants in concentrations that exceed the MDK. The test programme included the analysis of ten soil samples near substations in Ulcinj, Tivat, Podgorica, Berane and Pljevlja. The presence of PCB congeners found in soil samples in Tivat, Podgorica (Tološi), Pljevlja (T2) and Berane. The content of PCB congeners in a concentration above the MPC was recorded in soil sampled by the transformer at the substation Berane Mažina in Tivat.

§2. COMPETENCIES

638. Several ministries and other bodies and institutions are competent or important for various issues concerning the soil. According to the Decree on state administration organization and operations (OJ MNE, Nos 49/22, 52/22, 56/22, 82/22) most important institutions are MESPU (Article 12), Forest Administration (Article 37), Water Administration (Article 35), Administration for Food Security, Veterinary and Phytosanitary operation (Article 35), MCI (Article 9), Statistical Office of Montenegro (Article 26), Centre for Ecotoxicological Research (CETI), etc.

§3. LEGISLATION

639. Article 58 of the Constitution of Montenegro (OJ MNE, No. 1/2007) proclaims that 'natural wealth and goods in general use shall be owned by the state'.

640. There are provisions in several laws that are relevant to soil protection depending on the types of soil. Besides the regulations directly related to the protection of soil (a set of regulations in the field of agriculture, forestry, water, construction land, etc.) following environmental regulations are also very relevant: Law on the Environment, the Law on EIA, the Law on the strategic impact assessment, the Law on IPPC, the Law on Waste Management, Nature Protection Law, etc.

I. The Law on the Environment

641. According to Article 2 of the Law, soil is element of the definition of the notion of 'environment'. Besides that, soil is mentioned in following provisions of the Law: special laws (Article 6), protection of environmental segments (Article 15), soil protection (Article 16), monitoring (Articles 54, 55), national plan to combat desertification (Article 34) and environmental information (Article 67).

II. Specific Legislation

A. Agricultural Land

642. When agricultural land is concerned, the main law regulating soil protection in Montenegro is the Law on agricultural land (OJ RM, Nos 15/92, 59/92 and OJ MNE, No. 32/11).[709] It has seven following chapters: Chapter I – Basic Provisions (Articles 1–9), Chapter II – Exploitation of Agricultural Land (Articles 10–18), Chapter III – Exploitation of the Agricultural Land for Non-agricultural

709. The amendments have introduced new fines. *See also* Law on organic agriculture (Official Journal of RM, No. 49/2004) and several by-laws, including Regulations on permitted amounts of hazardous and harmful substances in soil and methods of their testing (Official Journal of RM, No. 18/97).

Purpose (Articles 19–31), Chapter IV – Agricultural land management (Articles 32–61), Chapter V – Protection of the Agricultural Land (Articles 62–74), Chapter VI – Supervision (Articles 75–78), Chapter VII – Penal Provisions (Articles 79–83) and Chapter VIII – Transitional and Final Provisions (Articles 84–88).

643. According to the Law, agricultural land[710] is a good of general interest that deserves special protection (Article 1). Agricultural land must be used for agricultural production, and for non-agricultural purposes, only in cases established by-law (Article 4).

644. Special provisions of the Law deal with soil protection (Articles 62–74). Measures prescribed by this law have to be taken in order to protect agricultural land from the harmful effects of erosion and flash flood, pollution by hazardous and harmful substances and protection from field damage[711] (Article 62). Implementation of the anti-erosion measures is prescribed by Article 63 of this Law[712] and the procedure for the implementation of prescribed anti-erosion measures have to be implemented by the competent authority of the municipality.

645. It is forbidden by the Law to emit dangerous and harmful substances in the amount of which can damage and change the characteristics of production of agricultural land and quality of agricultural culture.[713] Besides that, incorrect use of fertilizers and means for plant protection is prohibited (Article 67).[714]

646. The Law prescribes obligation of systematic control of fertility of arable agricultural land. Testing of soil fertility has to be made every fifth year (Article 69).[715]

---

710. Agricultural land, according to the Law, is considered, *inter alia*: ploughland, gardens, orchards, vineyards, meadows, pastures, swamps and other lands which, by its natural and economic conditions, can serve the general interests, if used or can be used for agricultural production. Arable land, in the sense of this law, is considered: ploughland, gardens, orchards, vineyards and meadows (Art. 2).
711. Measures for suppression of field damage have to be prescribed by decision of the Municipal Assembly (Art. 71).
712. Anti-erosion measures include, *inter alia*: temporary or permanent ban of plough of meadows, pastures and other surfaces in order to their transformation in the fields with annual crop; growing perennial crops; construction of buildings; manner of the processing of land; lifting and growing agricultural protection belts or planting perennial wooden plants; prohibition of pasture of cattle in the determined time or limitation for number of livestock that can be run on a certain surface, and prohibition of cutting of forests and forest plantations on and above the vulnerable plots (Art. 63, para. 1).
713. Governmental authority competent for agriculture, in agreement with authorities responsible for environment, determines the allowed quantity of hazardous and harmful substances in soil and methods for their investigation (Art. 67, para. 2).
714. Municipal Assembly may prescribe measures for the protection of agricultural land from frost, ice, fire and other natural disasters (Art. 74).
715. The company that makes the control of fertility of land has obligation to submit report on the results of investigation of fertility to legal or physical person whose land is controlled. Besides that the company that makes the control of fertility of land has to give instructions on how to use fertilizers (Art. 69, para. 2).

B. Forest Land

647. The Law on Forest (OJ MNE, Nos 74/10, 40/11) regulates silviculture, protection, conservation and forest improvement, planning, method and conditions of forest utilization, construction and maintenance of forest roads, monitoring of forests, as well as other issues of significance for forests, forest land and forestry. This Law shall also apply to protection, conservation and use of forest trees outside forests and forest land (trees outside forests) (Article 1).[716]

648. Pursuant to Article 3 of the Law, forest land shall be considered to be areas bigger than 50 ar (ars), covered by forest trees: forest trees higher than 5 m, or the trees capable of reaching that height in their maturity phase and the canopy of 5%–10% of the area; forest trees that are not capable of reaching the height of above 5 m, that is, covered by the combination of trees and low forest vegetation provided that their coverage is higher than 10% of the area (paragraph 2). Forest and other forest lands shall also be deemed temporarily barren areas where the natural regeneration of forest trees has started, fire protection lanes, areas covered with non-forest vegetation under 50 acres within forest and other forest land complexes, forest trees protection belts larger than 50 acres and wider than 20 m and forest roads not being portioned out and classified to cadastre parcels (paragraph 3).[717]

649. Protection of soil has been included in a number of the provisions of the Law, especially in provisions related to the protection of forest functions and purposes (Articles 26–32), measures of protection, conservation and monitoring of forests (Articles 33–49), forest infrastructure (Articles 58–62), utilization of non-wood forest products (Articles 63–65), organization of works in forestry (Articles 66–70), etc.

650. Forest and forest land, as goods of general interest, are used in the manner and under the conditions stipulated by the Law (Article 5). Forests, forest land and trees outside forests can only be used in the manner that ensures their commercial, ecological and social functions are in accordance with the Law.[718]

651. Land owner, that is holder of the land, shall be obliged to enable the owner or beneficiary of forest and forest land to have undisturbed access across their land,

---

716. For more details *see* Part II, Ch. 6 (Forest) of the Monograph.

717. The following shall not be deemed to be the forest and forest land: alleys and parks in residential areas, forest nurseries, seed and fast-growing species plantations on agricultural land (para. 5). Trees outside forests shall be considered to be individual trees or groups of trees on land not meeting the criteria referred to in paras 1 and 2 of this article (para. 6). In the event of a doubt or a dispute whether it is the forest, other forest land, trees outside forests or barren land the decision shall be made by the state administration authority competent for forest administration and management (hereinafter 'the Competent Administrative Authority') (para. 8).

718. Forest owners shall administer and manage their forests, forest land, trees outside forests and barren land in accordance with the law. Authorized administrative authority shall administer and manage the forests, forest land, trees outside forests and barren land in state ownership (Art. 6 paras 1 and 2). Forest and forest land in state ownership can be alienated only based on the Government's decision and if the relevant conditions are fulfilled (Art. 7).

that is, across the land it uses for purposes of harvesting and extraction of forest assortments (Article 8, paragraph 1).[719] C. Construction Land

652. The legislation relating to the construction land is basically laid down in the Law on spatial development and construction of buildings (OJ MNE, Nos 64/17, 44/18, 63/18, 11/19-corr, 82/20).[720]

§4. Priority of Future Activities

653. According to the National Strategy of Sustainable Development of Montenegro (NSSDM) improvement of soil management and prevention of the causes of land degradation and damages are priority objectives.[721]

719. For access from para. 1 of this article the owner, that is, forest beneficiary shall be obliged to pay the charges (para. 2). Mutual rights and duties from para. 1 of this article shall be stipulated by the Contract (para. 3). If forest owner, that is, forest beneficiary and land owner, that is, holder of land, do not reach the agreement about the time, method and charges for land utilization, the competent court shall adjudicate (para. 3).
720. For more details *see*: Part III of this Monograph (Zoning and Land-Use Planning).
721. *See*: MSDT (2016b), 179–191.

Chapter 6. Noise and Vibrations

§1. State of the Noise Pollution

654. Measurement of noise level in Montenegro started in 2004. The noise level is measured at locations where exceeding the level is expected.[722] The CETI has implemented programme of noise research which has been created in accordance with the Law on the Environment (96) and the Decree on noise protection (OJ RM, Nos 24/95, 42/2000, 25/2003). The programme of noise measurement included: intensity of noise at the crossroads locations in the cities of Montenegro; in hospitals; the background noise during the tourist season in cities of Budva and Kotor; noise level in NP.[723]

655. Values of measurement on the location of crossroads in the inhabited places in Montenegro are mostly exceeding highest permitted level. Measurements near hospitals show that the noise level is below the maximum allowed values in the case of hospitals in cities of Pljevlja, Bijelo Polje and Risan.[724] In NP, the results are significantly exceeding the highest allowed level because of the influence of natural factors (birds, wind).[725]

656. There are no specific characteristics of noise in the Coastal Zone if compared to the noise in other areas. However, increasing noise particularly in tourist complexes in the Zone, especially near the Adriatic highway, is evident. A special case is city of Tivat, where negative impact is generated by road traffic and aeroplane noise coming from the nearby airport.[726]

657. In the implementation of noise monitoring in Montenegro in 2011, the emphasis was put on examining traffic noise as one of the biggest causes of increasing levels of environmental noise. In this programme in the process of determining the level of noise, there have been included urban areas in the vicinity of the public interest, such as schools, kindergartens, hospitals and hotels, as well as near the traffic counter and on the beaches. The examinations showed a high percentage of exceeding a limit level, especially during night time. In all municipalities in the measurement sites located in the vicinity of hospitals, the allowable limits were exceeded.[727]

---

722. MEPP (2006) (assessment of the state of noise in Montenegro in 2005).
723. CETI (2006).
724. Relatively low values of noise in these locations can be explained by the fact that hospital buildings are situated far from the roads in these cities, with the data significantly exceeding the highest allowable level in the case of the Clinical Hospital Centre in city of Podgorica, because it is in the vicinity of frequent traffic.
725. Maximum value was registered in the case of NP Durmitor in the summer period.
726. GMNE (2007D), 70.
727. EPA (2012b), 44. The planned number and frequency of measurements are not yet sufficient to determine the actual noise level for the period – day, evening or night in some locations. This is especially true for the night period, as after midnight, the frequency of cars and noise levels is significantly lower than before midnight.

§2. Competencies

658. The MESPU and NEPA conduct administrative activities concerning, *inter alia*, 'the protection from noise', as prescribed by Articles 12, and 39 of the Decree on state administration organization and operations (OJ MNE, Nos 49/22, 52/22, 56/22, 82/22).[728]

659. Municipalities regulate streets, parts of streets and districts, squares and other locations for performing public meetings, parties and sport events, as well as other activities in open air or in closed space, which can lead to exceeding limited noise level (Article 22 of the Law on Environmental Noise Protection).

§3. Legislation

I. Law on Environmental Noise Protection

660. Basic legal act regulating noise protection in the environment in Montenegro is the Law on Environmental Noise Protection (OJ MNE, Nos 28/11, 01/14, 2/18). It has the following eight parts: Part I – General Provisions (Articles 1–4), Part II – Management of noise in the environment (Articles 5–10), Part III – Strategic noise maps[729] and action plans (Articles 11–18), Part IV – Measures for noise protection in the environment (Articles 19–22), Part V – Reporting to the EC (Articles 23–24), Part VI – Supervision (Articles 25–29), Part VII – Penalty Provisions (Articles 30–31) and Part VIII – Transitional and final provisions (Articles 32–37).

661. According to Article 1, the Law on Environmental Noise Protection determines measures for prevention or minimization of the adverse impact[730] of noise in the environment, as well as other issues of importance for the protection of the environment and human health from the impact of noise.

662. This law applies to the noise in the environment,[731] particularly in built areas, city parks and other quiet areas in agglomerations,[732] quiet areas in the countryside, near schools, hospitals and other facilities where populations, especially vulnerable groups (children, elderly, sick people, etc.), are exposed to the harmful

728. *See also* Arts 26–29 of the Law on Environmental Noise Protection. Inspection supervision affairs within the competence of the MHLSW are performed by the Sanitary Inspector, and within the competence of the local administration body Communal Inspector performs inspection supervision affairs.

729. *Strategic noise map* is a map made in order to examine the overall level of noise from various sources that the population is exposed on a certain area (Art. 4, point 17).

730. *Adverse impact of noise* is the negative impact of noise on human health (Art. 4, point 2).

731. *Noise in the environment* is unpleasant or harmful outdoor sound caused by human activity, including noise coming from road, railway and air traffic, as well as from industrial plants for which the integrated permit is issued (Art. 4, point 1).

732. *Agglomeration* is part of the territory, i.e., urbanized area with a population over 100,000 (Art. 4, point 10).

effects of noise (Article 2, paragraph 1). This law does not apply to noise that occurs indoors: at workplace, in transportation, in the household or noise from a neighbouring household, the noise that comes from military activities in the camp area, a military airport, a military vessel, or in barracks, military building or other military facilities, from the activities for the protection of natural disasters, natural and other accidents, as well as on the noise exposed on those who created it (Article 2, paragraph 2).

A. *The Sources of Environmental Noise and Protection from the Noise*

663. Noise source is any emitter of unwanted or harmful sound (machinery, appliance, installation, facility and means for work and transport, technological process, electro-acoustic and acoustic device for loud playing of music and speech, etc.) (Article 3, paragraph 1). As largest sources of environmental noise are considered: road, railway and air transport, including transportation and infrastructure, industrial facilities and equipment, labour and construction machines and other machinery and equipment used outdoors (Article 3, paragraph 2).

664. State governmental bodies, local governmental bodies, legal entities, companies, entrepreneurs and citizens are obliged to provide noise protection in accordance with this Law (Article 5, paragraph 1). State and local planning documents must contain the terms and noise protection measures (Article 5, paragraph 2). Companies, legal entities and entrepreneurs in carrying out activities which affect or might affect the excess of prescribed levels of noise limit values in the environment are required to provide (Article 5, paragraph 3): application of technical measures for the prevention or reducing of environmental noise, monitoring the impact of activities on the level of environmental noise and other protective measures in accordance with this Law and with other regulations.

B. *Acoustical Zoning and Limited Values*[733] *of Noise Levels in the Environment*

665. The responsible local authority is obliged to perform acoustic zoning for determining the acoustic zones of its territory in order to protect people from noise (Article 6, paragraph 1).[734] Acoustical zoning shall be based on documentation of existing or planned purpose of space and on the base of the noise level estimated in accordance with the noise sources located in a particular area and its immediate

733. *Limit noise value* is the highest possible value of environmental noise expressed by indicators L_{den} or L_{night} or L_{day} and $L_{evening}$ (Art. 4, point 18).
734. A fine of EUR 30 to EUR 2,000 shall be imposed on the responsible person in the competent local authorities, if they do not perform acoustic zoning in its territory within one year from the date of prescription of regulations referred to in Art. 7 para. 3 of this Law (Art. 31, para. 1 and Art. 33, para. 1).

vicinity (Article 6, paragraph 2).[735] Making noise above the prescribed limit values in the acoustic zones referred to in paragraph 1 of this article is prohibited (Article 6, paragraph 3). The noise from electro-acoustic and acoustic devices in open spaces from restaurants and the noise from construction work and other outdoor activities shall not exceed the prescribed limit values of noise levels in certain acoustic zones (Article 6, paragraph 4). The use of electro-acoustic and acoustic devices in open spaces and from restaurants is allowed in the period from nine to twenty-four hours, provided that it does not exceed the prescribed limit values of noise levels (Article 6, paragraph 5).

666. It is prohibited to cause noise in the environment above the prescribed limit values (Article 7, paragraph 2). The limit values of noise levels are expressed by a noise indicator[736] in accordance with this Law (Article 7, paragraph 1). The limit values of noise and the method of determining noise indicators in the environment and the acoustic zones in accordance with the purpose of open space, and assessment methods of harmful effects of noise, are prescribed by the state administration responsible for environmental protection (hereinafter 'Ministry') (Article 7, paragraph 3).

C. *Indicators of Noise*

667. Noise indicators are used to determine the level of noise in the environment, for the assessment and prediction of noise level and its impact on the environment, development of strategic noise maps[737] and for planning measures for noise protection (Article 8, paragraph 1).

668. Indicators L_{den}[738] and L_{night}[739] are used for preparation of strategic noise maps, while for the acoustic planning and zoning can be used additional indicators ($L_{day,}$[740] $L_{evening}$)[741] and prescribed noise limit values (Article 8, paragraph 2). The values of indicators L_{den} and L_{night} shall be determined by the prescribed methods

735. The responsible local authority is obliged to submit to the authority responsible for environmental protection (hereinafter 'the Agency') information about certain acoustic zones within one month from the date of determination of the acoustic zones (Art. 6, para. 6).

736. *Noise indicator* expresses a level of the noise in the environment compared to the adverse impact (Art. 4, point 4).

737. *Preparation of strategic noise maps* is presentation of data on existing or projected noise levels by determined indicators, including exceeding of prescribed limit values, the number of people exposed to the noise in an area or number of households exposed to certain values of a noise indicators in a certain area (Art. 4, point 16).

738. L_{den} is an overall indicator of the noise level during the day, evening and night (Art. 4, point 6).

739. L_{night} is an indicator of night noise level and is related to the period of time from 11 PM to 7 AM (Art. 4, point 9).

740. L_{day} s the indicator of daily noise level and is related to the period of time from 7 AP to 7 PM (Art. 4, point 7).

741. $L_{evening}$ is a noise level indicator during the evening and is related to the period of time from 7 PM to 11 PM. (Art. 4, point 8).

of calculation and measurement of noise levels (Article 8, paragraph 3). Only methods of calculation are used for the prediction of noise levels in the environment (Article 8, paragraph 4). Methods of calculating and measuring the noise level and content of report on calculating or measuring the noise in the environment are specified by the Ministry (Article 8, paragraph 5).

D. Monitoring of Environmental Noise

669. Monitoring of noise levels in the environment is based on the annual programme of noise monitoring (hereinafter referred to as 'Programme monitoring') adopted by the GMNE at the proposal of the Agency (Article 9, paragraph 1).[742] The monitoring programme shall be adopted by the end of the year for next year. It makes an integral part of the Programme for the environmental assessment (Article 9, paragraph 2).

670. The Agency is in charge for implementation of the monitoring programme (Article 9, paragraph 3). Based on the results determined by conducting the monitoring programme, the Agency constitutes information on the noise in the environment, which makes an integral part of the information on the state of the environment (Article 9, paragraph 4).

671. The local government unit may, in accordance with the Law, organize monitoring of noise levels (noise monitoring) on its territory (Article 9, paragraph 5). The local authority submits to the Agency monitoring data determined under paragraph 5 of this Article (Article 9, paragraph 6).[743]

E. Professional Activities in Noise Protection

672. Measuring the environmental noise level may be conducted by domestic and foreign legal entities and entrepreneurs, based on permits issued by the Agency (Article 10, paragraph 1). The permit may be issued to domestic or foreign legal entity or entrepreneur registered at the authority responsible for the registration of legal entities, i.e., in the appropriate register, at the competent authority of the home state of a foreign legal entity or entrepreneurs, accredited in accordance to the standards of MEST ISO/IEC 17025 (Article 10, paragraph 3).

673. Development of strategic maps and calculation of the noise level can be performed by domestic and foreign legal entities and entrepreneurs, based on permit issued by the Agency (Article 10, paragraph 4). The permit may be issued to

742. Funds for monitoring programme implementation referred to in para. 1 of this Article shall be provided from the budget of Montenegro (Art. 9, para. 7).

743. Funds for monitoring programme implementation on local self-government territory shall be provided from the budget of local governments (Art. 9, para. 8).

domestic or foreign legal entities or entrepreneurs registered at the authority responsible for the registration of legal entities, i.e., at the appropriate register of the competent authority of home state of foreign legal persons or entrepreneurs, accredited under the standards of MEST ISO/IEC 17020 (Article 10, paragraph 6).[744]

F. Strategic Noise Maps

674. Strategic noise maps are made for agglomerations, main roads,[745] main railway[746] and main airport[747] (Article 11, paragraph 1).[748] Strategic noise maps referred to in Article 11 paragraph 1 of this Law relating to the areas near the borders are drafted in cooperation with the competent authorities of neighbouring countries (Article 12, paragraph 1).

675. Development of strategic noise maps for agglomeration provides local authority in its territory (Article 11, paragraph 2). For main roads, main railway and the main airport, operated by a concessionaire, the preparation of strategic noise maps is done by the concessionaire (Article 11, paragraph 3).[749] Strategic noise maps are reviewed and, if necessary, revised every fifth year (Article 11, paragraph 5).[750]

676. Strategic noise maps prepared by local governments or Concessionaire shall be submitted electronically to the Agency (Article 13, paragraph 1), together with used input data and metadata,[751] for the purpose of entering data into the environmental information system (Article 13, paragraph 2).[752]

---

744. Report on performed measurements, i.e., calculation shall be made in accordance with the provisions of Art. 8, para. 5 of this Law (Art. 10, para. 7).
745. *Main road* is the road with the average annual flow of traffic exceeding three million units (Art. 4, point 13).
746. *Main railway* is the railway with the average annual flow of traffic greater than 30,000 trains (Art. 4, point 14).
747. *Main airport* is an airport with more than 50,000 take-off or landings per year, excluding the airport for training (Art. 4, point 15).
748. Strategic noise maps for agglomerations, main roads, main railway and the main airport will be prepared no later than 30 Jun. 2017 year (Art. 34, para. 1).
749. For main roads, main railway and the main airport, operated by the state, preparation of strategic noise maps provides the Agency in cooperation with state authorities in charge for traffic (Art. 11, para. 4).
750. The development and detailed content of strategic noise maps are prescribed by the Ministry, with the prior opinion of the state administration in charge for traffic (Art. 11, para. 6).
751. *Metadata* information to describe, explain and locate data for strategic noise maps and which allows easier data management (Art. 4, point 25).
752. Data of noise levels in the environment and the strategic noise maps are published on the Agency website (Art. 15, para. 1).

677. Strategic noise maps are used for the preparation of action plans[753] against noise in the environment (hereinafter referred to as 'an action plan'), reports on the noise level in the environment under Article 23 of this Law and for informing the public (Article 14, paragraph 2). The data from strategic noise maps are the basis for producing national and local planning documents and project-technical documentation (Article 14, paragraph 3).

678. Legal entities and entrepreneurs in charge of measuring noise levels in the environment, making strategic maps and calculation of noise levels are required to harmonize their business with this Law within two years from the date of entry into force of this Law (Article 35, paragraph 1).[754]

G. Action Plan

679. Action plans are made based on strategic noise maps for main roads, main railway, main airport and agglomerations (Article 16, paragraph 1). Action plans for main roads, main railway and main airport are developed by the Government (Article 16, paragraph 2) and are prepared by the state administration responsible for traffic, with the prior obtaining opinion of the Ministry (Article 16, paragraph 3). The local government unit on its territory develops Action plan for the agglomeration (Article 16, paragraph 4).[755] Action plans from paragraphs 2 and 4 of this Article related to the border areas are prepared by the state administration authority in charge of Transportation and the Ministry, i.e., local government unit, in cooperation with the Ministry and with the competent authorities of neighbouring countries (Article 16, paragraph 5). Action plans from paragraphs 2 and 4 of this Article shall be adopted for a period of five years (Article 16, paragraph 6).[756]

H. Public Discussion

680. The authorities responsible for the preparation of action plans from Article 16 of this Law shall inform authorities, organizations and the interested public about the manner and terms of insight into the draft action plans, delivering of opinions,

753. *Action Plan* is a plan that includes measures for protection against noise and its effects in the environment, as well as measures to reduce noise in case of exceeding the limit values (Art. 4, point 20).
754. Legal entities and entrepreneurs, using noise sources for which there is no data on emitting noise values, are required to harmonize noise sources with this Law, within three years from the date of entry into force of this Law (Art. 35, para. 2).
755. Funds for the development and implementation of action plans referred to in para. 2 of this Article shall be provided from the budget of Montenegro, while means for the implementation of action plans referred to in para. 4 of this Article shall be provided from the budget of local governments (Art. 16, para. 8).
756. The Action Plan can be revised before the expiration of the period for which the document was adopted, in case of the significant changes of environmental noise level (Art. 16, para. 7). Action plans from the Art. 16 of this Law are to be adopted within two years from the date of making strategic maps referred to in para. 1 of this Article (Art. 34, para. 2).

as well as about time and place of the public discussion[757] through the media (Article 18, paragraph 1). A public discussion has to be conducted by the competent authority for preparation of an action plan, and the competent authority has the obligation to prepare a report on a conducted public discussion (Article 18, paragraph 3).[758]

I. The Noise Protection Measures

681. In the process of strategic impact assessment on the environment, i.e., EIA shall determine the conditions and measures to prevent, reduce and eliminate the harmful effects of noise in accordance with the Law (Article 19, paragraph 1). For facilities that are not assessed for environmental impact, the authority responsible for building permits issuing is obliged to determine in the technical documentation satisfying conditions and noise protection measures (Article 19, paragraph 2). Integrated permit[759] must contain noise protection measures in accordance with the Law (Article 19, paragraph 3).

682. In the process of determining of airworthiness of the aircraft in terms of generated noise, the authority responsible for air traffic duties is required to comply with the conditions laid down in Annex 16, Part III, Volume 1, of the Convention on International Civil Aviation (Article 20, paragraph 1).[760] During the registration and renewal of vehicle registration, state authority responsible for internal affairs may reject issuance of traffic permit if documentation on vehicle technical condition does not contain data from paragraph 2 of this Article or if it is determined that the vehicle is exceeding limited values of outside noise, i.e., malfunction of the unit for diminishing the sound (Article 20, paragraph 3).

683. The Agency gives approval in the procedure of EIA on the technical documentation for construction, reconstruction or expansion of airports on the basis of strategic noise maps and/or action plans (Article 21, paragraph 1).[761] Placing on the market and usage of permitted noise sources from paragraph 1 of this Article have to be marked by prescribed conformity signs in accordance with the technical regulation issued by the Ministry (Article 22, paragraph 2).

---

757. Public discussion may be held, the earliest, ten days from the date of notification of authorities, organizations and interested public (Art. 18, para. 2).
758. The adopted action plans are published on the website of the authority competent for adoption of the action plan (Art. 18, para. 4). The adopted action plans are submitted to the Agency for preparation of reports under Art. 23 of this Law (Art. 18, para. 5).
759. *Integrated permit* is a permit issued in accordance with the Law governing the integrated prevention and control of environmental pollution (Art. 4, point 21).
760. In the process of technical inspection of vehicles, authorized legal entity is required to determine the level of vehicle outside emitted noise and the safety of the devices to diminish the sound in the documentation technical soundness of the vehicle (Art. 20, para. 2).
761. It is forbidden to trade in and use of noise sources used for performing business (machinery, non-road machinery, appliances), recreation boats and equipment used outdoors, if their sound power exceeds the prescribed limit values (Art. 22, para. 1).

J. Supervision and Reporting

684. The monitoring of implementation of this Law shall be conducted by the Ministry and the competent local authority[762] unless otherwise prescribed by this Law (Article 25, paragraph 1). Inspection supervision of implementation of this Law and the regulations adopted on the base of this Law shall be conducted by the Agency, through the Environmental Inspector, in accordance with this Law and the Law regulating the inspection supervision (Article 25, paragraph 2).

685. The Agency prepares a report on the level of noise in the environment (hereinafter 'Report') and submits it to the Ministry (Article 23, paragraph 1), while the Ministry submits the report to the EC (Article 23, paragraph 3).[763]

II. Other Regulations

686. Following by-laws have been adopted:

- Rulebook on threshold noise levels in the environment, the manner of estimation of noise indicators and acoustic zones and methods of assessment of harmful effects of noise (OJ MNE, Nos 60/2011, 94/21).
- Rulebook on methods and instruments of measuring noise and conditions which must fulfil organization for noise measuring (OJ RM, No. 37/2003).

§4. Harmonization with EU Legislation

687. Regarding noise, 'Montenegro has fully aligned with the Noise Directive and works on the preparation of strategic noise maps'.[764] In addition, the capital city of Podgorica has started the implementation of noise monitoring programmes at eleven resident locations.[765]

762. Inspection Supervision within the jurisdiction of local government performs local governmental body in charge for communal police, in accordance with the Law (Art. 25, para. 3).
763. The report shall be made for a period of five years and includes data on the level of noise in agglomerations and noise caused by road, railway and air traffic in the areas around main roads, main railway and main airport (Art. 23, para. 2).
764. EC (2018). p. 81.
765. EC (2022). p. 113.

Chapter 7. Radiation

§1. Levels of Radiation in Montenegro

688. Only sources of radiation of low and medium degrees are used in Montenegro since the country has no nuclear reactors.[766] Law on Ionizing Radiation Protection and Safety (OJ MNE, Nos 56/09, 58/09, 40/11) in Article 17 prohibits the construction of nuclear power plants, plants for production of nuclear fuels and plants for spent nuclear fuel processing. The same Law in Article 19 prohibits all research and activities with an aim to develop, manufacture and use nuclear weapons, as well as to use radioactive and nuclear material for production of weapons of mass destruction.[767]

689. Measurements of contamination with radioactive pollutants are regularly conducted, by a network of measuring stations, established by the Decision on Systematic Examination of Contents of Radionuclide in Environment (OJ FRY, No. 45/1997). Besides that, the preparation of a radon map for Montenegro is being carried out by the CETI under the initiative of the Ministry of Tourism and Environmental Protection (MTEP).[768] According to the relevant data collected by the CETI radioactive burden of inhabitants, as the consequence of the exposure to radon, is at the level of the European average. The existence of the natural and long-lasting artificial radio nuclides is at low level, that is, far below maximum allowed quantity, so it could be concluded that the state of environment, concerning radioactive safety, is satisfactory in Montenegro.[769]

690. Monitoring programme for environmental radioactivity in Montenegro that is required by Article 35 of the Euratom Treaty does not fully comply with it. Only the absorbed gamma radiation dose rate in the air is continuously being measured, while it is not measured in water or soil. The problem is lack of equipment necessary for the implementation of continuous monitoring. … Online network of radioactivity dose rate measuring stations does not exist in Montenegro. One site for online measuring of the absorbed dose rate is located in Podgorica, within the Public Institution 'Centre for Ecotoxicological Research of Montenegro ….'[770]

---

766. The Energy Development Strategy does not envisage construction of nuclear facilities by 2025. MED (2007), 63.
767. 'The Government of Montenegro has no plans regarding nuclear energy, including the financial aspect.' GMNE, ME (2009), 114.
768. In order to detect and report on radioactive contamination of the environment as a result of transboundary transport, the Hydrometeorological Institute measures the absorbed dose of gamma radiation in the air in Žabljak and Herceg Novi. Measurements are taken periodically using methods prescribed by the Rulebook on Network Determination and the Programme on the Performance of Meteorological Stations of National Interest (Official Journal of SFRY, No. 50/1990), and the authorized bodies are informed accordingly. UNECE (2007), 32.
769. MTEP (2008a), 11–13. For more details *see also* CETI (2008b); GMNE (2008C). 93.
770. GMNE, ME, 48.

691. Montenegro has no capacity for disposal of spent fuel and radioactive waste.[771] There is temporary storage for radioactive waste, managed by the CETI. International Atomic Energy Agency (IAEA) supported establishment of this storage by providing the required equipment.[772]

692. There are no reliable data on contamination levels resulting from natural and artificial nuclides in the region of Coastal area. Nevertheless, during the last few years detailed measurements of beta-activity and its spectrometry have been performed (the experts of the Hydromet and Moscow University have been in charge of this research, on behalf of the MTEP).[773]

§2. Competencies

693. Regulatory jurisdiction in the field of protection from ionizing radiation is, according to the Decree on state administration organization and operations (OJ MNE, Nos 49/22, 52/22, 56/22, 82/22), shared between the MESPU and NEPA (Articles 12 and 39).

694. Control of radioactive material trade is performed through Environmental Inspection. In addition, the Environmental Inspection controls the fulfilment of the conditions under which the licence was issued. In addition, the internal transport of radioactive material is regulated by Law on the Transport of Dangerous Goods (2008). While the trade of radioactive material is defined within national legislation/regulation, the trade of nuclear materials in the territory of Montenegro is prohibited by the Law on Protection against Ionizing Radiation and Radiation Safety.[774] In the control of goods radioactivity and preventing illegal trafficking of radioactive and nuclear materials, apart from Environmental Inspection, an important role is played by the Customs Administration and Directorate of Police.

695. Ministry of Interior and Public Administration is competent in the case of accident that can cause a state of emergency in the country.[775]

696. The Centre for Ecotoxicological Testing of Montenegro (CETI), University of Montenegro, Faculty of Natural Science and Mathematics and Institute for

771. GMNE, ME (2009), 119.
772. GMNE (2008b), 318.
773. According to this research, the Littoral is one of the cleanest areas in Montenegro with respect to the level of radioactivity. Besides that, the Herceg Novi Monitoring Station is included in the Mediterranean pollution monitoring and research programme dealing with pollution from land-based sources (MEDPOL). The levels of gamma radiation exponential dosage have been within the usual natural radiation thresholds for air and precipitations. GMNE (2007D), 69.
774. Permanent Mission of Montenegro to the UN, OSCE and other International Organizations in Vienna (2012), 11.
775. GMNE, ME (2009), 117.

Ferrous Metallurgy are providing necessary technical support services as well as expertise to assist the EPA.

§3. Legislation: Ionizing Radiation

I. International Treaties

697. Montenegro is, through the succession, a contracting party of the following international treaties: Vienna Convention on Civil Liability for Nuclear Damage, 1963, Convention on Physical Protection of Nuclear Material, 1979,[776] Convention on Assistance in the Case of Nuclear Accident or Radiology Emergency, Vienna, 26 September 1986, Convention on Early Notification of a Nuclear Accident, 1986, and Technical Assistance Agreement signed in 1983.

698. In 2006, Montenegro accepted also following international agreements: Treaty Banning Nuclear Weapon Tests in the Atmosphere, in Outer Space and Under Water of 5 August 1963, Treaty on Non-Proliferation of Nuclear Weapons, 1 July 1968, Treaty on the Prohibition of the Emplacement of Nuclear Weapons and Other Weapons of Mass Destruction on the Sea-Bed and the Ocean Floor and in the Subsoil Thereof, London, Moscow, Washington of 11 February 1971, Treaty on the Prohibition of the Emplacement of Nuclear Weapons and Other Weapons of Mass Destruction on the Sea-Bed and the Ocean Floor and in the Subsoil Thereof of 11 February 1971, and Treaty Banning Nuclear Weapon Tests in the Atmosphere, in Outer Space and Under Water, Moscow, of 5 August 1963.

699. Moreover, Montenegro ratified following international treaties: Joint Convention on Safety of Spent Fuel Management and on Safety of Radioactive Waste (OJ MNE – International Treaties, No. 3/1010), the Protocol to Amend the Vienna Convention on Civil Liability for Nuclear Damage (OJ MNE – International Treaties, No. 16/2010) and the Convention on Supplementary Compensation for Nuclear Damage (1997) (OJ MNE – International Treaties, No. 3/2011). 'At the same time, Montenegro still does not participate in some binding and non-binding instruments that belong to the nuclear safety and security regimes: Convention on Nuclear Safety (planned in 2014), Code of Conduct on the Safety and Security of Radioactive Sources, Supplementary Guidance on the Import and Export of Radioactive Sources'.[777]

700. The Agreement on the implementation of protection measures in relation to the Treaty on Non-proliferation of Nuclear Weapon between Montenegro and

776. The amendments to the Convention on the Physical Protection of Nuclear Material were ratified in 2016 (OJ MNE – IT, No. 4/16).
777. Permanent Mission of Montenegro to the UN, OSCE and other International Organizations in Vienna (2012), 11.

International Atomic Energy Agency has been ratified (OJ MNE – International Treaties, No. 16/2010.[778]

II. National Legislation

701. In the Law on Environment (OJ MNE, No. 52/16, 73/19), radiation has mentioned in Article 26 (Protection against ionizing radiation), and in Article 67 (Environmental information). The Law on ionizing radiation protection and radiation safety (OJ MNE, Nos 56/09, 58/09, 40/11, 55/16) has been adopted. This Law stipulates, *inter alia*, the adoption of Strategy for Protection against Ionizing Radiation, Radiation Safety and Radioactive Waste Management.[779]

A. The Law on Protection from Ionizing Radiation and Radiation Safety

702. Basic legal act regulating ionizing radiation[780] protection and radiation safety in Montenegro is the Law on protection from ionizing radiation and radiation safety (OJ MNE, Nos 56/09, 58/09, 40/11, and 55/16).[781] It has the following ten parts: Part I – General Provisions (Articles 1–5), Part II – Protection against ionizing radiation (Articles 6–16), Part III – Bans (Articles 17–19), Part IV – Performing radiation activity (Articles 20–33), Part V – Actions taken in case of radiation accident (Articles 34–36), Part VI – Radioactive waste management (Articles 37–40), Part VII – Trade in ionizing radiation sources and radioactive materials (Articles 41–46), Part VIII – Supervision (Articles 47–48), Part IX – Penalties (Article 49) and Part X – Transitional and final provisions (Articles 50–55).

703. According to Article 1, this Law regulates[782] protection of human life and health as well as protection of the environment against harmful effects of ionizing radiation, performing radiation activities, trade of ionizing radiation sources and

778. Montenegro submitted its application for membership in the International Atomic Energy Agency on 14 Jun. 2006 and became a member on 30 Oct. 2006. The Country Programme Framework for the period 2009–2013, as the key document for defining priorities of a country in cooperation with the International Atomic Energy Agency, is in preparatory phase. GMNE (2008b), 328.

779. For more details *see*: MSDT, Strategy for Protection against Ionizing Radiation, Radiation Safety and Radioactive Waste Management for 2017–2021 with Action Plan. December 2016.

780. *Ionizing radiation* is electromagnetic or particle radiation that may produce ion pairs in biological material (Art. 5, point 13).

781. The Parliament of Montenegro adopted new Law on ionizing radiation protection and radiation safety on 27 Jul. 2009. On the day of this Law entering into force Law on Establishment of Authorities for Performing Activities in the Field of Ionizing Radiation Protection (Official Journal of SRM, No. 13/89) shall seize to have effect and Law on Ban on Construction of Nuclear Power Plants (Official Journal of FRY, No. 12/95) shall seize to apply as well as Law on Protection against Ionizing Radiation (Official Journal of FRY, No. 46/96) (Art. 54).

782. This Law does not relate to ionizing radiation of natural origin from the space on the level of ground, earth crust and human organisms, if such radiation is not altered by human action (Art. 1, para. 2).

radioactive materials,[783] radioactive waste management, actions taken in case of radiation accidents,[784] as well as other relevant issues for protection against ionizing radiation[785] and radiation safety[786] (Article 1, paragraph 1).

704. Protection against ionizing radiation and radiation safety[787] is carried out through the following objectives (Article 2, paragraph 1): preservation and protection of life and health of present and future generations; working and living environment protection; security[788] and safety of ionizing radiation sources; ensuring conditions for professional and rational usage of ionizing radiation sources; and increasing the level of knowledge and awareness in the field of ionizing radiation protection and radiation safety.

1. Objectives, Achievements and Basic Principles

705. Objectives of ionizing radiation protection and achievement of radiation safety laid down in Article 2 of this Law shall be achieved by (Article 3, paragraph 1): application of ionizing radiation in all activities for peaceful purposes; establishing a control system for ionizing radiation sources and radioactive materials; planning, monitoring,[789] rational and professional restriction of ionizing radiation source utilization; control of trade in ionizing radiation sources and radioactive materials; control of imported items and goods; ban on import of radioactive waste;[790] radioactive waste management; providing working conditions for persons professionally exposed[791] to harmful effects of ionizing radiation; providing objective and timely information to the public; and enforcement of approved international conventions and other agreements from the field of ionizing radiation protection and radiation safety.

---

783. *Radioactive material* is material containing one or more radionuclides whose total and specific activity exceeds prescribed limits (Art. 5, point 34).
784. *Radiation accident* is any unintentional or unexpected event, including human mistake, equipment failure of other irregularities whose possible consequences are not neglectable regarding ionizing radiation protection and radiation safety (Art. 5, point 32).
785. *Protection against ionizing radiation* is a group of measures for preventing harmful effects of exposure to ionizing radiation (Art. 5, point 42).
786. *Safety* encompasses measures that foresee reducing to least possible measure the probability of radiation accident including radioactive sources, and in case such an accident occurs, mitigation of its consequences (Art. 5, point 36).
787. *Radiation safety* presents a group of operating conditions, technical and organizational measures taken for prevention of radiation accidents or reducing the consequences of accidents, i.e., protection of professionally exposed persons, population and environment against radiation risk (Art. 5, point 31).
788. *Security* consists of: prevention, detection and action in case of theft, sabotage, unauthorized access, illegal trade or other malevolent activities including nuclear material, radioactive material or their facilities (Art. 5, point 4).
789. *Monitoring* is measuring of dose of contamination with the purpose of estimation or control of exposure to ionizing radiation and radioactive materials, processing and interpretation of the results (Art. 5, point 19).
790. *Radioactive waste* is radioactive material not planned for further use (Art. 5, point 35).
791. *Professionally exposed persons* are persons working with sources of ionizing radiation or, who are within the field of ionizing radiation while performing their work (Art. 5, point 25).

706. Basic principles applied when performing radiation activities are the following (Article 4, paragraph 1): (1) justifiability of application,[792] (2) optimization of ionizing radiation protection[793] and (3) limitation of individual exposure.[794]

2. Protection Against Ionizing Radiation and Competence of the EPA

707. For the purpose of providing conditions for implementation of the policy in the area of protection against ionizing radiation and radiation safety, the GMNE adopts the Strategy for Protection against Ionizing Radiation, Radiation Safety and Radioactive Waste Management,[795] with Action plan for its realization, at the proposal of the Ministry competent for the affairs of environmental protection[796] (hereinafter 'the Ministry') (Article 6, paragraph 1). Activities and measures for implementation of Strategy laid down in paragraph 1 of this Article shall be provided from the Budget of Montenegro in accordance with the Law (Article 6, paragraph 3).

708. Professional management operation in the field of protection against ionizing radiation and radiation safety shall be carried out by the administrative body competent for environmental protection (hereinafter 'the Agency') (Article 7, paragraph 1). Measures for the purpose of protection of human life and health as well as environmental protection against harmful effects of ionizing radiation are prescribed in Article 8, paragraph 1.

3. Systematic Radioactivity Level Analysis in the Environment

709. Systematic analysis of radioactivity level in the environment (hereinafter 'radioactivity monitoring')[797] shall be performed for determination of radionuclide presence in the environment and estimation of ionizing radiation exposure level of the population under normal conditions, in case of a suspected radiation accident,

792. Each radiation activity should be planned and implemented in such manner that the use of ionizing radiation sources provides more benefit than the overall damage (Art. 4, point 1).
793. Each radiation activity must be performed in such manner that the exposure to ionizing radiation shall be as low as objectively possible, considering economical and social factors (Art. 4, point 2).
794. Radiation activity must be planned in such manner that the individual exposures shall always be under prescribed limits (Art. 4, point 3).
795. This strategy determines plans and objectives regarding protection against ionizing radiation, radiation safety and radioactive waste management in accordance with standards and principles of international organization in this field, as well as undertaken international obligations (Art. 6, para. 2). *Radioactive waste management* consists of administrative and operative activities regarding handling, treatment, storage, transport and disposal of waste (Art. 5, point 39).
796. *Environmental protection* is taking measures and actions for prevention of ionizing radiation harmful effects to the environment and elimination of consequences of the radiation (Art. 5, point 43).
797. Radioactivity monitoring shall be performed in accordance with the Systematic Radioactivity Level Analysis in the Environment Programme adopted by the Government, at the proposal of the Ministry, at latest till 1 December of current year for the next year (Art. 9, para. 2). The Programme referred to in para. 2 hereof determines locations, time intervals, types and manners of systematic radioactivity level analysis in the environment (Art. 9, para. 3).

as well as during the course of a radiation accident (Article 9, paragraph 1). Allowed content of radionuclides in the environment shall be prescribed by the Ministry (Article 9, paragraph 5).

710. Costs of radioactivity monitoring activities and estimation of ionizing radiation exposure level of the population shall be covered in the Budget of Montenegro (Article 9, paragraph 4). According to the results of radioactivity monitoring referred to in Article 9 of this Law, the Agency shall monitor ionizing radiation exposure of population, order measures in case of increased radioactivity and perform evaluation of effective dose[798] at the population (Article 10, paragraph 2).

4. Exposure Limits

711. Professionally exposed persons, persons attending schools and performing scientific research and population must not be exposed to ionizing radiation above the prescribed limits (Article 12, paragraph 1). For purpose of making estimation of ionizing radiation medical exposure,[799] holder of licence for performing radiation activity referred to in Article 21 of this Law shall perform the prescribed measurements[800] (Article 13, paragraph 1).

712. The legal entity laid down in Article 32 of this Law performing measurements referred to in Articles 11 and 13 of this Law is bound to keep records on measurements and to submit the Report on the measurements to the Agency (Article 14, paragraph 1). The contents of the Reports on the measurements referred to in paragraph 1 of this Article, manner of keeping and period of saving the records, as well as procedure of informing the competent authorities shall be prescribed by the Ministry (Article 14, paragraph 2). Depending on type of business, professionally exposed persons must have prescribed professional qualifications and be trained for providing ionizing radiation safety measures (Article 15, paragraph 1).[801]

798. *Effective dose* is the sum of products of equivalent dose in the tissue or an organ of respective weight factor, throughout all exposed tissues and organs (Art. 5, point 7). *Dose equivalent* is the product of the absorbed dose in the tissue or organ and so-called quality factor reflecting biologically harmful effect caused by particular type of ionizing radiation (Art. 5, point 8).

799. *Medical exposure* is the exposure of patients and persons helping patients with medical application of ionizing radiation sources, and are not professionally exposed persons, as well as persons voluntarily included in medical research programmes with application of ionizing radiation sources (Art. 5, point 18).

800. Types, exposure limits and manner of measurement for making estimate on ionizing radiation medical exposure shall be prescribed by the Ministry, in cooperation with the Ministry competent for health-related affairs (Art. 13, para. 2).

801. For the purpose of additional training and periodic updating of knowledge in the field of ionizing radiation protection, the Ministry, in cooperation with the ministry competent for health-related affairs and ministry competent for educational affairs, adopts the Additional Training Programme and training of professionally exposed persons responsible for implementation of ionizing radiation protection measures laid down in Art. 15 of this Law (Art. 16, para. 1).

5. Bans

713. Construction of nuclear power plants, plants for production of nuclear fuel and plants for treatment of used nuclear fuel is banned (Article 17, paragraph 1). Work with ionizing radiation sources is prohibited to (Article 18, paragraph 1): (1) persons under 18 years of age; (2) women during pregnancy; (3) women while breastfeeding; and (4) work with open sources of ionizing radiation.[802]

714. Every research and activity with the aim of development, production and use of nuclear weapons as well as use of radioactive or nuclear material for production of mass destruction weapons is banned (Article 19, paragraph 1). Import of radioactive waste, as well as processing, storing and disposal of radioactive waste[803] of foreign origin in the territory of Montenegro is banned (Article 19, paragraph 2). Trade of nuclear material on the territory of Montenegro is banned (Article 19, paragraph 3). Installation of radioactive lightning rods on the territory of Montenegro is banned (Article 19, paragraph 4). Installation of ionizing smoke detectors having a source of ionizing radiation in the gaseous state or ionizing radiation source whose break-up products in gaseous state are banned (Article 19, paragraph 5). Adding radioactive substances in food, drinking water, medicines, tobacco and tobacco products, toys, jewellery, cosmetics, toiletries, construction material, animal fodder, ores, primary form metal products, mineral raw materials and consumer goods, as well as import, export and release of such products is banned (Article 19, paragraph 6).

6. Performing of Radiation Activity

715. Any user owning an ionizing radiation source with low radiation risk[804] is bound to inform the Agency about it and obtain a Certificate of Registration from the Agency (Article 20, paragraph 1).

716. Radiation activity may be performed exclusively by users of ionizing radiation sources possessing Radiation Activity Licence issued by the Agency (Article 21, paragraph 1). The holder of licence for performing radiation activity is obliged to keep records on ionizing radiation sources, on professionally exposed persons, as well as on radioactive waste (Article 26, paragraph 1).[805]

---

802. *Open source* of ionizing radiation is such ionizing radiation source that is not a sealed source of ionizing radiation, and can be in solid, liquid or gaseous state (Art. 5, point 24). *Sealed source* of ionizing radiation is an ionizing radiation source sealed by impermeable coating of non-radioactive material (encapsulated) so that the radioactive material cannot get in contact with the environment (Art. 5, point 41).

803. *Radioactive waste disposal* is permanent disposing of radioactive waste (Art. 5, point 22).

804. *Radiation risk* is the probability of causing harmful effect to the health of an individual or a group of people and environment due to exposure to ionizing radiation (Art. 5, point 30).

805. The holder of licence for performing radiation activity in medical purposes is obliged to, besides keeping records referred to in para. 1 of this Article, to keep evidence on patients' exposure to ionizing radiation (Art. 26, para. 2).

717. The holder of licence for performing radiation activity[806] referred to in Article 21 of this Law is bound to perform the prescribed measurements[807] for purpose of making an estimate of the level of ionizing radiation exposure of professionally exposed persons, persons attending schools and performing scientific research, patients and inhabitants (Article 11, paragraph 1).

7. Quality Control[808] and Decontamination

718. The holder of licence for performing radiation activity is obliged to establish and implement Programme for quality security and control of measures for ionizing radiation protection (Article 27, paragraph 1). In case a holder of licence for performing radiation activity causes contamination,[809] he is obliged to inform the Agency immediately and to implement decontamination[810] engaging the legal entity for performing decontamination laid down in Article 32 of this Law and bear the expenses of such decontamination procedure (Article 28, paragraph 1). The Agency shall inform professionally exposed persons and public about possible harmful consequences of contamination (Article 28, paragraph 3). Manner of carrying out decontamination as well as requirements that must be satisfied by legal entities performing decontamination shall be prescribed by the Ministry (Article 28, paragraph 4).

8. Limitations in Use of Ionizing Radiation in Medical Purposes and Protection Level

719. Ionizing radiation sources may be used for medical purposes in prescribed manner if a medical doctor of appropriate specialization performs estimation of medical justifiability of their use and approve the diagnostic or therapeutic procedure (Article 29, paragraph 1).[811]

---

806. *Holder of licence for performing radiation activity* may be a company, any other legal entity or entrepreneur, holding the radiation activity licence (Art. 5, point 20). *Radiation activity* is each human activity dealing with ionizing radiation sources that may lead to increase of ionizing radiation exposure level or increase the number of people exposed to ionizing radiation (Art. 5, point 29).
807. Costs of measurements for purpose of ionizing radiation exposure level estimation referred to in para. 1 of this Article shall be covered by the holder of licence for performing radiation activity (Art. 11, para. 2).
808. *Quality control* is technical–technological control of system structure and components corresponding to requests previously determined by quality security programme (Art. 5, point 14).
809. *Contamination* is an unplanned and undesired presence of radioactive material, as well as process leading to its presence on surfaces or inside solid, liquid or gaseous bodies (including human organism) above the prescribed limits (Art. 5, point 14).
810. *Decontamination* is removal or reduction of contamination level by physical, chemical and biological processes (Art. 5, point 6).
811. Conditions for use of ionizing radiation sources in medical purposes as well as protection measures for the patients during medical exposure for implementation of diagnostic or therapeutic procedure shall be prescribed by the Ministry, in cooperation with the ministry authorized for health-related affairs.

720. The holder of licence for performing radiation activity is obliged to provide such protection level that will prevent exposure above the limits prescribed for population (Article 30, paragraph 1).

9. Role of Legal Entities

721. A legal entity or entrepreneur performing such technical-technological procedures that increase natural radionuclide[812] concentration above the prescribed limits is obliged to keep records thereof and submit these records to the Agency annually (Article 31, paragraph 1).[813] Contents and time limits for submission of evidence referred to in paragraph 1 of this Article shall be prescribed by the Ministry (Article 31, paragraph 4). The costs for implementation of ionizing radiation protection measures shall be borne by the legal entity or entrepreneur referred to in paragraph 1 of this Article (Article 31, paragraph 5).

722. All the testing, measurements, control and other expert activities laid down in Articles 9, 11, 13, 27, 28 and 44 of this Law can be performed by legal entity holding the licence for performing ionizing radiation protection[814] (Article 32, paragraph 1).

10. Actions Taken in Case of Radiation Accident

723. Any person, who finds out about possible danger of increased ionizing radiation exposure to population and environment, is obliged, without postponing, to inform the Ministry authorized for emergency situation and civilian safety, the Agency and other authorities (Article 34, paragraph 1). A legal entity or entrepreneur responsible for radiation accident is obliged, without postponing, to organize and carry out foreseen measures and procedures in case of an accident, as well as to mobilize people and means (Article 34, paragraph 2).

724. For the purpose of timely discovery of radiation accidents that may produce a state of emergency, and puts in danger or may endanger people's health and life as well as the environment, the Ministry authorized for emergency situations and civilian safety shall establish the system of early warning, ensuring continuous measurement of gamma radiation ambient dose[815] rate in the air (Article 35, paragraph 1). According to the National Strategy for states of emergency, the Ministry

---

812. *Natural radionuclides* are radionuclides occurring in nature in significant quantities, i.e., not produced by human activity (uranium-235, uranium-238, thorium-232, potassium-40 and products of their degradation) (Art. 5, point 26).
813. The Agency shall define the list of legal entities and entrepreneurs referred to in para. 1 of this Article (Art. 31, para. 2).
814. The licence shall be issued in the form of decision and shall be published in the 'Official Journal of Montenegro' (Art. 33, para. 1).
815. *Dose* is deposited energy of ionizing radiation within a facility (Art. 5, point 5).

authorized for emergency situations and civilian safety, in cooperation with competent authorities, shall issue the National Action Plan for actions taken in the event of such radiation accident that may cause a state of emergency (Article 35, paragraph 2).[816]

11. Radioactive Waste Management

725. The holder of licence for performing radiation activities is obliged to collect, store, treat, record and dispose radioactive waste in the prescribed manner and under prescribed conditions, till its delivery to the legal entity laid down in Article 38 of this Law (Article 37, paragraph 1).[817]

726. Radioactive waste, till establishing conditions for its disposal, shall be stored with a legal entity holding the licence for radioactive waste storage[818] management (Article 38, paragraph 1).[819] The legal entity referred to in paragraph 1 of this Article is obliged to submit to the Agency the request for issuing the licence (Article 38, paragraph 2).

727. It is not allowed: to import, own and use such radiation sources that after expiry of exploitation time present highly radioactive waste unless an indisputable evidence is obtained that the source after the expiry of the time shall be returned to the supplier outside Montenegro or shall abandon Montenegro in some other way (Article 40).

---

816. 'Ministry of Interior and Public Administration – Department for Emergency Situations and Civil Security, as authority competent for protection and rescue, in accordance with Article 37 of the Law on protection and rescue (Official Journal of MNE, No. 13/07 and 5/08) paragraph 1 indent 2 … and upon the recommendation of the International Atomic Energy Agency (IAEA), started activities on development of National Action Plan for nuclear/radiological (radiation accidents), chemicals and biological protection (CBRN) during 2009, as very important document for security of citizens and protection of material goods and environment.' GMNE, ME (2009), 116.
817. The holder of the licence is obliged to: (1) assure that the radioactive waste developed during the radiation activity is the least possible regarding activity and volume; (2) assure that facilities and rooms where radioactive waste is collected, kept, recorded and stored conform with technical, safety and other prescribed conditions providing ionizing radiation protection to people and the environment; (3) take measures for prevention of radioactive waste causing environmental contamination; (4) provide stored radioactive waste; (5) apply protection measures for radioactive waste management in Montenegro respecting internationally acknowledged criteria, standards and guidelines (Art. 37, para. 2).
818. *Radioactive waste storage* is storing of radioactive waste at a place under supervision of an authorized legal entity (Art. 5, point 37).
819. The licence holder referred to in para. 1 of this Article is obliged to keep records on radioactive waste and to submit data from these records to the Agency within time limits and in manner prescribed by the Agency (Art. 38, para. 5). The expenses of maintaining the storage referred to in para. 1 of this Article shall be covered from the Budget of Montenegro (Art. 38, para. 6).

12. Trade in Ionizing Radiation Sources[820] and Radioactive Materials

728. Trade in ionizing radiation sources and radioactive materials may be performed by such legal entity or entrepreneur to whom the Agency issues the licence for trade in ionizing radiation sources and radioactive materials (Article 41, paragraph 1).[821]

729. The Agency shall issue the licence to a legal entity or entrepreneur trading in ionizing radiation and radioactive materials if measures prescribed by this Law are taken, and if such trade is performed in accordance with acknowledged international conventions (Article 42, paragraph 1).[822]

730. The Agency shall issue the licence to a legal entity or entrepreneur performing export of ionizing radiation sources and radioactive materials only if the importer obtains approval for such import from the competent authority of the state into which such export is performed (Article 43, paragraph 1).[823]

13. Radioactivity Control of Goods and Administrative Supervision

731. Drinking water, food, animal fodder, medicines, tobacco and tobacco products, cosmetics, toiletries and other general use products, as well as construction

820. *Ionizing radiation sources* are substances, equipment or facilities emitting or able to emit ionizing radiation (Art. 5, point 12).
821. The legal person or entrepreneur is obliged to submit to the Agency a request for issuing licence to perform trade in ionizing radiation sources and radioactive materials. Based on meeting the prescribed requirements, the Agency shall issue the licence. The licence shall be issued by decision, within thirty days from the day of submittal of the request for licence issuing.
822. The Agency shall issue the Licence for trade in ionizing radiation sources and radioactive materials to a legal person or entrepreneur if: (1) facilities and rooms where trading in ionizing radiation sources or radioactive material is performed comply with technical, security and safety, sanitary and other prescribed requirements ensuring health protection of people and the environment against ionizing radiation; (2) there is an employee in charge with protection against ionizing radiation; (3) persons operating ionizing radiation sources are provided with adequate ionizing radiation means of protection, as well as equipment for radiation measurements; (4) all persons operating ionizing radiation sources are provided with prescribed professional qualification and satisfy prescribed health requirements for work with ionizing radiation sources; (5) certificate on technical/technological integrity of ionizing radiation source is obtained by the competent authority; (6) there is an Instruction for action in case of radiation accident; (7) radioactive materials, X-ray devices or other devices producing ionizing radiation are secured in accordance with prescribed requirements for their trading.
823. Trading in ionizing radiation sources and radioactive materials may be performed solely across such border crossings where inspection monitoring is organized. The importer of ionizing radiation sources and radioactive material is obliged to inform the Agency about arrival of goods at the border-crossing within time period not shorter than five days and not longer than sixty days from the day of receipt of the goods (Art. 43 paras 3, 4).

materials, ores, metal products, raw materials and other goods should not be marketed if they contain radionuclide content exceeding prescribed limits (Article 44, paragraph 1).[824]

732. Supervision over implementation of this Law and of regulations adopted based on this Law shall be performed by the Ministry unless differently regulated by this Law (Article 47, paragraph 1).[825]

B. Other Relevant Regulations[826]

733. The following by-laws have been enacted relating to the protection against radioactive radiation:

- Rulebook on methods of application of sources of ionizing radiation in medicine (OJ FRY, Nos 32/98 and 33/98).
- Rulebook on conditions to be fulfilled by legal persons for performing systematic investigations of radionuclide contents in the environment (OJ FRY, Nos 32/98, 67/02 and 70/02).
- Rulebook on limits of exposure to ionizing radiation (OJ FRJ, No. 32/98).
- Rulebook on limit values for exposure to ionizing radiation (OJ FRY, No. 32/98).
- Rulebook on conditions for putting in circulation food supplies and objects of general use that are preserved by ionizing radiation (OJ FRY, No. 42/98).
- Rulebook on limit values of radioactive contamination of the environment and on method of performing decontamination (OJ FRY, No. 9/99 and OJ SRM, No. 1/2003).
- Rulebook on conditions to be fulfilled by legal persons for performing decontamination (OJ FRY, No. 9/99 and OJ SRM, No. 1/2003).
- Rulebook on the requirements for trading and use of radioactive materials, x-ray devices and other devices that generate ionizing radiation ('OJ FRY', No. 32/98).
- Rulebook on application of the ionizing radiation sources in medicine ('OJ FRY', Nos 32/98 and 33/98 – corr.).
- Rulebook on methodology for compilation of assessment study on imperilment by Natural, Technical-Technological and other accidents (OJ MNE, No. 41/08).
- Rulebook on methodology for development of plans for protection and rescue (OJ MNE, No. 44/08).
- Rulebook on method of collecting, keeping, treatment and storing of radioactive waste ('OJ MNE' No. 58/11).

---

824. For the purpose of detection and prevention of unauthorized trade of radioactive and nuclear material across the Montenegrin border, ionizing radiation monitors shall be placed at border crossings, in accordance with the Act issued by competent authority for internal affairs and public management (Art. 45, para. 1).
825. Inspection supervision over implementation of this Law and of regulations adopted based on this Law shall be performed by the Agency and other inspection authorities within their competences, in accordance with this Law and the Law regulating inspection supervision (Art. 47, para. 2).
826. For more details *see also* GMNE, ME (2009), 127–130.

- Rulebook on detailed conditions for obtaining a permit for management of radioactive waste storage (OJ MNE, No. 56/11).
- Decision on qualifications and health conditions of persons working with sources of ionizing radiation (OJ FRY, No. 45/97).
- Decision on keeping the record of sources of ionizing radiation and irradiation of population, patients and persons exposed to effects of ionizing radiation at work (OJ FRY, No. 45/97).
- Decision on systematic investigations of radionuclide contents in the environment (OJ FRY, No. 45/97 and OJ SRM, No. 1/2003).
- Decision on conditions to be fulfilled by legal persons for performing measuring for assessing the level of exposure to ionizing radiation of persons working with radiation sources, patients and population (OJ FRY, No. 45/97).
- Decision on the control list for export, import and transit of goods (OJ MNE, No. 10/11).

III. Enforcement and Control

734. In 2008,[827] the Environmental Inspection has conducted 37,755 controls of commodities, as well as thirty shipments of transport of sources of ionizing radiation on border-crossing points and 208 imports of used electrical and electronic devices.[828]

IV. Harmonization with EU Legislation

735. 'The 2009 Radiation Protection Act provides the legal framework for the nuclear sector in accordance with international standards. However, Montenegro needs to develop implementing regulations and working procedures in line with the EU *acquis*. The regulatory body has been integrated into the Environmental Protection Agency, but there is no specific department within the EPA that has been assigned to nuclear issues. Neither has the EPA sufficient manpower to fulfil the tasks assigned in the nuclear field. There is no separate/dedicated budget for regulation in this area. The EPA's capability for review and assessment needs to be enhanced. There is no programme of environmental monitoring of radioactivity that is in full compliance with Articles 35 and 36 of the Euratom Treaty. There is no national emergency plan for radiation/nuclear accidents. The licencing of the storage facility for radioactive waste needs to be licensed following international standards and EU Directives, with special reference to environmental impact assessment'.[829]

---

827. During 2006, the ecological inspectorate carried out 15,305 controls of radioactivity on imported goods. UNECE (2007), 25.
828. GMNE (2008a), 42.
829. EC (2010), 81. This was also emphasized in the report for 2011 Year. *See*: EC (2011), 48.

736. Montenegrin legislation is not yet aligned with the Directive on the supervision and control of shipments of radioactive waste and spent fuel.[830] The Comprehensive Law on protection against ionizing radiation, radiation and nuclear safety and security, which will align with thirteen relevant EU legislative acts, is pending adoption.[831]

§4. Legislation: Non-ionizing Radiation

I. The Law on Protection from Non-ionizing Radiation

737. The basic legal act regulating non-ionizing radiation in Montenegro is the Law on non-ionizing radiation (OJM, No. 035/13 of July. 23, 2013.). It has the following eleven parts: Part I – General Provisions (Articles 1–4), Part II – Non-ionizing radiation protection (Articles 5–7), Part III – Professional protection against non-ionizing radiation (Articles 8–11), Part IV – Sources of electromagnetic fields (Articles 12–21), Part V – Devices and sources that emit optical radiation and ultrasound (Articles 22–31), Part VI – Minimal health and safety conditions (Articles 32–39), Part VII – Evidence sources of non-ionizing radiation (Articles 40–45), Part VIII – Publicity of data (Article 46), Part IX – Supervision (Articles 47–49), Part X – Penalties (Article 50) and Part XI – Transitory and final provisions (Articles 51–55).

738. According to Article 1, the Law regulates the protection of the lives and health of people, persons working with sources of non-ionizing radiation[832] or those who are exposed to non-ionizing radiation during the work (hereinafter referred to as 'professionally exposed persons') and protection of the environment against the harmful effects of non-ionizing radiation, conditions for the use of non-ionizing radiation sources and other issues of importance for protection against non-ionizing radiation.[833]

830. EC (2018), p. 68.
831. EC (2020b), p. 93). Proposal of the Law on the Protection against Ionizing Radiation, Nuclear and Radiation Safety was adopted by the Government of Montenegro in November 2022. https://www.gov.me/dokumenta/c2933ef7-f644-498a-b676-adfe63850a2b (3 Jan. 2023).
832. Non-ionizing radiation is electromagnetic fields and electromagnetic waves of frequency less than 300 GHz, optical radiation and ultrasound frequency less than 500 MHz, which in the interaction with the substance do not create ions. Non-ionizing radiation sources are devices, installations or objects that emit one or more types of non-ionizing radiation (Art. 5, paras 1–2).
833. Protection against non-ionizing radiation is based on the following principles: (1) *the justification of use* is the use of sources of non-ionizing radiation which is justified if it gives greater benefit than the estimated damage; (2) *optimization* of protection means the application of protection measures for each use of non-ionizing radiation sources that prevent or reduce adverse effects to the life and health of people and professionally exposed persons; (3) *limiting exposure to non-ionizing radiation* means the determination of the upper limit of the permitted exposure of humans to non-ionizing radiation and the level of non-ionizing radiation that may emit the source of non-ionizing radiation; (4) *informing the public about non-ionizing radiation* are data on non-ionizing radiation that are published in accordance with this Law for the purpose of informing the public (Art. 3, para. 1).

A. Systematic Research of Non-ionizing Radiation

739. In order to monitor the presence, determine the danger, notify and take measures for protection against non-ionizing radiation, a systematic examination level of non-ionizing radiation is performed (hereinafter 'monitoring'). Monitoring is carried out on the basis of the annual programme of systematic testing of non-ionizing radiation levels (hereinafter 'the Programme'), which is adopted by the GMNE (Article 6, paragraph 1).[834]

740. Monitoring is carried out by the Agency. For the implementation of the Programme, the Agency may hire an authorized professional referred to in Article 9 of this Law.[835] The authorized professional shall be obliged to submit to the Agency a report on the systematic examination level of non-ionizing radiation no later than 31 March of the current year for the previous year (Article 7, paragraphs 1–3).

B. Sources of Electromagnetic Fields

741. Sources of electromagnetic fields can be used only if, in their normal use, the population and professionally exposed persons are not exposed to radiation above the prescribed exposure limits to electromagnetic fields. The stationary source of the electromagnetic field, which does not fulfil the prescribed conditions regarding the exposure limits, must be reconstructed or adapted (Article 12, paragraphs 1–2).

742. Sources of electromagnetic fields can be used only on the basis of a licence for the use of electromagnetic field sources issued by the Agency for a period of four years. The permit shall be issued before release of the source into regular work, at the request of the holder of the source of non-ionizing radiation (Article 13, paragraphs 1–2). The first measurements of electromagnetic fields in the vicinity of stationary sources shall be carried out before obtaining the permit, as well as after each reconstruction of the stationary source.[836]

743. The operator to whom the licence for the use of sources of electromagnetic fields is issued shall be obliged to provide periodic measurement levels of electromagnetic fields in the vicinity of the source. Periodical measurement shall be carried out by an authorized professional (Article 15, paragraph 1).[837]

834. The costs for implementing the Programme are provided from the budget of Montenegro (Art. 6, para. 5).
835. Professional activities may be performed by a company, entrepreneur or other legal entity that has a licence for performing professional activities for protection against non-ionizing radiation (hereinafter: authorized professional) issued by the Agency (Art. 9, para. 1).
836. The measurements shall be performed by an authorized professional referred to in Art. 9 of this Law at the request of the holder of the source of non-ionizing radiation (Art. 14, paras 1–2).
837. The method of first and periodical measurements, criteria for determining the frequency of periodic measurements, content and form of reports on performed first and periodical measurements shall be prescribed by the Ministry (Art. 15, para. 6).

744. Permit for using sources of electromagnetic fields shall be suspended by the agency if the operator: (1) ceases to fulfil the conditions on the basis of which the licence was issued to him; (2) fails to submit the report and expert opinion referred to in Article 15 paragraph 2 of this Law; and (3) fails to submit evidence of periodic examination of professional qualifications in accordance to this Law (Article 16).

II. Devices and Sources that Emit Optical Radiation and Ultrasound

745. Devices emitting ultrasound or devices emitting optical radiation or containing optical radiation sources may be used only if they do not adversely affect human health, professionally exposed persons and the environment, in accordance with the prescribed limits (Article 22, paragraph 1).

746. Devices emitting ultrasound and devices that emit optical radiation or contain optical radiation sources and are intended for use (medicine, dentistry, economy, etc.) must be labelled with the prescribed labels and accompanied by conformity certificates in accordance with a special regulation (Article 24, paragraph 1).[838]

A. *Licences*

747. Devices emitting ultrasound can only be used on the basis of a licence for use issued by the Agency. The licence shall be issued for a period of four years (Article 26, paragraph 1). Devices emitting optical radiation or containing optical radiation sources may be used only on the basis of an operating licence issued by the Agency for a period of four years (Article 27, paragraphs 1–2).[839]

748. The Agency shall suspend the licence if the operator: (1) ceases to fulfil the conditions on the basis of which the licence was issued; (2) fails to submit a report to the Agency on performed inspection and/or examination of the device within eight days from the day the report is written; (3) does not perform the check and/or testing of the device after the repair or reconstruction of the device, and before reuse, in accordance with this Law; (4) does not provide periodic examination of professional competence for professionally exposed persons and persons responsible for the implementation of non-ionizing radiation protection measures; and (5) fails to submit the data to the Agency from the records referred to in Article 40 of this Law (Article 30).

838. Devices emitting optical radiation or containing optical radiation sources for which a licence is issued in accordance with this Law shall be labelled according to the degree of danger and shall meet the requirements for safe use. The manner of labelling and the requirements for safe use of the devices shall be prescribed by the Ministry, with the previously obtained opinion of the state administration body in charge for quality infrastructure (Art. 24, paras 1–3).
839. The types of devices for which licences for use are issued shall be prescribed by the Ministry, with the consent of the state administration body in charge of health (Art. 27, para. 3).

B. Checking and/or Testing the Device

749. The operator is obliged to ensure that every device that emits an ultrasound or optical radiation or contains a source of optical radiation provides a check and/or test of the device every two years (Article 28, paragraph 1).[840]

C. Minimal Health and Safety Conditions

750. The holder of the non-ionizing radiation source shall prepare an exposure risk assessment of the professionally exposed persons and persons responsible for the implementation of non-ionizing radiation protection measures against electromagnetic fields and optical radiation (hereinafter 'Risk assessment').[841]

751. If, on the basis of the Risk Assessment, it is determined that the values of the electromagnetic field warning, i.e., the maximum permitted levels of exposure to optical radiation above the permitted levels, the holder of the development of non-ionizing radiation is obliged to develop and implement the Action Programme on the implementation of protection measures (hereinafter 'the Action Programme') (Article 33, paragraph 1).[842]

752. Professionally exposed persons and persons responsible for implementation of non-ionizing radiation protection measures should have an appropriate education level and should be professionally qualified for the implementation of non-ionizing radiation protection measures. The operator is obliged to provide a periodical examination of professional qualifications of these persons. Professional training and proficiency checking are carried out by a legal entity that has a licence for vocational training issued by the Agency. Permit for vocational training is issued for a period of four years based on the request of a legal entity that meets the requirements for personnel, equipment and space (Article 34, paragraphs 1–4).[843]

753. In order to prevent and timely detect all harmful effects on health, as well as to prevent all long-term health risks and all risks of chronic diseases that result from exposure to electromagnetic fields and optical radiation, health examinations

---

840. The operator shall submit a report on the performed inspection and/or examination of the device to the Agency, within eight days from the day the report is written. The manner of checking and/or testing of devices shall be prescribed by the Ministry. The costs for conducting the check and/or testing of the device shall be borne by the operator (Art. 28, paras 3–5).
841. Risk assessment includes: assessment, measurement and/or calculation of exposure levels to non-ionizing radiation in order to eliminate or reduce the risk of exposure and for the safety and health of professionally exposed persons and persons responsible for the implementation of non-ionizing radiation protection measures. (Art. 32, para. 1).
842. The Ministry shall prescribe the contents of the Action Program, the manner of labelling of jobs and access to workplaces, the manner of informing, training, counselling and participation in the discussions of professionally exposed persons and persons responsible for protection against non-ionizing radiation (Art. 33, para. 9).
843. The licence shall be seized by the Agency to a legal entity if it ceases to fulfil the conditions on the basis of which the licence was issued (Art. 36, para. 1).

for professionally exposed persons and persons responsible for implementation measure of protection against non-ionizing radiation are conducted. The operator is obliged to provide a check of the medical conditions of these persons (Article 37, paragraph 1).[844]

D. Evidence Sources of Non-ionizing Radiations

754. The operator is obliged to keep record of sources of non-ionizing radiation (Article 40, paragraph 1).[845]

755. The register of non-ionizing radiation is kept by the Agency in electronic form (Article 41, paragraph 1).[846]

756. The operator is obliged to label the source of non-ionizing radiation. The manner of labelling and layout of the source of non-ionizing radiation is prescribed by the Ministry (Article 42, paragraphs 1–2).[847]

757. The operator is obliged to inform the authority responsible for inspection activities and the Agency about the accident that caused or could have caused harmful effects of non-ionizing radiation to human health and the environment, immediately and within twenty-four hours from the occurrence of the accident (Article 44, paragraph 1).[848]

E. Supervision

758. Supervision over the implementation of this Law and regulations adopted pursuant to this Law shall be carried out by the Ministry. Inspection supervision

844. When using sources of non-ionizing radiation, personal protective equipment and equipment at work must be used and protective measures must be implemented (Art. 38, para. 1). The holder of the non-ionizing radiation source shall be obliged to designate a person responsible for the implementation of non-ionizing radiation protection measures (Art. 39, para. 1).
845. The operator shall be obliged to submit data from the records to the Agency no later than 1 March of the current year for the previous year. The manner for keeping records shall be prescribed by the Ministry (Art. 40, paras 3–4).
846. The register shall contain information on: (1) Issued permits in accordance to this Law; (2) Sources of non-ionizing radiation; (3) Professionally exposed persons; (4) Persons responsible for implementation of non-ionizing radiation protection measures; (5) Performed measurements in accordance to this Law; (6) Reports in accordance to this Law; (7) Other data on non-ionizing radiation (Art. 41, para. 2).
847. The operator shall be obliged, to notify in writing the Agency and the administrative authority responsible for inspection activities about all significant changes in the technical characteristics of the sources of non-ionizing radiation and termination of use sources of non-ionizing radiation, within seven days from the date of the change or the termination of use sources of non-ionizing radiation (Art. 43, para. 1).
848. The notification shall comprise: the circumstances under which the accident occurred, the place, the time, the imminent danger to human health and the environment and a brief description of the measures taken (para. 2).

over implementation of this Law and the regulations adopted pursuant to this Law shall be performed by the administrative authority responsible for inspection issues through the environmental inspection, in accordance with this Law and the Law regulating inspection supervision.

759. The Agency is obliged to submit the data necessary for the implementation of the inspection supervision to the administrative body competent for inspection activities (Article 47, paragraphs 1–3).[849]

III. Other Relevant Legislation

760.

- Rulebook on conditions for means and equipment for personal protection at work when using sources of non-ionizing radiation (OJ MNE, No. 4/17).
- Rulebook on the method of professional training of professionally exposed persons and persons responsible for the implementation of the protection measure against non-invasive radiation (OJ MNE, No. 21/16).
- Rulebook on Conditions for Performing Professional Activities in Non-Ionizing Radiation Protection (OJ MNE, No. 21/16).
- Rulebook on the manner of verification and/or examination of devices emitting ultrasound and optical radiation (OJ MNE, No. 66/2015).
- Rulebook on the manner of designation and appearance of the mark of the source of non-ionizing radiation (OJ MNE, No. 65/2015).
- Rulebook on the types of significant sources of non-ionizing radiation for which the study is being developed (OJ MNE, No. 42/2015).
- Rulebook on the content of the action programme on the implementation of non-ionizing radiation protection measures (OJ MNE, No. 23/14).
- Rulebook on content and method of submitting reports on systematic testing of non-ionizing radiation levels (OJ MNE, No. 56/2013).
- Rulebook on keeping records on sources of non-ionizing radiation (OJ MNE, No. 56/13).

849. The Agency, ex officio, shall obtain evidence of enrolment in the Central Registry of Business Entities for performing non-ionizing radiation protection activities in the procedure for issuing licences, in accordance to this Law (Art. 47, para. 4).

Chapter 8. Other Sectors

§1. Noxious Substances

761. Noxious substances are related to various areas and in their management are involved different subjects in different fields (health, environment, water, soil, agriculture, transport, waste, etc.).

I. Competencies

762. Pursuant to Article 13 of the Decree on state administration organization and operations (OJ MNE, Nos 49/22, 52/22, 56/22, 82/22) the Ministry of Environment, Spatial Planning and Urbanism is competent for the policy in the field of chemicals. Protection from chemicals is in competence of NEPA (Article 39).

763. CETI, according to the Decision on Establishment of PI Centre for Ecotoxicological Research of Montenegro (OJ RM, No. 40/96), performs ecotoxicological research of air, water, sea, soil, flora and fauna, climate change, ionizing and non-ionizing radiation, noise and vibrations. It also organizes special toxicological studies, analyses and programmes and other undertakings.[850]

II. Legal Framework

A. *International Treaties*

764. Montenegro has ratified PIC (OJ MNE – International Treaties, No. 3/2011) and Convention on Persistent Organic Pollutants (POPs) (OJ MNE – International Treaties, No. 16/2010). Montenegro adopted the law ratifying the amendments to the Stockholm Convention on Persistent Organic Pollutants (POPs) (Official Journal of Montenegro – International Treaties (OJ MNE – IT), No. 9/17).

B. *National Legislation*

1. A Law on Chemicals

765. On 26 July 2017, the Parliament of Montenegro adopted new Law on chemicals (OJ MNE, No. 51/17). It has the following twelve parts: Part I – General Provisions (Articles 1–4), Part II – Classification, labelling and packaging (Articles 5–17), Part III – Notification within the chemical supply chain (Articles 18–25), Part IV – Registration of chemicals (Articles 26–36), Part V – Free trade of hazardous chemicals (Articles 37–40), Part VI – Export and import of chemicals

850. *See*: https://eng.ceti.me/ (16 Jan. 2023).

(Articles 41–48), Part VII –Detergents (Articles 49–55), Part VIII – Good laboratory Practice (GLP) (Articles 56–59), IX – Management of chemicals (Articles 60–66), Part X –Supervision (Articles 67–70), Part XI – Penalties (Article 71) and Part XII – Transitional and final provisions (Articles 72–75).

766. The Law regulates the classification, labelling, packaging, traffic, import and export of dangerous chemicals,[851] and other issues of importance for the protection of human health and environment from harmful influence of chemicals (Article 1).

a. Classification, Labelling and Packaging

767. Classification of chemicals is based on the assessment of their physical and chemical properties, properties that affect human health, and the environment, in accordance with the criteria for the classification in certain risk classes[852] (Article 5, paragraph 1). The chemicals are classified into the following classes: explosive, oxidizing, extremely flammable, highly flammable, flammable, very toxic, toxic, harmful, corrosive, irritant, chemicals that lead to hypersensitivity, carcinogenic, mutagenic, reproductive toxic and chemicals dangerous to the environment (Article 5, paragraph 2).[853]

768. The manufacturer, importer, distributor and another user who place the chemical on the market shall be obliged to classify, mark and package chemicals in accordance with this Law (Article 6, paragraph 1). The exporter is obliged to label and pack a chemical or product that exports, in accordance with this Law, unless it is necessary to label and package the chemical in accordance with international standards at the request of the country in which the chemical is exported (Article 6, paragraph 2).[854]

b. Storage

769. The supplier is obliged to store hazardous chemicals in a manner that does not endanger the human health and the environment (Article 16, paragraph 1). The supplier is obliged to store and safely dispose chemical waste, including the rest of the chemicals and the used packaging in accordance with the law governing waste management (Article 16, paragraph 2).

851. A chemical is a substance in an individual form or in a mixture or mixture, obtained by a production process or in a natural state. (Art. 2).
852. The hazard class of chemicals is determined based on the properties of the chemical that affect the life and health of people and the environment or on the basis of the effects of the chemical (Art. 5, para. 3).
853. The method of classification, labelling and packaging of chemicals is prescribed by the Ministry in accordance with the Globally Harmonized System of the UN (Art. 5, para. 4), see further the Rulebook on the method of classification, labelling and packaging of chemicals in accordance with the Globally Harmonized System of the UN (OJ MNE, 85/17, 117/21).
854. A further user who does not change the composition of the chemicals during use can use the classification, labelling and packaging of chemicals of one of the entities in the supply chain (para. 3).

c. Notification Within the Chemical Supply Chain

770. The supplier of chemicals is obliged to submit to the recipient of the chemical a safety data sheet for hazardous chemicals, chemicals containing substances identified as persistent – bioaccumulative – toxic (hereinafter referred to as 'PBT') or highly persistent – highly bioaccumulative (hereinafter 'vPvB') and other chemicals that have the properties referred to in Article 33, paragraphs 1 and 2 of this Law which are placed on the market (Article 18. paragraph 1).[855]

771. The supplier is obliged to submit a safety data sheet to any distributor or to a further user in the supply chain in the Montenegrin language in printed or electronic form (Article 18. paragraph 3). The exporter of chemicals referred to in paragraph 1 of this Article shall be obliged to submit the safety data sheet to the importer, in the language of the country in which it is exported or in the English language.[856]

d. Registration of Chemicals

772. Substances individually, in mixtures or in a product that are produced or marketed in total quantities over 1 t per year (in a calendar year), have to be registered in a publicly available register (Article 26, paragraph 1).[857]

773. Registration of chemicals into the register shall be made on the basis of a request for registration in the register (hereinafter 'the application'), submitted by the producer or importer which is registered in the Central Register of Economic Entities to the Agency by 31 March of the current year for the chemicals he has produced, in the previous year (Article 27, paragraph 1).[858]

774. Substances produced or imported for research and development are exempted from registration in the register for a period of five years, for quantities less than 1 t per year (Article 29).

775. Substances that are carcinogenic, mutagenic, toxic after reproduction and identified as PBT or vPvB substances have to be registered in the list of substances that cause high concern (Article 33, paragraph 1).[859] The list of substances that

855. The safety data sheet shall in particular include: chemical name (substance/substance identification), data on physico-chemical properties of the chemical, methods of use, preventive measures, risk mitigation measures and chemical supplier data (Art. 18. para. 2).

856. The criteria for identifying the substance as PBT or vPvB and content of the safety data sheet are prescribed by the Ministry, with the consent of the state administration body competent for health (Art. 18. para. 5).

857. The register is kept by the Agency in electronic form (Art. 26, para. 3).

858. The content of the dossier and register is prescribed by the Ministry, with the consent of the state administration body competent for health (Art. 27, para. 9).

859. The dossier for substances that cause high concern, or mixture containing that substance, in addition to the data from Art. 33, para. 3 of this Law, contains: (1) information on the use of that substance or mixture containing the substance; (2) measures to reduce risk when used; (3) systematic monitoring of the use of substances or mixtures containing the substance (Art. 34).

cause serious concern is prescribed by the Ministry, with the consent of the state administration body competent for health (Article 33, paragraph 4).

e. Free Trade of Hazardous Chemicals

776. Free Trade of Hazardous Chemicals is performed by the supplier on the basis of the Licence for free trade of dangerous chemicals, issued by the Agency for nature and environmental protection (hereinafter 'permits'). The licence is issued at the request of the supplier who places the chemical in free trade (Article 37).[860] More detailed conditions for storage and measures for safe storage, i.e., use of hazardous chemicals shall be prescribed by the Ministry (Article 38, paragraph 3).

777. The records on issued licences are kept by the Agency. The manner of keeping records shall be prescribed by the Ministry (Article 39, paragraphs 1 and 2). Chemicals that represent an unacceptable risk to human health and the environment can be used in the manner, under the conditions and within the deadlines prescribed by the GMNE (Article 40, paragraph 1).

f. Export and Import of Chemicals

778. Export of chemicals from the List of chemicals subject to the prior notification procedure shall be done on the basis of a notification submitted by the Agency in the country where the chemical is exported (Article 41, paragraph 1).[861]

779. Chemicals and products whose use is prohibited, in order to protect human health and the environment, must not be exported (Article 48, paragraph 1).[862]

780. For the import of chemicals from the List of chemicals subject to prior notification procedure the Agency has to receive an export notification from the competent authority of the country from which the chemical is exported (Article 42).[863]

781. The PIC procedure is carried out for the export of chemicals found on the Chemicals List for the PIC procedure and for the chemicals from the Rotterdam Convention List (Article 43).[864] Exporters and importers of chemicals referred to in

860. A licence may be issued to a supplier who has the appropriate storage and guarding facilities for hazardous chemicals in a way that prevents persons from accessing it for unauthorized use (para. 3).
861. The provision of para. 1 of this Article shall not apply to the manufacture, placing on the market and the use of substances for scientific research and development and use of substances for cosmetic products in accordance with the regulation governing cosmetic products (para. 2).
862. List of hazardous chemicals and products for which the export is prohibited shall be prescribed by the Ministry (Art. 48 para. 3).
863. Upon receipt of the notification of export, the Agency shall inform the authority referred to in para. 1 of this Article that it has received the notification.
864. For the import of chemicals from the Chemistry List for the PIC procedure and for the chemicals from the Rotterdam Convention List the Agency issue consent on the basis of a prior notification from the competent body of the exporting country (Art. 44).

Articles 41–44 of this Law shall be obliged to submit until 31 March to the Agency information on exported or imported quantities of chemicals and products, of the countries from which the chemicals are imported or imported, as well as data on the exporter or importer of chemicals (Article 45, paragraph 1).[865] The Agency electronically keeps records of imported and exported chemicals or products (Article 45, paragraph 3).

782. The exporter of chemicals is obliged to provide the Agency with the information required by the competent authority of the transit country for the chemicals from the Rotterdam Convention (no later than thirty days before the transit day) (Article 47).[866]

783. List of hazardous chemicals and products for which the export is prohibited shall be prescribed by the Ministry (Article 48, paragraph 3).

g. Detergents

784. Detergents can be placed on the market only if they fulfil the conditions of complete aerobic biodegradability and if the chemicals and surfactants contained in detergents meet the conditions relating to the classification, packaging and labelling prescribed by this Law (Article 49).

785. Industrial detergents and detergents for professional use containing surface-active substances which do not meet the conditions of full aerobic biodegradability as well as detergents for home use, containing as an active ingredient a chemical from the Classified Substances List in per cent greater than 1%, can be placed on the market on the basis of a permit the use of a surfactant substance issued by the Agency (Article 50).[867] The permit shall be issued on the basis of a request submitted to the Agency by the manufacturer of the detergent (Article 51, paragraph 1).

h. Good Laboratory Practice

786. Non-clinical testing of chemicals is carried out to evaluate the chemicals and the risk assessment of their potential threat to human health and the environment (Article 56, paragraph 1). Non-clinical testing of chemicals may be carried out by laboratories whose work complies with the GLP guidelines (Article 56, paragraph 2).[868] Fulfilment of the GLP conditions is determined by the Agency and

865. The manner of submission of data shall be prescribed by the Ministry (Art. 45, para. 5).
866. The Agency shall submit to the competent authority of the transit country data on chemicals, at least fifteen days before the date of transit (Art. 47, para. 2).
867. The permit referred to in Art. 50 of this Law shall be issued within six months (Art. 53 para. 1).
868. Guidelines and conditions for the GLP are prescribed by the Ministry (Art. 50, para. 3).

issued a certificate of GLP. A GLP certificate is issued on the basis of a request submitted by the laboratory (Article 57, paragraphs 1–2).

787. Laboratory that has GLP certificate can perform non-clinical testing on the basis of the authorization issued by the Ministry's decision[869] (Article 58).

i. Chemicals Management

788. In order to protect the human health and the environment from the harmful effects of chemicals, the Agency monitors the use and placing on the market of chemicals (Article 60, paragraph 1). Based on chemical monitoring, the Agency makes a report on chemical management (the Report) and submits it to the Ministry by 31 March of the current year for the previous year.[870]

789. The Agency performs data exchange on chemicals with international organizations and foreign countries in accordance with the ratified international treaties and agreements, as well as with relevant bodies and organizations of the EU (Article 62).

790. The National Strategy for chemical management (hereinafter 'National Strategy')[871] is adopted for the purpose of adequate management of chemicals, from the manufacture or importation to the disposal, which contributes to sustainable development of Montenegro (Article 63, paragraph 1).[872] The Agency is obliged to inform the public through the media about the risks arising from the use of chemicals, in order to protect the health of the people and the environment (Article 64, paragraph 1).

791. Supervision over the implementation of this Law and regulations adopted pursuant to this Law shall be carried out by the Ministry. Inspection supervision over the implementation of this Law is performed by the administrative authority responsible for inspection work through environmental and sanitary inspectors (Article 67, paragraphs 1–2).

869. The decision under para. 1 of this Article shall be issued on the basis of public invitation announced by the competent Ministry (Art. 58, para. 3).
870. The report is an integral part of the Report on the state of the environment in accordance with the Law on Environment (Art. 60, para. 3).
871. National Strategy for the period of four years is adopted by the Government (Art. 58, para. 2). Annual report on the implementation of the National strategy is designed by the Ministry and submitted to the Government by 31 March of the current year for the previous year (Art. 63, para. 4).
872. For more information on the National Strategy for Chemicals Management for the period 2019–2022. *See*: https://www.gov.me/dokumenta/874a5afd-6b90-448c-9875-edf445dfb861 (3 Dec. 2022).

2. Other Relevant Legislations

792. Other relevant laws to be mentioned are following: Law on flammable liquids and gases (OJ MNE, Nos 26/10 and 31/10-Corr, 48/15),[873] Law on transport of dangerous substances (OJ MNE, Nos 33/14, 13/18),[874] Law on Explosive Substances (OJ MNE, Nos 49/08, 58/2008, 31/14, 31/17), Law on the Protection and Rescue (OJ MNE, Nos 13/07, 5/08, 86/09, 32/11, 54/16, 146/21), Law on Traffic Security on Roads (OJ MNE, Nos 33/12, 58/14, 14/17-CC, 66/19), Law on Railways (OJ MNE, Nos 27/13, 43/13), Law on Railway Transport Safety, Organization and Efficiency(OJ MNE, Nos 1/14, 6/14), Law on Maritime Navigation Safety (OJ MNE, Nos 62/13, 6/14, 47/15, 71/17, 34/19, 77/20), Law on Maritime and Inland Navigation (OJ SRM, Nos 19/78, 8/79, 19/87, 22/90, 13/91; OJ RM, Nos 48/91, 17/92, 59/92, 4/93, 27/92; OJ MNE, Nos 51/08, 40/11, 62/13), Law on Yachts (OJ RM, No. 46/07, OJ MNE, Nos 73/10, 40/11, 42/15, 16/16), Law of the Sea (OJ MNE, Nos 17/07, 6/08, 40/11) and Law on Air traffic (OJ MNE, Nos 30/12, 30/17, 82/20), etc.

793. Besides above-mentioned laws, a number of by-laws are relevant for chemical management issues. These are the following:

- Rulebook on the criteria and method of classification, packaging and labelling of chemicals and certain products in the hazard class (OJ MNE, No. 53/12).
- List of Classified Substances (OJ MNE, No. 58/12).
- Rulebook on the prior notification procedure and the procedure for granting consent on the basis of the prior notification for the export of chemicals (OJ MNE, Nos 13/13 and 27/14).
- Rulebook on the closer content of the dossier and the register of chemicals (OJ MNE, Nos 96/20, 63/22).
- Rulebook on the manner of preparation and content of the Chemical Safety Report (OJ MNE, No. 28/13).
- Rulebook on the manner of keeping records on chemicals and issued permits for the performance of the activities of the traffic in hazardous chemicals (OJ MNE, No. 28/13).
- Rulebook on storage conditions, measures for the safe storage and use of hazardous chemicals (OJ MNE, No. 28/13).
- Rulebook on determining the list of surface-active substances that can be used in the detergent (OJ MNE, No. 36/13).

873. It has the following six parts: Part I – General Provisions (Arts 1–6), Part II – Safety measures (Arts 7–20), Part III – Conditions for storage and transport of flammable liquids and gases (Arts 21–36), Part IV – Supervision (Arts 37–38), Part V – Penalties (Arts 39–40) and Part VI – Transitional and final provisions (Arts 41–44).

874. In January 2020, the Government of Montenegro submitted to the Assembly a proposal for amendments to this law. *See*: https://zakoni.skupstina.me/zakoni/web/dokumenta/zakoni-i-drugi-akti/925/2225-13232-14-1-20-1.pdf (16 Jan. 2023).

- Rulebook on the content of the requirements and certificates of good laboratory practice (OJ MNE, No. 48/13).
- Rulebook on the prohibition and restriction of the use, placing on the market and production of chemicals that constitute an unacceptable risk to human health and the environment (OJ MNE, Nos 49/13, 12/16).
- Rulebook on the methods for testing the biodegradability of surfactants, the manner of collecting and the composition of detergents (OJ MNE, No. 50/13).
- Rulebook on methods for testing hazardous properties of chemicals (OJ MNE, Nos 16/14 and 44/15).
- Rulebook on Guidelines and Conditions of Good Laboratory Practice (OJ MNE, No. 24/14).
- Regulation on the list of hazardous chemicals and products whose export is prohibited (OJ MNE, Nos 71/18, 68/20, 99/20).
- Rulebook on the list of substances that cause high concern (OJ MNE, Nos 65/17, 37/21, 64722).
- Rulebook on the contents of the safety data sheet for chemicals (OJ MNE, No. 28/20).
- Rulebook on criteria for identification of substances as persistent, bioaccumulative and toxic and very persistent and very bioaccumulative substances (OJ MNE, Nos 84/17 42/20).
- Regulation on the manner of classification, packaging and labelling of chemicals and certain products in accordance with the UN Globally Harmonized System for the Classification and Labelling of Chemicals (OJ MNE, No. 85/17).
- Regulation on prohibited or allowed manners of usage, production and marketing of chemicals that present an unacceptable risk for human health and the environment (OJ MNE, Nos 70/18, 76/20, 134/22).

3. Law on Biocidal Products

794. The basic act regulating biocidal products in Montenegro is the Law on biocidal products (Official Journal of Montenegro (OJ MNE), No. 54/2016). It has the following eight parts: Part I – General Provisions (Articles 1–4), Part II – Biocides and active substances in biocides (Articles 5–6), Part III – Permits for putting biocides on the market and in use (Articles 7–30), Part IV – Classification, packaging, labelling and advertising of the biocides (Articles 31–36), Part V – Conditions for import and export of the biocides (Articles 37–48), Part VI – Supervision (Articles 49–56), Part VII – Penalties (Article 57) and Part VIII – Transitory and final provisions (Articles 58–60).

795. This Law regulates the method of placing on the market and the use of a biocidal product (hereinafter 'biocide'),[875] import, export, as well as other important issues for the use of biocides (Article 1, paragraph 1).[876]

875. *Biocide*, for the purposes of this Law, is: (1) a substance or mixture of substances containing one or more active substances, prepared in the form in which users are supplied, whose purpose is to destroy, prevent the action, make it harmless or control unwanted organisms on any way other than

796. Regulation of the state administration body competent for environmental protection (hereinafter 'the Ministry') determines the types of biocides depending on the manner of use, the organisms to which they operate, the facilities in which they are used and the objects and areas treated with biocides (Article 5, paragraph 1). The biocide contains the active substances allowed for use in biocides and allowed for use in low-risk biocidal products (Article 6, paragraph 1).[877]

4. Permit for Putting Biocides on the Market and in Use

797. Biocide can be placed into circulation and in use, if it is classified, packaged and labelled in accordance with this Law and the Law regulating chemicals, only on the basis of the marketing and use Permit (hereinafter 'permit'). The permit is issued by an administrative body competent for environmental protection (hereinafter 'the Agency') (Article 7, paragraphs 1 and 2).

798. The Permit is issued on the basis of a Request[878] submitted by the manufacturer, or importer of a biocide with the status of a legal entity based in Montenegro and registered for performing this activity in the Central Registry of Business Entities (hereinafter 'the applicant') (Article 8, paragraph 1).[879] The Agency issues a permit within ninety days from the date of submission of the complete permit application (Article 9, paragraph 3). The permit is issued for a period of up to ten years. The permit may also contain special conditions for the placing of biocides on the market and use as well as the place of sale depending on the characteristics of the biocide (Article 14, paragraphs 2 and 3).[880]

---

physical or mechanical action; (2) the substance or mixture obtained from substances and mixtures which do not belong to substances and mixtures referred to in para. 1 of this Article and whose purpose is to destroy, prevent the activity, make it harmless or control unwanted organisms in any way, other than by physical or mechanical action; and (3) a treated product that has a primary biocidal function.

876. This Law shall not apply to: (1) medicines and medical devices used in human and veterinary medicine; (2) food products, food additives, spices and raw materials for production in the food industry, materials and products that come in contact with food; (3) animal feed, animal feed additives and other products used in animal nutrition; (4) substances and products considered as waste; (5) detergents, other than detergents having biocidal activity; (6) cosmetic products; (7) plant protection products; (8) biocides used as ancillary technological means; and (9) treated products used for storage or transportation and where no residues are expected after use (fumigation or disinfection of space or storage) (Art. 3, para. 1).

877. Lists of active substances referred to in para. 1 of this Article in accordance with the list of the European Union shall be determined by a Regulation of the Ministry (Art. 6, para. 2).

878. The Request may be submitted by several importers together (Art. 8, para. 2).

879. The applicant for a Permit may submit a request for the determination of a group of biocidal products (Art. 15, para. 1). The Agency, in the procedure for issuing the permit, informs the applicant about the group of biocidal products for which the permits has already been issued (Art. 15, para. 3). The conditions for placing on the market and use, the validity period of the permit and other conditions for biocide must be the same for all biocides within the group of biocidal products (Art. 15, para. 5).

880. The conditions for placing biocides on the market and use and the content of the licence shall be determined by a regulation of the Ministry with the consent of the state administration body in charge of health affairs (Art. 14, para. 4).

799. Based on the request of the authorized representative of the biocide producer, the Agency may issue a permit for a biocide for which the permit has already been issued in accordance with the regulations of the EU, from the competent authority of a Member State of the EU; EC; countries of the European Economic Community and Switzerland (Article 21, paragraph 1).[881]

800. The Agency may allow to place on the market and use biocides that do not meet the conditions for obtaining a permit in accordance with this Law for limited and controlled use, if necessary due to public health, animal health or the environment, and if the harmful organism cannot be suppressed by other means. The permit shall be issued for a period not exceeding 180 days. The Agency may allow to place on the market and use a biocide containing a new active substance for a period not exceeding three years (Article 23, paragraphs 1–3).

801. The Agency may issue a temporary permit for placing on the marketing and the use of biocides (hereinafter 'temporary permit') within thirty days from the date of submission of the application, in case of an unexpected occurrence of a harmful organism, which cannot be suppressed by the biocides for which the licence was issued (Article 24, paragraph 1). The period of validity of the provisional licence cannot be longer than 180 days from the date of issue of the licence. The holder of the temporary permit after the expiration of the period for which the licence was issued or after the termination of the use of that biocide is obliged to submit to the Agency a report on the amount of biocides used and the results of the systematic monitoring of the use of biocides (Article 24, paragraphs 3–4).

802. The Permit holder may submit a request to the Agency for special approval for placing on the market and use of biocides which are in composition, purity of active substances and efficacy similar to the biocide for which the licence has already been issued and the determined biocidal products group (Article 16, paragraph 1). The special approval referred to in paragraph 1 of this Article shall be issued for the same validity period of the biocide permit for which a group of biocidal products has been established (Article 16, paragraph 4).

5. Register of Biocides

803. The biocide for which the licence is issued shall be entered in the biocide register (hereinafter 'the register'). The Registry is an integral part of the Chemicals Registry kept by the Agency. The content and manner of keeping the register shall be determined by the Ministry's Regulation (Article 18, paragraph 1).

---

881. The expert evaluation of data from the dossier summary is done by the Agency (Art. 21, para. 3). The permit is issued for the period of validity of the licence issued by the competent authority of the Member State of the European Union (Art. 21, para. 6).

6. Abolition of the Decision on Entry into the Provisional List and Permits

804. The Agency shall annul the Decision[882] on entry in the provisional list if: (1) based on the submitted data, it is estimated that the cancellation is aimed to protect the health of people, animals and the environment or (2) it is determined that the holder of the Decision on entry in the provisional list does not comply with the prescribed conditions for placing biocides on the market and in use (Article 26, paragraph 1).[883]

805. In the case of reasonable doubt that the placing on the market and the use of a biocide or an active substance pose a significant risk to human, animal and environmental health, the Agency may, with the consent of the state administration body competent for health, temporarily prohibit placing of biocides or active substances on the market and use and order the holder of the permit to carry out further tests on the biocide or the active substance (Article 28, paragraph 1).

7. Research and Development

806. Scientific research and development of biocides is scientific experimentation, analysis or research of biocides, which is carried out under controlled conditions and imports in quantities less than 10 kg. No permission is required for biocides or active substances used for scientific research (Article 29, paragraph 1).[884] If, when using a biocide or an active substance for the purposes referred to in Article 29, paragraph 1 of this Law, the release of a biocide or an active substance into the environment is required, the Agency shall issue a permit for the use of the biocide or the active substance for that purpose (Article 30, paragraph 1).

8. Classification, Packaging, Labelling and Advertising of the Biocides

807. Classification, packaging and labelling of biocides shall be carried out in accordance with the Law governing chemicals.[885] Biocides containing microorganisms are classified in accordance with the Law regulating healthcare (Article 31, paragraphs 1–2).

808. When advertising biocides, each advertisement should contain the following text: 'Use the biocide product carefully' and 'Always read the declaration and information on the biocide product before use'. The biocide application must not be

882. The Decision shall determine the method of withdrawal of biocides and the deadline by which the biocide may be found in circulation and in use (Art. 26, para. 3).
883. The Agency shall abolish the issued licence in accordance with the conditions set forth in para. 2.
884. Based on the assessment of the data, the Agency shall issue consent for the import of biocide or active substance and use for scientific research and development, upon previously obtained opinion of the state administration body in charge of veterinary affairs and health affairs (Art. 29, para. 4).
885. The provision referred to in para. 1 of this Article shall not apply to the transport of biocides by rail, road, water and air traffic (Art. 31, para. 3).

misled in relation to the risks to human, animal and environmental health and its effectiveness (Article 36, paragraphs 1–2). Advertising and giving recommendations to users of biocides can be done only for biocides for which the licence is issued (Article 36, paragraph 4).

9. Conditions for Biocides Import and Export

809. The biocide may be imported by the holder of the licence, provisional permit and holder of consent or permit for the use of biocides for the purpose of scientific research. Biocides classified as dangerous may be imported by legal entities that meet the conditions for placing on the market dangerous chemicals in accordance with the Law regulating chemicals. An active substance may be imported by the holder of an authorization or permission to use an active substance for the purpose of scientific research or consent for the production of biocides (Article 37, paragraphs 1–3).[886]

810. The activities of production, transport, use and storage of biocides can be performed by legal entities registered for performing this activity in the Central Registry of Economic Entities and that meet the requirements regarding personnel, space and equipment. The fulfilment of the conditions shall be determined by the Agency with a Decision and issue an approval for performing the activity (Article 40, paragraphs 1–2).[887]

10. Biocides Record

811. Manufacturers, importers or exporters who place on the market and use biocides are obliged to keep records of biocides and store data from the records for five years from the date of their entry in the records. The subjects referred to in paragraph 1 of this Article shall submit to the Agency, by 31 March of the current year for the previous year, a report from the records of the biocide containing data on: quantities of produce, imported and used biocides, volumes of biocides and quantities of biocides withdrawn from traffic and use with the situation on 31 December (Article 43, paragraphs 1–2).

---

886. Biocides for which the licence and active substances have been issued may be exported. The holder of the licence referred to in para. 1 of this Article shall be obliged to submit to the Agency a notification of the performed export (Art. 38, para. 1).
887. No import licence is required for the active substance used for the production of biocides (Art. 42, para. 1).

11. Biocide Waste

812. Manufacturers, importers or exporters that produce, place on the market and use or store biocides are obliged to collect and safely dispose empty containers of biocides and residues of biocides after use, in accordance with the Law governing waste management (Article 45).

12. Damage to the Environment

813. Manufacturers, importers or exporters that produce, place on the market and use or store biocides are obliged to compensate for the damage caused in connection with the biocide due to non-compliance in accordance with this Law and due to the biocidal properties that could be affected by this person (Article 46).

13. Supervision

814. Supervision over the implementation of this Law and regulations adopted pursuant to this Law shall be carried out by the Ministry. Inspection supervision over implementation of this Law shall be performed by the administrative authority responsible for inspection work through sanitary, veterinary, phytosanitary and environmental inspectors (Article 49, paragraphs 1–2).

III. Other Relevant Legislations

815. Pursuant to the Law on Biocidal Products, the following by-laws were adopted:

- Rulebook on types of biocidal products (OJ MNE, No. 66/16).
- Rulebook on the lists of active substances that are allowed for use in biocidal products and low-risk biocidal products (OJ MNE, No. 72/16).
- Rulebook on the manner of risk assessment of biocidal products (OJ MNE, Nos 62/16, 60/19).
- Rulebook on conditions for putting biocidal products on market and use (OJ MNE, No. 59/16).
- Rulebook on the content and manner of keeping the register of biocidal products (OJ MNE, No. 62/16).
- Rulebook on the contents of the report on the import of biocidal products (OJ MNE, No. 69/16).
- Rulebook on the contents of the technical dossier and the basic data on biocides (OJ MNE, No. 5/17).
- Rulebook on methods for testing the efficacy of biocidal products (OJ MNE, No. 5/17).

- Rulebook on the content of the application for issuing a license for biocidal products (OJ MNE, No. 17/17).
- Rulebook on conditions in respect of personnel, premises and equipment for legal entities which professionally use biocidal products (OJ MNE, No. 26/17).

IV. Harmonization with EU Legislation

816. According to the EC Progress Monitoring Report for 2021 'on chemicals, Montenegro is partially aligned with the EU acquis. Further secondary legislation was adopted.'[888] However, the government adopted implementation reports as concerns the Stockholm Convention 2019–2023 and the Minamata Convention, jointly with the action plan 2022–2023 and the Minamata initial assessment.[889]

§2. Rational Use of Energy

817. One of the basic problems of the sustainable development of Montenegro is law level of energy efficiency,[890] as a consequence of non-economic prices, obsolete and energy-inefficient technologies and equipment and other reasons.[891] Besides that, there are other problems in energy sector as, for example, very high electricity losses in the transmission and distribution systems which contribute to law energy efficiency; unfavourable structure of energy consumption, with high participation of electricity and primary sources of energy (coal, oil, etc.); low level of use of own natural energy resources, especially of hydro-potential. In Montenegro, the dominant source of energy in the final energy consumption of households is biomass accounting for 54% followed by electricity at 44%. Coal (lignite) and oil derivatives (LPG) each represent approx. 1% of final energy consumption of households.[892]

818. It should be added that Montenegro has significant potential for energy generation from small hydropower plants and alternative sources[893] (solar energy,

888. EC (2021), p. 104.
889. EC (2022), p. 113. *See*: MSDT (2019).
890. For more information, *see*: ME (2019). However, 'in the period 2016–2021, several energy efficiency programmes were implemented that targeted various sectors, including the residential and public sectors.' GMNE (2022d), 97.
891. 'The energy intensity ratio (use of energy per unit of gross domestic product) was 0.432 kgoe/EUR in Montenegro in 2003, while in the developed countries this indicator is on average 0.205 kgoe/EUR. According to the IEA (International Energy Agency) calculations, this ratio was 0.13 kgoe/EUR for EU countries in 2001. This means that approximately 2.1 times more energy is consumed per unit of domestic product in Montenegro than in the developed countries, or 3.3 times more than in the EU, which shows that there is a large room for improvements in energy efficiency.' GMNE (2007C), 31–32.
892. Energy Community (2021), 192.
893. *See*: MED (2007), 30–32; 36–37. *See also* GMNE (2008b), 33.

wind power and biomass, etc.) that are already being used in Montenegro, but still not enough.[894]

I. Competencies

819. In accordance with Article 14 of the Decree on state administration organization and operations (OJ MNE, Nos 49/22, 52/22, 56/22, 82/22) the Ministry of Capital Investments (MCI) is responsible for the activities in the field of energy, including 'energy policy; establishment of directions and dynamics of development of energy; preparation of energy balance sheet of the Republic'. Directorate for Energy and Energy Efficiency as a part of the MCI performs planning and evaluation of developmental investment projects of interest for Montenegro, as well as the developmental policy in general, monitoring and actions in the field of energy and energy efficiency.[895]

The Energy Regulatory Agency must also be mentioned.[896] It is an independent, functionally autonomous and non-profit organization which functions according to the Energy Law. Its goal is to ensure, *inter alia*: that energy entities promote preservation of stability, capability and efficiency.[897]

II. Strategic Documents

820. Besides the Energy Efficiency Strategy of the RM (2005),[898] the Strategy for development of energy sector in the RM by 2030[899] was adopted, and the Strategy for development of small hydropower plants was adopted in April 2006, as well as the Action Plan for its implementation.[900]

894. GMNE (2008C), 86.
895. https://www.gov.me/mki/energetika (9 Dec. 2022).
896. *See*: https://regagen.co.me/ (14 Dec. 2022).
897. Based on the obligations given by the Law, the Agency issued the following secondary legislation, *inter alia*: Interim methodology for use of TS and DS charge, Methodology for setting of tariffs, Interim methodology for supply of tariff customers and for regulated public supply, Methodology for setting prices for supply of tariff customers and for public supply, Methodology for setting prices for ancillary and system services and balancing services, Rules for dispute settlement via arbitrage, Rules for tariff changes upon request of a regulated undertaking, Rules for procedure and conditions for licencing, Rules for market operator unbundling, Rules for functioning public supplier, Rules on condition and procedure for supplier of last resort, Rulebook on safeguard of confidential information by system operators.
898. The Action Plan for 2007 included drafting of the Programme for development of basic legislation in the field of energy efficiency; strengthening of Energy Efficiency Unit; drafting Programme for improvement of legislation and regulations, as well as of institutional requirements in the field of energy efficiency in building construction and drafting Programme for development of the energy data basis in Montenegro in compliance with the EU standards in this area.
899. *See*: ME (2014).
900. According to this Action plan the following documents have been adopted: Decree on terms and conditions for awarding concessions for exploration of water streams and techno-economic use of the water energy potential for electricity generation in small hydropower plants (Official Journal of RM, No. 70/06), Regulation on technical requirements for connection of small hydropower plants

821. A number of documents important for development of energy efficiency in Montenegro were adopted within the EAR project of technical assistance to Montenegrin Energy Efficiency Unit (2006–2007),[901] but little has been done for their implementation.

822. The current Energy Efficiency Action Plan was adopted for the period 2019–2021 by the GMNE in June 2019.[902]

III. Legislative Framework

A. *Energy Law*

823. The Parliament of Montenegro adopted the new Law on energy on 20 January 2016 (OJ MNE, Nos 5/16, 51/17, and 82/20).[903] The Law regulates: energy activities and prescribes conditions and methods for their performance, with an intention to secure quality and safe supply of final customers with energy;[904] conditions and methods of utilization of renewable sources of energy and of

---

to electric distribution network (Official Journal of RM, No. 25/07) and Instruction on establishing methodology for calculation of the selling price of electricity from small hydropower plants (Official Journal of RM, No. 46/07).

901. Action Plan for Implementation of Energy Efficiency Strategy in 2008; Long-term Action Plan for Energy Efficiency by 2012; Action Plan for Energy Efficiency in the Public Sector and Strategy of Heating and Cooling Space in Housing Sector. Data basis for energy efficiency in public sector has also been made.

902. *See*: ME (2019).

903. After entry into force of this Law, the Energy Law ('Official Journal of the RM' No. 28/10, 6/13 and 10/15) shall cease to apply (Art. 261).

904. Energy activities, according to this law are: (1) production of electric energy; (2) transmission of electric energy; (3) distribution of electric energy; (4) supply of electric energy; (5) organization and management of electric energy market; (6) storage of gas; (7) transmission of gas; (8) distribution of gas; (9) supply of gas; (10) transport of oil by pipelines and other forms of oil transport which are not regulated by special regulations; (11) transport of products from oil derivatives and other forms of transport of oil derivatives which are not regulated by special regulations; (12) transport of petroleum products by product lines; (13) transport of petroleum products by means of transport, other than product pipelines; (14) wholesale trade in oil derivatives; (15) retail trade in oil derivatives; (16) storage of oil and oil derivatives; (17) production of heat for distant heating and/or cooling; (18) distribution of heat for distant heating and/or cooling; (19) supply of heat for distant heating and/or cooling; (20) trade, go between and representation on the energy market; (21) transport and storage of liquid natural gas (hereinafter: LNG); (22) management of installation for LNG; (23) management of installations for liquid oil gas (hereinafter: LOG); (24) wholesale trade and supply of final buyers of LNG; (25) electricity and heat cogeneration; (26) production of biofuels and biodiversity; (27) transport of biofuels and biosecurity; (28) Wholesale of biofuels and biotechnologies; (29) retail trade in biofuels and biodiversity; (30) storage of biofuels and biodiversity (Art. 3). Energy activities may be performed only on the basis of licences, unless otherwise provided by this Law (Art. 65, para. 1).

cogeneration; organizing and managing the electricity and gas market, as well as other issues of importance for the energy (Article 1).[905]

824. The Law contains 261 articles divided into following 24 chapters: I Basic provisions, II Planning of the energy development, III Renewable energy sources, highly efficient cogeneration and incentive measures, IV Regulatory Energy Agency, V Prices and fees, VI Licences, certificates and energy permits, VII Renewal of energy activity, VIII Performance of electricity activity, IX Access to the transmission and distribution system of electricity, X Separation of the electricity system operators, XI Conducting activities regarding gas, XII Link to the transmission or distributive system, XIII Direct lines, XIV Supply with electricity and gas, XV Conducting activities concerning heat energy, XVI Safety of supply and measures in case of disturbance on the electricity and gas market, XVII Trade of petroleum products and biofuel, XVIII Reserves of oil and/or oil derivatives, XIX Coal delivery, XX Protection of energy objects, XXI Unauthorized use of energy, XXII Supervision, XXIII Penalties and XXIV Transitory and final provisions.

825. Long-term goals, economic and institutional-organizational framework of energy development are determined by the energy development plan of Montenegro (hereinafter 'Energy Development Plan'), adopted by the GMNE (Article 7, paragraph 1).[906] Energy development plan is regulated in more detail and implemented by the Development energy strategy of Montenegro (hereinafter 'Development energy strategy'), Action plan for implementation of Development energy strategy[907] (hereinafter 'Action plan'), the action plan for the use of energy from renewable sources, the action plan for the development and use of district heating and/or cooling and high-efficiency cogeneration and the action plan for energy efficiency, local energy plans and the energy balance (Article 7, paragraph 2). These documents are published on the internet page of state administration responsible for energy affairs (hereinafter 'Ministry').

905. This law is not applied to activities concerning exploration and exploitation of coal, other than exploitation for the production of electricity and heat; prospecting and exploitation of coal, oil and gas, development, production or refining crude oil or gas, as well as to energy efficiency and to final consumption of energy (Art. 2).

906. Energy development is planned with the aim to: (1) provide permanent, safe and quality supply of energy; (2) provide sustainable and efficient production and use of electric energy; (3) develop and use different sources of energy; (4) increase production of energy from renewable sources; (5) efficient performance of energy activities and public services on sustainable development; (6) protect the environment in all fields of energy activities; (7) introduce competition on the energy market based on principles of impartiality, transparency and non-discrimination; (8) create stable conditions for private sector and stimulate private sector in the field of energy; (9) protect final buyers of energy; (10) link the Montenegrin energy system to European energy systems and systems of states in the region in accordance with energy needs and needs of economic development; (11) develop energy market and its connection with regional and internal EU markets; (12) create conditions for investment in energy, (13) the development of the gas system and its connections with neighbouring gas systems, regarding the need to meet domestic demand for natural gas and the diversification of energy sources. (Art. 8, para. 1).

907. With the aim to realize goals from the Development energy strategy, the Government adopts the Action plan for period of five years (Art. 10).

826. Following the need to align the law with newly adopted legislation in the field of climate change, Article 8a was introduced in the latest amendments in 2020. It introduces another strategic document – National Energetic and Climate Plan (NECP). It aims to give an overview of the state of current policies and sets national aims in the field of greenhouse gasses emissions, renewable energy consumption, energy efficiency, energy security, internal energy market, research-innovations and competition. Furthermore, the NECP should allocate required financial resources for its realization and give an assessment of the effects of planned policies and measures. The NECP is still in preparation at the time of this writing (December 2022). Bodies responsible for its adoption are the MESPU and the state authority responsible for the control of state aid (only in consultative function). It should be adopted for ten years and reviewed regularly every four years.

Renewable energy sources, Highly efficient cogeneration and Incentive Measures

827. Realizing the mandatory share of energy from renewable sources[908] in gross final consumption of energy in accordance with the obligations under a ratified international treaty is of public interest. The sources and scope for the use of energy from renewable sources shall be determined by NECP in accordance with the General directives of energy policy and the regulations on energy efficiency and greenhouse gasses emissions mitigation (Article 18, paragraphs 1 and 2).[909]

828. The development and use of high-efficiency cogeneration[910] in accordance with the NECP are determined by the action plan for the development and use of remote heating and/or cooling and high-efficiency cogeneration, adopted by the Government for a period of up to ten years (Article 20, paragraph 4).[911]

829. At the latest, by the expiration of the fifth year from the adoption, the Ministry proposes implementation of an action plan for the development and use of remote heating and/or cooling and high-efficiency cogeneration, followed by its alignment with the Energy Development Strategy. The Ministry submits to the Government a statement on its implementation for the previous two calendar years,

908. Renewable sources of energy are non-fossil energy sources such as: watercourses, biomass, wind, sun, biogas, landfill gas, geothermal energy sources, waves, tides and oscillations, gas and solid wastes from waste water treatment plants and solid municipal waste (Art. 6, point 41).

909. The goals for using renewable energy sources with the action shall be determined on the basis of energy needs, economic opportunities and obligations of Montenegro taken over by a ratified international agreement (para. 3).

910. High-efficiency cogeneration, for the purposes of this law, is cogeneration that generates primary energy savings of at least 10% compared to the reference values for separate heat and power generation and cogeneration in small and micro-cogeneration facilities that provide savings of primary energy (Art. 20, para. 3). High-efficiency cogeneration, for the purposes of this law, is cogeneration that generates primary energy savings of at least 10% compared to the reference values for separate heat and power generation and cogeneration in small and micro-cogeneration facilities that provide savings of primary energy (Art. 20, para. 3).

911. Cogeneration, for the purposes of this Law, is a combined and simultaneous production of heat energy for remote heating and/or cooling and electricity or heat for remote heating and/or cooling and mechanical energy in a unique process (Art. 20, para. 1).

which in particular contains: the degree of achievement of the objectives, the implemented incentive measures and the proposal for the improvement of measures for the next period (Article 20, paragraph 7).

830. An energy entity engaged in the trade of petroleum products used in transport is obliged to place biofuels on the market in order to achieve a mandatory share of renewable energy sources in the transport sector (Article 22, paragraph 1).[912]

831. The use of renewable energy sources and high-efficiency cogeneration promotes promotional and incentive measures[913] in accordance with the Law (Article 23, paragraph 1).[914]

832. In addition to the price of electricity, the final electricity purchaser is obliged to pay compensation for stimulating the production of electricity from renewable sources and high-efficiency cogeneration. In addition to the price of oil derivatives, the final customer of petroleum products is obliged to pay the fee for encouraging the incineration of biofuels (Article 24, paragraph 1).[915]

833. In order to achieve a mandatory share of energy from renewable sources in the total final energy consumption, cooperation mechanisms may be agreed upon with other countries in accordance with established international agreements. The cooperation mechanisms are forms of cooperation between the countries that include joint projects, statistical transfers of a certain amount of energy from renewable sources, cooperative incentive measures and other forms of cooperation that enable the reduction of costs of the parties achieving the required share of renewable energy in the total final energy consumption (Article 25, paragraphs 1 and 2).[916]

912. The types, content, quality and share of biofuels being placed on the market, measures for achieving the two-link share of biofuels in petroleum products, the obligations of the energy entity from para. 1 of this Article, the manner of reporting, as well as the manner of informing the public about the characteristics of biofuels available on the market and advantages in the protection of the environment are determined by the regulation of the Government (Art. 22, para. 2).
913. The incentive measures referred to in para. 1 of this Article include: obligatory purchase of electricity, incentive prices for which this energy is purchased, the period of validity of obligatory purchase of electricity, exemption from payment of services of system balancing, priority in taking over of the produced electricity into the system, as well as other measures in accordance with this Law (Art. 23, para. 5).
914. The Ministry shall make publicly available information on the advantages and specificities for using renewable energy sources, as well as the incentive measures that are applied for the utilization of renewable energy sources (Art. 23, para. 2).
915. The supplier or retail seller of petroleum products shall be obliged on the invoice for consumed electricity, i.e., on the invoice for the sold quantity of oil derivatives delivered to the final customer, to separately charge a fee for stimulating the production of electricity from renewable energy and high-efficiency cogeneration, i.e., the fee for boosting the use of biofuels (Art. 24, para. 2).
916. The cooperation mechanisms may be contracted for one or more years (Art. 25, para. 3).

834. Installation of small boilers and stoves on biomass, solar photovoltaic systems and solar thermal systems, shallow geothermal systems and heat pumps may be performed by a physical person who has a certificate for performing these tasks (Article 26, paragraph 1).

Regulatory Agency for Energy and Regulated Communal Activities

835. The activities stipulated by the law in the field of energy and regulated communal activities are performed by the Regulatory Agency for Energy and Regulated Communal Activities (hereinafter 'the Agency') as an independent, non-profit organization, legally and functionally independent of the state authorities and energy entities (Article 27, paragraph 1).[917]

836. The Agency shall perform direct control functioning of the electricity and gas market and shall impose the measures necessary for the elimination of established irregularities in the functioning of the market (Article 49, paragraph 1). The Agency's resources shall be provided from licence fees, annual fees for the use of licences, fees for determining the status of a closed distribution system, annual fees for using the status of the closed distribution system, fees for resolving disputes, and other fees determined in accordance with this Law (Article 51, paragraph 1).[918]

837. The work of the Agency shall be public in accordance with the law. General acts of the Agency shall be adopted after a public hearing, which lasts at least fifteen days (Article 53, paragraphs 1 and 2).[919]

838. In the area of renewable energy sources and high-efficiency cogeneration the Agency: (1) performs annual analysis and publishes data on the share of renewable energy sources and high-efficiency cogeneration in total production and consumption of electricity; (2) keeps a register of issued guarantees of origin; (3) approves and changes the temporary status of the privileged manufacturer; (4) approves, modifies and revokes the status of the privileged manufacturer; (5) keeps a register of privileged producers; (6) informs the Ministry, the market operator, the distribution system operator and the electricity transmission system operator about the issued decisions on obtaining the status of the privileged producer (Article 55).

839. The Agency may resolve disputes between energy entities or between energy co-owners and users of their services, arising from their contractual relations arranged in accordance with this Law if the contracting parties entrust the resolution of the dispute (Article 57, paragraph 1).

---

917. The Agency shall have the status of a legal entity. The Agency shall be registered in the Central Registry of Enterprises. The Agency operates under the name Regulatory Agency for Energy and Regulated Communal Activities. The Agency's head office is in Podgorica (Art. 28, paras 1–4).
918. The Agency's resources shall be determined by the financial plan of the Agency which is adopted by the Assembly in accordance with the law and which is published on the Agency's website (Art. 51, para. 2).
919. The Agency shall submit to the Assembly for adoption the report on the state of the energy sector of Montenegro, no later than 31 July of the current year, for the previous year (Art. 54, para. 1).

Licences, Certificates and Energy Licences

840. The Agency shall determine the fulfilment of conditions for issuing licences determined by this Law. The Agency shall issue a licence at the request of a company, a legal entity or a natural person (Article 65, paragraphs 2 and 3).[920] The licence shall be issued for a period of up to ten years (Article 66, paragraph 1).

841. The energy entity shall be obliged to pay the fee for issuing the licence and pay the annual fee for the use of the licence for the period of licence issuance, in the amount determined by the Agency in the decision referred to in Article 51 paragraph 5 of this Law. The Registry of licences in which data on issued and withdrawn licences are entered shall be kept by the Agency (Article 67, paragraphs 1 and 2).[921]

842. Energy facilities shall be constructed in accordance with the law governing the construction of facilities and the regulation of space and technical regulations, with the previously obtained energy permit in accordance with this Law, without the implementation of a public tender procedure (Article 78, paragraph 1). An energy permit shall be obtained for the construction of: (1) facilities for electricity generation up to 1 MW[922] and (2) facilities for the production of heat for remote heating and/or cooling or industrial use and facilities for the distribution of heat for remote heating and/or cooling or industrial use[923] (Article 78, paragraph 2).[924]

B. Law on Efficient Energy Usage

843. The Law on efficient energy usage (OJ MNE, Nos 57/2014, 3/15, and 25/19)[925] has sixty-one articles divided into following ten chapters: Chapter I – Basic Principles (Articles 1–4), Chapter II – Planning of energy efficiency[926]

---

920. The licence issued for distribution of electricity or gas, the gas storage operator and the TPG plant is at the same time the act on the appointment of the operator of a distribution system of electricity or gas, a gas storage operator and a TPG plant (Art. 65, para. 6).
921. Data from the licence registry are public (Art. 67, para. 3).
922. The Energy permit referred to in para. 2, item 1 of Art. 78 shall be issued by the Ministry at the request of a company, legal entity or natural person or entrepreneur (Art. 78, para. 3). On the basis of the issued energy permit the Government shall issue a decision on granting the use of state property, on the basis of which the contract is concluded (Art. 78, para. 5).
923. The energy permit referred to in para. 2, item 2 of Art. 78, at the request of a company, legal entity or natural person, i.e., entrepreneur, shall be issued by the competent local authority (Art. 78, para. 4).
924. Energy facilities built on the basis of public bidding conducted in accordance with the law and for the construction of facilities referred to in Art. 96, para. 1 of this Law shall not be required to obtain an energy permit (Art. 78, para. 6).
925. According to the Art. 60 on the day of entry into force of the present Law, the Law on Energy Efficiency (OJ MNE, No. 29/10) shall be repealed.
926. Efficient use of energy, in terms of this Law, is considered as an increase in degree of energy efficiency in final consumption. The energy efficiency shall be the ratio between the energy consumption and the effect achieved in services, goods or energy (Art. 2, paras 1 and 2).

(Articles 5–18), Chapter III – Measures of energy efficiency (Articles 19–29), Chapter IV – Performing of energy audit (Articles 30–38), Chapter V – Certification of buildings (Articles 39–43), Chapter VI – Labeling of the energy efficiency of products (Articles 44–48), Chapter VII – Energy services (Articles 49–50), Chapter VIII – Supervision (Articles 51–52), Chapter IX – Penalties (Articles 53–54) and Chapter X – Transitional and Final provisions (Articles 55–61).

844. This Law regulates the way of efficient use of energy, measures for improvement of energy efficiency and other issues of importance for energy efficiency in final consumption. This Law does not apply to the energy efficiency of the facilities for production, transmission and energy distribution (Article 1, paragraphs 1–2).

845. Energy efficiency policy is defined and implemented in accordance with: Energy development strategy, which is adopted in accordance with the Law regulating the field of energy; Action Plan for Energy Efficiency;[927] Annual operational plan for improving energy efficiency; and Programmes and plans for improving energy efficiency (Article 5).

846. Energy efficiency measures, for the purposes of this Law, are actions and activities that improve energy efficiency, which can be checked, measured or evaluated; production of electric and/or thermal energy using renewable sources provided that the produced electricity or heat is used for own needs; and educational or informative activities aimed at raising the awareness of legal and natural persons about importance, effects and possibilities for improving energy efficiency (Article 3).[928]

C. Other Regulations

847. In addition to the general regulations in the field of energy,[929] several specific by-laws have been adopted:

- Rulebook on the designation of energy-efficient vehicle tyres and other parameters (OJ MNE No. 119/22).[930]

927. *See*: ME (2019); MCI (2021).

928. Energy efficiency measures include the following: obligations of the public sector (Art. 19), public procurement of goods and services (Art. 20), obligations in case of the purchase or leasing of buildings (Art. 21), obligations of large consumers (Art. 22), submission of data on annual energy consumption (Art. 23), energy consumption measurement (Art. 24), submission of data of energy supplier and energy distributors (Art. 25), energy efficiency of buildings (Art. 26), energy audit (Art. 27), regular energy audit of the system (Art. 28) and financing and incentives (Art. 29).

929. For example, Decision of the energy balance of Montenegro for 2012. (Official Journal of MNE, No. 7/12), Rulebook on the criteria for issuing energy permit, contents of application and register of energy permits (Official Journal of MNE, No. 49/10), etc.

930. For the list of relevant legislation, *see*: https://energetska-efikasnost.me/en/documents/ (15 Jan. 2023).

- Rulebook on technical standards of the eco-design for household clothes washing and drying appliances (OJ MNE No. 119/22).
- Rulebook on technical requirements of eco-design for ovens, hobs, and hoods (OJ MNE, No. 62/20).
- Rulebook on energy labelling of residential ventilation units (OJ MNE, No. 63/20).
- Rulebook on energy labelling of ovens and hoods (OJ MNE, No. 63/20).
- The Rulebook on minimum energy efficiency requirements of buildings (OJ MNE, No. 23/13).
- Decision on determining indicative energy savings target (OJ MNE, No. 48/11).
- Instructions on definition of methodology for calculating indicative energy savings target (OJ MNE, No. 18/11).
- Rulebook on the content of the report on implementation of the Energy Efficiency Improvement Plan by local self-government unit (OJ MNE, No. 61/11).
- Rulebook on the information system of energy consumption and on the manner of submission of data on annual consumption of energy (OJ MNE, No. 6/12).
- Regulation on determining limit for energy consumption to define big consumers, the content of the energy efficiency improvement plan and report on the plan implementation (OJ MNE, No. 10/12).

Furthermore, according to Article 6 of the Law on Energy Efficiency the Government of Montenegro has obligation to adopt the annual Energy Efficiency Operational Plan of Public Administration Institutions.[931]

D. International Treaties

848. The Treaty Establishing Energy Community between the European Community and the RM[932] was ratified in October 2006 (OJ RM, No. 66/06). The treaty entered into force on 1 July 2006, creating the largest internal market in the world. Basic goals of the Energy Community are securing supply of the single regulatory space; improving the environmental situation in relation to Network Energy and related energy efficiency, fostering the use of renewable energy, setting out the conditions for energy trade in the single regulatory space, etc.[933]

931. *See*: Energy Efficiency Operational Plan shall set forth: measures to be implemented where the public administration institutions operate; dynamics and methodology of implementation of measures and required resources for implementation of measures, sources and methods for providing sources. *See*: https://energetska-efikasnost.me/en/annual-energy-efficiency-operational-plan-of-public-administration-institutions/ (15 Jan. 2023). *See also*: Plan for the reconstruction of state-owned official buildings for the period 2020–2022 year. https://energetska-efikasnost.me/en/download/strateska_dokumenta/4.-Plan-rekonstrukcije-drzavnih-sluzbenih-zgrada-za-period-2020-2022.-godina.pdf (15 Jan. 2023).
932. Apart from Montenegro, members of the Treaty are following countries: Albania, Bosnia and Herzegovina, Bulgaria, Croatia, Macedonia, Romania Serbia and United Nations Interim Administration Mission in Kosovo (UNMIK) on behalf of Kosovo, too. *See*: https://eur-lex.europa.eu/legal-content/EN/TXT/PDF/?uri=CELEX:22006A0720(01)&from=HR (13 Dec. 2022).
933. The treaty aims at creation of a stable regulatory and market framework which will be able to attract investments into the natural gas and electricity sectors and ensure reliable power sources. This

849. Montenegro ratified the Kyoto Protocol (OJ RM, No. 17/2007) and started the process of creating conditions to start with the implementation of the projects within the Clean Development Mechanism (CDM). In addition, Montenegro ratified the Paris Agreement.[934] The country is contracting party of the Energy Charter Treaty and Energy Charter Protocol on Energy Efficiency and Related Environmental Aspects.[935]

850. Statute of the International Renewable Energy Agency (IRENA) has been ratified by the Parliament of Montenegro (OJ MNE – International Treaties, No. 6/2010).

IV. Harmonization with EU Legislation

851. 'The national action plan on the use of renewable energy sources by 2020 was adopted in December 2014. According to Montenegro's targets, by 2020, 33% of its energy should come from renewable sources in gross final consumption, although the preliminary 2014 energy balance figure showed it had already reached this target. Montenegro has partially transposed the Renewable Energy Directive, implementing legislation still has to be adopted. There are incentives for the use of renewable sources. … However, their development, in particular on hydropower, should be in conformity with the relevant EU legislation on environment. Sustainability criteria for biofuels and bioliquids are yet to be implemented'.[936]

852. Regarding energy efficiency, 'some progress was made in alignment with the EU *acquis*, with the adoption of implementing legislation on requirements for eco-design and energy efficiency labelling of energy-related products'.[937]

should be achieved with the gradual implementation of the *Acquis communautaire* in the areas of energy, environment, competition, etc., by the contracting parties. Environmental Policy in South-Eastern Europe, 178. *See also* Todić, Dimitrijević (2012), 715–716.

934. *See*: https://treaties.un.org/Pages/ViewDetails.aspx?src=TREATY&mtdsg_no=XXVII-7-d&chapter=27&clang=_en (13 Dec. 2022).

935. *See*: https://energycharter.org/who-we-are/members-observers/countries/montenegro/ (13 Dec. 2022).

936. EC (2016). p. 45.

937. EC (2022). p. 110.

Part II. Nature Conservation and Management

Chapter 1. Monuments and Landscapes

§1. Monuments

I. Monuments in Montenegro

853. 'The nature of Montenegro, including biological diversity, as well as characteristic landscapes and cultural values are some of the greatest treasures of Montenegro'.[938]

854. In accordance with the current Montenegrin legislation, cultural heritage is made of 357 archaeological, historical, artistic, building, ethnological and technical monuments of culture in Montenegro. Monuments of exceptional significance (e.g., the monuments registered in the List of World Cultural Heritage etc.) are in the first category and there are presently thirty-five of them. Monuments of great importance form the second category and there are 135 of them. Finally, there are 187 monuments in the third category (monuments of local significance).[939]

855. Existing archaeological research is not comprehensive and the issue of underwater archaeology is practically undeveloped.[940]

856. The monumental heritage located along the Montenegrin coast comprises around ninety monuments with following characteristics: urban entities and

938. GMNE, NCSD (2011), 9.
939. It should be stressed that cultural heritage in Montenegro is mainly in a very bad condition and unfavourable position, 'due to the fact that at its larger part, as well as at its most important monument units, basic monument values have been jeopardized, with the tendency of the further change of integrity, loss of the monument values and historical origins'. GMNE (2008C), 95.
940. A special danger for immovable cultural heritage and in the first place for the protected area of the city of Kotor represents more and more uncontrolled urbanization that can endanger the values because of which Kotor has been included in the List of World Cultural Heritage (UNESCO). GMNE (2008C), 96.

agglomerations (seven), sacral monuments (thirty-nine), profane monuments (twenty-six), fortification monuments (six), archaeological sites on the land (ten) and in the submarine area (two).[941]

II. Competencies

857. The Ministry of Culture (MC) and Media is responsible for cultural heritage protection, according to Article 13 of the Decree on state administration organization and operations (OJ MNE, Nos 49/22, 52/22, 56/22, 82/22).[942]

858. The Law on Local Self-Government (OJ MNE, Nos 2/18, 34/19, 34/20, 50/22) provides, *inter alia*, that the municipality 'creates and provides conditions for development of culture and protection of cultural goods' (Article 27, point 11).

III. Strategic Documents and Legislation

859. Montenegro is currently drafting the Strategy for Sustainable Development of Cultural Heritage 2023–2028, as well as the National Strategy for Conservation and Sustainable Use of Cultural Heritage. It demonstrates the government's intention to include key instruments and protect World Heritage sites within its strategic planning efforts.[943]

860. Natural and cultural heritage is protected by the Constitution. Its Article 78[944] stipulates that 'everyone shall be obliged to preserve natural and cultural heritage of general interest'. By virtue of paragraph 2 of the aforementioned article, protection of the natural and cultural heritage is obligation of State. Besides that, Cultural rights are defined in Chapter IV of the Constitution (Economic, Social and Cultural Rights and Freedoms).

A. *Environmental Legislation*

861. In the key environmental legal act the Law on the environment (OJ MNE, No. 52/16) notion 'environment' is defined (in Article 2) so to include 'cultural and historical heritage' apart from the 'natural environment: air, land, water and sea, wildlife, features and activities: climate, ionizing and nonionizing radiation, noise

941. Besides the protected cultural monuments, directly along Montenegrin coast there have also been recorded around seventy buildings/facilities of different types, that also possess certain monumental features, on the basis of which they can be considered to be potential candidates for registration, as following categories: ambience entities (six), sacral facilities (thirty-four), profane facilities (nineteen), fortification facilities (five), archaeological sites on land (six). GMNE (2007D), 74–77.
942. *See*: https://www.gov.me/dokumenta/091d5e55-3917-4d7f-b30f-6faa2ae292e4 (3 Dec. 2022).
943. GMNE (2022d), p. 102. At the international level, these efforts include participation in UNESCO conventions, European conventions and directives and other forms of international cooperation.
944. Constitution of Montenegro (Official Journal of MNE, No. 01/07).

and vibration, as well as the environment that has created man: cities and other settlements, … infrastructure, industrial and other facilities' (Article 2). Apart from that, the notion 'natural good' has been defined and includes 'cultural' element. 'Natural good' is preserved natural part of nature, which has a permanent ecological, scientific, and cultural, apart from educational, health-recreational and tourist importance (Article 7, point 32).

862. Also relevant for cultural heritage is the Law on EIA (OJ RM, No. 80/05, OJ MNE, Nos 40/10, 73/10, 40/11, 27/13, 52/16). The aims of EIA, according to it, include determination, description and assessment of the possible direct and indirect impacts of the planned project to, *inter alia*: material resources and cultural heritage (Article 2).

863. According to Article 3, paragraph 2, of the same Law, EIAs have to be carried out for projects within the protected surroundings of national monuments in addition to projects on industry, mining, energy production, transport, tourism, agriculture, forestry, water management and utilities, and for all the projects that are planned in protected natural zones.

B. Specific Legislation

864. The Montenegrin legislation relating to the protection of cultural heritage[945] is mainly laid down in the following laws:

- Law on Culture (OJ MNE, Nos 49/08, 16/11, 40/11, 38/12).
- Law on the Protection of Cultural Property (OJ MNE, Nos 49/10, 44/17, 18/19).
- Law on Museum Activities (OJ MNE, No. 49/10).
- Law on Archiving Activities (OJ MNE, Nos 49/10, 40/11).
- Law on Librarian Activities (OJ MNE, Nos 49/10, 40/11).
- Law on Monuments (OJ MNE, No. 48/08), etc.[946]

945. 'The modern practice of treatment and care for the cultural heritage was established in the second half of XIX century, with the following legal acts: 1868. – National Parliament of Principality of Montenegro proclaimed Financial Reform which is considered to be the first legal act in Montenegro that partially related to the conservation of cultural heritage, 1896 – the Law about the Library and Museum of the Principality of Montenegro was proclaimed, 1945 – The Law about the protection of cultural monuments and natural rarities was proclaimed.' (http://www.seeheritage.net/index.php/montenegro/heritage-conservation, 3 Dec. 2022).

946. Moreover, several other laws and by-laws regulate specific aspects of the cultural activities. For example: The Law on publishing activities (Official Journal of MNE, No. 30/12), The Law on cinematography (Official Journal of RM, No. 45/93), The Law on theatrical activities (Official Journal of RM, No. 60/2001), Law on rehabilitation of the monumental area of Kotor (1991), Law on rehabilitation and revitalization of old towns damaged in the disastrous earthquake on 15 Apr. 1979 (1984, 1986), etc.

865. The Law on Culture (OJ MNE, Nos 49/08, 16/11, 40/11, 38/12) establishes general elements of cultural policy. It defines the public interest in culture and regulates institutions of culture, status and rights of artists and experts in culture, incentives and supports the development of culture, the financing of culture and other issues of importance for the culture (Article 1). According to Article 4 of the Law, some areas of cultural and artistic creativity and cultural activities have to be regulated by the special laws.

C. The Law on the Protection of Cultural Property

866. On 27 July 2010, the Montenegrin Parliament passed new Law on protection of cultural property (OJ MNE, Nos 49/10, 040/11, 044/17, 018/19). It has the following eleven parts: Part I – General Provisions (Articles 1–11), Part II – Types of cultural property (Articles 12–17), Part III – Establishing of protection, categories and registration of the cultural property (Articles 18–36), Part IV – Regime of cultural property protection (Articles 37–69), Part V – Measures of cultural property protection (Articles 70–110), Part VI – Rights and obligations of the owners and cultural property holders (Articles 111–119), Part VII – Conducting activities of cultural property protection (Articles 120–124), Part VIII – Financing of protection and preservation of cultural property (Articles 125–130), IX Supervision on Law implementation (Articles 131–133), X Penalty provisions (Articles 134–140) and Part XI – Transitional and final provisions (Articles 141–150).

867. According to Article 1, the Law regulates the types and categories of cultural properties,[947] ways of establishing protection, regime and protection measures, rights and obligations of owners and keepers of cultural property, as well as other issues of importance for protection and preservation of cultural property.

868. Cultural property, as valorised part of the cultural heritage[948] of general interest, shall be protected in accordance with this Law and in accordance with international regulations, regardless of the time, place and way of creation, origin, current ownership and their secular or religious character (Article 3, paragraph 1). Protection of cultural property is of public interest (Article 3, paragraph 2).

947. *Cultural property* is any immovable, movable and immaterial property for which, in accordance with this Law, is determined that it is of permanent historical, artistic, scientific, archaeological, architectural, anthropological, technical or other social importance (Art. 2, para. 1). Cultural property may be public or private ownership (Art. 2, para. 2).

948. *Cultural heritage* is a set of properties inherited from the past that people recognize as a reflection and expression of their values, beliefs and traditions, which are constantly evolving, including all aspects of their environment arising from the interaction between people and nature over time, regardless of ownership (Art. 11, point 9).

1. The Objectives of the Protection and General Obligations

869. The objectives of protection of cultural property are the following (Article 4, paragraph 1): (1) preservation and improvement of cultural properties and their transmission to future generations in an authentic form; (2) ensuring conditions for the survival of cultural properties and for preservation of their integrity; (3) ensuring of sustainable use of cultural property, in accordance to their traditional or new relevant purposes, for human development and quality of life; (4) dissemination of knowledge about the value[949] and importance of cultural property; (5) preservation of cultural diversity through improvement of the condition and values of all types of cultural property, fostering of creativity and understanding of different cultures and cultural layers and improving the dialogue among cultures and religions; (6) providing conditions for cultural property, according to their purpose, are used to meet the cultural, scientific and educational needs of individuals and society; (7) the prevention of actions and activities that can alter the appearance, characteristics, specificity, meaning or significance of cultural property; and (8) prevention of illegal trade and transfer of cultural property.

870. Everyone has the right, under equal conditions, individually or collectively, to use cultural property for participation in cultural life, enjoyment, scientific progress or other benefits resulting from it, as well as to contribute to its enrichment and preservation, in accordance with this Law (Article 5, paragraph 1).

871. Montenegro is obliged to provide protection and preservation of all cultural property situated within its territory, including internal waters and territorial sea, as well as to take care of protection and preservation of property located abroad if they are relevant to its history or culture (Article 6, paragraph 1). Owners and keepers of cultural property, including religious communities, are obliged to preserve, respect, maintain and properly use the cultural property that they possess (Article 6, paragraph 2).

872. Administrative and related professional activities on protection of cultural property are performed by the administrative authority in charge of the protection of cultural property (hereinafter 'the Administration') (Article 8, paragraph 1).[950]

2. Types of Cultural Property

873. Immovable cultural property is a profane, religious, memorial, fortification or infrastructural building, a group of buildings or areas with characteristic

949. *Cultural values* are determined characteristic feature and characteristics of cultural goods that are of lasting historical, artistic, scientific, archaeological, architectural, anthropological, technical or other social significance (Art. 11, point 13).

950. Professional work on the protection of cultural property, which are not under the jurisdiction of the Administration, may be conducted by a legal entity and a natural person who meets the requirements for conservation, museum, library, archive and cinematheque activities, in accordance with this and special Laws (Art. 8, para. 2).

interactions of man and nature (Article 12, paragraph 1). Immovable cultural property may be cultural – historical building,[951] cultural-historical unit,[952] site or area[953] (Article 12, paragraph 2).

874. Movable cultural property is the single archaeological, artistic, ethnographic, technical or documentary item or a natural specimen or a collection of these items, which is a witness of human creativity and evolution of nature (Article 16, paragraph 1). Immaterial cultural heritage is a human skill, expression or performance, as well as the item, crafts, instrument or space that is associated with it, which communities, groups and in some cases individuals recognize as part of their cultural heritage (Article 17, paragraph 1).

3. Establishing of Protection, Categories and Registration of Cultural Property

875. Protection of cultural property is established by determining previous protection[954] and determining the status of cultural property (Article 18, paragraph 1). Any person may launch the initiative with the Administration for establishing protection of a cultural property and Administration is obliged to consider the initiative and to inform the submitter in writing, within ninety days of the initial submission (Article 19).

876. Cultural value of the immovable, movable and immaterial property shall be determined by a professional body of at least three members, formed by the Management Board[955] (Article 23, paragraph 1).

877. The Law also regulates following: criteria for determining cultural values (Article 24), decision on establishing the status of a cultural property (Article 26), delivering a decision (Article 27), publishing decision (Article 28), registering with a real estate cadastre (Article 29), monitoring situation and revalorization of cultural values (Article 30), cessation of the status of cultural values (Article 31)[956] and the file of the cultural property (Article 32).

---

951. *Cultural–historical building* is a single immovable object of architectural, archaeological, artistic, technical, palaeontological or of other social importance (Art. 13, para. 1).
952. *Cultural and historic unit* is an urban or rural settlement or part thereof, including associated infrastructure and isolated or related group of buildings that are by its characteristic peculiarities unique enough to represent the topographic unit (Art. 14, para. 1).
953. *Locality or area* represents the joint work of man and nature, which is partially built, sufficiently especial and homogeneous to be topographically defined (Art. 15, para. 1).
954. Previous protection is established on the immovable and movable property that is reliably believed to have cultural value, to prevent the risk of damage, destruction or disappearance (Art. 20, para. 1). Previous protection shall cease: on the day of issuance of decision establishing status of cultural property, by the expiration of a previous protection period and on the day of establishing that a property has no cultural values (Art. 22).
955. The Management Board is required to regularly monitor the situation and that at least once every five years make revaluation of cultural value of cultural property (Art. 30, para. 1).
956. Administration shall pass a decision on the cessation of the status of a cultural property, if a cultural property is: (1) completely destroyed of seriously damaged and there is no possibilities for its

878. There are three categories of cultural property: cultural property of international importance, cultural property of national importance and cultural property of local importance (Articles 33–35). Cultural properties are recorded in the Register of Cultural Property (hereinafter 'the Register') (Article 36, paragraph 1).

4. System of Protection of Cultural Property

879. In this part of the law the following issues have been regulated: (1) Managing cultural property: establishing the state property (Article 37), prohibition of acquiring of ownership (Article 38), managing a state-owned cultural property (Article 39), managing a privately owned cultural property (Article 40), temporary guardian cultural property (Article 41); (2) Flow of cultural property: alienation of a state-owned property and its temporary loan (Article 42), liability for state-owned cultural property (Article 43), sale of privately owned cultural property (Article 44), pre-emptive right (Article 45), sale in a direct agreement (Article 46), sale at a public auction (Article 47), sale of a cultural property in the enforcement (Article 48), sales contract for a cultural property (Article 49), liability of a seller, real estate agent and purchaser (Article 50), purchase and sale of antiquities and object d'art (Article 51), taking cultural property out of country (Article 52), monitoring or taking cultural property out of country (Article 53), taking out of antiquities and objects d'art (Article 54), taking a cultural property into a country (Article 55), relocation of a cultural property (Article 56); (3) The using of cultural property: purpose of a cultural property (Article 57), usage of cultural property for special purposes (Article 58); (4) Concession on cultural property: the scope of concession (Article 59), a concessionaire (Article 60), concession act and concession contract (Article 61), giving a cultural property for use without public advertisement (Article 62); (5) Return of cultural property: return of cultural property to EU Member State (Article 63),[957] procedure to return a cultural property (Article 64), court proceedings (Article 65), cooperation with Member States (Article 66), return of cultural property illicitly taken out from the territory of the state, a non-EU member (Article 67), return of cultural property illicitly taken from the territory of Montenegro (Article 68), activities on return of cultural property (Article 69).

---

reconstruction due to lack of adequate documentation, that is relevant data or critical quantity of the remnant of its structure; (2) completely destroyed of seriously damaged and there is no possibilities for its reconstruction on the location where it was, and the location is of significance for its cultural and historical significance and (3) an archaeological find which is completely explored, movable findings excavated and housed out a find, and there are no immovable findings at the find (Art. 31, para. 1).

957. Certain types of cultural goods – 'national treasures', are exempted from this obligation as well as from the general EU principle of freedom of movement for goods, by the provisions on the Treaty on the functioning of the EU (see more in Pavićević, Vučić 2021).

5. Measures for Protection of Cultural Property

880. Preventive measures for protection of cultural property are research, documentation, labelling, storage, maintenance, education, presentation and popularization of cultural property and cooperation with owners and keepers of cultural property, NGOs and other entities (Article 70, paragraph 2). Furthermore, following issues have been regulated: documenting cultural property (Article 71), information system of cultural property (Article 72), marking cultural property (Article 73), preserving cultural property (Article 74), maintaining cultural property (Article 75), education (Article 76), presentation and popularization of cultural property (Article 77), cooperation with owners and holders of cultural property (Article 78) and cooperation with NGOs (Article 79).

881. Research of the cultural property is made for the purpose of (1) detection, identification, documentation, study and determination of the characteristics, qualities, significance and meaning; (2) establishing and implementing measures for the protection and conservation; (3) expansion and deepening of professional and scientific knowledge; (4) building construction or carrying out of other actions which result in changes in space (Article 80, paragraph 1).[958] In connection with this following issues have been regulated in more detail: research approval (Article 81), obligations of the approval holder (Article 82), suspension of research and revocation of the approval (Article 83), research licence (Article 84), foreign researchers (Article 85) and priority rights to scientific processing (Article 86).

882. Obligations of the discoverer at accidental findings and obligations of the Administration and investor are prescribed in Articles 87 and 88. Integrated protection of cultural property is achieved through (1) protection of cultural property in planning documents (Article 89);[959] (2) The study of cultural property protection (Article 90); (3) Management plan (Article 91); (4) Geological exploration and exploitation of mineral resources (Article 92); and (5) Protection of cultural property from the factors of environmental impact (Article 93).

883. Conservation measures on the cultural properties are the following: conservation (Article 95),[960] restoration (Article 96), reconstruction (Article 97), anastylosis (Article 98), consolidation, rehabilitation, adaptation (Articles 99–108) and other works and activities that maintain or change the current state of cultural property (Articles 109–110).

958. Research of cultural property shall be performed as (Art. 80, para. 2): (1) archaeological research; (2) conservation research; and (3) other professional and scientific researches.

959. *Planning documents* are state and local planning documents prepared and adopted in accordance with the Law regulating the space (Art. 11, point 16).

960. *Preservation of cultural property* is the extension of the duration of the properties feature and characteristics of cultural property, which represent its cultural value, and prevention deterioration of cultural heritage and ensuring its purposes and functions (Art. 11, point 15).

6. Rights and Obligations of Owners and Holders of Cultural Property

884. In this section of the law following issues have been regulated: (1) Rights of owners and holders:[961] right to expert assistance (Article 111), the right to public presentation (Article 112), right to deposit (Article 113), right to financial support (Article 114), right to compensation for damage (Article 115); (2) Obligations of owners and holders: reporting changes (Article 116), guarding, maintaining and implementing protective measures (Article 117), allowing research and implementation of protective measures (Article 118) and providing accessibility of a cultural property to public (Article 119).

7. Performing the Activities on Protection of Cultural Property

885. The protection and preservation of cultural property are achieved by performing conservation, museum, archives, library and cinematheque activities, in accordance with the Law and professional rules (Article 120, paragraph 1). Conservation services include expert tasks referring to research, study, documenting, marking, presentation, valorisation and revalorization of cultural property and implementation of conservation measures (Article 121, paragraph 1).[962]

8. Financing of Protection and Preservation of Cultural Property

886. The protection and preservation of cultural property are financed by (1) owner and the holders of cultural heritage; (2) the general budget revenues of Montenegro; (3) rent for the preservation of cultural property; (4) the municipality's budget; (5) grants; (6) other sources in accordance with the Law (Article 125, paragraph 1).[963] Apart from that, in this part of the law following issues have been regulated: cultural property owners fund (Article 126), Montenegro budget fund (Article 127), programme of protection and preservation of cultural property (Article 128), municipal budget's fund (Article 129) and return of invested funds (Article 130). Furthermore, the law regulates role of the public institutions in conservation service (Article 131), performing professional tasks (Article 132) and professional titles (Article 133).

---

961. *Holder of the cultural property* is a legal entity or natural person who owns cultural property, but is not its owner (Art. 11, point 5).
962. Certain tasks from conservation service may be performed by expert and scientific institutions and other legal and natural persons which fulfil prescribed spatial, staffing, technical, technological and material conditions (Art. 121 para. 3).
963. Rent for the preservation of cultural property is determined by tax laws (Art. 125, para. 2).

9. Inspection Supervision

887. Inspection supervision over the implementation of this law is performed by the Ministry and Administration through inspector for cultural heritage and inspector for cultural property (hereinafter 'inspector') (Article 131, paragraph 1). Obligations and authorizations of inspections and obligations of subjects of supervision have been precisely regulated by Articles 132 and 133.[964]

D. International Treaties

888. Montenegrin legislation concerning monuments contains principles and standards from the following international treaties:[965]

- Hague Convention for the protection of cultural property in the event of armed conflict from 1954.
- Convention on means of prohibiting and preventing the illicit import, export and transfer of ownership of cultural property (Paris, 1970).
- Convention on the protection of world cultural and natural heritage (Paris, 1972).
- European Convention on the protection of architectural heritage (Granada, 1985).
- European Convention on violations regarding cultural property (Delfi, 1985).
- United Nations Educational, Scientific and Cultural Organization (UNESCO) recommendation on international principles of exchange of cultural property (Nairobi, 1976).
- UNESCO recommendation on the protection of mobile cultural property (Paris, 1978), etc.[966]

964. Penalties are prescribed in Arts 134–140.

965. The Government of the Republic of Montenegro has also become a contracting party to several treaties of the United Nations Educational, Scientific and Cultural Organization 'as from 3 Jun. 2006, the date on which the Republic of Montenegro assumed responsibility for its international relations'. These are, *inter alia*, Convention for the Protection of Cultural Property in the Event of Armed Conflict – The Hague, 14 May 1954; First Protocol to the Convention for the Protection of Cultural Property in the Event of Armed Conflict – The Hague, 14 May 1954; Second Protocol to the Convention for the Protection of Cultural Property in the Event of Armed Conflict – The Hague, 26 Mar. 1999; Convention on the Means of Prohibiting and Preventing the Illicit Import, Export and Transfer of Ownership of Cultural Property – Paris, 14 Nov. 1970; Convention for the Protection of the World Cultural and Natural Heritage – Paris, 16 Nov. 1972 https://whc.unesco.org/en/conventiontext (3 Dec. 2022). In addition, list of Council of Europe conventions signed and ratified by the Montenegro includes, *inter alia*, European Cultural Convention (1954) and Convention for the Protection of the Architectural Heritage of Europe (1985); *see*: https://www.coe.int/en/web/culture-and-heritage/granada-convention (3 Dec. 2022).

966. GMNE (2008b), 509–511. Moreover, the Parliament of Montenegro has adopted the Law on Ratification of the UNESCO Convention on the Protection and Promotion of the Diversity of Cultural Expressions on 19 May 2008 and Law on Ratification of the Framework Convention on the Values of Cultural Heritage for Society (Official Journal of MNE, No. 1/08).

889. Montenegro is a State Party of the UNESCO Convention on the Protection of the Underwater Cultural Heritage.[967]

890. In November 2011, Montenegrin Parliament ratified the European Convention on the protection of archaeological heritage (revised) (Valetta, 1992) (OJ MNE – International Treaties, No. 14/11).

IV. Harmonization with EU Legislation

891. According to the EC Report for 2022, Montenegro has a good level of preparation[968] in the field of education and culture (Chapter 26). Besides that:

> in December 2021 Montenegro signed an agreement with the European Commission for its participation in the EU Creative Europe 2021–2027 programme. However, Montenegro still needs to establish an overall management system to implement protection measures for the preservation of Kotor's (Boka Kotorska Bay) UNESCO World Heritage status.[969] However, Montenegro needs to adopt implementing legislation on the export control of cultural goods.[970]

§2. LANDSCAPES

I. Landscape Diversity of Montenegro

892. Landscape diversity of Montenegro stems from a combination of exceptional natural values alongside different local traditions in spatial use, which resulted from reflection of cultural-historical and socio-economic circumstances.[971] Having in mind the biogeographical and environmental criteria, ten landscape types (E-Mediterranean, lower sub-Mediterranean, Mediterranean flysch, flat land-swampy, higher sub-Mediterranean, hilly silicate, mezophile, mountainous, high mountainous and anthropogenic landscape type)[972] and twenty-one basic landscape units can be recognized.

---

967. *See*: http://www.unesco.org/eri/la/convention.asp?order=alpha&language=E&KO=13520 (3 Dec. 2022). 'Concerning underwater cultural heritage, Montenegro has many archaeological sites that are still *in situ* and protected by the law, and there are many more that have not yet been explored or discovered. … Montenegro has two underwater archaeological sites that are protected by the law, the Bay of Bigovica in Bar and the under-ocean area between cape Strpački and cape Murove in Risan. However, there is a list of registered underwater archaeological sites which are not protected by the law, but whose cultural importance is recognized through a new group of Laws protecting cultural heritage.' *See* extensively, UNESCO (2010), 2.
968. EC (2022), 102.
969. *Ibid.*, 104.
970. EC (2020). p. 115.
971. 'The area of Montenegro is very complex in terms of landscape and has many natural contrasts, which together form a unique geographical whole.' MSDT (2020), p. 18.
972. GMNE (2008C), 47.

893. According to the accepted classification, the Montenegrin Littoral belongs to the Mediterranean landscape type.[973] Landscape values of the coastal region suffer from pressure of increasing tourism and urbanization that cause degradation of natural areas and also endanger certain components of biodiversity.[974]

894. According to the NSDSM landscape quality has been significantly affected by insufficiently developed awareness, state of the regulations and inadequate expert bases combined with impacts of urbanization, etc.[975]

II. Legislation

895. Several legal acts and international treaties in the field of environmental protection, protection of nature, agriculture, forestry and other related fields, are relevant or could be relevant in the domain of landscape protection.

896. Law on Environment (OJ MNE, Nos 52/16, 73/19) mentions landscapes in the following three provisions: Article 5 (Principle of Environmental Protection), Article 7, point 9 (definition of the notion 'integral coastal zone management') and Article 7, point 43 (definition of the notion 'natural protected goods'). Landscape (in addition to human life and health, flora and fauna, land, water, air, climate, material resources and cultural heritage) should be, as already mentioned, identified, described and assessed in the EIA procedure, in accordance with Article 3 of the Law on EIA (OJ MNE, No. 75/18). Law on spatial development and construction of buildings (OJ MNE, 74/17, 44/18, 63/18, 11/19-corr, 82/20) contains several provisions related to landscape protection.

897. 'Landscape' and 'landscape diversity' are mentioned in several provisions of the recently adopted Law on Nature Protection (OJ MNE, Nos 54/16, 18/19).[976]

898. A special regime for the landscape of exceptional characteristics[977] is also defined by the Law (Article 26). In the landscape of exceptional characteristics, it is forbidden to carry out activities that distort the characteristics due to which the area was declared protected (Article 26, paragraph 2).

973. Eight types of landscape are distinguished in this area. These are: hygrophilous forests and thickets, marshes landscape, dune landscape, pebbled sandy beaches, coastal reefs and rocky coasts, muddy coasts, the Boka Kotorska Bay landscape, and anthropogenic landscape. GMNE (2007D), 40.

974. GMNE (2008C), 47–48. Similarly, UNECE (2007), 75, 81.

975. MSDT (2016b), 139.

976. According to Art. 6, para. 46, 'Landscape' is 'the site of a visual experience, whose structure and character are the result of the interaction of natural and anthropogenic elements'. 'Landscape diversity' is defined as 'the structure of space created in the interaction of natural and constructed landscape elements of certain biological, climatological, geological, geomorphologic, pedagogical, hydrological, cultural–historical and sociological characteristics' (Art. 6, para. 45).

977. A landscape of exceptional characteristics is the land or sea, i.e., land and sea, where the interaction of people and nature over time has shaped the recognizable features of the site with significant aesthetic, ecological and cultural values, followed by high biological diversity (Art. 26. para. 1).

899. According to Article 3 nature protection is being carried out in order to, *inter alia*, preserve and improve biological (genetic, species, ecosystem), geological and landscape diversity. In addition, Article 11 prescribes that the Biodiversity strategy has to define, *inter alia*, long-term goals and guidelines for the preservation of biological and landscape diversities (paragraph 3).[978]

900. A general obligation of the Government to adopt the annual monitoring programme, which includes, *inter alia*, monitoring of the state of protected areas, is prescribed by Article 100 of the Law.

901. It is stated in the NSSDM that the implementation of the European Convention on Areas is not at a satisfactory level. Harmonization of legal regulations in spatial planning, nature protection and cultural heritage has not been fully implemented. Landscape policy is not adopted.[979] Montenegro is a member of the European Landscape Convention (2003) since 1 May 2009.[980]

978. The strategy should include measures to preserve landscape diversity, in addition to the description of the state of nature and natural values, strategic objectives of nature protection with indicators of implementation, guidelines for the conservation of protected natural assets, guidelines for the protection of ecosystems, habitat types and wildlife, plants and fungi, guidelines for research and monitoring, guidelines for informing the public and public participation in decision-making on nature protection, manner of implementation of international obligations in the field of nature protection, etc (para. 4).
979. MSDT (2016b), 139.
980. *See*: https://www.coe.int/en/web/conventions/full-list/-/conventions/treaty/176/signatures (18 Apr. 2018).

Chapter 2. Parks and Reserves

§1. The Physical Context

902. National network of protected nature areas currently counts seventy-three areas and covers 185,269.69 ha, or 13.414% of the land territory of Montenegro, of which the largest part (100,427 ha or 72,71%) belongs to five NP.[981] In accordance with provision of Article 2 of the Law on National Parks (OJ MNE, No. 56/09) these are Skadar Lake, Lovćen, Durmitor, Biogradska gora and Prokletije.[982] The remaining part consists of sixty-eight protected areas within the following categories: strict nature reserve (three), special nature reserve (one), nature park (six), nature monument (fifty-six), and a region of exceptional qualities.

903. Internationally protected areas include the Tara River Basin, the M&B UNESCO Biosphere Reserve, including Durmitor National Park with the Tara River Canyon (182,889 ha), Skadar Lake National Park – a Ramsar site (List of wetland areas of international importance, especially as a habitat for waterfowl – 20,000 ha), Tivat salt pans also Ramsar site (150 ha), Bay of Kotor-Risan, Municipality of Kotor (UNESCO – 15,000 ha) and Ulcinj Salt Flats as Ramsar site (1,477 ha) since 2019.[983] In addition to areas previously referred to, in Montenegro, there are also many other areas of nature with significant and valuable biological diversity which meet the criteria of international agreements. The rest consists of over forty protected areas within the categories: natural monument, a region of special natural characteristics and the (general and special) reserves.[984]

904. Generally, 'the state of biodiversity can be described as satisfactory, with some reasons for concern'.[985] There was no proclamation of new protected areas since 2010, even though there are ongoing efforts to improve representativeness and extend coverage of the protected area system.

---

981. EPA (2021), p. 133. *See also* GMNE (2007C), 35–37; MSDT (2014), p. 5.
982. SY MNE-2008, 24. For further information concerning national parks in Montenegro, *see* http://nparkovi.me/sajt/ (3 Dec. 2022).
983. EPA (2021), p. 133.
984. On the territory of Montenegro 156 habitat types, five plant species, five mosses species and 162 species of invertebrates and vertebrates were identified having protection/conservation importance based on the criteria of Resolutions 4 and 6 of the Convention on the Conservation of European Wildlife and Natural Habitats (Bern Convention) and Annexes I and II of the Habitats Directive and the Birds Directive. Some thirty-two Emerald areas were proposed for conservation using criteria compatible with the Natura 2000. Government adopted a proposal for defining fifteen areas. GMNE (2008b), 514. Montenegro is one of the biodiversity 'hot spots' in the Mediterranean. 'Together with mountainous region of Bulgaria, Montenegrin territory is one of the 153 globally significant floristic biodiversity centres. Mountain areas of Lovćen and Prokletije stand out as herpetofauna "hot spots".' *National Report to the United Nations Convention on Biological Diversity*, 2014. https://www.cbd.int/doc/world/me/me-nr-05-en.pdf (3 Dec. 2022), 5.
985. MSDT (2014), p. 6.

§2. Competencies

905. Several bodies and organizations have the competence to implement relevant regulations and carry out activities related to nature protection and management of protected areas. Pursuant to Article 12 of the Decree on state administration organization and operations (OJ MNE, Nos 49/22, 52/22, 56/22, 82/22). the MESPU conducts administrative activities with regard to, *inter alia*, the protection of nature.

906. Additionally, protections of nature imply measures implemented by the following authorities and institutions: MAFWM (Forest Management Directorate),[986] NEPA,[987] The Institute of Marine Biology[988] and The Public Enterprise for National Parks.[989] The role of local government institutions and professional organizations in parks and reserve protection is particularly important, too.

§3. Strategic Documents

907. Montenegro has adopted several strategic documents relevant to nature protection including parks and reserves. General importance has the following documents: Spatial plan of Montenegro until 2020 (SPM), Spatial plan for special-purpose coastal zone, National Forest and Forest Land Administration Policy, Agriculture and Rural Development Strategy, Montenegro Tourism Development Strategy to 2020, et al. National Strategy for Sustainable Development of Montenegro with the Action Plan 'stipulates international standards integration within the national legal framework and protected areas management system'.[990]

908. In 2010, National Biodiversity Strategy and Action Plan for the period 2010–2015 has been adopted. Since 2016, the National Strategy and Action Plan for the period 2016–2020 has been implemented.[991] In accordance with the provisions of Article 11 of the Law on nature protection (OJ MNE, Nos 54/16, 18/19), the strategy contains several elements. These are: Description of the state of nature and natural values; Strategic goals of nature protection with implementation indicators; Guidelines for the preservation of protected natural resources; Guidelines for the protection of ecosystems, habitat types and wild species of animals, plants and fungi; Guidelines for research and monitoring of the state of nature; Guidelines for the inclusion of protection of nature in the other sectors; Guidelines for public notice and public participation in decision-making in nature protection; Action plans

986. For more information *see*: http://www.upravazasume.me/kontakt.php?main_id=6# (9 Dec. 2022).
987. *See*: https://epa.org.me/opste-informacije/ (3 Dec. 2022).
988. Institute of Marine Biology carries out monitoring and research programmes on the biological resources of the continental shelf and slope of the Montenegrin Coast. *See*: http://www.ucg.ac.me/ibm (3 Dec. 2022).
989. Cadastres of plants and animals as well as their habitats and ecosystems are the responsibility of the Public Enterprise for National Parks.
990. *See*: GMNE (2007C), 35.
991. *See*: https://www.cbd.int/doc/world/me/me-nbsap-v2-en.pdf (3 Dec. 2022).

for the implementation of the Strategy, with establishing priorities and possible funding sources; Manner of implementation of international obligations in the field of nature protection; Measures to preserve landscape diversity; Measures for the protection and sustainable management of protected areas; Indicators of successful implementation of the action plan; Maps which show the measures for preserving biological and landscape diversity and protection of natural resources; and Other elements of importance for the nature protection.[992] Generally, the management of the five national parks is funded from their own revenues, grants and transfers from the state budget. However 'total revenues are barely sufficient to finance operating costs and basic maintenance works. There is significant public underinvestment in the national parks'.[993]

909. According to the National Report of Montenegro to the United Nations Convention on Biological Diversity, the country has defined seven strategic targets when it comes to the protection and conservation of biodiversity. The targets have been defined in accordance with the national needs recognised through implementation of the NBSAP 2010–2015, as well as with other strategic documents, assessment of the situation in the field and consultations with a wide array of stakeholder.[994]

§4. Legislation

910. A number of provisions of the Constitution of Montenegro (OJ MNE, No. 1/2007) refer to nature. The conviction that the state is responsible for the preservation of nature, sound environment, sustainable development, balanced development of all its regions and the establishment of social justice has been stipulated in the preamble of the Constitution (paragraph 4). Pursuant to Article 58 'natural wealth and goods in general use shall be owned by the state' (paragraph 3),[995] and protection of natural and cultural heritage has been guaranteed by Article 78.

I. Law on the Environment

911. Law on the environment (OJ MNE, Nos 52/16, 73/19) could be relevant for the protection of parks and reserve only in a general way. For example, aims of

992. It has to be mentioned that some activities has been conducted in the framework of several other projects. *See*: GMNE (2008b), 533.
993. UNECE (2015), xxi.
994. *See*: MSDT (2018). Although the targets have been defined at the national level, taking into account specific national situation, needs and priorities, they also comply with global targets defined in the Strategic Plan for Biodiversity 2011–2020 and Aichi targets, which were one of the inputs for defining the national targets.
995. Freedom of entrepreneurship may be limited only if so necessary in order to protect the, *inter alia*, natural resources of Montenegro (Art. 59, para. 2). Otherwise, freedoms of entrepreneurship are guaranteed (Art. 59, para. 1).

environmental protection (Article 4, points 2, 3, 5, 7), principle of sustainable development (Article 5, point 1), principle of natural resources protection (Article 5, point 3), principle use-pay (Article 5, point 6), definition of 'environment' (Article 2), definition of 'sustainable use and management of natural resources' (Article 7, point 23), definition of 'environmental pollution' (Article 7, point 39), definition of 'monitoring' (Article 7, point 18, Articles 54–59), information system (Articles 62–65), obligations of legal and natural entities (Article 9), nature protection (Article 20) and sustainable development and nature protection documents (Articles 29–37).

912. According to Article 7, point 43 of the Law on the Environment 'protected natural good is natural good which, because of its special values and characteristics (geodiversity, biodiversity, landscape), is under special protection'.[996]

II. Law on Nature Protection

913. Several chapters of the Law on Nature Protection (OJ MNE, Nos 52/16, 18/19) relate to the protected natural areas implicitly and Law could be considered a basic source of law in this field. In addition to general provisions these are following chapters: Chapter V – Protected Natural Goods (Articles 20–54); Chapter VI – Management of Protected Areas and Areas of Ecological Networks (Articles 55–67); Chapter VII – Speleological, Geological, and Paleontological objects (Articles 68–72); Chapter VIII – Protection of Wild Species (Articles 73–96); Chapter IX – Preservation of Genetic Diversity (Articles 97–99); Chapter X – Monitoring of the State of Nature (Articles 100–101); Chapter XII – Financing Nature Protection (Article 104); Chapter XIII – Protection of the Protected Natural Goods (Articles 105–106), etc. However, it should be kept in mind that the concept of protected natural resources has been based on a wider approach and includes different elements.[997]

A. Subjects of the Nature Protection

914. Protection of nature, within their rights and obligations, is provided and actively implemented by: state administration bodies, local self-government bodies and local authorities, legal entities and natural persons, international organizations, NGOs and citizens (hereinafter 'subjects of protection') (Article 7).

915. Regarding nature protection, in carrying out their activities subjects of protection are obliged to provide, within the framework of their rights and obligations: applying the regulations on nature protection; respecting the objectives of nature protection; implementing measures and conditions of nature protection; obtaining

996. Natural good is a preserved part of nature, which has a permanent ecological, scientific, cultural, educational, health–recreational, tourist and other character; (Art. 7, point 32).
997. *See also* the next Chapter relating to the wildlife protection.

licences for activities in protected areas; conducting the procedure for assessing eligibility for the ecological network; using protected natural assets in accordance to this Law; controlling and preventing the degradation of natural values, i.e., reducing them to the smallest possible extent measure; and other measures in accordance to the Law (Article 8, paragraph 1).[998]

B. Nature Protection Documents

916. Nature protection documents are Biodiversity strategy; Management plans for protected natural resources and annual programmes for the management of protected natural values; and Local action plans for biodiversity (Article 10, paragraph 1).[999]

917. The Strategy is adopted for a period of five years. The Strategy is adopted by the GMNE (hereinafter 'the Government'). The Strategy defines long-term goals and guidelines for the preservation of biological and landscape diversity (Article 11, paragraphs 1 and 3).[1000]

918. The Report on the implementation of the Strategy is prepared by the administrative authority responsible for environmental protection (administrative body) and submitted to the Government. The Report shall be prepared every second year on the basis of data on the implemented measures from Strategies and reports on the implementation of Local Action Plans (Article 12, paragraphs 1–4).

919. Competent local self-government bodies prepare Local action plans for biodiversity in order to implement the Strategy and conservation and protection of nature at the local level. A local action plan for biodiversity is adopted for a period of five years and submitted to the administrative body (Article 13, paragraphs 1, 2 and 4).

998. Non-governmental organizations participate in the preservation of nature protection in accordance with their programmes. The state encourages the participation of non-governmental organizations in the adoption and implementation of decisions and measures of importance for nature protection (Art. 9, paras 1–2).

999. Plans and programmes referred to in para. 1 indents 2 and 3 of this Article must be harmonized with the Strategy (Art. 10, para. 2).

1000. The Strategy contains: Description of the state of nature and natural values; Strategic objectives of nature protection with indicators of implementation; Guidelines for the conservation of protected natural assets; Guidelines for the protection of ecosystems, habitat types and wildlife, plants and fungi; Guidelines for research and monitoring of the situation in the countryside; Guidelines for inclusion of nature protection in other sectors; Guidelines for informing the public and public participation in decision-making on nature protection; Manner of meeting international obligations in the field of nature protection; An action plan for implementing the Strategy, with priorities and funding sources, etc. (Art. 11, para. 2).

C. Protection and Conservation of Nature

920. Measures for protection and conservation of nature are protection of natural assets; sustainable use of natural resources, natural assets and control of their use; preservation of the ecological network area; implementation of the documents referred to in Article 10 of this Law; mitigation of harmful effects of natural disasters, harmful consequences caused by nature activities and using of natural resources; and implementation of incentive measures for the protection and preservation of natural assets (Article 14, paragraph 1).

921. The arrangement and use of space and natural resources and assets can be done only on the basis of spatial planning and technical documentation, plans and programmes of management and use of natural resources in mining, energy, transport, maritime affairs, water management, agriculture, forestry, hunting, fishing, tourism and other activities that may have an impact on nature (Article 15, paragraph 1).[1001] It is forbidden to use space and natural resources and assets in a way that permanently violates biodiversity. Spatial plans, development plans, management plans and/or management plans for protected areas and areas of the ecological network must be harmonized (Article 15, paragraphs 3–4).

922. Activities and actions in nature are planned in a way to avoid or minimize nature endangering and damage (Article 16, paragraph 1).[1002] A legal entity or natural person who, by performing activities and actions, causes damage to protected species of plants, animals and mushrooms and natural habitats is obliged to implement remedial measures in accordance with the Law that regulates environmental damage (Article 17, paragraph 1).

923. Strategies, spatial plans, plans on placement of temporary facilities, plans and programmes of management and use of natural resources (mining, energy, transport, maritime affairs, water management, agriculture, forestry, hunting, fishing, tourism and other activities that may have an impact on nature) and Strategic development plans and programmes must include guidelines and conditions for the protection of nature (Article 18, paragraph 1).[1003]

924. It is forbidden at sea and underwater to perform acts and perform activities that destroy marine habitats significant for the survival of endangered species of plants and animals, threatened with extinction or endemic species, or protected species (Article 19, paragraph 1).

1001. In order to preserve natural values, these documents shall include guidelines and conditions for the protection of nature (Art. 15, para. 2).

1002. A legal and natural person using natural resources and goods is obliged to perform activities in a way that avoids the damage to nature or minimizes it (Art. 16, para. 2).

1003. Prior to the preparation of the documents referred to in para. 1 of this Article, the holder of the preparatory work on drafting of documents shall be obliged to obtain from the administrative body the act on the conditions and guidelines for nature protection (Art. 18, para. 2).

D. Protected Natural Goods

925. Protected natural goods can be proclaimed as parts of nature's extraordinary values, which are characterized by biological, geological, ecosystem and landscape diversity (Article 20, paragraph 1). Protected natural assets are: (1) protected areas: strict nature reserve, national park, a special nature reserve, nature park, a monument of nature, an area of exceptional features and (2) areas of the ecological network (Article 20, paragraph 2).[1004]

Protected Areas

926. Protected areas can be used in accordance with the protection study, i.e., the special-purpose spatial plan, the protected area management plan and on the basis of permits in accordance with this Law (Article 39, paragraph 1).

927. In the strict nature reserve, it is forbidden to perform operations and activities, and to perform activities other than visits for the purpose of education, conducting research and monitoring the state of nature (Article 21, paragraph 1).[1005]

928. In the national park, it is forbidden to perform acts and activities that endanger the originality of nature (Article 22, paragraph 1).

929. In a special nature reserve, it is forbidden to perform acts and activities that may impair the properties for which it was declared as protected area (Article 23, paragraph 3).[1006]

930. It is forbidden to perform acts and activities in Nature Park that endanger the characteristics, value and role of the park (Article 24, paragraph 2).

931. On a monument of nature and in its immediate surroundings, which forms an integral part of protected natural values, it is forbidden to perform acts and activities which endanger the characteristics, value and role of the monument of nature (Article 25, paragraph 3).[1007]

932. In the area of exceptional features, it is forbidden to perform actions and activities that violate the characteristics that made this area declared protected (Article 26, paragraph 2).

The Procedure for Declaring Protected Areas

933. The procedure for declaring protected areas shall be initiated by the request for the preparation of an expert study (hereinafter 'protection studies'). The request

1004. Protected areas may be linked to protected areas of another state in accordance with an international agreement (Art. 27).
1005. In the strict nature reserve, it is forbidden to carry out activities other than visiting for the purpose of education, conducting research and monitoring the state of nature (Art. 21, para. 2).
1006. A special nature reserve may be at natural, semi-natural or anthropogenic area (Art. 23, para. 2).
1007. The monument of nature can be in a natural, semi-natural or anthropogenic area (Art. 25, para. 2).

shall be submitted by the Ministry or the competent body of the local self-government unit. The study of protection is made by the administrative body (Article 28, paragraphs 1–3).[1008]

Zones and Protection Regimes

934. The protection zones are defined in the protected area. The following protection regimes are implemented in protection zones: protection zone I – strict protection regime;[1009] protection zone II – active protection regime;[1010] and protection zone III – regime of sustainable use[1011] (Article 31, paragraph 1). Outside the boundaries of the protected area, a protected belt can also be identified if necessary (Article 31, paragraph 7).

Act on Designation of a Protected Area

935. The act on the designation of the protected area is passed for the natural assets for which it is determined that it has the properties of the protected area on the basis of the protection study (Article 32, paragraph 1). In order to prevent the endangering of the protected area, an act of proclamation of a protected area may define protective belt with measures for its protection (Article 32, paragraph 3).[1012]

Public Participation

936. The proposer of the act informs the public about the proposal of the act on the proclamation of a protected area. The proposer of the act provides public insight into the study of protection and the proposal of the act on the designation of the protected area and organizes the public hearing (Article 33, paragraphs 1–2).

937. The proposer of the act on the designation of a protected area is obliged to inform the owners of the real estate in writing about the intention of placing under the protection of the area and to provide insight into the protection study (Article 33, paragraph 4).[1013]

1008. Funds for the preparation of a study of protection shall be provided from the budget of Montenegro, European Union funds, donations from international organizations and other sources in accordance to this Law (Art. 28, para. 4).
1009. Protection zone I – a strict protection regime, is carried out in a protected area or part thereof with slightly changed habitats of exceptional ecological importance, which enable natural biological processes, preservation of the integrity of habitats and life communities, including extremely valuable cultural assets (Art. 31, para. 2).
1010. Protection zone II – active protection regime, is carried out in a protected area in which the properties of natural habitats are partially changed but not to the extent that they threaten their ecological significance, including valuable geographical areas and facilities (Art. 31, para. 4).
1011. In the protection zone III with a sustainable use regime it is allowed to carry out interventions aimed at restoration, revitalization and overall improvement of the protected area; to develop settlements and supporting infrastructure to the extent that no disturbance of core values is caused areas; to perform works on the arrangement of cultural and historical heritage objects and traditional works; to preserve the traditional activities of the local population; selective and limited use of natural resources (Art. 31, para. 6).
1012. The act on the designation of a protected area is published in the 'Official Journal of Montenegro', i.e., in the 'Official Journal of Montenegro – Municipal Regulations' (Art. 32, para. 4).
1013. A public insight into the protection study and the act on the designation of a protected area may last at least twenty days from the date of publication of the notice (Art. 33, para. 4).

Proclamation of Protected Areas

938. The National Park is proclaimed by the Assembly of Montenegro by Law. Strict and special nature reserves are proclaimed by the Government (Article 34, paragraphs 1–2).[1014] The Nature Park, a monument of nature and an area of exceptional features located in the area of several local self-government units, is proclaimed by the Government on the proposal of the local self-government units in whose territory it is located, with the previously obtained opinion of the Ministry and the state administration bodies in charge of agriculture, forestry and water management and cultural affairs (Article 34, paragraph 4).

939. Marine protected areas whose territory partly or completely lies in the zone of the sea property is proclaimed by the Government, except the national park (Article 34, paragraph 5).

Revision of Protected Areas

940. If on the bases of scientific knowledge is determined that there has been a change in certain types of protected areas, the revision procedure is initiated. The procedure shall be initiated on the basis of a request from the Ministry, the local authority or the Manager (Article 35, paragraphs 1–2).

941. The audit of the protected area is initiated by the preparation of the audit study (Article 35, paragraph 6).[1015]

942. If the audit study finds that the protected area has lost the characteristics for which it was declared a protected area, the administrative body proposes the adoption of an act on the cessation of protection of the area to the body competent for adoption of the act on the proclamation of that protected area. The Act on Termination of Protection of the Area shall be published in the 'Official Gazette of Montenegro', i.e., in the 'Official Gazette of Montenegro – Municipal Regulations' (Article 36, paragraphs 2–3).[1016]

1014. A local self-government unit shall be proclaimed the Nature Park, a monument of nature and an area of exceptional characteristics located in the area, by the Assembly of the local self-government unit, upon the previously obtained approval of the Ministry and the opinion of the state administration bodies in charge of agriculture, forestry and water management and cultural affairs (Art. 34, para. 3).

1015. The funds for the preparation of the audit study shall be provided from the budget of Montenegro, European Union funds, donations from international organizations and other sources in accordance to the Art. 28, para. 4 of this Law (Art. 35, para. 7).

1016. Protected area for which an act on the cessation of protection of the area has been passed shall be deleted from the register within one month from the date of publication of the act on termination of protection of the area in the Official Gazette of Montenegro, or in the Official Gazette of Montenegro – Municipal Regulations (Art. 36, para. 4).

Preventive Protection

943. For an area for which the administrative authority, on the basis of expert analysis, assesses that it has a protected area property or has initiated a procedure for placing under protection of that area, the act on preventive protection of the area is adopted (Article 37, paragraph 1).

944. The area for which the act on preventive protection of the area has been adopted or the procedure for putting it under protection has been initiated is considered protected in accordance with this Law (Article 37, paragraph 5).

Register

945. Protected areas and areas under preventive protection are recorded in the register. The register is administered by the administrative body (Article 38, paragraphs 1–2).[1017]

Ecological Network Area

946. The area of the ecological network is declared in order to protect and preserve certain habitat types and species of interest for Montenegro and the EU in accordance with the Law and ratified international agreements. The areas of the ecological network also include natural corridors for the passage of certain wildlife species (Article 41, paragraphs 1–2).

947. The areas of the ecological network are:

- areas important for the conservation of bird habitats and bird species;
- areas important for the conservation of habitats and wild plants and animals (Article 41, paragraph 3).

948. The areas of the ecological network are declared by the Government (Article 43, paragraph 1). The act defines the areas of an ecological network with boundaries for each area, data on target species and habitats, and the name of the management, as well as the measures for protection and preservation of the ecological network area (Article 43, paragraph 5).[1018]

949. If it is found that some areas of the ecological network have lost the characteristics for which it was proclaimed, the administrative body shall propose to the Ministry the adoption of an act on the cessation of protection of the area (Article 44, paragraph 1). The Ministry informs the EC and conducts negotiations on

1017. The manner of keeping the register is prescribed by the Ministry (Art. 38, para. 7).

1018. The act on proclamation of the ecological network is published in the 'Official Gazette of Montenegro' (Art. 43, para. 6).

termination of the protection of the area of the ecological network. If the negotiations permit the termination of the protection of the area of the ecological network, the act on termination of protection of the ecological network area shall be adopted (Article 44, paragraphs 2–4).[1019]

E. Management of Protected Areas and Areas of Ecological Network

950. Protected areas and areas of the ecological network are managed by a manager who meets the requirements for personnel, and organizational capacity to perform protection, promotion, and sustainable development of the protected area and the area of the ecological network. The fulfilment of these conditions shall be determined by the Ministry or by the local authority (Article 55, paragraphs 1–2).

951. In accordance with Article 56 of the Law, duties of the Protected Area Manager and/or of the Ecological Network Area Manager are, *inter alia*, the following: adopt the annual management programme and internal order act; provide protection service; adopt a financial plan for the protection and development of the area; adopt an annual plan for the development and training of personnel; ensure the implementation of nature protection measures in accordance with the protection objectives, zones and protection regimes; preserve, improve and promote the protected area and/or areas of the ecological network; mark the protected area and/or the area of the ecological network, etc.

952. Means for the operation of the Manager are provided from the budget of Montenegro, or budget of the local self-government units in accordance with the annual programme and management plan; fee for the use of the protected area and/or the area of the ecological network; donation; and other sources in accordance to the Law (Article 57).

Management Plan

953. The Management plan is a planning document that plans measures and activities for the protection and conservation of a protected natural property, which is a planned basis for the management and use of a natural good for ecological, economic and social purposes. The management plan is adopted for a period of five years (Article 58, paragraphs 1–2).[1020]

954. The annual management programme is drawn up and adopted by the Manager, with the approval of the Ministry, or the competent local authority. The annual management programme shall be submitted to the Ministry, or to the competent local authority, by 30 November of the current year for the next year. The report on the implementation of the annual management programme of management shall be

1019. The act on the cessation of protection of the area of the ecological network is passed by the Government and published in the 'Official Gazette of Montenegro' (Art. 44, para. 5).

1020. National Park Management Plan is adopted by the Government. The Management plan for a strict and special reservation is adopted by the Ministry (Art. 58, paras. 5–6).

submitted to the Ministry, or to the competent local authority, by 1 March of the current year for the previous year (Article 58, paragraphs 16–18).

955. The fee for the use of the protected area and the area of the ecological network

956. For the use of a protected area and/or an area of an ecological network, the legal entity or natural person (the user) shall pay compensation to the managed protected area or the area of the ecological network for entering the protected area; providing services to visitors (use of guides, sightseeing of natural collections, parking and informative educational materials); catering, sales, accommodation and infrastructure facilities; collecting, reading and purchasing forest fruits; sports and commercial fishing; camping; rafting; firefighting in specially organized places; other activities and activities in accordance with the Law (Article 60, paragraph 1).[1021]

F. Speleological, Geological and Palaeontological Objects

957. Speleological objects: potholes, cave, cave jewellery and other parts of the cave are good of general interest. For speleological objects, a register of speleological objects is created as a digital geographic information system (hereinafter 'the register') (Article 68, paragraphs 1–2).

958. Protected geological and palaeontological objects (fossils, minerals, crystals and cave jewellery) are parts of the geoheritage that, due to their rarity, have outstanding scientific significance (Article 70, paragraph 1).[1022]

959. It is forbidden to take from nature protected geological and palaeontological objects that have been declared protected or located on a geoscientific object, on a protected site or mineral resource deposit. It is forbidden to export geological and palaeontological objects that have been declared protected (Article 72, paragraphs 1–2).[1023]

1021. The amount, method of calculation and payment of the fee referred to in para. 1 of this Article shall be determined by the controller of the protected area or the area of the ecological network, subject to prior agreement of the Government (Art. 60, para. 2).

1022. Protected geological and palaeontological facilities are determined and proclaimed by the Ministry of Natural Resources at the request of expert and scientific institutions engaged in geological and palaeontological research (Art. 70, para. 2).

1023. Kind of habitat types, criteria for determining habitat types, list of types and ecological habitat significant sites from Art. 32 of this Law, protection measures for the preservation of habitat types, a way of making maps of habitat, as well as ways of monitoring and vulnerability of habitat and content of annual report have to be prescribed by the Ministry (Art. 30, para. 10).

III. Law on NP

960. The basic legal act regulating national parks in Montenegro is the Law on national parks (OJ MNE, Nos 28/14 and 39/16). It has the following nine parts: Part I – General Provisions (Articles 1–7), Part II – Borders (Articles 8–13), Part III – Protecting, developing and improvement measures (Articles 14–17), Part IV – Using resources of national parks (Articles 18–30), Part V – Funds for the work of the Managers (Article 31), Part VI – Access to the information and public participation (Articles 32–33), Part VII – Supervision (Article 34), Part VIII – Penalties (Articles 35–37) and Part IX – Transitory and final provisions (Articles 38–44).

961. National parks as protected natural resources have special protection (Article 1).[1024] Nature protection regulations shall apply to national parks unless otherwise provided by this Law (Article 2).

A. *National Parks in Montenegro: Borders*

962. National parks on the territory of Montenegro are the following: National park 'Biogradska gora', National park 'Durmitor', National Park 'Lovćen', National Park 'Skadar Lake' and National Park 'Prokletije' (hereinafter 'National parks'). National parks are protected natural goods of category II (Article 3, paragraphs 1–2).

963. The national park 'Biogradska gora' includes parts of the municipalities: Kolasin, Mojkovac, Berane, within border lines established by this Law (Article 8, paragraph 1). The national park 'Durmitor' includes parts of the municipalities: Zabljak, Mojkovac, Pljevlja, Pluzine and Savnik, within border lines established by this Law (Article 9, paragraph 1). The national park 'Lovcen' includes parts of the municipalities: Budva and Cetinje, within border lines established by this Law (Article 10, paragraph 1). The national park 'Skadarsko jezero' includes parts of the municipalities: Podgorica, Cetinje and Bar, within border lines established by this Law (Article 11, paragraph 1). The national park 'Prokletije' includes parts of the municipalities Plav and Gusinje, within border lines established by this Law (Article 12, paragraph 1).[1025]

964. The borders of national parks are marked by a commission comprised of the following representatives: a business company, a state body administration

1024. The protection, improvement and development of national parks are activities of the public interest (Art. 4).

1025. Marking of the borders from Arts 7, 8, 9, 10 and 11 of this Law performs the commission formed by the Montenegro Government (hereafter: Government), on the proposal of the Ministry in charge for environmental protection (hereafter refers as Ministry) (Art. 12, part. 2). The cartographic presentation with marked borders of national parks is attached to this Law and makes its integral part (Art. 12, part. 1).

responsible for forestry and environmental affairs, administration bodies responsible for cadastre affairs, city municipalities and municipalities on whose territory the national park is located (Article 13, paragraph 1).[1026]

965. The protection, improvement and development of national parks are activities of public interest (Article 4). National parks are managed by a company with the status of a legal entity, which should fulfil the conditions for management of protected natural goods prescribed by the Law regulating nature protection (hereinafter 'Business company') (Article 5, paragraph 1).[1027]

966. The company manages national parks on the basis of a management plan and annual management programmes and performs activities in accordance with the founding act and the Law (Article 6, paragraph 1).[1028]

B. Measures for Protection, Development and Improvement

967. The protection, improvement and development of national parks shall be based on: a spatial plan of special purpose;[1029] management plan;[1030] and annual management programme[1031] (Article 14, paragraph 1).

968. Legal and physical persons performing activities and acts in the area of the national park are obliged to implement activities and acts in accordance with the

1026. Funds for marking the borders are provided from the budget of Montenegro and other sources in accordance with the Law. The cartographic presentation of the marked borders of national parks is prepared by the administrative body in charge for cadastral affairs. The manner of marking the borders of national parks is prescribed by the state administration body in charge for environmental protection activities (hereinafter: the Ministry) (Art. 13, paras 2–4).

1027. The company is founded by the Government of Montenegro (hereinafter: Government) (para. 2). According to the Art. 31, Funds for the work of the company are provided from: Budget of Montenegro; fees for the use of the property of national parks referred to in Art. 21 of this Law; donation; loans; and other sources in accordance with the law.

1028. In conducting the management of national parks, the company carries out the following activities: undertakes measures and activities for achieving the established policy in the management, use, protection, development and improvement of national parks; takes care on implementation of the management plan and adopts the annual management programme; implement protective measures in accordance with the protection regime; performs other duties as stipulated by the Law and the founding act (Art. 6, para. 2).

1029. *The spatial plan for special purposes* determines the protection zones with the boundaries, the conditions and protection measures (Art. 14, para. 2).

1030. *The management plan* is adopted by the Government for a period of five years in accordance with the Law. The management plan is drawn up by a company, with the previously obtained opinion of the Ministry. (Art. 14, paras 3–4).

1031. *The annual management programme* is adopted by a company in accordance with the spatial plan of special purpose and management plan, with the previously obtained approval of the Ministry. The annual programme shall be submitted to the Ministry in accordance with the Law regulating nature protection (Art. 14, paras 5–6).

management plan and the annual management programme. A report on the implementation of the annual management programme shall be submitted by the company to the Ministry by 1 March of the current year for the previous year (Article 15, paragraphs 2–3).

C. *Prohibitions*

969. In the area of national parks, it is prohibited: (1) contraction and pure felling; (2) the introduction of allochthonous plant species, as well as the collection of rare, endemic and hardened plant species, except for the purpose of scientific research; (3) the introduction of allochthonous animal species, as well as the supply of lakes, rivers and other watercourses with allochthonous fish species; (4) capture or kill endangered animal species living in the area of the national park; (5) harassment of endangered animal species; (10) reading, collecting and using unprotected plants and mushrooms, or capturing and killing unprotected animal species to the extent that the population may be endangered; (12) capture, keep, kill or disturb strictly protected wild animal species; (13) capture or kill wildlife in the area of a national park using non-selective means; (14) killing or capturing severely protected birds, especially migratory birds; (15) picking, collecting, cutting, uprooting or destruction of endangered species and fungi whose habitat is in the area of a national park; (16) the deposit of industrial, construction and municipal waste and its temporary disposal in places not designated for such purposes; (17) discharge of untreated industrial and other waste water into the waters of the lake, river, stream and other natural recipients; (18) build nuclear facilities and radioactive and hazardous substances disposal; (19) perform fishing without a fishing licence; (20) performing underwater activities without authorization; (21) throwing away waste out of the place designated for such purposes (Article 16, paragraph 1).[1032]

D. *Using Resources of National Parks*

1. Protection During Using Goods of National Parks

970. In accordance with the management plan and the annual management programme, in the use of national parks goods, protection of waters and their shores, land and forests, wild plants, animals and fungi, fish fund, air, landscape and ambient values, the work of created values, as well as protection of other natural resources must be ensured. The use of natural resources is done in a way that ensures sustainability for present and future generations (Article 20, paragraph 1).

1032. In the protection zone of the national park, in accordance with the spatial plan of special purpose, no allochthonous species and genetically modified organisms should be introduced and shall not be taken other actions that are contrary to the protection measures laid down in the spatial plan of special purpose (Art. 16, para. 2).

2. Fees

971. For the use of the national park property, the legal entity or natural person (hereinafter 'the user') pays the fee for: entry into the national park; providing services to visitors (use of guides, viewing of the collection, use of informative-educational materials, etc.); catering, sales, accommodation and infrastructure facilities (permanent and temporary); renting and/or using facilities and premises of a national park; use of mineral resources; renting of assets and equipment for sport and recreation (boats, ships, kayaks, bicycles, etc.); organized observation of birds; camping; floating and rafting; burning of fire at specially arranged places, etc. (Article 21, paragraph 1).[1033]

3. Construction of Facilities

972. Construction of facilities and other works in the area of national parks can be carried out in accordance with spatial plan of special purpose, management plan and other planning documents (Article 22, paragraph 1).[1034]

973. In the area of national parks, temporary facilities may be placed in locations in accordance with the plan of temporary facility. The plan shall be adopted by the state administration body competent for spatial planning for a period of three years, in accordance with the Law (Article 23, paragraphs 1–2).

4. Forests in National Parks

974. Forests in national parks are special-purpose forests. Forests and forest land in national parks are managed by a company in accordance with the management plan and annual management programme, which ensures the realization of the forest functions established by the Law (Article 24, paragraphs 1–2).

5. Management of Land and Management of Other Real Estate

975. Business company manages land and other state-owned natural assets located in the area of national parks (Article 25, paragraph 1).[1035] The owner of the

1033. The amount, method for calculation and payment of compensation shall be determined by the general act of the company, with the approval of the Ministry. The fee shall be the income of the company. Funds from benefits are used to protect, develop and improve national parks (Art. 21, paras 3–5).

1034. Construction of facilities and other works in national parks can be done on the basis of a building permit, in accordance with the Law (Art. 22, para. 2).

1035. Land and other natural resources in national parks owned by the private persons are managed by the owner in accordance with the spatial plan of special purpose, management plan and annual management programme (para. 2).

real estate in the national park who is limited in the use of property (by the measures of protection) is entitled to compensation for damages in proportion to the reduction of income (Article 26, paragraph 1).[1036]

E. Access to the Information and Public Participation

976. Information on the state of nature in national parks is provided by the business company at the request of interested legal and natural persons (Article 32). The business company is obliged to inform the interested authorities, organizations and the interested public on beginning preparation of the management plan by publishing the notice in at least one printed medium (Article 33, paragraph 1).

F. Supervision

977. Supervision over the implementation of this Law and regulations adopted pursuant to this Law shall be performed by the Ministry and other competent state administration bodies, in accordance with the Law. Inspection supervision over the implementation of this Law and regulations adopted pursuant to this Law shall be carried out by the administrative authority competent for inspection work through competent inspections in accordance with this Law and the Law regulating inspection supervision (Article 34, paragraphs 1–2).

IV. Other Legislation

978.

- Rulebook on internal order in National Parks 'Biogradska gora', 'Durmitor', 'Lovćen' and 'Skadarsko jezero' ('OJ the RM', 32/05).
- Decision on designation of protection of certain species of plants and animals ('OJ RM', 76/06).
- Decision on the manner, conditions and time period relating to the allowed use of assets of national parks ('OJ RM', 53/06).
- Decision on determined level of compensation for destroyed specimens of protected species of animals and plants and wild animals which are prohibited to hunt, and their nests, litters, eggs and young in the territory of National Parks of Montenegro ('OJ RM', 38/97).
- Decision on organization of rafting, boat and kayak rides down the Tara River ('OJ RM', 25/07).

1036. The owner of the real estate in the area of a national park that intends to sell the real estate is obliged to offer it to the Government, through the body of the administration responsible for the property (Art. 27, para. 1).

- Decision on the amount and method of payment of fees for the use of goods of National parks, performing business activities and doing services ('OJ MNE', Nos 52/19, 55/20, 79/20).
- Statute of the Public Enterprise for National Parks of Montenegro (2011).[1037]
- Durmitor National Park Management Plan 2021–2025.
- Biogradska gora National Park Management Plan 2011–2015 Biogradska gora.[1038]
- Lovćen National Park Management Plan 2021–2025.[1039]
- Management Plan for Lake Skadar 2021–2025.[1040]

V. International Treaties

979. Montenegro is a member of the following international treaties: Convention on Biological Diversity,[1041] Cartagena Protocol on Biosafety, Convention on Wetlands of International Importance (Ramsar Convention), CITES Convention, Convention Concerning the Protection of the World Cultural and Natural Heritage. Apart from that, the UN Convention to Combat Desertification in Those Countries Experiencing Serious Drought and/or Desertification, Particularly in Africa, has been ratified in March 2007 as well as Revised Convention for the Protection of The Mediterranean Sea Against Pollution with additional four protocols.

980. Furthermore, Montenegro is a party to the following international treaties: Convention on the Conservation of European Wildlife and Natural Habitats (Bern Convention),[1042] the Convention on the Conservation of Migratory Species of Wild Animals (Bonn Convention),[1043] the Agreement on the Conservation of Cetaceans of the Black Sea, Mediterranean Sea and Contiguous Atlantic Area (ACCOBAMS),[1044] the European Landscape Convention,[1045] the Convention on the Protection of Underwater Cultural Heritage,[1046] the Agreement on the conservation of African-Eurasian migratory water birds and Agreement on the conservation of bats in Europe (EUROBATS).

1037. http://nparkovi.me/wp-content/uploads/2019/11/STATUT.pdf (9 Dec. 2022).
1038. http://nparkovi.me/wp-content/uploads/2022/05/Plan-upravljanja-2021-2025NP-Biogradsko.pdf (9 Dec. 2022).
1039. http://nparkovi.me/wp-content/uploads/2022/05/Plan-upravljanja-2021-2025NP-Lovcen.pdf (9 Dec. 2022).
1040. *See*: http://nparkovi.me/wp-content/uploads/2022/05/Plan-upravljanja-2021-2025NP-Skadarsko.pdf (3 Dec. 2022).
1041. For more details, *see* MSPE (2010a).
1042. http://conventions.coe.int/Treaty/Commun/ChercheSig.asp?NT=104&CM=8&DF=&CL=ENG (3 Dec. 2022). For more details, *see*: CE (2010).
1043. https://www.cms.int/en/parties-range-states (3 Dec. 2022).
1044. https://www.cms.int/en/legalinstrument/accobams (9 Dec. 2022).
1045. http://conventions.coe.int/Treaty/Commun/ChercheSig.asp?NT=176&CM=8&DF=&CL=ENG (9 Dec. 2022).
1046. http://www.unesco.org/eri/la/convention.asp?KO=13520&language=E&order=alpha (3 Dec. 2022).

981. In addition, Montenegro ratified the European Convention for the Protection of Animals during International Transport (Revised) (OJ MNE-IT, No. 4/17). In March 2020, the Parliament ratified the Law on Nagoya Protocol on access to genetic resources and the fair and equitable sharing of benefits arising from their utilization to the Convention on biological diversity (OJ MNE-IT, No. 3/20).

§5. Harmonization with EU Legislation

982. 'For reason of incomplete harmonisation of national legislation with the EU acquis,'[1047] it is not possible now to implement the requirements under several Directives and Regulations. These are following: Directive 1992/22/EC concerning keeping wild animals in zoos, Regulation 3254/91/EEC concerning wild animal trapping, Directive 83/129/EEC and Regulation (EC) No. 1007/2009 concerning products of marine mammals known under the name of Pinnipedae, Directive 1999/22/EC concerning the protection of animals used in science, Regulation (EC) 2173/2005 (FLEGT) and Regulation (EC) 995/2010 defining the obligations of operators who place timber and timber products on the market. 'In the field of nature protection, Montenegro is partially aligned with the EU acquis'.[1048] Activities regarding Natura 2000 have continued over the reporting period, funded by the national budget. Recommendations of the Bern Convention related to Skadar Lake still need to be addressed. Montenegro should use support provided to establish its Emerald network based on Natura 2000 mapping information.[1049]

1047. MSDT (2016a). p. 39. In addition, 'the implementation of Montenegro's international obligations arising from CITES Convention and requirements stemming from the EU legislation governing the implementation of the CITES convention is not entirely governed in adequate manner by the national legislation.' *Ibid.*

1048. EC (2022). p. 113.

1049. *Ibid.* During 2021 the government declared the two marine nature parks 'Katič' and 'Stari Ulcinj' as protected areas. Following decision of the government's privatisation council on Ulcinj Salina (July 2021) land as state-owned, the adoption of the privatisation council decision by the Government is pending.

Chapter 3. Wildlife Protection

§1. Biodiversity in Montenegro

983. Montenegro is among the leading countries in Europe where biodiversity of the ecosystem is concerned[1050] due to the geographical position, distribution and heterogeneity of habitat, topographic variations, geological history and climate variation.[1051]

984. Since 2000 monitoring of biological diversity in Montenegro is carried out, within the framework of National Programme of monitoring the state of the environment.[1052] Due to financing problems, the information collected until now still does not provide enough data for serious analysis of trends or state of population of relevant species and changes in selected habitat types. Pursuant to the results of the research on biological diversity revision of old and adoption of new List of protected species has been carried out. The mentioned list includes 454 plant and 430 animal species, as well as entire line of bats (Decision on protection of some plant and animal species (OJ RM, No. 76/06)).

985. It can be concluded, according to the available information, that following main factors represent threat to biological diversity: uncontrolled urban and tourist, especially in the Littoral and in Podgorica; modification of purposes of land; uncontrolled and unsustainable use of natural resources; introducing a new invasive species and climate changes.[1053]

986. 'Assessment of biodiversity status and trends as well as of the changes that have taken place since 2010 (since the submission of the Fourth National Report) is hampered by a limited (in its scope and time span) biodiversity monitoring and insufficient number of biodiversity research projects. Red lists and books of flora and fauna as an important tool for assessing the state and status of species have not been developed yet'. Annual biodiversity monitoring programmes (introduced in

---

1050. Montenegro is considered to be among the most important biodiversities in Europe, according to the index size S/A = 0.837, which represents the proportion between species of vascular flora and size of state territory. Approximately 20% of overall flora belongs to endemic and sub-endemic herbs that occur only in Montenegro and in some neighbouring countries. GMNE (2008c), 46–47.

1051. *See*: MSPE (2010b), 13.

1052. It was concluded, on the basis of the results obtained through the Programme, that the most negative consequences happened to the aquatic ecosystems and forests, and then in the urban and agrarian areas. The coastal system is exposed to pressure because of the transformation of natural habitats in the built spaces and buildings. Water ecosystems are under pressure of various forms of pollution, which reduce their productivity. *Ibid.*, 11. For characteristics of flora and fauna in Costal Zone, *see*: GMNE (2007D), 31–36.

1053. The main causes of threats to biological diversity come from various factors, like: (1) low political priority of environmental protection issues; (2) promotion of policies that are not compatible with sustainable use of natural resources; (3) low level of restrictions and incentives related to protection of biological diversity/Nature protection; (4) demographic, social and economic changes that affect biodiversity; and (5) minimum participation of stakeholders. MSPE (2010b), 39–42. *See also* GMNE, NCSD (2011), 8.

2000 and often subjected to substantial financial restrictions) were conducted for a limited (and declining) number of locations/species during the past few years.[1054]

§2. Competencies

987. Pursuant to Article 11 of the Decree on state administration organization and operations (OJ MNE, Nos 49/22, 52/22, 56/22, 82/22) the MAFWM conducts administrative activities with regard to, *inter alia*: the protection of nature, sustainable use of natural resources, etc.

988. The inventory of protected areas is kept by the EPA, the institution which also provides research services on nature protection. The Institute of Marine Biology carries out monitoring and research programmes on the biological resources of the continental shelf and slope of the Montenegrin Coast, while cadastres of plants, animals, their habitats and ecosystems are in competence of the Public Enterprise for National Parks.

989. The forest cadastres are maintained by the Forest Management Directorate within the MAFWM and its fifteen local management units.[1055]

§3. Legislation

990. Some general obligations and rights concerning protection of wildlife are contained in the Constitution of Montenegro (OJ MNE, No. 1/2007) and in the Law on the environment (OJ MNE, Nos 52/16, 73/19).[1056] More concrete obligations and rights are prescribed by specific laws and by-laws.

I. Law on Nature Protection

991. The basic legal act regulating nature protection in Montenegro is the Law on nature protection (OJ MNE, Nos 54/2016, 18/19), adopted on 15 August 2016. It has the following sixteen parts: Part I – General Provisions (Articles 1–6), Part II – Subject of the nature protection (Articles 7–9), Part III – Documents of the nature protection (Articles 10–13), Part IV – Protection and conservation of nature (Articles 14–19), Part V – Protected natural assets (Articles 20–54), Part VI – Management of protected areas and areas of ecological network (Articles 55–67), Part VII – Speleological, geological and palentological objects (Articles 68–72), Part

1054. MSDT (2014) p. 16. The key problems in planning and executing annual monitoring programmes included lack of baseline data for certain areas, habitats and species, insufficient coverage (reduced and changing scope from one year to another) due to financial restrictions, and insufficient human resources (limited number of experts for some species groups). Nevertheless some general trends have emerged from gathered data.

1055. UNECE (2007), 32.

1056. For more details *see* Ch. 2 of this part.

VIII – Protection of wild species (Articles 73–96), Part IX – Conservation of genetic diversity (Articles 97–99), Part X – Monitoring the state of nature (Articles 100–101), Part XI – Access to information and promotion of nature protection (Articles 102–103), Part XII – Financing of nature protection (Article 104), Part XIII – Protection of protected nature assets (Articles 105–106), Part XIV – Supervision (Articles 107–110), Part XV – Penalties (Article 111), Part XVI – Transitory and final provisions (Articles 112–121).

992. This Law regulates the conditions and manner of protection and conservation of nature[1057] (Article 1).

993. Nature protection includes protection of flora, fauna and geomorphological phenomena; proclamation of protected natural values and their conservation and management; protection of all endangered, rare and indigenous species; identification and assessment of the state of phenomena and processes in nature; implementation of nature protection measures; determination of guidelines and conditions for nature protection in spatial planning documents; establishing a system for managing protected natural values; linking and harmonizing nature protection system with international nature protection system; encouraging scientific and professional works in the field of nature protection; emphasizing the importance and necessity of nature protection through the education system from preschool education to the University (Article 4).[1058]

994. Nature protection is being carried out due to: preservation and improvement of biological (genetic, species, ecosystem), geological and landscape diversity; conservation and improvement of individual natural assets; identification and monitoring of the state of nature; harmonization of human activities, economic and social development plans, programmes and projects with sustainable use of renewable and rational use of non-renewable natural values and resources, in order to their permanent preservation; prevention of activities with adverse impacts on nature that are a consequence of the linear dependence of economic growth and the use of natural resources; protection and preservation of cross-border valuable parts of nature and protected natural assets; preserving the natural properties of the land, preserving the quality, quantity and availability of water, including quality of seawater (Article 3).

1057. *Nature* is the unity of the geosphere and the biosphere, including the species of wild plants, animals, fungi and natural values. They are distinguished by biological, geological, geomorphological and frontal diversity. Nature is of interest to Montenegro and is protected in accordance to this Law (Art. 2, paras 1–2).

1058. This Law shall not apply in case of suppression and prevention of imminent danger to life and health of people or property, or rescue of people and property, only during the duration of these circumstances which are determined by the act of the competent authority (Art. 5).

A. Protection of Wild Spaces

1. Protection of Wild Species of Plants, Animals and Fungi

995. It is forbidden to exterminate the indigenous wild species of plants, animals and fungi (Article 73, paragraph 2).[1059] It is forbidden to pick, collect and use wild plants and mushrooms, i.e., to capture and kill wildlife species to the extent that their population numbers and the favourable status of conservation can be endangered (paragraph 3).[1060] It is forbidden to deliberately harass and kill wildlife, except for hunting in accordance with the Law governing game and hunting (paragraph 4).

996. Import, export and transit of wild species of plants, animals and mushrooms can only be carried out with the permission of the administration body, in accordance with confirmed international treaties (Article 73, paragraph 7).[1061]

997. The transit of wild species of plants, animals and fungi through the territory of Montenegro is done on the basis of the export or import permit issued by the competent authority of the exporting or importing country (Article 73, paragraph 9).[1062]

2. Measures for the Protection of Migratory Wildlife

998. Public roads, other roads and other facilities must be built in such a way as to reduce the negative effect on the migratory wildlife pathways and enable the safe movement of wild animals at appropriate spatial intervals (Article 76, paragraph 1). The measures referred to in paragraph 1 of this Article shall be secured by the application of special construction and technical-technological solutions (ecological

1059. Wild species of plants, animals and fungi are: specimens of wild plants, fungi and wildlife and their breeding specimens; their developmental forms (eggs, seeds, fruits, mycelium); their parts and derivatives; their easily recognizable products (Art. 73, para. 1). However, according to Art. 6, wild species of plants, animals and fungi are species and subtypes that are not originated by man's influence as a result of artificial selection (selection and breeding for the purpose of obtaining breeds of domesticated animals and varieties of cultivated plants) or genetic modification of hereditary material by techniques of modern biotechnology (item 9).

1060. Physical and legal entities may gather, collect and use wild plants and fungi, or catch and kill wild animal species referred to in para. 3 of this Article for commercial purposes only on the basis of a permit issued by an administrative body (Art. 73, para. 5).

1061. During transport and transit of live animals, they must be transported and kept in a way that ensures the safety of the animals from being infected, damaged by health or inhumane treatment (Art. 73, para. 8).

1062. The manner and conditions for use and collection with quantities that can be used and put into market, the manner of monitoring the status of populations and a list of wildlife, plants and fungi that can be used for commercial purposes shall be determined by the Ministry, in cooperation with the state administration authority in charge of forestry (Art. 73, para. 10).

bridges, built passes, tunnels, permeable pipes, channels, safety and directional facilities, fish trails, elevators) at the facilities and in their surroundings (paragraph 2).[1063]

3. The Reintroduction of Missing Indigenous Species

999. The reintroduction of missing indigenous wild species of plants, animals and mushrooms and their breeding grounds into ecosystems may be carried out with the permission of the administrative authorities (Article 79, paragraph 1). The permit referred to in paragraph 1 of this Article shall be issued by the administration body on the basis of a previously prepared risk assessment (paragraph 2).[1064]

4. Protected Wild Species of Plants, Animals and Fungi

1000. Wild species of plants, animals and fungi that are endangered or can become endangered, rare and endemic, and which have special significance from the genetic, ecological, ecosystem, scientific, health and economic aspects are protected wild species (Article 89, paragraph 1).[1065] The list of protected wild species of plants, animals and fungi is determined by the Ministry on the basis of an assessment of the endangerment of certain species, and obligations from the confirmed international treaties, and on the basis of national and international red lists and other professional documentation, at the proposal of the administrative body and with previously obtained opinion of the state administration organs responsible for agriculture, forestry and game (Article 89, paragraph 6).

5. Red List of Species of Wild Plants, Animals and Fungi

1001. Red lists of wild species of plants, animals and fungi[1066] are determined by the administration authority on the basis of international red lists and scientific data according to the degree of vulnerability, distribution, population numbers and other characteristics of individual wild species of plants, animals and fungi (Article 90, paragraph 1). On the basis of the red list referred to in paragraph 1 of this Article, the administrative body may draw up a red book, which shall also include

1063. The measures of protection and the manner of maintaining technical–technological solutions referred to in para. 2 of this Article shall be prescribed by the Ministry, with the consent of the state administration authority in charge of traffic affairs (Art. 76, para. 3).

1064. The costs of assessing the risk of reintroduction of indigenous species into the wild shall be borne by the legal or natural person who has applied for the licence (Art. 79, para. 3).

1065. Protected wild species of plants, animals and fungi are protected in a way that achieves or maintains their favourable status of preservation (Art. 89, para. 4).

1066. The Red List is a list of endangered wild species of plants, animals and fungi on a given territory according to threat categories and threat factors classified in vulnerability categories in accordance with the categorization of the International Union for Conservation of Nature (IUCN) (Art. 6, para. 7).

measures to protect and improve the status of the endangered species, the manner of treatment and the area of spread of protected wild species of plants, animals and fungi and measures to protect their habitats (paragraph 2).

6. The Trade of Protected Wild Species of Plants, Animals and Fungi

1002. The trade of certain protected wildlife species of plants, animals and fungi, their parts and derivatives that are protected in accordance with this Law and ratified international agreements, may be carried out on the basis of a permit issued by an administrative authority according to the previously obtained opinion of the Institute if the introduction of wild species is done from the sea, in accordance with the Law and confirmed international agreements (Article 94, paragraph 1).[1067]

B. Conservation of Genetic Diversity

1. Establishing a Gene Bank

1003. In order to preserve the genetic diversity of wild plants, animals and fungi, a gene bank is established (Article 97, paragraph 1).[1068] Taking genetic material from nature for use should not endanger the survival of the ecosystem or the population of wildlife, plant and animal species in their habitats (paragraph 2).

1004. Genetic material from nature can be used in accordance with this law (Article 98, paragraph 1). The property cannot be acquired from genetic material created from the genetic material of wild plant species, animals and mushrooms (Article 98, paragraph 2).[1069]

II. Law on Alien and Invasive Alien Species of Plants, Animals and Funghi

1005. The most recent addition to existing legislation in this field is the Law on alien and invasive alien species of plants, animals and fungi (OJ MNE 18/19). This law regulates the manner of prevention of the introduction of alien and invasive

1067. The permit referred to in para. 1 of this Article shall be issued only if the administrative body determines that the transport does not endanger the wild population of plants, animals or fungi (Art. 94, para. 3).
1068. In the gene banks, the biological material of the controlled or cultivated population or parts of plants, animals and fungi, seeds, spores, cell bodies and other biological materials, used to preserve the genus and their genetic resources and potentials, are stored (Art. 99, para. 1). The bank of genes referred to in para. 1 of this Article may be founded by a legal or natural person who meets the conditions in terms of space, equipment and personnel, on the basis of a permit issued by the administrative body (para. 2).
1069. As 'protected species of wild plants, animals and fungi' can be also determined vulnerable autochthonous plant species and animal which has been developed as a consequence of traditional breeding and represent part of natural and ethno-cultural heritage (Art. 44, para. 4).

alien species to minimize or mitigate as much as possible the negative impact on biodiversity, ecosystem services and human health (Article 1). The alien species are defined as species introduced into areas where they are not naturally distributed (Article 2). Excluded from this definition are species that change their habitats through natural processes – changes in environmental conditions or climate change (Article 3) and other specified species.[1070]

1006. Alien species must be listed as allowed to be imported, marketed or grown, or a special permit under the law must be obtained for these purposes. The list of allowed species is made by the MESPU. The person responsible for import, marketing or growth shall enable strictly controlled conditions to prevent their escape or discharge into nature and is liable for any damage caused (Article 5).[1071]

1007. The alien species listed as allowed or invasive species that cause anxiety might be introduced into nature if they do not represent a danger to biodiversity, ecosystem services or human health. The application for the Permit for the introduction of alien species into nature can be submitted by a company or another legal entity, an entrepreneur or a natural person.[1072] The application is submitted to the Commission for the evaluation of the invasiveness of the alien species which has to deliver an opinion on possible dangers in twenty days. In case the Commission finds some inherent dangers in the introduction of alien species, the administrative organ will deny the request, and the applicant can then initiate the risk assessment procedure from Article 9 (Article 6).[1073]

1008. The species from Article 6 can also be introduced for breeding purposes. The procedure is analogous to the one described above. Necessary elements of the application include also the location of the breeding grounds, its capacity, description of measures intended to prevent their spread into nature and their removal from the closed breeding system, conditions for management and holding of species in the closed breeding system, transport condition to and from the system, the method of risk management in cases of breakout or spread or illegal removal of a specie, the method of supervision.[1074] (Article 7).

1070. E.g., – genetically modified organisms, pathogenes, alien aquatic organisms used for aquaculture, domesticated animals, microorganisms used in biocides, planting seeds and sorts (Art. 3).

1071. Articles 6–8 of the Law define procedures for obtaining different types of permits for alien species: the permit for import into nature (Art. 6); the permit for its growth in the closed system (Art. 7); the permit for its marketing (Art. 8).

1072. The application must contain the basic information of the applicant (name and seat, identification number, address); the name, quantity and origin of the species with the description of its form/or development phase; the purpose and method of introduction, its time period and location; and finally the reasons for the introduction. The maximum number of species is 10.

1073. The species from Art. 6 can also be marketed inside the territory of Montenegro. The procedure is analogous to the previous two cases. The application must contain the description of the marketing purpose. Maximum number of species is 50 (Art. 8).

1074. Maximum number of species is 20.

1009. Article 9 defines the procedure for invasiveness risk assessment. The Commission responsible for the procedure is formed from employees of the administrative organ and relevant experts. It evaluates several criteria: dynamics and conditions of reproduction and spread; possible paths of import and spread of species including products especially related to the species; dependence of risk on the foreseeable climate change and biogeographical regional factors; description of harmful impacts on biodiversity and ecosystem services, on autochtonous species, protected areas, vulnerable habitats and human health, including possible future impacts based on accessible scientific data; assessment of possible costs of harm; social and economic benefits of alien species, etc.

1010. The alien invasive species is defined as a species whose introduction or spread might endanger or harmfully impact biodiversity, ecosystem services or human health (Article 10). The list of alien invasive species is defined by the Ministry with the consent of the state authority responsible for agriculture and is formed by the species that cause anxiety in Montenegro or the EU. These species must not be introduced to Montenegro's territory, kept in closed systems, bred or raised, marketed, transported (except to the facilities for extermination), used or exchanged, or let into nature.

1011. The exception to this ban are the species used: (1) for scientific purposes, ex-situ preservation or production of medical products licenced by the state authorities (Article 11);[1075] (2) in public interest, for the protection of health, security, establishment of more agreeable environmental conditions, economics or social public interest, if no other options exist (Article 12). A special permit is then issued to a legal entity that requests it and fulfils conditions in terms of personnel, equipment and facilities.

1012. The principle of precaution in the management of alien species is contained in Article 14 (Emergency measures) – if the administrative organ establishes the introduction of an alien species previously non-existent on Montenegro's territory, or the introduction of an alien invasive species not listed on the 'anxiety list' from Article 10, it must assess on the basis of available scientific evidence whether

1075. The invasive alien species can be used in scientific purposes, ex-situ preservation and medicines production. The legal entity that satisfies conditions in terms of personnel, equipment and facilities can submit the application for the permit to the administrative organ. The procedure is analogous to the previously described ones. The application must be followed by the documentation on the proof of fulfilment of the prescribed conditions and the plan and measures in case of breakout or spread, including the plan of extermination. The invasive species have to be properly marked, according to the Law on the nature protection. The administrative organ has to inform the public on the application and leave ten days for possible opinions of stakeholders to be submitted. The Commission must adopt its report on the application in twenty days, and the administrative organ can then, if the report is positive, issue the permit. The permit is valid for five years. The permit holder must inform the administrative organ periodically on the activities performed. The reports are used to form the evidence on the activities that must be published on the administrative organ's website (Art. 11).

the species might cause the risk for biodiversity and promptly inform the Commission to propose emergency measures for its extermination, control of further spread or prevention of introduction.

1013. Any natural or legal person that spots the introduction of invasive alien species that causes anxiety must inform promptly the administrative organ and the responsible inspectionary organ (Article 15). This so-called early discovery system enables the administrative organ to define the extermination measures in the early phase of invasion. The polluter-pays principle is applied in the provision that puts the burden of costs of these measures on the person that caused the invasion. Only if it is not possible to pinpoint the responsible person, the state budget of Montenegro would cover the costs (or the manager of protected area if the invasion occurred inside of such area).

1014. The law further defines several important documents and procedures for the management of invasive and alien invasive species: The Action Plan for the control of inadvertent introduction and spread of alien invasive species (Article 18); The Plan of Management of invasive alien species that cause anxiety (Article 19); Recovery of damaged ecosystems (Article 20); Monitoring of the alien invasive species' condition (Article 21); Reporting on the monitoring results (Articles 22–23); Database on alien and invasive species (Article 24); Transboundary cooperation (Article 25); The procedure of the responsible authorities (Article 26).

1015. Furthermore, the law provides for supervision by the customs authorities (Articles 27 and 31) concerning the introduction of alien species into Montenegro's territory and supervision by the environmental inspection (Articles 29–30).[1076]

III. Other Relevant Legislation

1016. Besides the Law on Nature Protection and Law on alien and invasive alien species of plants, animals and funghi, relevant provisions concerning protection of wildlife can be found in the following laws: Law on National Parks (OJ MNE, Nos 28/14, 39/16), Law on Forests (OJ MNE, No. 74/10),[1077] Law on Forest Trees Reproductive Materials (OJ RM, No. 37/07), Law on Game and Hunting (Official Journal MNE, Nos 51/08, 48/15), Law on Animal Welfare Protection (OJ MNE, Nos 14/2008, 40/2011),[1078] Law on the Marine Fisheries (Official Journal MNE, Nos 56/09, 40/11), Law on the Freshwater Fisheries (Official Journal MNE, Nos 11/07, 40/11), Law on Plant Health Protection (Official Journal RM, No. 28/06, OJ

1076. The law provides for monetary sanctions for persons found to be in breach of its provisions, ranging from EUR 2.000 to EUR 40.000 (Art. 32 – Penal provisions).

1077. *See* Chapter devoted to Forest Protection.

1078. This law regulates the rights, obligations and responsibilities of natural and legal persons for the protection of animal welfare with regard to the protection of animals from torture. It refers to the keeping, breeding, killing, slaughter of animals and performing procedures on animals, during transport and experiments as well as other issues of importance for the protection of animal welfare (Art. 1).

MNE, No. 28/11), Law on Agricultural Plant Seeds (OJ RM, No. 28/06, OJ MNE, Nos 73/10, 40/11, 61/11, 48/15), The Law on Means for Plant Nutrition (Official Journal RM, No. 48/07, OJ MNE, Nos 76/08, 73/10, 40/11), Law on Veterinary Medicine (OJ MNE, Nos 30/12, 48/15, 52/16, 43/18), Law on Animal Identification and Registration (OJ RM, No. 48/07, OJ MNE, No. 73/10), etc.

1017. Following by-laws were adopted on the basis of the Law on alien and invasive alien species of plants, animals and fungi:

- The Rulebook on conditions expected from the legal entity that conducts the emergency measures and extermination measures of invasive alien species (OJ MNE, No. 114/20).
- The Rulebook on closer conditions expected from the legal entity that submits a request for permit, the form of the request for permit and the form of the permit for the use of invasive alien species that causes anxiety in Montenegro and/or the EU (OJ MNE, No. 114/20)

1018. In addition, several sub-legal acts also regulate protection of wildlife:

- Rulebook on the methodology for determining and monitoring the numerous state of game (OJ MNE, No. 86/17).
- Decision on establishment of the Nature Protection Office of Montenegro ('OJ MNE', 15/09).
- Rulebook on types and criteria for determining the habitat types, method of development of habitat map, manner of monitoring the state and endangerment of habitats, content of the annual report, measures to protect and conserve habitat types ('OJ MNE', 80/08).
- Rulebook on more detailed content and manner of keeping the register of protected natural assets ('OJ MNE', 79/09).
- Rulebook on more detailed conditions which must be fulfilled by a manager of a protected natural asset ('OJ MNE', 35/10).
- Rulebook on more detailed content of annual monitoring programme of the state of conservation of nature and conditions which must be fulfilled by a legal entity conducting monitoring ('OJ MNE', 35/10).
- Rulebook on more detailed conditions which must be met by legal and natural person for keeping temporarily seized protected wild species of plants, animals and fungi ('OJ MNE' 46/10).
- Rulebook on the method of conducting risk assessment for introduction of alien wild species of plants, animals and fungi ('OJ MNE' 46/10).
- Rulebook on criteria for classification of mountain paths ('OJ MNE' 20/11).
- Rulebook on more detailed conditions of keeping and breeding of protected wild species of animals ('OJ MNE', 67/10).
- Rulebook on more detailed manner and conditions of collecting, using and trade in unprotected wild species of plants, animals and fungi used for commercial purposes ('MNE', 62/10).
- Rulebook on more detailed conditions which must be met by legal or natural person in order to establish a bank of genes ('OJ MNE', 77/10).

- Rulebook on protective measures and manner of maintaining passageways for wild animals ('OJ MNE', 80/10).
- Rulebook on manner of monitoring of the size and state of the populations of protected wild birds ('OJ MNE', 62/10).
- Rulebook on conditions of circulation and manner of treatment of protected wild species during transport ('OJ MNE', 67/10).

§4. Harmonization with EU Legislation

1019. In order to prevent illegal trade in species, in addition to CITES Convention, the following EU legislation needs to be implemented: Regulation (EC) No. 338/97 (protection of wild species of flora and fauna by way of regulating the trading in them); Regulation (EC) No. 865/2006 (detailed rules for the implementation of Regulation (EC) No. 338/97); Regulation (EU) No. 792/2012 (permits and certificates); Regulation (EU) No. 791/2012 (amendments to Regulation (EC) No. 865/2006 and Regulation (EC) No. 338/97).[1079]

1079. MSDT (2016a), p. 38.

Chapter 4. Agricultural Resources

§1. Agriculture in Montenegro

1020. 'Montenegro has scarce natural conditions for development of particularly intensive agriculture, because a very small amount of agricultural land can be cultivated in order to organize intensive agricultural production, without significant investments in land amelioration and infrastructure. Still, even these scarce natural conditions with their production potential provide opportunities for a lot larger and quality agricultural production, and food provision for double as much people than at the moment'.[1080] However, agriculture in Montenegro has higher economic significance than in most EU Member States. Its share in the GDP is 13.5% (together with processing sector).[1081] 'The drought of 2011 evolved into a social and economic challenge that affected the whole country and led to an extreme hydrological deficit in the Zeta–Bjelopavlići region, which includes the largest agricultural area in Montenegro.'[1082]

1021. Application of chemical means and artificial fertilizers in Montenegro is 'well below average'.[1083] Agricultural households belong to small-scale, traditionally extensive households, implying that chemical usage is at the lowest possible level. The economic crises in the last fifteen years influenced the level of pesticide usage and artificial fertilizers which is still declining. With regard to intensity level, agriculture cannot be considered to significantly pollute the environment.[1084]

§2. Competencies

1022. Pursuant to Article 11 of the Decree on state administration organization and operations (OJ MNE, Nos 49/22, 52/22, 56/22, 82/22) the MAFWM shall conduct administrative activities regarding, *inter alia*: current and development policy in the agriculture area; protection, agricultural terrain usage and improvement; floral production (farming, fruit growing, viticulture and plant protection); cattle raising (the production, raising, protection and development of all kinds of livestock); veterinary; development of apiculture; freshwater and saltwater fishing; villages development; the application of modern technique and technology in agriculture; provision of loans for current production and development; balance of basic agricultural products; agro-industry; and international cooperation, establishment of quality standards and administrative supervision, and other activities delegated to its competency.[1085]

1080. GMNE, NCSD (2011), 9.
1081. MARD (2012), 8. *See also* GMNE (2008b), 225. GMNE (2007C), 30–31.
1082. MSDT (2020), p. 166. In 2017 and 2018 the intensity of the drought varied from moderate, very arid to extremely arid.
1083. MAFWM (2006a), 49. *See also* MARD (2012), 8.
1084. *Ibid.*, 50. *See also* MONSTAT (2011g), 66, 67.
1085. In regard to professional and technical assistance (laboratory testing) plant health protection is provided by the Plant Protection Centre of the Biotechnical Institute Podgorica, which is part of

§3. Strategic Documents

1023. The Strategy entitled: 'Montenegro's Agriculture and the EU – Food Production and Rural Development Strategy' adopted in mid-2006, was considered a document of crucial importance for the further development of agriculture. The Strategy defined the following development objectives: (a) sustainable resource management; (b) stable and acceptable supply of safe food; (c) providing an appropriate standard of living for the rural population; and (d) increasing competitiveness of food producers. The New Strategy for Agriculture and Rural Development (June 2015) has been developed in order to properly define the path of the future reform process in the sector.[1086]

§4. Legislation

1024. Many laws are applied in the agriculture field or can be relevant to agriculture. Some of the most important are the following:

- Law on Agriculture and Rural Development (OJ MNE, Nos 56/09, 34/14, 1/15, 30/17, 51/17, 59/21).
- Law on Plant Health Protection (OJ RM, No. 28/06, OJ MNE, Nos 73/10, 28/11, 48/15).
- Law on Plant Protection Products (OJ MNE, Nos 51/08, 40/11, 18/14).
- Law on Agricultural Plant Seeds (OJ RM, No. 28/06, OJ MNE, Nos 73/10, 40/11, 61/11, 48/15).
- Law on Plant Variety Protection (OJ RM, No. 48/07).
- Law on Organic Agriculture (OJ RM, No. 56/13).
- Law on Veterinary Medicine (OJ MNE, Nos 30/12, 48/15, 52/16, 43/18).
- Law on Protection of Animal Welfare (OJ MNE, Nos 14/08, 40/11, 47/15).
- Law on Agricultural Land (OJ RM, Nos 15/92 and 59/92, OJ MNE, No. 32/11).
- Law on the Forest Trees Reproductive Material (OJ RM, No. 37/2007, OJ MNE, No. 57/15).
- Food Safety Law (OJ MNE, No. 57/15).
- Law on Animal Identification and Registration (OJ RM, No. 48/07, OJ MNE, No. 73/10).
- Law on Livestock (OJ MNE 72/2010, 40/2011, 48/2015).
- Law on Olive Growing (OJ MNE, Nos 45/14, 39/16).
- Law on Wine (OJ MNE, No. 41/16).
- Law on Designations of Geographical Origin (OJ MNE, No. 48/08), etc.

In addition, a number of by-laws have been adopted.

---

the University of Montenegro. Regarding expert and technical support the seeds and planting materials are delivered to the Ministry by the Biotechnical Institute of Podgorica and its regional Centres.

1086. *See*: https://www.eu.me/download/1650/11-poljoprivreda-i-ruralni-razvoj/20264/strategija-razvoja-poljoprivrede-i-ruralnih-podrucja.pdf (3 Dec. 2022). *See also*: https://www.gov.me/dokumenta/8d4d0d4c-7d01-4e5d-b328-598862ebe753 (13 Jan. 2022).

I. Law on Agriculture and Rural Development

1025. Law on Agriculture and Rural Development (OJ MNE, Nos 56/09, 34/14, 1/15, 30/17, 51/17, 59/21) is the basic legal document for defining and implementing the agricultural policy. The Law consists of eighty articles divided into sixteen chapters: Chapter I – Basic provisions (Articles 1 and 2), Chapter II – Agricultural and rural development planning (Articles 3–7), Chapter III – Agricultural Policy Measures (Articles 8–24), Chapter IV – Incentives to Agriculture and Rural Development (Articles 25–33), Chapter V – Agricultural Producers Organizations (Articles 34–38), Chapter VI – Quality and Marking of Agricultural Products and Food (Articles 39–45), Chapter VII – Good Agricultural Practice (Article 46), Chapter VIII – Trade in Agricultural Products and Food (Articles 47–48), Chapter IX – Supplementary Activity (Articles 49–51), Chapter X – Activities of Public Interest (Articles 52–59), Chapter XI – Certificates of Merit (Article 60), Chapter XII – Registers and Records (Articles 61–68), Chapter XIII – Council of Agriculture and Rural Development (Articles 69–71), Chapter XIV – Inspection (Articles 72–74), Chapter XV – Penalty provisions (Article 75) and Chapter XVI – Transitional and Final Provisions (Articles 76–80).

1026. The law regulates the development of agriculture and rural areas, objectives and measures of the agricultural policy,[1087] support in agriculture and eligibility requirements, support to beneficiaries, supplementary activities in agriculture,[1088] organization in agriculture, as well as other issues of relevance for agriculture and rural development (Article 1). Several provisions of the Law directly relate to the environment.

1027. Sustainable agriculture resource management shall be ensured by implementation of the following measures: (a) support to development of areas with limited opportunities for agricultural production, (b) support to agriculture programmes harmonized with the principles of environmental protection – agro-environmental measures,[1089] (c) agroforestry programmes (Article 14, paragraph 1). The criteria and method for implementation of measures shall be laid down by the agro-budget (Article 14, paragraph 2).

1087. Pursuant to the Art. 3 the main objectives of agriculture and rural development (hereinafter referred to as 'agricultural policy') are, as follows: (1) Agricultural resource management sustainable on a long term, with preservation of the environment, (2) ensuring a stable supply of safe food affordable in terms of quality and price, (3) improving the standard of living of the rural population and rural development in general, with preservation of traditional values, (4) strengthening of competitiveness of food producers.

1088. *Agriculture* means an economic activity, including plant and livestock production and related activities, in compliance with the regulations laying down the classification of activities and register of organizational units; (Art. 2, para. 1 point 1).

1089. Agriculture programmes harmonized with the principles of environmental protection shall be supported through agro-environmental measures, aimed at the following: protection and development of natural resources (land, water, air) with particular emphasis on development of organic and integral agriculture, preservation and sustainable use of genetic resources in plant and livestock

1028. According to Article 34, the measures of agricultural and fisheries policy shall encourage organization of producers in agriculture and fisheries into cooperatives and other forms of organizations of producers (hereinafter referred to as 'producer organizations') (paragraph 1). Producers may be organized into a producer organization based on one product or a group of products, with a view to planning the production in line with market demand in terms of quality and quantity, marketing the products produced by members of the producers organization, optimization of production costs and stabilization of the producer price, conservation of the environment by implementation of Good Producers Practice, waste management and biodiversity conservation (paragraph 2).[1090]

1029. Producer organization (referred to in Article 34, paragraph 2 of this Law) may be established only at the initiative of producers and in case it complies with the following conditions: that it has at least five members, that it has established the minimum volume and value of the production, that it places the total quantity of products produced by members of the producers organization on the market, that it has its rules of organization and operation and that it has the capacity of a legal person (Article 35, paragraph 1). More detailed conditions referred to in paragraph 1 of this Article shall be laid down by the Ministry (Article 35, paragraph 2).[1091] Members of the producers organization shall abide by the rules of the producers organization referred to in paragraph 1 indent 5 of this Article laying down, in particular, the following: production planning, submitting of reports on production, method and conditions of production, sale of products, environmental protection, financial obligations of the members of the producers organization (Article 35, paragraph 3).[1092]

1030. In carrying out the activities, the supplementary activity holder[1093] shall meet the minimum criteria as laid down by laws governing environmental protection, public health, animal and plant health, animal welfare and safety at work (Article 50, paragraph 2). A supplementary activity at family agricultural holdings may be carried out solely on the basis of an approval (Article 51, paragraph 1).[1094]

---

production, preservation of natural habitats and the environment, with particular emphasis on sustainable use of mountain pastureland. The Agro-budget may lay down other measures for support to sustainable agricultural resource management (Art. 16).

1090. A product or a group of products that producers' organizations may be organized for shall be laid down by the Ministry (Art. 34, para. 3).

1091. The founders of the organization shall submit the application for recognition of producers' organization to the Ministry (Art. 36 para. 1).

1092. More detailed contents of the rules referred to in the para. 3 of this Article shall be laid down by the Ministry (Art. 35 para. 4).

1093. A holder of supplementary activity is a natural person who is the owner, lessee or other person authorized to use the agricultural holding concerned and to engage in agriculture (hereinafter referred to as 'supplementary activity holder') (Art. 50 para. 1). (1) Supplementary activity of a family agricultural holding is an activity related to agriculture and forestry, carried out at the family agricultural holding and makes possible better utilization of its production opportunities and workforce (Art. 49, para. 1).

1094. The approval for carrying out a supplementary activity shall be issued by the Ministry, following an application from the holder of the supplementary activity (Art. 51, para. 2).

1031. By virtue of Article 52, paragraph 2 of the Law activities of public interest in the field of agriculture and rural development[1095] are the following: (a) extension activities,[1096] (b) professional activities in livestock production, (c) professional activities in plant production, (d) professional activities in preservation of genetic resources – gene bank, (e) analytical-developmental activities, (f) activities of education and training of human resources for the purpose of agriculture and rural development and (g) research activities in agriculture.

II. Law on Plant Health Protection

1032. The legal basis for plant health protection system is established by the enactment of the Law on Plant Health Protection (OJ RM, Nos 28/06, 28/11, 48/15). The law contains seventy-two articles and following twelve chapters: Chapter I – Basic Provisions (Articles 1–3), Chapter II – Performance of Plant Health Care Activities (Articles 4–7), Chapter III – Prevention of Importation and Spread of Harmful Organisms and their Suppression (Articles 8–38), Chapter IV – Import, Export and Transit of Plant Shipments (Articles 26–38), Chapter V – Move Package of Plant (Articles 39–48), Chapter VI – Biological Plant Health Care (Articles 49–50), Chapter VII – Ensuring Performance of Activities in the Public Interest (Articles 51–53), Chapter VIII – Financing, Fees and Compensation for Damages (Articles 54–56), Chapter IX – Collection, Use and Exchange of Data and Information (Articles 57–58), Chapter X – Inspection Supervisions (Articles 59–61), Chapter XI – Penal Provisions (Articles 62–64) and Chapter XII – Transitional and Final Provisions (Articles 65–72).

1033. The Law regulates the plants' health protection and plant products against harmful organisms; prevention measures of introduction and spreading and measures for control of harmful organisms; and health surveillance of plants in national trade and of plant consignments during import, export and transit.

1034. The legal basis for a single service for plant health protection establishment was provided (it is the competent authority for enforcement and monitoring of

1095. Activities of public interest in the field of agriculture and rural development shall be carried out by authorized scientific research institutions and other legal and natural persons in the field of agriculture that meet the conditions for carrying out these activities (Art. 52 para. 1).

1096. Extension activities in the field of agriculture and rural development are the following: organization of organic, integrated and conventional agricultural production, implementation of new scientific developments, technologies and techniques, etc, development of programmes for rational use of agricultural land and plant nutrition products in line with the principles of sustainable development, implementation of Good Agricultural Practice, environmental protection, drawing up developmental and investment programmes for agricultural holdings, training related to management of agricultural holdings, including economic analyzes, incentive applications, development of supplementary activities in agricultural holdings and extending the scope of economic activities (diversification) in rural areas, farmers' organizations, interpretation of regulations in the field of agriculture and related activities (Art. 53).

Law enforcement), a structure of responsibility has been established and a phytosanitary inspectorate was set up with precise and defined authority as regards the borders, national trade and the site of production.

1035. The Law introduces the term of plant passports (Articles 40–48), protected zones (Articles 14–17, etc.), records of producers, processors, distributors and importers of certain plant species (Articles 21–25), etc.

III. Law on the Plant Protection Products

1036. The protection of plants has been regulated by the Law on Plant Protection Products (OJ MNE, Nos 51/08, 40/11, 18/14).

1037. The Law on plant protection products regulates manner of classification, registration, trade and use of plant protection products[1097] and active substances, maximum permitted level of residues of plant protection products, manner of keeping registers and records, information exchange and other issues relevant to plant protection products (Article 1). The Law has following thirteen parts: Part I – General provisions (Articles 1–2); Part II – Trade in Plant Protection Products (Articles 3–13); Part III – Registration of Plant Protection Products (Articles 14–33); Part IV – Authorized Legal Persons (Articles 34–36); Part V – Provision of Services (Article 37); Part VI – Devices for Use of Plant Protection Products (Articles 38–40); Part VII – Importation (Article 41); Part VIII – Responsibility of Administration Body (Article 41); Part IX – Information and Record Keeping (Articles 43–44) and Part X – Fees and Costs (Article 45); Part XI – Inspection Supervision (Articles 46–52); Part XII – Penal Provisions (Articles 53–54); and Part XIII – Transitional and Final Provisions (Articles 55–58).[1098]

1038. According to Article 3 Plant protection products may not be placed on the market nor used in the territory of Montenegro unless they are registered in accordance with this Law, except for scientific and research purposes.[1099] Plant protection products may be placed on the market only if they are registered, classified, packed or marked and if they are accompanied by a declaration and instruction for use, in accordance with regulations governing dangerous substances, and chemicals

1097. Plant protection products shall mean active substances and preparations that contain one or more active substances in a form in which they are delivered to the end user, and are intended for: protection of plants or plant products from harmful organisms or for preventing influence of such organisms unless such substances or preparations are intended for other purposes, in accordance with this Law; exercising influence on life processes of plants, except nutrition (growth control and the like); conservation of plant products, unless otherwise regulated by separate regulations; destruction of unfavourable plants; destruction of parts of plants or preventing of unfavourable plants growth (Art. 2, Item 1).

1098. Provisions of the Law on Plant Protection (OJ FRY, No. 24/98) related to the plant protection products shall not apply from the day this Law comes into force (Art. 57).

1099. Notwithstanding para. 1 of this Article, plant protection products that are not registered may be produced, stored or shipped only if they are intended for use in another country and if they were registered in another country (para. 2).

and in accordance with this Law. Registered plant protection products shall be classified according to their intended use (Article 4).[1100]

1039. Trade in plant protection products may be performed by a company, other legal person and entrepreneur registered for performing these activities in the Central Register of the Commercial Court (hereinafter referred to as 'the CRCC') with corporate domicile in Montenegro and which is entered in the Register for Wholesale Trade in Plant Protection Products and the Register for Retail Trade in Plant Protection Products (hereinafter referred to as 'the Register') (Article 6, paragraph 1). Wholesale and retail trade in plant protection products may be performed by a company, other legal person and entrepreneur, if: it has a full-time employed person responsible for purchase, trade, storage, keeping and issuing plant protection products that have completed specialist studies, that has faculty of agriculture degree (department – plant protection), or specialist studies or faculty of agriculture degree (department – plant production) with completed specialist course in plant protection products; it has appropriate equipment and facilities for storage or sale of plant production products (paragraph 2).[1101]

1040. Plant protection products registered in Montenegro may be imported by companies, other legal persons or entrepreneurs entered in the Register of Importers (Article 41, paragraph 1).[1102]

IV. Law on Veterinary Medicine

1041. The Law on Veterinary Medicine is the main veterinary regulation in Montenegro (OJ MNE, Nos 30/12, 48/15, 52/16). This law regulates conditions and methods of performing veterinary activity, health protection of animals, measures of veterinary public health, veterinary protection of the environment, as well as other issues important for performing veterinary activity. Organization and implementation of protection of animal health as well as application of measures of veterinary public health are of interest to Montenegro (Article 1).

1042. Veterinary activity, according to this law, comprises protection and control of health and welfare of animals, repulsing zoonosis, control of safety and health quality of products of animal origin and food for animals and other activities concerning veterinary public health, improvement of reproduction of animals taking into account health protection of animals and veterinary protection of the environment (hereinafter 'veterinary activity') (Article 2).

1100. List of classified plant protection products referred to in para. 2 of this Article shall be determined by the ministry responsible for agriculture (the Ministry) (para. 3).

1101. Administration authority responsible for plant protection products (hereinafter referred to as: the administration body) shall determine the fulfilment of requirements referred to in paras 1 and 2 of this Article in a decision (para. 3).

1102. Persons referred to in para. 1 of this Article shall deliver imported plant protection products registered in Montenegro only to persons entered in the Register referred to in Art. 6 of this Law. Entry in the Register of Importers shall be made upon request (paras 2, and 3).

1043. Veterinary protection of the environment is regulated by: Article 13 paragraph 1 point 13, Article 17 point 5, Article 22 paragraph 2 point 21, Article 44, Article 53, point 13, Article 62 paragraph 2, Articles 98, 99, Article 108, Article 126, Article 144, Article 150, Article 162, points 34, 35, 58, Article 163, point 17.

V. Other Regulations

1044. The most important by-laws adopted by the competent organs in the field of agriculture are, *inter alia*, as follows:

- -The Rulebook on the closer content of the Plan of action in crisis situations for certain harmful organisms (OJ MNE No. 118/22).[1103]
- The Rulebook on maximally allowed amounts of residues of pharmacologically active substances of veterinary medicines in the products of animal origin (OJ MNE Nos 75/18, 47/20, 135/21, 120/22).
- The Rulebook on phytosanitary measures for prevention of introduction and spread of harmful organism Phyllosticta citricarpa (McAlpine) Van der Aa (OJ MNE No. 119/22).
- The Rulebook on phytosanitary measures for introduction of plants and plant products that present an unacceptable risk from harmful organisms (OJ MNE No. 135/22).
- The Rulebook on phytosanitary measures for prevention of introduction and spread of harmful plant and plant product organisms and objects under surveillance (OJ MNE No. 135/22).
- The Rulebook on phytosanitary measures for prevention of introduction and spread of tomato brown rugose fruit virus (OJ MNE No. 135/22).
- The List of Harmful Plant and Plant Product Organisms and Objects under Surveillance (OJ MNE No. 135/22).
- Phytosanitary Measures Programme for 2018 (OJ MNE, No. 10/18).
- List of Active Substances Permissible for Use in Plant Protection Products for 2018 (OJ MNE, No. 12/18).
- Programme for nitrate monitoring in food of plant origin for 2018 (OJ MNE, No. 12/18).
- Seed Testing Control Programme for 2018 (OJ MNE, No. 9/18).
- List of Registered Plant Protection Products (OJ MNE, No. 43/17).
- List of active substances for use in plant protection products for 2017 (OJ MNE, No. 7/2017).
- National Plan for Sustainable Use of Plant Protection Products (OJ MNE, No. 57/16).
- Regulation on Notification Procedure in the Field of Sanitary and Phytosanitary Measures (OJ MNE, No. 13/08).
- Rulebook on Integrated Plant Protection (OJ MNE, No. 68/15).

1103. For the full list of regulations in the phytosanitary field, *see*: https://www.gov.me/pretraga?page=1&sort=published_at&q=fitosanitarni&dt=5 (3 Dec. 2022).

- Rulebook on Precautionary Measures Relating to Plant Protection Products (OJ MNE, No. 69/2016).
- Rulebook on the manner of storing and handling ammonium nitrate fertilizers with high nitrogen content (OJ MEN, No. 45/15).
- Rulebook on sampling methods for determining residues of plant protection products (OJ MNE, No. 48/14).
- Programme of Compulsory Animal Health Measures in 2018 (OJ MNE, No. 9/18).[1104]
- Rulebook on conditions for facilities and equipment for keeping and breeding animals for production (OJ MNE, No. 64/17).
- Rulebook on Measures for the Prevention, Detection and Suppression of Certain Animal Diseases (OJ MNE, No. 33/2017).
- Programme of Food and Feed Safety Measures for 2018 (OJ MNE, No. 9/18).[1105]
- The Regulation on Food Hygiene (OJ MNE, Nos 13/16, 80/16).

§5. Organic Agriculture

1045. Development of organic agriculture is at a very early stage and up to now, all activities were directed towards creating normative and institutional prerequisites for complete affirmation of this type of production, and through it for affirmation of the comparative advantages of ecologically pure, natural and agricultural resources of Montenegro.[1106]

1046. According to the Strategy for Development of Agriculture and Rural Areas 2015–2020 'organic production is a key development opportunity for Montenegrin agriculture, especially taking into account the availability of very favourable natural conditions that are reflected in the country's uncontaminated soil, water and air'.[1107] Although organic producers are still not in the habit of registering their activities, they are slowly improving. Compared with 2013, the number of registered producers has increased by 4.38%, the number of certified producers has increased by 28.57% and the number of issued certificates for organic production has increased by 10%. All of this implies that there are 167 producers in Montenegro, of which twenty-seven have certified products.[1108]

1104. For the list of veterinary regulations *see*: https://www.gov.me/pretraga?page=1&sort=published_at&q=veterina&dt=5 (3 Dec. 2022).
1105. For the list of regulations in the food safety field *see*: https://www.gov.me/pretraga?page=1&sort=published_at&q=bezbednost%20hrane&dt=5 (3 Dec. 2022).
1106. MAFWM (2006a) 50. According to the European Commission Report for 2010 'the organic farming sector in Montenegro is relatively small but expected to grow due to domestic support, ongoing international projects and trends. There are eighty-eight producers involved in organic production but no precise data are available on the area planted'. EC (2010), 72. For more details, *see* GMNE, MAFWM (2009a), 163–173.
1107. MARD. Strategy for Development of Agriculture and Rural Areas 2015–2020, p. 47.
1108. *Ibid.*

I. Competencies

1047. The MAFWM performs administrative affairs related to, *inter alia*, organic production (Article 11 of the Decree on state administration organization and operations, OJ MNE, Nos 49/22, 52/22, 56/22, 82/22).

1048. The enforcement control of the Law on Organic Agriculture and relevant secondary legislation is performed by the agricultural inspectorate.

1049. The national certification body, named Monteorganica, was established in 2005. Experts from internationally recognized certification agencies were involved in functional development and establishment of this certification body.[1109] Monteorganica is accredited and certified to perform controls and certify organic products according to the requirements of standard MEST EN 45011.2004. The Accreditation Body of Montenegro has issued a Certificate of Accreditation ATCG – 0021 to Monteorganica. The MARD authorize this body.[1110]

II. Law on Organic Agriculture

1050. The Montenegrin legislation relating to organic agriculture is mainly laid down in the Law on Organic Agriculture (OJ MNE, No. 56/13), while the specific aspects of organic agriculture are regulated by secondary legislation. The Law consists of nine chapters. These are Chapter I – Basic Provision (Articles 1–3), Chapter II – Goals and principles of organic productions (Articles 4–8), Chapter III – Rules of production (Articles 9–10), Chapter IV – Production in agricultural economy (Articles 12–23), Chapter V – Labeling (Articles 24–27), Chapter VI – Control (Articles 28–41), Chapter VII – Supervision (Articles 42–44), Chapter VIII – Penalty Provisions (Articles 45–49) and Chapter IX – Transitional and Final Provisions (Articles 50–55). This law regulates organic production, labelling of organic, ecological and biological products, control over organic production and other issues of importance for organic production (Article 1).

1051. This Law regulates organic production,[1111] labelling of organic, ecological and biological products,[1112] control over organic production and other issues of importance for organic production (Article 1).

1109. Funds for organic agricultural production development are allocated from the Agro-budget under the rural development measures.

1110. MARD. Strategy for Development of Agriculture and Rural Areas 2015–2020, p. 12.

1111. *Organic production* is the production of agricultural and other products, based on the application of organic production methods at all stages of production, preparation and distribution, in accordance to this Law (Art. 3, para. 1, point 1).

1112. *Marking* are letters, words, details, trade names, trademarks, image displays or symbols relating to an organic product and contained on the packaging, document, notice, label, ring, pendant, wrapper, etc., that accompany or they relate to that product (Art. 3, para. 1, point 11).

A. Application of the Law

1052. This Law shall apply to products placed on the market or intended for placing on the market, as follows: (1) live or unprocessed agricultural products; (2) processed agricultural products used as food; (3) products of aquaculture; (4) animal feed; (5) seeds and planting material; and (6) yeasts used for food and animal feed (Article 2, paragraph 1).[1113]

B. Rules of Production

1053. Entities producing organic products must comply with the production rules established by this Law (Article 9). GMOs and products produced from or using GMOs must not be used in organic products such as food, animal feed, auxiliary processing substances, plant protection products, fertilizers, soil improvement substances, seeds, vegetative propagating material, microorganisms or animals (Article 10, paragraph 1). The origin of a product used as food or animal feed shall be determined on the basis of the mark on the product or on the basis of the accompanying document that is attached or delivered with the product, in accordance with the law governing food safety (paragraph 2).[1114]

1054. It is forbidden to use ionizing radiation in the processing of organic food or animal feed, or raw materials used in organic food or animal feed (Article 11).

C. Production in Agricultural Economy

1055. The entire agricultural farm that is used for organic production is managed in accordance with the rules of organic farming (Article 12, paragraph 1). Exceptionally, an agricultural farm may be divided into production units or aquaculture farms, but not all aquaculture production units or aquaculture farms are managed in accordance with organic production rules (paragraph 2).[1115] In addition, the law prescribes, *inter alia*, rules on organic plant production (Article 13), rules for organic livestock production (Article 14), aquaculture production rules (Article 15) and rules for sea algae production (Article 16).

1113. This Law shall apply to legal entities and natural persons (hereinafter referred to as: entities) involved in all stages of production, preparation and distribution of products (Art. 2, para. 2).

1114. Entities that use non-organic products and which are not food or animal feed during the purchase must ask the supplier to confirm that the products delivered are not GMOs or products produced from GMOs or manufactured using GMOs (para. 3).

1115. On separate production units, i.e., the aquaculture farms referred to in para. 2 of this Article: in the case of animal production, different types of animals must be grown in parallel; in aquaculture farms, the same species may be cultivated, provided that the locations of the breeding sites are appropriately separated; in plant production, different plant varieties must be grown in parallel, which can easily be distinguished from one another (para. 3).

1056. The Ministry determines the list of products and substances that can be used in organic production (hereinafter 'List'): (1) for the protection of plants, (2) as fertilizer and soil cultivators, (3) as ingredients for food for animals of plant, animal and mineral origin and certain products used in animal nutrition, which are not organic, (4) as additives for animal feed and processing aids, (5) as products for cleaning and disinfection of swimming pools, cages, buildings and facilities for breeding animal and (6) as products for cleaning and disinfecting the objects and devices used in plant production, including warehouses in agricultural holdings (Article 17, paragraph 1). Approval of the products and substances referred to in paragraph 1 of this Article shall be made by the Ministry (paragraph 2).[1116]

1057. The law also prescribes, *inter alia*, the transition period (conversion) (Article 18), processing of organic animal feed (Article 19), organic food processing (Article 20), rules for the production of organic yeast (Article 21), criteria for certain products and substances in processing (Article 22) and exceptions to the rules of production (Article 23).

D. Marking

1058. In accordance with Article 25 of the Law the organic production symbol (hereinafter 'logo') is used in the marking, advertising and presentation of products that meet the requirements set forth in this Law. The logo shall not be used for products in the transitional period and food referred to in Article 24, paragraph 6, points 2 and 3 of this Law.[1117] The law also regulates the use of terms relating to organic production (Article 24), labelling obligations (Article 26) and special labelling requirements (Article 27).

E. Control

1059. Organic production is subject to expert control (Article 28). The frequency of expert control shall be determined on the basis of the assessment of the risk of non-compliance with the rules laid down by this Law (paragraph 2).[1118]

1116. The use of the products and substances referred to in para. 1 of this Article, the manner of their use, the dosage and the time limit for use in agricultural products shall be prescribed by the Ministry (para. 3).

1117. The content, size and form of the logo referred to in para. 1 of this Article shall be prescribed by the Ministry (para. 3).

1118. Professional control is carried out at least once a year, with the exception of those subjects engaged in wholesale trade and selling the products to the final consumer or user in accordance with Art. 35 para. 4 of this Law (para. 3).

1060. Expert control and certification of organic production can be carried out by a control authority that meets the requirements laid down by this Law and authorized by the Ministry (Article 29, paragraph 1). The control authority must meet several conditions (paragraph 2).[1119]

1061. The control authority or control body shall issue a certificate to the subject under its control whose product meets the organic production requirements established by this Law. The certificate must contain the name of the entity, the type or list of products and the validity period of the certificate (Article 36, paragraphs 1 and 2).[1120]

1062. Organic production and import of organic products may be conducted by entities registered in the Register of organic production entities (hereinafter 'the Registry'). The Register shall be kept by the Ministry. Entities that have concluded the contract on control and certification in organic production referred to in Article 18, paragraph 2 of this Law shall be entered in the Register (Article 39, paragraphs 1–3).[1121]

F. Import of Organic Products

1063. Organic products may be imported if there is a certificate issued by the control authority, i.e., the control body which is on the official list of control authorities, i.e., the EU control bodies or the official list of the EU of control authorities, i.e., control bodies of third countries (Article 40, paragraph 1).[1122]

1064. Organic products to be imported must be packed and closed in such a way as to prevent the replacement of their contents and have a clearly visible mark marking the organic product in the country of origin (paragraph 4).

1065. Pursuant to Article 41 certified organic products (referred to in Article 40, paragraph 2 of this Law) may be placed on the market if the control authority or control body, in the process of recognition of the certificate, determines that: (1) the

1119. For example, control authority must be registered in Central register of economic entities (Art. 29, para. 2, point 1).
1120. A content and certificate form shall be prescribed by the Ministry (Art. 36, para. 3).
1121. The Ministry shall prescribe the contents, the manner of registration and keeping of the Registry (para. 4).
1122. Entities that import organic products that are accompanied by a certificate of control authority, i.e., control bodies that are not on the official lists referred to in para. 1 of this Article are obliged to initiate the procedure for granting a certificate to the control authority or control body for the purpose of obtaining a certificate of equivalence, in accordance with Art. 41 of this Law (para. 2).

product is manufactured in accordance with the rules of production that are equivalent to the rules laid down in Articles 9–24 of this Law and (2) entities were subject to a control system that is equivalent to the control system referred to in Articles 28, 29 and 35 of this Law.[1123]

III. Other Regulations in the Field of Organic Agriculture

1066. Based on the Law on organic production (OJ MNE, No. 56/13) the following by-laws have been adopted:

- Rulebook on Conditions and Rules for Processing, Packaging, Transport and Storage of Organic Products (29 December 2016).
- Rulebook on Conditions for Plant and Livestock Organic Breeding (15 December 2014).
- Rulebook on the Content and Management of the Register of Subjects in Organic Production (14 May 2015).
- Rulebook on the Manner and Methodology of Professional Control in Organic Production (30 December 2015).
- Rulebook on the Content and Size of the Sign of Organic Production (16 September 2016).
- Rulebook on Rules and Conditions for Organic Production of the Aquaculture Animals and Sea Algae (7 December 2017).

§6. Harmonization with EU Legislation

1067. According to the EC Progress Report for 2022, 'Montenegro remains moderately prepared in the area of agriculture and rural development.'[1124] The potential for further development of organic farming and expansion of the sector remains to be supported. The law on organic production, to align with the EU acquis, is being drafted.[1125]

1123. In the process of recognition of the certificate, the importer is obliged to submit to the control authority the documentation on the basis of which it can determine whether that product meets the conditions prescribed in para. 1, item. 1 and para. 2 of this Article (Art. 41. para. 2).
1124. EC (2022). p. 114.
1125. *Ibid*, p. 115.

Chapter 5. Biotechnology

1068. Biotechnology is still not sufficiently developed in Montenegro. 'At the moment there is no comprehensive or detailed information on the presence of either plant or animal GMOs in Montenegro. Also, there are no specialized devices for testing of GMOs and for testing of suspicious samples institutions from Serbia are engaged'.[1126]

§1. Competencies

1069. According to Articles 10 and 11 of the Law on Genetically Modified Organisms (OJ MNE, Nos 22/08, 40/11),[1127] competencies concerning the GMO belong to following institutions: ministry competent for agriculture, ministry competent for environmental protection, ministry competent for health, state organ for veterinary medicine, state organ for sanitary matters and state organ for environmental protection.[1128]

1070. National Bio Safety Council (NSBS) is planned to be established in order to monitor state and development in the area of GMO and to provide expert assistance to competent bodies for the implementation of this Law (Articles 15–19 of the Law on GMO).[1129]

§2. Legislation

I. Law on GMO

1071. The new Law on GMO[1130] (OJ MNE, Nos 22/08, 40/11) regulates the use of GMO in closed systems (laboratory work and greenhouses), their deliberate release into the environment (experimental fieldwork or commercial growing), commercial release of products that contain or consist of or are derived from GMO (import, export or internal trade), handling, transport, packaging, transit through

1126. MSPE (2010b), 32.
1127. *See also* Arts 21, 46 of the Decree on Organization and Manner of Work of the Public Administration (Official Journal of MNE, Nos 5/12, 25/12, 61/12, 20/13, 17/14, 35/16, 73/16, 3/17, 19/17).
1128. In accordance with the Law (Art. 10, para. 2), certain tasks of public interest can be entrusted to authorized legal entities.
1129. It will be composed of members who are prominent public, scientific and professional workers in the field of biology, agriculture, medicine, veterinary microbiology, genetics, ecology, evolutionary biology, population biology, toxicology, allergology, forestry, biochemical, molecular biology and other relevant scientific areas. Council has a president and ten members. The members have to be appointed by the Government on proposal by the competent authorities of state administration for a period of four years (Art. 16, paras 1–3).
1130. After this Law had entered into force the Law on Genetically Modified Organisms (Official Journal of FRY, No. 21/01) ceased to be in force (Art. 74). Regulations adopted on the basis of this Law are, however, to be implemented if they are not in contradiction with the new Law (Art. 74).

Montenegro, labelling and processing of products that either contain or consist of or are derived from GMO, conditions and measures for prevention and elimination of potentially adverse effects in work with GMO, liability for illegal utilization of GMO, inspection supervision over the implementation of this Law, etc.

1072. Obtaining pre-announced import permits, risk assessment procedures, conditions for contained use in laboratories and other matters are to be regulated in detail by sub-legal acts.[1131]

A. Principles of GMO Management

1073. The second chapter of the Law (Articles 6–9) defined the following principles of GMO management: the principle of integration, principle of precautionary, principle of assessment of risk and principle of publicity.[1132]

1074. According to Article 6 of the Law, the basis and goals of GMO management policy (as well as measures aimed at prevention of the harmful effects of products that contain, consist or are obtained from GMO to human health and the environment) comprise strategy, planning and programme documents concerning development, finance, education, information and scientific research activities.

1075. Competent authorities, in accordance with the principle of precaution, are obliged to ensure that appropriate measures are undertaken aimed at avoiding harmful effects to human health and the environment that may be caused by intentional introduction into the closed systems, products which contain or which consist of or which were obtained from the GMO. This includes putting on market these kinds of products (Article 7).[1133]

1131. Sub-legal acts on the basis of the new Law will be adopted within two years from the date of entry into force of this Law (Art. 73). *See also* Arts 13 and 14 of the Law.

1132. When management of GMO is concerned, the public has the right to be informed and to be included in the decision-making process in accordance with Art. 9 of the Law. In addition, state authorities responsible for health issues, veterinary medicine, phytosanitary affairs and environmental protection have the obligation to publish in the 'Official Journal of Montenegro' a list of GMO or products that contain GMO, consist of GMO or produced from GMO, for which is issued approval for intentionally introducing in the environment, for commercial purposes, that is placing on the market (Art. 60).

1133. According to Art. 12, the competent authority may temporarily restrict or prohibit the import, use and placing on the market, and the introduction of GMO in the environment or products which contain, which consist of or which are obtained from the GMO, in the case of a lack of scientific information and knowledge about the possible scale of harmful effects on human health, biological diversity and the environment, or if there is new scientific knowledge about harmful effects to human health, biological diversity and life environment of the product.

1076. The risk of potential harmful effects to human health and the environment that may arise due to the transfer of genes of the GMO to other organisms is to be assessed according to individual cases as prescribed by this law (Article 8).[1134]

1077. Use of GMO in closed systems, deliberate introduction in the environment, putting on marked and transit of GMO are allowed under conditions and in the manner determined by this law (Article 21).[1135]

1078. Putting GMO on the market or keeping them for commercial purposes is prohibited if experimental data and research results do not exist concerning the direct and indirect impacts on the ecosystem that may be affected. These data and results are to be acquired by the experiment carried out in Montenegro (Article 22).[1136]

1079. The competent authority is obliged to publish notification in at least one daily newspaper distributed in the territory of Montenegro, in electronic media and on the web page of the authority. In addition, it has obligation to organize and conduct a public hearing that must be at least forty-five days from the date of publication of information (Article 25).[1137]

B. Authority for Testing and Control of GMO

1080. Testing and control of GMO, or products that contain them, consist of or obtained from the GMO, can be performed only by an authorized laboratory, in accordance with Article 20.[1138]

1134. The GMO containing gene resistant to antibiotics for human and veterinary use, which can cause harmful effect to human health and the environment, has to be particularly identified and excluded (Art. 8, para. 2).
1135. The procedure for the approval starts on the basis of applications which have to be submitted in written or electronic form (Art. 21, para. 2). The applicant may identify specific information in the report as a business secret, or as confidential in accordance with the law governing the protection of confidential data (Art. 23, para. 1).
1136. Content of the application for obtaining approval for the experiments, the method and conditions of conducting experiments and monitoring of the use of GMO in the experimental purposes shall be determined by regulation issued by the Ministry competent for agriculture with opinion of the Ministry in charge for environmental protection (Art. 22, para. 2).
1137. Decision of the competent authority must be published in the 'Official Journal of Montenegro' (Art. 25, para. 3).
1138. According to Art. 20, para. 3 provides that authorization for carrying out the testing has to be issued by the Ministry of Agriculture with the approval of the Ministry of Environmental Protection.

1081. After completing testing of GMO or the products containing them, the authorized laboratory has the obligation to submit a report and results to a competent organ of state administration (Article 20, paragraph 4).[1139]

C. Use of GMO in the Closed System

1082. By virtue of Article 26, use of GMO or products containing them in closed systems is classified into following four levels of risk: first level is related to the limited use when the risks are negligible; the second level refers to the limited use when the risks are small; the third level refers to the limited use when the risks are significant; and the fourth level refers to the limited use when the risks are great.[1140] Risk level classification of the use of GMO in closed systems is done by the authorities responsible for sanitary issues and is based on the fulfilment of the prescribed security measures and other conditions in accordance with the law (Article 26, paragraph 3).[1141]

1083. Use of GMO in a closed system is allowed only if the prescribed requirements for the level of risk are met (Article 27). Before the first use, the applicant is obliged to inform the organ of state administration competent for sanitary work.[1142] The organ checks whether the closed system meets the prescribed conditions and, after obtaining opinion of the NSBS, enters it in the register of closed system[1143] if the conditions prescribed are met.[1144]

1084. The application for the first and each subsequent limited use of GMO, or products that contain, consist of or are produced from the GMO, classified in the

1139. Obligation of the authorized laboratory and its employees is to respect confidentiality of data that are marked as confidential in accordance with this law, as well as the confidentiality of results obtained on the basis of testing and controls performed at the request of the competent authorities (Art. 20, para. 5).
1140. The Law provides requirements and procedures for the beginning of the use of first and second level of risk (Art. 30) and for the beginning of the use of the third and fourth level of risk (Art. 31).
1141. Criteria for classification, conditions for facilities and level of risk have to be established by regulation adopted by the Ministry of Agriculture and with opinion of the Ministry of Environmental Protection (Art. 26, para. 3).
1142. The applicant has obligation to develop risk assessment for the intended use of GMO, prior to the commencement of their use in a closed system (Art. 28, para. 1). Conditions, content and scope of risk assessment of GMO use in closed systems have to be prescribed by regulation issued by the Ministry of Agriculture in accordance with the Ministry of Environmental Protection (Art. 28, para. 4).
1143. Registration in the Registry and deletion from the register are regulated by Arts 58 and 59.
1144. The competent authority has, besides that, the obligation to issue decision on registration, within sixty days of receipt of application (Art. 27, para. 5).

first and second level of risk, must be submitted to the organ responsible for sanitary issues (Article 30). If a closed system is registered in the Register, it can start with activities only after obtaining approval from the competent authorities.[1145]

1085. The competent organ has an obligation to consider the application and to decide[1146] within forty-five days from the day of receipt of application (for the first and second level of risk), that is, within sixty days from the day of receipt of application (for the third and fourth level of risk) (Article 30, paragraph 5 and Article 31, paragraph 5).

1086. Article 29 establishes the obligation of the applicant to develop a plan of measures in case of an incident[1147] prior to the commencement of the use of GMO in a closed system.

D. Deliberate Introduction of GMO in Environment

1087. Article 34 prescribes that introduction of GMO in the environment in protected areas and in the areas intended for organic production of agricultural products and areas for development of ecotourism is prohibited.

1088. The applicant is obliged, before the deliberate introduction of GMO in the environment to obtain the approval of competent authority for the protection of the environment (Article 32). On the other hand, the organ of the state administration responsible for environmental protection is obliged to obtain consent from the MAFWM (Article 32, paragraph 3).

1089. The subject who obtained the approval (subject in business with GMO)[1148] is obliged to submit to state authorities responsible for environmental protection a report on progress concerning the intentional introduction of GMO in the environment, within sixty days from the date of introduction (Article 36). Besides that, the subject has obligation to submit periodic reports, in written or electronic form, meeting the terms established by the approval. The report contains the

1145. Organ of the state administration is obliged to submit, without delay, a copy of the application and accompanying documentation to the NSBS for obtaining opinions (Art. 30, para. 3). Similar procedure is in the case of the commencement of the use of GMO classified in the third and fourth level of risk (*See* Art. 31).

1146. Renewal of the approval is regulated by Art. 47 of the Law.

1147. Moreover, the applicant has obligation to provide information on planned measures in case of incidents, which have to be approved by Ministry of Agriculture after having obtained opinion of the Ministry of Environmental Protection and the Ministry of Health (Art. 29, para. 2).

1148. Subject in business with the GMO is the business firm, other legal entity, entrepreneur or a physical person who uses, intentionally introduced into the environment or closed systems, puts on the market, or transport GMO products that contain, consist of or obtained from the GMO (Art. 2, point 16).

results of the introduction and in particular observations relevant to the potential risk to human health and the environment.[1149]

E. Trade and Transboundary Transfer

1090. According to Article 37, subject who intends (first time) to put on the market GMO is obliged to obtain approval from the competent authority for placing it on the market.[1150] The authority may, according to Article 43, recognize the approval for putting on market GMO issued in another state, if conditions prescribed by the law are fulfilled.[1151]

1091. If subject in the business with GMO suspects or knows of existence of a higher degree risk for human health and the environment than it was estimated,[1152] when the approval was issued, he must undertake measures for protection of human health and the environment, start the process of withdrawal from the trade and inform the authority which issued the permit (Article 44).

1092. Cross-border transfer of GMO or products containing them can be done only on the basis of approval in accordance with this law (Article 46).[1153]

1093. Import and use of GMO or products containing, consisting of or derived from the GMO can be restricted or prohibited by the Government, in the case of a lack of scientific information and knowledge about the scale of possible harmful effects on human health, biological diversity and living environment or if new or additional scientific information about harmful effects on human health, biological diversity and the environment exists.

F. Marking, Handling and Actions in the Case of Incident

1094. One of the obligations of the subject in the business with GMO relates to marking packages and accompanying documentation of GMO or products which contain them, with a legible and visible sign (Article 48). Packaged GMO has to be marked by the label on the packaging. If not packed, the product should be marked

1149. The content and form of reports will be prescribed by the regulation of Ministry of Environmental Protection (Art. 36, para. 3).
1150. The procedure of the competent bodies of state administration is regulated by Arts 39–43.
1151. The competent authorities may, after obtaining reports from NSBS or the National Council for Food Security Assessment, temporarily prohibit or restrict the placing on the market GMO or product containing, consisting of or derived from GMO (Art. 43, para. 3).
1152. Each subject in the business with the GMO must, without delay, submit new information about the risks to human health and the environment to the competent authority (Art. 44, para. 3). In this case subject in the work with GMO is obliged to submit a new application (Art. 44, para. 2).
1153. Detailed conditions for cross-border transfer of GMO are to be established by the Ministry of Agriculture in cooperation with the Ministry of Environmental Protection (Art. 46, para. 3).

by a mark on the product or by a sign set directly with the product (Article 48, paragraph 2).[1154] According to Article 48, paragraph 3, the label must contain the following phrases: 'genetically modified organism', 'this product contains genetically modified organism', 'this product consists of a genetically modified organism' or 'this product is derived from genetically modified organism'.[1155]

1095. In addition, subject in the business with GMO has the obligation, when advertising a GMO product, to clearly and unequivocally state that the advertised product contains, consists of or is produced from a GMO (Article 51).[1156]

1096. As prescribed by Article 50, paragraph 1, the supporting documentation during the handling, transportation and packaging of GMO, or products that contain them, must contain prescribed information.[1157]

1097. In the case of the incident subject in GMO business has the obligation to promptly act in accordance with the plan of measures in the event of incident. It must inform the competent authority on following issues: circumstances of the incident; type and quantity of GMO which is the unintentional introduction in the environment; procedure undertaken for the necessary actions and measures to protect human health and the environment; and other information necessary to assess the impact of incidents on the health, biological diversity and the environment.[1158]

1098. It must be added that the subject in the business with GMO is also obliged to destroy waste containing GMO in a way that it becomes ineffective to reproduce or transfer genetic material to other organisms.[1159]

II. Other Relevant Regulations

1099. The following sub-legal acts have been adopted on the basis of the Law on GMO (2001):[1160]

1154. Detailed way of labelling of GMO or products shall be determined by regulation issued by the Ministry of Agriculture in cooperation with the Ministry of Environmental Protection and the Ministry of Health (Art. 48, para. 5). Government determines the level of random and technological unavoidable trace of GMO under which these products need not be marked (Art. 48, para. 6).
1155. It is forbidden to put on the market GMO or products containing, consisting of or derived from GMO, which is not marked in accordance with Art. 48, para. 3 of this Law (Art. 49). *See also* Art. 71, point 20.
1156. The Law prescribes penalty for violation of this provision. Business society, other legal person or entrepreneur will be punished in accordance with Art. 71, point 21.
1157. Conditions regarding the handling, packaging and transport of GMO have to be defined by the regulation issued by the Ministry of Agriculture with the opinion of the Ministry of Environmental Protection (Art. 50, para. 2).
1158. Penalty for violation of this provision is prescribed by Art. 71, point 22.
1159. Procedure of the destruction of waste has to be prescribed by the Ministry of Environmental Protection with the consent of the Ministry of Agriculture (Art. 56, para. 2).
1160. In accordance with Art. 74 of the Law (Official Journal of MNE, No. 22/08, 40/11) until the adoption of regulations based on the authority of this Law the regulations adopted by the Law on GMO (Official Journal of FRY, No. 21/01), if not in contradiction with this law, will be applied.

- Rulebook on Production Release of Genetically Modified Organisms and Products Derived from Genetically Modified Organisms (OJ FRY, No. 62/2002).
- Rulebook on Commercial Release of Genetically Modified Organisms and Products Derived from Genetically Modified Organisms (OJ FRY, No. 62/2002).
- Rulebook on Contained use of Genetically Modified Organisms (OJ FRY, No. 62/2002).
- Rulebook on Manner of Labelling of Agricultural and Food Products derived from Genetically Modified Organisms (OJ FRY, No. 62/2002).
- Rulebook on Content and Data of the Register of Genetically Modified Organisms and Products Derived from Genetically Modified Organisms (OJ FRY, No. 62/2002).
- Pursuant to Article 91, paragraph 4 of the Law on Food Safety (OJ MNE, No. 57/15), the MARD adopted the Rulebook on methods for sampling and laboratory testing of animal feed regarding the presence of genetically modified material ('Official Gazette of Montenegro' No. 69/2016).

§3. Harmonization with EU Legislation

1100. According to the NPI,[1161] during the process of drafting the new Law on Genetically Modified Organisms provisions of following EU legal and other acts have been transposed, *inter alia*: Regulation 1829/2003 on placing on the market genetically modified food and feed, as well as food and feed containing and/or consisting of GMO, Regulation 1946/2003 on transboundary movements of GMO (intentional and unintentional movement of GMO among EU member countries and countries outside of EU), Regulation 1830/2003 concerning the traceability and labelling of GMO and the traceability of food and feed products produced from GMO, Regulation 50/2000/EC, Regulation 641/2004/EC, Regulation 65/2004/EC, Regulation 258/97, Directive on the Contained Use of Genetically Modified Microorganisms, Directive on the Deliberate Release into the Environment of Genetically Modified Organisms, etc. From 2010 to 2012 further activities will be carried out with the objective of complete harmonization with the EU legislation.[1162]

1101. 'The Law on GMO adopted the EU legislation in the area of GMO, while complete harmonization with EU legislation will be secured through the adoption of secondary legislation'.[1163] According to the EC reports since 2012, no progress has been made with regard to alignment and implementation of the acquis in the area of GMOs.[1164] However, the 2021 programme for genetically modified food and feed monitoring was implemented and the programme for 2022 was adopted and is being implemented.[1165]

1161. GMNE (2008b), 539.
1162. It should be added that, however, there is no development concerning legal framework for the issue of 'intellectual property rights' over the development of biodiversity and/or agrobiodiversity. MSPE (2010b) 34.
1163. GMNE, MPPEP (2009), 202.
1164. *See,* e.g.,: EC (2016)., p. 42.
1165. EC (2022), p. 17.

Chapter 6. Forests

1102. 'Forests and forest lands cover 54% of the overall territory of Montenegro. Of the total area of the state territory, forests cover 621,000 ha, whereas bare forest land covers 123,000 ha of the land territory. Overall wood volume in Montenegro's forests is estimated at around 72 million m^3, of which conifers account for 29.5 million m^3 or 41%, and deciduous 42.5 million m^3 or 59%. Based on their purpose, forests intended for wood protection cover 348,000 ha or 81% of all forests. Protective forests cover 66,000 ha or 16%, and forests in national parks 12,975 ha or 3%. Overall growth in all forests is estimated at 1.5 million m^3. According to the data around 700,000 m^3 of our forests are logged annually'.[1166]

1103. Between 2005 and 2015, there were around 800 large forest fires in Montenegro, and more than 18,000 ha of forests and over 800,000 m3 of wood mass were damaged or destroyed. 'Montenegro's fire season was the worst in 2017. There were 124 fires covering over 30 ha, affecting a total of 51,661 ha, six times the area mapped in 2016'.[1167] In addition, illegal logging is a threat to forests of high ecological value, some of which are under national protection.[1168]

§1. Strategic Documents

1104. A number of strategic documents relevant to forest issues have been adopted in Montenegro which are following:

- The Spatial Plan of Montenegro.[1169]
- National Strategy of Sustainable Development by 2020.[1170]
- National Biodiversity Strategy with Action Plan for 2016–2020.[1171]
- National Forest Strategy (Strategy with Forestry Development Plan 2014–2023 years).[1172]
- The Hunting Development Programme of Montenegro for the period 2014–2024.[1173]

1166. GMNE, NCSD (2011), 10, 11. *See also* MAFWM (2008); GMNE (2008c), 71; For the identified problems which have negative impacts on the state of forests in Montenegro, *see* GMNE (2007), 42. However, forest area (forest and forest land) had expanded from 7,180 km2 in 2007 to 9,640 km2 in 2013 (i.e., by 34.3%). In 2013, forests covered 69.8% of Montenegro's land area. UNECE (2015), xix, and 6. *See also* MSDT (2020), p. 169.
1167. MSDT (2020), p. 169.
1168. GMNE (2022d), p. 84. Additionaly, the system of concessions has led to the destruction of entire areas, some of which have turned into barren land. 'There is no wood processing and this has led to the export of huge quantities of round wood and timber assortments to neighbouring countries.' *Ibid.*
1169. *See*: https://www.gov.me/dokumenta/c53c7c1d-1c2c-4c4d-b29c-9bd4aabce2b6 (3 Dec. 2022).
1170. https://www.gov.me/dokumenta/632aa485-839f-47a6-aa10-9b180aba31bc (3 Dec. 2022).
1171. https://www.gov.me/dokumenta/47673bc4-b66d-45f2-975e-db4743bf81a6 (3 Dec. 2022).
1172. *See*: https://www.gov.me/clanak/nacionalna-sumarska-strategija (13 Jan. 2023).
1173. *See*: https://wapi.gov.me/download/789dc4ac-1373-4456-b2ea-580610dea035?version=1.0 (3 Dec. 2022).

§2. Competencies

1105. There are a number of institutions with certain competencies concerning forests. Pursuant to Article 11 of the Decree on state administration organization and operations (OJ MNE, Nos 49/22, 52/22, 56/22, 82/22) the MAFWM conducts following activities: 'forest husbandry, protection, development, economic use and improvement; utilization of forests, forest land and forest products; management, protection, use and improvement of game; and hunting and managing the hunting areas'. Article 34 of the same Decree establishes competencies of the Forest Administration and Article 37 prescribes competencies of the Nature and Environment Protection Agency.

1106. Competencies of local self-governments concerning forests and forestry have not been defined by the Law on Local Self-Government (OJ MNE, Nos 22/18, 34/19, 38/20, 50/22).

§3. Legislation

1107. There is a long tradition in Montenegro concerning legal regulation in the field of forestry.[1174] Presently, provisions relevant to forests and forestry are contained in a number of legal regulations including most of the regulations in the field of environment.[1175]

1108. Several general provisions concerning forests are contained in the Law on the environment (OJ MNE, Nos 52/16, 73/19). The most important of them are Article 21 (forest protection), Article 15 (protection of environmental segments), etc.

I. Law on Forests

1109. New Law on forests (OJ MNE, No. 74/10) was adopted in December 2010, by which act the previous Law on forests from 2000 (OJ RM, No. 55/00) ceased to be in force. The new Law contains ninety-eight Articles divided into following fifteen chapters: Chapter I Basic provisions (Articles 1–4), Chapter II Rights and duties of forest owners (Articles 5–8), Chapter III Inventory of forests and planning (Articles 9–25), Chapter IV Functions and purpose of forests (Articles 26–32), Chapter V Protection measures, conservation and monitoring of forests (Articles 33–49), Chapter VI Growing and upbringing of new forests (Articles 50–52), Chapter VII Marking, cutting trunks and turnover of wooden products (Articles 53–57), Chapter VIII Forest infrastructure (Articles 58–62), Chapter IX Use of non-wooden

1174. *See* extensively, MAFWM (2008b), 8. The Circular (order) on forests which was adopted in 1904 is the first comprehensive state act on regulation of forest-related activities. *Ibid.*, 9.
1175. *See also* Chapters 2 (Parks and Reserves) and 3 (Wildlife Protection).

forest products of forest and function of forest (Articles 63–65), Chapter X Organization of work in forestry (Articles 66–70), Chapter XI Ways and conditions for use of forests in state ownership (Articles 71–80), Chapter XII Providing of means for implementation of planning documents in forestry (Articles 81–85), Chapter XIII Supervision (Articles 86–87),[1176] Chapter XIV Penal provisions (Articles 88–90) and Chapter XV Transitional and final provisions (Articles 91–98).

1110. By this law are regulated growing, protection, conservation and improvement of forests, planning, ways and conditions of use of forests, building and maintenance of forest roads, monitoring of forests, as well as other issues of importance for forests, forest soil and forestry.[1177]

1111. Forests[1178] and forest soil,[1179] as goods of public interest, are under special protection that is realized by: permanent conservation and improvement of forests and forest soil and their function; sustainable and multifunctional forest management; and conservation and improvement of biological and landscape diversities of forests, as well as of the quality of their environment (Article 2).

A. *Rights and Obligations of Forest Owners*

1112. Forests and forest soil, as goods of public interest, are used in a way and under conditions prescribed by law. Forests, forest soil and trees out of forests may be used only in a way that provides their economic, ecological and social function in accordance with the law (Article 5).

1113. Article 6 prescribes that forests, forest soil, trees out of forests and treeless soil in private ownership are managed by their owners in accordance with

1176. Supervision over implementation of this law and regulations based on this law, within the prescribed competences is performed by the Ministry, ministries competent for financial affaires, protection of the environment, spatial management and transport, as well as the competent organ of administration (Art. 86, para. 1).

1177. This law also regulates protection, conservation and use of forest trees which are out of forests and forest soil (hereinafter 'trees out of forest').

1178. Forest, according to this law, is soil greater than 50 ares, that is covered with forest trees which treetops cover at least 10% of the soil and height of dominant trees is above 5 m, or trees able to reach that height in their ripe physiological age (Art. 3, para. 1).

1179. Forest soil, according to this law, is soil greater then 50 ares, that is covered by forest trees: of height taller than 5 m, or trees able to reach that height in their ripe physiological age which treetops cover at least 5%–10% of the soil; which is not able to reach the height above 5 m, or which is covered by combination of trees and low forest vegetation, if overgrowth is greater than 10% of the soil (Art. 3, para. 2). As forest or forest soil are regarded also temporary bare areas of soil on which natural growth of forest trees has begun; antifire belts, soil overgrown with non-forest vegetation of area less than 50 ares, if it is within forest complex or on forest soil; protective belts of forest trees greater than 50 ares and wider than 20 m and forest roads. As forest or forest soil are not regarded: trees lining paths, parks in populated places, forest nurseries, seed producing plantations and plantations of fast growing species of trees on agricultural soil (Art. 3, para. 3 i 5).

law.[1180] Forest, forest soil, trees out of forests and treeless soil in state ownership are managed by competent organ of administration in accordance with law.[1181] Forest and forest soil, as ecosystems, are managed in sustainable and multifunctional way in accordance with criteria and indicators prescribed by the Ministry (Article 6, paragraph 5).

1114. Forest or forest soil in state ownership may change ownership only on the basis of decision of the Government, in case it is: on the territory which is by spatial plan planned for change of purpose because of building objects of public interest, exchange of forest parcels, or forest soil in state ownership with private with an intention of uniting forest parcels, or forest soil in state ownership, under conditions, that value of state forests or forest soil is not reduced (Article 7).[1182]

B. Planning Documents in Forestry

1115. According to Article 19 of the Law, planning documents in forestry are:

(1) National forestry policy.[1183]
(2) Strategy with development plan of forests and forestry (hereinafter 'strategy').[1184]

1180. Owners and users of forest are obliged, *inter alia*, to organize work on upbringing of forest proportionally to kind and intensity of wood cutting. Works from para. 1 of this Article are ordered to owners of private forests by a decision by which is allowed wood cutting, to users of state forest by the forest works project, or by annual programme of forest management in accordance with this law and with the contract (Art. 50, para. 1 i 2).
1181. Management from para. 2 of this Article includes preparation and decision-making regarding management of forests and forest soil in state ownership, as well as monitoring and control over management of forests in accordance with law. Management of forests from para. 1 i 2 of this Article includes afforestation, or upbringing of new forests, upbringing (care, renewal and conversion) of forests, protection, conservation and rehabilitation of forests, use of forests (wood cutting, processing, export, towing and other forms of transport of wooden products), use of non-wooden forest products, building and upkeeping of forest infrastructure, marketing and selling of forest products, as well as maintenance and improvement of function of forests (Art. 6, paras 3, 4).
1182. Owner or user of soil is obliged to allow owner or user of forest or forest soil free passing across his soil, or soil he uses for wood cutting and export of forest assortment (Art. 8, para. 1).
1183. National forestry policy is adopted by the Assembly of Montenegro, for period of ten years. National forestry policy is regulated in more details and implemented by the strategy, development plan of forests and programme of forest management (Art. 11, paras 3, 4). National forestry policy is to be adopted in the period of five years from the day of coming in force of this law (Art. 92, para. 2).
1184. The Strategy prescribes goals and directions for development of forest and forestry, in accordance with national forestry policy, measures for improvement of forests, as well as approximate amount of financial means for implementation of strategy and method of their procurement. Strategy is adopted by the Government, for a period of ten years (Art. 12). Upbringing of new forests is done in accordance with the strategy, or by forest development plan (Art. 51, para. 2).

(3) Forest development plan (hereinafter 'forest development plan').[1185]
(4) Programme of forest management for a management unit (hereinafter 'programme of forest management').[1186]

C. *Function and Use of Forest*

1116. Functions of forest and forest soil (hereinafter 'functions of forest') are productive,[1187] ecological[1188] and social[1189] (Article 26).

1117. Forests, according to purpose, in accordance with function of the forest, are divided into commercial, protected and forests of special use. Forest purpose is prescribed by the Forest development plan.[1190]

D. *Protection Measures, Conservation and Monitoring of Forest*

1118. It is forbidden, except in cases and under conditions prescribed by this law: (1) irregular cutting and forest clearing; (2) regular wood cutting of forest and wood cutting of great intensity which is not planned as a regular way of forest renewal;[1191] (3) wood cutting that is not in accordance with the programme of forest management; (4) wood cutting of protected and strictly protected species of

1185. Forest development plan, with previously obtained opinion of the organ of state administration competent for protection of the environment and for tourism and unit of local self-government whose territory is included in the plan, is adopted by the Government, for period of ten years (Art. 13, para. 4).
1186. Programme of forest management is adopted by the competent organ of administration, with agreement of the Ministry, after it previously obtained opinion of the organ of state administration competent for protection of the environment and the association of owners of forests which are included in the Programme of forest management. (Art. 14, para. 4).
1187. Productive functions of forest are especially: (1) production of wooden forest products; (2) production of non-wooden forest products.
1188. Ecological functions of forest are, especially: (1) protection of forest soil of washing away and of erosion; (2) conservation of water regime; (3) conservation of biological and landscape diversity; (4) lessening of macro climate changes, regulation and improvement of micro climate; (5) absorption of carbon from the air; (6) production of oxygen; and (7) conservation of habitat conditions for development of wild flora and fauna.
1189. Social functions of forests are, especially: (1) protection of settlements and infrastructural objects from erosion and slides; (2) favourable influence to water supply for various purposes; (3) reserve areas for rest and recreation; (4) development of ecotourism; (5) favourable influence to pasture and hunting; (6) research and education; (7) protection natural heritage; (8) protection of cultural heritage; (9) supply of local population with timber; (10) conservation of rural areas; and (11) defence of the country.
1190. A more precise regulation on ways of evaluation of function and purpose of forests is passed by the Ministry, with previously obtained opinion of the organ of state administration competent for protection of the environment. (Art. 28, para. 3).
1191. Trunks may be cut only after they are selected, marked and put in evidence (hereinafter 'marking'), in accordance with the programme of forest management and forest works project (Art. 53, para. 1). Wood cutting forests in private ownership can be done only on the basis of decision of the competent organ of administration by which wood cutting is allowed (Art. 55, para. 1).

trees; (5) whitewashing of trunks; (6) collection of non-wooden forest products;[1192] (7) wood cutting of trees with seed which were not included in the programme of forest management, or forest works project; (8) illegal possession of forest and forest soil, destruction, damaging of planted forest, signs and border signs; (9) disposal of waste, harmful and dangerous materials and waste, as well as pollution of forest in any other way; and (10) undertaking of other activities by which is weakened productive capacity of forest or imperils function of forests (Article 33).

1119. Besides that, the Law regulates protection of forests and forest soil (Article 34), duties of forest guards (Article 35), obligation of rehabilitation of degraded forests and forest soil (Article 36), regular wood cutting and wood cutting of great intensity (Article 37), change of purpose of forest by clearing (Article 38), wood cutting that is not in accordance with the programme of forest management (Article 39), pasture, branch cutting and use of fallen leaves in forest (Article 40), prohibition of building objects in the forest (Article 41), prohibition of waste disposal in the forest (Article 42),[1193] use of means of plant protection in forests (Article 43), general measures of protection of forests (Article 44), extraordinary measures protection of forest (Article 45), protection of forests from fire (Article 46), monitoring of forests (Article 47) and plan of forest rehabilitation (Article 48).

E. Forest Infrastructure

1120. In forests and on forest soil may be built forest infrastructure only in accordance with the programme of forest management and forest works project, in accordance with law. Planning, projecting, building and maintaining forest

---

The Ministry prescribes more precise regulation on:

(1) marking and cutting of trunks, method of receiving and marking of wooden assortment, which contains: methods and conditions for cutting of trunks and evidence of trunks marked for cutting, form of application for issuance of decision by which is allowed wood cutting, procedure of information on performed cutting, method of marking and of evidencing wood cutting, wooden mass, marking of stumps of illegally cut trunks and form and content of stumps (2) proof of origin of wooden assortment, and which contains: proof of origin of wooden assortment, way of information on sending the assortment, keeping register of documents, as well as evidence of trading with wooden assortment (Art. 57).

1192. Non-wooden forest products from forest in state ownership may be used in commercial and non-commercial purposes, in accordance with the programme of forest management, in a way that does not imperil ecosystems and functions of forest. Commercial use of non-wooden forest products comprises their collection, for sake of putting them on the market, on the basis of the contract (Art. 63, paras 1 and 2).

1193. It is prohibited to dispose waste in forest, on forest soil and on treeless areas, except on sites designated for that purpose. The person who has committed waste disposal in forest, on forest soil or on treeless areas, on a site which was not intended for waste disposal, is obliged to take away the waste on his own expense. Owners and users of forest are obliged to remove, from forest or from forest soil, waste disposed by unknown persons (Art. 42).

infrastructure may be done only in accordance with principles of nature protection, needs of forest management and technical regulations, in a way that does not: endanger water sources and water courses; cause erosion; harm forest ecosystems; harm habitats of rare and protected plant and animal species; block normal water flow of rain streams; destabilizing soil and increasing danger of slides; and endanger generally useful functions of forests (Article 58).

1121. Roads that are in function of forest management are regarded as forest roads. Forest roads may be used by legal and physical persons under conditions prescribed by the competent organ of administration.[1194]

F. Organization of Work in Forestry

1122. Competent organ of administration performs administrative and expert activities in forestry, related to: (1) preparation and production of plans in forestry; (2) implementation of national forest inventory; (3) concession of works in forests in state ownership; (4) collection of data regarding state of the forest; (5) mapping of forest habitats and forest types; (6) implementation of monitoring of forest health, sustainable forest management and illegal activities in forests; (7) growing of new forests, including afforestation and care of new cultures; (8) establishment and maintenance of information system on forests; (9) maintenance and rehabilitation of forest roads in accordance with this law; (10) preparation of expert basis for regulations, plans and programmes, that are, on the basis of competences prescribed by this law, passed by the Government and the Ministry; (11) implementation of measures of conservation biodiversity and natural value of forest; (12) implementation of protection of forest from biotic and abiotic factors and from fire, including diagnostic forecasting activities; (13) protection of forest and forest soil from illegal activities; (14) marking trunks for cutting, stamping assortments and acceptance of cutting grounds, or forest works; (15) expert help to owners of forests in private ownership regarding use and protection of forest; (16) control of finished works from forest works project; (17) cooperation with scientific research institutions in the field of forestry; and (18) other activities in accordance with law.[1195]

1123. The Law prescribes conditions for performing expert jobs in forestry (Article 67), regulates compensation for performing certain expert jobs in forestry (Article 68), prescribes expert jobs in forestry that can be performed by legal

1194. The Government can transfer management to the unit of local self administration of built forest roads, which serve for communication with rural farms, tourist and other objects, that are of public character (Art. 59, para. 3).

1195. For expert jobs from para. 1 points 1, 2 and 4 to 10 of this Article competent organ of administration can engage other legal person who fulfils prescribed conditions in accordance with law.

persons and entrepreneurs (Article 69) and regulates establishment and competence of the Forest council (Article 70).

G. Methods and Conditions for Use of Forests in State Ownership

1124. In accordance with Article 71 forests in state ownership can be given for use on the basis of contract on concession concluded in accordance with law. Concession is granted for one or more managerial units, for a period of five to thirty years.[1196]

1125. The Law regulates in more detail conditions for concessionaire and conditions for concession granting (Article 72), contents of concession (Article 73), obligations of concessionaire (Article 74),[1197] compensation for concession (Article 75), control of realization of concession and other contracts concerning forests in state ownership (Article 76), selling of timber (Article 77), supply with timber population in rural areas, or method and conditions for providing timber (Article 78), procedure for providing timber (Article 79) and registration of private forest farms (Article 80).

H. Securing Means for Implementation of Planning Documents in Forestry

1126. Means for implementation of the programme of forest management and forestry projects are provided from the state budget on the basis of annual programme of forest management. Annual programme of forest management is produced by the competent organ of administration (Article 81). Means for realization of incentive measures in forestry and co-financing of forest works can be provided, in accordance with the annual programme of forest management, from the state budget for strengthening competition in forestry; improving conditions of the environment; and improving quality of life of rural population in diversification of rural economy (Article 82).[1198] Means for financing implementation of measures for conservation of certain types of forests (NATURA 2000) are provided in accordance with the law (Article 84).

1196. Procedure of granting concessions is conducted by the competent organ of administration in accordance with law (Art. 71, para. 3).

1197. Besides duties prescribed by the law concessionaire is obliged to: apply measures established by the programme of forest management, undertake measures set by the forest works project and keep evidence on quantity of produced and sold wooden assortments; fulfil obligations from the contract (keeps evidence of forest works, works of building and maintenance of forest roads, expenses of his own processing of wooden products etc.,).

1198. Allocation of financial means is done by the competent organ of administration according to the public procedure on the basis of criteria established by the Ministry (Art. 82, para. 3). Control purposeful use of incentive means for co-financing of works and of incentive measures is done by the competent organ of administration (Art. 85).

II. The Law on Game and Hunting

1127. The Game and hunting management in Montenegro is regulated by the Law on Game and Hunting (OJ MNE, Nos 52/08, 40/11, 48/15).[1199] This legal act contains following fourteen chapters: Chapter I – General Provisions (Articles 1–10), Chapter II – Physical Units for Planning and Management (Articles 11–13), Chapter III – Assignment of Hunting Area for Using (Articles 14–22), Chapter IV – Planning Documents for Game Management (Articles 23–33),[1200] Chapter V – Protection and Breeding of Game (Articles 34–49),[1201] Chapter VI – Public Interest in the Field of Protection of Wild Game and Hunting (Articles 50–55), Chapter VII – Hunting and Use of Game (Articles 56–72), Chapter VIII – Limitations of Interventions in Space Where Game Live (Articles 73–75), Chapter IX – Prevention and Compensation of Damage (Articles 76–78), Chapter X – The Means for the Protection and Breeding Game and Improvement of Wildlife Management (Article 79), Chapter XI – Council for Hunting (Articles 80–81), Chapter XII – Supervision (Articles 82–83), Chapter XIII – Penal Provisions (Articles 84–87) and Chapter XIV – Transitional and Final Provisions (Articles 88–95).

III. Law on Forest Trees Reproductive Material

1128. Law on Forest Trees Reproductive Material (OJ RM, Nos 37/07, 57/15) regulates the conditions and manner of recognition of the basic material for the production of forest reproductive material trees (the reproductive material),[1202] production, control of production, finishing, quality and use of reproductive material, collection, use and change data and information; jurisdiction and inspection (Article 1).

IV. Law on Mountain Paths

1129. Basic legal act regulating mountain paths in Montenegro is the Law on mountain paths (OJ RM, No. 51/08).[1203] It has the following five parts: Part I – General Provisions (Articles 1–2), Part II – Mountain paths (Articles 3–22), Part III –

1199. Game management includes the breeding, protection, hunting as well as the use of game and its parts. Hunting, as an organized activity, is in the 'public interest' (Art. 2).

1200. Including following: programme of hunting development, hunting basis, year plan of hunting, cadastre of hunting area and central hunting evidence.

1201. The hunting season for certain types of game is determined by the Ministry based on the reproductive and life cycle development, hunting zones, needs for tourism, etc. (Art. 35). By Art. 36 the list of species which are under permanent protection is prescribed.

1202. According to Art. 6 of the Law, categories of reproductive material are: (1) reproductive material of known origin; (2) selected reproductive material; (3) qualified reproductive material; and (4) tested reproductive material.

1203. *See also* Rulebook on the criteria for classification of mountain paths ('Official Journal of MNE', 20/11).

Supervision (Article 23),[1204] Part IV – Penalties (Articles 24–25) and Part V – Transitional and final provisions (Articles 26–27).

1130. This Law regulates the conditions and manner of determining the mountain paths network, their regulation and maintenance, classification and categorization, as well as other issues relevant to the use of mountain paths[1205] (Article 1, paragraph 1).

1131. The regulations related to transport, the forests use, hiking and physical planning, construction and environmental protection are applied to decoration, marking and maintenance[1206] of mountain paths and their safe use (Article 1, paragraph 2). The components of mountain paths are (Article 3, paragraph 1) the beginning of mountain path (portal), tracks of mountain path (itinerary), the purpose of mountain path and infrastructure.

1132. The mountain paths are organized in a system of (Article 4, paragraph 1) National mountain paths network[1207] and Local mountain paths network.[1208] National network of mountain paths represents the basis of mountain paths network (Article 4, paragraph 3).

1133. According to the purpose, mountain paths are divided into hiking,[1209] walking paths[1210] in the nature, paths for mountain bicycling[1211] and special-purpose paths[1212] (Article 13, paragraph 2).

1134. Mountaineering Association of Montenegro keeps a single register of mountain paths, on the basis of the spatial display of the national network of mountain trails and the information that is obliged to submit to the competent local authorities (Article 6, paragraph 1). Notwithstanding paragraph 1 of this Article, the

---

1204. The supervision of implementation of this Law performs the Ministry in charge for environmental affairs and the Ministry in charge for agriculture, forestry and water management through competent inspectors, as well as the Police Administration, in accordance to the Law (Art. 23, para. 1). The Ministry is in charge for monitoring of arrangements and maintenance of mountain paths in the National network of mountain paths (Art. 12, para. 1).

1205. *The mountain path* is a peace of land, usually in hilly or mountainous area, which can be spread through the territory of national parks (Art. 2, point 1).

1206. *Maintenance* is providing the necessary conditions to keep the mountain paths and transversal passable and arranged, and ongoing maintenance of infrastructure on them (Art. 2, point 6).

1207. The National network of mountain paths is determined by the Montenegro Government on the proposal of the Ministry (Art. 5, para. 1).

1208. The criteria for the classification of mountain paths shall be prescribed by the Ministry responsible for tourism (hereinafter 'the Ministry') (Art. 4, para. 2).

1209. *Hiking path* is the arranged mountain path, which use requires physical fitness and training of users, but not the use of special auxiliary equipment used for climbing (Art. 13, para. 3).

1210. *Walking path* in the nature is the path which use, by the characteristics of the land, does not require special physical fitness and training of the users (Art. 13, para. 4).

1211. *Paths for mountain bicycling* is the path in the nature intended for riding a bike through the hilly and mountainous regions (Art. 13, para. 5).

1212. *Special-purpose paths* are recreational, ecological, educational, athletic, caving and research paths (Art. 13, para. 6).

register of mountain paths that are primarily used for mountain biking is kept with the Cycling Association of Montenegro (Article 6, paragraph 2).[1213]

1135. Regulation and maintenance of the National network of mountain paths keeping of the register and other tasks stipulated in this Law shall be financed from the budget of Montenegro, from donations and other sources in accordance with the Law (Article 21, paragraph 4).[1214]

V. International Treaties

1136. Montenegro is a contracting party to following international agreements relevant, *inter alia*, to the protection and use of forests: Convention on biodiversity (1992), UN Convention to Combat Desertification in Those Countries Experiencing Serious Drought and/or Desertification, Particularly in Africa UN Framework Convention on Climate Change (UNFCCC) (1992), Convention on Long-Range Transboundary Air Pollution (1979), Convention on the Conservation of European Wildlife and Natural Habitats (Bern Convention), Convention on the Conservation of Migratory Species and Wild Animals (Bonn Convention), Convention Concerning the Protection of the World Cultural and Natural Heritage (1972), Convention on Wetlands of International Importance (Ramsar Convention) and Convention on International Trade of Endangered Species of Wild Fauna and Flora – CITES (2001).

1137. Montenegro signed the Decision 'Forests of Europe 2020' and Ministers' authorization for negotiation on legally binding agreement on forests in Europe at the VI Ministerial Conference on the Protection of Forests in Europe.[1215]

VI. Other Regulations

1138. A large number of by-laws in the area of forestry have been adopted. Following deserve to be mentioned:

- Rulebook on uniform and official identity card of forest guards (OJ MNE, No. 30/17).[1216]
- Rulebook on the method of allocation of trees for cutting, receiving and marking wood assortments (OJ MNE, No. 11/2017).
- Rulebook on the methodology for determining and monitoring the numerous state of game (OJ MNE, No. 86/17).

1213. The detailed contents and the way of keeping of the registries from paras 1 and 2 of this Article are determined by the Ministry in the appropriate regulation (Art. 6, para. 3).
1214. The local government provides financing of arrangement and maintenance of local network of mountain paths (Art. 21, para. 5).
1215. GMNE (2012), 99.
1216. For the list of rulebooks *see*: https://www.gov.me/en/mpsv (26 Dec. 2022).

- Rulebook on the amount of the fee for the remittance of trees, survey and stamping of wood assortments and preparation of the execution project (OJ MNE, No. 74/2016).
- Rulebook on the content and manner of development of forest management programmes and plans and the manner of marking forest borders (OJ MNE, No. 57/2016).
- Rulebook on the allocation of trees for cutting, methods of reception and marking of wood assortments and certificate of origin of timber assortments (OJ MNE, Nos 55/15, 15/16).
- Rulebook on manner of evaluation of forest functions and uses (OJ MNE, No. 9/13).
- Rulebook on the list of forest trees and other forest vegetation (OJ MNE, No. 3/12).
- Rulebook on the content and method of development of the forest management programme (OJ MNE, No. 40/13).
- Rulebook on the method of design, and technical conditions for the construction, maintenance and technical reception of forest infrastructure (OJ MNE, No. 38/12).
- Rulebook on conditions that, in terms of equipment and number of employees, should be fulfilled by a legal entity or entrepreneur for performing professional activities in forestry (OJ MNE, No. 50/12).
- Rulebook on the conditions under which grazing, cropping of branches and gathering of fallen leaves may be carried out (OJ MNE, No. 59/12).
- Rulebook on Criteria and Indicators for Management of Forests and Forest Land in a Sustainable and Multifunctional Way (OJ MNE, No. 63/12).
- Decision on Determining Forest Areas (OJ RM, No. 53/03).
- Rulebook on Programme, Manner and Requirements for Passing Hunter's Exam (OJ RM, No. 01/01).
- Rulebook on contents and manner of keeping the central hunting records ('OJ MNE', No. 53/11).
- Rulebook on the trophy list forms and shipping document, their content, way of issue, the amount of fees for the issue and records ('OJ MNE', No. 09/12).
- The decision on granting of hunting area on utilization for sixteen hunting grounds ('OJ MNE', No. 11/12).
- Rulebook on fines for damage compensation caused by physical and legal persons on the hunting ground by illegal hunting or by any other illegal way (OJ MNE, No. 45/11).
- Rulebook on contents of the evidence book and method of submitting data on shot and found dead game and their parts (OJ MNE, No. 32/11).
- Rulebook on the form and contents of permit for hunting and the hunting card, more precise conditions and procedure of their issuance and their revoke, as well as on amount of charge for issuance of the hunting card (OJ MNE, No. 20/10).
- Rulebook on hunting seasons (OJ MNE, Nos 34/09, 48/09, 60/10).
- Decision on establishment of hunting ground and establishment of hunting ground with special purpose (OJ MNE, No. 62/10).
- Rulebook on Requirements and Manner for Issuing Hunting Card/License (OJ RM, No. 54/01).

– Rulebook on Establishing Prize for Catch of Some Unprotected Game Species (OJ RM, No. 22/01).

§4. Harmonization with EU Legislation

1139. The Law on Forest Trees Reproductive Material is, however, fully harmonized with the EU legislation (Council Directive on Marketing of Forest Reproductive Material). Two currently applicable rulebooks were not harmonized and aligned with the existing EU regulations, and thus development of new secondary regulations is forthcoming.[1217]

1140. According to the Statement on the harmonization of Montenegro's legislation with EU legislation, the level of the harmonization of the Law on forests (OJ MNE, No. 74/10, 47/15) has been assessed with regard to the following EU regulations: Directive 2003/35/EC, Regulation (EC) No. 1367/2006, Commission Regulation (EC) No. 1737/2006, Council Regulation (EC) No. 1698/2005 and Proposal for a Regulation of the European Parliament and of the Council laying down the obligations of operators who place timber and timber products on the market (COM/2008/0644 final) (fully harmonized) as well as with the following international treaties: UN Framework Convention on Climate Change (UNFCCC) (1992), Convention on Biological Diversity (1992) and Convention on Long-range Transboundary Air Pollution (1979).[1218]

1217. GMNE (2008b), 527.
1218. *See* https://www.gov.me/dokumenta/a166d7d6-9bf2-4b2f-bb51-06e40deb3c8c (13 Jan. 2023).

Chapter 7. Fishery

§1. Fishery as Economic Activity

1141. The fisheries sector is important for the national economy and livelihoods of coastal communities in Montenegro. According to the most recent fish assessment, 407 fish species and subspecies were recorded in the Adriatic Sea, and in the meantime, the number has increased.[1219] The assessment of the climate sensitivity of the marine shows the vulnerability of natural (indigenous) populations of marine organisms that inhabit the Adriatic Sea. The Adriatic Sea has experienced increasing temperatures in the last decade.[1220]

1142. Fishery sector is not very developed in Montenegro in spite of the fact that it has significant water sources in the Adriatic Sea, lakes and rivers. Fishing is one of the most neglected economic sectors, and even fish consummation per capita is only somewhat more than 1 kg/year.[1221] 'According to the data published by MONSTAT, there were 269 persons employed in marine fisheries in 2013, most of whom (179) on a part-time basis'.[1222] For the same period, the study undertaken in the framework of MAREA project indicates that the number of employees in marine fisheries was 273. Freshwater fisheries employed 49 persons. However, both (MONSTAT and MAREA data) are considered to be estimates, but they do give an indication of the relatively low overall level of employment in the sector.

1143. The Montenegrin fishing fleet had 290 vessels in 2020, of which 91% were less than 12 metres long; two-thirds of the vessels are equipped with small-scale coastal fishing tools (the source of data on catches and the fishing fleet is Monstat).[1223]

§2. Strategic Documents

1144. Elements of the strategic approach to the fishery are contained in all basic strategic documents of Montenegro, including SPM, Spatial Plan for Special-Purpose Costal zone, National Strategy on Sustainable Development by 2030, and NPI 2008–2012. Nevertheless, the basic document dealing with this issue is the

1219. MSDT (2020), p. 211.
1220. In the last twenty years, there have been quantitative and qualitative changes in the Adriatic ichthyofauna, which are a consequence of climate change. *Ibid.*
1221. GMNE (2007D), 50. The total value of the annual production in the fishery sector is EUR 7.4 million, so its share in the Gross Domestic Product (GDP) is about 0.5%. MAFWM (2006b), 1.
1222. MARD. *Fisheries Strategy of Montenegro 2015–2020 with an Action Plan (for Transposition, Implementation and Enforcement of EU Acquis)*, Podgorica, June 2015, p. 13.
1223. GMNE (2022d), p. 75. *See also*: http://www.monstat.org/eng/page.php?id=1795&pageid=162 (13 Jan. 2023).

Fisheries' strategy of Montenegro 2015–2020 with an Action plan (for transposition, implementation and enforcement of EU acquis).[1224]

1145. Fisheries' strategy of Montenegro is in line with other national strategic documents, particularly those related to agriculture, rural and regional development. It gives an overall strategic framework and identifies the key steps that Montenegro intends to take in order to prepare for full discharge of its obligations stemming from the Common Fisheries' Policy.

§3. COMPETENCES

1146. Pursuant to Article 11 of the Decree on state administration organization and operations (OJ MNE, Nos 49/22, 52/22, 56/22, 82/22) the MAFWM conducts administrative activities with regard to, *inter alia*: freshwater and saltwater fishing. It is the competent authority for administrative and technical issues concerning fisheries; it proposes, develops and implements relevant legal and sub-legal acts and monitors and controls legislation enforcement of the fishing and aquaculture sectors. When technical services in fisheries are concerned, the Ministry relies on the technical and scientific recommendations given by the Marine Biology Institute[1225] and by the Department of Biology of the Faculty of Science and Mathematics.

1147. Certain competencies in relation to fishing also have following institutions: Veterinary Directorate, The Veterinary Diagnostic Laboratory, CETI, the Institute of Public Health, The Public Enterprise National Parks of Montenegro,[1226] The Statistics Institute of Montenegro, etc.

§4. LEGISLATION

1148. Two key legal acts that regulate fishing, fish farming and protection of fish and other aquatic organisms in the sea and freshwaters are the Law on the Marine Fisheries and Mariculture (OJ MNE, Nos 56/09, 47/15) and the Law on the Freshwater Fisheries and Aquaculture (OJ MNE, No. 17/18).

1224. *See*: https://wapi.gov.me/download/6ad8575b-1cd1-4e77-bd9a-5fd2d8bfdba3?version=1.0 (3 Dec. 2022. This Strategy can be seen as the continuation of the 2006 Strategy, with a more pronounced focus on the elements necessary for harmonization with the acquis in the area of fisheries policy, particularly having in mind the overhaul of the EU Common Fisheries Policy.

1225. *See*: http://www.ucg.ac.me/ibm (3 Dec. 2022).

1226. The National Park Lake Skadar is responsible for issuing licences and for control of fishermen on the Lake, while others are responsible for rivers on the territory of respective national parks.

I. Law on Marine Fisheries and Mariculture

1149. Basic legal act regulating marine fisheries and mariculture[1227] in Montenegro is the Law on marine fisheries and mariculture (OJ MNE, Nos 56/09, 40/11). It has the following twelve parts: Part I – General Provisions (Articles 1–4), Part II – Management of the living marine resources (Articles 5–28), Part III – Fisheries policy measures (Articles 29–36), Part IV – Competencies (Articles 37–39), Part V – Marine fishing (Articles 40–66), Part VI – Mariculture (Articles 67–88), Part VII – Producers organization in the fishery (Articles 89–93), Part VIII – Foreign fishing vessels and international relations (Articles 94–98) and Part IX – Monitoring and surveillance (Articles 99–111), Part X – Inspection (Articles 112–115), Part XI – Penalty provisions (Articles 116–120) and Part XII – Transitional and final provisions (Articles 121–129).

1150. According to Article 1, Marine fisheries, in the terms of this Law, mean the management of living marine resources and applies to fishing,[1228] collecting[1229] and protecting fish[1230] and other marine organisms based on the principles of sustainable development within the fishery sea of Montenegro.[1231] (Article 1, paragraph 1). This Law regulates mariculture as well (Article 1, paragraph 2).

1151. Marine fisheries (hereinafter referred to as 'fishery') can be performed by companies and entrepreneurs, as well as by other domestic or foreign legal entities or natural persons under the conditions stipulated herein (Article 3, paragraphs 1 and 2). This Law also applies to Montenegrin-flagged fishery vessels[1232] fishing beyond the boundaries of the fishery sea referred to in Article 98 of this Law (Article 3, paragraph 3).

1227. *Mariculture* means the rearing or cultivation of fish and other marine organisms in the fishing sea using the techniques designed to increase the production of such organisms beyond the natural capacity of the environment (Art. 4, point 1). *Capacity* means the capacity of an ecosystem to support healthy organisms, maintain productivity, adaptability and renewal capability (Art. 4, point 8). *Fish and other marine organism* means a marine animal or a plant and includes any shellfish or other molluscs, crustacean, coral, sponge, sea urchin or their echinoderm, turtle and marine mammal, their eggs, spawn, spat and juvenile stages (Art. 4, point 22).

1228. *Fishing* means activities related to preparation, searching for, catching, treatment and dispatching of caught fish (Art. 4, point 28). *Fishing* also means a group of activities related to management of living marine resources, including activities related to: (a) fish species and description; (b) fishing area; (c) fishing method; and (d) type of fishing vessel (Art. 4, point 32).

1229. *Collecting* means the process of collecting marine organisms without the use of fishing gear (Art. 4, point 58).

1230. Fish and other marine organisms in the fishery sea of Montenegro, being a resource of common interest, have special protection and are used in the way and under the terms stipulated by this Law and by other regulations (Art. 1, para. 3).

1231. The fishery sea of Montenegro (hereinafter referred to as 'the fishery sea') includes marine and submarine area of internal seawaters, territorial sea and epicontinental area of Montenegro as defined by the Law governing the sea (Art. 2, para. 1). The fishery sea includes also the exclusive marine economic zones in accordance with the Law (Art. 2, para. 2).

1232. *Fishing vessel* is: a boat, ship or other vessel equipped for fishing, including fishing tool, equipment or stores for fish (Art. 4, point 26).

A. Management of the Leaving Marine Resources[1233]

1152. The exploitation of living marine aquatic resources is consistent with sustainable economic, environmental and social development (Article 5, paragraph 1). The management of living resources in the fishing sea and protection of the marine environment shall be carried out in accordance with the Strategy for the Development of Fisheries and Aquaculture (hereinafter 'the Strategy') (Article 8, paragraph 1). The strategy contains in particular: long-term directions, priorities and objectives of fisheries development, financial resources required and deadlines for their implementation, as well as obligations assumed under international agreements.[1234]

1153. Fishing is conducted in accordance with the management plans (Article 11, paragraph 1). Management plans contain following: a description of the resource status, biological characteristics and types of fish stock to which the plan relates, the species and characteristics of the fisheries, economic indicators for exploiting the fish stock, the type and volume of fishing gear used, guidelines for issuing special permits for performing fisheries for certain fish species using certain fishing gear and equipment with the areas and time of fishing (paragraph 2). Management plans must be based on scientific and economic data and contain protection measures to restore fish resources in order to ensure sustainable fisheries management.[1235]

B. Protection Measures

1154. Fish and other marine organisms, as well as marine biodiversity,[1236] must be protected from threat to their vital environment and overexploitation (Article 6, paragraph 1). The protection shall be obtained by implementing measures aimed at preserving the bio-ecological reproduction potentials and environmental conditions (Article 6, paragraph 2).

1155. In order to protect the biodiversity and conditions of the environment (Article 7, paragraph 1) it is prohibited, *inter alia*, following: (1) to dispose of or discharge liquid or solid wastes from production or processing or any other materials that have adverse effects on the quality of marine environment; (2) to restock,

1233. *Living marine resources* means available and living species of fish and other marine organisms, including anadromous and catadromous species during their marine life (Art. 4, point 52).

1234. The Strategy is adopted by the Government of Montenegro for a period of seven years (Art. 8, para. 3). For the text of Fisheries strategy of Montenegro 2015–2020 with an Action Plan (for transposition, implementation and enforcement of EU acquis), *see*: https://wapi.gov.me/download/6ad8575b-1cd1-4e77-bd9a-5fd2d8bfdba3?version=1.0 (3 Dec. 2022).

1235. Management plans are made by the Ministry for a period of three years. The manner of issuing and the content of the permit referred to in para. 2 of this Article shall be prescribed by the Ministry (paras 4 and 5).

1236. *Biodiversity (biological diversity)* means the variability among living organisms, including terrestrial, sea and other aquatic ecosystems and the ecological complexes, as well as the diversity within a species, between species and ecosystems (Art. 4, point 2).

to introduce[1237] allochthonous species of fish[1238] and other marine organisms, genetically modified species of fish or other marine organisms into the sea; (3) underwater activities are prohibited in locations for which the permit from the Ministry had not been obtained; (4) fishing, collecting and marketing of protected species of fish and other marine organisms, etc[1239]

1156. If there is scientific evidence of serious and unforeseen threats to the marine resources of the sea or the marine ecosystem due to fishing activities in the Montenegrin fishing sea, the Ministry is obliged to undertake urgent measures to address the causes of the threat (Article 12, paragraph 1).

1157. For the purpose of protecting fish and other marine organisms, the Ministry shall designate protected fishing areas (Article 13, paragraph 1). The protected fishing areas are, in terms of this Law, parts of fishing sea favourable for natural reproduction of fish and for feeding young fish, as well as other marine organisms (Article 13, paragraph 2). In protected fishing areas, it is prohibited[1240] to (Article 14, paragraph 1): (1) perform fishing or attempt to fish; (2) take or destroy fauna or flora; (3) place or exploit sand or gravel, leave or dispose of waste or any other polluting material, or disturb, change or destroy the environment in any way; (4) build or place structures on the ground or across water; (5) engage in other activities which may have an adverse effect on the ecosystem of the protected fishing area.

1158. The species[1241] of marine fish and other marine organisms, including anadromous and catadromous species,[1242] shall be declared to be protected species by the Government, at the proposal of the Ministry, based on the approval previously obtained from the Ministry in charge of environmental protection (Article 15, paragraph 1).

1159. The minimum size of fish and other marine organisms, including anadromous and catadromous species, below which catch and trade are prohibited, shall be set by the Ministry (Article 16, paragraph 1). Exceptionally from paragraph 1 of this Article, the administration authority may, at proposal of the Institute, and for

1237. *Introduction* means the process by which allochthonous fish species is moved, i.e., introduced into areas that are not their natural habitats (Art. 4, point 35).
1238. *Allochthonous fish species* means species whose historically known natural habitat is beyond the fishing sea (Art. 4, point 45).
1239. To protect biodiversity and environmental conditions, underwater artificial reefs are placed at the place where new biological habitats could be formed (Art. 7, para. 2).
1240. The prohibited activities referred to in para. 1 of this Article may be performed based on the permit of the administration authority where such activities are needed for protected fishing areas management (Art. 14, para. 3). The time, fishing equipment and specific technical rules for fishing in protected fishing areas shall be prescribed by the Ministry (Art. 14, para. 4).
1241. The list of protected species of fish and other marine organisms shall be published in the 'Official Journal of Montenegro' (Art. 15, para. 2).
1242. *Anadromous species* means fish species which move from the sea to freshwaters for spawning (Art. 4, point 39). *Catadromous species* means species of fish which move from the freshwaters into the sea for spawning (Art. 4, point 40).

the purpose of cultivation, restocking[1243] and research activities, allow the catch of young fish, reproductively immature species of fish and other marine organisms in specific localities, at a specific period of time and using the specific fishing tools (Article 16, paragraph 2).

1160. For the purpose of protecting fish and other marine organisms or parts of fishing sea which are favourable for natural fish reproduction and feeding of young fish and other marine organisms or vulnerable areas, the Ministry may prohibit fishing for a certain period of time[1244] (Article 17, paragraph 1).

1161. Fishing is prohibited in the area of ports, their entrance and access to the port and anchorage (Article 19, paragraph 1).[1245] Fishing is prohibited in areas of managed and marked bathing areas in the period 1 May–1 October from sunrise to sunset (Article 19, paragraph 4).

1162. For the purpose of protecting general marine biodiversity in shallower zones of the littoral, it shall be prohibited to fish with bottom trawls and floating trawls at a distance of 3 NM that follows the configuration of the shore, or at the depth of 50 m in case the isobaths of 50 m are reached at a distance shorter than 3 NM (Article 25, paragraph 1).[1246]

1163. In order to protect rocky shores as a special habitat in the fishery sea, catching, marketing or exporting of date shells (Litophaga litophaga) is prohibited on the whole territory of Montenegro (Article 26).

C. Fishermen's Post and Fish-Gathering Devices

1164. The Fishermen's post[1247] in the Bay of Boka Kotorska is an area in the sea where the net is towed and a part of the shore up to 150 m in length, with gravel and sandy bottom, which is not fenced and which does not have a dock or where a

1243. *Restocking* means releasing of permitted species of fish and other marine organisms in waters where they occur naturally, in order to use natural aquatic environment to increase the number of fish and increase the natural offspring (Art. 4, point 15).

1244. It shall be prohibited to trade in fish and other marine organisms during the prohibition of fishing and from the prohibited areas (Art. 17, para. 3). However, under conditions stipulated in Art. 17, para. 4, the administration authority may permit the fishing on the proposal of the Institute.

1245. Notwithstanding the para. 1 of this Article, fishing in the area of port, entrance and access ways and anchorages is permitted only where the port user, with approval from the Port Master's Office and approval from the Institute, permits fishing in these areas (Art. 19, para. 2). Fishing is permitted in the areas of channels and internal marine routes if it does not hinder the navigation of other ships and vessels (Art. 19, para. 3).

1246. Notwithstanding para. 1 of this Article, in case of damage, a fishing vessel with a net overboard can approach the shore to the depth lesser that the one prescribed, if it had previously notified the nearest Port authority (Art. 25, para. 2).

1247. The method of use, maintenance, protection, marking and the length of the shore, name and the location of the fishermen's post shall be laid down by the Ministry (Art. 27, para. 5).

net with the catch can be towed onto the shore (Article 27, paragraph 1). The fishermen's post is used exclusively at night and early in the morning (Article 27, paragraph 2).

1165. Placing of a fish-gathering device in a certain location in the fishing sea shall be done based on the approval issued by the administration authority based on an application (Article 28, paragraph 1).[1248] It shall be prohibited to remove and move fish devices from the approved place (Article 28, paragraph 6).

D. Fisheries' Policy Measures

1166. The fisheries' policy measures shall be set for the purpose of accomplishing the objectives referred to in Article 5 of this Law (Article 29, paragraph 1). The fisheries' policy measures include the following measures: (1) for development of the fishing fleet; (2) for development of aquaculture, processing, and marketing of fish and fish products and aquaculture products; (3) for collective actions; (4) for the sustainable development of fishing areas; and (5) for technical support (Article 29, paragraph 2).

1167. The terms, methods and timetable for implementation of the fisheries' policy measures set by the Strategy and by the management plans shall be determined more precisely by the beginning of the fiscal year by Governmental regulation (hereinafter referred to as 'agriculture budget'), in accordance with the Law (Article 35, paragraph 1).[1249]

E. Administration Authority and Financing

1168. The administrative and the related professional activities in marine fishery shall be implemented by the administration authority in accordance with the Law (Article 37, paragraph 1). The funds from the budget of Montenegro are provided for development of the following (Article 39, paragraph 1): (1) the strategy; (2) the management plan; (3) the programme for monitoring the quality of seawater and parts of the sea used for fishing and mariculture; (4) the national programme, as well as for monitoring, control and supervision of fishing vessels, financing or co-financing of Fishery Policy measures and measures related to organization of common fish market and market of fish products and producers organization.

1248. Technical characteristics of the fish-gathering devices and terms for fishing in the area of one nautical mile diameter from the place where the devices or several devices are installed shall be laid down by the Ministry (Art. 28, paras 2 and 3).

1249. Annual report on the disbursement of agricultural budget is developed by the Ministry and submitted to the Government for adoption not later than 31 March of the current year for the previous year (Art. 36, para. 1). This report shall also contain the assessment of effects of the fisheries policy for the year it refers to (Art. 36, para. 2).

F. Marine Fishing and Commercial Fishing

1169. Fishing[1250] can be commercial, sport-recreational and for scientific research purposes (Article 40, paragraph 2). Permits for fishing in parts of the fishing sea, designated as areas of defence, may be issued based on the approval obtained from the Ministry of Defence (Article 42, paragraph 1). Fishing in territorial water within the boundaries of the RM is not permitted for fishing vessels sailing under the flag of a foreign country (Article 42, paragraph 2). Fishing is prohibited for the fishing vessels under foreign flag in the fishing sea of Montenegro.

1170. Commercial fishing[1251] is the catch of economically significant species of fish and other marine organisms by using permitted tools and equipment for the selling purpose (Article 44, paragraph 1), which could be done under the terms and with fishing tools and equipment in accordance with the Law (Article 44, paragraph 2).

1171. [1252] Commercial fishing may be done by companies and entrepreneurs if they are: registered for performing this activity in the Central Register of Business Entities (hereinafter 'CRPS'), registered in the Register of Professional Fishermen (hereinafter 'Fisher Register') and are licensed by the Ministry (Article 45, paragraph 1). It is forbidden to conduct commercial fishing, to hold fishing tools and equipment on vessels, in ports and on shores to companies, entrepreneurs and natural persons who do not have a licence to conduct commercial fishing (paragraph 2).

1172. Based on the criteria referred to in Article 46 of this Law, commercial fishing is classified into large-scale[1253] and small-scale[1254] (Article 48, paragraph 1).

G. Permit for Commercial Fishing

1173. The permit for commercial fishing shall be issued by the administration authority based on a public advertisement published in at least one printed media distributed throughout Montenegro (Article 53, paragraph 1) over a period of five

1250. Marine fishing (hereinafter 'the fishing') means catching and collecting fish and other marine organisms (Art. 40, para. 1).
1251. A fee shall be paid for carrying out commercial fishing (Art. 44, para. 3) which shall be the revenue of the budget of Montenegro (Art. 44, para. 4).
1252. Small-scale commercial fishing shall be conducted in the period of three years following the date of entry of this Law into force (Art. 122).
1253. Large-scale commercial fishing is the fishing carried out by using fishing vessel shorter than 12 and longer than 12 m over all, with the fishing tools and equipment stipulated in Art. 49, para. 1 of this Law. Purpose, technical characteristics and the quantity of fishing tools and equipment allowed to be used in large-scale commercial fishing shall be prescribed by the Ministry (Art. 49, para. 2).
1254. Small-scale commercial fishing is the fishing carried out by fishing vessels shorter than 12 m overall, with fishing tools and equipment stipulated in Art. 49, para. 1 of this Law. Purpose, type, technical characteristics and the quantity of fishing tools and equipment allowed for use in small-scale commercial fishing is prescribed by the Ministry (Art. 50, para. 2).

years (Article 55, paragraph 4). The permit for commercial fishing may be issued to a holder of the permit after the fee for commercial fishing is paid (Article 55, paragraph 2).[1255] The amount of the fee shall be determined by the Government, following the proposal of the Ministry (Article 55, paragraph 3).

1174. Based on the permit for commercial fishing, the administration authority shall register fishing vessels in the Register of Fishing Vessels (hereinafter 'the Register')[1256] (Article 57, paragraph 1).

H. Sport: Recreational Fishing

1175. Sport-recreational fishing may be practised by natural persons holding a permit for sport-recreational fishing (Article 59, paragraph 1), issued by sport-recreational clubs that are members of the Association (Article 59, paragraph 3).

1176. The form of the permit for sport-recreational fishing shall be distributed by the administration authority to the Sport Fishing Association for the fishing sea of Montenegro (hereinafter 'the Association') (Article 59, paragraph 2). The permit for sport-recreational fishing may be permanent[1257] or temporary (Article 60, paragraph 1). A fee is paid for sport-recreational fishing (Article 61, paragraph 1) and the amount of the fee shall be determined by the Ministry, depending on the validity period of the permit (Article 61, paragraph 1). Sport-recreational fishing must not hinder commercial fishing (Article 63, paragraph 1).[1258]

I. Mariculture Development Plan

1177. At the proposal of the Ministry, the Government adopts the Mariculture Development Plan, based on the analysis of sustainable development of mariculture, taking into account the biological, typographic, hydromorphological and physico-chemical characteristics of mariculture zones set by the Spatial Plan for special-purpose areas of coastal zone (Article 67, paragraph 1). The administration authority, at the proposal of the Institute, defines locations for mariculture activities

1255. In case of a change of the company, in accordance with prescribed conditions, new permit for commercial fishing shall be issued to the owner or to the lessee of the vessel (Art. 55, para. 1).
1256. The Register of Vessels shall be kept by the administration authority (Art. 57, para. 2). The fishing vessel registered in the Register of Vessels shall bear an identification mark (Art. 57, para. 3). The content and the method of keeping the Register of Vessels and the identification mark referred to in para. 2 of this Article shall be laid down by the Ministry (Art. 57, para. 4).
1257. The permanent permit for sport–recreational fishing shall be issued for the current calendar year, and the temporary permit shall be issued for the period not exceeding thirty days (Art. 60, para. 2).
1258. The method, the type and the number of fishing tools and equipment permitted for use in sport–recreational fishing, the form and the content of the permit for sport–recreational fishing shall be prescribed by the Ministry (Art. 66, para. 1).

(hereinafter referred to as 'farm')[1259] based on the species of fish and other marine organisms farmed, the designed economic profitability, farming technology, etc (Article 68, paragraph 1).

J. Mariculture Activities and Permits for Mariculture

1178. Companies and entrepreneurs may engage in mariculture and processing of mariculture products provided that: (1) they are registered for mariculture activities; (2) they obtained approval on the Project for technical and technological requirements of mariculture together with the study on the economic viability of the investment; and (3) they hold a mariculture permit (Article 69, paragraph 1). The administration authority shall keep The Register of farms and The Register of processors of fish and other marine organisms (Article 69, paragraph 2).[1260] Mariculture activities shall be executed in line with the principles of good manufacturing practice in the field of mariculture and the principles shall be set by the Ministry (Article 74).

1179. The permit for mariculture shall be issued based on the application for each farm separately (Article 70, paragraph 1) and shall at all times be kept at the registered farm (Article 72, paragraph 2).[1261] The permit may be issued after payment of the fee for mariculture is made[1262] (Article 72, paragraph 3). It shall be registered in the Register of Permits kept by the administration authority (Article 72, paragraph 6) and could be issued for a maximum of five years, with the possibility of extension, depending on the results achieved in the planned farming (Article 73, paragraph 2).

1180. The administration authority issues the mariculture permit for the purpose of scientific research work (Article 71).

1181. A holder of a mariculture permit cannot change terms related to the structure, equipment and maintenance of the farm without prior consent of the administration authority. The administration authority may, without request from the

1259. Determination of farm boundaries is done by the holder of the mariculture permit, using marks in accordance with the sailing safety regulations (Art. 68, para. 2).
1260. The form, the content and the method for keeping the registers referred to in para. 2 of this Article shall be defined by the Ministry (Art. 69, para. 3).
1261. A mariculture permit is not transferable from the holder to any other company or entrepreneur without approval from the administration authority (Art. 77, para. 1).
1262. The amount of the fee is to be determined by the Government at proposal of the Ministry (Art. 72, para. 4). The funds collected from fees referred to in the para. 4 of this Article shall be the income of the budget of Montenegro (Art. 72, para. 5). The form of the permit, the method for paying the fee, the form, content and the method of keeping the Register of Permits shall be defined by the Ministry (Art. 72, para. 7).

permit holder, change or amend the terms if it establishes that it is in the interest of good manufacturing practice in mariculture or environmental protection (Article 75).[1263]

K. Ownership of Mariculture Products

1182. Fish and other marine organisms specified in a mariculture permit, within the farm boundaries, shall be the ownership of the permit holder (Article 80, paragraph 1).[1264]

1183. Without an approval[1265] from the administration authority, it is prohibited to introduce into the fishing sea of Montenegro allochthonous species of fish and other marine organisms or genetically modified fish and other marine organisms, as well as their transfer from one farm into another, or from one place in Montenegro to another (Article 81, paragraph 1).

L. Water Quality Monitoring and Biomonitoring in Fishing Sea

1184. For the purpose of public health and mariculture protection, the Ministry shall at proposal of the administration authority adopt Water Quality Monitoring and Biomonitoring Programme for the fishing sea, which shall ensure timely notification of mariculture permit holders[1266] of the occurrence or upcoming occurrence of pollution or a natural phenomenon that may have a harmful or detrimental effect on the mariculture zone or mariculture products (Article 88, paragraph 1).

M. Producers Organizations in Fishery and National Marine Fishery and Mariculture Council

1185. The companies and entrepreneurs registered in the fishermen register, the farm register and the register of processors of fish and other marine organisms are

1263. Permit extension shall be done by the administration authority based on the request of the permit holder (Art. 76, para. 1). The request referred to in para. 1 of this Article shall be submitted no less than three months prior to the expiration of the permit validity period (Art. 76, para. 2).

1264. Fish and other marine organisms referred to in para. 1 of this Article that leave the farm are the property of the permit holder of that farm while they are within the range of 100 metres from the farm (Art. 80, para. 2).

1265. The approval shall be issued by the administration authority with prior approval on the environmental impact assessment from the public administration authority in charge of the environmental protection (Art. 81, para. 2).

1266. A mariculture permit holder shall provide timely notification to the administration authority or a fishery inspector of the occurrence or a suspected occurrence of pollution or a natural phenomenon (Art. 88, para. 5). The monitoring shall be performed by an accredited laboratory of the Institute (Art. 88, para. 6). The procedure of timely notification on the phenomena for the purpose of monitoring and the closing of mariculture zones shall be prescribed by the Ministry (Art. 88, para. 6).

organized into producers organizations in the fishery sector, in accordance with the Law. The catch plan and the production plan referred to in Article 89 of this Law shall be approved by the Ministry (Article 90, paragraph 1).

N. Foreign Fishing Vessels and International Relations

1186. For the purpose of implementation of ratified international agreements in fisheries, the Ministry may adopt measures for implementation of such agreements (Article 94). A foreign fishing vessel may fish within the fishing sea of Montenegro if it has a fishing permit issued by the administration authority (Article 95, paragraph 1). A foreign fishing vessel that fishes in accordance with a ratified international agreements may fish in the fishing sea of Montenegro based on the permit issued in accordance with the agreement providing that: (1) it carries at all times on board the fishing permit issued by the administration authority in accordance with the terms of that agreement, (2) the fishing vessel is marked in accordance with the agreement, (3) where the agreement does not provide for the obligation to mark the vessel, the vessel shall be marked in accordance with this Law (Article 95, paragraph 2).[1267]

1187. The administration authority may, in addition to the measures prescribed by this Law for performing fishing, and in accordance with international measures for conservation and management of living marine resources and marine environment, to foreign fishing vessels: (1) inspect documents, fishing tools and equipment and catch on board of fishing vessels when such vessels are in a port or in a coastal zone and (2) prohibit landings and transhipments when it has been determined that the fish and other marine organisms were caught in a manner which undermines the efficiency of measures referred to in paragraph 1 of this Article (Article 97).

1188. In addition to the measures prescribed by this Law, for fishing vessels registered in Montenegro, the Ministry shall also prescribe the measures necessary for ensuring monitoring of the catch of fish and other marine organisms by such fishing vessels in the waters of third countries and in the open sea, as well as in order to ensure control of records on landings and transhipment of the catch. In order to implement the measures (referred to in paragraph 1) the owner or the captain of the fishing vessels shall: (1) keep on board the fishing vessel a logbook in which the captain shall record the quantity of fish and other marine organisms caught; (2) submit a landing declaration to the competent authorities of states where landing would like to place, in accordance with the agreement; and (3) inform the administration

1267. Where there is no ratified international agreement on fishing a foreign fishing vessels may engage in fishing in the fishing sea of Montenegro only for scientific research purposes in accordance with the approved scientific research project of national interest, with permission from the administration authority (Art. 95 para. 3).

authority or an inspector for marine fisheries on every landing of fish on a fishing vessel of third countries and of landing carried out directly in third countries (Article 98, paragraphs 1 and 2).[1268]

O. Recording and Reporting

1189. The administration authority shall (Article 99, paragraph 1):[1269] (1) collect the data necessary for monitoring the effects of the Strategy on the fisheries' development; (2) monitor the effects of fisheries' management plans adopted in accordance with this Law; (3) monitor the effects of the fisheries' policy measures in accordance with the national fisheries' policy or ratified international agreements; (4) establish the expenditures incurred by implementation of support measures for the fishery sector; and (5) submit to the Ministry reports on matters referred to in paragraph 1 Items from 1 to 3 of this Article.

1190. Holders of a permit issued in accordance with this Law shall provide and keep documentation, records and information and present them to the administration authority or fishery inspector, as appropriate (Article 102, paragraph 1). The documentation, in terms of this Law, shall be considered to be: (1) the catch logbook; (2) the declaration of landing of catch; (3) the report on catch; (4) written records and information; (5) a map, an overview, a graph or drawing; (6) a photograph; (7) a disc, a tape, a soundtrack or other means by which sounds or other data (non-visual) are recorded so that reproduction of sounds from them is possible (with or without the aid of some other equipment); (8) a film (including microfilm), a negative, a tape, a disc or other device in which one or more visual images are recorded so as reproduction of images from them is possible; and (9) the data reproduced and communicated via a satellite-based vessel monitoring system (Article 102, paragraph 2).[1270]

1191. A holder of a permit for commercial fishing with a fishing vessel of an overall length equal to, or more than, 10 m shall: (1) keep on board the fishing vessel the permit and fishing logbook; (2) enter daily records on the fishing activities into fishing logbook; (3) report in accordance with Article 104 of this Law; and (4) submit to the administration authority or a fishery inspector, within a period of forty-eight hours, a landing declaration for the total catch landed at the designated

1268. The measures referred to in para. 1 of this Article shall be implemented independently from the measures implemented under international fisheries agreements and conventions (Art. 98, para. 3).

1269. The method of publishing, usage or purchasing of data, the form, the content and time for delivery of reports referred to in para. 1, items 1) and 5) of this Article shall be prescribed by the Ministry (Art. 99, para. 2).

1270. The period of keeping, the form and the method of presentation of the documentation, records and information shall be prescribed by the Ministry (Art. 102, para. 4). The information on the data referred to in Art. 102 paras 1 and 2 of this Law may be kept electronically and submitted to the administration authority and other competent authorities, as well as by radio signals or in some other prescribed manner. The reporting method and the procedure, the devices for transfer of information and the reporting time shall be set by the Ministry (Art. 104, paras 1 and 2).

landing port. A holder of a permit for commercial fishing by fishing vessels of an overall length equal to, or longer than, 10 m shall report the total catch and landing of catch to the administration authority or the fisheries' inspector (Article 103, paragraphs 1 and 2).

1192. The administration authority shall establish a satellite fishing vessel monitoring system (Article 105, paragraph 1)[1271] within three years from the date of entry into force of this Law (Article 123, paragraph 1).

P. The First Landing Site and the First Sale Place

1193. The first landing[1272] of fish and other marine organisms shall be performed only in a port, harbour or another place meeting the prescribed technical conditions for inspection of fishing vessels (hereinafter referred as 'the first landing site') (Article 106, paragraph 1).[1273] The landing of fish and other marine organisms at the first landing site may be performed only by a holder of a permit for large-scale commercial fishing issued in accordance with this Law or in accordance with the ratified international agreement (Article 106, paragraph 3).[1274]

1194. The first sale of the fish and other marine organisms caught shall be performed only in a place meeting the prescribed technical conditions for sale, auction sale and marketing of fish (hereinafter referred to as 'the first sale place') (Article 107, paragraph 1).[1275]

1195. The trade in fish and other marine organisms at the first sale place may be performed by companies and entrepreneurs registered for wholesale in fish, and other marine organisms at the first sale place are entered into the register of wholesalers of fish and other marine organisms at the first sale place (referred to as 'the Register of fish wholesalers') (Article 108, paragraph 1).[1276]

1271. The type of the system, the way of establishing and the class of fishing vessels for which the system referred to in para. 1 of this Article is established shall be prescribed by the Ministry. The administration authority shall be responsible for management and operation of the system referred to in para. 1 of this Article (Art. 105, paras 2 and 3). In case of technical malfunction or non-functionality of the satellite monitoring system installed on a fishing vessel (hereinafter: device), the owner of the fishing vessel or the holder of a fishing licence may repair or replace the device with another device that is functional, based on the permission of the Ministry (Art. 105a, para. 1).

1272. *Place of the first landing* means an anchor, port or other place which meets the prescribed requirements for landing of fish (Art. 4, point 14).

1273. The technical requirements and the first landing site referred to in para. 1 of this Article shall be prescribed by the Ministry (Art. 106, para. 2).

1274. The method and conditions for landing of fish by a permit holder for small-scale commercial fishing shall be prescribed by the Ministry (Art. 106, para. 4).

1275. The technical requirements and the first sale place, the conditions and the method of sale at the first sale place shall be prescribed by the Ministry (Art. 107, para. 2). *The first sale fish* means fish being marketed for the first time at the first landing site (Art. 4, point 21).

1276. The Register of fish wholesalers shall be kept by the administration authority. The method of entry into and keeping of the Register of fish wholesalers, the form and the content of the applications

Q. Fish Transhipment

1196. When transhipment of fish and other marine organisms and fish products takes place, the captain of the vessel unloading and the captain of the vessel receiving the fish and other marine organisms and fish products are obliged to (Article 110, paragraph 1): (1) notify the administration authority or the fishery inspector of the time and the place of transhipment at least twenty-four hours in advance;[1277] (2) notify about the time when the transhipment was completed; and (3) keep records of the transhipment.

1197. A foreign fishing vessel when landing and transhipping fish and other marine organisms and fish products shall be treated in the same way as a third-country fishing vessel (Article 111, paragraph 1).[1278]

R. Inspection and Transitional Provisions

1198. Inspection supervision of this Law shall be conducted by the administration authority through inspectors for marine fisheries in accordance with the Law (Article 112, paragraph 1).[1279] In addition to the authority of inspectors provided by laws governing the inspection, an inspector for marine fisheries shall have the additional authorities prescribed by Article 113 of the Law. Apart from that, a fishery inspector shall take the additional administrative measures and actions prescribed by Article 114.

1199. Pending the adoption of regulations based on the authority from this Law, the regulations adopted under the Law on Marine Fisheries (OJ RM, No. 55/03) shall be applied unless they are in contradiction to this Law (Article 127).

---

referred to in para. 2 of this Article, and the List of traders in fish and other marine organisms shall be set by the Ministry (Art. 108, paras 3 and 4). A registered fish wholesaler referred to in Art. 108 of this Law shall keep records on the fish bought and/or sold and other marine organisms at the first sale place (Art. 109, para. 1).

1277. The method of notification and keeping of records referred to in para. 1, items 1 and 3 of this Article shall be prescribed by the Ministry (Art. 110, para. 2).

1278. Landing and transhipment from a foreign fishing vessel shall be performed only in a port, a harbour or other places meeting the technical requirements prescribed for inspection of foreign fishing vessels (hereinafter referred to as 'places for landing and transhipment') (Art. 111, para. 2). Technical requirements and the place for landing and transhipment referred to in para. 2 of this Article shall prescribed by the Ministry (Art. 111, para. 3).

1279. The authorizations of a fishery inspector in carrying out inspection governed by this Law and the Law on Inspection also applies to: (1) fishing vessels having Montenegrin flag within and beyond the fishing sea of Montenegro; (2) fishing vessels having a foreign flag in the fishing sea of Montenegro and within the authority laid down by ratified international agreement beyond the fishing sea of Montenegro (Art. 115, para. 1).

II. Law on Freshwater Fisheries and Aquaculture

1200. The Law on the Freshwater Fisheries and Aquaculture (OJ MNE, No. 17/18) was adopted in March 2018.[1280] It is divided into eleven chapters and contains eighty-six articles: Chapter I Basic Provisions (Articles 1–4), Chapter II Fishing Waters, Fishing Areas and Fishing Territories (Articles 5–8), Chapter III – The Manner of Assignment for Use of Fish and other Aquatic Organisms (Articles 9–18), Chapter IV – Protection and Conservation of Fish and other Aquatic Organisms (Articles 19–34), Chapter V – Fishery (Articles 35–52), Chapter VI – Aquaculture (Articles 53–63), Chapter VII – Marketing of Fish and other Aquatic Organisms (Article 64–67), Chapter VIII – Fishkeepers' authorizations (Articles 68–72), Chapter IX –Supervision (Articles 73–75), Chapter X – Penal Provisions (Articles 76–77) and Chapter XI – Transitional and Final Provisions (Articles 78–86).

A. *Basic Provisions*

1201. The Law regulates the manner of use, protection, conservation and fishing of fish, crabs, shells, frogs and other living aquatic organisms, aquaculture conditions and other relevant freshwater fisheries issues (Article 1). Aquaculture is defined as cultivation or breeding of aquatic organisms outside of their natural habitats, for the purpose of production enhancement (Article 2).

B. *Fishing Areas*

1202. The law differentiates between several types of areas suitable for fishing: (1) Fishing waters (Article 5) are suitable for sports and recreational fishing, for example, rivers, lakes, and other waters inhabited by aquatic organisms, with the exception of breeding grounds and water bodies intended for public water supply. (2) Fishing areas are specially designated by the competent Ministry and intended solely for economic fishing (Article 6). (3) Fishing territories serve as specially designated fishing areas where measures for protection and conservation of aquatic organisms are specifically provided by the Ministry (Article 7). (4) Fishing areas in specially protected natural areas might be established on the request of the authority that manages a natural area. The authority must submit the plan of use and the opinion of the relevant research institution for aquatic organisms to the Ministry for the authorization (Article 8).

1280. On the day when this Law entered into force the Law on fresh water fishery (Official Journal of SRM, Nos 39/76, 51/76, 34/88 and Official Journal of RM, No. 4/92) had been repealed.

C. Measures of Protection and Conservation

1203. The Law lists in Article 19 numerous measures of protection and conservation of aquatic organisms.

1204. The Ministry is obliged, according to define measures in order to protect and improve fish stocks and establish periods when fishing is banned for all or certain types of fish in the fishing waters and prohibition of fish that are not allowable size.

1205. This chapter includes provisions on logging (Article 20), import of aquatic species from other geographic areas (Article 21), fish-stocking (Articles 22–24), fish routes (Article 25),[1281] small hydroelectric power plants (Article 26),[1282] protected fishing areas (Articles 27–30), limits to fishing practices (Articles 31–32), damage compensation (Article 33) and migratory aquatic species (Article 34).

D. Fishing

1206. Fishing is divided into five categories: economic, sports, and recreational fishing, fishing for scientific research purposes, recovery fishing and selective fishing (Article 35). The economic societies and entrepreneurs registered for fishing can fish commercially, as prescribed, that is after obtaining a permit.[1283]

1207. Individuals who have permission for sports and recreational fishing can fish for sports and recreational purposes (Article 41). Article 42, paragraph 3 prescribes that permission for sports and recreational fishing is issued by the user of fish stocks for fish stock in fishing water that has the right to use, under the fishing grounds and the annual plan.[1284]

1208. Scientific institutions perform fishing for scientific purposes, with the approval of the Ministry (Article 49).

1209. Recovery fishing is performed for rescue purposes in certain fishing waters. If negative changes occur in physical, chemical or biological fishing water properties that can endanger aquatic organisms or a justified doubt exists that fishing waters might be drained, recovery fishing is performed on the Ministry's authorization. The aquatic organisms should be transferred to the fishing water of the

1281. Fish routes are hydrotechnical constructions that circle round the dams, hydropower plants and intake ducts, enter the breeding grounds and enable the free passage of aquatic organisms (Art. 4(21)).
1282. The Law prohibits pumping of water for the purpose of production of electricity in small hydroelectric power plants if the water level would become unacceptably low or the survival and development of aquatiac organisms would become impossible (so-called biological minimum defined by the Art. 4(5)).
1283. Permit is issued by the user of fish stocks, in accordance with the law (Art. 37, para. 5).
1284. For licence, a fee has to be paid (Art. 37).

same basin or provisionally to proper pools for feeding and conservation. After the end of negative changes, the organisms have to be returned to the original water. This type of fishing is performed by the manager of the natural good or the fishery association, with the obligatory presence of the agricultural inspector (Article 50).

1210. Selective fishing is performed for the protection of autochthonous aquatic species, with the Ministry's authorization. This type of fishing is performed by the manager of the natural good or the fishery association, with the obligatory presence of the agricultural inspector (Article 51).

E. Aquaculture

1211. According to Article 53, companies and entrepreneurs can deal with aquaculture[1285] based on approval for aquaculture issued by the Ministry.[1286] Holder of approval for aquaculture should provide health monitoring of fish and other aquatic fauna in ponds (Article 262).

III. Other Relevant Regulations

1212. Besides the mentioned laws, significant part of regulations relating to the water management and management and protection of sea and sea goods is also relevant to fishery.[1287] These are, *inter alia*:

- The Rulebook on the designation of fishing territories (OJ MNE, Nos 78/18, 36/20).
- The Rulebook on the content of the yearly plan of protection, conservation and improvement of fish and other aquatic organisms (OJ MNE, No. 8/19).
- Rulebook on the type of satellite system for monitoring fishing vessels and the type of fishing vessels for which the system is established (OJ MNE, No. 39/13).
- Rulebook on determining the line at which the water ceases to be permanently salted in rivers that flow into the sea and determining the boundaries of protected fishing areas (OJ MNE, No. 39/13).
- Regulation on register of fishing navigable objects (OJ MNE, No. 8/11).
- Regulation on conditions, restrictions and sequence of performing fishing in certain fishing areas (OJ MNE, No. 8/11).

1285. Freshwater fish breeding is done in twenty fish ponds and two cage systems for trout breeding. There are also conditions for cage fish breeding in hydro-accumulations. For more details, *see* GMNE (2008C), 88.
1286. Approval may be issued for a maximum of ten years, with possibility of extension in the same period, if the conditions for aquaculture are met and the results in the projected breeding are achieved (Art. 54, para. 2). The amount of annual fee has to be determined by the Ministry (Art. 54, para. 4).
1287. It also includes the regulations in the field of food safety, quality control, animal health, etc.

- Regulation on the form and contents of the fishing log, declaration on unloading, report on the catchments and the date of submitting the report on total catchments, of unloading the catchments and on the mode of information and of evidence keeping on the reload of fish and other sea organisms (OJ MNE, No. 8/11).
- Regulation on the mode of use, maintenance, protection, and marking, as well as the length of the coast, name and place of fishing post (OJ MNE, No. 8/11).
- Regulation on basic constructive-technical characteristics, method of application, time, purpose, quantity and kind of fishing tools and equipment that can be used in grand and in small-scale commercial fishing (OJ MNE, Nos 8/11, 27/14).
- Regulation on the form of permit, procedure of permit issuance, mode for paying the charge for performing commercial fishing and more precise conditions for transfer of the permit for commercial fishing (OJ MNE, No. 8/11).
- Regulation on conditions, fishing tools and equipment, period of performing fishing and procedure of permit issuance for performing small-scale commercial fishing of certain employed and retired persons (OJ MNE, No. 8/11).
- Rulebook on sporting and recreational fishing at sea (OJ MNE, Nos 34/10, 22/14).
- Order on Prohibition of Fishing and Marketing of Juvenile Fish, Fingerlings and other Sea Organisms (OJ RM, Nos 10/04 and 9/06).
- Rulebook on Manufacturing and Technical Requirements, Mesh Size, the Method of Use and Purposes of Certain Fishing Nets and Other Gear for Commercial and Leisure Fishing (OJ RM, Nos 10/04 and 9/06).
- Rulebook on the Form, Contents and Method of Keeping the Fishing and Fish Farming Logs (OJ RM, No. 10/04).
- Rulebook on the Method, Type and Quantity of Fishing Gear that May be Used in Leisure Fishing, as well as the Form, Number and Contents of the Leisure Fishing License (OJ RM, No. 10/04).
- Rulebook on Setting the Line where the Water Loses its Constant Salinity in the Rivers Flowing into the Sea, and on Setting the Limits to Fishing Reserve (OJ RM, No. 10/04).
- Rulebook on the Pricelist for Compensation of Damage caused by Illegal Fishing (OJ RM, No. 10/04).
- Rulebook on the Amount of the Fee for Commercial Fishing, Fishing and Fish Farming, as well as on the Form of the License, and on the Method of Keeping the Register of the Licenses Issued (OJ RM, No. 9/06).
- Order on the areas excluded for fishery, closing of fishing season and minimal sizes of fish and other aquatic organisms for fishery and for fishery purposes (OJ MNE, No. 69/21), etc.

§5. Harmonization with EU Legislation

1213. The Law on Marine Fisheries and Mariculture (OJ MNE, Nos 56/09, 40/11) is partly harmonized with relevant EU secondary legislation. However, Law is harmonized with the 1982 UN Convention on the Law of Sea, 1993 Food and Agriculture Organization (FAO) Agreement to Promote Compliance with international conservation and management measures by fishing vessels on the High Sea,

1995 Revised Convention on protection of sea environment and coastal area of Mediterranean, 1995 Agreement for the implementation of the provisions of the UN Convention of the Law of Sea of 10 December 1982 Relating to the Conservation and management of straddling fish stocks and highly migratory fish stocks, 1995 FAO Code of Conduct for responsible fisheries, 1995 International Convention on standards of training, certification and watch keeping for fishing vessels personnel, 1998 Arhus Convention and 1999 International Convention on Arrest of Ships.[1288]

1214. The Law contains basic legal framework for fleet and resource management and measures. However, with the reform of the CFP and the adoption of the new Basic Regulation (Regulation (EU) No. 1380/2013 of the European Parliament and of the Council of 11 December 2013 on the Common Fisheries' Policy, amending Council Regulations (EC) No. 1954/2003 and (EC) No. 1224/2009 and repealing Council Regulations (EC) No. 2371/2002 and (EC) No. 639/2004 and Council Decision 2004/585/EC), management measures foreseen by Montenegrin law will require further changes and harmonization.[1289]

1215. In its report for 2022, the EC has been noticed that: 'Montenegro has some level of preparation in this area. Limited progress was made on the recommendations of the last report, which remain valid.[1290] This means that Montenegro should finalise its work in preparation for the new fisheries and aquaculture strategy with the action plan on aligning with and enforcing the EU acquis; continue to strengthen administrative, data collection, scientific advice, inspection and control capacities; and continue the implementation of the multiannual plan for demersal species in the Adriatic.

1288. GMNE, MAFWM (2009b), 8, 9.

1289. Fisheries strategy of Montenegro 2015–2020 with an Action plan (for transposition, implementation and enforcement of EU acquis), Podgorica, June 2015, p. 31.

1290. EC.(2022), p. 117.

Chapter 8. Subsoil and Minerals

§1. State of Mineral Resources in Montenegro

1216. So far, twenty-eight types of mineral raw materials have been discovered in Montenegro, fifteen of which are exploited. It is estimated that twenty-three mineral raw materials are of significant economic importance. Metallic and non-metallic mineral raw materials, coals, sea salt and underground waters are significant, while oil and gas are still being researched. Besides these, technogenic raw materials should also be considered. Exploitation of mineral and other raw materials in Montenegro amounts to about 18,000 tonnes a year, and by the exploitation 25,000 m^3 of land is devastated.[1291]

1217. Numerous deposits of mineral raw materials including oil and gas are discovered on the territory of Montenegrin Littoral.[1292]

§2. Competencies

1218. The Ministry of Capital Investment is, according to Article 9 of the Decree on state administration organization and operations (49/22, 52/22, 56/22, 82/22) competent to conduct administrative activities with regard to: … exploitation of mineral and other raw materials; geological research; concession system and award of concessions from the competency of this Ministry. Besides that, following institutions are also involved in activities in this field: Geological Survey of Montenegro, CETI, Hydromet, Institute of Ferrous Metallurgy, etc. Administration for Hydrocarbons has been established by the Decree on changes of the Decree on Organization and Manner of Work of the Public Administration (25 December 2014) and has been kept in the latest Decree on state administration organization and operations.[1293]

§3. Legislation

1219. Several provisions in the Environmental Law (OJ MNE, Nos 52/16, 73/19) could be relevant for subsoil and minerals issues. These are Article 7 (definitions), Article 9 (obligations of legal and natural persons), Article 16 (land protection), Articles 54–59, (content and manner of performing monitoring), Article 34 (National Plan to Combat Desertification), Article 30 (National Strategy on Sustainable Development), etc. Worthy of mention is the Law on the Protection from Negative Impact of Climate Change in December 2019 (OJ MNE 73/19) which contains a part dedicated to Geological storage (Articles 23–27).

1291. GMNE (2008C), 102–104.

1292. *See*: extensively, GMNE (2007D), 19–21.

1293. Article 7 of the Law on research and production of hydrocarbons prescribes competences of this body.

I. Specific Legislation

1220. Besides the Law on geological research (OJ RM, Nos 28/93, 42/94, 26/07) there are following legal and sub-legal acts:

- Law on Mining (OJ MNE, Nos 65/08, 74/10).
- Law on Costal Zone (OJ RM, No. 14/92).
- Law on Sea (OJ RM, No. 17/07).
- Law on research and production of hydrocarbons (OJ MNE, Nos 41/10, 40/11, 62/13).
- Law on Concession (OJ MNE, Nos 8/09, 73/19).
- Regulation on the development of geological research projects (OJ SRM, No. 9/85).
- Regulation on the classification, categorization and calculation of solid mineral raw materials reserves and keeping records on them (OJ SFRY, No. 53/79).
- Regulation on the classification and categorization of reserves of underground water and keeping records on them (OJ SFRY, No. 34/79).
- Law on identifying and classifying reserves of mineral raw materials and displaying data on geological research (OJ SFRY, Nos 12/98, 13/98).
- Law on the participation of the private sector in performing public services (OJ RM, No. 30/02).
- Regulation on the manner and conditions for allocation of concessions for the performance of geological research and exploitation of mineral raw materials (OJ RM, No. 15/04), etc.

A. Law on Geological Research

1221. Law on geological research (OJ RM, Nos 28/93, 27/94, 42/94, 26/07)[1294] has following six chapters: Chapter I – Basic Provisions (Articles 1–3), Chapter II – Geological Research (Articles 4–38), Chapter III – Organization of Geological Research of Interest for the Republic (Articles 39–41), Chapter IV – Geological Inspection (Articles 42–44), Chapter V – Penal Provisions (Articles 45–46) and Chapter VI – Transitional and Final Provisions (Articles 47–51). The Law regulates the conditions and method of conducting geological research, funding, programming and organizations of geological research of interest to the RM, as well as the manner of exercising control over the implementation of the provisions of this law (Article 1).[1295]

1294. According to Art. 2 of the Law, geological research includes following: research the development, composition and materials of the Earth's crust, predicting, finding and establishing the deposit of mineral raw materials and assessment of economic effects of their use, establishing the geological and geo-mechanic characteristics of the soil for the purpose of construction of buildings, town planning, interior design and the protection and improvement of the environment (Art. 2).

1295. Article 3 stipulates that 'mineral raw materials include all types of coal, peat, hydrocarbons in the solid state, hydrocarbons in the liquid and gaseous state (oil and gas) and other natural gases, radioactive mineral raw materials, metallic mineral resources, mineral non-metallic raw materials,

1222. Pursuant to Article 4 of the Law there are two types of geological research: the basic and detailed research. Geological research can be done on the basis of the research project. Basic geological research is, according to Article 5, aimed at obtaining basic geological data on the development, composition and structure of the Earth's crust, the development of geological maps, determining the potentiality regarding the disclosure and to obtain the reserves of mineral raw materials, determining the state and characteristics of rock and soil, as well as to determine the geological conditions for detailed geological research project. The basic geological research and geological research of strategic importance are activities of interest for the RM and due to that are financed from the budget of the Republic.

1223. Detailed geological research can, according to Article 7 of the Law, only be carried out after the basic geological research is done,[1296] in the space where the existence of one or more mineral raw materials has been confirmed. Besides that, detailed geological research has to be done on the territory where the investment facilities are to be built (Article 6).[1297]

1224. Geological research and development of project research can be done by legal entities which meet prescribed conditions (Article 8). Research of mineral raw materials and soil for construction of facilities mentioned in Article 7 shall be on the basis of approval, issued by the Republic's government body responsible for geological research at the request of investors (Article 15).[1298]

1225. Governmental body competent for geological research can cancel approval under following conditions: (1) if the investigative work endangers or could endanger the future construction of buildings or exploitation of mineral raw materials or the neighbouring search space; (2) if the extent or type of investigative work from Article 17, point 3 of this law was not committed, and unforeseen difficulties appear; (3) if the investor does not start with the search works within a specific approval for research (Article 17, point 5); (4) if the investigative work obstructs or endangers other investigative work in the same or neighbouring areas (Article 18); (5) if it does not comply with the order of geological inspectors in

---

mineral raw materials for production of building materials, underground water (drinking, mineral and thermal) and all types of salt and salt water'.

1296. Article 7, para. 1 prescribes that detailed geological research of soil is obligatory before the creation of technical documentation for the construction of different facilities, including: public railway, roads, magisterial and regional roads, the port capacity of the receipt and dispatch of goods over 500,000 tonnes, the airport, accumulation of surface water whose volume is greater than 1,000,000 m3, dam height over 10 m, hydropower plants and thermal power over 10 MW, regional oil and water pipeline, buildings in protected areas, etc.

1297. Detailed geological research of soil is obligatory before the development of technical documentation for the construction of buildings and infrastructural plants with prescribed characteristics (railway, highways, accumulation of surface water, the main and regional roads, ports, nuclear power plants, gas stations, ski lifts, landfills, bridges, etc.) (Art. 7).

1298. According to Art. 17 by the approval for research following issues must be determined, *inter alia*: space where exploration will be carried out (investigation area), the largest amount of mineral raw materials that can be removed in order to test their quality and technological characteristics, environmental measures that must be taken in connection with the investigative work, etc.

accordance with the provisions of Article 28 of this Law; and (6) if the prescribed safety measures and security measures required of people, property and protection of human environment are not carried out (Article 26).

1226. Article 39 prescribes that the geological research of interest for the Republic is done by the public institution (legal person) if that kind of geological research is included in the research programme of geological research, made by the Republic's administration authority responsible for mining and geological research (Article 41).[1299] Article 41, paragraph 2, prescribes that programmes are made as mid-term and annual and are composed of parts that contain the basic geological research and parts that contain detailed geological research outside the approved field of exploitation.

B. *Law on Mining*

1. General Provisions

1227. Law on mining (OJ MNE, Nos 65/08, 74/10) contains 128 articles grouped into the following ten chapters: Chapter I – Basic Provisions (Articles 1–16), Chapter II – Competencies (Articles 17–20), Chapter III – Planning in the Field of Exploitation of Mineral Row Materials (Article 21), Chapter IV – Exploitation of Mineral Row Materials (Articles 22–81), Chapter V – Mining Measurements and Mining Plans (Articles 82–89), Chapter VI – Qualifications to Perform a Certain Affairs of Exploitation of Mineral Row Materials (Articles 90–110), Chapter VII – Protective Measures (Articles 94–111),[1300] Chapter VIII – Inspection's Supervision (Articles 112–117), Chapter IX – Penal Provisions (Articles 118–120) and Chapter X – Transitional and Final Provisions (Articles 121–128).

1228. The Law regulates conditions and manner of exploitation of mining wealth, measuring in mining, mining plans, degree of workers who manage the technical work in the exploitation, protection measures at work and measures of environmental protection in the performance of mining works as well as other issues of importance for the exploitation of mineral raw materials (Article 1).[1301] Mineral resources, as a wealth of general interest, are owned by the State and they can be used under conditions and in the manner provided by law.

1299. Detailed geological investigations which are not included in the programme referred to in para. 1 of this article can be carried out by the legal persons who meet the prescribed requirements.
1300. Protection measures are related to the obligations of the concessionaire regarding the protection of life and health of employees.
1301. Apart from the above-mentioned, the Law regulates exploitation of mineral raw materials and the construction, maintenance and use of facilities and plants for the exploitation of mineral raw materials (Art. 6). However, this Law does not apply to the extraction of sand and gravel on the soil water, which do not contain impurity of mineral raw materials of general interest, as well as to mineral raw materials that are used in medicinal purposes (Art. 7).

1229. By virtue of Article 10, exploitation of mineral raw materials has to be done in a way that ensures the rational use of mineral raw materials deposits. Article 13 prescribes that business Company has obligation to respect regulations concerning protection at work, environmental protection, protection from fire and explosion, technical regulations related to the type of works and objects and implement measures for the security of citizens, property and environmental protection.

1230. Exploitation of mineral raw materials can be performed by the business company on the basis of the contract of concession, and if it has a licence for mining works (Article 22).[1302] It will be done on the basis of the State plan[1303] (for a period not longer than ten years) composed of the general plan and plan for the exploitation of mineral raw materials (Article 21).

1231. The right to exploit deposits of mineral raw materials is acquired, according to Article 26, on the basis of the concession contract signed in accordance with the law and following approvals: (1) for the exploitation of mineral raw materials in the field of exploitation; (2) for the construction projects; and (3) for the use of mining facilities and plants. Approval for exploitation of mineral raw materials in the exploitation field is issued by the competent authority, at the request of the concessionaire (Article 33).[1304]

2. Technical Documentation

1232. Mining works must be carried out in accordance with technical documentation for the mining works, which in particular includes: (1) long-term programmes of exploitation of mineral raw materials; (2) mining projects, elaborates study solutions that are an integral part of mining projects; (3) annual plans of performance of works; (4) mining plans and maps; (5) geological documentation; and (6) documentation of monitoring the impact of mining works on the environment (Article 40).

1233. The construction of mining facilities and exploitation of mineral raw materials are done on the basis of the approved mining projects (Article 41).

1302. Licence can be obtained if the economic society is registered for the exploitation of mineral raw materials and which meets the requirements prescribed by the Law (Art. 22, para. 2).

1303. Government of Montenegro adopts the State plan of the exploitation of mineral raw materials and rules for the implementation of measures established by this plan; prescribes conditions for issuing permit for use of mineral row materials; makes decisions on mining concessions; prescribes criteria for determining the amount of funds for rehabilitation of space where is mining works are carried out, etc. (Art. 17).

1304. The competent authority will cancel the permit in following cases: if the concessionaire does not begin with the exploitation within the planned period; if the activities are not performed in accordance with the mining project; if exploitation endangers life and health of employees and third persons or property and other natural goods, and other measures under this law and other regulations are not sufficient to prevent it (Art. 38).

Approval and consent for the works are issued on the main mining project,[1305] an additional mining project and reduced mining project (Article 41, paragraph 2).

1234. Mining projects which are prepared abroad are technically controlled in accordance with the law (Article 48). The control includes, in addition to checking the fulfilment of the conditions of Article 47, checking whether regulations, measures and terms used for the project documentation are in accordance with appropriate regulations that apply in Montenegro.

1235. Pursuant to Article 51 licences which are issued in accordance with this Law are the following: (1) a licence for mining works and (2) a licence for the development of mining projects.[1306] The competent authority cancels the licence, if: (1) the licence holder received the licence on the basis of incorrect data; (2) the licence holder does not submit data before the deadline established in paragraph 6 of this article; and (3) the licence holder does not perform tasks in accordance with law (Article 51, paragraph 8).

3. Approval for Works

1236. It is prescribed by Article 52 that approval for works, in accordance with the main mining project and additional mining project, is issued by the competent authority. Execution of works on the exploitation of mineral raw materials and construction of mining facilities can be made only on the basis of the approved mining projects and after obtaining approval for exploitation (Article 53). With the application for issuing approval for the works according to the main and additional mining project, the necessary documentation has to be submitted.

1237. Approval for works for simplified mining projects is issued by the technical director of mining works employed by the concessionaires after obtaining consent of the competent authority (Article 54, paragraphs 1 and 2).[1307]

1238. The concessionaire has obligation to inform the competent authority, mining inspection and authority of local self-government about beginning of construction not later than fifteen days before the start of construction. Besides that, the

1305. The main mining project has to be made for the construction of new underground and surface mining facilities and for the reconstruction of the system of opening and preparation of mining facilities in order to exploitation of deposits of mineral raw materials, as well as for the opening of new ore deposits in the existing mines (Art. 42).

1306. Conditions for issuing licences, in terms of technical equipment and the required number of engineers respective professions, the form of licence, the fee for the issuance and certification of licences and the way of keeping the evidence of issued licence, are determined by the Ministry (Art. 51, para. 10).

1307. Nevertheless, if the works concerning simplified mining project affects the water regime and represent danger to the environment, the consent of the competent authorities for water and environmental protection has to be obtained (Art. 54, para. 3).

concessionaire is obliged to determine the persons who will perform the technical tasks of management mining works and professional supervision of the construction of mining facilities (Article 57).[1308]

1239. According to Article 58, necessary deviations concerning mining works and construction of mining facilities which are not significant can be carried out with the consent of the competent authorities.[1309]

1240. The concessionaire who exploits oil and natural gas may, due to geological conditions and configuration of the field, change the location determined by the project and plans. In this case, concessionaire has the obligation to notify the Ministry and submit study with justification for changes of location with opinion of organ of state administration competent for environmental protection.

4. Approval for the Use of Mining Facilities

1241. Already built mining facilities or parts of objects that can be used independently are subject to technical review, which depending on the type of object, includes following: mining and construction works, electrical installations, equipment and installations, and mining equipment and facilities (Article 59).[1310]

1242. According to Article 61 paragraph 1, technical review and approval for the use of mining facilities and plants built on the basis of the main and additional mining projects are done by the competent authority in accordance with the regulations on the construction of facilities, while approval for the use of mining facilities and plants built on the basis of reduced mining project is issued by the technical project manager responsible for the work of buildings and facilities built on the basis of reduced mining project.

1243. Technical review of mining object or part of the object (referred to in Article 59 of this Law) has to be done by the competent authority via expert Commission or a legal person in accordance with the regulations on the construction of facilities (Article 62). Technical review cannot be made by legal and natural persons who have participated in the design and technical control of mining projects.

1308. If the construction affects the water regime and if the environment concessionaire has the obligation to inform the Ministry responsible for water, and the Ministry responsible for environmental protection (Art. 57, para. 2).

1309. Concessionaire is obliged to submit application for issuance of approval for deviation from the approved project together with opinion of the author of project (Art. 58, para. 2).

1310. Article 60, para. 1 provides that technical review has to determine the compliance of these works with the technical documentation on the basis of which approval for construction is issued, with, *inter alia*, the measures and norms of the protection on the work and environmental protection.

5. Cessation of Exploitation's Works

1244. Articles 67–77 of the Law regulate cessation of exploitation works. If the works must be temporarily suspended due to unexpected circumstances (unexpected appearance of gas or water, fires, disorders of the main ways for ventilation, passage, drainage and transportation, slipping of ground, eruption, changes in water regime, etc.), concessionaire is obliged to temporarily suspend work and notify the mining inspection immediately, and no later than twenty-four hours of the suspension works (Article 67). The concessionaire has also several other obligations.

1245. Article 71 provides that during and after completion of construction works on the exploitation of mineral raw materials (no later than one year from the date of completion of works) the concessionaire is obliged to undertake measures relating to the land and environmental protection in accordance with the EIA study as well as water protection measures.[1311] According to Article 73, for rehabilitation and recultivation of land concessionaire is obliged to establish separate funds in accordance with approved projects of rehabilitation and recultivation.[1312]

C. The Law on Research and Production of Hydrocarbons

1246. Basic legal act regulating research[1313] in production of hydrocarbons[1314] in Montenegro is the Law on research and production of hydrocarbons (OJ MNE, Nos 41/10, 40/11, 62/13). It has the following ten parts: Part I – General Provisions (Articles 1–6), Part II – Administrative and professional services in hydrocarbons (Article 7), Part III – Blocks for exploration and production of hydrocarbons (Articles 8–10), Part IV – Award of concession contracts for research (Articles 11–18), Part V – Award of concession contracts for production (Articles 19–26), Part VI – Operations with hydrocarbons (Articles 27–46), Part VII – Obligations of concessionaire (Articles 47–69), Part VIII – Inspection supervision (Articles 70–71), Part IX – Penalty provisions (Article 72) and Part X – Transitional and final provisions (Articles 73–75).

1311. The Ministry and ministries competent for agriculture, water and environmental protection as well as organ of the local self-government have to be informed about measures (Art. 71, para. 2).

1312. Article 73, para. 2 stipulates that the amount of funds for rehabilitation and recultivation of space and other relevant elements has to be determined by government regulation.

1313. *Researches* are the operation of geological, geophysical or other forms of detailed examination of the Earth's crust, applying the appropriate method for determining the presence of hydrocarbon and characteristics of the reservoirs, except drilling of the wells (Art. 6, point 8).

1314. *Hydrocarbons* are all kinds of hydrocarbons which are in natural state located below the ground surface or seabed, in liquid or gaseous state, as well as raw mineral oil, natural gasoline, natural gas and other substances that can be extracted with it from the deposit (Art. 6, point 1). *Deposit* is an elementary and self-accumulation of the hydrocarbons in the Earth's crust, determined by the research and limited in structural and stratigraphic boundaries (Art. 6, point 4).

1247. According to Article 1 paragraph 1, this Law regulates the conditions, manner and procedure of research and production of hydrocarbons, and other issues important for the exploration and production of oil and gas.[1315] Hydrocarbons are the natural resources of the state.

1. Research and Production

1248. Research and production of hydrocarbons can be performed by a company, legal entity or natural person on the base of the concession contract concluded in accordance with this Law[1316] (Article 3, paragraph 1). The right to exploration and production of hydrocarbons can be given to one or more companies, legal entities or natural persons in the concession contract concluded in accordance with this Law (Article 4, paragraph 1).[1317]

1249. Provisions of the Law governing the concession shall not apply to the procedure for granting concessions and contracts for research and production of hydrocarbons (Article 5, paragraph 1). Also, provisions of the Law regulating geological research and mining shall not apply to research and hydrocarbon production (Article 5, paragraph 2).

2. Blocks for Exploration and Production of Hydrocarbons

1250. The block[1318] is usually determined in a rectangular shape and cannot exceed an area of 1,000 km^2 for the land part of Montenegro or 1,500 km^2 for seabed (Article 8, paragraph 1). Blocks for exploration and production of hydrocarbons are determined by the GMNE (Article 8, paragraph 2).[1319]

1315. *Oil* is a hydrocarbon which after removing from the deposit remains in liquid state at normal atmospheric pressure and temperature (Art. 6, point 2). *Gas* is a hydrocarbon that is free or bounds natural gas in its natural form in the Earth's crust (Art. 6, point 2).
1316. The activity referred to in para. 1 of this Article include the planning, preparation and activities related to research, development and production of hydrocarbons from the reservoir, as well as the construction, use, uninstallation and removal of plants (hereinafter referred to as 'operations') (Art. 3, para. 2).
1317. The right to explore and produce hydrocarbons can be given to a foreign legal or natural person, provided that the data on business, ownership, financial and fiscal records from the state where company has headquarters, i.e., residence, are available to the state authorities of Montenegro (Art. 4, para. 2).
1318. *Block* is part of the land or the sea intended for research and production, determined by the geographic coordinates (Art. 6, point 5).
1319. Concession contract for the production, including maximum 50% of total blocks area allocated for production, can be concluded with a single concessionaire (Art. 9, para. 1).

3. Award of the Concession Contracts for Research

1251. The subject of the concession contract for the research can be right to the geological, geophysical or other detailed studies of the Earth's crust, except in case of drilling with aim to determine the structural and tectonic features of the environment and to assess the presence of hydrocarbons (Article 11, paragraph 1).[1320]

1252. The concession contract for the research may be awarded to the company, legal entity or natural person that has experience in research and meets the financial and technical requirements determined in the public call for award of a concession for exploration (Article 13, paragraph 2).[1321]

4. Production of Hydrocarbons

1253. Production of hydrocarbons can only be made on the basis of the concession contract for oil and gas production (hereinafter 'concession contract for the production'), in accordance with this Law (Article 19, paragraph 1).[1322]

1254. The concessionaire is obliged to pay an annual fee for the area used under the concession contract for production. The fee is calculated on the basis of surface area for exploration and production, according to the criteria stipulated in the concession contract for the production (Article 26, paragraph 1). Apart from that, the concessionaire is obliged to pay compensation for the produced oil and gas for hydrocarbons extracted in a month, in the amount proportionate to produced and delivered oil and gas in accordance with the concession contract for the production (Article 26, paragraph 2).

5. Operations with Hydrocarbons

1255. The period of research phase and the phase of verification of reserves may not exceed six years for a block of land, or seven years for the offshore block from the day of signing of the concession contract for the production (Article 27, paragraph 1).

1320. The study of hydrocarbons is performed on the area bordered with block from Art. 8 of this Law on which previous level of exploration was not sufficient (Art. 11, para. 2). The right on hydrocarbon exploration is acquired by signing the concession contract for research, in accordance with this Law (Art. 11, para. 3).

1321. The concession contract for the research may be awarded for the period of up to two years (Art. 13, para. 1).

1322. The decision to grant the concession contract for the production makes the Parliament of Montenegro at the proposal of the Government (Art. 24, para. 1).

1256. The concessionaire is obliged to submit to the administrative authority detailed annual report on completed research with research results, in accordance with the timetable set out in the concession contract for the production (Article 28, paragraph 1).[1323]

1257. If the concessionaire in exploratory wells confirms the existence of hydrocarbons, it is obliged that without delay, the latest fifteen days after the discovery, notify the administrative authority in writing about the location and nature of findings and submit the available data (Article 31, paragraph 1). Exploration wells[1324] referred to in paragraph 1 of this Article are wells made to verify the research results and determine the presence of hydrocarbons (Article 31, paragraph 2).

1258. Production stage[1325] starts from the date of the first extraction of hydrocarbons from the reservoir and may last up to twenty years from the date of production (Article 36, paragraph 1 and Article 37, paragraph 1).[1326]

1259. Transport of oil and gas, in accordance with this Law, is by pipeline network from the manufacturing facilities to the last destination terminal (upstream pipeline network)[1327] (Article 40, paragraph 1).

6. Obligations of the Concessionaire

1260. After completing the research phase or after the abandonment of exploration activities, the Concessionaire is obliged to, within the time frame set out in the concession contract for the production, which cannot exceed six months: (1) remove the plants used in the research, unless they are necessary for the development phase, or production phase; (2) preserves the well and bring the entire area in the condition as it was before the research activities; and (3) realize other obligations in terms of environmental protection in accordance with the Law (Article 48,

1323. In addition, the concessionaire is obliged to, within six months from the completion of the research phase, submit to the administrative authority study on the results of the performed researches with interpretation of the data, analysis of the results and with documentation containing the source data and information obtained in the research process (Art. 28, para. 2).
1324. *Well* is the channel below the Earth surface made by drilling for the penetration to the layers containing hydrocarbons or for production, except shallow drilling for the seismic calibration needs (Art. 6, point 10).
1325. Production stage under Art. 36 of this Law may, at the request of the concessionaire, be extended for a maximum of half stages of production period laid down in the concession contract for the production (Art. 38, para. 1).
1326. Production stage, at the request of the concessionaire, may be extended for a maximum of half stages of production period laid down in the concession contract for the production (Art. 38, para. 1).
1327. *Upstream pipeline network* is a pipeline or pipeline network, which operates or has been constructed for production of hydrocarbons or is used for gas transport from one or more production plants to the processing plants, terminals or to the final terminal to the which the hydrocarbon is leaded, except parts of plants used for local production from the reservoirs at the place where gas is extracted (Art. 6, point 18).

paragraph 1). Furthermore, the concessionaire is obliged to prepare a plan of production termination and uninstallation of facilities (dismantling and disposal of facilities) (Article 49, paragraph 1) and to sell all or part of oil and gas produced in Montenegro, at the request of the Government or persons authorized by the Government (Article 55, paragraph 1).[1328]

1261. The concessionaire shall acquire ownership of extracted quantities of oil and gas in accordance with the Law and in accordance with the contract concession for the production (Article 56, paragraph 1).

7. Environmental Protection

1262. The concessionaire has the following obligations: to take all possible measures to prevent negative impacts on individual segments of the environment – air, atmosphere, land, water resources and sea, and the living world (Article 60, paragraph 1); to take all necessary steps to protect and preserve historical and cultural resources (Article 60, paragraph 2); and to implement measures for environmental protection during operations with hydrocarbons and control measurements of environmental parameters, in accordance with the Law, to prevent or reduce harmful effects and their consequences to the environment (Article 60, paragraph 3).[1329]

1263. It is forbidden to discharge or to burn oil or gas, pressure release or discharge water reservoirs except to eliminate immediate threats to people's lives, health and property (Article 61, paragraph 1).[1330]

8. Inspection Supervision

1264. The supervision over the implementation of this Law and the regulations adopted on the basis of this Law is to be conducted by the Ministry, if not otherwise specified in this Law (Article 70, paragraph 1). Inspection supervision performs an inspector for hydrocarbons, in accordance with the Law and the Law regulating the inspection (Article 70, paragraph 2).

1328. Oil and gas referred to in para. 1 of this Article shall be delivered at same prices valid at international market for the same quality and quantity (Art. 55, para. 2).
1329. Detailed terms of environmental protection from the paras 1 and 3 of this Article are determined by regulation of the state administration responsible for environmental protection (Art. 60, para. 4).
1330. Protection zone around and above the plants for research and production of hydrocarbons is determined by the state administrative authority responsible for trade and transport of flammable liquids and gases (Art. 62, para. 1).

D. The Law on Concessions

1265. A new Law on Concessions (OJ MNE, Nos 08/09, 73/19) was adopted by the Parliament on 26 January 2009. It has the following eight parts: Part I – General Provisions (Articles 1–4), Part II – Subject matter and terms of concessions award (Articles 5–8), Part III – Institutional structure (Articles 9–16), Part IV – Procedure for awarding concessions (Articles 17–41), Part V – Protection of the rights of participants in the public notice (Article 42), Part VI – Concession contract (Articles 43–57), Part VII – Concession fee (Articles 58–61) and Part VIII – Transitional and final provisions (Articles 62–69).

1266. According to Article 1, the Law on concessions regulates requirements, mode and procedure for awarding concessions, the subject of concessions and other issues of importance for the concession.[1331] It is prescribed in Article 2 that concessions shall be awarded under the equal, transparent and non-discriminatory requirements, for the usage of natural wealth, goods in general use and other goods of general interest, taking into consideration the public interest, and infrastructure development and functioning (Article 2, point 1). Concession award is based on the principles of transparency,[1332] non-discrimination[1333] and competitiveness[1334] (Article 3, point 1).

1. Terms of Concession Award

1267. Pursuant to Article 5 a concession may be awarded to a tenderer in the manner and under the requirements set forth under this Law. A subject matter of the concession may be: (1) exploration or exploitation, or exploration and exploitation of mineral resources; (2) usage of watercourses and other waters or the parts or certain quantities thereof, for the purposes provided for under a separate law; (3) construction or reconstruction, maintenance and usage of water-related facilities; (4) forests exploitation; (5) use of radio frequencies; (6) construction of hydro-amelioration systems and extraction of materials from waterlogged land; (7) construction, maintenance and usage, or reconstruction, modernization, maintenance

1331. *Concession* means the right (Art. 4, para. 1, point 1): to use the state-owned natural wealth, goods in general use and other goods of the general interest; or to perform activities of the public interest which include the payment of a concession fee by a concessionaire, or the delivery of a financial compensation or other support to a concessionaire for achieving relevant public interest; to fund, explore, design, construct or reconstruct, use, maintain, recover or sell structures, facilities or plants owned by a grantor within a contracted period, including also other similar forms thereof.

1332. Principle of transparency ensures that all parties in procedure for awarding of concession have complete, accurate and timely information on: process, standards and criteria for selection of the concessionaire, the bidder who has given concessions and conditions of its offer (Art. 3, point 2).

1333. Principle of non-discrimination in the procedure for awarding concession shall ensure that all tenderers have equal treatment in the procedure for awarding concession (Art. 3, point 3).

1334. By applying the principles of competition in the process of granting concessions shall ensure the conditions for the participation of higher number of the bidders (Art. 3, point 4).

and usage, or use of: roads, road-related and the accessory structures thereof, railroads, air traffic facilities and airports, water transport facilities and ports, telecommunication facilities, oil pipelines, gas pipelines, warehousing structures, structures for oil and gas transport and distribution, structures of healthcare and education institutes, structures of public utility services, for the delivery of public utility services; (8) designing, constructing, maintaining and using of the energy-related and other structures for generation, transmission and distribution of electrical energy, thermal energy and gas or the reconstruction, modernization, maintenance, and usage thereof; (9) use of the river banks and lake shores; (10) Carrying out state educational curricula; (11) organizing lottery games of chance and specific games of chance in casinos; and (12) construction, maintenance and usage of sport and recreation facilities, sport grounds and spaces designated for sport, recreation and cultural activities; (13) construction, maintenance and usage of facilities, or reconstruction, modernization, maintenance and usage of the existing structures in the areas with natural healing features and other natural values.[1335]

1268. Concessions shall be awarded pursuant to an annual plan adopted by the Government or the Municipality, and published on the website of the Government or of the Municipality (Article 7, point 1). The annual plan stipulates the areas, localities or the areas for which concessions are to be awarded, the subject matter of the concession and deadlines for publication of public notices for awarding concessions (Article 7, point 4).

1269. The period for which the concession is determined[1336] depends on the public interest, the subject of the concession, time needed for the return on investment and realization of adequate profit from the concession activities (Article 8, point 1).

2. Institutional Structure

1270. The decision on granting a concession to the subject of the concession on which property rights and authorization is owned by the state of Montenegro is adopted by the Government or the Assembly pursuant to Article 8, paragraph 2 of this Law (Article 9, point 1).[1337]

1335. In addition to the subject matter of the concession referred to in para. 1 of this Article, the usage of other natural wealth, goods in general use and other state-owned goods of the general interest may also be the subject matter of the concession, in accordance with law, as well as the performance of other activities provided for under law as activities of the public interest (Art. 6 para. 2).

1336. The term of the concession period may not exceed thirty years in case the decision on awarding concession is adopted by the Government and the Municipality, nor it may exceed sixty years in case the decision on awarding concessions is adopted by the Parliament (Art. 8, point 2). It may be extended following the expiry of initially contracted period and thus for a maximum of a half of the already contracted period which is prescribed by the Concession Contract (Art. 8, point 3).

1337. The same rule applies to Municipality for the concession to the subject of concession on which the Municipality has the property rights and authorizations (Art. 9, point 2).

1271. The Concession Commission of Montenegro (hereinafter referred to as 'the Commission') shall be autonomous and independent in performing the duties stipulated in this Law (Article 10, point 1). It consists of chairperson and eight members (Article 10, point 2) with Montenegrin citizenship (Article 10, point 3), appointed by the Government (Article 10, point 3).

1272. Competency of the Commission, Conflict of Interests Article and Termination of the Term of Office and Revocation from Duty are prescribed by Articles 11, 12 and 13.[1338]

1273. The funds for the work of the Commission shall be allocated in the Budget of Montenegro (Article 14, paragraph 1). Concession contracts, as well as changes related to the contract, shall be registered in the Register of Concession Contracts kept by the Commission (Article 15, points 1 and 2) and published on the website of the Commission (Article 15, point 5). No later than 31 March of the current year, the Commission shall submit to the Government annual report on its activities in the previous year (Article 16, point 1), which is also submitted to the Parliament and municipalities for consideration (Article 16, point 2).

3. Procedure for Awarding Concessions

1274. The procedure for awarding concessions shall be initiated by the Competent Authority upon development of a Concession Document,[1339] in accordance with the plan referred to in Article 7 of this Law (Article 17, paragraph 1).[1340]

1275. Prior to sending a Concession Document to be adopted, the Competent Authority shall organize and carry out a public consultation, within fifteen to thirty days of the day of submission of the public notice to such public consultation

1338. The Commission member must not have direct or indirect interests in the subject matter of the concession award, which could cause a conflict between his/her personal and business interests in awarding concession. In case the chairperson or a member of the Commission is in a conflict of interests, he/she shall be obliged to inform the Government thereof, and the Government shall appoint a person to replace such chairperson or member of the Commission having the conflict of interest (Art. 13).

1339. Contents of the Concession Document is prescribed by the Art. 19. The Competent Authority shall submit the Concession Document referred to in Art. 17 para. 1 of this Law to the Government, or to the competent authority of the Municipality, in accordance with law (Art. 18 para. 1). Along with the Concession Document, the following shall also be submitted: analysis of justifiability of achieving the public interest by awarding a concession, containing the indicators that such concession is capable of providing the public interests and the analysis of the possible alternatives in delivering the services concerned; indicators that a planned concession is capable of ensuring an appropriate value for money; analysis of the risk assessments and balance of risks between the Grantor and the Concessionaire; consideration of the need that the Grantor has to have a stake in a concession company concerned (type and scale of such stake); report from the public consultation. The Government or the competent authority of the Municipality shall adopt the Concession Document (Art. 18, point 6).

1340. The procedure may also be initiated upon an initiative presented by an interested party (Art. 17 para. 2).

(Article 18, paragraph 3). The Competent Authority may engage professional legal entities or natural persons to deliver support in drafting or for drafting the proposal of the Concession Document and tender documentation.[1341]

1276. Article 19 prescribes fifteen elements of the Concession Document.[1342] Among other things Concession Document includes (Article 19, paragraph 1, point 11): environmental protection measures and measures for the improvement of energy efficiency, in accordance with regulations.

1277. A concession shall be awarded based on a public notice, by (Article 20, point 1): (1) the public tender in open procedure (hereinafter referred to as 'the open procedure'), (2) two-stage procedure public tender (hereinafter referred to as 'the two-stage procedure') and (3) public tender in simplified procedure (hereinafter referred to as 'the simplified procedure').

1278. The Competent Authority shall publish a public notice upon the adoption of the Concession Document (Article 21, point 1). The Notice shall be published in the *OJ MNE,* in at least one daily printed media circulated on the entire territory of Montenegro and on the website of the Competent Authority.[1343]

1279. Pursuant to Article 23 the following shall be considered ineligible to participate in a public competition for concession award: (1) business organizations, other legal entities and entrepreneurs against which bankruptcy or liquidation procedure was initiated, except for the reorganization procedure in line with the law that governs insolvency of business organizations; (2) business organizations, other legal entities, entrepreneurs and natural persons that were convicted by a final and binding judgment for a crime in performance of the professional activity; and (3) business organizations, other legal entities, entrepreneurs and natural persons that have unsettled tax liabilities and liabilities arising from penalties pronounced in criminal or misdemeanour procedure in a period of at least three years prior to publishing of the public notice.[1344]

1341. The persons referred to in para. 4 of this Article may not be tenderers in any procedure for awarding concessions for which they have delivered support in development of the Concession Document or they have drafted the Concession Document (Art. 18 para. 5).

1342. *Concession Document* means the fundamental document based on which the procedure for awarding concession shall be initiated.

1343. In case that a subject of the concession is of strategic importance for Montenegro, for the subjects of the concession referred to in Art. 6, para. 1, items 7 and 8 of this Law it shall also be published in one representative international economic printed media (Art. 21, point 2).

1344. A business organization, other legal entity, entrepreneur or natural person may submit only one tender to a public notice, independently, under a consortium or under other form of business association (Art. 24).

1280. As a matter of security, a tenderer[1345] is obliged to submit, along with the tender, evidence of monetary deposit payment or bank guarantee, in the amount and for the period that is defined under a public notice (Article 25, point 1).

1281. The procedure of public competition, based on a public notice, shall be conducted by an ad hoc tender commission composed of odd number of members appointed by the Competent Authority (Article 26, point 1). The Commission shall consist of a chairperson and a minimum of four members appointed among the professionals in the area of concession subject (technical, legal, financial and other professions) (Article 26, point 3).[1346]

1282. Article 29 prescribes eleven tender evaluation criteria of which criterion nine prescribes programme and extent of environmental protection and measures for improving energy efficiency.[1347]

1283. The tender commission shall, within thirty days from the date of bid opening, submit to the competent authority ranking of bidders, a report on the conducted proceedings with an explanation of ranking bidders, the record of the proceedings, which shall include information on meeting the required conditions to be met by concessionaire[1348] and the basic elements from the offer according to the structure of criteria on which base the evaluation of tenders was carried out (Article 30, point 2).

1284. A ranking list of tenderers shall be posted on the bulletin board or on the website of the Competent Authority (Article 31, point 1).[1349] The Grantor shall decide on awarding concession within thirty days of the day of the receipt of the proposal referred to in Article 33 paragraph 1 of this Law if no appeals were presented to the ranking list of tenderers or to the evaluation procedure (Article 34, point 1).[1350] The Competent Authority shall inform the tenderers in writing of the results of public notice within five days from adoption of the decision on awarding

---

1345. *Tenderer* means a national or a foreign business organization or another legal entity, entrepreneur or natural person, consortium or other form of business association that participates in the procedure for awarding concession.
1346. The costs of the Tender Commission work shall be borne by the authority that has appointed the Tender Commission (Art. 26, point 6).
1347. The value of points shall be set under the tender documentation per each selected criterion for evaluation, whereat the sum of all points shall be 100 (Art. 29, para. 2).
1348. *Concessionaire* means a national or a foreign business organization or another legal entity, entrepreneur or natural person that acquired a concession right, as well as consortium or other form of business association that regulates their mutual relations under a separate contract.
1349. Tenderers shall be entitled to the following: to examine the documentation referred to in Art. 30 para. 2 of this Law, within eight days as of the day of the publishing of the ranking list of tenderers on the website of the Competent Authority, upon a written request; to lodge an appeal about the ranking list of tenderers within fifteen days as of the day of the publishing of the ranking list of tenderers on the website of the Competent Authority (Art. 31, paras 2 and 3).
1350. If the first ranked tenderer withdraws from the conclusion of the concession contract or fails to conclude the concession contract within the deadline stipulated under the decision on awarding concession, the Grantor may call the tenderers, as per the order on the ranking list, to conclude a contract or may annul the public notice (Art. 35).

concession (Article 36, point 1). The decision on awarding concession or a decision on public notice annulment shall be published in the OJ MNE and on the website of the Competent Authority (Article 36, point 2).

1285. Procedure when there is one Application upon the Public Notice, is prescribed by Article 37.[1351] Two-stage Procedure (Implementation of the procedure and Competitive Dialogue) is regulated by Articles 38 and 39 while the Accelerated Procedure is prescribed by Article 40.[1352] The Initiative of an Interested Party is defined by Article 41.[1353]

4. Protection of the Rights of Participants in Public Notice

1286. Rights of the Participants in the Public Notice Procedure are protected by the provisions of Article 42 of the Law (the right to attend the opening of tenders, to withdraw a tender at the latest by the expiration of the deadline established in the public notice).[1354]

1287. The Tenderer shall have the right to lodge an appeal to the Commission about the evaluation of tenders and ranking list of Tenderers (Article 42, paragraph 3).[1355] In addition, the Tenderer shall have the right to reimbursement of the monetary deposit or bank guarantee in the manner and within the deadline as established in the public notice (Article 42, paragraph 5).[1356]

1351. If one tenderer submits the tender upon a public notice, and the Tender Commission verifies that such tender meets the requirements and criteria of the public notice, the Competent Authority may annul the public notice or continue the procedure for awarding concession (Art. 37).
1352. Concessions with the term of validity of the award of up to three years shall be awarded in the procedure which is determined in Arts 17–37 and Art. 40 of this Law, whereas in the procedure for awarding concession: the public consultation referred to in Art. 7 of this Law does not need to take place; a Concession Document is prepared which, depending on the subject matter of the concession, includes items 1, 3, 8, 9, 10, 11, 12 and 13 of para. 1 of Art. 19 of this Law, as well as other elements as determined by the Competent Authority; the deadline for submission of tenders is determined, which cannot be shorter than fifteen days as of the day of publication of a public notice in the Official Journal of Montenegro; ranking list of tenderers which is determined by the Tender Commission referred to in Art. 26 of this Law is submitted to the Competent Authority within twenty days as of the day of opening of tenders (Art. 40, para. 1).
1353. An interested party may submit an initiative to the Competent Authority to commence the procedure of awarding concession which is not included in the plan referred to in Art. 7, para. 1 of this Law (Art. 41, para. 1).
1354. The tender shall be regarded as withdrawn upon the receipt of the request in writing for tender withdrawal, which should be returned unopened to a tenderer without any delay.
1355. An administrative dispute can be initiated against the Decision on awarding concession (Art. 42, para. 4).
1356. The tenderer who withdraws from the conclusion of the concession contract shall have no right to reimbursement of the monetary deposit or bank guarantee referred to in para. 5 of this Article (Art. 42, para. 7). No interest shall be calculated for the deposit reimbursed within the deadline established in the public notice (Art. 42, para. 6).

5. Concession Contract

1288. A Concession Contract[1357] shall be concluded within fifteen days from the decision adoption, or within the deadline, as determined in a decision on awarding concession, in line with tender documentation, submitted tender and decision on awarding concession (Article 43, point 1). Paragraph 2 of Article 43 prescribes content of Concession Contract of which point 19 prescribes rights and obligations with regard to undertaking measures for providing overall safety, health protection and environmental protection, improvement of the energy efficiency as well as responsibility for compensation of damage caused by jeopardizing overall safety and environmental protection.

1289. The Competent Authority shall monitor and control the execution of contractual obligations from the Concession Contract (Article 49, point 1).[1358]

1290. In addition, Law prescribes concessionaire's Rights (Article 50), concessionaire's obligations (Article 51), Assigning the Contract (Article 52),[1359] Cessation of the Concession Contract (Article 53),[1360] Transfer of the Structure (Article

1357. *Concession Contract* means a written contract concluded for a defined period of time, which governs mutual rights and obligations between a grantor and a concessionaire (Art. 4, para. 1, point 2). *Grantor* is the Parliament of Montenegro (hereinafter referred to as 'the Parliament'); the Government of Montenegro (hereinafter referred to as 'the Government'); local self-government, the Capital and the Historic Royal Capital (hereinafter referred to as 'the Municipality').

1358. The Competent Authority can engage experts or professional institutions for monitoring the execution of contractual obligations by the Concessionaire (Art. 49, point 2).

1359. A Concession Contract can be assigned to another concessionaire with a prior consent of the Grantor, provided that the new concessionaire meets at least the same requirements as the Concessionaire. Assigning the Concession without the consent of the Grantor shall be null and void (Art. 52).

1360. A concession-based relation shall cease: (1) by expiration of the term for which the Concession Contract was concluded; (2) by revoking of the Concession; (3) by cancellation of the Concession Contract; (4) based on an agreement between the Grantor and the Concessionaire. The Concession shall be revoked if: (1) the Concessionaire fails to carry out a concession-related activity in line with the schedule and in the scope as determined by the Concession Contract, except in the case of unforeseen circumstances or force majeure; (2) the Concessionaire fails to carry out preparatory activities within contracted deadline or fails to start the concession-related activity within the contracted deadline; (3) the Concessionaire fails to pay a Concession Fee; (4) bankruptcy or liquidation procedure is initiated of the Concessionaire, except in the case of a reorganization procedure under a law which governs insolvency of business organizations; (5) the Concession is awarded based on false data important for decision-making on awarding concession; (6) the execution of concession-related activity endangers the environment and people's health or areas and structures protected by law, which could not have been foreseen at the time of awarding of the Concession, and measures prescribed by special regulations are not sufficient to prevent that; and (7) the Concessionaire assigns the Concession without a consent of the Grantor (Art. 53, paras 1 and 2).

54), Rehabilitation and Reclamation of the Area (Article 55), Exemption (Article 56)[1361] and Stay of Rights and Obligations from the Concession Contract (Article 57).[1362]

6. Concession Fee

1291. A Concession Contract may determine the payment of a Concession Fee, which is paid for the granted Concession in line with regulations and the Concession Contract (Article 58, point 1).[1363] A portion of the Concession Fee for concessions awarded by the Government shall be allocated to the municipality at whose territory the subject matter of the Concession is located, in line with a law which governs the manner of financing of local self-government units (Article 59). A Concessionaire can be, pursuant to the contract, partially or completely exempted from the payment of the Concession Fee in the cases of unforeseen circumstances or force majeure, while such unforeseen circumstance or force majeure lasts (Article 60).[1364]

E. The Law on Sea

1292. The Law on Sea (OJ MNE, Nos 17/07, 6/08, 40/11) contains, as it is stated in Article 1, rules related to the research and exploitation of natural resources of the internal seawaters, territorial sea, exclusive economic zone and continental shelf. According to Article 2, the Republic has sovereign rights and jurisdiction in its exclusive economic zone and continental shelf for research, exploitation, protection, preservation and promotion of natural marine resources, including resources in the seabed and under it.

1361. The Concession cannot be the subject of bankruptcy proceeding or liquidation proceeding (Art. 56).

1362. In the case of force majeure or extraordinary event preventing the execution of the concession-related activity, which could not have been foreseen at the time the Concession Contract was concluded, the rights and obligations from the Concession Contract shall temporarily stay until the force majeure or extraordinary event ceases. The Grantor shall, based on the request of the Concessionaire in writing, make the decision on stay of rights and obligations from the Concession Contract (Art. 57).

1363. The Concession Fee for concessions awarded by the Government shall be the revenue of the Budget of Montenegro (Art. 58, point 2). A minimum Concession Fee shall be determined based on: (1) type, category, quantity, quality and market price of a resource which is the subject matter of a Concession Contract; (2) type of activity which is the subject matter of the Concession Contract and market conditions for its performance; (3) term of validity of the Concession; (4) a return on investment period; (5) expected gain; and (6) other criteria pursuant to law and the subject matter of the concession (Art. 61 para. 1).

1364. The Grantor shall adopt the decision referred to in para. 1 of this Article, based on a written request with explanatory note of the Concessioner (Art. 60, para. 2).

1293. Approval of the competent Ministry for Education and Science (MES)[1365] (Article 9) is needed for domestic and foreign legal and natural persons who intend to carry out research, recording and Hydrographic survey of the bottom of the seabed of the internal seawaters for scientific purposes.

1294. Legal or natural persons that participate in the research of exploitation of natural resources in the exclusive economic zone are obliged to respect international and domestic legal regulations, procedures and standards concerning protection of the sea, living marine resources and marine environment (Article 34, paragraph 2).

1295. Domestic and foreign legal and natural persons may carry out the research, recording and Hydrographic survey of the bottom of the sea and of internal seawaters for scientific purposes if they acquire approval of the competent MES.

1296. It is prescribed by Article 36 of the Law that the RM has sovereign rights for the exploration and exploitation of natural resources[1366] in the area of continental shelf. The rights are exclusive and that means that foreign legal and natural persons can use these resources only with explicit consent, that is, in cases established by international treaties.

1365. Approvals for other types of research have to be issued by other competent authorities (ministry competent for culture, ministry for environmental protection, fishing, Art. 9, paras 2–4).

1366. The natural resources means the mineral and other inanimate wealth of the sea bottom and the seabed, as well as sea creatures which can be hunted, if they are immobile on the sea bottom or below it. This applies also to the sea creatures which are unable to move if they are not in constant physical contact with the sea bottom and seabed (Art. 36, para. 2).

Part III. Zoning and Land-Use Planning

§1. Introduction

1297. In the 1980s, development and spatial planning in Montenegro were based on a self-governing social planning system. The regulations on development and spatial planning were based on the social planning system with complete planning of the social and economic development, mainly through the rules for planning development of activities in the space and protection of the public property.

1298. In spite of long-standing and significant tradition of spatial planning, the system for planning, adopting and implementing the plans has shown numerous limitations. Important element in spatial development of Montenegro is extensive illegal construction and inadequate land usage, creating great obstacles to sustainable development.[1367]

1299. The main characteristics of the spatial development system are the following:

- secondary legislation (supplementary regulations) for realization and supervision over the Law implementation is not completed and particularly inter-sector harmonization is lacking;
- the relation between development and normative contents of spatial and urban planning documents is insufficiently determined;
- there are often and long-lasting changes in municipal spatial plans and general urban plans;
- the criteria and indicators for monitoring of spatial conditions and changes, as well as criteria for the monitoring and evaluation of the legal and planning provisions realization are missing;
- the supervision of the plans' realization is insufficient, and the inspection services practice is inefficient; and
- indirect instruments for more efficient spatial development are missing.[1368]

1367. GMNE (2008C), 17. *See also* GMNE (2007d), 17, GMNE (2007C), 44–46, UNECE (2007), 76–79.
1368. GMNE (2008C), 29–30.

§2. STRATEGIC DOCUMENTS

I. Spatial Plan of Montenegro[1369]

1300. Pursuant to Article 15, paragraphs 1–3 of the Law on spatial development and construction of buildings (OJ MNE, Nos 64/17, 44/18, 63/18, 11/19-corr, 82/20), types of planning documents are (1) spatial plan of Montenegro; (2) Montenegro's general regulation plan. The adoption of the Spatial Plan of Montenegro and the general regulation plan of Montenegro is mandatory. The Spatial Plan of Montenegro and the General Regulatory Plan of Montenegro are passed by the Parliament of Montenegro (hereinafter 'Assembly').[1370]

II. Spatial Plan for Special-Purpose Coastal Zone

1301. Spatial plan of the Coastal Zone of Montenegro[1371] covers the local seawater (about 2,540 km^2); overall coast length is about 310 km as well as a narrow part of mainland defined according to the Law on the Coastal Zone (surface of about 58 km^2). Even though the Plan is formally made only for the previously mentioned area, all the previous analyses have shown that mainland of the coastal zone defined by the Law is not relevant enough for research and development of this type of plan document. A proposal for the new Spatial Plan of Special Purpose for the Coastal Area was drafted.[1372]

§3. COMPETENCIES

1302. By virtue of Article 12 of the Decree on state administration organization and operations (OJ MNE, Nos 49/22, 52/22, 56/22, 82/22) Ministry of Ecology, Spatial Planning and Urbanism shall conduct administrative activities with regard to, *inter alia*, strategic planning of space and environment; state plan documents; approvals of the local plans documents; sea good; plans for temporary objects in the area of the sea good and national parks; documentation bases for the space for the

1369. Adopted in 2008. by the Parliament of Montenegro (OJMNE, No. 24/08). *See*: https://www.gov.me/dokumenta/c53c7c1d-1c2c-4c4d-b29c-9bd4aabce2b6 (3 Dec. 2022). The Pprogram task for creating the Spatial Plan of Montenegro until 2040 was published on 22 Nov. 2019. *See:* https://www.gov.me/en/documents/0c22a56c-7d81-45cb-b28f-c934f89514f1 (11 Dec. 2022).

1370. The Spatial Plan of Montenegro is a strategic document and the general basis for organization and regulation of the territory of Montenegro, which determines state objectives and measures of spatial development, in accordance with the overall economic, social, ecological and cultural–historical development of Montenegro (Art. 16).

1371. Republic Montenegro initiated in June 1998 development of the Spatial Plan for the special-purpose area in the Coastal Zone of Montenegro, aiming to create a strategic document for organization and planning of this area. Also, the purpose was to obtain instructions for concrete actions through segregation of functions and zones for individual purposes as well as for joint standards of use. *See*: GMNE (2007D), 8.

1372. *See*: *Programme for space planning for 2017*, Government of Montenegro, 27 Apr. 2017.

purpose of monitoring the situation in the space and drafting of planning documents; reports on the state of space arrangement; creating a space planning programme; establishment and management of information space system in cooperation with the state administration body responsible for information society; urban technical conditions; permits for building and use; approvals and technical conditions for objects of temporary character; licences to carry out the activities of drawing up planning documents, producing technical documentation and building objects; and development and strategic policies in the field of civil engineering.

§4. LEGISLATION ON SPATIAL ORGANIZATION AND CONSTRUCTION

I. Environmental Legislation

1303. Since spatial planning is one very complex activity several regulations contain provisions relevant to spatial planning. Some regulations in the field of environment contain provisions that are directly related to the planning. Apart from the Law on Environment, several other sources of environmental law and legislation in other fields should be kept in mind (Law on EIA, Law on SEA, Law on nature protection, Law on self-government, etc.).

1304. According to Article 38 of the Law on Environment (OJ MNE, Nos 52/16, 73/19), instruments for environmental protection are, *inter alia*: spatial plans harmonized with the sustainable development and environmental protection documents (Article 38, point 9). In addition, information system of environmental protection contains data and information on the state of the environment, charges and impacts on the environment, and information on, *inter alia*: natural and spatial characteristics (Article 63, point 3).

II. Law on Spatial Development and Construction of Buildings

1305. The basic legal act regulating spatial development and construction of buildings in Montenegro is the Law on Spatial Development and Construction of Buildings (OJ MNE, Nos 64/17, 44/2018, 63/2018, 11/2019, 82/2020).[1373] It has the following fourteen parts: Part I – General Provisions (Articles 1–6), Part II – Space planning (Articles 7–56), Part III – Development of construction land (Articles 57–66), Part IV – Construction of buildings (Articles 67–111), Part V – Removing of buildings (Articles 112–114), Part VI – Temporary and auxiliary facilities (Articles 115–120), Part VII – Performing of activity (Articles 121–134), Part VIII – Licences (Articles 135–141), Part IX – Engineers Chamber of Montenegro

1373. As of the day of entry into force of the present Law, the Law on Regularisation of Informal Structures (OJ MNE, Nos 56/16, 13/17 and 47/17) and the Law on Spatial Development and Construction of Structures (OJ MNE, Nos 51/08, 34/11, 35/13 and 33/14) shall be repealed, except for the provisions of Arts 7, 16, 63, 64, 65, 67,67a and 162c which shall apply until the adoption of the General Regulation Plan of Montenegro (Art. 244).

(Articles 142–151), Part X – Legalization of illegal buildings (Articles 152–171), Part XI – Safe engineering facilities (Articles 172–195), Part XII – Supervision (Articles 196–202), Part XIII – Penalties (Articles 203–211) and Part XIV – Transitory and final provisions (Articles 212–245).[1374]

1306. The 'environment' is explicitly mentioned in several of the following articles of the law: Article 3 point 4 (Principles), Article 5 points 1, 16, and 27 (meaning of the notions), Article 16 (Spatial Plan of Montenegro), Article 17 (Plan of General Regulation of Montenegro), Article 55 (Content of urban-technical conditions), Article 68 (Basic Requirements for the Object), Article 100 (Obligation to Perform Professional Supervision), Article 109 (Contents of the object maintenance study) and Article 116 (Temporary objects programme).

A. *Principles*

1307. According to Article 3 of the Law, spatial development has to be based on, *inter alia*, the principles of: integral approach to the planning process; spatial sustainability of development and quality of planning and construction; alignment of planning documents with ratified international treaties, statements and conventions; horizontal integration;[1375] vertical integration; preventing or mitigating the impact of climate change; achieving and protection of the public and individual interests; reduction of seismic risk; public nature of work; and the prohibition of discrimination.

B. *Development and Adoption of Planning Documents*

1308. As already mentioned the planning documents are (1) spatial plan of Montenegro and (2) general regulation plan of Montenegro (Article 15).

1374. The objectives of planning and construction shall be, *inter alia*, (1) uniform and regionally balanced spatial development adjusted to the needs of society, economy and spatial capacities; (2) rational and efficient use and conservation of spatial potentials and resources on land, at sea and in the undersea and protection of natural resources; (3) developing regional spatial characteristics and preserving the identity and recognizability of the terrain; (4) mutually aligned distribution of various human activities and activities in space, while protecting the integral values of space; (5) protection and promotion of cultural property and protected environment while preserving the integrity and authenticity of cultural values, creating conditions for sustainable use of cultural property and creating a highly valuable built environment with respect for and development of specific characteristics, integrity and values of both the natural and urban terrain and the environment, etc (Art. 2).

1375. According to which, when developing, adopting and implementing development documents (strategies, plans, programmes, etc.), regulations and other general acts which affect the spatial development and space utilization, and which are adopted on the basis of separate regulations, the principles of planning must be respected, especially in terms of ensuring spatial sustainability in processes that affect the planning of settlements, use of natural resources, environmental protection, development of activities, infrastructure and their distribution in space (Art. 3, point 4).

1309. The affairs related to the development and adoption of the planning document shall be performed by the Ministry (Article 21, paragraph 1).[1376] The concept of the planning document shall be prepared by the Ministry after obtaining the opinion of the planning document reviewer (paragraph 3).[1377]

1310. Development of the spatial document shall be initiated on the basis of a decision to develop a planning document (hereinafter referred to as the 'decision to develop') adopted by the Government (Article 24, paragraph 1).[1378] Funds for developing the planning document shall be provided from the budget of Montenegro (Article 44).

1311. After the decision to develop has been issued and planning document concept developed, the Ministry shall organize information provision to the interested public regarding the objectives and purpose of developing the planning document, possible planning document designed solutions and effects of planning (hereinafter referred to as the 'prior public participation'). The Ministry shall publish the notification on prior public participation on the website and in one daily print media outlet which is issued and distributed in the territory of Montenegro (Article 27, paragraphs 1 and 2).[1379] Before review, the Ministry shall submit draft planning document to the local self-government unit and the body in charge of technical specifications, for the purpose of obtaining their opinions (Article 28).

1312. In the process of planning document development, review of the planning documents shall be mandatory (Article 29, paragraph 1). Review of the planning document shall be carried out by the Review Council (Article 30).

1313. The rules for a public hearing are prescribed in Articles 33–35 of the Law. The public debate set out in Article 32 of the present Law shall be announced in one daily print media outlet published and distributed in the territory of Montenegro and on the website of the Ministry and it shall last for a minimum term of thirty working days as of the date of announcement. The Ministry shall submit a separate notification about the public debate to the local self-government unit and body in charge of technical specifications, within two days of the date of announcing the

1376. The affairs set out in para. 1 of this Article, shall, in particular be deemed to be: preparing decisions to develop the planning document and design brief; provision of baseline studies, base maps and other documents necessary to develop the planning document; obtaining guidelines and specifications in accordance with the law governing environmental protection; organization of the planning document's development; drafting the planning document concept; implementation of the previous public participation process; planning document development; conducting public debates; preparing decisions on the planning document adoption; other affairs concerning the planning document's development and adoption (para. 2).

1377. The methodology for drafting the planning document shall be prescribed by the Ministry (para. 4).

1378. The decision to develop shall be published in the Official Journal of Montenegro. The Ministry shall publish the decision to develop on the website within seven days following that of its publication in the Official Journal of Montenegro (Art. 24, paras 9, and 10).

1379. More detailed manner of organization of prior public participation shall be prescribed by the Ministry (para. 7).

public debate in one daily print media outlet published and distributed in the territory of Montenegro (Article 33, paragraphs 1 and 2).[1380]

C. Construction of Structures

1314. The basic requirements for structures are the requirements that the structure, depending on its designated use, must fulfil during building and utilization, and which ensure its overall safety and the safety of each of its separate parts (Article 68, paragraph 1).[1381] The basic requirements for structures set out in paragraph 1 of this Article shall be, *inter alia*, following: (3) hygiene, human health and environmental protection which imply that the structure must be designed and built in such a way that it will not be a threat to hygiene or health and safety of workers, occupants or neighbours, nor cause the allowed *environmental or climate impact* limit values to be exceeded during their construction, use and demolition, or during their service time, in particular as a result of any of the following: (a) the giving-off of toxic gas; (b) emissions of dangerous substances, volatile organic compounds (VOC), greenhouse gases or dangerous particles into indoor or outdoor air; (c) emission of dangerous radiation; (d) the release of dangerous substances into groundwater, marine waters, surface waters or soil; (e) release of dangerous substances into drinking water or substances which have an otherwise negative impact on drinking water; (f) faulty discharge of waste water, emission of flue gases or faulty disposal of solid or liquid waste; (g) dampness in parts of the structure or on surfaces within the structure; (h) presence of radioactive gas radon within the structure; (5) protection against noise, which implies that structures must be designed and built in such a way that noise perceived by the occupants or neighbours is kept to a level that will not threaten their health and will allow them to sleep, rest and work in satisfactory conditions; (6) energy economy and heat retention; (7) sustainable use of natural resources, etc.

1315. Designs and studies of cultural property protection, landscape architecture, EIA, fire protection, thermal and sound insulation of the structure, energy efficiency, interior design, etc., shall be developed during the development of designs set out in Article 77 paragraph 5[1382] and Article 78 paragraph 3 of the present

1380. The Ministry shall prepare a proposed planning document on the basis of the public debate report (Art. 36).

1381. Construction of structures means a set of actions that include engineering documents development, engineering documents review, building of structures, performance of engineering supervision over the building of structures and creation of conditions for utilization of structures. Structure building means execution of works (preliminary works, works on building structures, fitting works, works on installation of construction products, installation of plant and equipment and other works) for the purpose of building a new structure, structure reconstruction or with a view to changing the status of space (Art. 67).

1382. The preliminary design, depending on the type and designated use of the structure, may comprise: (1) architectural design, (2) construction design, (3) electrotechnical design and (4) mechanical design (Art. 77, para. 5).

Law[1383] or after their development, in accordance with the present Law and separate regulations (Article 80, paragraph 2).

1316. During the execution of works, engineering supervisor shall make sure, *inter alia*, that the contractor: (1) is executing works in accordance with the reviewed final design; (2) is marking boundary and building lines, elevation points of the structure and terrain alignment, in compliance with the reviewed final design; (3) has a copy of the final design at the building site, in analogue form, stamped by the design engineer and responsible reviewer, bearing a stamp including the number, date and signature and a seal on each sheet of the final design; (4) is organizing the building site in a manner which ensures access to the location, unimpeded traffic and *protection of the environment* during the building;. . . (6) is ensuring the safety of the structure, health and safety at work of employed persons and *protection of the environment* (adjacent structures and infrastructure), etc. (Article 95, paragraph 1).

1317. Should the contractor notice deficiencies in the reviewed final design, which do not affect the change of horizontal and vertical dimensions of the structure, nor change in the faÇade of the structure, it cautions warning in writing the engineering supervisor thereof, within one day of the date of noticing the deficiencies (Article 97, paragraph 1). Should the deficiencies set out in paragraph 1 of this Article pose a threat to the lives and health of people, safety of the structure, *environment*, traffic and/or adjacent structures, the contractor shall suspend the execution of works as per the order of the engineering supervisor (paragraph 6).

1318. During the structure building, the employer shall provide for the performance of engineering supervision (Article 100, paragraph 1).[1384] Prior to drawing up the final report, the engineering supervisor shall notify the administrative authority competent for cultural property protection in case of building on or in the immediate environment of a structure which is a protected cultural property, which shall in turn determine if the structure has been constructed in compliance with the reviewed final design, i.e., the as-built design (Article 102, paragraph 6).[1385]

1319. Depending on the soil and structure features, the final engineering supervision report may include an obligation of the employer to carry out adequate observations of the soil and structure behaviour and of the impact of the structure on the

1383. The final design, depending on the type and designated use of the structure, may comprise: (1) architectural design, (2) construction design, (3) electrotechnical design and (4) mechanical design (Art. 78, para. 3).

1384. The supervision set out in para. 1 of this Article shall include *inter alia*, control of undertaking of environmental protection measures (Art. 100, para. 3).

1385. According to the Art. 206 (para. 1, point 15) legal entities shall be punished for a misdemeanour with a fine ranging from EUR 5,000 to EUR 40,000, if they: prior to drawing up the final report, fail to notify the administrative authority competent for cultural property protection in case of building on or in the immediate environment of a structure which is a protected cultural property, which shall in turn determine if the structure has been constructed in compliance with the reviewed final design, i.e., the as-built design (Art. 102 para. 6).

environment within the specified time limit and to inform the competent inspection authority of the results of such observations and measures undertaken (Article 106).[1386]

1320. Structure maintenance shall be conducted based on a structure maintenance study (Article 108, paragraph 2). The structure maintenance study shall specifically determine the taking of measures necessary for preservation of structure stability, *environmental protection*, fire protection, and energy efficiency of the structure as well as other measures necessary for the use of the structure (Article 109, paragraph 1).

D. *Removal of Structures*

1321. The study of structure removal or part of structure removal shall serve to technically elaborate the designed solutions, that is, the procedure and manner of removal of structure and items in the structure, to resolve in advance the disconnection of the structure from the energy and/or other infrastructure and safety measures (Article 114, paragraph 1).[1387] The study of structure removal or part of structure removal shall include, *inter alia*: (1) drawings, estimates and/or other engineering evidence that the removal will not lead to the loss of stability of the structure which would pose a threat to the lives and health of people or the *environment*, etc (paragraph 2).

E. *Temporary and Auxiliary Structures*

1322. Temporary structures may not be erected or built if their erection or building impairs utility operations, poses a threat to the traffic and green areas, impairs the integrity of cultural property with protected environment, threatens the environment, and at the locations in the immediate vicinity of primary hospitality facilities set forth in the Temporary Structures Programme (hereinafter referred to as the 'Programme'), regardless of the structure category, unless they operate as primary hospitality facilities (Article 115, paragraph 2).[1388]

1323. Temporary structures shall be erected or built in accordance with the Programme (Article 116, paragraph 1). The programme set out in paragraph 1 of this

---

1386. The manner and procedure of observing soil and structure behaviour during building and utilization shall be laid down by the Ministry (para. 2).
1387. The removal of structure shall be conducted on the basis of the study of removal (Art. 112, para. 3).
1388. Temporary structures shall be structures whose erection or building is not defined by a planning document (Art. 115, para. 1).

Article shall contain in particular: zones and guidelines with the zoning specifications for erecting temporary structures, and the types, form and dimensions of temporary structures (paragraph 2).[1389]

F. Complex Engineering Structures

1324. In addition to the activities set out in Article 67 of the present Law, construction of a complex engineering structure[1390] shall include the execution of investigative actions, installation and testing of built-in equipment, and testing and commissioning of the structure (Article 173).

1325. A building permit for the building of a complex engineering structure shall be issued by the Ministry (Article 181, paragraph 1). A building permit shall be issued within thirty days of the date of submission of the application (paragraph 7). Notwithstanding paragraph 7 of this Article, building permit for a complex engineering structure for which an *EIA study* is required shall be issued within sixty days from the date of submission of the application (paragraph 8).

1326. An employer may start preliminary works for building of a complex engineering structure after the issuance of a building permit (Article 185, paragraph 1). Notwithstanding paragraph 1 of this Article, preliminary works on the building of a complex engineering structure may also be initiated on the basis of the approval of the Government, provided that the employer provided the evidence set out in Article 183, paragraph 2, item 6 of the present Law,[1391] as well as evidence of acceptability of building in terms of *environmental impact* (conducted decision-making process on the need to assess impact, i.e., approval granting procedure for the impact assessment study, in accordance with separate regulations) (paragraph 2).

1389. The Programme shall be adopted by the local self-government unit for a five-year period, based on the previously obtained approval of the Ministry and the state administration body competent for cultural property protection and *environmental protection* (Art. 116, para. 3). Notwithstanding para. 3 of this Article, for maritime domain areas or national park, the Programme shall be adopted by the Ministry, after obtaining the opinion of the local self-government unit, state administration bodies responsible for cultural property protection and *environmental protection* (para. 4).

1390. Complex engineering structures, within the meaning of the present Law, shall be, *inter alia*, highways, fast roads, main roads, regional roads, tunnels longer than 200 m, bridges with a span exceeding 30 m, railway lines, airports, long-distance transmission lines and substations of voltage level of 10 kV and more, cable underground installations of a voltage level of 10 kV and above, power plants of 1 MVA and above (hydropower plants, thermal power plants, wind power plants, solar power plants, etc.), dams and reservoirs filled with tailings or ashes which require technical monitoring, liquefied natural gas storage and transfer plants, liquefied petroleum gas storage and transfer plants, structures producing and storing hazardous substances and similar structures and plants whose operations might expose *environment* to danger, buildings and plants for chemical and heavy industry, landfills, waste-to-energy plants, anaerobic digestion plants, water treatment plants, etc. (Art. 172).

1391. Evidence of ownership right over land or another right to build on land (property deed, concession contract, decision identifying public interest, etc.), or evidence of ownership right over the structure or another right to build, in cases of structure reconstruction (Art. 183, para. 2, point 6).

III. Law on Territorial Organization

1327. On 2 November 2011, Parliament of Montenegro adopted Law on territorial organization of Montenegro (OJ MNE, Nos 54/11, 26/12, 27/13, 62/13, 12/14, 3/16, 31/17, 86/18 – CC, 3/20, and 92/22). It has the following five parts: Part I – Basic Provisions (Articles 1–3), Part II – Territorial organization (Articles 4–14), Part III – Establishment, termination and change of the municipality territory (Articles 15–37a), Part IV – The Creation of Conditions for the Start of Activities of a Newly Established Municipality (Articles 38–50); Recently added subparts IVa and IVb on Supervision and Penal Provisions (Articles 50a and 50b); Part V – Transitional and final provisions (Articles 51–56).[1392]

1328. The territory of the municipality, the Major city (Podgorica) and the Capital city (Cetinje) (hereinafter referred to as 'the local government units') shall be determined by this law (Article 2).[1393]

A. *Territorial Organization*

1329. The territory of the local government unit consists of settlements[1394] (Article 4). The boundaries of local government units are bordered by settlement boundaries (Article 8, paragraph 1). The name of the settlement, the street and the square is determined by self-government unit, having obtained prior opinion of local communities at which territory is the settlement, street or square (Article 10, paragraph 1).

B. *Establishment, Termination and Change of the Territory of Municipality*

1330. The new municipality may be established in a territory representing natural and geographical units, as well as economically integrated space with municipality centre as a gravitational centre of the municipality (Article 15). The establishment of the municipality, termination and territory changes of the municipality (hereinafter referred to as 'territorial changes') is done by: (1) merging two or more municipalities in the new municipality; (2) dividing a municipality into two or more new municipalities; (3) the acquisition of part of one municipality to another; (4) combining parts of two or more municipalities in the new municipality; (5) the abolition of the municipality and the annexation of its territory to one or

1392. According to Art. 1, this Law regulates territorial organization of Montenegro, conditions, manner and procedure of territorial organization and other issues of importance for the territorial organization.
1393. The territory of local government units and the municipality name may be changed in accordance with this Law (Art. 31).
1394. The settlement is part of a local government territory unit that has built facilities for housing or economic activities, basic utilities infrastructure and other facilities to meet the needs of local people and economy (Art. 9, para. 1). Border areas of settlements shall be determined by decision of the local government unit assembly, in accordance with this Law (Art. 9, para. 2).

more municipalities; (6) separation of part of the municipality in the new municipality; and (7) separating the urban municipality in the new municipality (Article 16, paragraph 1)[1395]

§5. Harmonization with EU Legislation

1331. It is believed that new Law on spatial development and building construction (OJ MNE, Nos 64/17, 44/18, 63/18, 11/19-corr, 82/20, 86/22) has been harmonized with relevant EU legislation, that is, with 305/2011/EU CPR – Regulation on construction products, and with the Directive on services in the internal market 2006/123/EC.[1396]

1332. There are 'widespread illegal constructions and inadequate use of land as a threat to tourism development, and ultimately as obstacles to sustainable development. The spatial protection inspection within the Administration for Inspection Affairs is carrying out checks regarding this issue; for example, it made 3,656 visits in 2013. The spatial protection inspection also mentions the lack of capacity at the local level'.[1397] Although, legislative reforms, like the Law on spatial planning and construction of buildings, adopted in October 2017, were expected to improve the issuing of construction permits and the regulation of existing illegal constructions, implementation of the law is delayed by a number of factors.[1398] The overall impact of anti-corruption measures in particularly vulnerable areas (spatial planning, public procurement, privatization, healthcare and education) still has yet to be demonstrated by tangible results.[1399]

1333. Generally, 'there was no major progress in the implementation of NSSD 2030's measures related to spatial management and construction.' The coastal area, 'and especially valuable coastal ecosystems, remain exposed to significant pressures from the construction industry.'[1400]

1395. Territorial changes are done to encourage economic development of certain areas, providing a higher level of service, as well as efficiently performing of activities in order to meet the needs of local residents and legal entities in the area of the municipality (Art. 18, para. 1). Territorial changes must not endanger neither the economic development of an area, nor capacity of the municipality to successfully carry out their functions (Art. 18, para. 2).

1396. *See* the assessments in the explanations of the Proposal of the new Law on spatial planning and construction of buildings, https://www.gov.me/dokumenta/e8ef1532-febc-4824-8f82-91ea85e7b326 (3 Dec. 2022), p. 88.

1397. UNECE (2015), 148.

1398. EC (2019), 47. It includes the shortage of municipal architects to perform inspections, resulting in delays in processing some of the 50,000 requests to regularise informal constructions. In addition, the cost of construction permits remains high and the time taken to issue the permits has increased since the new law came into force.

1399. EC (2020), 29.

1400. GMNE (2022d), 75.

Part IV. Liability Questions

Chapter 1. Civil Liability

§1. International Treaties

1334. Through the succession procedure, Montenegro has become a party to the Vienna Convention on Civil Liability for Nuclear Damage (1963).[1401] Montenegro acceded to the Protocol to Amend the Vienna Convention on Civil Liability for Nuclear Damage, and the Convention on Supplementary Compensation for Nuclear Damage (1997). Montenegro did not ratify Convention on Civil Liability for Damage Resulting from Activities Dangerous to the Environment (Lugano, 1993).[1402]

§2. National Legislation

I. Law on Obligation Relationships

1335. The Law on obligation relationships (OJ MNE, Nos 47/2008, 4/2011, 22/2017)[1403] succeeds the system of the previous law of former Yugoslavia (OJ SFRY, Nos 29/78, 39/85, 45/89, 57/89, OJ SRY, Nos 31/93, 22/99, 23/99, 35/99 and 44/99) containing two basic parts. The first one establishes basic principles and regulates obligations relating to contracts, damage, acquisition without basis, unilateral declaration of will and other legal facts (general part). The second part deals with individual contracts and banking transactions (special section).[1404]

1336. The basic principle of liability is, according to Article 148, that everyone who causes harm to another is obliged to compensate it if he/she does not prove that

1401. *See*: https://www.iaea.org/resources/legal/country-factsheets (16 Jan. 2023); In addition, Montenegro is contracting party of the Civil Law Convention on Corruption (Strasbourg, 1999); *See*: http://conventions.coe.int/Treaty/Commun/ChercheSig.asp?NT=174&CM=8&DF=4/27/2009&CL=ENG (16 Jan. 2023).
1402. *See*: http://conventions.coe.int/Treaty/Commun/ChercheSig.asp?NT=150&CM=8&DF=4/27/2009&CL=ENG (16 Jan. 2023).
1403. *See* Art. 36 of the Law – 4/11-1.
1404. Although the Law contains formulations from the former federal law, it also introduces a few new institutes that have not existed in the old Law on Obligations relationships. New elements in Law on obligation relationships relate, *inter alia*, to the following issues: liability for damage from animals, liability for damage from buildings, liability of producers, etc.

the damage occurred without his/her guilt. For environmental damage, caused by the things or activities from which comes the increased risk, the liability exists regardless of guilt.[1405]

1337. It is important to mention that when the issue of liability for damage to the environment is concerned, Article 150 of the Law prescribes following:

(1) Everybody can claim from other persons to remove the source of danger which could cause more considerable damage to the claimant or indefinite number of other persons, as well as to abstinence from activities which causes disturbance or danger from damage if the disturbance or damage cannot be prevented by adequate measures.
(2) The Court, reacting to the claim of interested person, will order undertaking adequate measures for preventing the damage or disturbance, or to remove the source of danger. This will be done at the expense of the owner of the source of danger if he/she himself/herself does not do it.
(3) If the damage is caused in the course of activity which has general interest which is authorized by competent authority, only compensation for damage which surpasses normal thresholds could be demanded.
(4) But, even in that case it is possible to demand undertaking of socially acceptable measures for prevention of the damage or its minimizing.

1338. Rules on liability for damage caused by dangerous goods[1406] or dangerous activities[1407] are contained in Articles 167–172. Article 169 prescribes that for damage from dangerous goods their owner is liable, and for damage caused by hazardous activities the person who is doing them is liable.[1408]

II. Law on Ownership Rights

1339. Another important legal act to be mentioned is the Law on ownership rights (OJ MNE, No. 19/09).

1340. Its Article 9 prescribes following:

> the owner of property must not exercise his ownership rights outside the limit prescribed for all owners of such properties by this or a separate law, for a purpose of protecting the interests and the safety of the state, nature, environment and health of people. If the owner of property is subject to limitation for the

1405. For damages, regardless of guilt, one will be liable in the other cases prescribed by law, too (Art. 148, para. 3).
1406. According to Art. 167, para. 1, dangerous goods are considered to be movable or immovable things, whose position, way of use, characteristics or existence represent higher level of risk of damage to the environment.
1407. Dangerous activities are activities that represent increasing risk of damage to the environment (Art. 167, para. 2).
1408. General rules for the exception from liability are governed by Art. 172 of the Law.

purpose of protecting interests and safety of the state, nature, environment and health of people, which required that he, but not other owners of such property, suffers of greater damage, he shall be entitled to compensation as in the case of expropriation (para 2 and 3).

1341. Pursuant to Article 20 goods of general interest shall enjoy special attention (natural resources, goods in general use, cultural goods, coastal commons, national parks and other goods of general interest) in accordance with the law (paragraph 1). Goods of general interest such as construction land, agricultural land, forest and forest land, protected parts of nature, in exceptional cases coastal commons, flora and fauna, property of cultural, historical and ecological importance, and other goods with such purpose, may be in private ownership and subject to other property rights (paragraph 2).[1409]

III. Environmental Legislation

1342. Several provisions of the Law on Environment (OJ MNE, No. 52/16) relate to damage to the environment (Articles 5, 7, 9, 17, 18, 22–27, 44, 54, etc.). Nevertheless, Article 6 of the Law provides that, *inter alia*, specific laws will be adopted, including new law on liability for environmental damage.

A. *Law on Environmental Liability*[1410]

1343. The specific legal act regulating environmental damage is the Law on liability for environmental damage (OJ MNE, No. 27/14), adopted on 30 June 2014 and applied until 1 July 2017. It has the following seven parts: Part I – General Provisions (Articles 1–8), Part II – Determination of damage in environment (Articles 9–15), Part III – Measures for prevention and remediation of environmental damage (Articles 16–30), Part IV – Costs for implementation of preventive measures and measures of remediation of environmental damage (Articles 31–37), Part V – Supervision (Articles 38–40), Part VI – Penalties (Article 41) and Part VII – Final provisions (Articles 42–44).[1411]

1409. Owners and holders of other property rights on goods of general interest shall be obliged to exercise their rights in accordance with the manner of use prescribed by a separate law (para. 3).

1410. The implementation of the Environmental Liability and Environmental Crime Directives 'is at an early stage due to insufficient inspection and prosecution capacities.' EC. *Montenegro 2018 Report*, Accompanying the document Communication from the Commission to the European Parliament, the Council, the European Economic and Social Committee and the Committee of the Regions 2018 Communication on EU Enlargement Policy, Strasbourg, 17.4.2018, SWD(2018) 150 final, 79.

1411. This Law regulates the manner and procedure for determining liability for environmental damage, as well as application of preventive and remedial measures in order to prevent and eliminate environmental damage (Art. 1).

1344. *Damage* is any negative change in the natural good or damage to the natural resource that arises or may arise from the performance of the activities referred to in Article 7 of this Law and other activities and which can be assessed (Article 8, paragraph 1, point 1). Damage in the environment is the damage that can be caused to protected species of plants, animals and fungi (hereinafter 'protected species')[1412] and natural habitats; waters (Article 4).

1345. Legal and natural persons who, by performing actions or activities, cause damage or imminent danger to the environment, are liable for damage and are obliged to implement measures for the prevention and remedy of damages in accordance with this Law (Article 2).[1413]

1346. This Law applies to damage and imminent danger to environmental damage caused by the activities or activities referred to in Article 7 of this Law; damage and imminent threat of damage to protected species and natural habitats caused by the performance of other activities, or activities that are not activities referred to in Article 7 of this Law, which resulted from violation of Laws or professional standards, internal rules of business or gross negligence of the operator; damage and imminent danger of damage caused by diffuse pollution, provided that it is possible to identify an operator who caused damage or imminent danger to his activity (Article 5, paragraph 1).[1414]

1347. Actions and activities that pose a risk to human health and/or the environment are: (1) management of plants for which, in accordance to the Law, an integrated permit is issued, with the exception of plants or parts thereof intended for the research, development and testing of new products and processes; (2) waste management, including mining waste, includes: collection, transportation, processing and disposal of waste, supervision of these procedures and subsequent maintenance of landfills for which a permit is issued or is entered in the register in accordance to the Law; (3) use of sewage sludge for agricultural purposes, from municipal waste water treatment plants, processed in the prescribed manner; (4) discharge of pollutants into surface and groundwater and management of water facilities for water use (water intakes, reservoirs, etc.) for which a water consent is issued in accordance to the Law; (5) production, use, storage, inland transportation, processing, filling and discharging into the environment of dangerous substances and mixtures, as defined

1412. *Protected species* are wild species of plants, animals and fungi that are protected in accordance to the Law and confirmed international treaties (Art. 8, para. 1, point 3).

1413. Compensation for environmental damage is based on the following principles: (1) *the polluter pays principle* – legal and natural person who caused damage in the environment or imminent danger of damage must compensate for the implementation of preventive measures and remedial measures at his own expense; (2) *the principle of compulsory insurance* – legal and natural person performing the activities that pose a risk to human health and/or the environment, shall be obliged to ensure liability for damage to the environment (Art. 3).

1414. Legal entities and individuals cannot exercise the right to financial compensation for damage caused or imminent danger to environmental damage in accordance to this Law (Art. 5, para. 2).

by the Law regulating chemicals, plant protection products and biocides; (6) management of plants for which an integrated permit is issued and/or an EIA in accordance to the Law; (7) transport of dangerous goods on road, rail, sea and air traffic, on inland waterways, in accordance to the Law; (8) controlled use, including transport of GMOs and products containing, consisting of or derived from GMOs, in accordance to the Law; (9) any intentional introduction into the environment, transport and placing on the market of GMOs, in accordance to the Law; (10) cross-border movement of waste for which a permit is issued in accordance to the Law; (11) management of geological storage facilities for coal (IV)-oxide; and (12) exploration and production of hydrocarbons at sea, including installations and infrastructure (Article 7, paragraph 1).[1415]

B. Determination of Environmental Damage

1348. Damage in the environment or imminent danger of damage is determined by the administrative authority responsible for environmental protection (hereinafter 'administrative body'). The procedure for determining damage in the environment or imminent danger of damage shall be initiated ex officio or at the request of the interested public[1416] (the request). Any person who finds out that there has been damage in the environment or that there is an imminent danger of environmental damage is obliged to notify the administrative authority and the competent inspection without delay (Article 9, paragraphs 1–3).

1349. The administrative body shall inform the applicant, the operator, the local government authority in whose territory the damage was caused or there is an imminent threat of damage, the state administration authority responsible for environmental protection (hereinafter 'the Ministry') and the competent inspection, initiating proceedings or rejecting the application with justification, within five days from the date of initiation of the procedure for determining the damage (Article 14, paragraph 1).

1350. The significance of the damage that has a negative impact on the achievement or maintenance of a favourable protection status of habitat or protected species is determined on the basis of the preservation status at the time of damage, functions and services provided by those habitats or protected species and their capacity for natural recovery. The significance of the damage shall be determined on the basis of significant negative changes in relation to the original situation (Article 15, paragraphs 1–2).

1415. The operator performing the actions or activities referred to in Art. 7 of this Law shall be obliged to ensure liability for damage and immediate danger from environmental damage in accordance to this Law and the Law regulating the insurance or securing another financial security instrument (Art. 34, para. 1).

1416. *Public concerned* is a public affected by the damage or is likely to be affected by the damage, including non-governmental organizations dealing with environmental protection (Art. 8, para. 1, point 16).

C. Measures for Preventing and Remedying Environmental Damage

1351. If there is an imminent threat of damage to the environment, the operator is obliged, without delay, to implement the measures set forth in the plans for protection and rescue, in accordance with the Law on protection and rescue (Article 16, paragraph 1).[1417]

1352. When an environmental damage occurs, the operator is obliged, without delay, to notify the administrative body and the competent inspect and take the necessary remedial measures in order to limit and prevent further spread of environmental damage and negative impacts on human health. Remedial measures are measures aimed at restoring to the original state of damaged water, land, protected species and natural habitats by applying primary, complementary and compensatory remediation (Article 17, paragraphs 1–2).

1353. The operator who caused damage to the environment is obliged, within the deadline determined by the decision on initiating the procedure for determining the damage, to draft a remedial measure and submit it to the administrative authority for approval (Article 18, paragraph 1).[1418]

1354. When the environment causes such damage that all necessary remedial measures cannot be implemented at the same time, the authority determines the priorities for the application of remedial measures, taking into account the nature, extent and significance of damage done in different segments of the environment, the natural recovery possibilities and the risks to human health (Article 15, paragraph 5).

1355. The evaluation of the proposals for remedial measures is carried out by the Commission for the assessment of remedial measures (hereinafter 'the Commission'), established by the administrative body (Article 19, paragraph 1).[1419]

1356. The decision on the education of the Commission determines the number, composition, deadline and manner of work of the Commission. The costs for Commission work are borne by the operator (Article 19, paragraphs 4–5).[1420]

1417. In case of suspicion of immediate danger from environmental damage or in case of danger, the administrative authority is obliged to ask the operator the necessary information and implementation of the necessary preventive measures (Art. 16, para. 4).
1418. The proposal for remedial measures shall also include the monitoring programme the state of the environment after implementation of the remedial measures (Art. 18, para. 2).
1419. The Commission consists of experts in certain environmental areas, representatives of administrative bodies and the Ministry and representatives of relevant environmental institutions, as well as representatives of other competent administrative bodies. The Commission assesses the proposed remedial measures, gives its opinion and proposes new remedial measures if the proposed remedial measures do not achieve recovery in the original situation (Art. 19, paras 2, and 3).
1420. The administrative body decides to give consent on the proposal of the remedial measures within a period of five days from submission of the Commission's opinion (Art. 20, para. 1).

1357. Remedial measures can be primary, complementary and compensatory. Primary remediation measures[1421] are measures to eliminate damage that restores the damaged natural resource[1422] or its function to its original state (Article 21, paragraphs 1 and 2). Complementary remedial measures are measures that are implemented in cases where the damaged natural resource and/or services cannot fully restore the primary remediation to the primary remediation, in order to provide similar natural resources and/or services in the same or other areas. Compensatory remedial measures are measures that are being implemented to compensate for losses caused by damage to natural resources that can no longer perform their ecological functions or provide services to other natural resources or the public (Article 21, paragraphs 3, and 4).

1358. Land remediation measures include measures to ensure the control, restriction, reduction or elimination of all relevant pollution, so that contaminated land does not pose a significant risk to human health, taking into consideration its current or planned purpose (Article 27, paragraph 1).[1423]

1359. If the operator does not implement the determined remedial measures, the measures are implemented by the administrative body at the expense of the operator (Article 28, paragraph 1).[1424]

1360. In urgent cases, the operator is obliged, without delay, to carry out preventive measures and remedial measures, for the purpose of preventing or eliminating damage to the environment (Article 30, paragraph 1).[1425]

1361. Costs for implementation of preventive measures and measures for remediation of environmental damage

1421. *Remedial measures* are actions and measures for the recovery, rehabilitation or replacement of damaged natural resources and/or services, including measures to mitigate the consequences of damage, provisional measures and measures, which provide resources or services equal to the original (Art. 8, para. 1, point 15).
1422. *Natural resources* are parts of a nature that a person uses for economic purposes. They can be non-renewable and renewable, including protected species, natural habitats, water and water resources and land (Art. 8, para. 1, point 8).
1423. Determining the risk for human health is done based on the characteristics and purpose of the soil, the nature and concentration of the harmful substances, mixtures, organisms or microorganisms it is contaminated, as well as the possibilities for their spread and the danger they pose. Land use is determined on the basis of spatial planning documents (Art. 27, paras 2–3).
1424. Remedial measures are implemented by the administration body, as well as in case the operator is not known (Art. 28, para. 2).
1425. If the operator is not able to promptly implement preventive measures and remedial measures without delay, in order to prevent or eliminate damage in the environment, an administrative body may hire an authorized person to implement these measures at the operator's expense (Art. 30, para. 2).

1362. The operator who caused damage or imminent environmental damage is obliged to bear the costs for implementing preventive measures or remedial measures in accordance with the 'polluter pays' principle (Article 31).[1426]

1363. In case of damage or immediate danger of environmental damage, which may have significant adverse effects on the environment of another country, the Ministry shall notify the other State of the damage caused and the imminent danger of environmental damage and measures to eliminate damage (Article 35, paragraph 1).[1427]

1364. Data on the implementation of preventive measures and remedial measures, data on liability insurance for damage and immediate dangers for environmental damage and data on transboundary pollution are public, except for data classified as secret in accordance with a special regulation (Article 36).

D. Supervision

1365. Supervision over the implementation of this Law shall be performed by the Ministry and other competent state administration bodies, in accordance with the Law (Article 38, paragraph 1).[1428]

E. Other Relevant Regulations

1366. Pursuant to the Law on Responsibility for Environmental Damage (OJ MNE, No. 27/14), a special rulebook has been adopted (a Rulebook on detailed requirements for personnel and equipment to be fulfilled by an authorized person for the implementation of preventive measures and remedial environmental measures (OJ MNE, No. 48/16).[1429]

1426. The law also regulates: exemption from the obligation to pay for the costs of implementing remedial measures, damage caused by several persons, compulsory insurance (Arts 32–34).
1427. In case of damage or immediate danger to environmental damage in another country, which may have significant negative effects on the environment of Montenegro, the Ministry may request all relevant information on damage or imminent threat of damage, provide recommendations for the implementation of measures to prevent or eliminate damage and ask for a reimbursement of costs (Art. 35, para. 2).
1428. Inspection supervision over the implementation of this Law and regulations adopted pursuant to this Law shall be carried out by competent inspections, in accordance with this Law and the Law regulating inspection supervision (Art. 38 para. 2).
1429. During 2022, the EPA adopted two decisions based on this law. *See*: https://epa.org.me/wp-content/uploads/2022/01/steta_u_zivotnoj_sredini_sajt.pdf (10 Jan. 2023).

Chapter 2. Criminal Liability

§1. International Treaties

1367. Montenegro is not a contracting party of the Convention on the Protection of Environment through Criminal Law (Strasbourg, 1998).[1430] Within the framework of the reform in the judiciary, priority has been given to the reform of criminal legislation and harmonization with the EU in particular. Most important treaties that have already been ratified or are expected to be ratified soon are the European Convention on Human Rights Protection; the UN Convention on Fight against Trans-national Organized Crime with supplementing protocols; the UN Convention on Fight against Corruption; Convention on Laundering, Search, Seizure and Confiscation of the Proceeds from Crime; International Convention for the Suppression of the Financing of Terrorism; Rome Statute of the International Criminal Court (ICC).[1431]

§2. National Legislation

I. Criminal Code

1368. The Criminal Code of the RM (OJ RM, Nos 70/03, 13/04, 47/06 and OJ MNE, Nos 40/08, 25/10, 32/11, 64/11, 40/13, 56/13, 14/15, 42/15, 58/15, 44/17, 49/18, 3/20, and 145/21) has 488 articles divided into two parts. General part includes following thirteen chapters: General Part: Chapter I – General Provisions (Articles 1–4), Chapter II – Criminal Offence (Articles 5–31), Chapter III – Punishments (Articles 32–51), Chapter IV – Warning Measures (Articles 52–65), Chapter V – Security Measures (Articles 66–78), Chapter VI – Provisions on Juveniles (Articles 79–111), Chapter VII – Seizure of Material Gain (Articles 112–114), Chapter VIII – Legal Consequences of Conviction (Articles 115–117), Chapter IX – Rehabilitation, Discontinuance of Legal Consequences of Conviction and Disclosure of Data from Criminal Records (Articles 118–123), Chapter X – Barring by Time Limits (Articles 124–129), Chapter XI – Amnesty and Pardon (Articles 130–132), Chapter XII – Applicability of Criminal Legislation of the RM (Articles 133–141) and Chapter XIII – Definitions of the terms (Article 142).

1369. A Special part of the Code defines groups of criminal offences[1432] including, *inter alia*: Chapter XXII – Criminal Offences against Property (Articles 239–257), Chapter XXIV – Criminal Offences against Human Health (Articles 287–302), Chapter XXV – Criminal Offences against the Environment (Articles 303–326), Chapter XXVI – Criminal Offences against General Safety of People and

1430. *See* http://conventions.coe.int/Treaty/Commun/ChercheSig.asp?NT=172&CM=8&DF=4/27/2009&CL=ENG (10 Jan. 2023).
1431. GMNE (2008b), 441.
1432. Criminal offence is a socially dangerous act that the law prescribes as a criminal offence, which is unlawful and which has been committed with guilty mind (Art. 5).

Property (Articles 327–338), Chapter XXVII – Criminal Offences against Public Traffic Safety (Articles 339–348), Chapter XXIX – Criminal Offences against Constitutional Order and Security of Montenegro and S&M (Articles 357–374) and Chapter XXXVII – Transitional and Final Provisions (Articles 486–488).

A. *Criminal Offences Against the Environment*

1370. As already mentioned, the Criminal Code in Chapter XXV defines criminal offences against the environment and spatial planning. This chapter prescribes following criminal offences: pollution of the environment (Article 303), environmental pollution by waste (Article 303a), ozone depletion (Article 303b), failure to take measures for the protection of the environment (Article 304), unlawful construction and putting into function buildings and plants which pollute the environment (Article 305), damaging of buildings and plants for the protection of the environment (Article 306), damaging the environment (Article 307), abuse of GMOs (Article 307a), destruction of plants (Article 308), killing and torturing animals (Article 309), destroying and damaging protected natural goods (Article 310), stealing protected natural good (Article 311), taking abroad protected natural goods and especially protected plants and animals (Article 312), bringing dangerous substances into Montenegro (Article 313), unlawful processing, taking away and storing of dangerous substances (Article 314), unlawful construction of nuclear plants (Article 315), non-executing the decision pertaining to environmental protection measures (Article 316), violation of the right to be informed on the state of the environment (Article 317), transmitting of contagious animal and plant diseases (Article 318), non-conscientiously rendering veterinary services (Article 319), quack veterinary assistance (Article 320), producing harmful products for treating animals (Article 321), pollution of livestock fodder and water (Article 322), devastation of forests (Article 323), forest theft (Article 324), unlawful hunt (Article 325), unlawful fishing (Article 326), construction of building without a building permit (Article 326(a)) and illegal connection of the construction site to technical infrastructure (Article 326(b)).

1371. Article 303 of the Code defines basic criminal offence ('pollution of the environment'). According to the article, everyone can commit this criminal act which includes polluting air, water and soil[1433] 'to a larger extent or in a wider area'. Maximum penalty is three years of imprisonment. If the offence is committed out of negligence, the offender shall be liable to a fine or imprisonment for a maximum term not exceeding one year.[1434] If a suspended sentence is pronounced, the court

1433. Additional condition for the existence of criminal act is the violation of regulations in the field of environmental protection and development.

1434. The Law prescribes different sanctions depending on the way of commitment of the act and scale of destruction and damage. If animal or plant life is destroyed or damaged to a larger extent or the environment is polluted to such an extent that longer period of time and larger expenditures are needed for removing harmful consequences, the offender shall be punished by an imprisonment

may order the perpetrator to take particular measures for protection, preservation and development of the environment within a specified time limit (Article 303, paragraph 5).

1372. Apart from the above-mentioned, the Criminal Code provides a number of criminal offences which could be very relevant to environmental issues. These are, for example: causing general danger (Article 327), destroying and damaging public infrastructure (Article 328), jeopardizing safety at workplace (Article 329), construction work which does not comply with regulations and standards (Article 330), damage to dams and water supply facilities (Article 331), destroying, damaging or removing danger warning signs (Article 332), abuse of telecommunication signs (Article 333), failure to remove danger (Article 334), unauthorized handling of explosive and inflammable material (Article 335), unlawful acquisition and disposing of nuclear substances (Article 336), endangering safety with nuclear substances (Article 337), grave offences against general safety (Article 338)[1435] and war crimes against civil population (Article 428).[1436]

B. Criminal Sanctions

1373. Article 4 of the Criminal Code prescribes following criminal sanctions: punishments, warning measures, security measures and educational measures. Following kinds of punishment can be imposed on the perpetrators of criminal offences: (1) a forty-year imprisonment; (2) an imprisonment; (3) a fine; and (4) a community service (Article 33). According to Article 52, warning measures are suspended sentence and judicial admonition.[1437]

II. Liability of Legal Entities for Criminal Offences

1374. As a novelty in the legal system of Montenegro criminal liability of legal entities has been introduced. The Law on responsibility of legal entities for the criminal offence (OJ RM, Nos 02/07, 13/07 and OJ MNE, Nos 73/10, 30/12, 39/16)

---

sentence of one to eight years (Art. 303, para. 3). On the other side if same act is committed out of negligence the offender shall be punished by an imprisonment sentence of six months to five years (Art. 303, para. 4).

1435. This article is part of the Ch. XXVI – Criminal Acts against General Safety of People and Property.

1436. Chapter XXXV – Criminal Offences against Humanity and Rights Guaranteed under International Law.

1437. It is prescribed by Art. 67 of the Code that the following security measures can be imposed on persons who have committed a criminal offence: (1) mandatory psychiatric treatment and custody in a medical institution; (2) mandatory psychiatric treatment at liberty; (3) mandatory medical treatment of a drug addict; (4) mandatory medical treatment of an alcoholic; (5) prohibition from practising a profession, activity or duty; (6) prohibition of driving a motor vehicle; (7) confiscation of objects; (8) expulsion of a foreigner from the country; and (9) publishing of a judgment.

is the basic law regulating this issue.[1438] The Law contains sixty-six articles and following four chapters: Chapter I – General Provisions (Articles 1–4), Chapter II – General Part (Articles 5–44), Chapter III – Procedure (Articles 45–63) and Chapter IV – Transitional and Final Provisions (Articles 64–66).

1375. It regulates the conditions for liability of legal entities[1439] for criminal offences, criminal sanctions applied against legal entities, as well as criminal procedure within which such sanctions shall be imposed (Article 1).[1440] Legal entities may be held liable for criminal offences from the special section of the Criminal Code and for other criminal offences prescribed by special law, if the conditions for liability of a legal entity prescribed by this Law have been fulfilled (Article 3).[1441]

A. *Conditions for Liability of the Legal Entity for a Criminal Offence*

1376. According to Article 5 of the Law, the legal entity is liable for a criminal offence of a responsible person[1442] who, while acting within the scope of his/her competencies in the name of the legal entity, and with intention of obtaining some benefit for that legal entity, commits a criminal offence. The legal entity is liable even if that responsible person's action was contrary to the legal entity's business policy or orders.

1377. The liability of the legal entity does not exclude criminal liability of the responsible person for the committed criminal offence although the legal entity shall be liable for a criminal offence even if the responsible person who committed the criminal offence has not been convicted for that criminal offence (Article 6).

1438. In accordance with Art. 43 this Law shall apply to a following domestic and foreign legal entity: to a domestic and foreign legal entity liable for a criminal offence committed in the territory of Montenegro; to a foreign legal entity liable for a criminal offence committed abroad to the prejudice of Montenegro, its citizen or a domestic legal entity; to a domestic legal entity liable for committing a criminal offence abroad.(*See also* Art. 138, para. 3 of the Criminal Code Official Journal of RM, Nos 70/2003, 13/2004, 47/2006 and Official Journal of MNE, No. 40/2008).

1439. The legal entity shall be a business organization, foreign company and part of a foreign company, public utility company, public institution, domestic and foreign non-government organization, investment fund, other fund (with exception of a fund exclusively performing public authorities), sports organization, political party, as well as other association or organization that within its operations regularly or occasionally gains or obtains funds and manage them (Art. 4, para. 1).

1440. The Law on business offences (Official Journal of SFRJ, Nos 4/77, 14/85, 74/87, 57/89, 3/90 and Official Journal of FRY, Nos 27/92, 24/94, 28/96 and 64/01) is repealed by this Law (Art. 65). Business offences stipulated by special laws become violations (Art. 64).

1441. Republic of Montenegro, organs of state administration and local self-government cannot be responsible for the criminal offence. Legal person who has been entrusted by law to exercise of public authority cannot be responsible for the criminal offence that has been done in the performance of those powers (Art. 2).

1442. The responsible person shall be a natural person delegated with certain activities in the legal entity, a person authorized to act in the name of the legal entity, as well as a person who may reasonably be assumed to be authorized to act in the name of the legal entity. A natural person acting in the name of the legal entity as a shareholder shall also be deemed the responsible person (Art. 4, para. 2).

1378. Article 7 prescribes that the business organization under bankruptcy may be liable for a criminal offence regardless of whether such offence has been committed before the initiation or during the bankruptcy procedure, and in such a case no penalty shall be imposed but material benefit shall be confiscated or the security measure of confiscating objects shall be applied.[1443]

B. *Sanctions That May Be Imposed on a Legal Entity*

1379. According to Article 12, following sanctions may be imposed on a legal entity for a criminal offence: penalty, suspended sentence and safety measures.[1444] The following penalties may be imposed on a legal entity: fine and termination of a legal entity (Article 13). Mentioned penalties may be imposed only as main penalties.

1380. When the suspended sentence is concerned, the Court may determine a fine up to EUR 100,000 against the legal entity, under condition that it shall not be enforced if the convicted legal entity is not liable for committing a new criminal offence in terms of Article 5 of this Law during the period of time defined by the Court, which cannot be shorter than one year or longer than three years (probation period) (Article 24, paragraph 2).[1445]

III. Misdemeanour Liability

A. *Law on Misdemeanours*

1381. The Parliament of Montenegro has enacted the new Law on misdemeanour (OJ MNE, Nos 01/11, 6/11, 39/11, 32/14, 43/17-CC, and 51/17) on 22 December 2010.[1446] The Law has the following twenty-seven parts: Chapter I –

1443. If a legal entity ceases to exist before the termination of a criminal procedure, a fine, safety measures and seizure of material benefit may be imposed on a legal entity that is its legal successor. If a legal entity ceases to exist upon the termination of a criminal procedure, by a final decision, a fine, safety measures and seizure of material benefit shall be exercised on its legal successor (Art. 8).

1444. The following safety measures may be imposed for criminal offences that legal entities are liable for: design and implementation of the programme of effective, necessary and reasonable measures, confiscation of objects, and publication of the judgment, prohibition to conduct certain business or other activities (Art. 28).

1445. Under the suspended sentence, the Court may determine that the penalty shall also be enforced if the convicted legal entity fails to restore the material benefits acquired by committing the criminal offence within specified period of time, fails to compensate for the damage it caused by committing the criminal offence or fails to meet other obligations prescribed by criminal law provisions. The deadline for meeting these obligations shall be set by the Court within the specified probation period (Art. 24, para. 3).

1446. On the day this Law enters into force, the Law on misdemeanour (Official Journal of the RM, Nos 25/94, 48/99) shall be repealed, except provisions of the Arts 71, 72, 81–93, as well as the provisions of the Arts 208–290 of the Customs Law (Official Journal of RM, Nos 7/02, 38/02, 72/02, 105/02, 21/03, 29/05, 66/06, and Official Journal of MNE, No. 21/08) (Art. 244).

Substantive legal provisions: Part I – General Provisions (Articles 1–11), Part II – The way of the misdemeanours commitment (Articles 12–14), Part III – Misdemeanour liability (Articles 15–21), Part IV – Misdemeanour sanctions (Articles 22–49), Part V – Confiscation of property gain, rehabilitation, data from the records of misdemeanour and legal consequences of conviction (Articles 50–58), Part VI – Obsolescence (Articles 59–60), Part VII – Juveniles (Articles 61–97), Chapter II – Misdemeanour proceedings: Part VIII – Basic rules (Articles 98–105), Part IX – Jurisdiction and exemptions (Articles 106–109), Part X – The subjects of misdemeanour proceedings (Articles 110–117), Part XI – Court submissions and records (Articles 118–119), Part XII – Deadlines (Articles 120–121), Part XIII – Reinstatement (Articles 122–126), Part XIV – Property and legal requirements and offence proceedings costs (Article 127), Part XV – Adoption and disclosure of the decisions (Articles 128–130), Part XVI – Submission of written and review of the documents (Articles 131–142), Part XVII – Initiating of misdemeanour charges (Articles 143–161), Part XVIII – Measures to ensure the presence of the defendant and for the smooth conducting of infringement proceedings (Articles 162–170), Part XIX – Supervision measures (Articles 171–176), Part XX – The plea agreement (Articles 177–178), Part XXI – Search (Articles 179–189), Part XXII – Court decisions (Articles 190–198), Part XXIII – The complaint (Articles 199–216), Part XXIV – The extraordinary legal remedies (Articles 217–224), Part XXV – Special procedures (Articles 225–227), Part XXVI – Sanctions executions (Articles 228–239) and Part XXVII – Transitional and final provisions (Articles 240–245).[1447]

1382. This Law regulates the conditions for prescribing misdemeanour[1448] and misdemeanour sanctions, misdemeanour liability, infringement proceedings and the enforcement of misdemeanour sanctions (Article 1, paragraph 1). Misdemeanour sanctions may be prescribed only in accordance with this Law (Article 4, paragraph 1).[1449] For the misdemeanours may be prescribed (Article 22, paragraph 1): (1) imprisonment; (2) a fine;[1450] and (3) a fine or imprisonment. For the misdemeanour of a legal person and responsible person can be prescribed only a fine (Article 22, paragraph 2).[1451]

1447. According to the Progress Monitoring Report 'this law aims at aligning with the Directive on environmental crime but further efforts will be needed to align fully this law with the *acquis*, especially as regards criminalization of specific offences, criminal penalties and sanctions other than fines.' EC (2011), 67.

1448. *The misdemeanour* is an action which constitutes a violation of public policy established by Law and is mandated by the sanctions (Art. 2, para. 1).

1449. Misdemeanour sanctions are: punishments, warning measures, protective measures and educational measures (Art. 5, para. 1).

1450. The funds collected from fines imposed for violation are revenue of the state, except for funds collected from fines for offences that violate regulations, for which application supervision is done by a local authority, representing the local government revenue (Art. 7, para. 1).

1451. The general purpose of prescribing, imposition and application of sanctions is that people respect the legal system, to express social rebuke the offender because of the breach and to influence him and any other person that in the future does not make an offence (Art. 6, para. 1).

1383. For the offence prescribed by the Montenegro Laws the offender shall be punished if the offence is committed in the territory of Montenegro, or if it is done on a domestic vessel or aircraft while it is outside the territory of Montenegro (Article 9, paragraph 1).[1452]

IV. Environmental Legislation

1384. All four basic environmental laws (horizontal legislation) prescribe penal provisions for misdemeanours committed.[1453] Article 87 of the Law on Environment (OJ MNE, No. 52/16), for example, prescribes fiscal fines ranging from EUR 2,000– EUR 40,000 for offences of legal persons and entrepreneurs.[1454] Organ of the state authority and organ of local self-government (and responsible persons in these organs) could be punished for offences prescribed by Article 28 of Law on SEA (OJ RM, No. 80/05, OJ MNE, Nos 73/10, 40/11, 59/11, 52/16) and by Article 36 of the Law on EIA (OJ MNE, No. 75/18).

1452. Misdemeanour proceedings cannot be initiated or taken against a person having diplomatic immunity (Art. 10, para. 1).

1453. It should be added that several other environmental laws contain provisions relating to the misdemeanours. *See*: for example: Art. 90–91a of the Law on Waste Management (OJ MNE, Nos 64/11, 39/16), Arts 164–166 of the Law on Waters (Official Journal of RM, No. 27/07, Official Journal of MNE, Nos 32/11, 47/11-corr, 48/15, 52/16, 2/17, 80/17,), Arts 30–31 of the Law on Environmental Noise Protection (OJ MNE, Nos 28/11, 28/12, 1/14), Arts 43–44 of the Law on Air Protection (Official Journal of MNE, Nos 25/10, 40/11, 43/15), Arts 116–120 of the Law on the Marine Fisheries and Mariculture (OJ MNE, Nos 56/9, 40/11), Arts 50–51 of the Law on the Freshwater Fisheries (Official Journal of MNE, Nos 11/07, 40/11), Art. 71 of the Law on Chemicals (OJ MNE, No. 51/17,), Arts 231–233 of the Energy Law (OJ MNE, No. 5/16), Arts 84–87 of the Law on Game and Hunting (Official Journal MNE, Nos 52/08, 40/11, 48/15), Art. 111 of the Law on Nature Protection (OJ MNE, No. 54/16, 18/19), Arts 88–90 of the Law on Forests (Official Journal of MNE, Nos 74/10, 40/11, 47/15), etc.

1454. *See also* similar provisions of the Law on Environmental Impact Assessment and Law on Industrial Emissions.

Chapter 3. Administrative Liability

1385. Rules concerning administrative liability are contained in several legal acts. Different forms of responsibility for different entities that participate in the administrative proceedings are prescribed.

§1. Law on State Administration

1386. According to Article 9 of the Law on State Administration (OJ MNE, Nos 78/18, 70/21, 50/22), the work of state administration authorities is subject to control. The control is realized through administrative and other supervision, judicial control and other forms of control, in accordance with the law.

1387. Article 8 of the Law prescribes that the Republic shall be responsible for damage caused by unlawful or inaccurate work of a state administration authority.[1455]

1388. The state administration authorities are obliged to use the resources for operation in such a way as to provide as complete an execution of their functions as possible, respecting the satisfaction of specific social needs and execution of certain tasks (Article 91). The minister shall be responsible for the lawful use of resources of state administration authorities (Article 78).

§2. Law on Civil Servants and State Employees

1389. The Law on Civil Servants and State Employees (OJ MNE, Nos 2/18, 34/19, and 8/21)[1456] has several provisions concerning liability issues. Chapter VII of the Law is devoted to the liability of the civil servants and state employees (Articles 93–120).

1390. Fifth chapter VII of the Law regulates, *inter alia*, following issues: the basis of disciplinary responsibility (Article 93), offences of official duty (Articles 94, 95), Disciplinary measures (Article 96), launching disciplinary proceedings (Article 85), disciplinary proceedings (Article 88), enforcement and deletion of disciplinary measures (Article 92), temporary suspension of duty Article 111–113), the material liability of a civil servant or an employee (Article 114–120), damage to a third person (Article 119), responsibility of the state (Article 120), etc.

1455. The affairs of state administration shall be performed by the ministries and other administrative authorities (state administration authorities). Certain affairs of state administration may be performed, as public authorities, by local self-government authorities, institutions and other legal persons, when these affairs are delegated or entrusted to them (Art. 3).

1456. This law regulates the rights, obligations, responsibilities and other issues related to the status of civil servants and state employees (Art. 1).

Part V. Juridical Actions of Individuals

Chapter 1. Introduction

1391. Montenegrin legal regulation concerning juridical actions of individuals includes several different sources of law.[1457] They are, primarily, legal acts regulating administrative procedures and judicial procedures (civil procedure, criminal procedure, procedure before Constitutional Court, enforcement proceedings, inspection, etc.). Additionally, the procedure according to the Law on PHRF and Law on Mediation should be mentioned.

1392. Juridical actions are mentioned by several provisions of the Constitution (OJ MNE, No. 1/2007). According to Article 6, rights and liberties are protected in Montenegro. They must be exercised on the basis of the Constitution and ratified international agreements (Article 17).[1458] Article 19 guarantees that every citizen has equal protection of rights and liberties. Besides that, Article 20 prescribes that everyone has the right to legal remedy against the decision concerning the right or legally based interest thereof (Article 20).[1459]

1457. Article 57 of the Constitution establishes the right to recourse to the state body. This provision guarantees that everyone has the right to recourse to state body or organization exercising public authorities, individually or collectively with others, and to receive answer. No one may be held liable, or suffer other adverse consequences as a result of views presented in the recourse, unless she/he has committed a crime thereby. Art. 56 of the Constitution also prescribes that everyone has the right to address international organization for protection of personal rights and freedoms guaranteed by the Constitution.
1458. Article 17, para. 2, prescribes that all persons are deemed equal before the law, regardless of any particularity or personal feature (Art. 17, para. 2).
1459. In accordance with Art. 21, everyone has the right to legal aid. Legal aid has to be provided by the bar, as an independent and autonomous profession, and by other services. It may be provided free of charge, in accordance with the law. Basic legal act regulating legal aid is the Law on legal aid (Official Journal of RM, No. 20/11). It has the following twelve parts: Part I – General Provisions (Arts 1–11), Part II – Eligibility for legal aid (Arts 12–19), Part III – Forms of legal aid (Arts 20–26), Part IV – Competent authority granting legal aid (Arts 27–29), Part V – Persons authorized to provide legal aid (Arts 30–33), Part VI – Procedure for granting legal aid (Arts 34–52), Part VII – Changing circumstances and unduly granted legal aid (Arts 53–55), Part VIII – Payment of costs incurred in legal aid provision (Arts 56–57), Part IX – Records (Art. 58), Part X – Legal aid in disputes involving international elements (Arts 59–62), Part XI – Supervision (Arts 63–65), Part XII – Transitional and final provision (Arts 66–67). *See also* Decree on compensation of costs in judicial proceedings (Official Journal of MNE, No. 61/10).

1393. According to Article 23, everyone has the right to receive timely and full information about the status of the environment, to influence the decision-making regarding the issues of importance for the environment, and to legal protection of these rights.[1460] Article 32 stipulates that everyone has the right to fair and public trial within a reasonable time before an independent, impartial court established by the law.[1461]

1460. Article 73 of the Law on Environment (Official Journal of MNE, No. 52/16) regulates right to legal protection in environmental issues.
1461. It should be added that everyone has the right of recourse to international organizations for the protection of rights and freedoms guaranteed by the Constitution (Art. 56).

Chapter 2. Administrative Remedies

§1. General Legislation

1394. Article 4 of the Law on State Administration (OJ MNE, Nos 78/18, 70/21, 50/22) prescribes that state administration authorities have an obligation to provide for equal protection of rights and on law-founded interests to private as well as legal persons. (Article 4 – the principle of impartiality and political neutrality). In addition, state administration authorities are obliged to decide lawfully and timely in matters within their competence (Article 5 – the principle of efficiency).[1462]

1395. According to Article 165 of the Law on Local Self-Government (OJ MNE, Nos 2/18, 34/19, 38/20, 50/22) any person has the right to lodge a civil complaint or petition to local self-government bodies, as well as request information concerning the work of these bodies (Article 165, paragraph 1).[1463] The procedure for submitting civil complaints and petitions, as well as the methods of action to be taken by the competent bodies, has to be prescribed by municipal statutes (paragraph 4), but the law enables citizens to submit a complaint or petition electronically, where possible (paragraph 3).

1396. Article 172 of the Law on Local Self-Government stipulates that local self-government bodies should provide visitors' books and boxes for remarks, suggestions and complaints of citizens, while the head of the administrative body shall meet citizens for the purpose of hearing their remarks and complaints about improper work of the body or behaviour of civil servants.[1464]

§2. The Law on the Administrative Procedure

1397. The Law on the Administrative Procedure (OJ MNE, Nos 56/2014, 20/2015, 40/2016 and 37/2017) contains 164 articles divided into following sixteen chapters: Chapter I – Basic Principles (Articles 1–17), Chapter II – Administrative activities (Articles 18–35), Chapter III – Competencies (Articles 36–50), Chapter IV – Party and its proxy (Articles 51–58), Chapter V – Communication between

1462. Deciding in administrative procedures, concerning rights and obligations of private and legal persons, comprises of: commencement and the conduct of an administrative procedure, taking measures and actions in a procedure, passing of administrative acts as to the rights and obligations of private and legal persons and their immediate enforcement (Art. 15–16). By virtue of Art. 77, Ministry, i.e., an administrative authority decides on appeals against individual acts passed by the authorities in the first instance in performing the delegated or entrusted affairs, and exercises other rights that the second instance authority has in the administrative procedure.

1463. Authorities, to whom requests have been referred to, are obliged to make a decision, that is, provide information respectively within thirty days from the date that the request was received (Art. 165, para. 3).

1464. A competent body has to provide a written reply to complaints within fifteen days from the date a complaint was submitted, if required so by the citizens (Art. 172, para. 2).

Authorities and Parties (Articles 59–69), Chapter VI – Invitation, delivery and notification (Articles 70–87), Chapter VII – Deadlines (Articles 88–90), Chapter VIII – Restitutio in Integrum (Articles 91–93), Chapter IX –Costs of the Administrative Proceedings (Articles 94–97), Chapter X – Starting, management and completion of Administrative Proceeding (Articles 98–117), Chapter XI – Legal remedies (Articles 118–138), Chapter XII – Annulment and Abrogating of the Decision (Articles 139–143), Chapter XIII – Execution (Articles 144–157), Chapter XIV – Evidence (Articles 158–159), Chapter XV – Supervision (Article 160) and Chapter XVI – Transitional and Final provisions (Articles 161–164).

1398. This Law regulates the rules that, state bodies, state administration bodies, local self-government bodies, local government bodies, institutions and other entities performing public authority (hereinafter 'public authority') are obliged to apply in order to achieve protection of the rights and legal interests of physical persons, legal entities or other parties, as well as protection of the public interest when they directly apply the regulations decide and undertake other administrative activities[1465] in administrative matters[1466] (Article 1). This Law applies in all administrative matters (Article 4, paragraph 1).

§3. Environmental Legislation

1399. Pursuant to Article 73 of the Law on Environment (OJ MNE, Nos 52/16, 73/19) the interested public in the environmental decision-making process has the right to initiate the procedure for reviewing the decision before the competent authorities or the court in accordance with the law (paragraph 1). The interested public has the right to file an appeal against the decision of the competent body for environmental protection, that is, the right to file a complaint with the competent court in accordance with special regulations (paragraph 2).

1400. Articles 14 and 24 of the Law on EIA (OJ MNE, No. 75/18) guarantee the right to appeal. Article 14 establishes the right to appeal against decision on the need for impact assessment made by the competent authority referred to in Article 5.[1467] Article 24 prescribes that the right to appeal is guaranteed against the decision from Article 11, paragraph 8 (Decision on request) and Article 17, paragraph 1 (Decision on approval) made by the competent authority referred to in Article 4. In both cases, the appeal should be submitted to the main administrator.

1465. Administrative activities include the adoption of administrative acts, the conclusion of administrative contracts, the protection of users of services of general interest, as well as taking of other administrative activities in administrative matters, in accordance with the Law (Art. 3).

1466. Administrative matter is any specific situation in which a public law body, administrative act decides or otherwise determines or otherwise influences the rights, obligations or legal interests of a natural person, legal entity or other party for the purposes of this Law, as well as any other legal a situation that is legally prescribed as an administrative matter (Art. 2).

1467. It relates to the competent authority responsible for the implementation of EIA procedure (organ of the local administration responsible for environmental protection – for other projects for which consent, approval and permits are issued by other organs of local administration).

1401. Besides the above-mentioned provisions, the Law on Industrial Emissions (OJ MNE, No. 17/19) prescribes that right to appeal is guaranteed by Article 16, (Decision on the permit request).

Chapter 3. Judicial Remedies[1468]

§1. Introduction

1402. The Strategy on Judiciary Reform 2019–2022, adopted by the Government in September 2019,[1469] defines following key objectives of the further judiciary reforms for the five-year period: strengthening of independence, efficiency and availability of judiciary, and the increase of the public confidence in the judiciary. The Action Plan for the implementation of the Judiciary Reform Strategy for the period 2021–2022 envisages specific measures that should be undertaken for the implementation of these aims by responsible bodies, as well as implementation deadlines.[1470]

1403. Institutional framework of the Montenegrin judicial system consists of fifteen basic courts, two higher courts in Podgorica and Bijelo Polje, commercial court in Podgorica, Appellate Court, Administrative and Supreme Court.[1471]

1404. The Decision on the number of state prosecutors (OJ MNE No. 21/15) determined the total number of 131 state prosecutors, out of which 85 are in the basic state prosecutor's offices, 24 in two higher state prosecutors, 11 in the Special State Prosecutor's Office and 11 in the Supreme State Prosecutor's Office.[1472]

§2. Basic Legislation

1405. Basic legal acts concerning judicial protection in Montenegro are following:

– Constitution of Montenegro (OJ MNE, Nos 1/2007, 38/13).[1473]

1468. Judicial remedies in environmental cases including transboundary harm were multiple times the object of a dispute in front of the International Court of Justice. Of relevance to the topic at hand is the insight that the Court evaluates the remedies in front of municipal courts for the purpose of determining the amount of compensation awards (see extensively Vučić 2019a, 77–79; 128–129; 144–146).
1469. GMNE (2019).
1470. For more details *see*: GMNE (2021).
1471. Further information on the legal system can be found online at: https://www.sudovi.me/, 8 Dec. 2022).
1472. *See*: Strategy for Management and Development of Human Resource in Judicial Institutions 2016–2018, Ministry of Justice, Podgorica, June 2016, p. 3.
1473. Generally, 'the constitutional provision on the right to legal remedy does not fully comply with Article 13 of the European Convention on Human Rights'. EC (2011), 12. 'With regard to the *independence and impartiality* of the judiciary, procedures are ongoing for the adoption of constitutional amendments aimed at further enhancing judicial independence, in particular through depoliticized and merit-based appointments of the Judicial and Prosecutorial Councils' members and of state prosecutors. Draft constitutional amendments were adopted by the Parliament with the required two-thirds majority on 28 Sep. 2011. Following consultations held between the Government and the opposition parties, the Parliamentary Committee for Legal and Constitutional affairs adopted in March 2012 a set of constitutional amendments, to be submitted to a plenary

- Law on Courts (OJ MNE, Nos 11/15, 76/20).[1474]
- Law on the Court's Council and Judges (OJ MNE, Nos 11/15, 28/15, 42/18).
- Law on the Qualifying Examination for Judges (OJ RM, No. 52/04).
- Law on the State Prosecutor of Montenegro (OJ MNE, Nos 11/15, 42/15, 80/17, 10/18, 76/20, 59/21).
- Criminal Code (OJ RM, Nos 70/03, 47/06, OJ MNE, Nos 40/08, 25/10, 32/11, 64/11, 40/13, 56/13, 14/15, 42/15, 58/15, 44/17, 49/18, 3/20, 145/21).
- Criminal Procedure Code (OJ MNE, Nos 57/09, 49/10, 47/14-CC, 2/15-CC, 35/15, 58/15, 28/18-CC, 116/20-CC).
- Law on Witness Protection (OJ RM, Nos 65/04, 31/14).
- Law on Responsibilities for Criminal Acts of the Legal Entities (OJ RM, Nos 2/07, 13/07, OJ MNE, Nos 30/12, 39/16).
- Law on Civil Procedure (OJ RM, Nos 22/04, 76/06, OJ MNE, Nos 48/15, 1/17, 75/17-CC, 62/18-CC, 34/19, 42/19, 76/20).
- Law on Ownership Rights (OJ MNE, No. 19/09).[1475]
- Law on Executive Procedure (OJ MNE, Nos 36/11, 28/14, 20/15, 22/17, 76/17).
- Law on Misdemeanours (OJ MNE, Nos 1/11, 39/11, 32/14).
- Mediation Law (OJ M, No. 77/20).
- Law on Arbitration (OJ MNE, No. 47/15).
- Law on Notaries (OJ RM, No. 68/05, OJ MNE, Nos 49/08, 55/16, 84/18).
- Law on the Extra-Judicial Procedure (OJ RM, No. 27/06).
- Law on Advocacy (OJ RM, No. 79/06, OJ MNE, Nos 73/10, 22/17).
- Law on the Training Centre in the Judiciary and the State Prosecutor's Office (OJ MNE, No. 58/15).
- Law on Protection of the Right to a Trial in a Reasonable Period of Time (OJ RM, No. 11/07).
- Law on Courts Experts (OJ MNE, No. 54/16) etc.

---

vote. The initiated constitutional reform should bring the judicial system in line with European standards, in particular by safeguarding against political influence in appointments and strengthening judicial independence, notably through the replacement of MPs who were members of the Judicial Council by renowned lawyers and a new appointment procedure of the Supreme Court President by the Judicial Council.' EC (2012), 4. In July 2013, parliament adopted amendments to the Constitution, in the section on the judiciary, which are broadly in line with the Venice Commission recommendations. The amendments strengthen the independence of the judiciary. EC.(2013a), 35, 36. *See also Amendments to the Constitution of Montenegro* https://api.skupstina.me/media/files/1605826465-amandmani-i-do-xvi-na-ustav-crne-gore.pdf.(3 Dec. 2022).

1474. The most important sub-legal acts regulating organization of work in courts are: Court Internal Rules (Official Journal of MNE, No. 26/11); Regulation on costs compensation in courts procedures (Official Journal of MNE, No. 14/11); Decree on number of judges in Republic of Montenegro (Official Journal of MNE, No. 72/08); By-law on approximate parameter for assessment of the adequate number of judges and other employees in courts (Official Journal of MNE, No. 46/11); and By-law on permanent court interpreter (Official Journal of RM, No. 5/02, 49/04, and Official Journal of MNE, No. 22/08).

1475. According to the Art. 266 of the Law on Ownership Rights (Official Journal of MNE, No. 19/09) owners of immovables that are exposed to the excessive emissions shall be authorized to require from the owner of immovable property that emit them to remove the causes of these emissions and compensate the incurred damage, as well as refrain in the future from the activities that represent the cause of excessive emissions, until he undertakes all measures to make them impossible (para. 3).

§3. Procedure Before the Civil Court

1406. The Law on Civil Procedure (OJ RM, Nos 22/04, 28/05, 76/06, OJ MNE, Nos 73/10, 47/15, 48/15, 51/17, 75/17-CC, 62/18-CC, 34/19, 42/19, 76/20)[1476] defines rules of proceedings on the basis of which the court deliberates and decides on personal and family disputes, labour disputes and property and other civil disputes between natural and legal persons, if not prescribed differently by some other law (Article 1).

1407. Any natural and legal persons may be a party in the proceedings (Article 76).[1477] The civil court may, for purposes of the proceedings, exceptionally recognize the capacity of a party to have forms of association that are not eligible to be a party if the court determines that, with regard to the matter of dispute, they meet the crucial requirements for acquiring the capacity of a party, particularly if they possess the property which may be subject to enforcement.[1478]

1408. The civil proceeding is initiated by filing a complaint to a competent court (Article 186).[1479]

I. Ordinary Legal Remedies

1409. Ordinary legal remedies are appeals against judgment (regulated by Articles 361–392) and against decision (regulated by Articles 393–396). Parties may file an appeal against the judgment of first instance within fifteen days from the day[1480] of rendering the judgment, or from delivery of the judgment, as appropriate, unless a different deadline is set by this law.[1481] The second instance court decides on an appeal against the judgment.

1410. A judgment can be appealed in following cases: (1) violation of the provisions of the civil procedure law ('Procedural Errors' as defined by Article

1476. By virtue of Art. 511 on the day of entering into force of this Law, the Law on Civil Procedure (Official Journal of FRY, Nos 4/77, 36/77, 69/82, 58/87, 57/89, 20/90, 27/90, 35/91 and Official Journal of FRY, Nos 27/92, 31/93, 24/94, 12/98, 15/98 and 3/2002) ceased to be effective.
1477. Special regulations may define who may be a party in the proceedings apart from natural and legal persons (Art. 76, para. 2).
1478. A separate appeal shall not be allowed against the decision (referred to in para. 3 of this article) that recognizes the capacity of a party in litigation (Art. 76, para. 4).
1479. In order to be considered by court, a complaint and all other submissions should be understandable and must contain following: the name of court, name and surname of plaintiff, name of a legal person, residence or living address of parties, headquarters of legal entity, its legal representative or attorney, if any, that is the person who files a complaint on his behalf (Art. 103). A complaint should also contain certain request about the main subject and minor claims, facts on which a plaintiff's request is based and the evidence that makes a basis for the fact-finding. A plaintiff is, according to Art. 187, bound to attach to a complaint the receipt on paid court fee.
1480. In disputes concerning bills of exchange and check, the deadline is eight days.
1481. Appeal filed within the prescribed deadline prevents the finality of the judgment in the part contested by the appeal (Art. 361, para. 2).

367);[1482] (2) erroneously or incompletely determined state of facts (Article 368); and[1483] (3) misapplication of the substantive law (Article 369).[1484]

1411. Article 370 prescribes that an appeal should be filed with the first instance court with a sufficient number of copies for the court and the adversarial party. According to Article 364, paragraph 1, an untimely,[1485] incomplete or inadmissible[1486] appeal shall be rejected in the ruling of the first instance court without holding a hearing.

1412. The second instance court may, at the panel session or on the basis of a hearing, do following: (1) reject the appeal as untimely, incomplete or inadmissible; (2) dismiss the appeal as unjustified and confirm the first instance judgment; (3) reverse the judgment and remand the case to the first instance court; (4) reverse the first instance judgment and reject the complaint; or (5) overrule the first instance judgment (Article 380).

II. Extraordinary Legal Remedies

1413. Extraordinary legal remedies are the following: revision (regulated by Articles 397–415), request for protection of legality (regulated by Articles 416–420) and reopening of proceedings (regulated by Articles 421–428a).

1414. According to Article 397, the parties have the right to file the request for revision of the final second instance judgment within thirty days from the day of the delivery of the judgment. The Supreme Court decides on revision (Article 398).

1415. The public prosecutor may raise a request for protection of legality for procedural errors of the provisions in civil procedure from Article 367, paragraph 2; sub-paragraph 7 of the Code of Civil procedure in the deadline within three months (Article 416). Such request is not, however, allowed against a decision made upon

1482. A Procedural Error shall exist if the court, in the course of the proceedings, failed to apply or improperly applied a provision of this Law, which affected the rendering of a lawful and correct judgment (Art. 367).
1483. Erroneously or incompletely determined statement of the facts shall exist when the court has erroneously established or failed to determine a decisive fact. Incompletely determined statement of the facts shall also exist when the new evidence or facts so indicate (Art. 368).
1484. Misapplication of substantive law shall exists when the court failed to apply the provision of the substantive law, which has been applied or when such provision has not been properly applied (Art. 369).
1485. An appeal shall be considered untimely if filed after the expiration of the deadline prescribed for its submission (Art. 371, para. 2).
1486. An appeal shall be considered inadmissible if filed by a person who has not been authorized to file the appeal or person who waived or withdrew the appeal or if the person who filed an appeal does not have the legal interest to do so (Art. 372, para. 3).

a revision by the court competent to decide on that legal remedy (Article 416, paragraph 2). According to Article 417, the Supreme Court decides on the request for protection of legality.[1487]

1416. Article 421 provides that proceedings completed by a final court ruling may be reopened at the party's motion if: (1) a party was not given the possibility to be heard before the court by some illegal action, especially omission of delivery; (2) the personal delivery of the first pleadings has been made in accordance with Article 141 of this law, and the party was continually absent longer than three months; (3) a person who cannot be a party in the proceedings participated in the proceedings in capacity of plaintiff or defendant, a legal person in capacity of party has not been represented by an authorized person, a party which has no litigation capacity was not represented by a legal representative, a legal representative or an agent has not had necessary authorization for conducting the proceedings or performing particular procedural actions, unless conducting the proceedings or carrying out particular procedural actions has been subsequently approved; (4) the court decision has been based on a false testimony by a witness or an expert; (5) the court decision has been based on a false document or a document where the false content has been certified; (6) rendering the court decision involved a criminal act of the judge, the legal representative or the agent of a party, adversarial party or a third parties; (7) the party requests the possibility to use the final judgment of the court made on the same dispute and between the same parties; (8) the court decision has been made upon other decision of the court or some other body, and that other decision is final overruled, reversed and rejected; and (9) a party learns new facts, finds or gains the possibility to use new evidence that would have led to a more favourable ruling if those facts or evidence had been presented in the previous proceedings.[1488]

III. Proceedings in Litigation Concerning Trespassing

1417. Articles 439–445 of the Law (Chapter 29) regulate proceedings in litigation concerning trespassing.

1418. Deliberation on the complaint for trespassing is limited to deliberation and presentation of facts pertaining to the latest situation of possession and the disturbance thereof. Deliberation concerning the right to real estate, legal basis and possession in good and in bad faith or compensation claims shall be, according to Article 441, excluded.

1487. If both the revision and the request for protection of legality have been raised against the same decision, the court mentioned in Art. 398 of this Law shall decide on those legal remedies by passing a single decision (Art. 418).

1488. In addition, rules relating to the reopening of proceedings must be implemented in cases when European Court of Human Rights finds breaching of human rights and basic freedoms guaranteed by the European Convention for the Protection of Human Rights and Fundamental Freedoms (Art. 428(a)).

1419. During the course of proceedings, the court may determine security measures without hearing the adverse party, that are applied in enforcement law to prevent violently taken actions or to eliminate irreparable damage.[1489] An appeal is not allowed against this decision (Article 442).[1490]

§4. Criminal Procedure

I. Criminal Code Procedure

A. *Criminal Procedure Code*

1420. Pursuant to Article 18 of the Criminal Procedure Code (OJ MNE, Nos 57/09, 49/10, 47/14-CC, 2/15-CC, 35/15, 58/15, 18/18-CC, 116/20-CC, 145/21)[1491] criminal proceedings shall be initiated and conducted in line with the indictment of an authorized prosecutor.[1492] For criminal offences that are prosecuted ex officio, the authorized prosecutor shall be the State Prosecutor whereas, for criminal offences prosecuted upon a private action, the authorized prosecutor shall be a private prosecutor.[1493] Unless otherwise prescribed by the present Code, the State Prosecutor shall initiate prosecution when there is reasonable suspicion that a certain person has committed a criminal offence that is prosecuted ex officio (Article 19).

1421. When a State Prosecutor establishes that there is no basis for prosecution for a criminal offence that is prosecuted by virtue of office or that there is no basis to prosecute someone of reported accomplices, s/he shall inform the injured parties[1494] thereon within eight days, instruct them that they may take over the prosecution themselves and deliver them a decision on the rejection of the criminal

1489. Besides that, in setting the deadlines and hearings on complaints for trespassing, the court shall always have due regard to the necessity of expedited treatment considering the nature of every single case (Art. 440).

1490. Prescribed deadline for filing an appeal is eight days. However, the court may decide (due to extraordinary circumstances) that the appeal shall not stay the enforcement of the decision. The request for revision shall not be allowed against the decisions passed in the litigation concerning the trespassing (Art. 443).

1491. The present Code sets forth the rules with the objective to enable a fair conduct of the criminal proceedings and ensure that no innocent person be convicted and that a criminal sanction be imposed on a criminal offender under the conditions provided for in the Criminal Code and on the basis of legally conducted proceedings (Art. 1). By entry into force of the present Code, the Criminal Procedure Code (Official Journal of RM, Nos 71/03 and 47/06) shall cease to be valid except for the provisions of Chapter XXIX which shall apply until the adoption of a law regulating the proceedings against minors and other issues related to the position of juvenile offenders (Art. 515).

1492. *Prosecutors* are State Prosecutors, private prosecutors and subsidiary prosecutors (Art. 22 point 6).

1493. If a State Prosecutor determines that there are no grounds for the institution or conduct of criminal proceedings, the injured party acting as a subsidiary prosecutor may assume his/her role, under the terms stipulated by the present Code (Art. 18, para. 3).

1494. *Injured parties* are persons whose personal or property right of some type was violated or endangered by a criminal offence (Art. 22 point 5).

charge, with the exception of cases referred to in Article 272, paragraph 5 and Article 273 of the present Code[1495] (Article 59, paragraph 1).[1496] When a State Prosecutor abandons prosecution at the main hearing, injured parties shall declare immediately whether they intend to continue prosecution (Article 60, paragraph 1).

1422. As regards criminal offences prosecuted upon a private action, the complaint shall be filed within three months as of the day when the private prosecutor, i.e., person referred to in Article 54 of the present Code,[1497] learned about the criminal offence and the perpetrator (Article 51).

1423. Everyone shall report a criminal offence which is prosecuted by virtue of office and is obliged to report a criminal offence the commission of which has caused detriment to a minor (Article 255, paragraph 1).[1498]

1424. According to Article 254 persons acting in an official capacity and responsible persons in state authorities, local governance authorities, public companies and institutions shall file a charge for criminal offences, subject to prosecution by virtue of office, of which they have been informed or which they have learned while performing their office.[1499] This duty shall also be incumbent upon all natural and legal persons who are granted certain public powers pursuant to law, or are professionally involved in the protection and security provision to persons and property or in the healthcare of persons, as well as in jobs of minors care and education if they learn about a criminal offence while performing or in connection with their profession.

1495. These articles refer to 'Laying off Criminal Prosecution' (Art. 272) and 'Dismissal of Criminal Charge for Fairness' (Art. 273).

1496. Where an injured party assumes prosecution in compliance with Art. 59 of the present Code, s/he may a direct indictment (Art. 287).

1497. Article 54 (succession of a private prosecutor): If a private prosecutor dies within the deadline prescribed for submitting a private action or in the course of procedure, his/her spouse, extramarital partner, children, parents, adopted children, adoptive parents and siblings may, within three months after his/her death, file a complaint or make a statement that they will continue the procedure.

1498. When the court establishes in the course of criminal proceedings that reasonable suspicion exists that a person has failed to perform the duty referred to in para. 1 of this Article and that such omission results in a reasonable suspicion as to the commission of the criminal offence of neglecting and abuse of a minor, the court shall notify the competent State Prosecutor thereof (Art. 255 para. 2). Criminal charge shall be filed with the competent State Prosecutor whether in writing or orally. If the charge is filed orally, the informant shall be cautioned as to the consequences of false information. Oral charge shall be entered in a record, and where the information is filed over the phone or other means of electronic communication, an official annotation shall be made thereabout. The charge filed with a court, the police authority or a State Prosecutor lacking jurisdiction, they shall receive the information and immediately forward it to the State Prosecutor having the jurisdiction (Art. 256).

1499. Persons filing a criminal charge from para. 1 of this Article shall indicate evidence to the best of their knowledge and take measures to preserve traces of the criminal offence, the items upon which or by means of which the criminal offence has been committed, items resulting from the commission of criminal offence as well as other evidence (Art. 254, para. 3).

B. Regular Legal Remedies

1425. Regular legal remedies are following: an appeal against first instance judgment (Articles 381–412), an appeal against the second instance decision (Article 413), and an appeal against the ruling (Articles 414–419).

1426. An appeal against the first instance judgment may be filed within fifteen days from the date when the copy of the decision was delivered.[1500] An appeal filed in due time by an authorized person shall stay the execution of the judgment (Article 381). In accordance with Article 385 a judgment may be contested on the grounds of (1) substantive violation of the criminal proceedings provisions, (2) violation of the Criminal Code, (3) the state of the facts being erroneously or incompletely established and (4) the decision on criminal sanctions, forfeiture of property gain, costs of criminal proceedings, claims under property law.

1427. An appeal may be filed against the decision of a second instance court with a third instance court only in the following cases: (1) if the second instance court has imposed the most severe punishment of imprisonment or if it has confirmed the first instance decision that imposed such a punishment, (2) if the second instance court, upon conducting the main hearing, has established the state of facts differently from the first instance court and has based its decision on the newly established state of the facts and (3) if the second instance court has revised the decision of acquittal rendered by the first instance court and rendered a decision declaring the defendant guilty (Article 413, paragraph 1).[1501] Provisions of Article 402 of the present Code[1502] shall be applied to the co-defendant who was not entitled to file an appeal or did not file an appeal against the second instance decision.

1428. According to Article 414 parties and persons whose rights have been violated may file an appeal against a ruling of the investigating judge and against other rulings of the first instance court, unless the appeal is explicitly declared to be inadmissible by this Code. Unless otherwise prescribed by this Code, rulings rendered by the Panel prior to and in the course of the investigation are not subject to an appellate review. The investigating judge shall decide on appeals against the rulings

1500. An appeal may be filed by the parties, the defence attorney, the legal representative of the defendant and the injured party (Art. 382, para. 1). An appeal shall be filed with the court which rendered the decision at first instance in a sufficient number of copies for the court, the opposing party and the defence attorney (Art. 390, para. 1).

1501. A third instance court shall decide on the appeal filed against the second instance decision pursuant to the provisions of the present Code regulating the second instance proceedings (Art. 413, para. 2).

1502. If the second instance court, upon anybody's appeal, finds that the grounds on which the decision was rendered in favour of the defendant, are also of benefit to any of the co-defendants who did not file an appeal or did not file an appeal along the same lines, it shall proceed by virtue of an office as if such an appeal has been filed.

of the State Prosecutor if otherwise not provided by this Code. Rulings rendered for the purpose of preparing the main hearing and the decision may be contested solely in an appeal against the decision.[1503]

C. Extraordinary Legal Remedies

1429. Extraordinary legal remedies are following: reopening of criminal proceedings (Articles 420–432), extraordinary mitigation of punishment (Articles 433–436) and request for the protection of legality (Articles 437–445).

1430. A criminal proceeding that was completed with a final ruling or final judgment may be repeated at the petition of an authorized person only in cases and under the conditions provided by this Code (Article 420).[1504] A request for the reopening of criminal proceedings may be submitted by the parties and defence attorney and, after the death of the convicted person, in his favour, by the State Prosecutor and the persons referred to in Article 382, paragraph 2 of the present Code (Article 426, paragraph 1). The request for the reopening of the criminal proceedings to the benefit of the accused person may also be submitted after the convicted person has served a sentence, notwithstanding the statute of limitation, amnesty or pardon.[1505]

1431. Pursuant to Article 433 mitigation of a punishment pronounced by a final judgment which has not been executed or served shall be permitted when, after the decision becomes final, circumstances appear which did not exist at the time the decision was rendered or did exist but were unknown to the court, provided that they would clearly lead to a less severe sentence.[1506]

1503. Rulings rendered by the Supreme Court are not subject to an appellate review (Art. 414, para. 5).
1504. In this part the Law regulates following issues: Reversing a Judgment without a New Trial (Quasi Criminal Rehearing) (Art. 421), Resuming Proceedings (Art. 422), Reopening of the Proceedings Completed by the Ruling (Art. 423), Reopening of the Proceedings in Favour of the Accused Person (Art. 424), Reopening of the Proceedings to the Detriment of the Accused Person (Art. 425), Persons Entitled to Submit a Request for Reopening of Criminal Proceedings (Art. 426), Contents of Request and the court Competent to Decide on the Request (Art. 427), Deciding on a Request for Reopening of Criminal Proceedings (Art. 428), Permission to Reopen the Proceedings (Art. 429), Rules of the Reopened Proceedings (Art. 430), New Trial in Cases the Trial was Conducted in the Accused Person's Absence (Art. 431).
1505. If the court competent to decide on the reopening of the criminal proceedings referred to in Art. 427 of the present Code learns that reason for the reopening of the criminal proceedings exists, it shall notify the convicted person or person entitled to submit a request in favour of the convicted person thereon (Art. 426, para. 3).
1506. A request for extraordinary mitigation of punishment may be submitted by a State Prosecutor, convicted person and his/her attorney, as well as the persons referred to in Art. 382 para. 2 of the present Code.(2) A request for extraordinary mitigation of punishment shall not stay the execution of punishment (Art. 434).

1432. The Supreme State Prosecutor may submit a request for the protection of legality against final judgments and against the judicial proceedings which preceded such final decisions if the law has been violated.[1507] The Supreme State Prosecutor may submit the request if the European Court of Human Rights or another court established by a ratified international treaty has found that human rights and freedoms have been violated in the course of the criminal proceedings and that the judgment was based on such violations, and the competent court did not allow reopening of the criminal proceedings, or if the violation done by the judgment can be removed through the quashing of the decision or its reversal without retrial (Article 437, paragraphs 1 and 2).[1508]

II. Law on Misdemeanours[1509]

1433. The Law on misdemeanours (OJ MNE, Nos 1/11, 6/11, 39/11, 32/14, 43/17, 51/17) prescribes that the misdemeanour proceeding may be initiated on the basis of (1) request for a court decision on the issued misdemeanour warrant[1510] or

1507. The accused person who is sentenced to an unsuspended penalty of imprisonment of a year or more or to juvenile detention and the defence attorney of such an accused person may, within a month of receiving the final judgment, request from the Supreme State Prosecutor's Office, in a written and well-grounded proposal, to file a request for the protection of legality against the final judgment if they deem that the Criminal Code has been violated to the detriment of the accused person by that judgment or if in the criminal proceedings which preceded the judgment a right of the accused person to defence was violated and this violation affected the rendering of a lawful and proper judgment (Art. 438, para. 1).

1508. The Supreme State Prosecutor may also submit the request if a judgment is based on the law or other enactment which has been declared invalid by the Constitutional Court, in which case the request for the protection of legality may be submitted if the competent court did not allow reopening of the criminal proceedings, of if the violation done by the judgment can be removed through the quashing of the decision or its reversal without retrial (Art. 437 paras 1 and 3).

1509. 'The Law on Misdemeanour establishes a new and effective procedure for the prosecution of misdemeanour cases in line with the European Convention on Human Rights and introduce a new system of fines and misdemeanour records management … ' *See*: https://www.paragraf.me/dnevne-vijesti/10062020/10062020-vijest2.html (3 Dec. 2022). Four by-laws have been adopted by the Ministry of Justice with the aim to provide adequate implementation of the Law. These are following: Instruction for data input, control and modification of the data in the register of fines (5 Aug. 2011); Rules for access to the register of fines (5 Aug. 2011); Rulebook on contents and manner of keeping the register of fines (Official Journal of MNE, No. 48/2011); Rulebook on manner of keeping the misdemeanour records (Official Journal of MNE, No. 48/20).

1510. The authorized body shall issue a misdemeanour warrant if the misdemeanour is within its competences determined in: (1) direct observation by an authorized officer during inspection supervision, monitoring and review, as well as during insight into the official records of the competent authority; (2) based on data obtained using monitoring or measurement devices; (3) review of documentation, premises and the goods or on any other way prescribed by the Law; and (4) on the base of the admission on committed misdemeanour by the defendant on the spot, in front of the authorized body or during any other judicial or administrative proceedings (Art. 144, para. 1).

(2) request for initiating of misdemeanour proceedings[1511] (Article 143). Process procedure rules are regulated by the provisions of the Law.

1434. The provisions concerning the right to appeal are contained in Chapter XXIII of the Law on misdemeanours. According to the provisions of Article 199, against court decision reached in the first instance may be submitted an appeal within eight days from receiving of the court decision transcript, unless otherwise prescribed by this Law.[1512]

1435. The appeal may be filed by the parties, defence attorney, defendant's legal representative and the aggrieved party (Article 200).[1513] In favour of the defendant, the appeal may be filed by his spouse or common-law partner, blood relative in the direct line, adoptive parent or adopted child, brother, sister and foster parent.[1514] An appeal may be filed by a person to whom has been ordered protective measure of items seizure or from whom was seized the property obtained by an offence (Article 200, paragraph 4).

1436. Extraordinary legal remedies are regulated in Chapter XXIV of the Law on misdemeanour. These are the repetition of misdemeanour proceedings and the request for protection of the legality (Article 224).

1437. According to the provisions of Article 217 of the Law, misdemeanour proceedings that ended by a final court decision may be repeated, at the request of the convicted or punished person or his defender, only in cases and under conditions prescribed by this Law. Misdemeanour proceedings ended by a final decision may be repeated in favour of the defendant, if: (1) the court decision is based on a false document or on false testimony of a witness, court expert or interpreter; (2) the court decision was made due to criminal acts of a judge or other authorized person who participated in the process; (3) new facts are presented or new evidence submitted which, by themselves or in conjunction with previous evidence, could lead to different decisions if they were known in earlier proceedings; (4) it is determined that a person has legally imposed in misdemeanour proceedings for the same action or that is before a making decision on the misdemeanour found guilty in criminal

1511. When it is not possible to issue a misdemeanour warrant, in accordance with Art. 144 of this Law, the applicant shall submit a request for misdemeanour proceedings to the competent court, immediately upon learning for the misdemeanour and the offender, the latest in sixty days (Art. 153, para. 1).
1512. A timely lodged appeal shall postpone the execution of court decisions, unless otherwise prescribed by this Law (Art. 119, para. 2).
1513. The aggrieved party may refute the court decision only because of the court's decision on the costs of misdemeanour proceedings or if a acquittal is made, when the aggrieved party may file an appeal because of all basis from Art. 203 of this Law (Art. 200, para. 3).
1514. Also in this case, the deadline for filing an appeal starts from the date when the transcription of a court decision was delivered to defendant or to his counsel (Art. 200, para. 2).

proceedings for an offence which includes the characteristics of the offence; (5) in case of conviction for an offence in a prolonged period or for other offence which, according to the Law, encompass more the same or more different actions, present new facts or submit new evidence indicating that the convicted did not committed the action covered by the offence from the conviction, and the existence of these facts would lead to application of a more lenient law or would be of a significant impact on the sentencing imposing; and (6) it is by decision of the European Court for Human Rights or other court established by international agreement determined that there was violation of human rights and fundamental freedoms during the misdemeanour proceedings, and that the court's decision is based on such violation, and that is in repeating the procedure possible to correct committed violation (Article 218).[1515]

1438. The rules concerning the request for protection of legality are governed by Article 224. Against the final court decisions and against legal proceedings that proceeded to these final decisions, the Supreme Public Prosecutor's Office may raise the request for protection of legality, in case of violation of the Law.[1516] The provisions of the Code of Criminal Procedure relating to raising the request for protection of legality and deciding on it in an appropriate way will apply to a request for protection of legality in misdemeanour proceedings (Article 224, paragraph 3).

§5. Constitutional Court Procedure

1439. Article 149 of the Constitution (OJ MNE, No. 1/2007, 38/13) prescribes that the Constitutional Court[1517] decides on following issues: (1) conformity of laws with the Constitution and confirmed and published international agreements; (2) conformity of other regulations and general acts with the Constitution and the law; (3) constitutional appeal due to the violation of human rights and liberties granted by the Constitution, after all the effective legal remedies have been exhausted; (4) whether the President of Montenegro has violated the Constitution; (5) the conflict of responsibilities between courts and other state authorities, between state authorities and local self-government authorities, and between the authorities of the local

1515. The Law prescribes: request content (Art. 219), deciding on the request (Art. 220), the decision regarding the request for reopening of judicial proceedings (Art. 221), the rules of the reopened proceeding (Art. 222) and the application of the Code of Criminal Procedure (Art. 223).

1516. Supreme Public Prosecutor's Office does not have to raise the request for legality protection if it considers that there was law violation, but the violation of the law did not affected the correctness of the decision and it is not about a legal issue important for the uniform application of the law or for protection of human rights and freedoms (Art. 224, para. 3).

1517. For more details on Constitutional Court *see*: https://www.ustavnisud.me/ustavnisud/objava/blog/2/objava/16-nbsp-nbsp-nbsp-istorija-i-razvoj-crnogorskog-ustavnog-sudstva (3 Dec. 2022). 'Constitutional amendments enhancing the capacity and the independence of the Constitutional Court, and setting out clear grounds for dismissal of judges and prosecutors should also be adopted.' EC (2012), 4.

self-government units; (6) prohibition of work of a political party or a NGO; (7) electoral disputes and disputes related to the referendum, which are not the responsibility of other courts; (8) conformity with the Constitution of the measures and actions of state authorities taken during the state of war or the state of emergency; and (9) performs other tasks stipulated by the Constitution.

1440. Any person may, according to Article 150, file an initiative to start the procedure for the assessment of constitutionality and legality.[1518] Procedure before the Constitutional Court for the assessment of constitutionality and legality may be initiated by: the court, other state authority, local self-government authority and five Members of the Parliament. It should be added that the Constitutional Court itself may also initiate the procedure for the assessment of constitutionality and legality.[1519]

1441. According to Article 68 of the Law on constitutional Court (OJ MNE, No. 11/15), constitutional complaint can be lodged against an individual act of state authority, local self-government authority or organization vested with public powers, for the reason of violation of human rights and freedoms guaranteed by the Constitution, after all effective legal remedies have been exhausted.[1520]

1442. When the Constitutional Court establishes that a challenged individual act violated a human right or freedom guaranteed by the Constitution, it shall grant the constitutional complaint and repeal that act (entirely or partially) and remand the case for repeat procedure to the authority which enacted the repealed act (Article 76).[1521]

1518. According to Art. 68 of the Law on Constitutional Court (OJMNE, No. 11/15) constitutional complaints may be lodged by anyone who believes that his human right and freedom guaranteed by the Constitution was violated by an individual act of state authority, local self-government authority or organization vested with public powers. In addition, according to the Art. 19 of the Law on the Protector of Human Rights and Freedoms (OJMNE, No. 42/11, 32/14) the Protector may propose the initiation of proceedings before the Constitutional Court for the purpose of assessing the constitutionality and legality of the legislation and general enactment.

1519. The Constitutional Court may during the procedure by its order stop the enforcement of an individual act or actions that have been taken on the basis of the law, other regulation or general act, the constitutionality, that is legality of which is being assessed, if the enforcement thereof could cause irreparable damage (Art. 150, para. 4).

1520. A constitutional appeal can be submitted after the exhaustion of effective legal remedies, which imply that the applicant of the constitutional appeal has used all the legal remedies to which he was entitled in accordance with the law. This includes effective and extraordinary legal remedies and other special legal remedies that can lead to the amendment of an individual act in favour of the applicant of the constitutional appeal, i.e., to the cessation or correction of the action, i.e., to the termination of the inaction of the state body, state administration body, local self-government body, or local administration, legal entity or other entity that exercises public powers (Art. 68, para. 2). A constitutional appeal may be submitted even before the exhaustion of the effective legal remedies referred to in paragraph 2 of this article, if the applicant of the constitutional appeal proves that the legal remedy to which he is entitled in the specific case is not or would not be effective.

1521. If, during the decision-making process on a constitutional appeal, the legal effect of an individual act that is the subject of a constitutional appeal has ceased, and the Constitutional Court determines that this act violated a human right or freedom guaranteed by the Constitution, it will issue

§6. Administrative Court Procedure

1443. Article 1 of the Law on Administrative Dispute (Official Journal MNE, No. 54/16) prescribes that the competent authority decides on the legality of an administrative act and on the legality of other individual administrative acts, when it is so prescribed by the law. An administrative dispute may be instituted against an administrative or other act that has been passed in second instance (Article 12). An administrative dispute may as well be instituted against an administrative or other act passed in first instance, against which appeal is not permitted in an administrative or other procedure. Apart from that, an administrative dispute may also be initiated when the competent authority failed to pass an adequate administrative or other act upon the request of a party, under the conditions stipulated by this law.[1522]

1444. Article 14 stipulates that an administrative or other act may be disputed in following cases: (1) in the case of violation of the rules of procedure; (2) in the case of inaccurate and incomplete establishment of facts; and (3) in the case of inaccurate application of the material law.[1523]

1445. An administrative dispute has to be resolved by the Administrative Court of Montenegro and by the Supreme Court of Montenegro (Article 6).

I. The Right to Institute an Administrative Dispute

1446. By virtue of Article 10, paragraph 1 any natural or legal person, who believes that some of his/her rights or legally based interests have been violated by an administrative or other act, has the right to institute an administrative dispute. Besides that, a state authority, organization, settlement, group of persons or others who do not have the attribute of a legal person may institute an administrative dispute, if they are entitled to be holders of rights and obligations decided on in an administrative or other procedure (Article 10. paragraph 2).

---

a decision accepting the constitutional appeal and determine the way to fairly satisfy the applicant of the constitutional appeal due to suffered violation of human rights or freedoms guaranteed by the Constitution (Art. 76, para. 2).

1522. An administrative dispute cannot be conducted against following acts: (1) that have been passed in matters, in which judicial protection is provided beyond the administrative dispute and (2) that have been passed in matters decided on directly by the Parliament of Montenegro and the President of Montengro by virtue of constitutional authority (Art. 13).

1523. According to Art. 14, para. 2, there is no case of inaccurate application of regulations, if the competent authority had decided by free estimation on the basis of and in the framework of the authority conferred on it by legal regulations and in accordance with the objective, for which the authority has been conferred. This also applies to the situation when the competent authority decided in accordance with earlier decisions made by the public law authority in essentially identical administrative matters.

1447. In accordance with Article 16 an administrative dispute is initiated by a complaint.[1524] Complaints are resolved by the Administrative Court in a panel.

II. Examination of Court Decision and Repetition of Procedure

1448. The following may be submitted against the final decision of the Administrative Court: (1) a request for examination of the court decision; (2) request to repeat the procedure (Article 40).

1449. A request for examination of a court decision can be submitted by the parties in an administrative dispute. (Article 41).[1525]

1450. The request for examination of the court decision is submitted to the Supreme Court, within twenty days from the date of receipt of the final decision of the Administrative Court (Article 44).

1451. In accordance with Article 48, a procedure concluded by a judgment or a decision can be retried upon request of a party in following cases: (1) if the party discovers new facts, or finds or gets the possibility to use new evidence, on which grounds the dispute might have been settled more favourably for him/her, had these facts that is evidence been put forward or used in the previous court procedure; (2) if the court decision was reached due to a criminal act of the judge or an employee of the court, or the decision was reached through deceit by the legal representative or attorney of the party, the opposing party or his/her legal representative or attorney, and such an act represents a criminal act; (3) if the decision was based on a judgment passed in a criminal or civil matter, and this judgment was later nullified by another legally binding court decision; (4) if a document, on which the decision is based, is false or forged, or if a witness, assessor or party has given a false statement during the examination before court, and the court decision is based on that statement; (5) if a party finds or gets the possibility to make use of an earlier decision passed in the same administrative dispute; (6) if an interested party had not been given the possibility to participate in the administrative dispute; and (7) if the judgment of the Administrative Court contradicts the judgment of the European Court of Human Rights in the same matter.[1526]

1524. The complaint has to be submitted within twenty days from the delivery of the administrative act to the party submitting the complaint (Art. 17). The complaint has to be delivered personally to the Administrative Court or sent by post or electronically. The day of posting the complaint by registered mail shall be considered as the day of submission to the court (Art. 18). If the complaint is submitted electronically, it is considered to have been submitted on the date and time specified in the document receipt confirmation in electronic form, in accordance with the law regulating electronic administration.

1525. The request for examination of the court decision is decided by the Supreme Court, in a panel composed of three judges, as a rule, in a closed session (Art. 42).

1526. Due to the circumstances from paragraph 1 point. 1 and 5 of this article, the repetition of the procedure will be allowed only if the party, through no fault of his own, was not able to present these circumstances in the earlier procedure (Art. 48, para 2).

§7. The Law on Enforcement and Security of Claims

1452. According to the provisions of the Law, on enforcement and security of claims (OJ MNE, Nos 36/11, 28/14, 20/15, 22/17-CC, 25/19)[1527] procedure of the forced realization of the claims on the basis of the domestic or foreign executive or authentic document (hereinafter referred to as 'enforcement proceeding') and secure of the claims (hereinafter referred to as 'security procedure') is to be conducted in accordance to this Law, unless otherwise stipulated by special law. This Law also applies to the compulsory execution of the decision made in administration proceedings issued to meet financial obligations, if the execution is to be carried out on real estate, stocks and shares of the company members. This Law is to be applied to the compulsory execution of the notarial acts and other documents prescribed by the Law (Article 1).[1528]

1453. According to the provisions of Article 2, enforcement proceeding is to be initiated on the proposal of the enforcement creditor, while the security procedure is to be initiated on the proposal of the security proposer.[1529] Against the decision in enforcement and security procedure may be filed a complaint in accordance to this Law. The complaint is not allowed against conclusion (Article 8).[1530]

1454. On a decision of enforcement, decision on dismissing or denying the proposal for execution, may be filed a complaint within five days of decision receipt (Article 47).[1531]

1455. Following the entry into force of the Law on enforcement and security of claims, transferring powers for civil enforcement to the bailiffs, the Parliament enacted in December 2011 the Law on public bailiffs (OJ MNE, No. 61/11, and 22/17). In March 2019 amendments to the Law on public bailiffs (OJ MNE, No. 17/19) were adopted which introduced an obligation for bailiffs to submit asset

1527. In April 2019, amendments to the Law on enforcement and securing of claims were adopted, 'aiming to align with the EU acquis and address some challenges in the practice of enforcement proceedings.' EC. (2020), 25.

1528. This Law is to be applied on enforcement and security on the ship and in the aircraft only if it is prescribed by the special Law (para. 4).

1529. The procedures referred to the para. 1 of this Article are to be initiated ex officio when specified by the Law (para. 2). According to the provisions of the Art. 14, in the enforcement and security procedures are to be applied provisions of the Law regulating litigation procedure, unless this or another law provides otherwise.

1530. The rules regulating complaint are in detail prescribed in the Arts 47–60. Beside that, provisions about possibility of the complaint are regulated in Art. 65, paras 7–9; 67–69; 73 para. 4; 79, para. 3; 106, para. 5; 118, para. 3; 128 para. 3; 181 para. 4; 252 para. 2; 253; 270, point 1; 292, para. 2.

1531. The complaint is to be filed to the court, i.e., to the public executor who made decision on the enforcement proceeding. Public executor is obliged to submit to the court case files, in five days for the purpose of making decision regarding complaints (paras 2 and 3).

declarations to the Anti-Corruption Agency. In December 2019, the revised code of ethics for public bailiffs was adopted and the new commission for ethical conduct of public bailiffs formed.[1532]

1532. 'Additional steps are needed to promote professional and ethical standards among bailiffs, including appropriate training. EC.' (2020), p. 23.

Chapter 4. Other Forms of Juridical Actions of Individuals

§1. Human Rights and Freedoms Protector's Procedure[1533]

1456. In July 2011 the Parliament of Montenegro adopted a new Law on the PHRF of Montenegro (OJ MNE, Nos 42/2011, 32/14).[1534] According to Article 30, the complaint can be filed by anyone who believes that his/her rights and freedoms are violated. In the case of violation of the right of a child, the complaint may be filed by its parent or guardian or legal representative.[1535] In addition, the complaint may be filed through an MP, as well as an organization dealing with human rights and freedoms. The complaint may be filed orally on the record. A person deprived of liberty shall have the right to file a complaint in a sealed envelope.[1536]

1457. In 2009, a total of twelve complaints were filed by citizens about the violation of the right to environment.[1537] 'The complaints were predominantly in reference to the noise emission in coastal areas during the tourist season. According to those complaints, the noise was particularly loud at night. In relation to this, the Ombudsman received the notification from the competent authorities that the relevant inspections conducted regular controls, and that a large number of fines were imposed in light of the aforementioned problem'.[1538]

1458. During 2021, in the cases in which the proceedings were concluded, the complainants pointed to the violation of the right to a fair trial (87), to other civil rights (275), to economic, social and cultural rights (204), to the rights of the child (165) and the prohibition of discrimination (173). The complainants invoked the right to a healthy environment in 5 cases.[1539]

1533. ' … the proposal is to establish the institution of a protector of environment in Montenegro, i.e., the ecological ombudsman. This institution would contribute to the respect of commitment from the Parliament's Declaration on Montenegro as an Ecological State, Constitutional provisions on those matters, as well as the Laws related to the environment and protection of natural and cultural values. It would encourage the involvement of a broad public in the control and prevention of violation of regulations and threats to the environment, and make the governmental institutions on the national and local level more responsible when it comes to enforcement of laws in that area.' GMNE, NCSD (2011), 24.
1534. On the day of entering into force of this Law, the Law on Protector of Human Rights and Freedoms ('Official Journal of the RM', No. 41/03) shall cease to have effect (Art. 58).
1535. If the right of a child is violated by a person referred to in para. 2 of this Article, the complaint may be filed by the organization or authority that deals with the protection of child rights (Art. 30, para. 3).
1536. The authorized person from authority, organization or institution in which reside a person deprived of liberty, is required to immediately submit to the Protector unopened and unread complaint or other writing of such person (Art. 30, para. 7).
1537. In 2011–2012 complaints were filed. PHRF (2012), 81.
1538. PHRF (2010), 79.
1539. PHRF (2022), 45, 46.

1459. Pursuant to Article 3 the Protector can be addressed by anyone who believes that an act, action or failure to act of the authorities violated his/her rights or freedoms. The Protector shall, as well, act on his/her own initiative.[1540]

1460. The procedure of examination of violations of human rights and freedoms shall be initiated following a complaint or by the initiative of the Protector (Article 28, paragraph 1).[1541] Protector shall examine violations of human rights and freedoms by his/her own initiative after he/she finds out that the act, action or failure to act of authorities violated human rights and freedoms.

1461. The Law prescribed that Ombudsman may also represent the parties only in the proceedings related to discrimination. However, 'Ombudsman has no competencies to represent citizens when it comes to serious human rights violations such as abuse and torture'.[1542]

§2. Alternative Dispute Resolution

1462. The Law on Alternative Dispute Resolution (OJ MNE, No. 77/20) was adopted by the government in November 2019, and declared in the Parliament in July 2020, set rules relevant to compulsory recourse to alternative dispute resolution for certain types of cases.[1543] The Centre for Mediation was transformed into a Centre for Alternative Dispute Resolution (ADR).

1463. This law regulates alternative dispute resolution in civil matters (hereinafter: alternative dispute resolution) through mediation, early neutral assessment of disputes and other alternative dispute resolution methods, in accordance with internationally accepted standards (Article 1). Expert work related to mediation, early neutral assessment of disputes and other methods of alternative dispute resolution, as well as encouraging and improving the availability of alternative dispute

1540. Proceeding before the Protector shall be free of charge.
1541. In order for Protector to act by his/her own initiative the consent of the victim is required (Art. 28, para. 3).
1542. 'The Law has not clearly defined whether Ombudsman has the access to personal documents. In cases when it is important to find out whether human rights were violated by the insight into personal data, a problem whether Ombudsman has that right, may occur … Office of Ombudsman stated at Boards for human rights several times that the budget for 2012 was insufficient for implementation of new competencies of Ombudsman.' Youth Initiative for Human Rights, Montenegro (2012), 10.
1543. In addition, the Rulebook on the training programme for dispute evaluators (OJMNE, No. 105/20), as well as several other by-laws. *See*: https://centarzaars.me/nacionalni-propisi/ (15 Jan. 2023).

resolution is carried out by the Centre for Alternative Dispute Resolution (hereinafter: the Centre), as the holder of public powers (Article 4).[1544,1545]

1544. The number of cases referred to the Centre for ADR has significantly increased, both by courts and by citizens. By mid 2021, the number of cases referred to the Centre for ADR (3,744) already exceed the total number for 2020. EC. (2021), 22. 'However, the judicial system is not yet prepared to accommodate the increased use of ADR, since the implementation of the new ADR legislation is still not effective or being applied consistently in the competent courts. EC.' (2022), 25.

1545. 'In the aim of reinforcing the rule of law in Montenegro by means of providing better access to justice, decreasing backlog of court cases and strengthening human rights' observance through the provision of larger number of opportunities for pursuing justice and reducing the number of prison sentences, UNDP Montenegro launched the project 'Strengthening the capacities of the Centre for Mediation and Promotion of Alternative Sanctions'. The goal of the project is the development of alternative dispute resolution tools, with an emphasis on the institute of mediation and promotion of alternative sanctions. This goal will be achieved through the adoption of the amended Law on Mediation and its implementation, development of the capacities of the Mediation Centre and its territorial units in Bijelo Polje and Kotor as well as training of future mediators.' https://info.undp.org/docs/pdc/Documents/MNE/00060174_Mediation%20project%20proposal%20June%202010%20FINAL.doc (3 Dec. 2022).

Selected Bibliography and the List of Official Journals

Amann, W. & Kalezić, Dj. (2012). *National Action Plan of Montenegro for Energy Efficiency Measures in the Residential Sector.* Geneve: UNECE. http://www.unece.org/fileadmin/DAM/hlm/documents/Publications/ee.ap.montenegro.pdf. (17 December 2022).

APAWA, JUCETI, SNV Montenegro, GEF, WB. (2007). *Strategic Action Plan for Skadar/Shodra Lake, Albania & Montenegro.* https://iwlearn.net/documents/32104 (17 December 2022).

The Belgrade Centre for Human Rights. (2006). *Human Rights in Serbia and Montenegro 2005: Legal Provisions, Practice and Awareness in the State Union of Serbia and Montenegro Compared to International Human Rights Standards.* Belgrade. (2006) https://www.bgcentar.org.rs/bgcentar/eng-lat/wp-content/uploads/2013/04/Human-Rights-in-Serbia-and-Montenegro-%E2%80%93-A-Comprehensive-Report-for-2004-in-Serbian-and-English-2005.pdf (16 December 2022.

Bieber, F. (ed.). (2003). *Montenegro in Transition – Problems of Identity and Statehood.* Baden: Nomos Verlagsgesellschaft.

Bobić, M. & Todić, D. (2009). Saradnja civilnog društva i državnih institucija u procesu evropskih integracija i sprovođenju koncepta održivog razvoja, u Radojević, D., (ur) *Održivi razvoj: naša zajednička budućnost: nacionalna strategija održivog razvoja* (Cooperation Between Civil Societies and State Institutions in the Process of European Integration and Implementation of the Sustainable Development Concept, in Radojević, D. (ed.) *Sustainable Development: Our Common Future: National Strategy of Sustainable Development*, Beograd, Ministarstvo za nauku i tehnološki razvoj, 28–32.

Bogdanović, S. (1998). *Pravci razvoja Crne Gore ekološke države – finalna studija (Development Direction of Montenegro ecological state – final study); Poglavlje 6. 'Strateški pravci, institucionalni instrumenti i primena razvojnog modela' (Chapter 6 'Strategic Directions, Institutional Instruments and Application of Development Model'*). Beograd: Evropski centar za mir i razvoj Univerziteta UN [ECPD – European Centre for Peace and Development of the University of United Nations].

Bogdanović, S. & Lj. Dabić. (2005). *Uskladjivanje propisa Crne Gore o zastiti zivotne sredine sa zahtjevima Evropske Unije [Harmonization of the Montenegrin Environmental Legislation with the Requirements of EU].* Espoo: Ramboll –

Finnconsult; Stockholm: Ramboll – Natura; Beograd: REC; Podgorica: Ministrastvo zaštite životne sredine i uredenja prostora Republike Crne Gore [Ministry of Environmental Protection and Spatial Regulation of the Republic of Montenegro].

Bulić, Z. & B. Jovanović. (2004). 'ZaštiÇena prirodna baština u funkciji održivog turizma u Crnoj Gori' ('Protected Natural Heritage and Sustainable Tourism in Montenegro'). *Ekonomist*, br. 1, str. 107–114.

Callaway, J., M., Kašćelan, S., Marković, M. (2010). *The Economic Impacts of Climate Change in Montenegro: A First Look,* UNDP.

CE. (2010). *Introductory Report on Nature Conservation in Montenegro*. Strasbourg. https://rm.coe.int/16807465ef (12 December 2022).

CE. (2012). *The Honouring of Obligations and Commitments by Montenegro*, Report, Parliamentary Assembly, Doc. 12952, 8 June 2012. https://pace.coe.int/en/files/18947 (17 December 2022).

CE (2004). Steering Committee for Culture. *Cultural Policy in Serbia and Montenegro, Part II: Republic of Montenegro, National Report*. Council of Europe, CDCULT-BU (2004)7A.

CETI. (2006). *Report on the Investigation of Noise Level in Montenegro Environment – 2005*, JU Centre for Ecotoxical Testing, Podgorica.

CETI. (2008a). *Izveštaj o kvalitetu vazduha u Crnoj Gori u 2007. godini* (*Report on Air Quality in Montenegro 2007*). Podgorica.

CETI. (2008b). *Izveštaj o ispitivanju sadržaja radionuklida u životnoj sredini Crne Gore za 2007. godinu* (*Report on the Research of Content of Radionuclide in the Environment of Montenegro for 2007*). Podgorica.

CETI. (2008c). *Izveštaj o realizaciji programa ispitivanja opasnih i štetnih materija u zemljištu Republike Crne Gore za 2007. godinu* (*Report on Realisation of the Programme of Research of Dangerous and Harmful Substances in Soil for 2007*). Podgorica.

Coalition for monitoring of negotiation process within Chapter 27, *ANALYSIS: Chapter 27-Environment and Climate Change,* English version, February 2018. http://koalicija27.me/2018/02/08/analysis-chapter-27-environment-and-climate-change-english-version/ (17 December 2022).

Čok, V. (2004) 'Međunarodnopravna zaštita kulturnih dobara' ['International Law Protection of Cultural Property']. *Pravni život* (*Juridical Life*). 12 373–382.

Dašić-Raspopović, T. & S. Bajić. (2007). *Normativni okvir u Crnoj Gori za primjenu 'Trećeg stuba' Arhuske konvencije: pristup pravdi* [*Normative Framework in Montenegro for Implementation Third Pillars of the Aarhus Convention – Access to Justice*]. Podgorica: Regionalni centar za životnu sredinu za Centralnu i Istočnu Evropu (REC), Kancelarija u Crnoj Gori.

Djurović, M. (Ed). (2010). *Montenegro in the XXI Century – in the Era of Competitiveness.* Montenegro in Academy of Science and Arts, Podgorica. https://canupub.me/knjiga/montenegro-in-the-xxi-century-in-the-era-of-competitive ness/ (19 Dec. 2022). EAR. (2004). *Strategic Master Plan for Waste Management on the Republic Level.* An EU-Funded Project Managed by European Agency for Reconstruction (. Podgorica, Gopa. https://zerowastemontenegro.me /wp-content/uploads/2016/11/Montenegro-National-waste-master-plan.pdf. (17 December 2022).

EC. (2006). *Montenegro 2006 Progress Report,* Commission of the European Communities, (COM (2006) 649 final), Brussels. SEC (2006) 1388.

EC. (2007). *Montenegro 2007 Progress Report, Accompanying the Communication from the Commission to the European Parliament and the Council.* Enlargement Strategy and Main Challenges 2007–2008, (COM (2007) 663 final), Commission of the European Communities, Brussels. SEC (2007) 1434.

EC. (2008). *Montenegro 2008 Progress Report, Accompanying the Communication from the Commission to the European Parliament and the Council.* Enlargement Strategy and Main Challenges 2008–2009, (COM(2008) 674), Brussels. SEC (2008) 2696.

EC. (2009). *Montenegro 2009 Progress Report,* SEC (2009) 1336; *Accompanying the Communication from the Commission to the European Parliament and the Council,* Enlargement Strategy and Main Challenges 2009–2010, (COM(2009) 533), Brussels, 14 October 2009.

EC. (2010). *Analytical Report Accompanying the Communication from the Commission to the European Parliament and Council – Commission Opinion on Montenegro's application for membership of the European Union,* COM(2010) 670, Brussels, 9 November 2010.

EC. (2011). *Montenegro 2011 Progress Report,* SEC(2011) 1204 final, Accompanying the document Communication from the Commission to the European Parliament and the Council, Enlargement Strategy and Main Challenges 2011–2012, Brussels, 12 October 2011.

EC. (2012). *Report from the Commission to the European Parliament and the Council on Montenegro's progress in the implementation of reforms,* COM(2012) 222 final, Brussels, 22 May 2012.

EC. (2013a). *Montenegro 2013 Progress Report.* European Commission, SWD(2013) 411 final, Brussels, 16.10.2013. https://neighbourhood-enlargement.ec.europa.eu/system/files/2016-12/mn_rapport_2013.pdf (16 January 2023).

EC. (2013b). *Screening report Montenegro Chapter 27 – Environment and climate change,* 28 November 2013, https://gbc.me/wp-content/uploads/2014/10/EU-screening_report_montenegro_ch27.pdf (17 Dec. 2022). EC. (2015). *Montenegro 2015 Report,* Accompanying the document Communication from the Commission to the European Parliament, the Council, the European Economic and Social Committee and the Committee of the Regions, EU Enlargement Strategy, Brussels, 10.11.2015, SWD(2015) 210 final.

EC. (2016). *Montenegro 2016 Report,* Accompanying the document Communication from the Commission to the European Parliament, the Council, the European Economic and Social Committee and the Committee of the Regions, 2016 Communication on EU Enlargement Policy, Brussels, 9.11.2016, SWD(2016) 360 final.

EC. (2018). *Montenegro 2018 Report,* Accompanying the document Communication from the Commission to the European Parliament, the Council, the European Economic and Social Committee and the Committee of the Regions 2018 Communication on EU Enlargement Policy, Strasbourg, 17.4.2018, SWD(2018) 150 final.

Selected Bibliography and the List of Official Journals

EC. (2019). *Montenegro 2019 Report*. SWD(2019) 217 final, Brussels, 29.5.2019. https://neighbourhood-enlargement.ec.europa.eu/system/files/2019-05/20190529-montenegro-report.pdf (16 January 2023).

EC. (2020a). *Guidelines for the Implementation of the Green Agenda for the Western Balkans*. European Commission. SWD(2020) 223 final. Brussels, 6.10.2020.

EC. (2020b). *Montenegro 2020 Report*. SWD(2020) 353 final, Brussels, 6.10.2020. https://neighbourhood-enlargement.ec.europa.eu/system/files/2020-10/montenegro_report_2020.pdf (3 January 2023).

EC. (2022). *Montenegro 2022 Report*. SWD(2022) 335 final, Brussels, 12.10.2022. https://neighbourhood-enlargement.ec.europa.eu/system/files/2022-10/Montenegro%20Report%202022.pdf (19 December 2022).

Energy Community. (2021). *Study on Addressing Energy Poverty in the Energy Community Contracting Parties*. Zagreb. https://www.energy-community.org/documents/studies.html (15 January 2023).

EEA. (2007). *Sustainable consumption and production in Southeast Europe and Eastern Europe, Caucasus and Central Asia* – Joint UNEP-EEA report on the opportunities and lessons learned, EEA Report No. 3/2007. Copenhagen. http://www.eea.europa.eu/publications/eea_report_2007_3. (17 December 2022).

EEA. (2010). *Environmental trends and perspectives in the Western Balkans: future productions and consumption patterns*, EEA Report, No. 1/2010, European Environment Agency. Copenhagen.

EEA. (2011). *European bathing water quality in 2011*. Copenhagen. (2011). http://www.eea.europa.eu/publications/european-bathing-water-quality-in-2011. (17 December 2022).

EEA. (2021). Municipal Waste Management – Conuntry Fact Sheet, Montenegro.

EEA. (2022) *Country profile (Montenegro)*. https://www.eea.europa.eu/countries-and-regions/montenegro (17 December 2022).

EPA. (2021). *Izvještaj o stanju životne sredine u Crnoj Gori na bazi indikatora (2017–2020)* [Report on the state of the environment in Montenegro based on indicators (2017–2020)]. Podgorica. https://epa.org.me/wp-content/uploads/2022/07/izvjestaj-o-stanju-zivotne-sredine-u-crnoj-gori-na-bazi-indikatora-2017-2020-sa-akcionim-planom-za-unapredenje-stanja-zivotne-sredine-sa-predlogom-mjera-za-period-2022-2025-godina.pdf (23 December 2022).

EPA. (2013). *Indicator-based State of the Environment Report of Montenegro*. Environmental Protection Agency of Montengro. Podgorica. https://epa.org.me/wp-content/uploads/2018/03/Izvjestaj-final-engl.pdf (15 January 2023).

Federal Ministry for Development, Science and the Environment. (2000). *The Consequences of NATO bombing for the Environment in FR Yugoslavia*. Belgrade.

Galli, A., Đurović, G., Hanscom, L., Knežević, J. (2018). Think globally, act locally: Implementing the sustainable development goals in Montenegro, *Environmental Science & Policy*, 84: 159–169.

Glavonjić, B. et al. (2005). *Forest and Forest Products Country Profile: Serbia and Montenegro*. Geneva Timber and Forest Discussion Paper 40 www.unece.org/timber/docs/dp/dp-40.pdf. Geneva: UNECE/FAO. (17 December 2022).

GMNE. (2003a). *Public Administration Reform Strategy in Montenegro 2002–2009*. Podgorica. https://www.gov.me/en/documents/569f56fd-5fe4-4191-82ea-e8fda100f2ce (17 December 2022).

GMNE. (2003b) *Strategy for Health Care Development in Montenegro*. Podgorica. www.gov.me/files/1077189400.doc, 10 January 2009.

GMNE. (2005). *Energy Efficiency Strategy of Montenegro*, Podgorica. https://energetska-efikasnost.me/ee/uploads/file/Dokumenta/Energy%20Efficiency%20Strategy%20of%20Montenegro.pdf (17 December 2022).

GMNE. (2007). *Spatial Plan for Special Purpose Coastal Zone*. RZUP Republic Institute for Urban Planning and Development. Kotor, Podgorica: MonteCEP Centre for Urban Planning Development. https://www.gov.me/en/documents/74151f35-c5a3-4bfb-aa53-2a4b94f574a7 (20 December 2022).

GMNE. (2008a). *Brief on the Work of the Ministry in the Department for Environmental Protection*. Podgorica: Government of Montenegro, Ministry of Tourism and Environment.

GMNE. (2008b). *National Programme for Integration of Montenegro into the EU (NPI) for the period* 2008–2012. Podgorica. https://www.esiweb.org/pdf/montengro_National%20Program%20for%20Integration%202008%202012.pdf (20 December 2022).

GMNE. (2008c). *Spatial Plan of Montenegro until 2020*. Podgorica. https://www.gov.me/en/documents/b57f5f50-6f9c-4c27-ba86-122f5166b126, (20 December 2022).

GMNE. (2008d). *Initial Report on the Implementation of the Convention on the Rights of the Child for the Period 2006–2008,* Government of Montenegro, Podgorica.

GMNE. (2009). *The Strategy of Cooperation of the Government of Montenegro and Non-Governmental Organizations,* Podgorica: Office for Cooperation with NGOs within the General Secretariat of the Government of Montenegro.

GMNE. (2011a). *Montenegro report: preparations for RIO + 20.* https://kipdf.com/montenegro-report-preparations-for-rio20_5ab469a91723dd329c63f5a6.html. (20 December 2022).

GMNE. (2011b). *Strategy of public administration reform in Montenegro 2011.-2016. 'Aururm'.* Podgorica.

GMNE. (2012). Prilog izveštaju Evropske komisije o napretku Crne Gore za 2012. za period 1 septembra – 25 aprila 2012. Podgorica: Vlada Crne Gore, Ministarstvo vanjskih poslova i evropskih integracija. (Annex to the Report of the European Commission on progress of Montenegro in 2012, for the period from 1 September to 25 April 2012, Podgorica: Government of Montenegro, Ministry of Foreign Affairs and European integration) https://www.gov.me/dokumenta/96170465-aedf-4c77-a5c0-74000c85de07 (21 December 2022).

GMNE. (2019). *The Strategy on Judiciary Reform 2019-2022.* https://wapi.gov.me/download-preview/6174402a-e27c-4858-a60e-3307d4332fbc?version=1.0 (8 December 2022).

GMNE. (2021) *The Action Plan for the implementation of the Judiciary Reform Strategy for the period 2021-2022.* https://wapi.gov.me/download-preview/180d621b-3d92-4304-981f-702ca00c0c19?version=1.0 (8 December 2022).GMNE. (2021). *Montenegro's Programme of Accession to the European Union 2021 – 2023.* Government of Montenegro, Prime Minister's Office, European Integration Office, Podgorica, March 2021. https://www.eu.me/wpfd_file/montenegros-programme-of-accession-to-the-european-union-2021-2023/ (3 January 2023).

GMNE. (2022a). *Predlog Programa pristupanja Crne Gore Evropskoji uniji 2022-2023. [Program for the Accession of Montenegro to the European Union 2022-2023 – proposal].* Vlada Crne Gore, Kabinet Predsjednika, Kancelarija za evropske integracije, Podgorica, Januar 2022. https://www.gov.me/en/documents/201269a4-2301-4e15-bd22-be4d8a542830 (3 January 2023).

GMNE. (2022b). *Izvještaj o realizaciji Programa pristupanja Crne Gore Evropskoj uniji 2021-2023, za 2021. godinu [Report on the implementation of the Program for the Accession of Montenegro to the European Union 2021-2023, for the year 2021].* Government of the Montenegro, Cabinet of the President, Office for European Integration Podgorica, January 2022. https://www.gov.me/dokumenta/a4fb6c49-bdc4-4880-b978-4b92805d859a (3 January 2023).

GMNE. (2022c). *The Economic Reform Programme for period 2022-2024.* Podgorica. https://www.gov.me/en/documents/e75a225c-375c-47bb-af21-5b595523b305 (23 December 2022).

GMNE. (2022d). *The Second Voluntary National Review: Montenegro and Sustainable Development Goals 2016–2021.* https://www.gov.me/en/article/montenegro-presents-second-voluntary-national-review (13 January 2023).

GMNE, GEF, UNDP. (2021). *Third biennial update report of Montenegro to the United Nations Framework Convention on Climate Change.* Podgorica. https://unfccc.int/sites/default/files/resource/BUR3_Montenegro%20-%2024.%20Jan%20-%20FINAL.pdf (21 December 2022).

GMNE, MAFWM. (2009a). *Questionnaire – Information Requested by the European Commission to the Government of Montenegro for the preparation of the Opinion on the application of Montenegro for membership of the European Union – 11 Agriculture and rural development.* Podgorica: Government of Montenegro, Ministry of Agriculture, Forest and Water Management.

GMNE, MAFWM. (2009b). *Questionnaire – Information Requested by the European Commission to the Government of Montenegro for the preparation of the Opinion on the application of Montenegro for membership of the European Union – 13 Fisheries.* Podgorica: Government of Montenegro, Ministry of Agriculture, Forest and Water Management.

GMNE, MARD. (2017). *Strategija upravljanja vodama Crne Gore.* (Water Management Strategy of Montenegro). Podgorica. https://javnepolitike.me/wp-content/uploads/2020/07/Strategija-upravljanja-vodama-2017-2035.pdf (23 December 2022).

GMNE, ME. (2009). *Questionnaire – Information Requested by the European Commission to the Government of Montenegro for the preparation of the Opinion on the application of Montenegro for membership of the European Union – 15 Energy.* Podgorica: Government of Montenegro, Ministry of Economy GMNE, MPPEP. (2009). *Questionnaire – Information Requested by the European Commission to the Government of Montenegro for the preparation of the Opinion on the application of Montenegro for membership of the European Union – 27 Environment.* Podgorica: Government of Montenegro, Ministry of Physical Planning and Environmental Protection.

GMNE, MPPEP.(….) *Questionnaire – Information Requested by the European Commission to the Government of Montenegro for the preparation of the Opinion on the application of Montenegro for membership of the European Union –*

27 Environment – Additional Questions. Podgorica: Government of Montenegro, Ministry of Physical Planning and Environmental Protection.

GMNE, MSDT. (2019). *Plan upravljanja komunalnim otpadnim vodama Crne Gore (2020-2035) (Municipal wastewater management plan of Montenegro (2020-2035)*. Podgorica. https://www.gov.me/en/documents/0e52a4d6-e200-4e20-b721-01bec2a7eb10 (23 December 2022).

GMNE, MSDT. (2015). *Rezime nacionalne strategije u oblasti klimatskih promjena do 2030. godine (Summary of the National strategy in the field of climate change until 2030)*, Podgorica. https://www.gov.me/dokumenta/cd1130f8-668b-4fbd-a094-20a04af536aa (23 December 2022).

GMNE, NCSD. (2011). *Analysis of Achievements and Challenges of the Ecological State – 20 years of the Ecological State of Montenegro*. Podgorica. https://www.gov.me/en/article/108441--20-years-of-ecological-state-of-montenegro-main-challenges-and-living-up-to-set-goals (21 December 2022).

GMNE, OSD. (2009). *Drugi godišnji izvještaj o implementaciji Nacionalne strategije održivog razvoja Crne Gore za period april 2008 – septembar 2009. godine*. [*The second annual report on implementation of National Strategy of Sustainable Development of Montenegro for the period April 2008 – September 2009 year*]. https://www.gov.me/en/documents/0bcaf317-1012-4d53-b283-6ed9195a50b9 (21 Dec. 2022). Golubovic, V., Mirkovic, M., & Kaludjerovic, J. (2022). In-work poverty in Montenegro. *Journal of International and Comparative Social Policy*, 38(2), 180–191. doi:10.1017/ics.2022.8.

Freedom House. (2012). *Report – Montenegro*.

Freedom House. (2021). *Report – Montenegro*. https://freedomhouse.org/country/montenegro/nations-transit/2021 (21 December 2022).

IFC. (2006). *Izveštaj o stanju u sektoru reciklaže u Srbiji i Crnoj Gori* (*Report on state in recycling sector in Serbia and Montenegro*). Predicament Consulting.

IMF. (2004). *Serbia and Montenegro: Poverty Reduction Strategy Paper*. Washington DC. www.imf.org/external/pubs/ft/scr/2004/cr04120.pdf. (22 December 2022).

IMPP. (1987). *Pregled medjunarodnih ugovora i drugih akata značajnih za medjunarodne odnose Crne Gore 1700–1918. godine* [*Repertoire de traites international et d'autres actes relatifs au relations international de Montenegro depuis 1700 jusqu'a 1918*], VI sveska 'Pregled razvoja medjunarodnopravnih odnosa jugoslovenskih zemalja', Beograd-Titograd.

Joldžić, V. (1995). *Ekološki kriminalitet u pravu i stvarnosti* [*Ecology Crime in Law and Reality*]. Beograd: Ecologica.

Joldžić, V. & G. Miličević. (1995). *Životna sredina i medjunarodni ugovori od znacaja za Saveznu Republiku Jugoslaviju* [*Environment and International Treaties Relevant for FR Yugoslavia*®. Beograd: Savezno ministarstvo za razvoj, nauku i životnu sredinu.

Jovanović, J. (2001). *Istorija Crne Gore* (History of Montenegro), Podgorica: CID.

Jovanović, M., *et. al*. (2017). *Invest in Montenegro 2018 – 111 Frequently Asked Questions*. MIPA, Podgorica.

Kavran, D. & G. Petković (eds). (1997). *Pravo i zivotna sredina* [*Law and the Environment*]. Beograd: Udruzenje pravnika Jugoslavije.

Selected Bibliography and the List of Official Journals

Kokel, P. (1998). *Istorija Crne Gore i Bosne* [Histoire de Montenegro et de la Bosnie], Podgorica: CID.

Komar O., Gegaj, P. (2015). *The Montenegro I Want*, Report on Post-2015 National Consultations in Montenegro, The United Nations System in Montenegro, Podgorica.

Koprivica, D. & Kovačević, M. (2010). *Guide through the Government of Montenegro*, Podgorica: Centre for Democratic Transition (CDT).

Kostić-Mandić, M. & M. Katić. (2004). *Strategija za primjenu Arhuske konvencije u Crnoj Gori.* [Strategy on Implementation of Aarhus Convention in Montenegro]. Beograd: REC Kancelarija u Srbiji i Crnoj Gori.

Kostić-Mandić, M. (2011). Harmonization of the Montenegrin Environmental Legislation with the European Union Law, *Natura Montenegrina*, Podgorica: 10(3): 323–333.

Matijas, M. (2007). 'Razvoj jugoistočne Evrope iz evropske perspektive u 19. i 20. veku' ['Development of South-Eastern Europe from European Perspective in XIX and XX Century']. *Megatrend Revija* (*Megatrend Review*). Belgrade, no. 1: 5–29.

MAFWM. (2006a). *Montenegro's Agriculture and European Union – Agriculture and Rural Development Strategy.* Final Report of the EU Funded Project, Podgorica.

MAFWM. (2006b). *Montenegro's Fisheries Development Strategy and Capacity Building for Implementation of EU Common Fisheries Policy.* Podgorica.

MAFWM. (2008a). *Razvoj ribarskog sektora Crne Gore 2009–2013 godine – Nacionalni strategijski plan, Nacrt* [*Development of Fishing Sector in Montenegro Year, 2009–2013 – National Strategic Plan, Draft*]. Podgorica https://www.gov.me/dokumenta/a78c616c-eee1-4a56-bf9f-990905cf1541 (23 December 2022).

MAFWM. (2008b). *Forest for the Future of Montenegro, National Forest and Forest Land Administration Policy*, https://www.lse.ac.uk/GranthamInstitute/wp-content/uploads/laws/8450.pdf (23 December 2022).

MARD. (2015). *Fisheries strategy of Montenegro 2015–2020 with an Action plan (for transposition, implementation and enforcement of EU acquis)*, Podgorica,. https://javnepolitike.me/wp-content/uploads/2020/07/15.-Strategija-ribarstva-Crne-Gore-2015-2020.pdf (23 December 2022).

MARD. (2012). *Annual Report on activities in 2011.* Podgorica.

MCI. (2021). *Fifth Annual Report under the Energy Efficency Directive.* https://www.energy-community.org/documents/parties/EE.html (15 January 2023).

ME. (2019). *Akcioni plan energetske efikasnosti Crne Gore za period 2019-2021.* [Energy Efficency Action Plan of Montenegro – for the period 2019 – 2021]. Ministarstvo ekonomije. https://energetska-efikasnost.me/en/download/strateska_dokumenta/3.-Akcioni-plan-energetske-efikasnosti-Crne-Gore-za-period-2019-2021.-godina.pdf. (15 January 2023).

ME. (2014). *Strategija razvoja energetike Crne Gore do 2030. godine (Bijela knjiga)* [Energy development strategy of Montenegro until 2030 (White Book)]. Ministarstvo ekonomije. https://www.gov.me/dokumenta/eac811f8-4b13-46ce-97c4-412b8d1ebb8a (15 January 2023).

ME. (2010). *Energy Efficiency Action Plan – for the period 2010–2012*, Podgorica, https://energetska-efikasnost.me/wp-content/uploads/2018/12/Energy-Efficiency-Action-Plan-for-Period-2010-2012.pdf. (22 December 2022).

MED. (2007). *The Energy Development Strategy of Montenegro by 2025 – White Book*. Podgorica: Ministry of Economic Development of Montenegro.

MED. (2008). *Energy Development Strategy of Montenegro by 2025, Action plan 2008–2012*. Ministry for Economic Development of Montenegro, Podgorica.

MEDT. (2022). *Montenegro Tourism Development Strategy 2022-2025 with the Action Plan*. Ministry of Economic Development. Podgorica. https://www.gov.me/en/documents/22c74c2f-ab37-4937-b1ee-d3ce2669e4d1 (20 December 2022).

MESPU. (2021). *Nacrt Strategije upravljanja kvalitetom vazduha za period 2021-2029*. [Draft Air Quality Management Strategy for the period 2021–2029]. Ministarstvo ekologije, prostornog planiranja i urbanizma. https://www.gov.me/dokumenta/11674b76-fe5c-4fcc-b0ac-9b3f681e633b (15 January 2023).

MESPU, EPA. (2022a). *Informacija o stanju životne sredine u Crnoj Gori za 2021. godinu* [Information on the state of environment in Montenegro for 2021], Ministarstvo ekologije, prostornog planiranja i urbanizma, Agencija za zaštitu životne sredine, Podgorica. https://epa.org.me/wp-content/uploads/2022/11/Informacija-o-stanju-%C5%BEivotne-sredine-jun-2022.pdf (19 decembar 2022).

MESPU, EPA. (2022b). *Informacija o stanju životne sredine u Crnoj Gori za 2021. godinu – REZIME* [Information on the state of environment in Montenegro for 2021 – RESUME], Ministarstvo ekologije, prostornog planiranja i urbanizma, Agencija za zaštitu životne sredine, Podgorica. https://epa.org.me/wp-content/uploads/2022/11/Rezime-2021-INFORMACIJAFINAL.pdf (19 December 2022). MESPU, EPA. (2021). Informacija o stanju životne sredine u Crnoj Gori za 2020. godinu [Information on the state of environment in Montenegro for 2020], Ministarstvo ekologije, prostornog planiranja i urbanizma, Agencija za zaštitu životne sredine, Podgorica. https://epa.org.me/wp-content/uploads/2021/11/Informacija-o-stanju-zivotne-sredine-za-2020.-godinu.pdf (10 January 2023).

MF. (2018). *Medium-Term Debt Management Strategy 2018–2020*. Ministry of Finance.

MHLSW. (2007). *Poverty Alleviation and Social Inclusion Strategy*. Podgorica. https://www.gov.me/en/documents/d2e71a97-3074-43f1-8249-851159f22af0 (2007).

MHLSW. (2008). *Nacionalna strategija upravljanja medicinskim otpadom* [*National Strategy on Medical Waste Management*]. Podgorica. https://wapi.gov.me/download-preview/9c5cd896-cb9e-49b6-8373-4fe5959d2f84?version=1.0 (22 December 2022).

MI (2021). *Strategy on migration and reintegration of returnees in Montenegro, for the period 2021-2025 year, with Action plan for 2021-2022*. https://javnepolitike.me/strateski-dokumenti/ (23 December 2022).

Milojević, M. (2005). Constitutional Competences for Conclusion and Enactment of International Treaties, *Facta Universitatis, Series: Law and Politics* 3, no. 1.

MLSW. (2011). *The Strategy for Durable Solutions of Issues Regarding Displaced and Internally Displaced Persons in Montenegro, with special emphasis on the Konik area.* https://www.gov.me/cyr/dokumenta/a7d782a4-ae4c-4d4f-bb9f-d3e003a6294d (22 December 2002).

MONSTAT. (2011a). *Population of Montenegro by sex, type of settlement, ethnicity, religion and mother tongue, per municipalities*, Census of Population, Households and Dwellings in Montenegro 2011. Podgorica. http://www.monstat.org/userfiles/file/popis2011/saopstenje/saopstenje(1).pdf. (20 December 2022).

MONSTAT. (2011b). *Agricultural Census 2010, Structure of Agricultural Holdings – Key variables – Land and Livestock Resources.* Podgorica. http://www.monstat.org/userfiles/file/popis%20poljoprivrede/knjiga_I%20POLJ%2015.4.pdf (20 December 2022).

MONSTAT. (2011c). *Poverty analysis in Montenegro in 2010*. Release No. 186. Podgorica. http://www.monstat.org/userfiles/file/analiza%20siromastva/POVERTY%20ANALYSIS%20IN%20MONTENEGRO%20IN%202010-2.pdf. (20 December 2022).

MONSTAT. (2011d). *Gross domestic product of Montenegro in 2010*, Release No. 119. Podgorica. http://www.monstat.org/userfiles/file/GDP/GDP%202010_eng.pdf. (20 December 2022).

MONSTAT. (2011e). Natural movement of population and internal migration flows in 2010. Release No. 98. Podgorica. http://www.monstat.org/userfiles/file/demografija/eng/saopstenje%20demografija%202010%20ENG.pdf. (20 December 2022).

MONSTAT. (2011f). *Population by age, sex, and type of settlement per municipality, as well as the most frequent name in Montenegro*, Release No. 117. Podgorica. https://www.monstat.org/userfiles/file/popis2011/saopstenje/saopstenje%20starost%204%2009%202011%20prevod.pdf (20 December 2022).

MONSTAT. (2011g). *Agricultural Census 2010, Structure of Agricultural Holdings – Livestock Resources.* Podgorica. http://monstat.org/userfiles/file/popis%20poljoprivrede/knjiga%20iii%20za%20sajt,%2029.07.2011.2.pdf (20 December 2022).

MONSTAT. (2012a). *Population by activity status in Montenegro*, Census of Population, Households, and Dwellings in Montenegro 2011. Podgorica. http://monstat.org/userfiles/file/popis2011/saopstenje/aktivnost%20saoptenje%20%2005%2003%202012%20eng-3.pdf. (22 December 2022).

MONSTAT. (2012b). *Educational structure of population in Montenegro,* Census of Population, Households and Dwellings in Montenegro in 2011. Podgorica. http://www.monstat.org/userfiles/file/popis2011/Saop%20obrazovanje11%2006%202012%20ENG%20PDF.pdf. (22 December 2022).

MONSTAT. (2012c). *Labour Force Survey 2011.* Release No. 60. Podgorica. http://www.monstat.org/userfiles/file/ars/ARS%20-%20Godisnje%20saopstenje,%202011.pdf. (22 December 2022).

MONSTAT. (2012d). Harmonized Index of Consumer Prices (HICP) February 2012, Release No. 56. Podgorica. http://monstat.org/userfiles/file/cijene/hicp/Saopstenja%202012/Harmonized%20index%20of%20consumer%20prices%20HICP,%20February%202012.pdf. (22 December 2022).

MONSTAT. (2012e). *Amount of waste generated from industry 2011*. Release No. 186. Podgorica.

MONSTAT. (2012f). *Municipal waste in Montenegro*. Release No. 185. Podgorica). https://www.monstat.org/userfiles/file/ziv%20sredina/eng%20OT%20KOM-03%2029%2006%202012%20%20PDF.pdf (20 December 2022).

MONSTAT. (2021). *Public Water Suply and Water Protection. 2020.* Release 66/2021. https://www.monstat.org/uploads/files/vode/2020/Public_water%20_supply_and%20_water_%20protection%20_2020.pdf (9 January 2023).

MONSTAT. (2022a). *Generated and Treated Waste*. Release 140/2022. https://www.monstat.org/uploads/files/otpad/2021/Generated%20and%20treated%20waste_2021.pdf (9 January 2023).

MONSTAT. (2022b). *Water use and protection against pollution in the industry*. Release 153/2022. https://www.monstat.org/uploads/files/vode/2021/Water%20use%20and%20protection%20against%20pollution%20in%20the%20industry%20(005).pdf (9 January 2023).

MSDT, NEPA. (2017). Informacija o stanju životne sredine u Crnoj Gori za 2016. godinu [*Information on the state of environment in Montenegro 2016]*. Podgorica. https://epa.org.me/wp-content/uploads/2018/04/Informacija-o-stanju-zivotne-sredine-za-2016.pdf (19 December 2022).

MSDT. (2020). *Montenergro Third National Communication on Climate Change*. Ministry of Sustainable Development and Tourism, GEF, UNDP, Podgorica, 2020. https://unfccc.int/documents/254489 (17. December 2022). MSDT. (2019). *National Plan for Implementation of Stockholm Convention, with an Action Plan for 2019-2023*. MSDT, GEF, UNEP. July 2019.

MSDT. (2018). *The Sixth National Report of Montenegro to the United Nations Convention on Biological Diversity*. Ministry of Sustainable Development and Tourism, UNEP, GEF, Montenegro, December 2018. https://www.cbd.int/doc/nr/nr-06/me-nr-06-en.pdf (3 January 2023).MSDT. (2017). *Plan of Institutional Adjustment and Strengthening of Administrative Capacities for Environment and Climate Change Sectors in Montenegro – for the period 2017–2020,* Podgorica.

MSDT. (2016a). *National Strategy with Action Plan for Transposition, Implementation, and Enforcement of the EU Acquis on Environment and Climate Change 2016–2020*, Podgorica.

MSDT. (2016b). *Nacionalna strategija održivog razvoja do 2030. godine.* [National Strategy for Sustainable Development by 2030]. Podgorica. https://javnepolitike.me/wp-content/uploads/2020/07/NSORdo2030FINALNA-3.pdf (17 December 2022); https://faolex.fao.org/docs/pdf/mne180387.pdf (17 December 2022).

MSDT. (2016c). *Voluntary national reviews at the HLPF 2016 Montenegro*, Montenegro https://sdgs.un.org/sites/default/files/documents/10695Montenegro%2520-%2520HLPF%2520Report.pdf (17 December 2022).

MSDT. (2015). *The Second National Communication on Climate Change of Montenegro to the United Nations Framework Convention on Climate Change (UNFCCC)*, 2015. https://unfccc.int/sites/default/files/resource/mnenc2_eng.pdf (17 December 2022).

Selected Bibliography and the List of Official Journals

MSDT. (2014). *The Fifth National Report to the United Nations Convention on Biological Diversity*, 2014. https://www.cbd.int/doc/world/me/me-nr-05-en.pdf (17 December 2022).

MSDT. (2011a). *Aarhus Convention Implementation Report*, Podgorica: Ministry of Sustainable Development and Tourism. http://www.unece.org/fileadmin/DAM/env/pp/reporting/NIRs%202011/Montenegro_-_National_Implementation_Report_2011_e.pdf. (17 December 2022).

MSDT. (2011b). *Prvi godišnji izveštaj o sprovođenju Milenijumskih razvojnih ciljeva u Crnoj Gori*. Podgorica. Ministry of Sustainable Development and Tourism, [*First Annual Report on the Implementation of the Millennium Development Goals in Montenegro]*. http://www.kor.gov.me/rubrike/milenijumski-razvojni-ciljevi/110941/Prvi-godisnji-i.html. (17 December 2022).

MSPE. (2009). *Report on status of spatial development for 2009*. Podgorica.

MSPE. (2010a). *Fourth National Report of Montenegro to the Convention on Biological Diversity*. Vasilije Bušković & Milena Kapa (eds). Podgorica.

MSPE. (2010b). *National Biodiversity Strategy with the Action Plan for the period 2010 – 2015*. Podgorica.

MSPE. (2010c). *The Initial National Communication on Climate Change of Montenegro to the United Nations Framework Convention on Climate Change (UNFCCC)*. http://unfccc.int/resource/docs/natc/mnenc1.pdf. (20 December 2022).

Nadić, D. (2012). Komparativna analiza nacionalnih strategija održivog razvoja Srbije, Crne Gore i Hrvatske [Comparative Analysis of National Sustainable Development Strategies in the Republic of Serbia, Montenegro and Croatia], *Teme*, 2: 501–523.

Parliament of Montenegro. (2018). *Performance Report 2018*. Podgorica: Parliament of Montenegro. https://api.skupstina.me/media/files/1638357453-2018-performance-report-of-the-parliament-of-montenegro.pdf (19 December 2022).

Permanent Mission of Montenegro to the UN, OSCE and other International Organizations in Vienna. (2012). *Questionnaires on the Code of Conduct on Politico-Military Aspects of Security*, FSC.EMI/124/12. 20 April 2012. http://www.osce.org/fsc/90092 (19 December 2022).

PHRF. (2005). *Annual Report for 2004*. Protector of Human Rights and Freedoms, Republic of Montenegro, Podgorica. https://www.ombudsman.co.me/doc.php?categ=godisnji&sector=&year=&find2=&page=3 (19 December 2022).

PHRF. (2010). *Annual Report 2009*, Podgorica: The Protector of Human Rights and Freedoms. https://www.ombudsman.co.me/doc.php?categ=godisnji&sector=&year=&find2=&page=2 (19 December 2022).

PHRF. (2012). *Izveštaj o radu za 2011. godinu*. Podgorica: Zaštitnik ljudskih prava i sloboda. [The Protector of Human Rights and Freedoms, *Annual Report 2011*]. https://www.ombudsman.co.me/doc.php?categ=godisnji&sector=&year=&find2=&page=2 (19 December 2022). .

PHRF. (2022). *Izveštaj o radu za 2021. godinu*. Podgorica: Zaštitnik ljudskih prava i sloboda. [The Protector of Human Rights and Freedoms, *Annual Report 2021*]. https://www.ombudsman.co.me/docs/1652269181_final_izvjestaj_05052022.pdf (19 December 2022).

Radunović, Lj. M. (2008). *Water Right in Montenegro*. Podgorica: Water Management of Montenegro. http://www.meteo.co.me/publikacije/VodnopravoEn.pdf (19 December 2022).

Rakić-Vodinelić, V. (1995). Ekološko pravo kao pravo čoveka [Ecology Law as Right of Man]. *Pravni život* [*Juridical Life*], 9: 245–266.

Stec, S. (ed.). (2003). *Handbook on Access to Justice under the Aarhus Convention*. Szentendre, Hungary: The Regional Environmental Centre for Central and Eastern Europe. http://pdc.ceu.hu/archive/00002416/01/accesstojustice.pdf (19 December 2022).

Stivenson S. Frensis. (2001). *Istorija Crne Gore* [History of Montenegro], Podgorica: CID.

SY MNE. (2008). *Statistical Yearbook of Montenegro 2008*. Podgorica. http://www.monstat.org/cg/page.php?id=216&pageid=101 (19 December 2022).

SY MNE. (2009). *Statistical Yearbook of Montenegro 2009*. Podgorica. http://www.monstat.org/cg/page.php?id=216&pageid=101. (19 December 2022).

SY MNE. (2010). *Statistical Yearbook of Montenegro 2010*. Podgorica. http://www.monstat.org/cg/page.php?id=335&pageid=101. (19 December 2022).

SY MNE. (2011). *Statistical Yearbook of Montenegro 2011*. Podgorica. http://www.monstat.org/userfiles/file/publikacije/godisnjak%202011/GODISNJAK%20%202011-%20new.pdf. (19 December 2022).

SY MNE. (2021). *Statistical Yearbook of Montenegro 2021. Podgorica.* https://monstat.org/uploads/files/publikacije/godisnjak%202021/STATISTI%C4%8CKI%20GODISNJAK%202021.pdf (19 December 2022).

TACSO. (2016). *CSO Needs Assessment Report Montenegro*, updated 2016. Technical Assistance to Civil Society Organizations. Podgorica. http://tacso.eu/wp-content/uploads/2019/05/doc2016_nar_mn.pdf (19 December 2022).

Todić, D. (2002). *Medjunarodne konvencije u oblasti zivotne sredine i SR Jugoslavija* [*International Conventions in the Field of Environment and FR Yugoslavia*]. Belgrade: REC.

Todić, D. (2008). *Savremena politika i pravo životne sredine* [*Contemporary Environmental Policy and Law*]. Beograd: Megatrend Univerzitet.

Todić, D. (2011a). *Vodič kroz EU politike – životna sredine [EU policy guide – Environment],* Belgrade, European Movement in Serbia.

Todić, D. (2011b). Social and Environmental Issues Related to the Security in *SEE* Countries, in Montini, M., Bogdanovic, S., (ed.) *Environmental Security in South – Eastern Europe*, Springer Science + Business Media B.V. 43–58.

Todić, D. (2014). Komparativna politika i pravo klimatskih promena: Bosna i Herzegovina, Crna Gora, Hrvatska i Srbija (osnovni elementi) [Comparative Politics and Climate Change Law: Bosnia and Herzegovina, Montenegro, Croatia and Serbia (Basic Elements)], *Strani pravni život* [Foreign Legal Life], 1 181–194.

Todić, D. (2014). *Klimatske promene u pravu i reforma sistema upravljanja* [Climate change in law and governance system reform]. Institutu za međunarodnu politiku i privredu, Beograd.

Todić, D. (2017). Članstvo u međunarodnim multilateralnim ugovorima u oblasti životne sredine i globalni bezbednosni izazovi [Membership in international multilateral environmental agreements and global security challenges], *Zbornik radova Pravnog fakulteta u Novom Sadu*, [Collected papers of the Faculty of law in Novi Sad], 3: 825-838.Todić, D. (2018). Zaključivanje i izvršavanje međunarodnih ugovora u pravnom sistemu BiH, Crne Gore i Hrvatske [Conclusion and implementation of international treaties in the legal systems of BiH, Montenegro, and Croatia]. *Strani pravni život* [Foreign Legal Life], 2: 103–119.

Todić, D. (2018). *Ujedinjene nacije, međunarodni ugovori i životna sredina* [United Nations, international treaties, and environment], Institut za međunarodnu politiku i privredu, Beograd.

Todić, D. (2019). Gde su granice prava klimatskih promena? [What are the boundaries of the Law on climate change?]. *Zbornik radova Pravnog fakulteta u Nišu* [Collection of papers, Faculty of law, Niš], 83: 41–59.Todić, D. (2019). Multilateral Environmental Agreements and EU Integration of Western Balkan States (Status of Bosnia and Herzegovina, Montenegro, Serbia and Croatia in Multilateral Environmental Agreemetns), *European Energy and Environmental Law Review*, 28, 1: 17–27.

Todić, D. (2021). Prirodni resursi u međunarodnim ugovorima – od suverenih prava država do zajedničke brige čovečanstva [Natural resources in international treaties – from the sovereign rights of states to the common concern of humankind]. *Strani pravni život* [Foreign Legal Life], 3:391-405.Todić, D. (2022). Klimatske promene, vanredne situacije i odgovor Srbije, Crne Gore i Hrvatske. [Climate Change, Emergency Situations and the Response of Serbia, Montenegro, and Croatia] *Zbornik radova Pravnog fakulteta u Nišu*, [Collection of papers, Faculty of law, Niš], 96: 29–43.

Todić, D. & Dimitrijević, D. (2012). Energetska bezbednost u međunarodnom pravu životne sredine [Energy security in international environmental law], Teme 2: 703–721.

Todić, D., Grbić, V. (2018). Natural disasters: Legal framework for cooperation between the Republic of Serbia and Bosnia and Herzegovina, In: Zlatić, M., Kostadinov, S. (Eds). Soil and water resources protection in the changing environment (Advances in Geoecology, Vol. 45) Catena Soil Sciences, Scheizerbat Science Publishers, Stutgart, Germany, 301–311.Todić, D., Ignjatić, M. (2015). Analiza zakonodavstva Republike Srbije, Bosne i Hercegovine (Republike Srpske i Federacije BiH) i Crne Gore u oblasti upravljanja otpadom – u svetlu evropskih integracija, [Comparative analysis of the Republic of Serbia, Bosnia and Herzegovina (The Republic of Srpska and Federationa of BiH), and Montenegro waste management legislation – in the light of European integration], *Evropsko zakonodavstvo*, 52–53: 222–239.Todić, D., Ignjatić, M., Vukaosović, V. (2022). *Environmental Law in Bosnia & Herzegovina*. Wolters Kluwer.

Todić, D. & Todić, J. (2022). Transboundary issues and cooperation in the domain of environmental protection in the legislation of Croatia, Serbia, Montenegro, and Bosnia and Herzegovina. *Glasnik of the Bar Association of Vojvodina*, 4.

Todić, D. & Vukasović, V. (2002). *Ekološka kriza u svetu i odgovor međunarodne zajednice – izbor najznačajnijih međunarodnih dokumenata i jugoslovenskih propisa* [*Environmental Crises and Responses of International Community*]. Savezni sekretarijat za rad, zdravstvo i socijalno staranje, Institut za medunarodnu politiku i privredu, Beograd.

Todić, D. Vukasović V., Ignjatić, M. & Čavoški, A. (2011). *Međunarodni ugovori u oblasti životne sredine u funkciji evropskih integracija i region jugoistočne*

Evrope, Evropski pokret u Srbiji, [*International environmental treaties and European integration of the Southeast Europe region, European movement in Serbia*], Beograd.

Todić, D., & Zlatić, M. (2018). Transboundary cooperation of Western Balkan states in the field of water resources management: Between the existing treaties and a new international treaty, *Environmental Science & Policy*, 89: 67–72.

Tomić, N. (2004). 'Odgovornost i efikasnost inspektora kao vršilaca upravnog nadzora u pravnom sistemu Srbije i Crne Gore' ['Responsibility and Efficiency of Inspectors as Administrative Supervisor in Legal System of Serbia and Montenegro']. *Pravni Život* (*Juridical Life*): 9.

UNDP. (2005a). *Diversities – Potential for Development, Montenegrin Human Development Report*. Podgorica: Institute for Strategic Studies and Prognoses.

UNDP. (2005b). *Millennium Development Goals Report 2004, Republic of Montenegro*. Podgorica. https://planipolis.iiep.unesco.org/sites/default/files/ressources/montenegro_mdg-2004-eng.pdf. (19 December 2022).

UNDP. (2007). *Environmental Policy in South-Eastern Europe*. https://unece.org/fileadmin/DAM/env/documents/2007/ece/ece.belgrade.conf.2007.inf.22.e.pdf. (19 December 2022).

UNDP. (2009). *National Human Development Report 2009 – Society for All*, Podgorica: United Nations Development in Montenegro. https://planipolis.iiep.unesco.org/sites/default/files/ressources/montenegro_nhdr_2009_en.pdf (19 December 2022).

UNDP. (2020). *Assessment of the impact of COVID-19 on the business sector and the growth prospects of the Montenegrin economy*. UNDP in Montenegro. Podgorica.

UNECE. (2003). *Environmental Performance Reviews, Yugoslavia*. United Nations, New York and Geneva.

UNECE. (2007). *Environmental Performance Reviews, Republic of Montenegro*. Second Review, United Nations, New York and Geneva.

UNECE. (2015). *Environmental Performance Reviews, Montenegro*, Third Review, United Nations, New York and Geneva.

UNECE, FAO. (2010). *Reporting on the pan-European Qualitative Indicators for Sustainable Forest Management and National Implementation of Commitments of the Ministerial Conference on the Protection of Forests in Europe*. http://www.unece.org/fileadmin/DAM/publications/timber/QL_SoEF_Montenegro_final.pdf. (19 December 2022).

UNEP. (2004). *From Conflict to Sustainable Development – Assessment of Environmental Hot Spots – Serbia and Montenegro*. Nairobi. https://www.unep.org/resources/report/conflict-sustainable-development-assessment-environmental-hot-spots-serbia-and (19 December 2022).

UNEP, GEF. (2006). *Development of National Biosafety Framework for Serbia and Montenegro*. Belgrade and Novi Sad. https://www.gmo-free-regions.org/fileadmin/files/gmo-free-regions/Montenegro/Development_of_National_Biosafety_Framework.pdf (19 December 2022).

UNESCO. (2010). *Montenegro National Report on underwater cultural heritage*. https://unesdoc.unesco.org/ark:/48223/pf0000189972 (19 December 2022).

United Nations Country Team in Montenegro. (2010). *Integrated United Nations Programme, Results and Budgetary Framework (2010 – 2015) for Montenegro.* United Nations Coordination Office Podgorica. http://www.unece.org/fileadmin/DAM/operact/Technical_Cooperation/Delivering_as_One/UNDAF_country_files/Montenegro_UNDAF_2010-2015_ENG.pdf. (19 December 2022).

Vučić. M. (2011). The Right to Environmental Information as a Technique for the Protection of the Environment. *Međunarodni problemi* [International Problems] 63(3): 449–465.

Vučić, M. (2012a). The Ecosystem Approach in the Environmental Protection of the Danube River Basin Wetlands. In: Jeftić-Šarčević, N. & Stojić-Karanović, E. (eds.): *Danube Strategy – Strategic Significance for Serbia*, Belgrade: Institute of International Politics and Economics, 197–212.

Vučić, M. (2012b). Seveso II Direktiva – ugaoni kamen industrijske bezbednosti [Seveso II Directive – A Cornerstone of Industrial Security]. *Evropsko zakonodavstvo* [European Legislation], 41: 187–202.

Vučić, M. (2016a). Integrated Pollution Prevention and Control in EU and Serbian Law. In Lazić, M. & Knežević S. (eds.): *Legal, Social and Political Control in National, International and EU Law*, Niš: Law Faculty of the Niš University, 293–306.

Vučić, M. (2016b). Procena uticaja na životnu sredinu u praksi Međunarodnog suda pravde [Environmental Impact Assessment in the Practice of the International Court of Justice]. *Međunarodni problemi* [International Problems] 68(1): 72–94.

Vučić, M. (2017). Ljudsko pravo na vodu – između plemenite ideje i surove realnosti [Human Right to Water – from a Noble Idea to the Harsh Reality]. *Pravni život* [Legal Life] 9: 515–528.

Vučić, M. (2018). *Mehanizmi ostvarivanja načela neuzrokovanja štete u praksi upravljanja međunarodnim vodotokovima* [The Mechanisms of the Implementation of the No-Harm Rule in the Practice of International Watercourses Management]. Belgrade, Institute of International Politics and Economics.

Vučić M. (2019a). *Korektivna pravda pred Međunarodnim sudom* [Remedial Justice in front of the International Court of Justice]. Belgrade, Institute of International Politics and Economics.

Vučić, M. (2019b). Access to Water in the Context of the International Watercourse: A Theory of the Community of Interest. *Belgrade Law Faculty Annals* 67(3): 73–94.

Vučić, M. & Pavićević, V. (2021). Zaštita nacionalnog blaga kao izuzetak od slobode kretanja u Evropskoj Uniji [Protection of National Treasures as the Exception from the Right of Freedom of Movement in the EU] *Evropsko zakonodavstvo* [European Legislation], 76: 119–144.

Vuković, B. & Perović, Lj. (2010) Building Institutional Framework for Sustainable Development in Montenegro. *Thermal Science*, 14, 3: 593–611.

Vujošević, M. (ed.). (2005). *Crnogorski ustavi 1905–2005* [*Constitutions of Montenegro 1905–2005*]. Podgorica: Službeni list Crne Gore.

Vukasović, V., Todić, D. (2021). *Environmenal Law in Serbia*, Wolters Kluwer.

WB. (2022). *Western Balkans Regular Economic Report No. 22, Fall 2022, Beyond the Crisis,* The World Bank Group, Washington, DC: 83–87. https://

openknowledge.worldbank.org/bitstream/handle/10986/38189/P17947818ec26c8c17fe014901194ac104a1b5d70a2a.pdf?sequence=1&isAllowed=y (19 December 2022).

Zoi Environment Network, EEA. (2012). *West Balkan Environmental Core Set of Indicator.* Beograd. http://www.epa.org.me/images/wb-indicators-2012.pdf. (19 December 2022).

Official Journals (Original titles are given in brackets):

Official Journal of SFRY – Official Journal of the Socialist Federal Republic of Yugoslavia [Službeni list Socijalisticke Federativne Republike Jugoslavije].

Official Journal of FRY – Official Journal of the Federal Republic of Yugoslavia [Službeni list Savezne Republike Jugoslavije].

Official Journal of SRM – Official Journal of the Socialist Republic of Montenegro [Službeni list Socijalisticke Republike Crne Gore].

Official Journal of RM – Official Journal of the Republic of Montenegro [Službeni list Republike Crne Gore].

Official Journal of MNE – Official Journal of Montenegro [Službeni list Crne Gore].

Selected Bibliography and the List of Official Journals

Index

The numbers here refer to paragraph numbers.

Index

Index

Index

Index

www.ingramcontent.com/pod-product-compliance
Lightning Source LLC
Chambersburg PA
CBHW071410230926
51846CB00001B/41